Mergers and Acquisitions

Qiusheng Zhang

Mergers and Acquisitions

Fundamental Theoretical Framework

中国财经出版传媒集团
经济科学出版社
Economic Science Press
·北京·

Springer

Qiusheng Zhang
School of Economics and Management
Beijing Jiaotong University
Beijing, China

ISBN 978-981-92-0121-1 ISBN 978-981-92-0122-8 (eBook)
https://doi.org/10.1007/978-981-92-0122-8

Jointly published with Economic Science Press
The print edition is not for sale in China (Mainland). Customers from China (Mainland) please order the print book from: Economic Science Press.
ISBN of the Co-Publisher's edition: 978-7-5218-0337-2

This Springer imprint is published by the registered company Springer Nature Singapore Pte Ltd.
The registered company address is: 152 Beach Road, #21-01/04 Gateway East, Singapore 189721, Singapore

Preface

As global capital continues to restructure the industrial landscape in cross-border flows, mergers and acquisitions have become a key force for promoting the optimization of resource allocation, industrial structure upgrading and global economic integration. Since the beginning of this century, after more than two decades of fluctuations and iterative evolution, the global M&A market, driven by the technological revolution, policy change and market competition, has set out a development path of scale and quality, innovation and risk. From the historical peak of US$6 trillion in 2021, to the second highest level of US$4.5 trillion in 2025,[1] M&A activity has always been a "barometer" of global economic vitality and industrial changes, and as an increasingly important player in market. During this period, China has become a key variable to reshape the global M&A market.

The trajectory of the global M&A wave since the turn of the century is a reflection of the synergistic impact of economic cycles, technological innovation and the institutional environment. In the first decade, driven by the dividends of globalization, cross-border M&A became the mainstream, and enterprises achieved scale expansion and market extension through cross-border integration, and M&A deals in information technology and financial services were particularly active. After the 2008 financial crisis, the M&A market underwent a brief adjustment, then gradually recovered under the support of quantitative easing policy, and the transaction structure exhibited the characteristics of "large-scale and professionalization." In recent years, with the rise of emerging technologies such as artificial intelligence and big data, mergers and acquisitions in the technology sector have continued to heat up. In 2025, the value of M&A in the global technology industry has reached US$1 trillion, accounting for more than one fifth of the total value of the transaction. Data enterprises, semiconductor manufacturers and network security solution providers have become the hot acquisition targets. At the same time, the leading role of large-scale transactions has become increasingly prominent. In 2025, the

[1] Li Wenxin, Global M&A Returns to Bull Market, French M&A Gradually Becoming a Driver of Overseas Activity [online]. Xinhua Finance Analyses, 2026-01-19. Available from: https://www.cnfin.com/gs-lb/detail/20260119/4367531_1.html.

world completed a total of 68 giant transactions of more than US$10 billion.[2] Cases such as the super merger between Union Pacific and Norfolk Southern and the battle between Netflix and Paramount over Warner Bros. Discovery have not only reshaped the competitive landscape of the industry, but also highlighted the core value of M&A as a strategic transformation tool for enterprises. In this dynamic market evolution, the scope of M&A has extended from simple scale expansion to multiple dimensions such as technology acquisition, industrial chain integration, and global layout, becoming an important choice for enterprises to cope with uncertainty and build core competitiveness.

China's rise and transformation in the global M&A market is the most remarkable chapter in the history of mergers and acquisitions of this century. At the beginning of this century, China's M&A activities were dominated by internal consolidation and restructuring of state-owned enterprises, and the scale and internationalization of transactions were relatively limited. With the rapid development of China's economy and the continuous improvement of corporate strength, especially the deep implementation of the "go global" strategy, Chinese companies began to actively participate in global mergers and acquisitions, gradually becoming important initiators of cross-border mergers and acquisitions since 2010. In energy resources, manufacturing, high technology and other fields, a number of landmark M&A cases have emerged, and Chinese enterprises have achieved the strategic transformation from "bringing in" to "going global" through M&A. In recent years, China's M&A market has shown a new characteristic of "two-way efforts": On the one hand, domestic M&A focuses on industrial upgrading and supply-side reform, resolves overcapacity through horizontal consolidation, and improves industrial chains through vertical M&A to promote high-quality development of the real economy. On the other hand, cross-border M&A pays more attention to strategic fit and technological synergy, shifting from traditional resource acquisition to technology-driven and market expansion, and deepening the layout of strategic emerging industrial fields such as artificial intelligence, biomedicine, high-end manufacturing and other strategic emerging industries. Today, China has become an indispensable core force in the global M&A market, not only as an important transaction initiator, but also as a key demander and market stabilizer of high-quality assets in the world. The rationalization and professional development of its M&A activities have injected lasting impetus into the global M&A market.

In contrast to the boom in global M&A practice, the evolution of M&A theory has always faced the challenge of "practice ahead of theory". Since the last century, the study of mergers and acquisitions theory has gradually deepened with the five global mergers and acquisitions waves. A companion has produced many influential academic achievements. Economics of scale and transaction cost hypotheses explained well the wave of horizontal mergers and acquisitions in the late 19th and early 20th centuries, and the wave of vertical mergers in the 20th century.

---

[2] Li Wenxin, Global M&A Returns to Bull Market, French M&A Gradually Becoming a Driver of Overseas Activity [online]. Xinhua Finance Analyses, 2026-01-19. Available from: https://www.cnfin.com/gs-lb/detail/20260119/4367531_1.html.

In the 1960s, diversification theory and financial synergy theory became the core framework for explaining hybrid mergers and acquisitions. In the 1980s, Tobin's Q-value theory and Jensen's free cash flow hypothesis provided theoretical support for the mercantile and innovation-driven mergers and acquisitions such as leveraged buyout. Since the 1990s, the theory of globalization and external shocks has focused on the analysis of the drivers and effects of cross-border mergers and acquisitions. These theories reveal the inherent logic of M&A from different perspectives, providing an important basis for understanding M&A behavior. However, there are still many areas where the existing theoretical system needs to be improved: First, the problem of theoretical fragmentation is acute, most studies focus on a single dimension, lack systematic integration of the entire process of M&A, and difficulty in explaining the "motivation-process-outcome" transmission mechanism in M&A practice. Second, there is insufficient explanation for emerging market mergers and acquisitions. Existing theories are mostly based on the experience of mature Western markets and fail to fully consider the institutional environment, corporate characteristics and cultural differences of emerging economies such as China. Third, there is a lack of in-depth answers to core contradictions in mergers and acquisitions, such as the path to achieving synergies in mergers, the key causes of mergers and takeovers failure, and the long-term evaluation of the performance of mergers. Fourth, in the face of new phenomena such as digital economy, platform mergers and green mergers, traditional theory is difficult to provide a full explanation framework, and theoretical innovation lags behind practical development. These theoretical gaps not only restrict the deepening of academic research on M&A, but also pose challenges for corporate M&A decision-making and policy formulation. Building a systematic, comprehensive basic theoretical system of M&A that is adapted to the characteristics of the new era has become a common aspiration of academia and the substantive circle.

It is based on the practical need for profound insight into global M&A practice and theoretical development that this book has been revised and adapted on the second edition of the Simplified Chinese language published by Economic Sciences Press in 2019, and finally introduced to global audiences by Springer Publishing in English. The core objective of this book is to build a logical, hierarchical, theoretical and practical framework for the basic theory of mergers and acquisitions, filling the fragmented deficiencies of the existing theoretical system. In its structure, the book takes the concept of mergers and acquisitions as a logical starting point and breaks down M&A activities into eight interrelated, step-by-step core dimensions. The eight-pillar theoretical system of "M&A motivation—M&A capability—M&A boundary—M&A direction—M&A matching—M&A synergy—M&A performance—M&A market" was constructed. This framework covers both strategic decision-making (motivation, capability and boundary) and execution elements in mergers and acquisitions (direction and matching), pays more attention to the value realization of M&A (synergy and performance) while placing M&A activities in a systematic market environment.

The framework also forms a multidimensional analysis perspective of "micro-enterprise behavior, meso-industry impact and macro-market environment". In its theoretical construction, the book incorporates the classic results of Western mergers and acquisitions theory, such as economics of scale, economics of scope, core concepts such as synergy and principal-agent theory integrate the characteristics of M&A practice in China and emerging markets, and explain innovatively issues such as the diversification of M&A motives, the dynamic evolution of M&A capabilities, and the paths to M&A synergies. In presentation, the book focuses on a combination of theory and practice, visualizing abstract theoretical concepts, providing readers with actionable analytical tools and decision references. It should be noted that the Simplified Chinese version of this book was finalized in 2018 and the data covered in this book have not been updated in order to be consistent with the scientific nature of the research.

The publication of this book could not be achieved without the support of many institutions and individuals. First of all, I would like to express my sincere thanks to Director Song Xuejun and Editor Li Bao of the Economic Sciences Press for their professional guidance and meticulous support in the publication of the second edition of the Chinese language and this book. At the same time, I sincerely thank Springer, who promote the successful publication of this book in English so that this system of mergers and acquisitions theory, which incorporates Chinese business wisdom, can go global as a benchmark. In addition, Li Xin'ao, Zhao Xiaofang, Li Chaofeng, Lin Jiayu and other doctoral students put in a lot of hard work in the translation, proofreading and material preparation of this book. Their meticulous attitude and academic level ensured the quality of the publication of this book, and I would like to express my sincere gratitude to them.

M&A activity is not only an important path for enterprise growth, but also a core driving force for industrial upgrading, and a key mechanism for optimizing the allocation of resources in the global economy. Today, with the deeply integrated digital economy and globalization, the M&A market will face more new opportunities and challenges, and the theory of M&A needs to be constantly enriched and developed in practice. The basic theoretical system of M&A developed in this book is not only a systematic summary of past M&A practice and theoretical research, but also a prospective exploration of future M&A development trends. It is hoped that this book will provide scholars engaged in M&A research with a clear theoretical framework, provide scientific guidance tools for corporate M&A decision-making, and provide useful reference for policy makers to regulate the M&A market and promote the healthy development of M&A. Due to the complexity of M&A theory and the diversity of practice, there are inevitably some omissions in this book. I hope readers to criticize and correct them at qszhang@bjtu.edu.cn.

I would like to dedicate this book to all those who are dedicated to the theoretical research and practical exploration of mergers and acquisitions.

Beijing, China
New Year's Day, 2026

Qiusheng Zhang

Contents

Chapter 1
Introduction

1.1 Mergers and Acquisitions Activity

Mergers and acquisitions (hereinafter referred to as M&A) are regular activities in the modern market economy and play an irreplaceable role in the market economy mechanism. The United States has always been the protagonist in M&A activity, having experienced six waves of M&A since 1893. In 2006, the value of M&A in the United States accounted for more than 10% of its GDP. According to preliminary statistics from Thomson Financial, global M&A amount reached a record US$4.38 trillion in 2007, an increase of 21 percent over 2006. In 2007, the value of M&A in Europe surpassed that of the United States for the first time, reaching US$1.781 trillion, compared with US$1.5697 trillion in the United States and US$0.5982 trillion in Asia.[1] The M&A wave in the United States and the M&A wave in Europe and Asia constitute another wave of global M&A under globalization.

Modern China's industry, commerce, and finance arose and developed under a relatively special economic and historical condition. It did not go through the general trajectory of the industrial development of the old capitalist countries, from simple cooperation to factory handicraft industry, then to large-scale machine industry, with the process of gradual specialization in industry and commerce, and financial services. However, during its development process, it still shows a relatively apparent trend of capital concentration. In the mid-1930s, the first signs of corporate M&A emerged. By 1949, competition and mergers among national capital, foreign capital, and bureaucratic capital had become a relatively common phenomenon. During this period, the economy was greatly influenced by politics and military affairs, and there were "privileged M&A" and other forms of "deformed M&A", which developed in three directions: M&A between national capitals, M&A of the national capital by bureaucratic capital, and M&A of the national capital by foreign capitalist enterprises.

[1] There is a statistics difference between Thomson Financial and Mergerstat. According to Mergerstat, the amount of European M&A in 2007 was US$1.7767 trillion, and the US M&A amounted to US$1.3453 trillion.

Q. Zhang, *Mergers and Acquisitions*, https://doi.org/10.1007/978-981-92-0122-8_1

During the transitional period of socialist construction (1949–1956), corporate M&A mainly represented the socialist transformation of private industrial and commercial enterprises. In China's highly planned economy (1955–1960), corporate M&A was manifested as administrative adjustments to industrial and commercial enterprises, namely closing, suspending, merging and transferring. From 1963 to 1966, the government also tried to set up professional companies with trust features through administrative means, and attempted to merge and reorganize the production capacity of enterprises. These policies included administrative adjustment and restructuring of the enterprise's human resources, asset resources, and management framework while maintaining the same ownership.[2]

After the reform and opening up, China's M&A, as an experiment, emerged in the mid-1980s, with the development of the socialist market economy, showing the characteristics of China both in theory and in practice. Reviewing China's M&A market from 2001 to 2016, the number and value of M&A transactions by Chinese companies showed a fluctuating upward trend. The wave of China's M&A is gradually integrating into the wave of global M&A and will become an essential part of the wave of global M&A.

1.2 Development of M&A Research

Although M&A has a history of more than a century, it is still a mystery.

M&A has a magical power that has always attracted entrepreneurs, but their possible endings are not a moth to a flame, at least as risky as gambling, with a 50/50 split between winners and losers. The research on M&A is long-term, in-depth, and fruitful. For the economic phenomenon of M&A, scholars have observed it from various perspectives, exploring it from the perspective of their respective disciplines, using economic, managerial, political, social, legal, and cultural theories and methods. A variety of practical explanations or conclusions are drawn.

Looking at the M&A research that emerged in the 1960s, M&A research has generally gone through four stages, namely the value creation stage, the strategic matching stage, the organizational matching stage, and the M&A process stage. Each stage represents the top research issues of the time.

Researchers naturally have a strong interest in whether M&A creates value, and initial research has focused on examining this topic. Jensen and Ruback (1983) summarize the findings of this stage as follows: the evidence shows that corporate takeovers generate positive returns, in which target shareholders benefit and acquirer shareholders do not lose. The research results of the value creation stage answer the question of whether M&A creates value and for whom, essentially examining the question of M&A performance. However, as later scholars commented, the research at this stage failed to explain the reasons behind the findings, which is related to the

[2] According to the definition of M&A, the activities of these stages are not M&A.

fact that the research results in this stage were mainly studied from the perspective of finance.

To explore what kinds of M&A can create value, scholars have turned to research from the perspective of corporate strategy. Scholars of corporate strategy have excavated the "correlation theory" in diversification research and advanced M&A research to the stage of strategic matching. Salter and Weinhold (1978) first introduced the concept of correlation into M&A research and put forward the hypothesis that related M&A should exhibit better performance. The strategic implication of this hypothesis is that related M&A creates value. Since then, many scholars have tested the correlation hypothesis, but the conclusions are inconsistent.

Singh and Montgomery (1987), in a case study of 203 target firms from 1970 to 1978, reported that correlated target firms had higher excess returns than uncorrelated target firms. Shelton (1988) reached a similar conclusion in a study of 218 M&A between 1962 and 1983 that horizontal mergers and related complementary mergers (selling the same product to new customers) can obtain huge returns, and the impact of unrelated M&A on performance is insignificant but negative. However, Lubatkin's (1987) research on 340 target firms from 1948 to 1975 concluded that related M&A did not create more value than unrelated M&A. In a case study involving a sample of 439 merging firms and 430 target firms, Elgers and Clark (1980) found that conglomerate M&A brought more wealth for shareholders of both parties than non-conglomerate M&A. Chatterjee (1986) also reported similar findings, in which he concluded that the target firm in unrelated mergers had better performance than the target firm in related mergers.

Correlation research is essentially the matching problem between the acquirer and the acquiree. The inconsistency of the empirical test results of the correlation hypothesis has prompted scholars to search for more profound reasons that affect value creation, thus opening the prelude to the stage of corporate matching. Scholars found that organizational factors, such as organizational culture, organizational structure, and organizational system, are essential factors affecting the success or failure of M&A (Lubatkin, 1987). Research on specific organizational factors such as management style (the core element of organizational culture) and compensation system showed that corporate matching determines the degree of difficulty in realizing potential value (Haspeslaph & Farquhar, 1987).

Exploring factors affecting value creation is simultaneously developed along the lines of the M&A process. M&A is composed of a series of activities, and which activities have an important impact on value creation is the problem that scholars consider. Overpayment (Serovo, 2001) and poor integration (Jemison & Sitkin, 1986) are considered important factors in destroying value, but the post- merger integration process has received prominent emphasis in recent years. The researchers' studies on the choice of integration strategies (Haspeslaph & Jemison, 1991) have provided important references for practice.

A summary of the M&A research results of the past 40 years may be missed from any perspective. Weston and Susan (1998) pointed out that M&A activity continued to stimulate the emergence of voluminous printed matter. Condensed abstracts or comprehensive articles based on these materials cannot adequately cover them.

Regarding the research focus of M&A theory, Weston and Susan (1998) summarized it into three questions. First, it is concerned with the motivations for M&A. Second, the theory should be able to predict the types of firms involved in M&A activity—which types of firms are likely to make acquisitions? What kind of firms is likely to be acquired? And so on. Third, the theory should include information about the entire activity—why do we observe more mergers in some periods than others? The summary of Weston and Susan can be seen as the three basic questions that M&A theory seeks to answer: the motivation behind M&A, the characteristics of the acquirer and the acquiree, and the determinants of the concentration of M&A activities.

Although scholars have carried out a lot of research and exploration on M&A, the results of M&A behaviors and activities are still unsatisfactory, and cases of failed M&A occur frequently. Professor Fred Weston, the most authoritative M&A research expert in the world, has to admit that there is no generally accepted theory that can explain the motivations behind mergers, the characteristics of the merging and the merged enterprises, and the determinants of the concentration of merger activity.

1.3 Definition of M&A

The scientific definition is a common language for communication among scientists, industry experts, and practitioners. Furthermore, it is the cornerstone of scientific development. However, there is currently no scientific definition of M&A. Since M&A is short for mergers and acquisitions, and mergers and acquisitions are legally different economic activities, they have separate definitions. Merger generally refers to the merger of two or more companies. The rights and obligations of the original company are assumed by the surviving (or newly established) company. Generally, it is carried out according to legal procedures with the consent of both parties' operators and shareholders' support. Mergers have two forms: absorption merger and new merger. An absorption merger is when one company merges with another, where one company disappears and the other becomes the surviving company. A new merger refers to the merger of two or more companies and the establishment of a new company to become a new legal entity. The original two companies no longer retain their legal personality. An acquisition is a transaction in which one company purchases another company's assets, business units, or stocks, thereby assuming a position of control. Acquisitions can be further divided into asset acquisitions and share acquisitions. Asset acquisitions refer to the purchase of part or all of the assets of the seller company by the buyer company; share acquisitions refer to the purchase of part or all of the shares of the seller company directly or indirectly by the buyer company and assume all the rights and obligations of the seller company jointly with other shareholders according to their interests.

Mergers and acquisitions are often intertwined and difficult to distinguish, such as stock-exchange acquisitions. Therefore, academia and practitioners are accustomed to using the two together, referred to as M&A. Unless otherwise specified, no distinction is made between the two. Because of the lack of distinction between mergers and acquisitions, there is no scientific definition of M&A, and people have different understandings of their connotation and extension. Therefore, the relationship between M&A, takeovers, reorganizations, divestitures, and spin-offs has become complicated. In the title of the second edition of Professor Weston's representative book *Mergers, Restructuring and Corporate Control*, the word mergers were abandoned and replaced by takeovers. He believes that mergers and acquisitions are two ways to achieve takeover form.

We believe that M&A are transactions targeted at business control. First, M&A is a transactional activity. Transactions are market economic activities. As a transaction, there are at least four essential elements: buyer, seller, subject, and price. M&A meets the requirements of the essential elements of a transaction. Second, M&A is a complex transaction activity with unique transaction objects. As a transaction, M&A is different from other transaction activities. The target of other transaction activities is a single resource, such as products (labor), human resources, technology, capital, etc., and the transaction venue is the product market or the factor market. The object of M&A is business control right. The business control right is the control right over the collection of factor resources.[3] The trading place is in the stock market and other property markets, the primary market for corporate control.[4] Third, M&A activity is one of the external development ways of enterprises, and it is a substitute for strategic activities such as new investments and alliances.

Business control rights aim at the combination of assets and capabilities, but capabilities do not exist separately from assets. Assets can be traded directly, and capability trades are achieved through asset trades. The activity of asset-based elements is low, so the leverage of transaction effect is low, and the degree of risk is also low; the activity of capability transaction is high, the degree of leverage of transaction effect is high, and the degree of risk is also high.

M&A is usually understood as a strategy for enterprise expansion. However, from the perspective of the transaction subject in the M&A market, an enterprise expanding through M&A must correspond to a company downsizing through sell-offs. Therefore, regardless of expansion or downsizing, as long as the downsizing activities that meet the definition of M&A are also the research objects of M&A, and the separation that is not within the scope of M&A is considered corporate restructuring. In M&A research, unless otherwise defined, it is the acquirer (investor) that is the subject of the research.

M&A is a huge corporate investment and a package of complete transactions. There is no rehearsal for M&A, and no chance of rehearsal. Therefore, M&A is corporate venture capital. The typical means to control risks before M&A are not to acquire directly, but first to take minority equity investments, joint ventures, strategic

---

[3] Enterprise resource elements are divided into six elements: human, material, financial, natural, knowledge, and ability. Human, material, financial, natural, and knowledge are asset elements. The human element and other asset elements make up the business. Asset elements and capability elements are transformed into each other, and their quality and quantity change over time.

[4] Market for corporate control is also a customary term. Since M&A can also be achieved through asset acquisitions, the accurate expression should be market for business control.

alliances, or agreements, or to control the scale of M&A. Once an acquisition target is identified, M&A risks can only be reduced through exhaustive due diligence, reasonable valuation, difficult negotiations, and careful integration. For M&A, people can only act carefully and cautiously, and no rule can be used boldly and safely yet.

Are M&A value-enhancing or value-destroying? If it is value-enhancing, is it value-discovery or value-creation? From the perspective of value, the acquisition of another enterprise by one enterprise can be considered that the acquirer has discovered the value of the target, and the target or the bidder also recognizes the value discovered by the acquirer. Due to the market mechanism, this value is shared equally. The target harvests most of the discovered value. If the acquisition can create new value that is not discovered or recognized by the target or the bidder, the value created can only be owned by the acquirer, or at least most of it will be obtained by the acquirer. So, while value discovery is good, the real challenge for M&A is value creation.

1.4 Fundamental Theoretical Problems of M&A

Just like the complex problem of the nature of the enterprise, what is the nature of M&A? The more basic the question, the more difficult it is to get an unambiguous answer. From the point of view of simple logical analysis, the reason why M&A is difficult to succeed can only be the lack of understanding of the laws of M&A behavior and activities. The motivation and performance of M&A are a pair of mutual causality, which is undoubtedly an essential part of M&A theoretical research. However, a black box of M&A is formed between motivation and performance. The M&A black box contains at least fundamental theoretical issues such as M&A capability, M&A boundary, M&A direction, M&A matching, and M&A synergy.

M&A motivation. Motivation is the starting point of behavior. The motivation for M&A can be described differently or explained by various theories from different disciplines. But in empirical research, can motivations and effects be consistently expressed? How can motivation and effect be expressed quantitatively and comprehensively? What is the relationship between M&A motivations and the actual effects achieved? Theories of M&A motivation must answer these questions.

M&A capability. Enterprises with M&A motivations cannot necessarily conduct M&A. What kind of companies are considered to have M&A capability? How is M&A capability expressed and judged? What are the relationship between M&A capability, enterprise scale, and enterprise competitiveness? M&A capability theory should answer these questions.

M&A boundary. Enterprises with M&A capabilities do not have to use M&A as a means of strategic development but can also achieve development through alliances, agreements, joint ventures, direct investment and other means. Then, under what environmental conditions M&A is applicable, and how M&A is carried out become the research object of M&A boundary theory.

M&A direction. If the actual situation of the enterprise is at the origin of the coordinates, what direction should the M&A take in a 360-degree circle around it? Simply put, should the M&A be horizontal or vertical, and specifically, in which quadrant should the M&A take place? Where are the coordinates of the target company? Considering more complex factors, where are the coordinates of other dimensions such as the industry, geographic location, scale, efficiency, and time to implement M&A? The theory of M&A direction should give answers to these questions.

M&A matching. If we follow the "map" of the direction of M&A, the next logical question will be whether the target company and the acquiring company can match. The goal of M&A is to obtain various capabilities of the target company, including R&D capabilities, manufacturing capabilities, marketing capabilities, and various auxiliary capabilities. The comprehensive performance of various capabilities is the company's sustainable ability to obtain free cash flow. But capabilities cannot be obtained directly through acquisitions. Acquisitions can only directly obtain the assets of the company. Obtaining the target company's assets does not mean possessing the company's capabilities, not to mention whether the intangible assets such as human resources and related assets of the target company will be preserved after the acquisition. Therefore, whether the resources of the acquirer and the target are matched, and whether the capabilities of the target can be preserved, transferred, and developed are the research objects of M&A matching theory.

M&A synergy. Even if the M&A parties are matched, it can only indicate that there is potential synergy between the M&A parties, and the matching constitutes a necessary condition for the expected M&A synergy. Based on M&A matching, what is the expected synergy between the two parties? How many are there? How are the sources of synergy explained? M&A synergy is expected to be reflected in what projects? If there is no M&A synergy, there must be no value-added, and the M&A transaction is a waste and loss of resources for the whole society. These pose the most direct challenge to M&A synergy theory.

M&A performance. The expected synergy of M&A produces the performance of M&A through post-merger integration, and M&A performance can be considered as the realization of the real synergy or the expected synergy of M&A. M&A is a strategic behavior, and its impact must be long-term and far-reaching. Financial performance may not be able to represent all the performance of M&A, and financial performance is certainly not all the performance generated by M&A. The M&A performance is not fully proportional to the starting point of M&A, that is, the connotation or extension of the motivation of M&A, because apart from realizing the individual motivation of the acquirer, the performance of M&A activities will objectively have an impact on the industrial structure and socio- economic structure. What is the relationship between M&A motivation and M&A performance even when M&A motivation and M&A micro-performance are matched? M&A performance theory must answer these questions.

M&A market. M&A starts with motivation and ends with a performance. M&A performance will induce M&A in turn, and the end point returns to the starting point, creating a succession of M&A activities. Many M&A activities constitute the M&A market, which is the environment for the M&A activities of enterprises. The M&A

market transactions in different periods contain the laws of its market operation. The mission of M&A market theoretical research is to reveal the law of the M&A market.

M&A evolution. From the perspective of history, M&A is not only the micro-level behaviors between enterprises, creating "smarter" and more complex enterprise organizations and behaviors. At the same time, M&A between enterprises has caused changes in the industrial and economic structure contributing to the difference of national competitiveness or the change of ability and way of human survival. M&A must have an evolutionary role for enterprises, just as marriage is for human beings. What M&A evolution theory wants to reveal is the law of the evolutionary effect of M&A behavior on enterprises, industries, countries, and even the whole society. It has been the law of the M&A market for an extended period.

The high risk of M&A and the development of M&A research require establishing a basic theoretical framework of M&A to explain and reveal the general laws of M&A activities, and guide M&A applied research and M&A practice activities. The main contents of the basic theory of M&A include M&A motivation, M&A capability, M&A boundary, M&A direction, M&A matching, M&A synergy, M&A performance, and M&A market. The gap between M&A performance and M&A motivation can be used as a criterion for the success of M&A. M&A motivation, M&A capability, M&A boundary, M&A direction, M&A matching, and M&A synergy are the key factors that affect scientific decision- making of M&A. The M&A market theory reveals the operation of the market for corporate control. While it has a positive evolutionary role, it is also a market that needs to be regulated as the environment for M&A activities. A cross-section of the fundamental theoretical problems of M&A is shown in Fig. 1.1. As a kind of independent economic activity, the fundamental theoretical problem of M&A becomes the problem of M&A evolution over time, which belongs to the category of M&A history research.

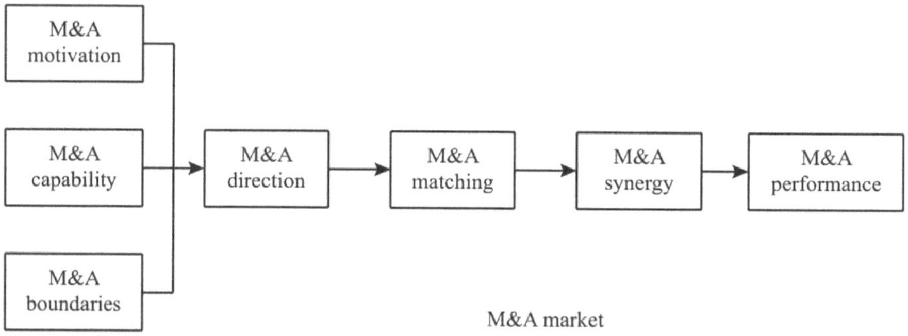

Fig. 1.1 Cross-section of the fundamental theoretical problems of M&A

1.5 The Disciplinary System and Epistemology of M&A

The word "science" comes from the medieval Latin "scientia", which originally means "learning" and "knowledge". In 1887, Darwin defined science: "Science consists in grouping facts so that general laws or conclusions may be drawn from them." Darwin's definition points out the connotation of science, that is, facts and laws. Science should discover facts unknown to man and use them as the basis for facts, rather than pure thinking and fantasy out of reality. As for the law, it refers to the inevitable connection of the intrinsic essence between objective things. Therefore, science is a knowledge system about the nature and laws of motion of various things in the objective world, which is based on practice, has been tested by practice, and demonstrated by logic rigorously.

A subject is an academic classification that refers to a certain scientific field or branch of science (Ci Hai Editorial Committee, 1999). M&A is the science of M&A activities and is the sum of knowledge systems about M&A. The different connections with practice include three levels: the basic theory of M&A, the basic M&A application theory, and the operational methods (techniques) of M&A. The basic theory of M&A is at the top of the M&A knowledge system. It is purely abstract M&A knowledge. It has the role of driving and guiding the M&A application basic theory. The M&A application basic theory is an extension and a practical application methodology of the basic theory of M&A. Its content is based on the main business links of M&A, including M&A strategy, M&A value assessment, M&A financing, merger accounting, M&A taxation, post-merger integration, acquisition defense, and M&A supervision, etc. The M&A operational methodology is a guide for M&A application basic theory-oriented to M&A practice, and it is also a summary of experience from long-term M&A practice activities. It seems that there is no verifiable history of M&A practice, but at least a hundred years of M&A has accumulated rich M&A techniques.

To answer the above basic theoretical questions on M&A, it is necessary to fully rely on and absorb the existing knowledge achievements of various fundamental disciplines, especially their research results on M&A. The basic theoretical disciplines of M&A include economics, management, law, sociology, history, etc., which are direct basic disciplines. The indirect basic disciplines of M&A include philosophy, mathematics, physics, and even biology. Disciplinary fields closely related to the M&A application basic theory include industrial organization, strategic management, financial management, accounting, human resource management, taxation, and commercial law. Due to the complexity and challenge of M&A activities, M&A has become an important research object in these disciplines. The research results also constitute an integral part of the knowledge system of these disciplines. In this sense, M&A is an interdisciplinary discipline, a specialized discipline enriched and developed by absorbing and integrating other discipline knowledge.

To answer the basic theoretical questions of M&A, it is necessary to rely on both theoretical derivation and practical verification, that is, with the help of normative and empirical research methods, to conduct research and exploration in two conduct corrections and different ways. Only by constantly exploring the fundamental theoretical issues of M&A, can we continuously deepen our understanding of the laws and the essence of M&A.

Chapter 2
Motivations of M&A

2.1 Concept of M&A Motivation

Motivation is the starting point of behavior. The motivation of the acquirer's stakeholders in the M&A activities is referred to as the motivations of M&A. M&A motivation is one of the most concentrated areas of M&A research. Weston (2006) classified M&A theory into four categories from the source of value increase: total value increase, arrogance, agency, and redistribution, which are essentially a generalization of M&A motivation, performance, and their causes. In general, arrogance and agency are essentially total value reductions, while redistribution does not increase or decrease firm value. Since the acquirer's M&A activities involve many stakeholders, such as shareholders, creditors, government, employees, and communities, each stakeholder has different motivations in M&A activities, and these different M&A motivations exert influence on M&A activities in different sizes and directions. Therefore, understanding the M&A motivations of various stakeholders in M&A activities, and expressing them quantitatively and comprehensively can help us to further understand corporate M&A motivations.

2.2 Related Theories of M&A Motivation

The theories of M&A motivation are the basis for studying the motivations of enterprises to carry out M&A behavior, mainly including scale effect theory, market power theory, tax saving theory, synergy theory, diversification theory, undervaluation theory, principal-agent theory, and new institutional economics theory of M&A.

Q. Zhang, *Mergers and Acquisitions*, https://doi.org/10.1007/978-981-92-0122-8_2

2.2.1 Scale Effect Theory

Scale effect, also known as economies of scale, means that under a certain output, the expansion of the company's scale will reduce the per-unit product cost, thereby increasing the operating profit level. The economies of scale effect are mainly applied to enterprises that require large production equipment or plants for production, that is, enterprises or industries with high fixed costs. This theory holds that M&A can increase the output of enterprises within a certain range, thereby reducing the fixed cost per unit product allocated, improving the market competitiveness of enterprises, and promoting the growth of enterprise net profits. This theory mainly expounds on the motivation of M&A from the perspectives of internal economies of scale and external economies of scale and believes that the internal economies of scale brought by M&A are mainly reflected in the internal optimization effect brought by enterprises through resource restructuring and M&A. Merging upstream companies can provide quality and price guarantees for the source of raw materials. Merging downstream companies can help companies control sales channels, understand market demand promptly, and improve the company's resilience. The external economies of scale brought to enterprises by M&A is mainly reflected in the fact that M&A can enhance the overall strength of enterprises, consolidate existing market shares, and help enterprises achieve professional and branded services.

2.2.2 Market Power Theory

Market power theory was put forward by Comanor (1967), which believes that the main motivation of M&A behavior is that companies can squeeze market competitors out of the market through M&A, enhance their ability to control the market, and then gain the excess benefits of oligopoly or monopoly. In market competition, enterprises obtain a dominant market position by merging with other enterprises in the same industry to capture market share. The expansion of scale will also increase the popularity of the enterprise among market consumers, thereby enhancing its brand effect. Market power is an intangible asset of an enterprise, which is a force that enhances the market competitiveness of an enterprise. Regarding the issue of market power, different scholars have different views. Most scholars believe that the hypothesis is valid only if the enterprises have achieved both an increase in market share and economies of scale through horizontal or vertical M&A. The improvement of market power alone does not mean that economies of scale and synergies are achieved.

2.2.3 Tax Saving Theory

The tax saving theory is based on the tax law, which holds that the M&A of enterprises is implemented to reduce taxes or reasonably avoid taxes. M&A mainly helps companies achieve reasonable tax avoidance through two forms. First, according to the loss deferral provision in the tax law, if a company has accumulated losses, its later profits should make up for its earlier losses, and pay taxes based on the offset profits. It motivates companies with high surpluses to aim at loss-making companies and achieve tax savings through M&A to a certain extent. On the contrary, this regulation also prompts loss-making companies to take advantage of their tax advantages to acquire a surplus company to expand the scale, save overall taxes, and improve operating profits. Second, based on the tax deductibility of debt interest payments, the theory believes that many surplus companies will increase their interest expense levels through leveraged M&A, exercising the tax avoidance function of corporate financial leverage. In addition, the tax rate on capital gains is lower than the income tax rate based on the tax law, and the tax law allows capital gains to be paid when they are realized, which forces surplus companies to invest in the form of M&A to reduce the dividend payout, such as mature stage companies acquiring growth stage companies. Enterprises in the mature stage have more funds. If these funds are used as dividends, it will increase the tax burden on shareholders. Therefore, generally speaking, companies in the mature stage will acquire a growth stage company and invest the surplus funds in the target company. After the company's growth period, it can be sold to obtain capital gains. The capital gains tax replaces the payment of income tax, which saves taxes and delays the time for tax collection.

2.2.4 Synergy Theory

The synergy hypothesis proposed by Weston (2003) is the most common form of efficiency theory, which holds that the net cash flow after a merger will be greater than the sum of the expected cash flows of two independent companies, or that the effect of a merger between two companies is greater than the effect of two independent companies, that is, the effect of $1+1>2$. The theory believes that companies generally pay a specific M&A price by reaching certain synergies. Because of this synergy, M&A between companies will become more common, and social efficiency will continue to increase. To a certain extent, this theory also implies that the government should encourage M&A. According to the source of synergy, the theory is divided into three categories: operational synergy, financial synergy, and management synergy.

The theory of operational synergy is similar to the theory of scale effect, mainly from the point of view of economies of scale. It is believed that when enterprises do not reach economies of scale, enterprises can expand the production scale through M&A, reduce the fixed cost-shared by unit products, and then reduce unit product cost, thus improving operating efficiency, and making production gradually reach the production range of economies of scale. This theory assumes that economies of scale exist in the industry and that companies have not yet achieved the potential requirements for economies of scale before M&A. Williamson (1981) pointed out that the economic synergies produced by different types of corporate M&A are different, and the impact of operating effects on transaction costs is mainly reflected in vertical M&A. Kentouris and Chris (1999) studied Deutsche Bank's HNA acquisition, and reached a different conclusion from Williamson, and found that Deutsche Bank can also obtain operational synergies from conglomerate M&A.

The theory of financial synergy believes that enterprises can obtain lower financing costs and investment costs through M&A. That's to say, both parties can use each other's borrowing advantages or scale advantages to improve the debt repayment ability, the enterprise rating, and then obtain the right of lower interest expenses. At the same time, both parties of the M&A can reasonably integrate their finances according to the tax law, to a certain extent, reducing the enterprise's tax burden and financial cost. Peterholl and Dimitris (1997) found that the financial synergies produced by the merger of upstream and downstream companies are different. Under the same circumstances, the management and financial synergies of corporate M&A are more significant than the operational synergy.

The theory of management synergy is based on the different management efficiency of two companies. It is believed that when a high-efficiency company merges a low-efficiency company, the management experience of the high- efficiency company will affect the low-efficiency company to a certain extent, which will make the low-efficiency company improve their management level. For the whole society, M&A can improve the operating efficiency of the entire capital market. Dodd and Ruback (1977) showed that the company's M&A could improve the management efficiency of enterprises to a certain extent and obtain positive excess market returns.

2.2.5 *Diversification Theory*

The theory of diversification starts from the perspective of how operators benefit from scope of economics and avoid business risks. It believes that corporate M&A can achieve diversified business operations and avoid operating risks due to a relatively single business scope. As we all know, a single business means not only higher costs but also a limited market size and increased business risk. For enterprises that invest funds to produce a single product, it is difficult for the enterprise to switch operations when the market consumption preferences deviate or even reverse. With the promotion of the shareholding reform, the ownership and operation of enterprises are separated. As a shareholder, they can diversify their investment through the securities market to diversify risks. However, as an operator responsible for the operation of the company, their interests are directly affected by the quality of the enterprise's operation and by the single business model of the enterprise, which forces the operators to adopt M&A to implement diversified operations, merging and acquiring relatively advantageous or complementary enterprises to maximize the value of the enterprise's advantageous resources. For the company, the centripetal force and sense of belonging of the employees will affect the efficiency and stability of the employees, and the diversified development of the enterprise can improve the sense of security and honor of the employees, which can avoid the loss of talents to a certain extent. The theory also believes that enterprises can use the target company's goodwill, customer groups, suppliers, and other resources through M&A to achieve rapid enterprise expansion.

2.2.6 Undervaluation Theory

The theory of undervaluation states that M&A occurs when a company's market value is lower than its intrinsic value for some reason. The core concept of the market undervaluation theory is Tobin's Q. When $Q > 1$, that is, when the market value of an enterprise is greater than the replacement cost, the enterprise is overvalued, and the possibility of M&A is relatively tiny; on the contrary, when $Q < 1$, when the market value of an enterprise is lower than the replacement cost value, the enterprise is undervalued, and it is easy to be acquired. The ultimate goal of an enterprise is to maximize profits, and all its behaviors exist to achieve this goal. To a certain extent, the generation of M&A is also a way to add value to the enterprise. The undervaluation theory believes that the undervaluation of an enterprise is mainly caused by the following factors: Firstly, the target company has not fully utilized its potential, and much potential value has not been tapped. Secondly, the value of the target company is known earlier by the acquiring company through news or research than the outside world. To seize the opportunity and achieve value-added benefits, the acquiring company will take action as soon as possible. Finally, when inflation occurs in the economy, the replacement cost of the company will be different from the company capital market value, and when the value of the capital market is less than the replacement value of the company, it will cause the phenomenon of underestimation of the enterprise value. When the target company is undervalued, the acquirer's M&A will generate positive returns.

2.2.7 Principal-Agent Theory

The principal-agent theory mainly refers to the fact that the owner of the company and the controller have a certain principal-agent relationship due to the separation of ownership and operation of the company. Due to the different interests of the two, there will be a certain amount of agency costs and moral hazard phenomenon. This theory holds that corporate M&A can reduce agency costs to a certain extent. The study of Manne (1965) shows that acquisitions can reduce the generation of agency problems for company managers. To prevent companies from being acquired, managers will work harder to operate, improve operating efficiency, and reduce operating costs. A representative hypothesis is a managerial hypothesis put forward by Mueller (1969), which holds that the size of the company is the main factor affecting the compensation of managers. Company managers hope to improve performance compensation through M&A, but this theory lacks a certain factual basis. The empirical research of Lewellen and Huntsman (1970) showed that the compensation of business managers is not related to the size of the company and the level of sales, rejecting this hypothesis. Fama and Jesen (1983) put forward the free cash flow hypothesis, pointing out that managers and owners have agency problems in free cash flow. Too much corporate cash flow can easily lead to adverse selection and a moral hazard for managers. The implementation of M&A can effectively reduce the free cash flow of enterprises and thus reduce the probability of adverse selection behavior of operators. Free cash flow is an important factor in the generation of corporate M&A.

2.2.8 New Institutional Economics Theory of M&A

Coase (1937) put forward the transaction cost theory, which provided a theoretical basis for the M&A behavior of enterprises, and put forward a more general enterprise boundary theory, arguing that the cost of a certain transaction placed internally by a firm should be the same as the transaction cost incurred by a firm placed into the market or within another firm. Based on Coase, Williamson (1985) made a further empirical study on transaction costs and further explored the issue of vertical integration. He believed that vertical M&A of companies can avoid the middlemen to earn price differences and reduce the uncertainty of the operating environment, thereby reducing the transaction costs of enterprises. Hart (1995) studied the aspect of enterprise rights allocation and believed that enterprise M&A is an important choice for enterprises to achieve the optimal allocation of rights under certain circumstances. Furubotn and Richter (2005) studied from the perspective of abstract level, trying to explain that the economic view of firm size frontier is derived based on a comparison of transaction costs.

2.3 Motivation for M&A from Inner Drive and External Incentive

Mergers and acquisitions are complex and mysterious. Theoretically and practically, there has been much interest in the question: What are the real motives for M&A? i. e., what are the real motives behind the complicated M&A activities? To unravel this question, scholars have conducted a lot of normative and empirical studies from different research perspectives, including economic, management, and legal perspectives, to explain the motives of M&A, and many mature theories have been formed. However, most existing theories focus on only one aspect of M&A motives, and firms' M&A motives are often not unique, so no single theory has yet been able to explain corporate M&A motives comprehensively.

The goal of an enterprise is to survive, grow, and make profits. As an extraordinary external development method for an enterprise, M&A should realize the enterprise's goal. Suppose M&A is an enterprise's behavior, and the motivation is the driving force that causes the behavior. In that case, an enterprise's motivation to conduct M&A should also be in line with the enterprise's goal. The existing theories of M&A motivation also focus on corporate motives for M&A, taking the firm as the subject of M&A behavior, but we should not ignore the point that corporate M&A behavior is the result of decisions made by various stakeholders, such as the firm's management department (including management and decision-making), regulators, and employees. Without considering the agency problem, the M&A decision made by management should serve the achievement of corporate goals, and then the management's M&A motivations are reflected as the firm's motivations.

Psychology is one of the foundations of management. Since M&A activities involve numerous games between companies and their stakeholders, management must analyze and process information from both inside and outside the company in a comprehensive manner. Hence, the M&A decision-making process of management is a psychological process of collecting and processing information related to M&A activities. Then, drawing on the research results of psychology research on motivation can help us gain a more comprehensive and in-depth understanding of M&A motivation.

Psychology defines motivation as the innate drive that causes, sustains, and moves an individual's activity toward a specific goal, manifested in the awareness that the individual has developed a need to initiate the occurrence of the individual's behavior. According to psychology, motivation is formed under the action of a need as the fundamental internal drive and various external incentives.

Psychology refers to the internal drive, an inner drive to restore homeostasis due to a lack or imbalance. For enterprises, Michael Porter's famous "Five Forces" model shows that enterprises competing in a fierce market are under constant pressure from new competitors, the threat of substitutes, buyer bargaining power, seller bargaining power, and competition among existing competitors. Each of these pressure leads to a state of imbalance, then the management is driven to change this imbalance to achieve its goals of survival, growth, and profitability, and M&A is one of the ways to change this imbalance. If the M&A is successfully implemented, the company will expand its scale, strengthen its products and services, have wider distribution channels, lower procurement costs, and gain an advantageous position in the competition. For monopolistic or oligopolistic, M&A can also reduce the number of competitors and thus gain monopoly gains. All these benefits make companies under the competition pressure have the will to change the imbalance and thus create an internal drive that gives rise to the M&A motivation.

However, whether or not a company goes through with an M&A is often determined not only by internal drivers but also by a comprehensive analysis of the company's internal and external environment, i.e., certain triggers are also needed. A trigger, in psychology, is a stimulus that satisfies an individual's needs. In the case of M&A motivation, inducements are those external conditions that can satisfy a firm's need to make an acquisition. For example, western scholars have found that inter-firm M&A increases when the capital markets are high and decreases when they are low, showing a homogeneous trend. This phenomenon occurs mainly due to the tendency of firms to be overvalued (undervalued) when the capital market is high (low), and this tendency affects the firm's M&A behavior.[1] A factor that positively influences a firm's M&A behavior is called a positive trigger for M&A motivation. Conversely, it is called a negative trigger for M&A motivation. In the above example, a high capital market is a positive trigger for M&A motivation, then a low capital market is a negative trigger for M&A motivation. For example, although M&A is a corporate behavior, it is often regulated by specific laws and policies, and once the laws and policies are changed or deregulated, it can objectively stimulate corporate M&A behavior. Then, deregulation is also a positive trigger for M&A motivation.

Based on the above analysis, enterprises, as the competition subjects in the market, are influenced by their drive and external inducements, and various factors determine the motivations of M&A. In the academic field of M&A, scholars have developed many mature research results on the various M&A motivations of enterprises. However, considering that the motivations of enterprises are often not unique, it is inevitable to "miss the forest for the trees" only from a certain aspect, which may lead to incomplete research conclusions. Therefore, referring to the research results of psychology, this chapter analyzes M&A motivation from the two aspects of drive and incentive, and comprehensively considers the factors affecting M&A motivation to build the motivation system for M&A.

2.3.1 Motivation Caused by Internal Drive

Business-level M&A and firm-level M&A will build a new economic network structure different from the original business or firm. With the help of the new economic network structure, internally driven motivations for M&A include the pursuit of synergies, the pursuit of market power, risk reduction, industrial organization, and the acquisition of premium assets of the target companies.

---

[1] When the capital markets are depressed, as listed companies become relatively cheap acquisitions of listed companies by non-listed companies increase as a result.

2.3.1.1 Pursuit Synergies

Typically, synergies from M&A are divided into operational synergies, management synergies, and financial synergies. M&A can also obtain intangible synergies, which we will discuss further in the section related to M&A synergies.

(1) Operational synergies

The pursuit of operational synergies is the most common motivation for M&A and is widely recognized by theoretical and practical communities. It is not only because the effects of M&A, such as lower operating costs and lower overhead, are often intuitive, but also because the synergies generated by M&A can be well explained by economic theory and methods. Neoclassical economic theory assumes that there are economies of scale and that, before M&A, a firm's activities do not meet the potential requirements for achieving economies of scale, including economies of scale in production that reduce costs horizontally, economies of scale that reduce transaction costs vertically, and economies of scale in specific management functions. The most classical economic answer to the motivation for M&A is that the firm's size can be expanded and adjusted to achieve optimal economies of scale or scope through M&A.

(i) Horizontal M&A to achieve economy of scale

The neoclassical theory of the firm assumes that the firm assumes the function of pooling and organizing social resources to produce socially desired goods. Firms produce according to the production and cost functions, and they always maximize output and minimize unit cost at a given level of inputs and technology. The activities of enterprises are characterized by the pursuit of efficiency, and social resources always flow to the most efficient enterprises. Therefore, in the allocation of social resources, enterprises always seek to obtain as many products as possible with fewer inputs.

The general form of the production function can be written as $Q = f\ (N, L, K, E)$ Among them:

N for land;

L for labor;

K for capital;

E for entrepreneurial talent.

The neoclassical theory of the firm assumes that land and entrepreneurial talent are given in the short run. The production function then takes the simplified form of $Q = f\ (L, K)$.

Given a firm's production function, if the market price of input factors of production and the production price of the produced product is assumed to be given, the firm will then make a choice between input and output levels based on the profit maximization principle. Since the cost theory of neoclassical economics defines the difference between constant cost and variable cost, variable cost increases year-on-year with the increase of production quantity, while constant cost is constant in the short term, so with the gradual increase of production quantity, there will be a gradual decreasing process of constant cost apportioned to individual products, and the average cost of products is also decreasing at this time. But this process will not be infinite, because there is a proportional relationship between the factors of production input of the neoclassical enterprise theory of production function. When the production quantity of the enterprise increases to a certain point, the average cost of the enterprise will begin to appear to rise again. From the above discussion, it can be seen that there exists a period in which the cost of production decreases as the size of the enterprise increases, and neoclassical enterprise theory refers to this phenomenon as economies of scale. With the development of the social division of labor and specialized cooperation, the importance of economies of scale has gradually emerged, and the pursuit of economies of scale increasingly permeates various economic activities.

Economies of scale can be divided into three levels according to the degree of concentration of production factors in enterprises and the number of inputs and outputs. The first level is the economy of scale for a single product; the second level is the economy of scale at the factory level; the third level is the economy of scale at the multi-factory level. The simplest multi-factory level economy of scale is where a firm or company replicates factory producing the same product one by one so that the scale expands and the level of output increases, resulting in a progressively lower cost for the firm or company. This is the case studied by neoclassical economics regarding the envelope where the long-run cost curve is the lowest point of the short-run cost curve. When multiple factories produce an increased variety of products, the economics of multiple factories is also often referred to as economies of scope. When there are economies of scale and scope at the multi-factory level, the total cost is greater when the products are produced separately in separate factories than when they are produced in multiple plants belonging to the same firm.

At the level of the factory-scale economy, enterprises can supplement and adjust the assets of factories through mergers to achieve the requirements of optimal economic scale; mergers can also concentrate on many single-variety production in one factory, thus achieving the requirements of specialized production. On some occasions, mergers can effectively solve the separation of various production processes caused by specialization, reduce losses in the production process, and make full use of production capacity. At the level of enterprise economies of scale, mergers can save management costs; individual enterprises can specialize production and services for different customers or markets, greatly reducing marketing costs; large enterprises can concentrate enough funds for research and development of new products and adoption of new technologies, and through mergers and expansion of enterprise-scale the enterprises have greater ability to control its cost, price, production technologies, the source of capital and customer's purchasing behavior, reduce business risks, improve its relationship with the government, thus improving the enterprise's ability of to survive and grow. It should be noted that economies of scale are not more economical the larger the scale is, when the scale is large enough, it will reduce management efficiency and increase management costs.

Neoclassical economics has strong explanatory power for horizontal M&A. To obtain scale economy, firms are motivated to expand their scale, and the faster way to expand their scale is through M&A. Since the economies of scale in neoclassical economics come from the expansion of the scale of production of the same product, neoclassical economics can only explain M&A behavior for horizontal M&A and lacks explanatory power for other types of M&A behavior. Neoclassical economics interprets M&A behavior based on non-economics of scale as firms seeking to achieve monopoly rather than efficiency (i.e., firms acquire to pursue, maintain, and strengthen their market position). This explanation also has its failings; real economic practice suggests that it is efficiency, not monopoly power, that ultimately determines the size of a firm. Economic historian Chandler's study of historical facts shows that if the expansion of scale does not increase the efficiency of a firm, then such expansion of scale cannot be maintained; and if the expansion of scale increases the efficiency of the firm, then the incentive to expand is unstoppable by any already existing monopoly power. Chandler's conclusion undoubtedly provides a counterfactual to the explanation of neoclassical economics for M&A behavior based on no-seeking economies of scale, which also suggests that neoclassical economics is only better able to explain the horizontal M&A phenomenon.

(ii) Vertical M&A to reduce transaction costs

Transaction cost theory began with Coase and was further developed by Williamson and others. Transaction cost theory suggests that M&A is due to efficiency reasons. Specifically, M&A is a replacement for market coordination by internal organizational coordination to reduce transaction costs. Transaction cost theory offers an explanation of vertically integrated M&A using the concepts of "asset specificity", "transaction uncertainty" and "transaction frequency": The higher the specificity of the assets involved, the higher the transaction cost. The higher the asset specificity, the stronger the uncertainty, the higher the transaction frequency, then the higher the potential cost of market transaction, and the greater the possibility of vertical merger and acquisition; when the cost of the market transactions is greater than the cost of coordination within the firm, vertical M&A will occur.

Most economists, Bain among them, have recognized to varying degrees that vertical mergers and acquisitions by firms, especially by large firms with market power, strengthen the market power of large firms and thus affirm the monopoly motive of vertical mergers and acquisitions. Bain (1968) argues that the apparent savings of integration come from the physical or technologies of the production process in individual plants, such as the thermal savings of iron and steel integration. Conversely, the apparent motive for vertical integration without material or technological aspects is a monopoly, and vertical integration can be employed as a strategic tool to disadvantage non-integrated competitors. Bain's "technological decision" explanation of vertical mergers has been challenged by several economists who argue that Bain is blind to the savings caused by non- technical factors and that the monopoly hypothesis is incomplete in explaining vertical M&A that lacks close technical ties. Based on this, transaction cost theory has reinterpreted the motivation for vertical M&A in terms of savings in transaction costs.

Transaction cost theory takes transaction costs as the basic concept and uses alternative and marginal approaches to study why firms exist, the scaling up and boundaries of firms, and the mutual substitution relationship between the firm system and the market mechanism. Transaction cost theory is divided into two main parts: the indirect pricing theory, which explains why firms can reduce their transaction costs, and the asset specificity theory, which explains how firms can reduce their transaction costs. M&As are a basic form of corporate expansion, usually accompanied by changes in corporate boundaries. According to the Coase School of thought, the creation of firms and their size (boundaries), division of labor, and degree of specialization can be explained by transaction costs. In particular, the expansion of a firm's size necessarily involves a method of expansion and corporate M&A is one of the available options, so transaction costs are linked to corporate M&A, and transaction cost theory has become the research tool to analyze the motives of vertical M&A.

There is a consensus in the transaction cost theory explanation of vertical mergers that considers the savings in transaction costs as the main motivation for vertical mergers, or vertical integration of firms, thus including the savings in non-technical factors. Under this analysis, monopoly acquisition is no longer an important motivation for vertical integration, but merely a by-product. Although transaction cost theory has been more successful in explaining the causes of this phenomenon of vertical integration of firms, the purpose of vertical integration is still one-sided only from the perspective of transaction cost savings, and the market behavior of enterprises is driven and influenced by the interests of many parties, whether the vertical merger will produce monopoly market consequences need to be further explored.

Theoretically, orthodox microeconomics before Coase was collectively known as price theory because it focused on the mechanism of price action, which was considered a signal for resource allocation, and the optimal allocation of resources could be achieved through the regulation of the price mechanism. Coase raised doubts about this, as the allocation of resources within the firm is not regulated by prices, and his 1937 article The Nature of the Firm explains why there exists an organization that does not use price regulation to allocate resources. Coase noted that "The main reason for the profitable establishment of the enterprise seems to be that there is a cost in using the price mechanism, and the most obvious cost of 'organizing' production through the price mechanism is all the work of discovering relative prices... by forming some authority ('entrepreneur') to dictate resources, certain market operating costs are saved." The market operating costs that Coase refers to here are transaction costs, which include at least the following four costs: (a) the information cost of discovering relative prices; (b) the negotiation cost of the contracting process; (c) the cost of long-term contracts that reduce flexibility and thus cause increased risk; and (d) the cost imposed by the government on market transactions, such as taxes.

Subsequently, in his article The Problem of Social Costs, Coase elaborated on the extent of transaction costs again in general, "To conduct market transactions, it is necessary to discover who wishes to conduct the negotiations that lead to the transaction, to conclude the contract, and to supervise the fulfillment of its terms. This work is often extremely costly." The empirical studies of John. J. Voorhees and North also show the magnitude of transaction costs; and 45% of the U. S. gross national product in 1970 was consumed in transaction costs. A large reason for generating vertical mergers and acquisitions lies in reducing the high transaction costs. Coase's explanation of the motivation for mergers and acquisitions is based on his understanding of the nature of the firm. According to Coase, the firm is a substitute for the market mechanism, and the market and the firm are two interchangeable means of resource allocation. Firms are created to save transaction costs and it is less expensive to use administrative means within the firm than to use impersonal price mechanisms for transactions. The expansion or contraction of the firm, i.e., the boundary between the firm and the market, depends on the comparison between the firm's internal organization costs and the market's transaction costs. It follows that vertical mergers and acquisitions can transform the original buyer–seller relationship in the factor or commodity markets into an administrative transaction relationship within the same enterprise group, thus reducing some market transaction costs. However, intra-firm market transactions and savings in transaction costs can increase internal administrative costs, but if the reduced market transaction costs are greater than the increased internal administrative costs, then vertical mergers are economically feasible. Based on Coase's understanding of the nature of the firm, we can assume that the motivation for vertical M&A is to reduce transaction costs and that the boundary condition for a firm's vertical M&A is that the reduced transaction costs are equal to the increased internal overhead costs.

Since Coase, Williamson's theory of transaction costs has been refined more systematically. These refined theories provide more detailed and convincing explanations of corporate mergers. Williamson divides transaction costs into two categories: one is "transaction elements" involving the market structure and environment, which refers to the size of market uncertainty and the number of potential counterparties arising from changes in market structure and environment. It includes two aspects, market uncertainty and fractional negotiation issues. The other category involves the "human elements" that are prevalent in human nature, i.e., limited rationality and opportunism.

Williamson develops Coase's theory that explains the relationship between firm-market substitution in terms of the concept of transaction costs, focusing on the motivations of firms for market substitution that constitute the motivation for mergers and acquisitions of competing firms. Williamson argues that the combined effects of market uncertainty and limited rationality increase the cost of long-term contracts; the combined effects of fractional bargaining and opportunism in turn increase the cost of a range of short-term contracts. Under these circumstances, firms then find that the cost of transfers through intra-firm may be lower than market transaction costs, thus motivating the choice of vertical integration. A comparative study of corporate mergers and acquisitions in several U. S. and European countries finds that uncertainty avoidance is a determinant of mergers and acquisitions, particularly in vertical and hybrid mergers and acquisitions.

Williamson analyzes the issue of asset specificity in detail. He summarizes the factors affecting transaction costs as asset specialization, transaction uncertainty, and frequency of transactions, while the main determinants of transaction costs lie in asset specialization and the opportunistic behavior it causes. Asset specialization refers to the dependence of one or both parties on a transaction that, as the transaction develops and becomes more closely tied to the other party, the scope of the product of the assets he or she possesses becomes increasingly narrow and gradually can only be adapted to the requirements of the other party. Asset specialization is a product of the specialized division of labor, which, while reducing production costs, causes an increase in transaction costs, and when asset specialization occurs to a very high degree in a particular transaction, both parties to the transaction are exposed to extremely high risk. The asset specialization counterparty, whose asset conversion costs and opportunity costs rise, forms a monopoly power over the counterparty for that kind of economic activity, raising the risk of contract default. In this case, the party with a high degree of specialization will increase transaction costs to be able to create a more rigid contract that will be more binding afterward. For this reason, both parties to the transaction will want to anticipate the future as much as possible before the contract is signed, sign the best possible transaction contract, and constantly monitor the transaction process, while at the end of the transaction process, they will promote the performance of the contract in their favor through various means. All of this will lead to significant transaction costs. In this case, firms that need certain intermediate inputs tend to turn outsourcing into in-house production, i.e., to perform mergers and acquisitions of firms that produce upstream products to gain complete domination over the transaction process. The higher the degree of asset specialization, the greater the potential transaction costs in the market and the greater the likelihood of vertical mergers and acquisitions.

In summary, we can argue that the motivation for vertical mergers is to eliminate or reduce opportunistic behavior due to asset specialization.

Grossman and Hart (1986) point out that it is the incompleteness of the contract that determines transaction cost. A perfect contract eliminates opportunistic behavior, but the reality of the economy is so full of uncertainty and the cost of achieving clear ownership is so high that contractual perfection is objectively impossible. The firm's emergence is because when contracts are incomplete, vertical integration can eliminate or reduce the opportunistic behavior caused by asset specificity. The firm's essence is a vertically integrated entity resulting from incomplete contracts between successive production processes. Based on the nature of the enterprise, it can be argued that the motivation of vertical M&A is not to sign a complete contract to eliminate the opportunistic behavior caused by asset specificity, but to eliminate the opportunistic behavior by transferring the transaction into the enterprise through M&A.

Zhang Wuchang further develops the transaction cost theory and gives new boundary conditions for M&A. He argues that firms are not created to replace markets, but merely to replace the product markets with factor markets, or to replace one contract with another. While vertical mergers eliminate the opportunistic behavior of the market that exists in the product market, they bring the opportunistic behavior of the firm that exists in the factor market into the firm.

When a firm acquires another firm and converts its purchase in the spot market into its production, the firm must purchase those factors of production that the target firm had purchased, thus creating new opportunistic behavior. It follows that the boundary condition for vertical M&A is that the reduction in costs associated with the reduction in the market equals the increase in costs required by the increase in the opportunistic behavior of the firm.

With the help of transaction cost theory in modern business theory, we have theoretically analyzed the motivations and boundary conditions of vertical mergers and acquisitions and concluded that the main motive of vertical mergers and acquisitions is to replace inter-firm transaction costs with inter-firm planning and coordination through vertical integration to reduce the total costs. This explanation of the motivation for vertical M&A is reasonable. However, from Williamson's transaction cost theory analysis of the motivation of vertical M&A, it can be seen that the traditional study of asset specialization is unilinear, mainly referring to the interdependence of assets between upstream and downstream firms. However, with the development of modern science and technology and the rapid industrialization of scientific and technological achievements, many industries are transforming from capital-intensive to technology-intensive, and the integration characteristics of the technological products and the fragmentation of the production of each part of the products have increased the difficulty and cost of product integration, and the complexity of asset specialization has been increasing. Therefore, the analysis of the motivation of vertical M&A by applying transaction cost theory needs to be further extended so that it can reasonably explain the vertical M&A behavior among enterprises occurring in reality.

Modern technology products are usually the integrated application of multiple technologies, a combination or integration of system products, whose production needs to be completed in a modern form of cooperation between multiple manufacturers of product collaboration. The product chain is no longer a simple "upstream" to "downstream" production and processing process, but a combination of several specific functions to form a comprehensive function of the final product or called system products. On the one hand, due to the possible existence of technical secrecy and monopoly, system products have the characteristics of multi- vendor product synergy, requiring a variety of technical standards and interfaces in a unified system, which increases the cost of information search and negotiation costs when signing contracts, and also increases the possibility of incomplete contracts. On the other hand, this multi-vendor cooperation model also aggravates the characteristics of asset specificity. The more vendors involved means more risk because, for any vendor, the asset exclusivity is more pronounced from being subject to one to being subject to multiple vendors. Combining these two reasons, the incentive of vertical integration is further reinforced by the fact that vendors try to reduce transaction costs caused by polyglot negotiations and weaken the risks associated with asset specialization through vertical mergers and acquisitions. From the perspective of benefits, the companies also have the dominance of the other party's monopoly technology when the M&A occurs, and the integration process of providing a full set of services after the M&A is easy to realize and reduces the cost of system products, thus increasing the vendor's benefits.

(iii) Complementary strengths

There is also a theory of complementary advantages in the theory of operational synergy, which believes that M&A can enable the mutual sharing of corporate advantages between the acquirer and the target to achieve complementary advantages and improve competitiveness. In a realistic, imperfectly competitive market, an enterprise may possess competitive advantages that others do not have, such as advanced management experience, proprietary technology, brand equity, product differentiation, and unique marketing technique. Corporate mergers and acquisitions may allow the acquired party to take advantage of the acquirer's competitive advantages or the acquirer to take advantage of the acquired party's competitive advantages. The purpose of M&A is to promote and facilitate the sharing of corporate advantages among enterprises, either to bring into play the acquirer's competitive advantages, to exploit the acquired party's competitive advantages, or to complement the advantages between enterprises and synergistic effects in management, finance, marketing, etc. Therefore, M&A can enable competitive advantages to be mutually utilized, brought into play among enterprises, and improve core competitiveness through resource sharing and complementary advantages.

The role of complementary advantages is most evident in the potent combination. When both parties conducting the merger occupy a considerable share in the industry, both have strong economic strength, the financial advantages, material advantages, talent advantages, technological advantages, and market advantages of both parties are combined and complimentary, making the merged enterprise more vital competitive ability and monopoly position. For example, in 1989, the merger of two U. S. electric utilities—Utah Power & Light and PacifiCorp. Utah Power's peak demand is for air conditioning in the summer, while PacifiCorp, which serves customers in California, is for heating in the winter. The network of the two companies' power generation systems generates an estimated US$45 million in annual synergies; then again, on September 13, 2000, Chase Manhattan Corporation, the third-largest bank in the United States, announced that it would acquire J. P. Morgan, the fifth-largest bank in the United States for US$33.2 billion, creating J. P. Morgan Chase & Co, with assets totaling more than US$660 billion, one of the largest U. S. financial industries at the time. Chase Manhattan specializes in commercial banking but is dwarfed by investment banking, in which J. P. Morgan has a large global presence and is particularly skilled. As a result, Chase's acquisition of J. P. Morgan is a complementary combination of strong business, particularly in Europe, where the combined firm's presence is strengthened, and J. P. Morgan Chase & Co.'s competitiveness is greatly enhanced.

(2) Management synergies

The concept of management synergy is derived from the theory of differential efficiency, which believes that the motivation of M&A lies in the difference in management efficiency between superior and inferior enterprises and that acquiring other enterprises to carry out "management release". By acquiring another company, the management resources of the company can be fully utilized, and the efficiency of the target company will not only be increased to the same level but also be greater than the sum of the output of the two companies, which is called "1+1 > 2". In layman's terms, if the management efficiency of company A is better than company B, then after company the merger of company A with company B, the management efficiency of company B will be raised to the standard of company A, and the efficiency of the two companies will be promoted due to the merging of the two into one. That is, the most efficient company will merge with the less efficient target company and gain by improving the efficiency of the target company, which implies that the acquirer has surplus management resources. The theory has two basic assumptions:

(i) If the acquirer has surplus management resources that can be easily spilled over, M&A activities will not be necessary; however, if its management as a team is efficient and indivisible, or if it has economies of scale, then it will be feasible to make full use of its surplus management resources through an M&A transaction.
(ii) For the target company, its management inefficiencies can be improved by the involvement of external managers and increased investment in management resources.

In M&A activity, if the acquirer has efficient management resources that can be easily spilled over, especially when the acquirer has an excess of efficient management resources, the acquiring companies will be motivated to acquire to fully utilize this resource. By acquiring companies with good assets that are only underperforming due to poor management, the acquirer's efficient management resources are imported, the target company's efficiency is increased, and the efficiency of both parties improved.

(3) Financial synergies

Financial synergies refer to the various financial benefits that the merger brings to the company. Such benefits are achieved not as a result of increased production efficiency, but as a purely pecuniary benefit resulting from capital efficiency and tax laws, accounting treatment practices, and the laws inherent in securities trading.

(i) Declining cost of capital

One theory of hybrid mergers suggests that a purely hybrid merger occurs when a firm in a low-demand growth industry (i.e., where demand growth in that industry is lower than that of the economy as a whole) acquires another firm operating in a high-demand growth industry and that the motivation for such a merger is to use the acquirer's lower-cost internal cash to lower the cost of capital for the acquiree, thereby capturing the opportunities available in the acquiree's industry. The theory implies a process of financial resource reallocation—a shift of resources from slow-growing demand industries in which the acquirer is located to high-demand-growing industries in which the acquiree is located.

There are three general reasons for the decrease in the cost of capital.

The first is the co-insurance effect. When the cash flows of two firms are not positively correlated, the likelihood of bankruptcy of the combined firm is not positively correlated, the likelihood of bankruptcy of the combined firm after the merger is greatly reduced, and the earnings stream tends to stabilize, making it less likely that leaders will suffer losses. The direct result of this effect is an increase in the ability of the firm to raise debt. Generally, the cost of debt financing is lower than that of common stock financing, bringing down the cost of capital for the firm.

The second is the difference between internal and external financing. Mergers and acquisitions can internalize investment opportunities in the target firm's industry and convert the firm's external financing into internal financing, which increases financing synergy and reduces financing risk because internal financing is less costly than external financing. Myers and Majluf (1984) studied the problem of corporate equity financing from the perspective of information asymmetry. In their model, investors do not know the value of the firm's assets and new projects in advance, while the firm's original shareholders know. If investors have less information about the value of the firm's assets than the firm's insiders, then equity is mispriced by the market. An underprice of equity can cause investors to seek a lower NPV for new projects, resulting in a net loss to the original shareholders. In this case, even a positive NPV investment project will be rejected by the original shareholders. This underinvestment can only be avoided by issuing securities not significantly undervalued by the market to finance the new project. Therefore, internal funds or riskless debt, or even less risky debt are preferable to equity financing. They obtained two important conclusions: in the case of information asymmetry, one is that corporate financing should follow a certain order, firstly, internal funds, followed by debt financing, and lastly, the option of issuing additional new shares; and the other is that financing by issuing additional new shares will cause the corporate stock price to fall. Myers (1984) refers to the ranking of the advantages and disadvantages of new project financing as a "pecking order".

The third is economies of scale in the cost of issuing and trading securities. Part of the economies of scale can be attributed to the fixed costs associated with the production and dissemination of information, and mergers can achieve economies of scale in information. More importantly, in the capital market, large firms have certain specific financing advantages over small firms, which lower their capital cost. While small companies have to pay higher risk premiums and liquidity premiums to obtain funds, large companies, which have proven their profitability over a long period and have won investors' trust, pay relatively lower premiums to raise funds and are more likely to obtain them.

Mergers and acquisitions of listed companies in China do not have a strong sequence of horizontal acquisitions, vertical acquisitions, and mixed acquisitions, but have strong mixed acquisition characteristics,[2] where the important reason is that the financing cost of non-listed companies is much higher than that of listed

[2] See Center for China Mergers & Acquisitions Research, Beijing Jiaotong University, *China Mergers & Acquisitions Yearbook* (2004 to 2016).

companies, and the savings in capital costs greatly exceed the operating synergies effect generated by the merger.

(ii) Reasonable tax avoidance

Taxation is a factor that has a significant impact on business decisions. Tax rates and tax brackets on capital gains, such as assets, dividend income, and interest income, vary greatly from country to country. This difference that allows companies to achieve reasonable tax avoidance and increase their free cash flow through mergers and acquisitions, which is an important source of financial synergies.

The financial synergy theory of reasonable tax avoidance is based on the fact that a firm with accumulated tax losses and tax deductions can merge with a profitable firm to make full use of the benefits of deferred taxation of losses, allowing the merged firm can achieve reasonable tax avoidance. The theory implicitly assumes the premium that the tax deductions generated by corporate M&A activities outweigh the costs of the merger, but this occurs only under certain conditions. Specifically, the merging firms use their higher financial leverage capabilities than they used before the merger, and the post-merger benefits more from tax shelter.

Lintner (1971) focuses on the situations that create an incentive for merger avoidance, i.e., when the acquirer or the acquiree has tax loss credits or tax credits that will not have a foreseeable opportunity to be utilized shortly.

Lewellen (1971) points out that the diversification of income sources, especially when the income of two firms is not perfectly correlated, can reduce risk and allow for the appropriate use of more liabilities, and that an increase in borrowed capital can also take advantage of interest charges. Due to the existence of interest tax shelters, an increase in a company's debt capital will lead to a consequent increase in the company's market value. Nevertheless, diversification of revenue sources is not considered a financial motivation for intra-industry M&A, but rather for inter-industry M&A. Kim and McConnell (1977) studied Lewellen's hypothesis using 39 M&As that occurred from January 1, 1960 to December 31, 1973. In the sample, the acquirer must acquire 100% of the target company's shares. Not only that, the target company's assets should be at least 10% of the acquirer's assets. The sample includes only the same publicly traded M&A examples before the M&A and between 24 months of the M&A completion. The mergers and acquisitions in the sample are all those classified by the Federal Trade Commission as conglomerates. Contrastive tests and least squares were used in the analysis to calculate excess returns for the overall sample and subsamples. Leverage was also measured to determine whether post-merger firms increased their leverage. Three leverage metrics were used: (a) long-term bond par value/average market share price; (b) all bond par value/average market share price; (c) all bond par value/total assets. Their study supports Lewellen's theory in that. First, they find no evidence that M&A completes the transfer of wealth from shareholders to bondholders, and do not find any excess return to bondholders at a statistically significant level; second, by applying the leverage metrics above, they find that the post-merger firms could take advantage of higher financial leverage compared to the simple sum of two firms. Since no positive or negative excess returns are found, Kim and McConnell argue that this is because the reduction in bond risk associated with the diversification of cash flows is offset by the increased risk associated with the use of higher leverage by the acquirer.

Asquith and Kim (1982) studied the returns on pre-and post-merger for 50 firms from January 1, 1960 to December 31, 1978. Their sample included only firms classified as conglomerates by the U. S. Federal Trade Commission, and such mergers typically occurred inter-industry rather than intra-industry. Asquith and Kim argue that many previous studies have explored returns to shareholders as a result of mergers and acquisitions rather than returns to bondholders and that these studies generally assume that any excess shareholders returns are the result of wealth transfer of wealth from bondholders to shareholders rather than any real increase in firm value due to synergies or financial effects. The results of study of Asquith and Kim do not provide any evidence that M&A has a positive or negative impact on bondholders. Not only that, but they also do not find any evidence of wealth transfer from shareholders to bondholders. Thus excess returns accrue to shareholders, but not at the expense of bondholders.

Bruner (1988) studied 75 takeover plans that occurred between 1955 and 1979 with the object of determining whether the capital structure was a motivating factor in mergers and acquisitions. Of the 75 acquisition plans, only 49 were successful. Bruner tested three hypotheses including the capital structure of the target firm and the acquirer: (a) he proposed that the acquirer's financial leverage is slack-rich and the target firm's financial leverage is slack-poor; (b) he wanted to examine whether the acquirer's financial leverage changes significantly during the acquisition period changes; and (c) he tries to determine whether there is a necessary link between the leverage of the target firm, the acquirer, and the financial gains obtained in the acquisition. The study results showed that the acquirer had less financial leverage before the acquisition compared to other firms in the same look. There is also no evidence found in the study to suggest that financial leverage decreases before attempted acquisitions. The acquirer becomes more leveraged and this high level of leverage is maintained for at least one year after the acquirer or the firm in the sample. The financial leverage of the target firm in a successful M&A is much greater than that of either the acquirer or the other firms in the sample. It can be seen that in a successful M&A, the acquirer has less financial leverage than his competitor, while the target company has more financial leverage than the equivalent company. It is found that as the financial leverage of the target company changes, the overall return to the target company's shareholders also differs significantly, but this only happens after the M&A announcement and not on the day of the M&A announcement. The study also found a significant relationship between the acquirer's total earnings and changes in the acquirer's level of financial leverage. In conclusion, the above findings support the theory that firms use capital structure development as a motivation for M&A.

Although the tax avoidance effect through M&A is very intuitive and readily accepted, there is also some evidence to support it. However, follow-up studies conducted by many scholars have shown that tax effects have a limited impact on M&A activity and are not the major motivation of M&A.

Gilson, Scholes and Wolfson (1988) comprehensively discuss this. When tax-related mergers are likely to occur (because TRA 1986 replaced the vast majority of merger tax benefits), they focus on three main acquisition tax benefits under the pre-1986 tax act. These three tax benefits include increased leverage, net operating loss carry forwards, and increased basis in acquired assets. Gilson, Scholes and Wolfson argue that in an efficient market with low transaction costs, mergers are not required to earn these types of tax benefits because companies can capture tax benefits through other means of asset and financing restructuring. For example, there is no clear answer to why a firm cannot achieve leverage on its own if it acquires without issuing bonds and repurchasing stock.

The empirical study of tax effects confirms the predictive analysis of Gilson, Scholes and Wolfson—less than 10% of merger transactions have significant tax factors. The case studies yielded similar results. Mergers do not increase leverage. While net operating losses are present in some mergers, they are a very small part of the merger. Finally, while an increase in asset base price can affect depreciation expense and subsequent cash flow increases, this appears to have little impact on merger activity. Moreover, even if the tax effect is significant, it is still not the main driver of merger transactions (Hayn, 1989).

A possible qualification of the tax role is in privately conducted M&A transactions, such as leveraged buyouts (LBOs) and management buyouts (MBOs). The study of Kaplan (1989) on the impact of tax factors on MBOs found that the tax benefits of MBOs can be explained as an important part of the premium paid to the target company's shareholders. Initially, LBOs and MBOs had up to 90% financial structure. While the tax savings resulting from such high debt ratios were caused by deductions of interest expense, subsequent studies have shown that the liabilities were paid off quickly. In some cases, some companies continue to remain privatized and pay down debt with retained earnings. In other cases, firms often go public again within 3 to 5 years (Muscarella & Vetsuypens, 1990). The proceeds obtained from the public listing are usually used to pay off forward liabilities. All this proves that tax savings due to high leverage do not significantly impact. It is also worth noting that due to the deduction of interest expense, companies that continue to operate privately can generate similar tax savings can be generated by financing the recapitalization of companies that continue to operate privately due to the deduction of interest charges.

2.3.1.2 Pursuit of Market Power

Market power is a firm's ability to influence and control the price of its products. A strong market force can enable enterprises to obtain a certain degree of monopoly rights, which is conducive to maintaining monopoly profits and original competitive advantages. Stigler (1950) argues that inter-firm mergers and acquisitions can increase control over the market. Firstly, by merging and acquiring enterprises in the same industry, the scale of the dominant enterprise is expanded while the competitors are reduced, and the dominant enterprise increases its control over the market, which leads to market monopoly; secondly, even if no monopoly is formed, the scale effect expanded due to M&A will become a barrier to market entry.

This theory suggests that after expanding their scale through M&A, firms form a certain degree of market monopoly regarding product output, sales, and raw material procurement, thereby increasing their market dominance. To ease the pressure of market competition, M&A can directly place competitors in the market under their control, increase industry concentration, improve industry structure, and enhance the firm's monopolistic control over the business environment. When an industry is controlled by one or a few companies, it can effectively reduce the intensity of competition and enable companies in the industry to maintain high- profit margins. As the scale of production expands, the demand of enterprises for raw materials, labor, and marketing intermediaries grows, causing the pattern of supply and demand in the market for these factors to change. A few enterprises monopolize the demand for these elements, thus increasing the ability of these enterprises to control their suppliers and sales channels. Mergers and acquisitions can also expand the field of branding and influence consumer perceptions, thereby increasing a company's market visibility.

The gain from M&A is the inevitable result of the requirements of capital concentration, which leads to inter-firm complicity and monopoly on the market. The expansion of the absolute size of the enterprise allows the enterprise to have sufficient financial resources to engage in price wars with the original market competitors, forcing the rivals to withdraw from the field and monopolize the market, achieving the purpose of obtaining monopoly profits.

In contrast to the efficiency motive (reducing unit costs), the direct aim of the market power-seeking motive is to increase unit revenues.

2.3.1.3 Reduce Risk

Companies competing in the marketplace need to control risk while pursuing revenue. One effective way to control risk is to diversify. While diversification may not always be achieved through acquisition, but can also be achieved through internal growth, time is often an important factor, and diversification and expansion can be achieved quickly through acquiring other companies.

Diversification strategy refers to the long-term business policy of seeking to expand and acquire markets and create benefits in multiple related and unrelated fields. Diversification is divided into related and unrelated diversification, and the concept of economy of scope is often used to explain related diversification. In contrast, unrelated diversification is generally motivated by the consideration of finding new opportunities, combining businesses, improving returns, and reducing risks. There are several reasons for companies to diversify their as follows.

(1) Making full use of and developing a company's existing resources is the most typical reason for a company to diversify and expand. At any given time, most companies have slack resources, which may be human resources, financial resources, physical resources, etc. At the same time, many of the valuable resources owned by a company are heterogeneous or contained within the firm,

making it difficult for a company to sell or lease its slack resources. Although there are some divisible resources in the company, the higher transaction costs or the uniqueness of the resources make them more valuable in the current environment than in other conditions. As a result, the company can only increase the level of return by keeping these resources within the business and applying them to new business areas through diversification and expansion.

(2) When a company operates several different but related products simultaneously, it may generate several improvements in economic efficiency. This savings resulting from increasing the variety of related products is an "economy of scope".

(3) Diversification can reduce risks and realize the comprehensive benefits of a diversified portfolio. The earnings of all enterprises always have a certain sensitivity to economic cycle fluctuations, but the products of various enterprises have different cycle changes. Therefore, an enterprise with large cycle changes can reduce the investment risk of the portfolio through a certain degree of risk offset under certain conditions, in addition to dispersing the risks specific to individual enterprises themselves, by merging with an enterprise with stable cycles.

(4) Another reason why companies pursue diversification is to seek new space for business growth. Within an industry, there are limits to business growth. The limits come from both market and legal aspects. In terms of market boundaries, when market concentration is high, it is very difficult for one company to continue to expand; from a legal perspective, government anti-monopoly legislation does not allow a single company to dominate within a certain market. Therefore, diversification is inevitable for a large company that wants to grow continuously. Mergers and acquisitions are the shortest routes to expansion and the most common way to diversify.

A mixed consortium formed by a mixed acquisition, characterized by diversified operations, is in more organizational parts on the factor market due to the common interests of the organizational parts, which are subordinated to the same entrepreneurial leadership, and the components change from multiple subjects to one subject on the factor market. Hybrid M&A provides an efficient and rapid way to diversify a company.

The third wave of mergers and acquisitions in the United States in the 1960s was characterized by a mix of mergers and acquisitions by large firms to diversify. After the first two waves of horizontal and vertical mergers and acquisitions, some large firms in the United States had achieved such a significant position and competitive advantage in the market that it was difficult for any other firm to enter or expand in the relevant industries. In addition, when the industry concentration is quite high, any one enterprise does not easily continue to expand because of the different enterprises in a certain industry, after the competition has formed a certain balance between the relationship. If one of them expands on its own, it is bound to affect other companies and cause retaliation from its rivals. Therefore, diversification through mixed mergers and acquisitions becomes a good option for companies in this situation. According to statistics, between 1948 and 1968, horizontal mergers between large manufacturing and mining companies fell from 31% to 6.8%, vertical mergers rose slightly from 10.3% to 11.4%, while mixed mergers rose from 5.2% to 24.3%. By injecting capital and key technologies (know-how) into the target companies, those well-managed acquirers established new sectors and achieved diversification goals.

2.3.1.4 Acquisition of Superior Assets of the Target Company

In the fierce market competition, successful enterprises often have advantages such as higher technology and management level, broad sales market, good brand, and even unique resources, etc. These advantages form the competitiveness that distinguishes them from other enterprises in the market and makes them invincible in the market competition.

However, suppose the advantages of enterprises in the aspects mentioned above only rely on their creation and accumulation. In that case, it is difficult to form them quickly, not to mention that an enterprise's premium assets, or core competencies, are unrepeatable and non-transferable. Establishing good brand requires long-term operation and a large amount of advertising investment, and the formation of enterprise proprietary technology and patents requires long- term technical accumulation and R&D support. Under the constraints of limited resources, enterprises need to rationally allocate existing resources to optimize benefits. When enterprises acquire advantageous assets through M&A more economical and faster than through internal cultivation, M&A is a more practical strategy.

In addition, the advantageous assets of enterprises are often integrated and exclusive, such as land use rights, mining rights, patented technologies, etc., which are challenging to acquire through market channels. At this time, the acquiring company can acquire the target company to acquire its advantageous assets.

The anti-M&A strategy of selling "crown jewels" can also illustrate from another perspective that acquiring the advantageous assets of the target company is a common motivation for M&A. Generally, the best-run companies or subsidiaries within a mixed company are known as "crown jewels". Such companies are in good condition in terms of asset value, profitability and development prospects, mainly including the following categories: assets that are quite profitable but seriously undervalued by the market, such as real estate, equipment, etc.; businesses or proprietary conditions that have promising growth prospects and are in a position to form mass production and have a high market share in a short period; and a business or division that poses a competitive threat to the acquirer's development or a threat to the supply and demand chain. In the face of the acquirer, if the target company cannot compete, to preserve the company's ownership, the best strategy is to sell the "crown jewels". Once the acquirer finds the acquisition unprofitable, it will lose interest in the target company.

2.3.1.5 Conducting Industrial Organization

According to the theory of industrial organization, companies often encounter many barriers to entry when seeking development in new production fields, such as sufficient funds to achieve an effective business scale necessary for new industry; technologies, professional information and patents required for effective entry; sales channels required for effective entry; after effective entry, it is faced with the high cost of user transposition due to product differences and cannot occupy the market; entering the international market needs to face high tariffs and various restrictions of the host country. These barriers are difficult to overcome in the short term using direct investment (greenfield), but can be effectively broken through by M&A. The M&A approach can also avoid the increase in market supply caused by the increase in production capacity brought about by new investments, ensure that the internal competition structure of the industry remains unchanged in the short term, and significantly reduce the possibility of price wars and mutual retaliation.

In explaining cross-border M&A activities, the theory of industrial organization has been widely used. In the international market, multinational companies often face high industrial barriers due to their unfamiliarity with the host country's market and the fierce competition in the existing international market; in the industrial policy, the host country's industrial policy has more restrictions on the entry of foreign capital, constituting a higher industrial entry policy barrier. For some industries that require a lot of capital investment, such as telecommunications, oil, etc., even large multinational companies with strong strength cannot enter the host country market through new construction but can only adopt the method of M&A investment (Yip,1982; Baldwin & Caves,1985). Here, although the industrial organization theory cannot fully explain the investment behavior of cross-border M&A (Yip,1982), this kind of exploration is great progress in theory, Because previous studies have focused only on the effects of firm characteristics, the host country's environmental characteristics, etc., on cross-border M&A, ignoring the research on the industry level.

2.3.2 Motivation Caused by External Incentive

2.3.2.1 The Emergence of Low-Priced Assets

M&A activity will occur when the market value of a target company does not reflect its intrinsic value or potential value for some reason. There are several general reasons why a company's market value is undervalued:

(1) The operation and management of the company fail to give full play to its potential;
(2) The acquirer has internal information about the true value of the target company that the external market does not have;

(3) The phenomenon of undervaluation of a company occurs due to the difference between the market value of an asset and its replacement cost caused by inflation. Two ratios are usually used to measure whether a company is undervalued: The first is the Tobin ratio, also known as the Q ratio, which is the ratio of the stock market value to the replacement cost. Tobin put forward this theory in 1977, which mainly clarified that M&A would be more likely to occur when the market value of corporate securities is lower than its replacement cost of capital without considering capital gains tax. If the Q ratio is less than 1, the acquisition will yield potential gains. For example, with a Q ratio of 0.6, even if the acquisition cost is 1.5 times the market value, and the total cost is only 90% of the asset's replacement cost, it is still profitable to acquire the company. The second is the value ratio, which is the ratio of the stock's market value to the asset's book value. If the market underestimates the value of the enterprise, it will become the target of acquisition by other enterprises.

In the early 1980s, it was cheaper for oil companies to acquire other oil companies to increase the reserves of oil wells than to explore oil fields separately, so Chevron Corporation purchased Gulf Oil Company, which not only reduced the investment cost, but also shortened the time of input and output. Compared with the cumbersome, time-consuming and labor-intensive application procedures for new construction, M&A show the characteristics of simple procedures. In this example, low-priced oil companies are the incentives for M&A activity, and the acquirer is more inclined to adopt the method of M&A.

2.3.2.2 The Emergence of Favorable Technical and Economic Conditions

In the book *Takeovers, Restructuring, and Corporate Governance*, J. Fred Weston et al. (2006) summarizes the revolutionary forces affecting merger activities from the perspective of primary technical and economic conditions, which give us good insights. Throughout history, it can be found that merger activities have always been related to the economic and cultural characteristics of specific periods and specific regions. The pace of growth in merger activity over the past 20 years has been closely linked to the top ten revolutionary forces.

(1) Technological change;
(2) The need for economies of scale, economies of scope, complementarity and technological catch-up;
(3) Globalization and free trade;
(4) Changes in industrial organization;
(5) New industries;
(6) Deregulation and new regulations;
(7) Most favorable economic and financial conditions over the past 20 years;
(8) Negative growth trends in certain individual economies and industries;
(9) Income and wealth spread unequally;

(10) Relatively high equity valuation during the 1990s.

Among all these revolutionary forces, the most important is technological change, which includes advances in computer technology, computer service technology, software, servers, and many information systems, including the Internet. Advances in communications and transportation have produced economic globalization. The euro, issued in 1999, became the sole currency of the 12 participating member states in 2002 and has continued to bring about the opening of borders and constraints throughout Europe. The growth of competitive forces has led to the deregulation of major industries such as financial services, aviation, broadcasting and medical services.

The second group of change factors is related to operational efficiency. Economies of scale allow many units to share large fixed-cost investments in machinery or computer systems. Economies of scope refer to the reduction of operating costs for related activities. In the information industry, economies of scope manifest themselves in the economization of microcomputer hardware, microcomputer software, server hardware, server software, the Internet, and other related business activities. Another type of efficiency is achieved by merging complementary businesses, for example, by combining companies specializing in R&D with companies specializing in marketing. While the series of acquisitions by AT&T in the 1990s were mergers that occurred to keep up with technological changes, AT&T has been trying to divest or spin off many of these businesses in the early 2000s.

The third group of revolutionary forces stimulating M&A and restructuring activity consists of changes in industrial organization. An example is the transformation of the computer industry from a vertically integrated enterprise to a horizontally independent business chain. As the industry continues to undergo rapid change, merger activity occurs frequently, and it is important to note that change does not end with mergers. Consolidating organizations is difficult when an industry is undergoing rapid change, often requiring multiple adjustment processes.

The fourth group of revolutionary forces is the result of favorable economic and financial conditions over the past 20 years. When corporate managers are optimistic about the future, they often make large investments through M&A. In 2001, with the ups and downs of the economy, the stock market also fell, and the scale of the company's internal and external investment through M&A also decreased significantly.

A summary of major merger activities in U. S. history suggests that slightly different forces were at work in the economic and financial environments of different historical periods. Weston makes two generalizations:

On the one hand, a significant merger movement reflects some underlying economic or technological factors. The early twentieth-century movement was triggered by the completion of the American Transcontinental Railroad, which made the United States the first large common market. This is the main force behind horizontal mergers, which combine regional companies into national companies. Automobiles and radios influenced the distribution system, spurring vertical merger activities in the 1920s. The conglomerate mergers of the 1960s reflected the idea that good managers were able to manage unrelated business activities. The deals of the 1980s were stimulated by the disintegration of diversification and financial innovation. The strategic M&A of the 1990s resulted from a combination of the seven factors described earlier. Thus, in some respects, each major merger movement was linked to strong economic and technological factors. However, the intensity and nature of the factors that influenced each merger movement were different.

On the other hand, some common economic factors are associated with different degrees of merger activity. Rising stock prices, low-interest rates, a suitable term structure of interest rates (formed by low short-term rates in contrast to long-term rates), and lower-risk option premiums (consisting of Treasury bills with nuances and corporate bonds with medium to low interest rates) favor higher levels of merger activity (Nielsen, 1959; Melicher, Ledolter & D'Antonio, 1983; Shughart & Tollison, 1984).

Combining the history of M&A in the U. S. market over the past 100 years and summarizing the factors mentioned before affecting merger activities, we can find that the emergence of favorable technical and economic conditions from the outside world has provided a good environment for enterprises to adopt merger activities, which gives them confidence in future development conditions and further generates the idea of expanding their businesses through M&A. For a specific enterprise, when a certain factor is strong enough, it may become an incentive for the enterprise to carry out M&A.

The most notable example in recent years is the Internet, whose explosive growth is driven by new technologies, new information systems, and new distribution systems. Many Internet companies, such as Yahoo and Amazon, have embraced this transformative trend and will rapidly expand through acquisitions. Although it has experienced the blow of the burst of the new economic bubble, in the long run, under the continuous stimulation of endless new technologies, M&A will still be a critical development method for companies in the Internet field.

2.3.2.3 Legal Permission and Deregulation

M&A activities involve the game of many stakeholders and can have an important impact on national economic development, market structure, etc., and need to be carried out under the framework of government laws, regulations and policies, especially, M&A between large companies often involve monopoly problems due to the considerable impact. For example, the rejection of General Electric Company's acquisition of Honeywell by the EU antitrust authorities is the most typical example of the impact of law on M&A activity. Therefore, the legal and regulatory situation is also a factor that must be considered in M&A.

As noted above, Weston also believes that deregulation has stimulated the acquisition process. Deregulation often reflects new technologies and increased competition, which puts pressure on existing companies to seek new opportunities through M&A. AT&T had to reinvent itself through M&A to accommodate new technologies, new competitive situations, and changing opportunities. In the auto industry, excess capacity and intense product competition have encouraged corporate alliances, joint ventures and mergers, such as the DaimlerChrysler deal. In addition, legal permission and deregulation mean that barriers to entry are removed, and firms can enter new areas to compete. In this case, M&A can make enterprises take the lead, reduce potential competitors, and achieve the purpose of quickly gaining a competitive advantage.

2.3.2.4 Capital Market-Driven

The idea that the market value of stocks affects corporate M&A activities can be traced back at least to Nelson's (1959) research on the trend of M&A in the United States: The unfolding of M&A appears to be more than a mere manifestation of economic prosperity; it is also closely related to the state of the capital markets. The two expansion cycles to be mentioned have not been accompanied by a substantial increase in stock prices, nor has there been a boom in mergers and acquisitions.

The stock market-driven M&A activity refers to the fact that the stock market's misestimation of the company's value is one of the motivations for companies to carry out M&A activities. This phenomenon has been noticed by the theoretical and academic circles for a long time. Many scholars have also studied the impact of the stock market on the company's financial decision-making and believe that the stock market has an impact on many decisions of the company. Regarding M&A activities, Shleifer and Vishny (2003) based on the history of U. S. corporate M&A activities and combined the research results of previous scholars, and for the first time, clearly put forward the view that the main driving force of M&A transactions is the market value of the acquirer's stock. They no longer assume that the market is efficient but argue that the stock market can misestimate the value of the acquirers, the target companies, and their integrated businesses. But corporate managers are perfectly rational, they know that markets are inefficient, and they take advantage of this through M&A decisions. This theory is contrary to the hubris assumption made by Roll (1986) when discussing corporate mergers and acquisitions. Roll's view is that the market is rational and business managers are irrational.

Based on the above considerations, they propose a stock market-driven M&A model, which belongs to the fast-growing field of behavioral corporate finance, arguing that corporate financial policies such as bond and equity issuance, stock buybacks, dividend policies, and investments are all responses to market mispricing. Furthermore, they argue that firms have an incentive to make their equity overvalued, allowing firms to make acquisitions with overvalued stocks. Under normal circumstances, companies with overvalued equity may survive and develop through mergers and acquisitions, while companies with undervalued equity may become acquisition targets. The benefits of M&A in which stocks are overvalued can even create incentives for companies to manipulate profits to boost stock prices.

Ang and Cheng (2006) build on the theory of stock market-driven M&A proposed by Shleifer and Vishny (2003) by using all publicly available M&A transactions in the U. S. domestic market from 1984 to 2001, selecting common stocks to measure and excluding negative book values of acquirers or targets, and selecting a sample of 9,334 for empirical study. The study finds that the acquirer's value is overvalued by the market on average, the market overestimates the acquirer's value much higher than the target company, and the successful acquirer is more overvalued than the unsuccessful acquirer. The study also finds that, after controlling for other potential factors influencing a firm's M&A decision, the likelihood of a firm becoming an acquirer increases significantly with the degree to which its stock is overvalued, with overvalued firms being more likely to be involved in M&A activities and tending to use the method of stock payment. This study provides evidence for the theory that the stock market-driven M&A activity, further proving that market driving (i.e., overvaluation of stocks) is also one of the motivations for corporate M&A.

2.3.3 *Enterprise M&A Motivation System Under the Combined Action of Drive and Incentive*

Enterprise M&A is a complex activity, and the formulation of a merger and acquisition decision needs to consider many internal and external factors of the enterprise. The motivation behind it is often multi-faceted. As the main body of competition in the market, the motive of enterprises' M&A is influenced by internal driving forces and incentives. The above summarizes the five internal driving forces and four incentives of enterprise M&A, which influence and interact with each other to form the motivation for M&A of enterprises.

The five internal drivers of corporate M&A, the pursuit of synergy, the pursuit of market power, the reduction of risk, the acquisition of superior assets of the target company, and the industrial organization, and the M&A motives generated by them up to the M&A behavior, are ultimately aimed at the survival, development and profitability of the enterprise in the competitive market and the creation of wealth for shareholders. The four corporate M&A incentives, namely the emergence of low-priced assets, the emergence of favorable technological and economic conditions, legal permission and deregulation and market-driven, can be considered as favorable external conditions for corporate M&A motives, which ultimately need to act on the companies themselves in order to function.

Firstly, the appearance of low-priced assets is unpredictable and uncontrollable by enterprises, and the transaction costs for enterprises to actively seek low-priced assets will also be high, which makes it difficult to purchase low-priced assets as a regular behavior of enterprises. Secondly, favorable technical and economic conditions and changes in laws and regulations act on the whole market, providing equal opportunities for competition to all enterprises in the market. When regulations are relaxed, the market is equal for all entrants, and if enterprises do not have the impulse to expand the market to improve their profits, they will not have the motivation for M&A, and certainly no M&A behaviors will occur. Finally, the market's overestimation of enterprise value is a favorable condition for M&A. However, enterprises cannot conduct blind M&A just because their value is overvalued. M&A still need to be carried out prudently under the overall arrangement of corporate strategy and finance.

The above analysis shows that considering the enterprises as the main body, the M&A incentives do not directly determine the M&A motivation of the enterprises but need to act on the internal driving forces and further combine with the internal driving forces of the M&A to finally form the M&A motivation. The motivation of an M&A activity can be summed up as the combined effect of one or more of the above five internal driving forces and four incentives. In this way, we can explain the M&A motivation of enterprises from the two aspects of motivation and incentives, integrate the current research results of M&A motivation into a unified analytical framework, and study the M&A motivation system more deeply.

The achievement motivation theory of psychology believes that individuals pursue higher goals, complete difficult tasks, compete and surpass others, all out of the need for achievement. Individuals with high achievement motivation tend to choose more difficult and riskier pioneering work, and obtain satisfaction from the process and results of reaching their goals. The further proposed achievement motivation model believes that whether a goal or incentive can arouse an individual's behavior depends on its value to the individual and the probability that the individual can successfully achieve it. The former is called valence and the latter is called expectancy. Psychologist Atkinson (1964) proposed that the size of behavioral motivation (intensity of motivation) can be expressed by the product of valence and expectancy, that is, the intensity of behavioral motivation = valence × expectancy. The valence and expectation here depend on the subjective evaluation of the individual, and different evaluation results exert different influences on the behavioral motivation of the individual.

Drawing on the results of the above psychological research, let us examine the M&A activity of companies by analogy. Professor Michael Porter said, "M&A are endlessly fascinating. It is a giant drama, a moving dance. With the stroke of a pen, your company can have hundreds of millions of dollars in the bank, make front page headlines in the newspapers and generate market excitement." M&A contain a lot of opportunities and risks, and it is a very challenging job, which has an irreplaceable role in promoting the development of enterprises. As mentioned above, the motivations of enterprises can be classified into five types of internal driving forces and four kinds of incentives, and both internal driving forces and incentives positively affect the enterprises' M&A motivation. Also, when making M&A decisions, firms assess the probability (expectancy) of success of the M&A activity; the higher the probability of success, the greater the motivation to acquire. Therefore, drawing on the motivational strength model proposed by psychologist Atkinson, we express the corporate M&A motivation as the product relationship of internal driving forces, incentives and expectancy, which is expressed by the following formula:

$$M = d \times c \times e$$

where M: the M&A motivation strength; d: the role of internal driving forces; c: the role of incentives; and e: the expectancy.

The above formula decomposes the M&A motivation of enterprises into the role of internal driving forces and the role of incentives, combined with the estimation of enterprises' expectancies of M&A activities, and obtains the strength of M&A motivation. Combined with M&A theory and practice, M&A should serve the achievement of corporate goals, and the incentives for M&A need to work through internal driving forces, which can ultimately be attributed to maximizing corporate value. It can be seen that the final effect of M&A internal driving forces and incentives in determining M&A motivation is consistent. An example can help us understand intuitively that firm A, which has enhanced market powers (internal driving forces), finds an undervalued firm B in the same industry (incentives), and then for firm A, that is its M&A motivation.

In addition, the strength of corporate M&A motivation is also positively correlated with the probability of successful M&A activities. If the management of company A believes that the probability (expectancy) of the successful merger is high, then the company's merger motivation is very large, and the merger is likely to occur. For example, in January 2003, BYD, the largest producer of secondary rechargeable batteries in China, acquired 77% of Xi'an Qinchuan Automobile, which produces Flair micro cars, for HK$254 million to achieve a related diversification from the secondary rechargeable battery industry to the automobile industry. In the preparation stage of this acquisition, BYD's growth space for rechargeable batteries was limited, and the industry's marginal profit declined. It was urgent to choose the company's new "star" business. Wang Chuanfu, president of BYD, believes that there is a good correlation between the rechargeable battery and the electric vehicle business, and the overall development momentum of the domestic auto industry is good, coupled with the company had RMB1.27 billion in cash, but also has the full financial capacity to implement the acquisition and development strategy. Wang Chuanfu said, "BYD's acquisition of Qinchuan was fully prepared, not on a whim, but part of the company's development strategy." As can be seen, when companies expect a high probability of M&A success, they will have good and optimistic expectations for the future, which in turn will make their M&A motivation enhanced accordingly.

2.4 Motivation for M&A from Stakeholder Perspective

2.4.1 M&A Motivation and Corporate Governance

In the above discussion, we mainly examine the enterprise's M&A motivations from the external perspective of the enterprises and regard the enterprise's M&A decision-making process as a black box. In the absence of the principal-agent problems, the enterprise's M&A motivation is reflected by the enterprise decision- makers (management and board of directors). However, under the modern enterprise system, the separation of ownership and control creates principal- agent problems, and the company's M&A decisions need to be made under the framework of corporate governance. Therefore, corporate governance becomes the most important issue to be considered when studying M&A motivations from an internal perspective.

Oliver Hart put forward the analytical framework of corporate governance theory in the article Corporate Governance: Some Theory and Implications. He believes that if the following two conditions exist, corporate governance problems will inevitably arise in an organization. The first condition is the agency problem, which is precisely the conflict of interest among the organization's members (which may be owners, workers or consumers); the second condition is that the agency problem cannot be solved contractually by the ambassador of transaction costs. Corporate governance structures are critical when there are agency issues and contracts are incomplete.

In their 1988 paper Corporate Governance: A Review of the Literature, Philip L. Cochran and Steven L. Wartick argue that corporate governance issues include specific problems arising from the interactions of senior management, shareholders, the board of directors, and other stakeholders in the company. At the core of what constitutes a corporate governance issue are: (1) who benefits from corporate decisions/senior management actions; (2) who should benefit from corporate decisions/ senior management actions? A corporate governance problem arises when there is an inconsistency between "what is" and "what should be". To further explain the issues involved in corporate governance, they cite Buckhoiz, who divides corporate governance into four elements, each of which has problems arising from inconsistencies between "what is" and "what should be" related to the interaction of senior management and other major relevant interest groups. Specifically, management has priority control, directors are subservient to management, workers have no say in corporate management, and government registration is too lenient. Each element focuses on one of these stakeholder groups, such as shareholders, boards, workers, and governments. Solutions to these problems could be enhanced shareholder participation, restructured boards, expanded worker democracy and tighter governance. They believe that "understanding the questions contained in corporate governance is one way of answering the question of what corporate governance is".

Corporate governance is also interpreted as an institutional arrangement. In his article Corporate Governance, Competition and Performance, Colin Meyer defines corporate governance as an organizational arrangement by which a company represents and serves its investors. It includes everything from the company's board of directors to the implementation of incentive programs for managers. The need for corporate governance arises with the separation of ownership and control of modern joint-stock companies in a market economy.

Based on the above viewpoints, it can be found that corporate governance is a multi-angle and multi-level concept, which is difficult to express in simple terms. But from the perspective of the emergence and development of corporate governance, it can be understood from both narrow and broad aspects.

In a narrow sense, corporate governance refers to a mechanism of supervision and checks and balances that owners, mainly shareholders, have over operators. That is, through an institutional arrangement, the rights and responsibilities between owners and operators can be reasonably allocated. The goal of corporate governance is to ensure the maximization of shareholders' interests and prevent operators from deviating from owners' interests. Its main feature is internal governance through the corporate governance structure constituted by the general meeting of shareholders, the board of directors, the board of supervisors and the management.

Corporate governance in a broad sense is not limited to the checks and balances between shareholders and operators, but involves a wide range of stakeholders, including shareholders, creditors, suppliers, employees, governments and communities, and other groups that have an interest in the company. Corporate governance is to coordinate the interest relation between the company and all stakeholders through a set of formal or informal, internal or external systems or mechanisms to ensure the scientific decision-making of the company, to ultimately maintain the interests of all aspects of the company. Because in a broad sense, a company is no longer just a shareholder's company, but a community of interests, and the company's governance mechanism is not limited to internal governance based on the governance structure, but stakeholders through a series of internal and external mechanisms to implement joint governance, the goal of governance is not only to maximize the interests of shareholders, but also to ensure the scientific of the company's decision-making, so as to maximize the interests of stakeholders in all aspects of the company.

Therefore, under the broad concept of corporate governance, we can go deep into the interior of corporate M&A decision-making for further analysis. M&A is an important decision of an enterprise, which will widely affect the interests of various stakeholders, and various stakeholders will also exert their own influence (big or small) on the decision-making process of corporate M&A through the corporate governance mechanism, and the interests of the parties will also compete. Therefore, from the perspective of each stakeholder, considering their own M&A motivations, and then exploring the mechanism of each stakeholder's motivation for corporate M&A motivations, can help us to have a deeper understanding of corporate M&A motivations.

2.4.2 Stakeholder Motivation for M&A

In 1984, Freeman clearly put forward the theory of stakeholder management in his book *Strategic Management: A Stakeholder Approach*. Stakeholder management theory refers to the management activities that enterprises' managers carry out to balance the interest requirements of various stakeholders comprehensively. Compared with traditional shareholder supremacy, this theory holds that corporate managers are not only concerned about the interests of corporate shareholders, but also the interests of other stakeholders. It is believed that the development of any enterprise is inseparable from the input or participation of various stakeholders, and the enterprise pursues the overall interests of the stakeholders, not just the interests of some subjects. The stakeholders' interests in the M&A activities are different, and finally, a balance is achieved in the game of the various stakeholders. Next, we analyze the motivation of the internal stakeholders of the enterprise.

2.4.2.1 Shareholder Motivation for M&A

Under the corporate governance mechanism, shareholders are the main body of corporate governance. As owners, shareholders invest their capital into the company and pass control to the management through the principal- agent mechanism. Shareholders then need to constrain the decision-making power and behavior of the management to ensure the safety and appreciation of capital. Shareholders have residual claims to the enterprise, M&A is the way of enterprise development, and the various benefits of enterprise development will eventually be returned to shareholders. In addition, M&A will lead to changes in the stock market's evaluation of the company's stocks, causing strong stock price fluctuations and forming stock speculation opportunities, which may also increase shareholders' capital gains. Therefore, in M&A decision-making, shareholders' M&A motivation is to control risks as much as possible while improving returns.

Of course, although we believe that shareholders are all rational, shareholders and shareholders have different preferences for risk. The risk-loving shareholders tend to be high-risk and high-return M&A projects, while the risk-averse shareholders are more willing to undertake those stable M&A projects. Some shareholders prefer long-term income projects, while others prefer short-term income projects; some shareholders prefer strategic projects, while others prefer strategic projects. For M&A projects, in addition to seeking residual income, controlling shareholders may also seek private interests of control rights, whether or not through related transactions. Different interest preferences and conflicts of interest are resolved through different corporate governance mechanisms, such as related parties in related transactions refraining from voting, and minority shareholders seeking entrusted voting rights.

2.4.2.2 Management Motivation for M&A

Under the modern enterprise system, the separation of ownership and control will inevitably lead to the problem of principal-agent. As an agent, the management owns the corporate property rights of the company rather than the ownership, but he directly controls the company and the company's surplus. Due to the inconsistency of corporate property rights and ultimate ownership, the interests of management and shareholders are inconsistent, which may make management's M&A motivation inconsistent with shareholders' M&A motivation, and then deviate from the company's M&A motivation, and ultimately make M&A activities damage the company's value.

The agency problems are more severe in public companies with extremely fragmented ownership. To solve the agency problems and reduce the agency costs, two ways can generally be considered: (1) Institutional arrangements of organizational mechanisms. Fama and Jensen point out that in the case of separation of ownership and control of the enterprise, separating decision management from decision control of the enterprise can limit the possibility of agents' erosion of shareholders' interests. Fama points out that agency problems can be mitigated through compensation arrangements and manager markets. (2) Institutional arrangements of market mechanisms. The stock market provides an external monitoring mechanism for corporate shareholders, because stock prices can reflect the merits of managers' decisions. Low stock prices can pressure managers to change their behaviors and be loyal to shareholder interests.

Manne (1965) pointed out that when all these mechanisms are insufficient to control the agency problems, the market for corporate control provides the last means of external control to solve the problem. He emphasized that if a company's management lags in its operations due to inefficiency or agency problems, the company may be taken over and thus face the threat of takeover.

A variant of agency theory is the managerialism theory proposed by Mueller (1969). Mueller uses managerialism theory to explain the conglomerate merger problems, and Mueller believes that management has an incentive to further expand the scale of the enterprise. He assumes that the management's compensation is a function of the size of the enterprise, and the management has a strong incentive to increase the size of the enterprise to increase the compensation, and believes that the management has adopted a meager return on investment. Agency theory shows that when the manager market fails to solve the agency problem, the inter-company market or the market on which mergers and acquisitions are conducted will play a role. That is, the theory believes that mergers are a way to solve the agency problem. Managerialism theory suggests that the agency problem is not solved and that merger activity is only one manifestation of the agency problem associated with inefficient outside investment by management. Managerialism theory holds that the management of M&A companies, when making M&A decisions, is not pursuing the maximization of the wealth of the company's shareholders, but pursuing the management's own interests, that is, spreading business risks and expanding control, specifically in the form of carrying out hybrid M&A and diversification. Therefore, management's interests are inversely related to the company's operating risks. Shleifer and Vishny (1989) believed that "expanding the scale of the company through M&A and thus increasing the company's dependence on the current management" is also one of the most important M&A motivations for management to make M&A decisions. However, diversification does not necessarily meet the requirements of shareholders. Because if a company's shareholders want to reduce their investment risks, they can simply diversify their own investments, that is, diversify into different companies' stocks to build their own portfolios, and there is no need to achieve this through diversification.

Overall, due to the existence of the principal-agent problems and the inconsistency of the interests of management and shareholders, the management has the motivation to maximize its own interests. In M&A activities, this may lead to the deviation of management's M&A decision and shareholders' interests, failing to maximize shareholders' interests, or even damaging shareholders' interests. In order to avoid the above situation, prevent the moral hazard and adverse selection behaviors of the management, and encourage them to operate in accordance with the company's goals, the enterprise needs to establish a set of formal or informal, internal or external systems or mechanisms to coordinate the interests between the company and all stakeholders, to coordinate management's M&A motivation with the company's M&A motivation by means of bonuses, management shareholding, equity incentives, etc., and to make management participate in sharing corporate residual income, etc., so as to ensure scientific M&A decisions and thus ultimately safeguard the interests of all parties in the company.

2.4.2.3 Creditor Motivation for M&A

In M&A activity, the company's creditors can also exert influence on M&A decisions. From the perspective of the bank, although it is not necessarily the asset owner of the company after it has issued a loan to the company, it is in consideration of preventing its risks, can request by contract the supervision or participation in the governance of the debtor's capital operations, a right that comes from the credit. The main concern of creditors is the safety of their invested assets and the possibility of repayment at maturity. In the co-guarantee effect of financial synergy, when a part of the merged enterprise fails, the creditors can be compensated from the profits of other parts of the enterprise, which can reduce the debt risks, thereby increasing the debt value, and the increased value comes from the transfer of wealth to shareholders of a merged enterprise. In the absence of M&A, no such enterprise would assume such a guarantee responsibility for the debt of another enterprise for free. Therefore, the creditor's M&A motivation is mainly due to the consideration of the changes in the solvency of the enterprise after the M&A.

2.4.2.4 Employee Motivation for M&A

According to Maslow's Hierarchy of Needs Theory, employees choose to work in an enterprise mainly concerned with remuneration, the degree of respect and the realization of self-worth. In a company that implements the employee stock ownership system and stock option incentives, if the management makes a M&A decision that can increase the value of the enterprise, it is equivalent to increasing the employees' salary, which the employees will support to a large extent. In successful strategic M&A, the acquisition direction is often accompanied by inputting the target company's corporate culture. Most of the employees want to work under the background of a sunny corporate culture full of entrepreneurial spirit. If the M&A is expected to create a more satisfactory working atmosphere and greater room for promotion, the employees will not object. If the target company's employees are not satisfied with their new roles at the acquirers, or if they are worried that their jobs or potential development opportunities will be affected after the M&A, the M&A

will be resisted, and excellent employees will be lost. A Portuguese bank (BCP) once forcibly acquired an investment management company against the wishes of its employees. As a result, all the company employees resigned immediately and established an investment management company with a similar name, which became a strong opponent of the original company.

In addition to the M&A motivations of the above four stakeholders, because consumers, suppliers, governments and other stakeholders have different degrees of interest relations with the company, these interest relations may be maintained through written or tacit contractual relations, which provides the possibility for them to participate in or influence corporate governance, but other conditions are needed for this possibility to become realistic, such as the specificity of the interest relationship, the institutional environment of the enterprise and so on. In enterprises with relatively large influence of customers, suppliers and governments, it is often very important to seek the opinions of these stakeholders in the process of M&A, and their attitudes towards M&A often determine the success or failure of M&A.

2.4.3 Enterprise M&A Motivation System Composed of Stakeholders

Under the corporate governance mechanisms, the M&A decisions of an enterprise are influenced by various stakeholders, and various forces can act on the M&A decisions, and the forces of all parties interact and compete with each other, so that it is often not a single motivation that determines the M&A behavior of enterprises, but is a motivational system.

From the static analysis of motivation, the M&A motivation of enterprises is jointly influenced by the M&A motivation of stakeholders. There are different types of motivations, different directions and different strengths, and they are interconnected to form the internal structure of the motivation system. In this internal structure, some motivations play a leading role and are the dominant motivations, which are often the strongest and have the greatest impact on the overall motivations, and are the main component that determines the internal structural characteristics of the motivation system, while the remaining non- dominant motives are in a relatively secondary position. However, what ultimately determines the M&A behavior of enterprises is often the resultant force generated by the M&A motivation system composed of various stakeholders. In other words, the final M&A motivation of a company is the result of the game of the motives of various stakeholders.

From the dynamic analysis of motivation, the various motivations in the M&A motivation system interact and change constantly. Its dynamic characteristics are manifested in three aspects: conflict, synthesis and transformation of motivation.

Motivational conflict refers to the inconsistency of the interests of various stakeholders and the possible differences in their value judgments on M&A activities, resulting in an inevitable conflict between the M&A motivations of various stakeholders. For example, under the proxy, the motivation of shareholders and management conflicts, and the motivation of management and employee conflicts.

Motivation synthesis means that when an enterprise conducts M&A activity to achieve a certain goal, its motivation is dominated by the combined force of the internal stakeholders' M&A motivation. This resultant force is composed of the internal driving forces, incentives, and various forces caused by various factors related to the motivations of various stakeholders. In motivation synthesis, the dominant motivation undoubtedly plays a significant role, but the power of the non-dominant motivation cannot be ignored. Successful M&A often overcomes the negative effects of the internal stakeholders' motivation in the corporate motivation system, and maximizes the coordination of various motivations to point in the same direction, thereby forming the greatest synergy.

Motivation transformation refers to the fact that corporate M&A motivation is constrained by various internal and external conditions. When the internal and external conditions change, the motivation of stakeholders within the corporate motivation system will also be transformed. This transformation can be divided into two situations: First, the types of motivations change, that is, some motivations may subside and new ones may emerge under changing circumstances. Second, the strength of each motivation is transformed, i.e., the strength of dominant motivation may weaken and decline to non-dominant motivation, while the strength of non-dominant motivation may increase and rise to dominant motivation. For example, if the terms of corporate M&A do not meet the interests of employees, employees will have incentives and behaviors against M&A, but when the terms change or compensation for losses, employees may have incentives to support M&A.

In the enterprise M&A motivation system, the conflict, synthesis and transformation among stakeholders' M&A motivation, mutual influence and mutual game, through the enterprise's management decision-making process, finally form the enterprise's M&A motivation. M&A is a way of developing enterprises, and the motivations of M&A of enterprises should be consistent with the development direction of enterprises under the framework of enterprise goals. The goal of an enterprise is to survive, develop and make profits, which are further specified by combining the M&A activities of enterprises. We can obtain five goals of the M&A activities of the enterprise, namely, increasing the rate of return, expanding the scale of the enterprise, pursuing stable development, acquiring core resources, and industrial restructuring. Therefore, the company's M&A motivation should also be consistent with the goals of these five M&A activities.

The relationship between the system of enterprise M&A motivation— enterprise motivation—and the objectives of M&A activities can be represented in Fig. 2.1.

To sum up, the game between the M&A motivations of various stakeholders in the enterprise M&A motivation system produces the M&A motivation. Enterprise M&A motivation needs to be consistent with the objectives of M&A activities within the framework of enterprise objectives. Enterprises with clear motives for M&A can

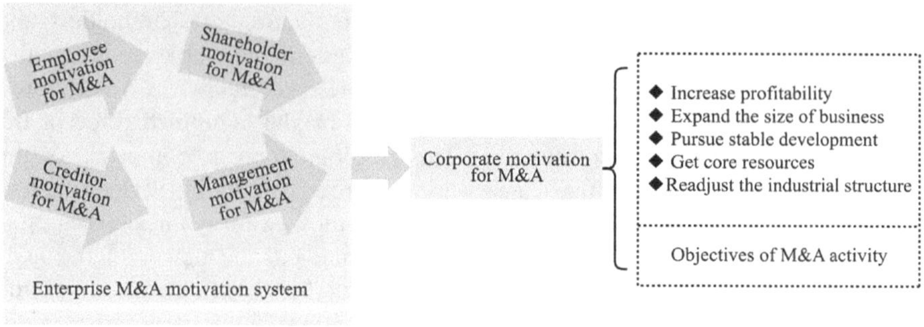

Fig. 2.1 The structure of enterprise M&A motivation

clearly evaluate the internal and external environment of the company, better coordinate the internal and external resources of the company, fully explore and cultivate their own competitive advantages, and realize the extraordinary development of enterprises through M&A.

Chapter 3
M&A Capability

3.1 Realistic and Theoretical Background

Mergers and acquisitions are an unconventional development model for enterprises, which can rapidly expand production scale, adjust industrial structure, increase profitability and avoid risks. At present, all the world's big companies have developed through mergers and acquisitions, and many well-known enterprises in China have also achieved leapfrog development through mergers and acquisitions. However, mergers and acquisitions are also highly risky, and the decision-making process is often complex. Many companies have the motive for mergers and acquisitions, but they are not very clear about how large-scale mergers and acquisitions they can implement, which often leads to the selection of target companies beyond the ability of the acquirer to implement the M&A, resulting in the final M&A failure.

In the process of M&A decision-making, enterprises with M&A motives cannot necessarily conduct M&A, and the methods or steps of M&A companies with M&A capabilities are not completely the same. The quality of acquisition decisions depends not only on how much information the acquirer has, but also on the ability it has accumulated to make M&A decisions (Sleptsov et al., 2013).

A series of questions are placed in front of us: what kind of enterprise can be said to have M&A capability? Is it true that the enterprises that have carried out mergers and acquisitions can acquire mergers and acquisitions? How to express and judge M&A capability? What is the relationship between M&A capability, enterprise scale and enterprise competitiveness? There is no good answer to these questions in the theoretical and practical circles. The book *Winning the Merger Endgam* Strategies (Deans et al., 2004) also mentioned at the beginning, "Even seasoned managers, after years of practice and due diligence, are often only marginally better than empirical guesses at choosing what to do and in which direction to go." Therefore, it has become a practical problem to study the M&A capabilities of enterprises to guide M&A decisions.

Q. Zhang, *Mergers and Acquisitions*, https://doi.org/10.1007/978-981-92-0122-8_3

Many research results at the theoretical level of M&A activities focus on why M&A occurs (M&A motivation) and whether M&A creates value (M&A performance). At the practical level, there is a lot of accumulation in M&A target identification and post-M&A integration, but no matter in the theoretical or practical circles, there are few issues related to the M&A capability of enterprises.

Penrose (1959) put forward the proposition that the enterprise is a collection of resources, which laid the foundation for the formation of Enterprise Resource Theory. After decades of development, Enterprise Resource Theory has evolved from resource-based view and competence-based view to knowledge-based view, the three share the same origin and form a theoretical development lineage. The above theories have conducted in-depth research and analysis on the fundamental driving force of the long-term development of enterprises from the perspective of resources in a broad sense, and provided a good theoretical basis for the study of M&A capability.

Enterprise M&A capability is undoubtedly a kind of enterprise capability. Scholars' discourses on M&A capability exist piecemeal in many enterprise capability and M&A research literature, resulting in certain research findings. Zhang Qiusheng (2005) first put forward the concept of enterprise M&A capability, arguing that enterprise M&A capability refers to the ability of acquirers with M&A motives to implement M&A, which is part of the basic theory of corporate mergers and acquisitions. Sleptsov et al. (2013) argue that the quality of acquisition decisions depends not only on how much information the acquirer has, but also on its ability to acquire. They also point out that investors are rational, and investors' expectations can reflect the M&A capability of enterprises from the side, so the mean and variance of the excess cumulative returns of historical M&A are used to control the heterogeneity of M&A capability. Ge Weijie et al. (2015) believe that M&A capability reflects the relative conversion efficiency of how a company converts resources into M&A value. They first use data envelopment analysis (DEA) to calculate relative conversion efficiency to measure a firm's M&A capability. The measurement results show that the mean value of the full sample M&A capability is 0.435, indicating that less than half of the input resources can be converted into M&A performance in general. For enterprises, market pressures and their own development requirements make them generate M&A motives, but enterprises with only M&A motives do not necessarily have the ability to M&A, nor do they necessarily have to choose M&A as an unconventional development option. Therefore, the implicit assumption of M&A capability research is that the enterprise has already generated M&A motivation, and in order to determine whether to proceed with M&A, it is necessary to conduct a comprehensive assessment of the enterprise's M&A capability in order to clarify the scale and scope of the M&A transaction that it can conduct and the influencing factors, so as to support the enterprise's M&A decision. It should be pointed out that the research on M&A capability here is only aimed at the acquirer itself, and the target company will not be an influencing factor in the M&A capability of the company.

3.2 Brief Review of Enterprise Resource Theory

Mergers and acquisitions are the behavior of the enterprise, and the ability of merger and acquisition is one of the capabilities of the enterprise. The research on enterprise capability in academia has rich results. With the continuous development of enterprise organization, it continues to deepen, from enterprise resource view, enterprise capability view to enterprise knowledge view, forming a complete theoretical system of enterprise resources. Therefore, a comprehensive review of enterprise resource theory can help us better understand M&A capabilities.

In studying the growth mechanism of enterprises, Selznick (1957) first proposed the concept of ability or special ability, thinking that ability or special ability is a special substance that can make an organization do better than other organizations. But the pioneering figure of enterprise resource theory is generally considered to be Penrose. Although there has been a long tradition in economics to look at economic units from the perspective of resource endowments, this analysis is limited to more abstract categories such as labor, capital, and land. In his article The Theory of the Growth of the Firm in 1959, Penrose constructed an analytical framework of enterprise resources-enterprise capability-enterprise growth, and explored the internal driving force of enterprise growth, marking the establishment of enterprise resource theory. He defines an enterprise as "a collection of resources coordinated and bounded by an administrative framework" and believes that the resource status of an enterprise is the basis for determining enterprise capabilities, and the process of producing productive services generated by resources promotes the growth of knowledge. The growth of knowledge will lead to the growth of management power, thereby promoting the evolution and growth of enterprises. Then, Richardson (1972) formally proposed the concept of "enterprise capability", thinking that capability reflects the knowledge, experience, and skills accumulated by an enterprise and is the basis of enterprise activities.

Wernerfelt and Penrose's research on corporate growth strategies is in the same line. Wernerfelt (1984) published Resource-Based View of the Firm, which has become iconic classic literature on enterprise resource theory. Wernerfelt put forward the concept of resource position barrier and the analysis tool of resource-product matrices to analyze strategic choices from a resource perspective rather than a traditional product perspective. He also listed the basic blank and unresearched issues in strategy implementation, such as how to identify resources, to what extent capabilities can be combined across departments, and how to establish a structure and system to support strategy implementation. These issues have become the focus of later discussions in strategic management.

In 1990, Prahalad and Hamel published the famous article The Core Competence of the Corporation, which proposed the concept of corporate core competence. They believe that the ability to determine the competitive advantage of an enterprise is the organic combination of the organization's accumulated knowledge and various skills and technology flow, rather than the pure enterprise resources. That is, the core competence is "the accumulated knowledge in the organization, especially about how to coordinate different production skills and knowledge in organically combining multiple technical streams".

Grant (1991) thinks that resources are the input of the production process. The individual resources of an enterprise include capital equipment, personal skills of employees, patents, brand names, funds, etc., which can be divided into six categories, namely financial resources, physical resources, human resources, technical resources, reputation, and organizational resources; and capability is the capacity of a group of resources to perform a certain task or activity, the capability is essentially many interacting norms, and can be through the enterprise classification of standard functions of activities to identify and evaluate. Grant proposes a resource-based approach to strategy formulation to pursue competitive advantage. This approach emphasizes capturing the relationship between resources, capabilities, competitive advantage, and profitability. He summarized the characteristics of resources and capabilities into four aspects, namely persistence, transparency, transferability, and reproducibility, which are of great reference for studying resources in mergers and acquisitions.

In the same year, Barney (1991) argued in a review article that sustainable competitive advantage comes from the resources and capabilities controlled by the firm, which have the following characteristics: valuable, scarce, inimitable, and irreplaceable. Resources and capabilities can be regarded as many tangible and intangible assets, including enterprise management skills, organizational processes and norms, and controlled information and knowledge. Grant and Barney initially answered the question of resource identification raised by Wernerfelt, but their greater contribution was to lead resources and capabilities to sustainable competitive advantage, the core theme of strategic management research, thus laying the foundation for the increasing role of enterprise resource view in the field of strategic management. Su Jingqin and Wang Hechun (2010) based on a review of domestic and foreign literature on enterprise resource theory, through the three dimensions of the form of resources, the relationship between resources and competition, and the relationship between resources and people, from the perspective of adaptation. Considering the entrepreneur's leading role, reclassify the enterprise's internal resources. According to the classification of enterprise resources, resources are divided into three categories: tangible resources, entrepreneur resources and intangible resources.

The classic literature on the enterprise resource view mentioned above either uses resources or uses both resources and capabilities as the basic unit of analysis. On the one hand, when resources and capabilities are used together, the concepts of resources and assets are similar. A resource is an asset with a semi-permanent connection to an enterprise (Maijoor & Witteloostuijn, 1996; Wernerfelt, 1984). On the other hand, the enterprise resource view also pays attention to the role of competence, which is essentially consistent with the very popular "core competence theory". Xia Qinghua (2002) pointed out more clearly that if the capability of an enterprise is also regarded as an enterprise resource, then the capability school belongs to the resource school in a broad sense. This reflects the consistency of the theoretical basis of the enterprise resource view and the capability view and the extension of development. This permanence is also shown in Prahalad and Hamer's paper, which also provides answers to the questions posed by Wernerfeldt. They give three principles for identifying core competencies, namely offering the potential to enter a wider market, helping to understand the interests of end-product customers, and being difficult for competitors to imitate. They also propose to develop a strategic architecture to guide the cultivation of core competencies and emphasize that senior managers should promote the flow of competencies within the company.

Some scholars believe that the distinction between competencies and the core competencies proposed by Prahalad and Hamel is ambiguous (Stalk, Evans & Schulman, 1992), so the two terms are used together (Wright, Dunford & Snell, 2001). But there are also scholars (Campbell, 1995; Xia Qinghua, 2002) who emphasize that the two are different, and believe that the concept of capability is broader than the concept of core competence. The former includes the entire value chain, while the latter is only reflected in one or several parts of the value chain a segment.

Grant (1997) put forward the framework of the knowledge-based view of the firm after summarizing previous research on internal enterprise knowledge. Grant himself is also a representative of the resource view. When talking about the origin of the knowledge view, he said, "The knowledge view is a fusion of many research schools, the most prominent of which is the resource view and epistemology." He also pointed out that "in terms of the contribution of value-added and its strategic importance, knowledge is the most important productive resource", clarifies the relationship between knowledge and resources. For the literature that contributed to the formation of the knowledge concept, he cites organizational learning, organizational capabilities and competencies, evolutionary economics, etc. It further states that "the view of knowledge provides a new understanding of the microstructure of capabilities, i.e., capabilities are the integration of individual expert knowledge based on teams. The complexity of capabilities depends critically on the scope of the integrated knowledge", clarifying the relationship between ability and knowledge. An important significance of the view of knowledge is to develop a method to recognize the nature of ability from the perspective of knowledge, not only the perspective of value activities (Porter, 1985) or the perspective of organizational capital (Weston, 1998).

The dynamic capabilities framework proposed by Teece, Pisano and Shuen (1997) provides an analytical method for the construction of competitive advantage in a changing environment. Dynamic capability is the ability of an enterprise to integrate, build and reconfigure its internal and external competitiveness in response to a rapidly changing environment. They believe that the competitive advantage comes from the norms of high performance in the internal operation of the enterprise, and the norms are determined by the process and the asset positions (such as hard-to-trade knowledge assets and a combination of complementary assets). It is worth noting that both Teece, Pisano and Shuen (1997) and Grant (1991) regard competence as a norm. For norm, Grant cites the definition of Nelson & Winter (1982): a regular, predictable pattern of activity, which consists of a series of coordinated activities of an individual. Teece, Pisano and Shuen (1997) further pointed out that norms are "soft assets", such as value, culture, and organizational experience. Su Zhiwen (2012) reviewed the literature on the dynamic capabilities of enterprises from the perspective of mergers and acquisitions and pointed out the advantages of dynamic theory. Resource view, capability view, and knowledge view have been questioned because of their static attributes, and none of them can fully explain how enterprises can achieve competitive advantage in a complex and changeable environment, while dynamic capability theory can reflect today's ever-changing competitive environment.

Synthesizing the above literature, we can see that the resource view, the ability view, and the knowledge view have the same origin and form a theoretical development thread. Their connection lies in the fact that the "capability" in the classification of assets and capabilities referred to by the enterprise resource view is closely related to the "core competence" of the core competency theory, and the capability view only focuses on explaining the long-term competitive advantage of enterprises. The proposition that "the essence of is knowledge" also makes the concept of enterprise capability inseparable from the concept of knowledge, but the concept of knowledge focuses on the interpretation of enterprise behavior from the perspective of knowledge resources. Based on recognizing the internal consistency of the resource view, capability view, and knowledge view, we use "enterprise resource theory" to describe the above three views.

Under the enterprise resource theory, many scholars have classified enterprise resources from different emphases. Here is a brief review to provide a reference for M&A capabilities.

Wernerfelt (1984) defines resources as tangible and intangible assets that have a semi-permanent relationship with an enterprise. For example, brand name, in-house technical knowledge, skilled employees, trade contracts, machinery, efficient procedures, capital, etc.

Barney (1991) believes that resources include all the assets, capabilities, organizational processes, enterprise characteristics, information, and knowledge controlled by the enterprise, and these resources can enable enterprises to conceive and implement strategies that can improve organizational efficiency and effectiveness. He further divides corporate resources into physical capital resources (including physical technology, plant, and equipment, geographic location, access to raw materials, etc.), human capital resources (including training, experience, judgment, intelligence, relationships, individual managers, and workers' insights power, etc.) and organizational capital resources (including formal reporting structures, formal and informal planning, control and coordination systems, and informal linkages between groups within and between enterprises).

Teece, Pisano and Shuen (1997) divide resources into technical resources, manufacturing resources, customer-related resources, and financial resources. Hofer and Schendel (1978) proposed that the composition of enterprise resources is more complex, including financial, physical, managerial, human, organizational, and technical resources.

Das and Teng (1998) also gave four classifications of corporate resources: financial, technical, physical, and management resources, but later they believed that all the above classification methods lacked sufficient theoretical basis. The method they advocated when they studied the problem of the strategic alliance was the classification of resources according to the imitability barrier proposed by Miller and Shamsie (1996), that is, property-based resources and knowledge- based resources. The resources based on property rights refer to the resources of legal property rights owned by enterprises, including financial capital, physical resources, human resources, etc. Knowledge-based resources refer to the intangible technical know-how and skills of the enterprise, which is tacit knowledge.

Capabilities are information-based, firm-specific, and inherently intangible processes that develop over time through complex interrelated interactions among firm resources (Amit & Schoemaker, 1993; Conner & Prahalad, 1996; Itami & Rohel, 1987; Kogut & Zander, 1992; Leonard-Barton, 1992; Winter, 1987). There are two important differences between resources and capabilities: First, capabilities are firm-specific because they are embedded in organizations and organizational processes, while resources are different (Makadok, 2001). The enterprise- specific nature of capabilities means that if an organization dissolves completely, its capabilities will also disappear. For example, if Intel were to be completely dissolved, its microprocessor patents (a resource) would likely remain in the hands of a new owner, but its skills to design a new generation of microprocessors (a capability) will likely disappear. Second, the main function of capabilities is to enhance the efficiency and productivity of the resources owned by the enterprise to achieve organizational goals, and capabilities act as "intermediate goods" in the process (Amit & Schoemaker, 1993). Third, unlike resources, capabilities are exercised through human capital and are based on developing, expressing, and exchanging information (Amit & Schoemaker, 1993). Table 3.1 shows that some scholars have differences in understanding resources and capabilities.

Table 3.1 Classification and summary of enterprise resources by previous scholars

Research scholar	Enterprise resources		
	Tangible asset	Intangible assets	Capacity
Wernerfelt (1989)	Fixed assets	Experience assets	Culture
Hall (1992)		Intangible assets	Capacity
Hall (1994)	Assets	Capacity	
Prahalad and Hamel (1990)		Core capacity	
Itami (1987)			Invisible assets
Amit and Schoemaker (1993)			Intermediate
Selznick (1957); Hitt and Ireland (1985); Hofer and Schendel (1978)			Unique capacity
Irvin and Michaels (1989)			Core skills

Source Wang Feng, Xuan Guoliang, Fan Wei, The Resource-Based Viewpoint and Its Application in Enterprise Theory, *Economic Theory and Business Management*, 2000 (4)

To sum up, after decades of development of enterprise resource theory, scholars have conducted comprehensive and in-depth research on important concepts such as enterprise resources and enterprise capabilities and have formed rich research results. In particular, the evolution of enterprise resource theory from the resource view, capability view, and knowledge view is not only the exploration of the law of enterprise development by scholars, but more importantly, they provide us with a way of thinking and understanding the "black box" of enterprises.

3.3 Definition of M&A Capability

The definition of capability in *Ci Hai*[1] is that capability usually refers to the ability to complete a certain activity, including the specific way to complete a certain activity and the psychological characteristics necessary for completing a particular activity. Capability is divided into general capability and special capability. The former refers to the basic abilities that must be possessed for various activities, such as observation, memory, abstract generalization, etc. The latter refers to the abilities necessary for engaging in certain professional activities, such as mathematical ability, music painting ability, or flying ability. Human abilities are formed and developed in acquired learning, life, and social practice based on quality. The degree of development and combination of the psychological characteristics necessary for various activities are different in individuals, so the ability characteristics differ from person to person. The definition of capability is the quality and ability to be able to do something in *Oxford Advanced Learner's English-Chinese Dictionary*.

The operation of enterprises requires the input and support of resources in five aspects: natural force, human resources, financial resources, material resources, and knowledge. The enterprise's production process needs to convert these inputs into products or services. To maximise profits, enterprises always need to coordinate the input ratio of various resources and carry out production under the optimal ratio of various resources. However, under realistic conditions, the pressure from all sides makes it impossible for the various resources of the enterprise to always be in the best configuration state. If the optimal allocation state of enterprise resources is taken as the benchmark, on the one hand, some resources will remain remaining because they are not fully utilized, such as the surplus management personnel of the enterprise, the annual retained earnings, etc. The part of these resources that exceed the optimally configured baseline state is the remaining resources. On the other hand, if a resource is in shortage relative to the baseline state, the resource is a shortage resource. Therefore, slack resources and shortage resources are relative and are two different perspectives of one thing.

In the modern market with an accelerated circulation of production factors, when a certain resource is in short supply, most enterprises can quickly replenish it by purchasing and other means. When there is a surplus of a certain resource, the

[1] An unabridged, comprehensive Chinese dictionary. -*Tr.*

remaining part of the resource cannot be combined with other resources in the production process, which will undoubtedly reduce the return on capital of the enterprise. Under the goal of maximizing enterprise value, the remaining resources should be invested in projects with good returns and risk characteristics to obtain future cash flow. At this time, mergers and acquisitions are a good way for enterprises to find investment opportunities for slack resources, and slack resources also become an internal driving force for enterprises to carry out mergers and acquisitions.

Mergers and acquisitions are an unconventional development method of an enterprise, which often have a huge impact on the enterprise and require the support of various enterprise resources. The normal business activities of the enterprise also require the investment of enterprise resources. The merger and acquisition activities of the enterprise should not affect the normal operation of the enterprise. It is difficult to imagine that a company with insufficient resources in terms of manpower and capital can successfully implement large-scale mergers and acquisitions. Therefore, having certain slack resources is also necessary for enterprises to carry out mergers and acquisitions, and the mergers and acquisitions activities of enterprises should be considered based on the remaining resources of the enterprise. Ge Weijie et al. (2014) verified this view through empirical research. The research finds that, whether it is a local state-owned enterprise or a private enterprise, slack resources are the precondition for launching mergers and acquisitions. Private enterprises store more slack resources before mergers and acquisitions and rely more on their mergers and acquisitions capabilities to complete transactions. For local state-owned enterprise mergers and acquisitions, government intervention partially replaces the role of remaining resources.

Yu Ying et al. (2004) said in *Three Principles to Manage Risks in M&A Operation*, "Some companies are good at mergers and acquisitions, while others are not good at mergers and acquisitions. Mergers and acquisitions may be based on the requirements of enhancing and improving core competitiveness, but mergers and acquisitions are also a kind of ability. Like people, the ability may be based on innate factors, but its formation often comes from acquired training. If we regard mergers and acquisitions as a kind of ability, we will look at a problem from a new angle. For example, when an enterprise first uses mergers and acquisitions as a means of development, it can take a tentative approach. It is best to control the number of mergers and acquisitions within a certain range and to estimate the various difficulties in the process of mergers and acquisitions more fully. When a company believes that M&A has become a part of its core competence, it can take more M&A means. This view is consistent with the research results of Western scholars. Western scholar research shows that statistically speaking, the more the number of times of M&A, the greater the probability of success, and the reason is that M&A capability is a process of continuous cultivation and improvement." This discussion regards M&A as an extension of corporate capability and involves the issue of M&A capability but does not define the concept of M&A capability. Laamanen and Keil (2008) argue that M&A capability can be defined as "the knowledge, skills, systems, structures, and processes that can be leveraged during M&A". M&A capabilities include organizational capabilities such as the ability to identify suitable acquisition targets, negotiate transactions and manage the integration process.

Combining the above definition of capability and the concept of enterprise resource-based theory, we define M&A capability as the ability of an enterprise to use its remaining resources to complete M&A activities.

3.4 Structural Analysis of M&A Capability

A modern enterprise is an economic organization that invests a certain combination of resources (tangible resources, intangible resources), produces products or services through the production process, obtains benefits through market transactions, and finally realizes the increase of enterprise value. Companies contemplating mergers and acquisitions need the necessary resources, and a lack of sufficient resources can hinder corporate strategic change (Iyer & Miller, 2008). Specifically, in M&A activities, enterprises not only need to invest tangible and intangible resources but also need to manage the entire M&A process to ensure the successful implementation of M&A activities. Therefore, clarifying the elements of M&A capability becomes the first step to understanding the structure of M&A capability.

3.4.1 Elements of M&A Capability

Enterprise resource theory reveals how an enterprise utilizes various resources for production and realizes the goal of maximizing enterprise value. The M&A capability of an enterprise is also closely related to the various resources that the enterprise possesses. Intuitively, mergers and acquisitions require investment in human, financial, material, natural, knowledge, and other aspects. It is difficult to carry out mergers and acquisitions without corresponding resources, but not all resources owned by an enterprise can constitute mergers and acquisitions capabilities. M&A capability is an abstract concept that should be refined through analysis. Therefore, identifying the constituent elements of enterprise M&A capability and extracting various representation dimensions of M&A capability has become a necessary part of our further study of M&A capability.

Capability is an abstract concept, but an enterprise's capability can be manifested through its behavior. By comprehensively examining the mergers and acquisitions activities of enterprises, through identification and refining, we can approach the essence through phenomena, identify which resources of the enterprise play a key role in the formation of mergers and acquisitions capabilities, and then summarize the constituent elements of mergers and acquisitions capabilities. Therefore, this section uses the multiple cases research method, by studying several actual merger cases, to achieve the above research purposes. The research method has the following characteristics: multiple cases should be regarded as multiple experiments, with the logic of replication rather than sampling (Yin, 1994); the evidence obtained by this method is generally considered to be strong and robust, and therefore the entire study is often considered to be relatively robust (Herriott & Fierstine, 1983).

Since the constituent elements of M&A capability are not single, six typical cases[2] are selected here to show various aspects of M&A capability constituent elements and reflect the four resource elements that must be possessed by the M&A capability: human resources, financial resources, practical and information resources, and the acquisition management capabilities to organize them.

Cisco Systems achieved high growth through mergers and acquisitions in the 1990s. The company's finance staff and the central business development team conducted all pre-acquisition negotiations without engaging an investment bank. In most acquisitions, 35 full-time employees were involved in all aspects of the transaction, from pre-acquisition due diligence to post-acquisition integration, demonstrating the company's excellent human resources. Cisco has always taken acquisitions as its development strategy. Between 1994 and 2000, Cisco acquired about 50 companies with a total consideration of about US$20 billion. During this period, the company's high stock price and abundant cash showed that the company has strong financial resources for acquisitions, making it possible to achieve high growth through mergers and acquisitions. Starting a business and then being acquired by Cisco is the dream of many small and mid-sized Silicon Valley startups. The rapid development of Internet technology has driven the continuous innovation of small- and medium-sized enterprises, and the tangible and intangible assets resources such as Cisco's good brand and product line make acquiring SMEs a win–win option. Cisco tends to focus on the 3 markets it wants to enter and pays close attention to 5 to 10 target companies in each market. Here, Cisco's brand and its insight into the Internet industry have become an important factor in Cisco's continued successful mergers and acquisitions.

Haier Electric eats "shock fish". Those enterprises with good equipment performance and debts that can be stripped, but only because of the inefficiency caused by vague property rights, no one responsible, or poor management, are considered by Haier Group as " shock fish" and can be merged. From the merger of Qingdao Electroplating Factory in 1988, the merger of Qingdao Air Conditioner Factory and Qingdao Refrigerator Factory in 1991, the merger of Condenser Factory in 1992, the merger of Qingdao Hongxing Electric Group in July 1995, and the merger of Laiyang Electric Iron Factory in July 1997, a total of 14 companies were merged, RMB70 million was invested, and RMB1.4 billion was revitalized. Through mergers, rapid expansion at a low cost was achieved. Starting from the merger of Hongxing Electric

[2] *Sources* Robert J. Borghese and Paul F. Borghese, M&A *from Planning to Integration*, translated by Wu Xuchuan and Wang Fen China Machine Press, 2004; Haier Group Website: Haier Concept; Steel King-Indian Rich Mittal the family history, Oriental Morning Post, 2006-2-8; Marion Devine, *Successful Mergers*, translated by Han Song, CITIC Publishing House, 2004; Mittal, the world's largest steel company, was approved to acquire the second largest steel company, Securities Times, 2006–5-19; Wang Dong and Zhang Qiusheng, Mergers and Acquisitions Cases, Tsinghua University Press, Beijing Jiaotong University Press, 2004.

Co., Ltd., Haier Group will send 3 managers to each merged enterprise. They will bring Haier's culture and management system to the merged enterprise and rejuvenate it. In the contract of merging Laiyang Iron Factory in July 1997, Haier Group invested RMB11 million in tangible and intangible assets such as technology, molds, and models, and became the largest shareholder of Laiyang Haier Electric Co., Ltd. (holding 55%). Human and financial resources are the basic capabilities that Haier must possess to carry out mergers and acquisitions in the early stage of development.

Mittal acquires Poland's Polskie Huty Stali Company, after the rapid asset injection, assigned a 15-person emergency management team to the factory to stabilize the operation of the factory. The team members included experts in management, finance, marketing, etc., and patiently improved the technology and capabilities of the factory, so that factory was under a Gross profit of US$121 million was achieved in the ninth month of the acquisition. In 2006, Mittal Steel acquired Arcelor, the second-largest steel group in the world. Through strong alliances, economies of scale will be better achieved, and companies will have stronger negotiating power over upstream suppliers and downstream consumers. The post-acquisition integration process demonstrated Mittal Steel's strong acquisition management ability to organize the human, financial, material, and information of both parties to serve the company's strategy.

Microsoft buys tech companies. Microsoft Corp., a giant in the software industry, claims to have US$50 billion in acquisition funding and has bought an average of 10 tech companies a year since 1995. Target companies mainly include software service and solution providers, Internet service providers, and companies developing new technologies. Strong financial strength guarantees the smooth implementation of its acquisition activities.

The acquisition of Revlon Cosmetics by Pantry Pride is a typical case of issuing junk bonds to finance leveraged buyouts. In 1985, Revlon was one of the largest health care products and beauty cosmetics companies in the United States, with a net worth of US$1 billion and stable operating income, while Pantry Pride was a company with total assets of only US$150 million. With the backing of junk bond founder Milken, Pantry Pride received a US$500 million bank loan, and the US$350 million junk bond issued was also subscribed by Drexel Burnham Lambert (DBL), and the acquisition was completed. Here, Milken's support played a crucial role in the merger case.

Theoretical and academic studies on M&A activities agree that M&A activities are hazardous, and no matter how wonderful the post-merger prospects of the company are, the results are often mixed. For most companies, few go through enough of the M&A process to form a set of patterns, as M&A activity tends to be a considerable effort. Managers who do not have enough experience in mergers and acquisitions, often only focus on how to complete the acquisition process rather than the merger event itself, ignoring the real play of expected synergies, resulting in unsatisfactory merger results.

Because the number of mergers and acquisitions continues to grow while the failure rate is high, focusing on the ability of companies to manage mergers and acquisitions throughout the merger process should be instructive. As mentioned in the previous case, Cisco Systems and Mittal Steel achieved high growth through mergers and acquisitions. Here, we introduce the example of General Electric Finance Company[3] to further interpret the key role of merger management capabilities in successful mergers and acquisitions.

In 1933, General Electric Company (GE) of the United States established a subsidiary, General Electric Finance Company, to provide loans to customers who purchased GE products. Now it has grown into a conglomerate that provides financial services. The company has been striving to turn the integration of merger and acquisition resources into a core capability and competitive advantage to maintain continuous growth in the future. The company has carried out more than 100 mergers and acquisitions between 1993 and 1998, of which more than half of the business is currently acquired through mergers and acquisitions.

During frequent M&A activities, GE Finance and its M&A consulting team created a complete set of M&A resource integration models from pre- M&A assessment to post-M&A integration, successfully guiding the company's M&A practice. The model divides the entire M&A process into four "action stages", covering the steps from the work done before the start of the M&A to the absorption and assimilation stage, and each action stage has 2 to 3 sub-processes. Although the model is the product of logic and reason, its creators also emphasize its artistry, and each acquisition and integration action can become a new interpretation. The model is a kind of structured knowledge, which is the refinement and summary of the company's M&A experience, and it is also becoming more and more perfect with the company's continuous M&A practice. Under managers with experience in mergers and acquisitions, using such a structured merger management model can significantly improve the success rate of mergers and acquisitions.

Similarly, Cisco Systems and Mittal Steel have their own set of summaries and refinements of the M&A process, forming their unique M&A management capabilities in their respective fields. Undoubtedly, this capability has become a core capability of these companies and a force multiplier for company development. The critical role of M&A management capability in M&A activities and its important position in M&A capability are highlighted.

3.4.2 Structure of M&A Capabilities

Using the method of multiple case studies, we have obtained the constituent elements of M&A capability. Further analysis shows that these elements are not arbitrarily combined, they need a certain structure to constitute M&A capability. The structure of M&A capability reflects the constituent elements of M&A capability and their interrelationships. Combined with the theory of enterprise capability and the particularity of M&A activities, we believe that the components of M&A capability

[3] Ronald N. Ashkenas, Lawrence J. DeMonaco, Suzanne C. Francis, Making the Deal Real: How GE Capital Integrates Acquisitions, *Harvard Business Review*, January/February 1998.

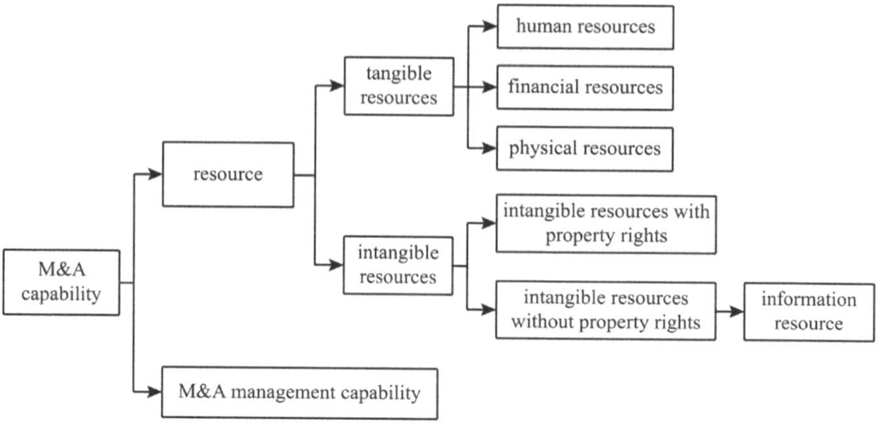

Fig. 3.1 Structure of M&A capability

include resources and skills. Resources are the preconditions, and capabilities act on resources to form M&A capabilities. Among them, resources include tangible resources (human resources, financial resources, and physical resources) and intangible resources, and skills refer to the skills of enterprises using the above resources to achieve the goals of mergers and acquisitions. Figure 3.1 illustrates the structure of M&A capability.

3.4.2.1 M&A Capability Elements—Resources

(1) Human resources

Firstly, M&A activities need the support of human resources. Mergers and acquisitions is a complex and highly specialized job, involving many issues such as strategy, finance, law, taxation, etc., which need to be handled prudently by companies. At the same time, mergers and acquisitions also involve stakeholders' interests such as shareholders, governments, creditors, and employees of both parties. Dealing with the interests of all parties also guarantees the success of mergers and acquisitions. All the above tasks require the enterprise to invest a certain number of human resources for overall planning and management. For some highly specialized links, hiring a qualified intermediary agency for support is often necessary.

Secondly, post-merger integration requires the support of human resources. Lajoux, an American M&A research expert, once cited the research results of fifteen well-known M&A experts or research institutions in the world on the reasons for the failure of M&A activities and believes that the reasons for the failure of M&A activities include strategic mistakes, improper valuation, poor integration, and other reasons. Through comprehensive analysis, it is found that poor integration is the main reason for the failure of mergers and acquisitions as high as 50%, which is much higher than other factors. The success or failure of post-merger integration is directly related to the success or failure of mergers and acquisitions and occupies a pivotal position in the entire process of mergers and acquisitions. It is precisely because the process of integration is the most complex and critical stage in the entire M&A process, it is often necessary to set up a special integration working group to formulate integration strategies, determine the content and scope of integration and implement them carefully. The integration process will involve many aspects such as strategy, business process, organizational structure, human resources, corporate culture, etc., which requires enterprises to invest a lot of manpower and material resources to ensure the smooth progress of the integration work. Integration efforts without adequately qualified human resources are unlikely to be successful.

Finally, managing a post-merger business requires the support of human resources. According to the different needs of the acquirer and the target company in terms of strategic dependence and organizational independence, integration can be divided into four types: full integration, coexistence integration, protection integration, and control integration. When the strategic dependence between enterprises is not strong, and the organizational independence is not strong, adopting protective integration can maintain the relative independence of the target company, and the acquirer does not need to invest too much management and human resources in implementing a larger integration. In other cases, M&A activities will bring about changes in the target company's organizational structure and human resources, often leading to the departure of target company employees, and may also lay off unqualified employees. To ensure the success of the integration and the normal operation of the integrated enterprise, the acquirer needs to input the management and human resources of the target enterprise. This also requires the acquirer to have a certain surplus of human resources.

(2) Financial resources

Mergers and acquisitions are transactions with business control as the target (Zhang Qiusheng, 2005). In an M&A transaction, to obtain business control, the acquirer must pay specific considerations to the target party. Mergers and acquisitions are an unconventional way of developing an enterprise. Once implemented, it will often bring about significant changes in the capital structure of both parties. In particular, the acquirer must carefully arrange its financial resources to maximize the success of the mergers and acquisitions. Currently, understanding the capital requirements of M&A activities and the payment method of M&A becomes a very critical issue.

(i) M&A funding needs

The capital requirement for M&A refers to the amount of capital required by the acquirer to complete the M&A. It is directly related to the amount of financing, financing method, and financing time arrangement, and is mainly composed of three components: consideration paid for mergers and acquisitions, direct costs of mergers and acquisitions, and expenditures required to undertake off-balance sheet liabilities and contingent liabilities of the target company. When financing capacity is insufficient, firms cannot integrate even if they have M&A incentives (Acemoglu et al., 2009). Therefore, to seize M&A opportunities, companies that intend to undertake mergers and acquisitions maintain loose financial resources by maintaining lower debt ratios and holding more cash (Almazan et al., 2010; Zhou Shouhua et al., 2016). Celikyurt et al. (2010) found that after the IPO, the mergers and acquisitions activities of enterprises are active, and the improvement of external financing ability promotes mergers and acquisitions.

First, M&A pays consideration. The consideration paid for mergers and acquisitions refers to the consideration paid by the acquirer to obtain business control. Depending on the payment method, this consideration can be the amount of cash or cash equivalents or the fair value of other relevant asset items or securities that the acquirer gave up on the acquisition date to obtain business control of the target enterprise, or it can be a mix of the two ways. The size of the consideration paid for mergers and acquisitions is related to the size of the target company's equity value, the holding ratio, and the payment premium rate, and there is the following relationship between them:

$$\text{M\&A payment consideration} = \text{target enterprise equity value} \times \text{shareholding ratio} \times (1 + \text{premium rate})$$

The premium rate is the rate at which the consideration paid is higher than the value of the acquiree's equity.

Second, the direct cost of mergers and acquisitions. Mergers and acquisitions often involve multiple interests. To complete the transaction, there will also be some direct costs associated with mergers and acquisitions, such as business fees paid to external investment banks, accountants, legal advisers, appraisal agencies, and other intermediaries. For listed companies that use securities financing, the fees for registration and issuance of equity securities are also included. The amount of M&A direct costs are often related to the consideration paid for the M&A. Generally, 1% to 5% of the consideration paid for the M&A.

Third, the expenditure required to undertake off-balance sheet liabilities and contingent liabilities of the target enterprise. Off-balance sheet liabilities refer to the obligations that the target enterprise does not reflect on the balance sheet but needs to undertake clearly, such as retirement expenses, severance expenses, and resettlement expenses of employees. Although these fees are not included on the target company's balance sheet, they are also expenses that the acquirer must bear in implementing the merger.

Contingent liabilities refer to potential obligations arising from past transactions or events, the existence of which must be confirmed by the occurrence or non-occurrence of uncertain future events, or actual obligations arising from past transactions or events, the performance of which is not likely to result in economic the outflow of benefits from the entity or the amount of the obligation cannot be measured reliably. Contingent liabilities mainly include endorsement transfer or discount of commercial paper, pending litigation or arbitration, debt guarantee, product quality assurance, etc. If these matters occur or are confirmed after the merger, the enterprise will be obliged to pay, which constitutes potential expenses for the acquirer. Whether or not the acquirer undertakes the off-balance sheet liabilities and contingent liabilities of the target enterprise depends on whether there are stipulations on these related matters in the acquisition agreement.

(ii) M&Apayment method

In mergers and acquisitions, cash and stocks are the two main means of payment, and the acquisition target can be assets and shares. In this way, there are four situations according to different payment methods and objects, namely, the acquisition of assets with cash, the acquisition of shares with cash, the acquisition of assets with shares, and the acquisition of shares with shares, as shown in Table 3.2. Under different payment methods, the acquirer's ability to pay for M&A transactions is different. In other words, the M&A payment method affects the size of the largest M&A transaction that the acquirer can complete, which will be discussed separately below.

The first is the case where cash is used as a payment method.

In the case of cash as the payment method, the acquirer needs to comprehensively examine its financial capabilities to determine whether the enterprise has sufficient financial resources to implement the merger and acquisition and how much the enterprise can bear the up-front debt of the target enterprise.

To evaluate a company's financial ability to undertake an acquisition, special interpretive tools should be used to analyze the company's financial statements and other relevant operating data statements. The four evaluation criteria for determining the financial capability of an enterprise under such conditions are:

Asset and Liability Quality Evaluation—Tests the ability of a company's assets and liabilities
Liquidity Evaluation—Evaluate the company's ability to use cash and current assets to complete current tasks
Solvency Evaluation—Determines the company's ability to repay long-term debt
Leverage Capability Evaluation—Determines the Company's Ability to Use Financial Leverage

It should be noted that the use of these evaluation tools described in the Fig. 3.2 is not fixed and should be changed according to the different needs of different industries.

The acquirer generally considers its funds first when deciding. If the acquirer has sufficient or even remaining cash, it can consider adopting cash payment during M&A. However, if it is difficult for its funds to meet the full consideration of the acquisition, the acquirer must raise the required cash through external debt financing. Bank borrowing and the issuance of corporate bonds are very common methods.

Table 3.2 M&A target and payment method

M&apayment method	Assets	Shares
Cash	Acquire assets for cash	Acquire shares for cash
Shares	Acquiring assets with shares	Buy-out shares

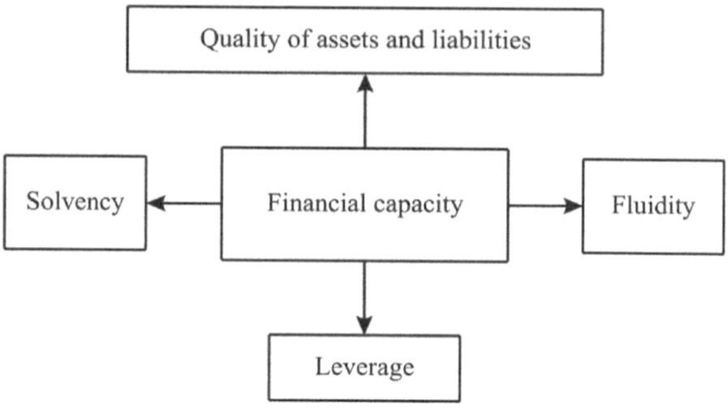

Fig. 3.2 Enterprise financial capability evaluation

When the acquirer chooses the debt financing method, the enterprise should consider the impact of debt on the enterprise's capital structure and capital cost, as well as the changes in the structure of the enterprise's consolidated financial statements caused by mergers and acquisitions.

The acquirer can also issue new shares on the stock market or place new shares to the original shareholders. That is, the company issues the shares and uses the proceeds from the sale of the shares to pay the consideration for the M&A transaction. In this case, the acquirer is equivalent to using its funds to carry out the acquisition, avoiding the dilution of the acquirer's control. However, after the merger, the net assets per share will not necessarily increase, because the change in the net assets per share after the merger depends on the relationship between the price-to-book ratios of both parties. The same is true for the impact on earnings per share.

Many companies will choose to implement acquisitions through subsidiaries. In this case, the assessment of the company's financial capabilities also needs to comprehensively consider the relevant financial capabilities of the parent and subsidiary companies.

The second is the case where shares are used as payment methods.

In the fifth wave of mergers and acquisitions in the 1990s, several super enterprises were created in the global financial, communications, petroleum, electrical, pharmaceutical, and other industries. In the context of global industrial integration, mergers among large enterprises are mostly voluntary combinations and rarely hostile takeovers. Since the amount involved is often huge, the payment method of the stock exchange between the two parties has become the mainstream.

When the acquirer uses shares as the payment method, the first point is to clarify the acquirer's company value, which can be obtained through valuation techniques such as cash flow discounting. In an acquisition process, the purchase price is determined based on the company's stock price. If the value of the acquirer's stock is overvalued by the market, it will be beneficial for the acquirer to use stock as a payment method for M&A; on the contrary, if the acquirer's stock price is undervalued, whether to use stock as a payment method needs to be carefully considered in conjunction with the transaction. Therefore, the use of stock as a means of payment is seen as a signal that management believes that the company's stock is not undervalued by the market.

Taking stock as a means of payment for mergers and acquisitions, that is, to achieve acquisitions through share swaps. According to the different ways of the stock exchange, it can be divided into directional capital increase and stock exchange, treasury stock exchange, and cross-share exchange between parent company and subsidiary. It is more common for the acquirer to realize financing through the targeted issuance of new shares or the repurchase of shares from the original shareholders. If the price-earnings ratio of the acquirer's stock is higher than that of the target company, the new company's earnings per share after the merger can be higher than the acquirer's original level. From the perspective of the target company's shareholders, this can delay the realization of earnings, resulting in tax benefits. At the same time, due to the continued ownership of equity, shareholders of the target company can also share in the value appreciation brought about by the synergistic effect of mergers and acquisitions. However, this method will be restricted by the relevant provisions in the securities laws of various countries, and it will take a long time for approval, which will easily provide opportunities for competitors. More importantly, the issuance of new shares will affect the acquirer's original equity structure, which in turn affects the equity value, so this method is often used in good faith mergers and acquisitions.

The determination of the stock exchange ratio in the payment method of purchasing shares by shares can be determined by the L-G model proposed by Larson and Gonedes (1969), which is currently a relatively recognized model for determining the stock exchange ratio.

Table 3.3 compares the factors that need to be considered and the application conditions of cash and stock payment methods.

Table 3.3 Comparison of M&A payment methods

Payment method	Considerations	Conditions of use
Cash	Provide tangible value to acquirer shareholders; May affect the acquirer's credit rating and financing flexibility; Target shareholders can cash out but have tax implications	The acquirer has strong financing ability and lower financing costs; Target shareholders wish to cash out; Targets have a higher tax base and shareholders enjoy lower tax rates
Stock	Calculated based on changes in share price; Requires a long-term assessment of the acquirer's share price; There is a risk that the target shareholder's share price will fall; The acquirer runs the risk of overpaying for the stock price	The price-earnings ratio of the acquirer's stock is relatively high, and there is a small dilution risk; The stock price is not very liquid, or the price limit is adopted to reduce the risk of stock price fluctuation; Target shareholders wish to continue to participate in business operations or avoid current taxation

Source Global M&A Research Center, Economic and Technological Commission of All-China Federation of Industry and Commerce *M&A Handbook*, China Times Economic Press, 2002 (6)

There is no need to stick to one payment method for mergers and acquisitions. In practice, two methods are often used in combination. According to statistics, in 1998, more than half of the M&A transactions in the United States were paid in cash, and the rest were either paid in stock (about 29%) or paid in both stock and cash (about 17%). In the previous 10 years, almost 70% of transactions were made in cash, only 8% were paid in stock, and the rest were a mix of the two. However, most of the mega deals are by way of the stock exchange, from 1995 to 2000, 90% of the mega deals of more than US$1 billion were completed by the two parties' stock exchange acquisition.[4] It can be predicted that in large and mega transactions, share-for-stock acquisitions will be the main trend in the future.

(3) Physical resources

The physical resources here mainly refer to fixed assets such as factory buildings, equipment, land, resource reserves, and information systems. In previous resource analyses of the competitive advantage of a single enterprise, physical assets have often received little attention, because they can generally be acquired directly in the factor market and therefore are generally not used as a source of competitive advantage. But there are at least four reasons why physical assets should be given attention in M&A.

First, M&A can acquire physical assets relatively quickly compared to purchasing from the factor markets, thereby gaining a time advantage.

Second, due to the volatility of the capital markets, sometimes there is an undervaluation of the assets of the acquiree, allowing M&A to gain a more favorable price advantage than buying directly from the factor markets.

Third, some physical assets may not be special in themselves, but if their performance depends on a particular environment, their value may exceed the value of similar assets. For example, a vacuum tube plant depends on the gas supply facilities of the industrial park in which it is located to provide production functions, which makes a plant in an industrial park more valuable than an independent plant. In fact, there are many such examples under the conditions of what Marshall (1965) calls external economies of scale.

Fourth, certain equipment developed by the target party alone (such as an information system developed especially for the enterprise) actually integrates the target party's proprietary knowledge, and the target party's capabilities cannot be exercised without the support of these proprietary assets, so it may also become a unique and valuable resource.

Moreover, if the value of a resource such as a management information system is measured by the value of hardware equipment or application software, it may be the same as using physical assets to measure a human capital-intensive enterprise, ignoring the most important value elements, so classifying management information systems as a physical asset is largely reluctant.

---

[4] Zhang Zelai, Hu Xuanneng, Song Linfeng, *M&A Financing*, China Finance & Economic Publishing House, 2004.

Because of the strong connection between these particular types of physical assets and the internal knowledge of the enterprise, they are often more difficult to transfer. Borghese and Borgese (2004) point out that unifying the IT systems of two companies is extremely difficult and usually takes more time and cost than expected. In fact, the information management system reflects the enterprise's business process, so the greater difficulty in integrating the information system lies in changing the operating way that the users of the information system are accustomed to.

(4) Information resources

Enterprises not only have the above-mentioned human resources, financial resources, and physical resources, but also have many information resources, including intangible assets with property rights, such as trademark rights, land use rights, and goodwill, and intangible resources without property rights, that is, information resources that can bring benefits to the enterprise although they do not have clear property rights, such as brand, social capital (relationship) and know- how.

Robert Kaplan and David Norton (2005) believe that more than 75% of a company's market value is derived from intangible assets that cannot be captured by traditional financial indicators, that is, the information resources referred to here. The focus on information resources in M&A is due to the following factors: first, the value amount of information resources is often difficult to assess accurately, which has become an important factor affecting the value of the target enterprise; second, information resources are not consumed in use and can even add value in some certain cases, so they can be a value base for expansion.

(i) Intangible assets

Intangible assets under the conceptual framework of financial accounting refer to identifiable non-monetary assets without physical form owned or controlled by an enterprise. The enterprise's self-created goodwill and internally generated brands, and newspaper names should not be recognized as intangible assets because their cost cannot be distinguished. This definition clearly reflects the connotation and extension of intangible asset items, and its main characteristics are recognizability and measurability for accounting purposes, and these two attributes are also the main characteristics that distinguish them from other information resources owned by enterprises.

(ii) Other intangible resources

Compared with intangible assets, companies also have many other intangible resources, such as brands, practices, processes, procurement, and sales networks. Although they cannot be specifically reflected in the statement because they cannot meet the conditions for recognition and measurement, they are often crucial to the business management activities of enterprises. Essentially, they are collections of some information and belong to the most important part of information resources.

Debra Emmington (1998), an American knowledge management expert, pointed out the difference between knowledge and related concepts: data is the element of analysis, information is data with content, knowledge is meaningful information, and wisdom is the combination of knowledge and insight. For companies competing in a specific market, not all information is valuable. The company needs to decide for itself what kind of information is meaningful, and those that are meaningful to the company are its information assets. For enterprise M&A activities, the information assets that constitute the company's M&A capability mainly refer to the brand, social capital (relationship), know-how, and know-who.

A brand is recognized as an important company-specific resource (Amit & Schoemaker, 1993; Dierickx & Cool, 1989; Wernerfelt, 1984) and is critical to a company's success in the marketplace (Kapferer, 1992; Shocker et al., 1994). Srivastava et al. (1998) pointed out that market-based intangible resources like brands can reduce costs or increase profits. A brand is also scarce, difficult to imitate, and replaces a resource, which requires long-term construction (Reddy et al., 1994; Bergen et al., 1996). For example, the brand of Coca-Cola cannot be built or replicated with thousands of advertisements, and it is derived from decades of consumers' experience drinking Coke and the resulting identification. Building a brand requires cumulative investment in advertising and marketing (Rossiter & Percy, 1997) so that customers are aware of it and generate positive associations. And once customers have established brand loyalty, they will be reluctant to switch brands due to usage habits (Wernerfelt, 1985). These characteristics of brands sometimes make acquiring a brand more attractive than building one, especially when operating across borders (Anand & Delios, 2002).

In M&A, a good brand of the acquirer can enhance the recognition of the target shareholders, reduce the concerns of the target stakeholders, and help ensure that the M&A process receives good cooperation from the target. At the same time, a good brand is also conducive to the market's better expectations of the post-merger companies, which is more conducive to realizing the expected synergy effect. It can be considered that the M&A capability of a company with a good brand is greater than that of a company without a good brand under other conditions being the same.

Social capital represents the relational resources available to individuals through the networks of social relationships (Baker, 1990; Bourdieu & Wacquant, 1992; Coleman, 1990; Portes, 1998; Portes & Sensenbrenner, 1993; Putnam, 1995). The social capital theory believes that an enterprise's network of external relationships is an important factor affecting its performance (Leenders & Gabbay, 1999). Enterprises trade with suppliers and other partners through networks to obtain external resources and produce products or services at competitive prices to attract or retain customers (Burt, 1992; Pennings & Lee, 1999; Pennings et al., 1998; Uzzi, 1996). That is, external linkages play a very important role in procuring those assets and identifying business opportunities because economic activity is embedded in a larger inter-organizational network and social relationships constitute the medium of the economic transaction (Burt, 1992; Granovetter, 1985).

Social relations are the carriers of social capital, so the analysis of social capital generally starts with analyzing relationships. Relationships with suppliers or channels are what Porter calls vertical linkages. Porter (1997) pointed out that although vertical linkages can be an important source of competitive advantage as cost drivers or uniqueness drivers, vertical linkages are often overlooked. The benefits of vertical linkages are achieved through the coordination or overall optimal design of the value activities of the parties involved in the linkage. The optimal arrangement of vertical linkages is related to specific production methods, commercial policies, and peer competition linkages. Changes resulting from M&A may upset the balance of the target's previous vertical linkages, causing suppliers or channels to expect to renegotiate to obtain or retain favorable business interests. Ignoring such changes may lead to the loss of suppliers or sales channels. For example, after the horizontal merger of aircraft manufacturer Boeing with McDonnell Douglas, one of McDonnell Douglas' suppliers stopped supplying, because the supplier had a competitive relationship with Boeing.

In contrast, horizontal linkages, that is, the linkages between companies and competitors, have received less attention in strategy research than vertical linkages. This is in stark contrast to the attention horizontal linkages receive in- game research and popular media reporting. The horizontal linkages should be given due attention because (a) competitors may become the target of horizontal M&A; and (b) M&A may cause the equilibrium of the industry to be disrupted: a company's M&A may cause retaliatory reactions from competitors. After PeopleSoft acquired J. D. Edwards in 2003, its scale and strength challenged its competitor Oracle (the second-largest player in the enterprise software market), and Oracle's announcement of a hostile takeover of PeopleSoft was an example of a chain reaction of M&A.

What Porter calls vertical linkages and the horizontal linkages mentioned above correspond exactly to vertical and horizontal mergers and acquisitions in M&A research. But in the study of social capital, both vertical and horizontal linkages are one kind of partnership-based linkages, which also include linkages with universities and research institutions and linkages with business associations. The opposite of partnership-based linkages is sponsorship-based linkages, such as government agencies, and commercial banks that provide policy-based loans. The criterion for distinguishing between partnership-based and sponsorship-based linkages is whether the linkages involve a clear two-way resource transaction.

The influence of the acquirer's social capital on M&A activities is often significant, and the acquirer should conduct a comprehensive examination and assessment of its social capital before M&A. When examining social capital, it should focus on the value of social capital such as vertical linkages (suppliers, channels, customers), horizontal linkages (competitors), and sponsorship-based linkages (government relations, creditor relations).

Know-how usually refers to practical knowledge, skills, and tricks, which are part of knowledge. The more authoritative classification of knowledge comes from the Organisation for Economic Cooperation and Development (OECD). In 1996, the OECD classified knowledge into four types in its annual report The Knowledge-Based Economy: know-why, which refers to the knowledge of objective principles and regularities of things; know-how, which refers to the knowledge of skills, techniques, and abilities to satisfy people's needs; know- what, which refers to knowledge about facts and know-who, which refers to the knowledge of who knows something or fact and who knows how to do something (see Fig. 3.3).

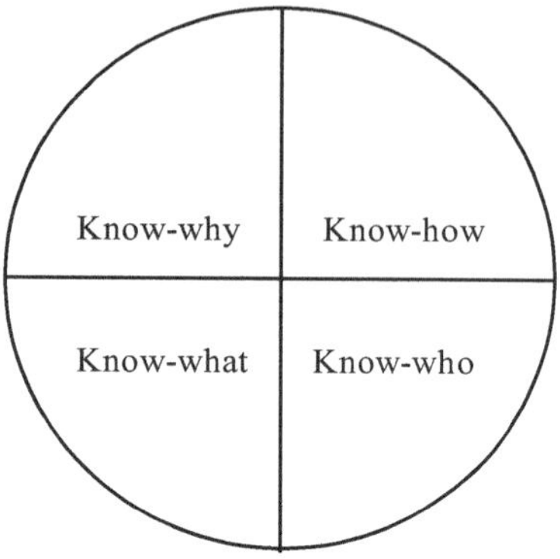

Fig. 3.3 Four types of knowledge

Know-how as a type of knowledge is produced by "learning-by-doing" (Argote & Epple, 1990; Arrow, 1962; Dutton & Thomas, 1985). Learning-by-doing is a process of accumulation, summarization, and improvement based on previous experiences. The previous experiences often have an impact on the subsequent learning process, so its formation process often shows a gradual accumulation and path dependence phenomenon (Arthur, 1988; David, 1993; Levitt & March, 1988).

Jin Yunhui and Jia Changjie (2003) studied the influence of inertia on the M&A strategy choice of listed companies. Inertia theory holds that every organization is controlled by powerful inertial forces, and when faced with the shock of environmental changes, they are rarely successful in making fundamental changes in strategy and organizational structure. Through the event analysis of M&A data from 210 listed companies in China's securities market over 4 years, the study concluded that there is inertia in the formulation and implementation of M&A strategies of enterprises, and enterprises tend to repeat the types of M&A that they have been implemented before, regardless of whether the environment has changed. The more times a certain type of M&A has been executed previously, the more likely that the company will execute that type of M&Anext time.

Know-how mainly refers to that technical and practical knowledge, which exists in many forms in individuals, organizational routines (Nelson & Winter, 1982), and organizational processes. Part of know-how can be made explicit by summarizing and distilling, which is manifested as operation manuals and templates. It is explicit know-how. However, what is easy to understand, distill and summarize is often only the information that is formed, mature, and easy to express in words or language, not all the information. There is also some information such as skills and tricks that are difficult to express, and often need to be obtained through observation, imitation, and practice. This part of the information is implicit know-how.

A lot of operational knowledge on M&A is in the ever-renewing guides, templates, and business instructions of investment banks and other intermediaries on M&A, and a large amount of information has been accumulated. However, due to the complexity and confidentiality of M&A activities, it is often difficult for written information to convey the full picture of M&A activities, and M&A involves the interests of multiple stakeholders on both sides of the M&A, which places high demands on the management capabilities of the acquirer. In this case, implicit know-how is often more important. M&A experience can improve and strengthen M&A capabilities because experience helps to accumulate M&A knowledge, especially tacit knowledge that is difficult to externalize. For example, Cisco is a typical company using M&A to achieve rapid development. The company has an internal team specializing in M&A. They have completed most of the M&A activities without hiring external investment banks. Continuous M&A allows the team to accumulate rich M&A experience, providing strong support for the company's development.

The know-how about M&A, that is, M&A know-how, plays a very important role in M&A capability. All other things being equal, having M&A know-how tends to perform better. The M&A know-how here includes explicit know-how and implicit know-how. As mentioned above, implicit M&A know-how plays an important role in M&A, and implicit M&A know-how mainly comes from M&A experience, so how do you understand the role of M&A experience? Combined with real M&A cases, some companies without M&A experience also made successful M&A when other conditions were present. It can be seen that M&A experience is not a necessary condition for forming M&A capability, but rather an enhancement factor. However, it has also been proved that companies with M&A experience have a higher probability of M&A success compared to companies without M&A experience. Therefore, the M&A experience plays an enhanced role in forming M&A capability, and the M&A know-how behind it is the internal determinant of M&A capability formation.

Know-who is also a type of knowledge that involves information about who knows and knows who can do something. It involves the formation of specific social relationships, that is, the possibility of accessing relevant experts and using their knowledge effectively. In M&A activity, this type of knowledge is concentrated in the choice of intermediaries by both parties. In today's business society, where the division of labor is becoming more and more meticulous, the importance of know-who is also increasingly reflected. For example, regarding the selection of intermediaries, many acquirers hire financial advisors to design M&A plans and control the pace of implementation. Financial advisors often play the role of coordinating lawyers, accountants, and other intermediaries in M&A activities. In developed countries, when intermediaries act as financial advisors to acquirer companies, they often act as financing advisors, responsible for the design of financing plans and the raising of funds, to support the acquirer in successfully completing the M&A plan. Therefore, it is also very necessary for acquirers to understand and choose M&A financial advisors suitable for their own companies.

3.4.2.2 M&A Capability Elements—M&A Management Capability

M&A management capability is a process in which the acquirer obtains knowledge of the internal laws of M&A activities by summarizing previous M&A experiences and integrating organizational knowledge based on comprehensively examining the company's resources, and applying it to M&A activities through management means.

Knowledge as the basis of competence here refers to organizational knowledge rather than individual knowledge. Based on this understanding, M&A management capabilities include M&A resource management capability and M&A knowledge management capability. The former refers to the acquirer's capability to manage the human resources, physical resources, and financial resources owned by the enterprise, while the latter refers to the acquirer's capability to achieve effective use of enterprise resources for M&A through a series of management methods based on the acquired knowledge of the internal laws of M&A activities. M&A management capability is the fundamental reason for the success or failure of M&A (Xie Jigang et al., 2009).

(1) M&A resource management capability

M&A resource management capability is a fundamental aspect of M&A management capability and a basic capability requirement for conducting M&A activities. Combined with the elements of enterprise M&A capability, the M&A resource management capability here mainly refers to the management capability of an enterprise on its human resources, physical resources, and financial resources.

(i) Human resource management capability

With the changes in the nature of work, organization and organizational structure, and the needs of global economic competition, competency-based human resource management has become the development trend of human resource management (Song Heyi & Shang Yufan, 2000). Competency-based human resource management means that the competencies of employees are first assessed to determine the competencies that they possess. Then, according to the needs of the job, the competency requirements of each job for the job holder are determined and compared with the competencies possessed by the employee to determine the best candidate for the job (Wang Dongmin & Jin Zemin, 2003). In this process, enterprises need to pay attention to two important links. The first is to establish an employee capability evaluation model by defining capabilities. The second is to build procedures and processes for competency-oriented human resource management practices.

For residual human resource management in enterprise M&A, enterprises need to first investigate the quantity of residual human resources and classify and evaluate the residual human resources according to the quality requirements of enterprise M&A activities. The evaluation should include both quantity and quality. Then, based on sufficient research and analysis, the residual human resources are allocated to appropriate positions according to the quantity and quality of the residual human resources and in accordance with the needs of M&A activities. In addition, due to the particularity and complexity of M&A, enterprises should fully explore the unique knowledge, technology, and behavior of residual human resources suitable for M&A activities, so as to improve the efficiency of personnel in general.

(ii) Financial resource management capability

From the perspective of enterprise core competence theory, enterprise financial resource management capability is an organic combination of the unique knowledge and experience about financial management work possessed by the enterprise.

Uniqueness refers to the unique financial management method of the enterprise created by financial managers according to the business environment of the enterprise by applying the basic principles of financial management (Zhang Dade, 2004).

Financial resource management capability and financial capability are two different concepts. It is generally considered that financial capability is a comprehensive evaluation of the financing capability, investment capability, and profitability possessed by the enterprise itself. The difference between financial resource management capability and financial capability is expressed as follows: financial capability is a tangible resource, and financial management capability is an intangible resource. Financial capability is the concentrated performance of the overall business activities of the enterprise, and financial management capability is the concentrated performance of the knowledge related to financial management accumulated by the enterprise. The internal relationship between the two is expressed as follows: financial capability is the result of the joint action of various capabilities possessed by the enterprise in past business activities, and financial management capability is one of the foundations for the formation of financial capability, and its ultimate value is reflected in the future financial capability of the enterprise. The direct goal of financial management capability is to form a good financial capability (Cheng Hongwei, 2002).

The high-risk characteristics of M&A activities place higher requirements on the management capability of enterprise financial resources. In the preparation stage of M&A activities, enterprises need to fully assess their financial capabilities, especially those directly related to M&A activities, such as financing capabilities, financial risk control capabilities, and profitability of existing assets. Under the goal of maximizing enterprise value, the enterprise finance departments should use their financial resource management capabilities to support the smooth implementation of M&A activities.

(iii) Physical resource management capability

Physical resources of an enterprise mainly refer to tangible assets such as plants, equipment, land, resource reserves, and information systems. In M&A activities, enterprises need to fully grasp the quantity, value, usage, characteristics, and location of the physical resources owned by the enterprise, formulate physical resource management plans based on historical records, predict growth trends and market price trends, and control the residual physical resources within a reasonable range to provide a basis for M&A decisions.

(2) M&A knowledge management capability

Since the development of the enterprise capability theory, scholars have formed a unified understanding that capability is the source of the enterprise's competitive advantage. With the rise of the new economy represented by computers, software, and networks, more and more scholars recognize that knowledge is the key factor that determines the competitive advantage of enterprises hidden behind the capabilities of enterprises, especially the tacit knowledge that is difficult to be imitated by competitors and the cognitive learning that is closely related to knowledge.

Almost all enterprise theories use the concept of knowledge, but traditional enterprise theories focus only on explicit knowledge that can be clearly described, rather than tacit knowledge that is generally only comprehensible. In traditional enterprise theory, knowledge is assumed to be homogenized, and all knowledge can be transferred, communicated, and shared. In comparison, the enterprise knowledge theory believes that enterprise knowledge is highly contextualized and has the characteristics of intentionality and discrete distribution. The intentionality of knowledge refers to the incomplete expressiveness of knowledge, which means that enterprise knowledge is a routine formed through specific practices, and its use is highly dependent on the internal environment of the enterprise; the discrete distribution of knowledge refers to the enterprise knowledge cannot exist in a centralized form in one person's head, but can only be mastered in a decentralized manner by individuals or teams in specific situations. The intentionality and discrete distribution of enterprise knowledge determine its difficulty of transferability and imitability and also determine the heterogeneity of enterprises, and thus the theory regards it as the source of competitive advantage.

In M&A activities, tacit knowledge often plays a crucial role, which is determined by several characteristics of M&A activities. Firstly, the complexity of M&A activities determines that M&A knowledge is difficult to be fully expressed, and tacit knowledge is stored in each M&A participant. Secondly, the confidentiality of M&A activities often makes certain aspects of M&A highly contextualized, and only a few participants can understand the most real information. Thirdly, for most enterprises, M&A is just an unconventional development method, which makes it difficult to continuously acquire and accumulate tacit knowledge of M&A. Although tacit knowledge of M&A is difficult to transfer and cannot be imitated, enterprises can still acquire, accumulate and diffuse such knowledge in certain ways to cultivate their M&A capabilities.

Grant, Spender, and Ikujiro Nonaka are representatives of the knowledge- based view of the enterprise. Among them, Nonaka mainly studied knowledge- based enterprise theory from the perspective of knowledge management. He emphasized the dependence of knowledge on the situation and insisted on the unification of cognition and action. He viewed the enterprise as an institution for knowledge creation. Nonaka believes that an organization is not the synthesis of much individual knowledge, and it can create knowledge through the interactive learning of individuals within the organization. He deeply studied the knowledge innovation experience of Japanese enterprises and proposed the famous knowledge creation transformation model (1991, 1995), which has become the classic foundation theory of knowledge management research. Nonaka especially emphasized the importance of tacit knowledge and a knowledge environment for enterprise knowledge innovation and knowledge sharing. He believes that new knowledge always comes from individuals, and the core activity of knowledge innovation companies is to spread individual knowledge to others. He created four basic modes of knowledge innovation in organizations, which form a "knowledge spiral", which reflects the knowledge evolution process of enterprises.

Table 3.4 Ikujiro Nonaka's transformation models of knowledge creation

Items	Tacit knowledge	Explicit knowledge
Tacit knowledge	Socialization	Externalization
Explicit knowledge	Internalization	Combination

The four transformation models of knowledge creation proposed by Nonaka are socialization, externalization, combination, and internalization, which together form the SECI model (see Table 3.4). These four aspects constantly interact with each other and transform, and finally achieve the creation of knowledge.

The first mode: "Socialization" refers to the transformation of tacit knowledge into tacit knowledge. It is a process of building tacit knowledge through shared experiences, and the key to acquiring tacit knowledge is through observation, imitation, and practice, not words. For example, apprentices that work with masters can learn the craft without speaking, only by observation, imitation, and practice.

The second mode: "Externalization" refers to the transformation of tacit knowledge into explicit knowledge. It is a process of expressing tacit knowledge clearly in explicit concepts and language, and its transformation techniques include metaphors, analogies, concepts, and models. This is a crucial link in the knowledge creation process.

The third mode: " Combination" refers to the combination of explicit knowledge and explicit knowledge. It is a process of combining and systematizing various explicit concepts by generating language or digital symbols through various media. New knowledge can be generated by sifting, adding, combining, and analyzing explicit knowledge (e.g., data, historical information) through tools or forms such as documents, meetings, telephone records, or computer technology.

The fourth mode: "Internalization" refers to the transformation of explicit knowledge into tacit knowledge. It is a process of visualizing and concretizing explicit knowledge, and through "combination", new explicit knowledge is absorbed and digested by employees within the organization, and sublimated into their own tacit knowledge.

Nonaka's transformation model of knowledge creation provides useful ideas for the study of M&A knowledge. Knowledge is acquired, processed, accumulated, and diffused within the enterprise through four modes: socialization, externalization, combination, and internalization, and then becomes the driving force for the sustainable development of the enterprise. The above four modes are a highly abstract summary of the process of knowledge creation and transformation, but in the enterprise, the above four modes are embodied through specific management means. For M&A knowledge, the enterprise's M&A knowledge management capability is reflected in a series of specific management means for M&A knowledge, and it is these specific management means focusing on M&A knowledge and making it socialized, externalized, combined, and internalized that promote the strengthening of M&A knowledge management capabilities, which can be expressed in M&A management functions, M&A management tools, M&A management processes, and management systems, and the employment of external intermediaries. M&A

knowledge management capability is an important part of M&A element capability. Amiryany et al. (2012) proposed that M&A reallocation capability consists of M&A experience, M&A-specific tools, and knowledge management tools.

(i) M&Amanagement function

The M&A management functions are mainly defined from the company's organizational structure and functional settings that require the management functions of planning, organizing, leading, and controlling M&A activities. Exercising these functions can promote the acquisition, processing, accumulation, and diffusion of M&A knowledge within the company in the following three aspects:

The general manager in charge of M&A is the representative of the company's decision-making level in charge of M&A, and directly affects the decision-making process and support of the company's decision-making bodies for M&A activities.

The M&A office, which is responsible for managing the specific matters of M&A activities, directly affects the socialization, externalization, internalization, and combination of M&A knowledge by coordinating the operation of various functional departments to achieve the purpose of operating the M&A management capabilities of the company.

The M&A manager is responsible for the day-to-day implementation of M&A activities and the operation of the management team. It needs to be held by managers with experience in various departments. Depending on the company's M&A business situation, an M&A manager can be a permanent or short-term position.

(ii) M&Amanagement tool

M&A knowledge requires the necessary management tools to achieve creation and transformation, and enterprises can use various M&A management tools to achieve this process. Different management tools may focus on one or several aspects of M&A knowledge transformation, and their functions are different. For enterprise M&A activities, the commonly used M&A management tools and their effects on M&A knowledge can be expressed in Table 3.5.

Each of the above-mentioned M&A management tools is not isolated. Enterprises can combine the above-mentioned tools in combination with enterprise strategies, highlight key points, cultivate advantages, and give full play to the functions of various management tools to achieve the best results.

(iii) M&A management process and management system

The management process and management system are important parts of the company's management activities and are the practices formed by the company's management experience through long-term accumulation and improvement. The M&A management process and management system can not only help the diffusion of M&A knowledge, but more importantly, they can accumulate M&A knowledge in the form of structured processes and specific systems, and continuously improve it during the accumulation. It can be reflected in the following aspects:

The M&A decision-making process refers to an enterprise's decision-making procedure to carry out an M&A. The details include whether the decision-making

Table 3.5 M&A management tools and knowledge process

M&Amanagement tools	Knowledge creation and transformation model	Process of knowledge
Internal M&A training	Externalization, combination	Diffusion
External M&A training	Combination	Obtain
Own strategy and capability assessment tool	Externalization	Deal with
Standardized target direction selection tool	Internalization	Deal with
Standardized M&A direction selection tool	Externalization	Deal with
M&A database	Combination	Accumulation
M&A internship	Socialization	Obtain

procedure is reasonably designed, whether there is a clear division of authority and responsibilities, whether there are sufficient checks and balances of power, and the final decision-making power. A scientific and rational M&A decision-making process provides an institutional guarantee for the success of M&A activities.

The division of responsibilities for M&A events among managers at all levels mainly refers to the division of responsibilities for M&A activities among the senior, middle and functional departments at all levels. In many cases, cooperation based on the division of labor is also very necessary.

Self-strategy and capability assessment is the standard internal condition evaluation for company strategy formulation. Fully understanding one's own strategic needs and the current situation is the primary prerequisite for conducting M&A.

Incentives for M&A event leaders. Human factors often play a key role in M&A activities. Reasonable incentives for M&A event leaders can inspire them to explore the potential of the company, promote the transformation of expected synergy into real synergy, and achieve more value for the company. Of course, the principal-agent problem is also an issue that requires special attention from enterprises in this process.

M&A experience and knowledge exchange, which can be achieved by holding seminars and training courses, is a simple and effective way to acquire and transform M&A knowledge.

(iv) Employment of external intermediary

The role of external intermediaries for M&A activities is recognized by many companies, and the professional knowledge and operational experience of intermediaries in the field of M&A are also one of the important sources of M&A knowledge. By hiring intermediaries, including consulting agencies, financial advisors, legal advisors, and M&A stakeholder coordinators, companies can quickly obtain the support of professional M&A knowledge, which is a good way to facilitate the socialization, externalization, internalization, and combination of their own M&A knowledge. The employment of intermediaries must grasp the specialties of intermediaries, and it is essential to understand and select the right M&A intermediaries for your own company. Therefore, companies need to formulate certain standards for the selection of intermediaries, and hiring the right intermediaries can achieve multiplier effects with half the effort.

3.4.2.3 The Relationship Between M&A Capability Elements and M&A Capability

(1) Residual resource is the necessary condition for the formation of M&A capability

The M&A capability of an enterprise is formed by the residual resources of the enterprise. M&A activity is an unconventional development way of the enterprise, but the M&A of an enterprise cannot affect the normal operation of the enterprise and cannot be at the expense of the efficiency of normal operation. The resources of the enterprise always need to meet the needs of normal production and operation first, and the residual resources can be used for M&A activities under the condition of ensuring the profitability of the existing business. Under the goal of maximizing enterprise value, the opportunity cost of residual resources needs to be avoided as much as possible. Therefore, seeking reasonable returns for residual enterprise resources has also become one of the internal driving forces of M&A activities. Theoretically, an enterprise whose resources have been fully utilized will not carry out M&A because there are no residual resources, and M&A capabilities will not be available. Therefore, the residual resource is a necessary condition for the formation of M&A capability.

(2) The logical relationship between the M&A capability elements and M&A capability

For the different constituent M&A capability elements, their logical relationship with M&A capability is different because each element has different attributes.

Firstly, the residual human resources are the basis for conducting M&A activities. It is easy to understand that for any business organization and business behavior, people are the primary condition. For the acquirer, if there are no residual human resources, the M&A process is unplanned, unorganized, and unimplemented, and the company's M&A activities cannot begin, and it is certainly impossible to develop M&A capabilities. Therefore, the residual human resource is a necessary condition to constitute the M&A capability.

Secondly, as a transaction with business control as the subject, whether the acquirer can pay the consideration of the M&A transaction becomes a key issue for whether the M&A can be completed. In M&A transactions, the acquirer can use the residual financial resources, such as cash and cash equivalents, as the payment method for the transaction consideration. The acquirer often can also use physical assets to pay, and the listed company can also pay with stocks. Essentially, in an active market, financial resources and physical resources can be easily exchanged for each other, and there is only a difference in liquidity between the two. Therefore, when they are used as payment methods for M&A transactions, there is an alternative relationship between the two, and through making liquidity discounts, physical resources can be converted into financial resources. As a payment condition for completing the M&A transaction, the residual financial resource or the residual physical resource is also a necessary condition to constitute the M&A capability.

Finally, M&A activities are numerous and complex. If you only have the resources but do not know how to manage and use them, M&A activities will be difficult to succeed in, so the role of an enterprise's M&A management capabilities in M&A cannot be ignored. The M&A resource management capability and M&A knowledge management capability can manage and guide the M&A activities of enterprises to ensure the smooth progress of all aspects of M&A activities. Even enterprises with no M&A experience can implement successful M&A through good planning and prudent execution, provided that other resources are adequate. Here, good M&A management capability is not only the basic component of M&A capability, but also a multiplier of M&A capability. Therefore, the M&A management capability of the enterprise is also an indispensable condition for the M&A capability.

In addition, there are some resources in the enterprise, such as brand, social capital, and M&A know-how, whose existence can enhance the M&A capability of the enterprise. Many M&A cases show that acquirers with a good brand, social capital, and other intangible resources are more likely to implement successful M&A than other companies. In many cases, the enhancing effect of these factors cannot be ignored, and these factors are not necessary conditions for M&A capability.

Based on the above discussion, the logical relationships between M&A elements and M&A capability are shown in Table 3.6.

(3) The residual amount of resources affects the level of M&A capacity

The M&A capability is composed of the residual of the above-mentioned several resource elements. It is easy to understand that the residual amount of resources will directly affect the level of the M&A capability, and the two are positively correlated.

Table 3.6 The logical relationships between each resource element and M&A capability

<table>
<tr><td rowspan="11">M&A capability</td><td rowspan="9">Resource</td><td colspan="2">Human resource</td><td>Necessary conditions</td></tr>
<tr><td colspan="2">Financial resource</td><td rowspan="2">Necessary conditions</td></tr>
<tr><td colspan="2">Physical resource</td></tr>
<tr><td colspan="2">Intangible asset</td><td>Enhancement</td></tr>
<tr><td rowspan="4">Other information resources</td><td>Brand</td><td>Enhancement</td></tr>
<tr><td>Social capital</td><td>Enhancement</td></tr>
<tr><td>Know-how</td><td>Enhancement</td></tr>
<tr><td>Know-who</td><td>Enhancement</td></tr>
<tr style="display:none"></tr>
<tr><td rowspan="2">M&A management capability</td><td colspan="2">M&A resource management capability</td><td>Necessary conditions</td></tr>
<tr><td colspan="2">M&A knowledge management capability</td><td>Necessary conditions</td></tr>
</table>

That is, the more residual resources, the greater the M&A capability of the company. For example, if a company has more residual financial resources, which can be used to pay the consideration for M&A transactions, its M&A capability will be greater; for another example, a company has a residual management team that has rich experience and competence in M&A in the telecommunications industry, then combined with other residual resources, the company will also have strong M&A capabilities in the telecommunications industry.

(4) The marginal contribution of resources to M&A capability varies

The positive effect of the residual amount of resources on M&A capability is easy to understand, but it is not the only determinant. M&A capability is formed by a combination of several residual resources, and there is not one unit of capability output for one unit of resource input. For example, adding one unit of human resource and adding one unit of financial resource have different effects on M&A capability, while adding one unit of physical resource and adding one unit of M&A management capability also have different effects on M&A capability. Therefore, the marginal contribution of a company's residual resources to M&A capability varies. For a resource, its residual quantity and marginal contribution together determine the importance of that resource to M&A capability.

3.5 M&A Capability Model

For both M&A theory and the M&A practice community, M&A capability is a new concept. This book defines it as the capability of a company to complete M&A activities with its residual resources. Focusing on the structure of M&A capability, the previous section has analyzed the constituent elements of M&A capability and the relationship between these elements and M&A capability, laying a theoretical foundation for building an M&A capability model. Based on the above discussion, this part proposes the M&A capability model to clarify the relationship between the elements of M&A capability, so as to further understand the M&A capability.

3.5.1 Basic Assumptions of the Model

In order to make the discussion clearer, before proposing the M&A capability model, here are some basic descriptions and assumptions about the resource situation of the enterprise.

It is assumed that the human resource, financial resource, and physical resource owned by the enterprise are H, K, M. Under the goal of maximizing the value of the enterprise, the enterprise needs to coordinate the input ratio of various resources. When the inputs of various resources reach the optimal allocation, the enterprise obtains the maximum outputs. Assuming that the input of human resource in the

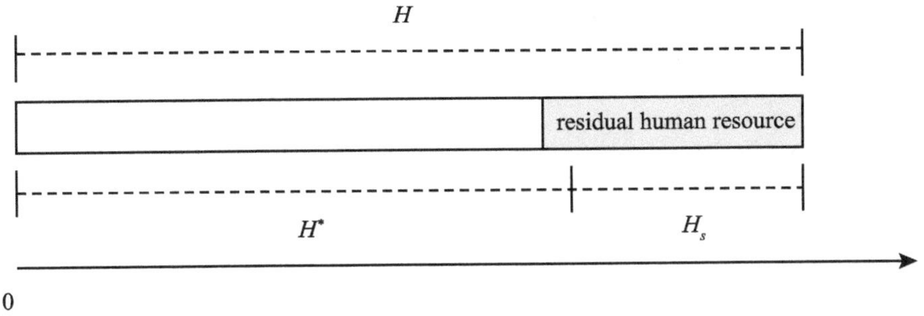

Fig. 3.4 Enterprise human resource residual

optimal resource allocation state is H_s, if the residual of human resource is H^*, then the following relationship exists:

$$H_s = H - H^*$$

When $H > H^*$, that is, $H_s > 0$, H_s means that there is a residual of human resource relative to the optimal allocation state; when $H < H^*$, that is, $H_s < 0$, H_s means that there is a negative residual of human resource relative to the optimal allocation state, a relative shortage of human resource. The residual human resource in the enterprise is shown in Fig. 3.4.

Similarly, for financial resource and physical resource, assuming that their inputs in the optimal resource allocation state are respectively K^* and M^*, K_s and M_s respectively represent the residual of the two resources, the following relationship also exists $K_s = K - K^*$, $M_s = M - M^*$, and there are two states of residual and shortage of financial resource and physical resource as well.

It is of great significance to examine the residual and shortage of enterprise resources for M&A activities. It is difficult to imagine that an enterprise with a shortage of human resource and cash flow can carry out M&A activities. Only if the enterprise has the residual resource can it use those residual resource for M&A activities, thus forming the M&A capability.

3.5.2 M&A Capability Theory Model

Based on the analysis conclusion of this chapter, it can be considered that the enterprise's M&A capability is a function of the enterprise's residual human resource, residual financial resource or physical resource, and residual M&A management capability. Thus, we obtain the basic theoretical model of M&A capability:

$$C = f(H_S, K_S, M_S, S_S)$$

where C: M&A capability; H_s: residual human resource; K_s: residual financial resource; M_s: residual physical resource; S_s: residual M&A management capability. Based on the basic model of M&A capability, combined with the previous structural analysis of M&A capability and the Cobb–Douglas function for reference, the basic model of M&A capability can be further expanded as follows:

$$C = \lambda H_s^\alpha (K_s + M_s)^\beta S_s^\gamma$$

where:

C: M&A capability, $C > 0$ and $C \subset R$;
H_s: residual human resource, $H_s > 0$ and $H_s \subset R$;
K_s: residual financial resource, M_s: residual physical resource, $K_s \geq 0$, $M_s \geq 0$, and $K_s + M_s > 0$;
S_s: residual M&A management capacity, $S_s > 0$ and $S_s \subset R$;
λ is a constant greater than zero;
α, β, γ represent the elasticity coefficients of residual human resource, residual financial resource, and residual M&A management capability to M&A capability, respectively. They are generally positive numbers. R is the collection of enterprise resources.

Since the residual physical resources can be transformed into financial resource in an active market, and after the liquidity discount, they can also be regarded as a kind of financial resource, in essence, so the above formula can be further simplified as follows:

$$C = \lambda H_s^\alpha K_s^\beta S_s^\gamma$$

3.5.3 Nature of the M&A Capability Function

3.5.3.1 Marginal Contribution of the Elements of M&A Capability Function

The marginal contribution of a element refers to the amount of increase in M&A capability generated by each additional unit of input of the element. Taking residual human resource as an example, the marginal contribution of residual human resource to M&A capability can be expressed as the derivative of this factor to M&A capability, that is

$$MC_{H_s} = \frac{\partial C}{\partial H_s}$$

This indicator reflects the marginal contribution of residual human resource H_s to M&A capability. Similarly, we can obtain the marginal contributions of residual financial resource and residual M&A management capability to M&A capability as follows:

$$MC_{K_s} = \frac{\partial C}{\partial K_s}, \quad MC_{S_s} = \frac{\partial C}{\partial S_s}$$

An important problem of the M&A capability function is that the marginal contribution of the capability element increases first and then decreases, which means that the amount of M&A capability obtained by each additional unit of factor input is not the same as the previous unit of factor input. In the case of M&A activities, when a company appoints a person in charge of M&A activities and forms an M&A management team, the M&A human resource invested at the beginning will be more efficient due to the more detailed division of labor, and the marginal contribution of M&A human resource to M&A capability is increasing. When the marginal contribution reaches zero if the enterprise continues to increase the M&A human resource, the inefficiency caused by the poor communication and the confusion in the division of labor due to the expansion of the team size will appear, and thus the marginal contribution of M&A human resource to the M&A capability will decrease.

3.5.3.2 Elasticity of M&A Capability Elements Contribution

If the input of other capability elements is kept constant, and the input of a certain capability element is changed alone, the ratio of the change rate of M&A capability to the change rate of the input of a certain capability element is called the contribution elasticity of the capability element. Its mathematical form is expressed as:

$$E_{H_s} = \frac{\frac{\partial C}{\partial H_s}}{\frac{C}{H_s}} = \alpha, \quad E_{K_s} = \frac{\frac{\partial C}{\partial K_s}}{\frac{C}{K_s}} = \beta, \quad E_{S_s} = \frac{\frac{\partial C}{\partial S_s}}{\frac{C}{S_s}} = \gamma$$

It can be seen from the above formula that the contribution elasticity of the M&A capability element is the index of each element in the M&A function. The larger the index, the greater the contribution elasticity of the M&A capability elements, and the greater the change rate of M&A capability caused by the change rate of M&A capability factor input. In M&A activities, enterprises can combine their own conditions and invest corresponding resources into elements with greater contribution elasticity to obtain better results.

3.5.3.3 M&A Capability Function and Returns to Scale

If we increase all the inputs of M&A capability elements by η times ($\eta > 1$) and substitute them into (the theoretical model ofM&A capability), we can get the scale return characteristics of the M&A capability function. That is

$$C' = \lambda(\eta H_s)^{\alpha}(\eta K_s)^{\beta}(\eta S_s)^{\gamma} = \lambda\eta^{\alpha+\beta+\gamma}H_s^{\alpha}K_s^{\beta}S_s^{\gamma} = \eta^{\alpha+\beta+\gamma}\cdot C$$

It is clear from the above equation that when $\eta > 1$, the scale return of the M&A capability function is directly related to the value of $\alpha + \beta + \gamma$.

When, $\alpha + \beta + \gamma > 1$, $C' > C$ the M&A capability function has increasing returns to scale;
When, $\alpha + \beta + \gamma = 1$, $C' = C$, the M&A capability function has a fixed return to scale;
When, $\alpha + \beta + \gamma < 1$, $C' < C$, the M&A capability function has diminishing returns to scale.

Return to scale reflects the relationship between the scale of inputs of M&A capability elements and M&A capability. What are the elements that lead to increasing or decreasing returns to scale of M&A capabilities? We believe that a firm's experience in M&A activities is the determinant of returns to scale of M&A capabilities. Companies with rich M&A experience, such as Cisco Systems and General Electric, have accumulated M&A experience through successful or unsuccessful M&A events and have further grasped the inner rules of M&A activities. With the same M&A capability and resources, these experiences have led to an incremental increase in the scale return of the company's M&A capabilities. On the contrary, for firms with no M&A experience, the complexity and high uncertainty of M&A activities will affect the role of their M&A resource input element, so that their M&A capacities eventually tend to show diminishing returns to scale.

3.5.3.4 Marginal Rate of Substitution of the M&A Capability Elements

The marginal rate of substitution of a capacity element is the amount of reduction of another element caused by increasing one unit of a element input to maintain the same level of M&A capability. It can be expressed as:

$$MRS_{ij} = \frac{\Delta x}{\Delta x}$$

where: MRE_{ij} is the marginal rate of substitution; Δx_i is the decrease in element input; Δx_j is the increase in element input.

The phenomenon of substitution of elements is most common in the practice of M&A activities in the form of payment of M&A consideration, such as cash, shares, physical assets or a combination of them are often used as M&A payment methods, and they can be translated into financial assets for measurement. For the substitution effect between M&A capability elements, the substitution effect between financial and physical resources is the most obvious; in the case of a lack of human resource, companies can supplement the human resource gap by recruiting the required personnel through the open market; M&A management capability can also be supplemented by hiring intermediaries such as investment banks with M&A business experience from outside.

It should be noted that the company's financial resource is the main resource for paying the M&A transaction consideration and are necessary for completing the M&A transaction payment process. When financial resource is lacking, it is difficult to replace them with residual human resource and M&A management capability, which means that M&A human resource and M&A management capability have the worst substitution effect on M&A financial resource.

3.6 M&A Capability Based on Resource Attributes

The M&A capability model portrays the functional relationship between M&A capability elements and M&A capability through a function, which provides a perspective for studying M&A capability. M&A is a way to achieve corporate strategy. When formulating overall strategy, enterprises must have conducted a comprehensive and in-depth analysis of their internal conditions and external environment, on this basis of which they can evaluate their M&A capability by assessing the number of slack resources based on the status of their internal resources, combined with the M&A capability function.

However, for firms, slack resources are not only similar or different in quantity, but also in attributes. If the quantity of a firm's slack resources determines the level of its M&A capability, then the attributes of the slack resources determine the firm's M&A capability in terms of that attribute. The attributes of slack resources mentioned here mainly refer to the directional attributes (including industry and geography) and process attributes (including procurement, R&D, manufacturing, marketing, and services) of slack resources. In many cases, the attributes of a firm's slack resources are often more decisive for M&A decisions. For example, a firm with more slack resources in the manufacturing area of China's telecom industry can be considered to have strong M&A capabilities in the manufacturing area of China's telecom industry. Based on the above understanding, further research on the attributes of slack resources becomes another important issue in understanding M&A capabilities.

3.6.1 Directional Attributes of Slack Resources

The directional attributes of the slack resources include both the industry dimension and the geographic dimension, which influence the M&A capability of firms in specific industries and specific regions, respectively.

3.6.1.1 Industry Dimension

A resource's industrial dimension mainly reflects the resource's industrial attributes and the information related to the industry it belongs to. Enterprises always compete in specific industries, which often have different life cycles, profit levels, market structures, etc. To achieve the goal of survival, development, and profitability in the fierce competition, enterprises must invest various resources, and these invested resources can be divided into two categories according to whether they have industrial attributes.

One category is resources with industrial attributes, such as human resource, physical resource, and intangible resource exclusive to the industry, including managers and technicians who are familiar with industry conditions, industry-specific equipment, industry patents, technical know-how, sales and customers relationship network, etc. These resources with industrial attributes can only be most effective if they are applied to their corresponding industries, and it is difficult to function if their industrial attributes are ignored. For example, it is difficult to imagine that applying pharmaceutical production equipment to the energy extraction industry can achieve economic benefits.

Another category is resources that do not have industrial attributes. These resources are common to all industries and can play the same role in any industry. The most typical one is financial resource, which have better liquidity in the effective market and their roles are not limited by the industries. In addition, general management talents can often be considered as human resource that do not have industrial attributes due to their general management capabilities.

For a firm's surplus resources, identifying whether and what industrial attributes they have provides useful information for understanding a firm's M&A capability in a particular industry. If a firm's slack resources have industry-specific attributes, then the firm's M&A capability in that industry is greater than the firm's M&A capability in other industries. It can be further inferred that if a firm has industry-specific slack resources, the probability of a firm's success in conducting M&A in that specific industry is greater than that of its success in other industries. Therefore, an in-depth analysis of the industrial attributes of the residual resources becomes a very important dimension of the M&A decisions for companies conducting M&A activities in a specific industry.

3.6.1.2 Geographical Dimension

Corresponding to the industrial dimension of resources, the geographical dimension of resources reflects the information related to the geographic attributes of resources and the geographical regions to which they belong. In today's increasingly accelerated economic globalization, the scope of business operations is no longer limited to the local region or country. But international companies have long been integrating resources and providing products and services on a global scale. M&A activities are also accelerating along with the process of economic globalization, and overseas acquisitions and cross-border mergers and acquisitions are on the rise.

The American scholar Green (1990) has studied corporate M&A from a geographical perspective. He found that the more prosperous the economy is, the more frequently M&A activities are conducted and the higher the rate of external control over other regions, that is, the ratio of acquirers to acquirees in a region. After mergers and acquisitions of enterprises from economically developed regions in the underdeveloped region, they import capital and technology to the acquirees, improve production and management, increase the productivity of the acquirees, eliminate or reduce regional disparities, produce resource reallocation effects, and promote the overall development of the regional economy and the overall economy.

Geographical factors here include natural geographical location and economic geographical location, including the distribution of local natural resources, the level of economic development, economic and legal policies, the degree of market development, the state of transportation and communication conditions, the state of the environment, the state of public security, the cultural quality of the public and ideological and moral concepts and many other factors.

A firm's slack resources also have geographic attributes, which can be further classified into physical geographic attributes and economic geographical attributes. For a slack resource, we can carve out its geographical attributes, e.g., firm A owns an idle piece of land in Beijing, China, which is 5 km from the Beijing Capital International Airport; firm B has a strong M&A management team in Lyon, France, etc. Understanding the geographic attributes of a firm's slack resources is a guide to understanding the firm's M&A capabilities.

First, one of the main motivations for vertical M&A is transaction cost savings. Vertical M&A internalizes the market, converting transaction costs into internal organizational costs, and can only generate benefits if the saving in transaction costs are greater than the resulting increase in internal organizational costs. For companies with good physical and economic geographical locations, acquiring target companies in the same region can result in better synergies in terms of internal and external logistics, with a corresponding reduction in their management costs.

Second, due to the similarity of customs, human environment, value orientation, and spirituality of enterprises in the same region, it is, respectively, much easier to organize and coordinate after internalization, and the increased organization coordination costs of enterprises for this purpose are much less. Therefore, it is appropriate to use enterprises in the same geographical area as the target enterprise.

Therefore, all other conditions being equal, a firm's slack resources have better M&A capabilities in regions that match its geographic attributes than in other regions.

3.6.2 Process Attributes of Slack Resources

Slack resources not only have directional properties, but also have process attributes, i.e., slack resources are often in a specific process of the enterprise value chain, or slack resources exist in a specific process of the enterprise value chain. The process attributes of the slack resources are equally important to the M&A capability of an enterprise.

In a modern market economy, the competition among enterprises has been increasingly reflected as the competition in the value chain, and value chain analysis tools provide a good way to identify assets and capabilities that can create a competitive advantage. The concept of the value chain was first introduced by Professor Michael Porter in 1985 in his book *Competitive Advantage*. He described the value chain as a collection of activities used by an enterprise to design, produce, sell, deliver and play a supporting role in the product, which is a series of continuously completed activities and the process of converting raw materials into a series of final products. It consists of basic activities, which are the activities involved in the physical creation of products and their sale, transfers to buyers, and after-sales services, including internal logistics, production operations, external logistics, marketing and services, and auxiliary activities, which are activities that support the basic activities and are mutually supportive within each other, including corporate infrastructure, human resource management, technology development, and procurement.

In each process of the value chain, enterprises need to invest corresponding human resources, financial resources, physical resources, information resources and capabilities, and other elements. In other words, it is precisely these resources that operate and support each relevant process in the enterprise value chain, and the value of the final output of the enterprise's products and services is the result of the joint action of resources in each functional process. Zhou Lin (2006) re- examined the relationship of each process in the value chain from the perspective of enterprise resources and established a resource-based value chain model, as shown in Fig. 3.5.

The model consists of two parts. At the bottom of the model are the various functional activities such as procurement, R&D, manufacturing, marketing, and service of the enterprise, and here the basic and auxiliary activities are not distinguished as in Porter's proposed value chain, but they are integrated. The upper part of the model is the main components of resources, including human resources, financial resources, physical resources, intangible resources, general capabilities, and specialized capabilities, and this division of resources is consistent with the division of resources in the structural part of M&A capabilities. As can be seen from Fig. 3.5, different categories of resources play an important role in the value creation of a company at all stages of its business process. The right side of the model values is also not

Financial assets/human capital/General ability						Value
Physical resources	Raw materials	Equipment	Workshop, production line	Product	Stock	
Intangible resources		Patent, Proprietary technology	Industry license	Trademark	Reputation	
Dedicated capabilities	Bargaining power	Creativity	Production capacity, quality management	Public relations ability, promotion ability	Service ability, Information feedback ability	
Functional process	Purchase	Research and development	Manufacture	Marketing	Service	

Fig. 3.5 Resource-based enterprise value chain model

represented by profit as in Porter's proposed value chain, but by the more connotative value instead. The model combines a company's resources with a functional process, providing a clear and effective framework for companies to identify the process attributes of their resources.

Drawing on the findings of the above models, it is possible to fully grasp the processes to which a company's slack resources belong, and thus understand the process attributes of each slack resource. A company with slack resources in a specific process will have greater M&A capabilities in that process. For example, if a company has slack physical resources such as slack plants and production lines in the manufacturing process, it can acquire a company with slack productive human resources and a shortage of plants and production lines in the manufacturing process, and the complementary nature of the two resources can make the transaction go more smoothly and the company will get good synergies effects after the acquisition. Therefore, the process attribute of slack resources of enterprises can not only increase the M&A capability of enterprises in this process but also point out the direction for enterprise M&A activities.

3.6.3 Resource Factors Affecting M&A Capability

In M&A activities, a firm's slack human resource, financial resource, physical resource, information resource, and M&A management capability interact with each other and together constitute the firm's M&A capability. If a firm does not have enough slack resources, it will focus more on internal production activities (Iyer & Miller, 2008) and will not focus too much on M&A, and other foreign investments. Whether for SOEs or private firms, slack resources are a prerequisite for firms to initiate M&A (Ge Weijie et al., 2014). From different dimensions, the slack resources have different attributes, but the directional and process attributes of the resources have the most profound impact on a firm's M&A capability. Bradley (1988) pointed out that M&A allows the acquirer to effectively control the target firm's resources and reconfigure the resources of both firms, thus increasing the return on assets and firm value. The directional and process attributes of resources are not only of great significance to the M&A capability but also will be very important in guiding the direction of the firm's M&A. It should be noted that although there are sometimes directional and process attributes of financial resources of enterprises, such as foreign exchange resources subject to foreign exchange control, the role of financial resources in resource direction and process are consistent in most cases, so no attribute classification is made for financial resources.

Based on the above analysis, the concept of "M&A capability based on resource attributes" is proposed here to represent the M&A capability of a firm consisting of slack resources with specific attributes. This concept can reflect not only the quantity of M&A capability but also the role of resource attributes on M&A capability, to fully grasp the essence of M&A capability of enterprises.

3.6.3.1 Prerequisite Assumptions for M&A Capability Based on Resource Attributes

It is assumed that A is used to represent the directional attributes of the slack resources and represents the industrial and geographical dimensions of the directional attributes of the resources, respectively. The specific attributes represented by A_1, A_2 here can be further refined based on national industry- standard codes and regional codes.

It is assumed that B is used to represent the process attributes of the slack resources, and B_1, B_2, B_3, B_4, B_5, represents the five dimensions of the resource process attributes of procurement, R&D, manufacturing, marketing, and service, respectively. Then combining the two, (A, B) can represent all attributes of the firm's remaining resources for M&A capability. For example, $H_s\ (A_1, B_2)$ would represent the surplus of a firm's remaining resources for the R&D process in A_1 industry; $S_s\ (A_2,\ B_1,\ B_4)$ would represent the surplus of a firm's M&A management capability for the procurement and marketing processing A_2 eographical region.

3.6.3.2 Rectangle Diagram of M&A Capability Based on Resource Attributes

Based on the above assumptions, this book proposes a "resource-attribute- based M&A capability rectangle diagram" to provide a more comprehensive picture of a company's M&A capability through graphics. The specific implications can be discussed as follows:

(1) The total area of the rectangular graph of M&A capability based on resource attributes represents the overall M&A capability of the firm;

(2) The three rectangles from left to right represent the M&A capability composed of human resources, the M&A capability composed of financial resources, and the M&A capability composed of M&A management capability, respectively, and the size of their area is determined by the degree of contribution of their corresponding slack resources to the overall M&A capability, with larger areas indicating the greater contribution of the corresponding elements to the M&A capability;
(3) Within each rectangle, the slack resources can be further divided according to their orientation and process attributes, and the area of each small rectangle represents the proportion of the slack resources for a specific attribute out of the total slack resources.

Through the above process, we can get the rectangle diagram of an enterprise's M&A capability based on resource attributes. Figures 3.6 and 3.7 show the rectangular diagram of the M&A capability of a firm based on resource direction attributes (including both industry and geographic dimensions), respectively.

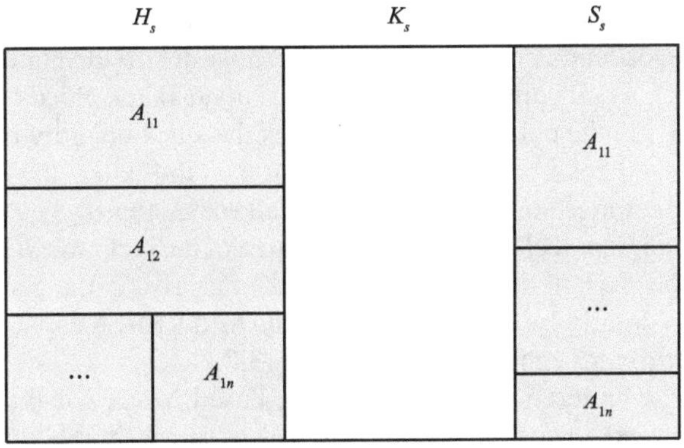

Fig. 3.6 Rectangle diagram of M&A capability based on industry attributes of resources

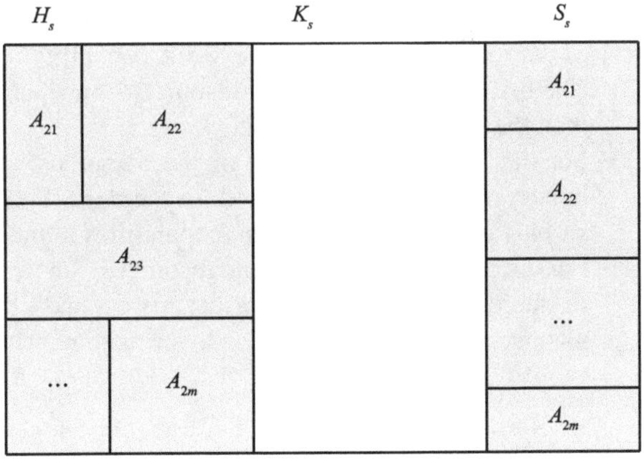

Fig. 3.7 Rectangle diagram of M&A capability based on geographic attributes of resources

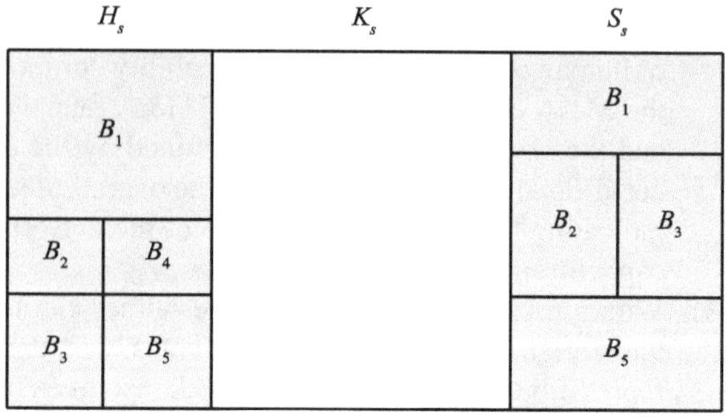

Fig. 3.8 Rectangle diagram of M&A capability based on process attributes of resources

The above two figures represent the M&A capability of the same firm, so the total area of both graphs is the same, and their slack human resources, slack financial resources, and slack M&A management capability account for the same proportion of the overall M&A capability. The difference between the two figures is that the former reflects the M&A capability of resource industry attributes, while the latter reflects the M&A capability of resource geographical attributes. For the former, the slack human resources of an enterprise are divided into n small rectangles of A_{11}, A_{12}, ..., A_{1n} according to their industrial attributes. Specifically, the area of the rectangle A_{11} in the column of H_s indicates the slack quantity of the enterprise's slack human resources in the industry of A_{11}. For the latter, the slack human resources of the enterprise are divided into m small rectangles of $A_{21}, A_{22}, \ldots, A_{2m}$ according to their geographical attributes, and the area of the rectangle A_{21} in the column of H_s indicates the slack human resources of the enterprise in the geographical area of A_{21}.

Similarly, the rectangular of the firm's M&A capability based on resource process attributes can be depicted in Fig. 3.8.

The three resources attribute-based M&A capability rectangle diagrams above provide a more specific illustration of the magnitude and attributes of the firm's M&A capability and allow the following useful inferences to be drawn.

(1) The size of the firm's overall M&A capability is represented by the total area of the rectangles in the above M&A capability rectangle diagram;
(2) The firm's residual financial resources contribute more to the M&A capability than the other two elements;
(3) For the directional attribute of the resources, the firm has a high surplus of human resources in the A_{11} industry and the A_{23} region, and the firm had a high surplus of M&A management capabilities in the A_{11} industry;
(4) For the process attribute of the resources, the firm has a high surplus of human resources in the B_1 (procurement) process and a high surplus of the firm's M&A management capability in the B_1 (procurement) and B_5 (service) processes.

3.6.4 M&A Capability Rectangle Chart and M&A Decision Making

The purpose of M&A capability research is to provide scientific analysis ideas and tools for corporate M&A decisions. The M&A capability rectangle not only helps companies understand their M&A capabilities intuitively and effectively, but more importantly, the process of completing the M&A capability rectangle itself is a comprehensive and in-depth logical thinking process about the company's M&A capability. Companies can follow the M&A capability rectangle to identify and evaluate M&A capability elements, build M&A capability models, determine the slack resource attributes, and finally obtain the M&A capability rectangle.

The significance of the M&A capability rectangle map for M&A decisions also lies in its clarification of resource constraints in the direction of a firm's M&A. Through the resource-based M&A capability rectangle diagram, companies can extract detailed information about their slack resources in specific industries, specific geographic regions and specific process, which is very important for companies to understand their M&A capabilities in relevant industries, regions, and processes. The more slack resources a company has in a specific industry, the greater its M&A capability in that industry should be, and thus the probability of its M&A success will increase, as will those companies that have slack resources in specific regions and specific processes. Therefore, companies need to consider the attributes of their slack resources when making M&A decisions, and only when slack resources with specific attributes are invested in M&A activities with their corresponding attributes can the effect of M&A be the best and the companies can obtain the greatest value.

Chapter 4
M&A Boundary

4.1 The Concept of M&A Boundary

The only way for a company to achieve growth is through internal growth, mergers and acquisitions, and alliances for continuous scale expansion and capacity enhancement. In the process of growth, enterprises can use their internal resources and production capacity to achieve the expansion of enterprise-scale and increase production capacity, i.e., internal growth such as new investment, or they can use the external resources and production capacity to achieve the expansion of enterprise-scale and increase of the production capacity, i.e., external growth, such as M&A and alliances. However, different enterprises, different industries, different institutional environments, and even the special circumstances of the same enterprise at different stages of development can affect the choice of enterprise growth methods, and the correct choice of enterprise growth mode is related to future enterprise performance and enterprise development, which determining the boundaries of M&As, new investment, and strategic alliances.

Boundaries of M&A is the boundary of application of M&A activities, and which addresses the question of whether or not a company's development strategy should be carried out through M&A as a form of external investment, i.e., the choice between two forms of strategic development, such as new investments and alliances. Companies with M&A capabilities do not necessarily have to use M&A as a way or means of strategic development, but can also achieve its development through such means as alliances and internal investment. In the process of expansion and growth, the method used is not only limited by the company's conditions but also by the external environment. Different expansion methods have different advantages and disadvantages and are suitable for different companies, different development periods, and different strategic goals.

Therefore, it is necessary to study when and under what conditions companies use M&A, under what conditions they use new investments, and under what conditions

Q. Zhang, *Mergers and Acquisitions*, https://doi.org/10.1007/978-981-92-0122-8_4

they use strategic alliances, and to distinguish what factors determine that it is advantageous and which factors are disadvantageous for companies to achieve expansion through M&A; and what factors in the external environment of companies constrain the choice of investment methods and what factors facilitate the choice of investment methods. This is a realistic and unavoidable choice for a company's decision-making. "In what environment to use M&A and in what way to carry out M&A becomes the object of research on corporate M&A boundary theory" (Zhang Qiusheng, 2005).

4.2 The Boundary Between M&A and New Investment

4.2.1 Concept and Comparison of M&A and New Investment

M&A is an transaction targeted at business control (Zhang Qiusheng, 2005). New investment, also known as "greenfield investment" in international investment, refers to the establishment of a new enterprise by an investor who invests capital and other factors of production, and generally, the enterprise produced by the new investment is fully owned by the investor. New investment includes the formation of new production capacity through the purchase of production materials, as well as the formation of new marketing capabilities and R&D capabilities through the establishment of new departments.

Mergers and acquisitions and new investments have different characteristics. The strengths of M&A are often the weakness of new investments, and vice versa, the weakness of M&A are often the strengths of new investments. Compared to M&A, new investments have the following advantages:

First, it is inductive to the selection of production scale and investment location in line with the foreign expansion objectives of the investment company. Direct investment is the main way for the investment company to achieve foreign expansion, and choosing the new investment method is beneficial for the investment company to accurately locate the production scale and investment location according to the needs of strategic objectives, while choosing the M&A method may not be realized because it is difficult to find the target enterprises whose production scale and investment location are in line with the wishes of the investment company. In the new investment method, the investor can also try to build the production, sales, and management model according to its wishes and requirements, so that the operation of the enterprise implements the investors' preferred business philosophy.

Second, investment costs are usually lower. Generally speaking, under the condition of forming the same scale of production scale, the cost of new investment is lower than that of M&A. In recent M&As, most of the target companies are highly competitive companies, and the transaction price is generally higher than the investment in a new enterprise of the same scale. In addition, M&A must rely more on the external market, and the acquirer must complete the investment process through the stock market where the target company is located or through negotiations with the target company, which may be sold at a price. Especially in the case of hostile M&A, the acquirers have to pay a high price. In addition to the direct payment, the acquirer in an M&A has to pay indirect costs, such as integrating the target's existing assets, downsizing existing employees, and dealing with external debts. In a new investment, all of these overhead costs are not present.

Third, it is easy to obtain the support of the government and the community in which the target market is located. New investment directly creates new production capacity, and as long as it is not a complete replacement for domestic investment, it will provide new jobs and is generally welcomed by the government and the community in the target market. Mergers and acquisitions do not create new production capacity and may reduce employment if the target company has a significant redundancy problem. In addition, governments and communities in many target markets are concerned that M&A entry may lead to a monopolistic market structure dominated by foreign firms. In particular, some developing countries view a large number of M&As by foreign investment firms in their own countries as an erosion of national sovereignty. Many developed countries have also shown the same concern about foreign investment companies entering their markets in the form of M&A on a large scale. Generally speaking, it is easier to obtain the support of the government and the society in the target market by choosing the new investment method than the M&A method.

Compared with new investment, M&A features are mainly focused on the following aspects:

First, rapid entry into the target market is possible. The biggest advantage of M&A over new investments is that there is no construction period and the time to enter is fast. Typically, without taking into account the lead time, an M&A can take only three to five months to reach production scale, and even if it is modified, it takes only one to two years at most. Since the 1990s, M&A transactions amounting to tens of billions of dollars have been commonplace, and such large investments can take years, decades, or more to build if realized through new construction. Increased market competition and a shorter product life cycle have made it more necessary than ever for investment companies to respond quickly to market changes. To achieve their global growth strategy goals and rapidly expand their production scale and market share, more and more investment companies are choosing M&A as a direct investment entry method.

Second, we acquire strategic assets. Strategic assets are resources of strategic importance to the survival and long-term development of an enterprise, mainly research and development capabilities, trademarks, goodwill, franchises, and marketing networks. Strategic assets are the most important ownership advantages of a company, which are generally difficult to obtain in the external market and take a long time to develop internally. Through M&A, the investor company can acquire the strategic assets of the target company in a very short period, and can also reduce the number of competitors and further enhance their ownership advantages. In addition, if the target of the investor's M&A is its competitor, it can also achieve the goal of eliminating the competitor.

Third, to avoid the control of the government of the investment country. Some mega multinational investment companies have a monopolistic position in the specific product market of the investing country, and the governments of the investing countries often use tools such as "anti-monopoly law" to interfere. For this reason, the investment company may transfer the core assets of the company to the foreign target enterprise through mergers and acquisitions to avoid the control of the government of the investing country.

Whether it is M&A or new investment, no one method can occupy an absolute advantage in any situation. In this chapter, we take into account the respective characteristics of the two approaches and various influencing factors when selecting the way of direct investment, and try to make use of their advantages and compensate for their shortcomings, to provide a theoretical analysis tool for the strategic investment of enterprises.

4.2.2 Theoretical Explanation of Outward Foreign Direct Investment

The study of direct investment by multinational corporations today has become the mainstream economic theory of investment research in a globalized economy. The main explanations for foreign direct investment are theories such as the theory of monopoly advantage, the theory of product life cycle, the eclectic theory of international production, etc.

4.2.2.1 The Theory of Monopoly Advantage

The theory of monopoly advantage, also known as the theory of specific advantage, is considered to be the basis and mainstream of the theory of western multinational corporations. International Operations of National Firms: A Study of Direct Foreign Investment written by Stephen Hymer in 1960. Hymer's mentor, Charles Kindleberger, elaborated and supplemented Hymer's theory in his later writings, making it the earliest and most influential systematic and independent study of multinational corporations and outward foreign direct investment (OFDI), which is why some literature refers to their research as the H–K Tradition.

The core elements of this theory are "market incompleteness" and "monopoly advantage". Hymer believes that the market's incompleteness is reflected in the following four aspects: (1) incomplete commodity market, i.e., commodity specialization, trademarks, special market skills, and price alliances, etc.; (2) incomplete factor markets, which are manifested in different levels of difficulty in accessing capital and differences in technology levels, etc.; (3) market incompleteness caused by economies of scale, i.e., enterprises obtain incremental returns to scale due to significant increases in production; (4) the market incompleteness formed by government intervention, such as tariffs, taxes, interest rates, and exchange rates, and other policies. Hymer argues that market incompleteness is the basis of OFDI because under the conditions of the perfectly competitive market, enterprises do not have the power to dominate the market. They produce the same products and obtain the same factors of production, so OFDI will not bring any special benefits to enterprises, while under the conditions of market incompleteness, enterprises may obtain monopoly advantages at home and through OFDI in foreign production and exploit it.

On this basis, Hymer believes that when an enterprise is in an imperfectly competitive market, the motivation for OFDI is to make full use of its "exclusive factors of production", i.e., monopoly advantage, which is sufficient to offset the disadvantages faced by cross-border competition and foreign operations and put the enterprise in a favorable position. With their monopoly advantages, enterprises exclude competition from host country enterprises and maintain high monopoly prices, leading to imperfect competition and oligopoly market pattern, which is the main reason for enterprises to make OFDI.

Through the empirical analysis of OFDI of U. S. multinational corporations, Hymer believes that investors entering the host country do not take indirect investment through capital market portfolio investment, etc., but make a direct investment through running enterprises, the reason is that under the conditions of non-perfect competition, investors have corporate advantages that local competitors in the host country do not have, and these advantages can ensure that investors get higher rates of return and profit than in the parent company. These advantages are expressed in the following aspects: capital advantages, currency advantages, management advantages, technological advantages, marketing advantages, advantages in terms of access to resources, advantages in terms of economies of scale, and advantages in terms of political power.

The theory of monopoly advantage answers the question of whether a firm should make OFDI through the conditions that a firm should have to make OFDI, which are adapted to any OFDI mode and are common to different investment modes (in this case, M&A and new investment). However, the theory does not answer the question of under what conditions to invest in what way, i.e., it does not explain the choice of OFDI methods. What the monopoly dominance theory has to offer for M&A and new investment is that it provides some influencing factors that can be used to analyze the choice of M&A and new investment, such as the level of management (management advantages), the tendency of government policy (advantage of political power), and the technical level (technical advantages).

4.2.2.2 The Theory of Product Life Cycle

In his article International Investment and International Trade in the Product Cycle in 1966, Vernon proposed the theory of product life cycle, which divides the product life cycle into innovation, maturity, and standardization stages, and explains the different positions of countries in international trade at different stages of the product life cycle and combines the location choice of enterprises with overseas production and export for a systematic dynamic analysis. The theory broadly classifies countries in the world into three types, namely, innovative countries (generally developed countries), sub-developed countries, and less developed countries.

In the innovation stage, the innovative countries' enterprises rely on their strong research and development strength to carry out technological innovation, develop new products, and put them on the national market. The products are highly technology-intensive and costly because of the need to invest a lot of R&D efforts and human capital, and because of the unstable production technology and low output. Production is mainly concentrated in innovative countries because the price elasticity of demand for new products is low, and the innovating companies can obtain high monopoly profits at home through their monopoly position on the technical process of new products. The occasional small demand from sub- developed countries with similar levels of economic development can be met by the innovating firms through exports, so there is no need for direct investment abroad at this stage.

In the mature stage, with the development of new product production and market competition, a series of changes have occurred in the market: the production technology of new products has become increasingly mature and mass production has begun; the value of products has been recognized by consumers in sub-developed countries with similar levels of economic development and foreign demand is strong; the price elasticity of demand has increased and companies have begun to focus on reducing production costs; production processes and methods have matured and spread abroad and the importance of R&D declines, and products gradually shift from technology-intensive to capital-intensive. At the same time, with the increasing exports from innovative countries to sub-developed countries, local enterprises in importing countries started to copy production while importing countries started to implement import barriers to restrict the import of products from innovative nations to protect the newly-growing infant industries, thus greatly limiting the foreign export capacity of innovative countries. As a result, firms from innovative countries began to invest in sub-developed countries to establish overseas subsidiaries and engage in local production and sales directly to reduce production costs, break through market barriers and capture the local market.

In the standardization stage, further development of production technology has led to complete standardization of products and production, the share of R&D costs in production costs has decreased, and capital and unskilled skilled labor become the main part of product costs. The competition of enterprises is mainly expressed as price competition, and the innovative countries have completely lost their monopoly advantage. As a result, firms in the innovative countries transfer standardized production processes to less developed countries with low-cost comparative advantages by way of OFDI, offshore production, and repatriation to home markets and sub-developed markets. Finally, when the technology is no longer profitable, the innovator firm transfers it through licensing.

The theory of product life cycle combines monopoly advantage and location selection, and provides a dynamic analysis of the motivation, timing, and location choice of firms entering foreign markets, but also does not address the specific ways of OFDI. The impact of the theory of product life cycle on M&A and new investment in terms of investment timing is common, and the theory is useful for M&A and new investment selection by providing some locational influences such as technological innovation advantages (technical level), market growth and competition in the host country, and host government policies.

4.2.2.3 The Eclectic Theory of International Production

In his paper in 1977, Trade, Location of Economic Activity and the MNE: A Search for an Eclectic Approach, Dunning proposed the eclectic theory of international production. Dunning argues that the various theories of OFDI in the past have only provided one-sided explanations from a certain perspective and have failed to analyze them in an integrated and comprehensive manner, so it is necessary to use a compromise theory to comprehensively explain the motivation of enterprises' OFDI. The core of the theory is that the multinational operation of an enterprise is the result of the combined effect of the three advantages of the enterprise: ownership specific advantage, internalization advantage, and location specific advantage.

First, ownership specific advantage, also known as monopolistic advantage, is an advantage unique to the company. The ownership specific advantage include:

(1) Asset-based ownership advantage, which refers to the advantages in tangible and intangible assets, the former refers to the monopolistic advantage in production equipment, plants, capital, energy, and raw materials, and the latter refers to the advantage in strategic assets such as patents, proprietary technology, trademarks and goodwill, technology development and innovation capabilities, management, and marketing technology, etc.; reflecting the asset-based ownership advantage of the enterprise is the size of the enterprise. (2) Transactional ownership advantage, refers to the advantages gained by enterprises in global cross-border operations, rational allocation of various resources, and risk avoidance, thus reducing the overall transaction cost of the enterprise, and it is the investment experience of the enterprise that reflects the transactional ownership advantage of the enterprise. Enterprises' OFDI is to take advantage of their advantages on the one hand and gain ownership advantages of other enterprises on the other hand.

Second, internalization advantage refers to the ability of a firm with an ownership specific advantage to keep the firm's advantage within the firm to avoid the impact of an incomplete external market on the firm's interests. Internal transactions save transaction costs and are more cost-efficient than non-equity transactions, especially for technology and knowledge products whose value is difficult to determine. Moreover, internalization brings all aspects of transaction activities under the unified management of the enterprise, so that the production and sales, and resource allocation of the enterprise tend to be stable and the ownership specific advantages ofthe enterprise can be fully utilized.

Third, location specific advantage refers to the favorable degree of a foreign market relative to the enterprise's home market in terms of the market environment for the enterprise's production and operation, that is, the host country's investment environment factors have the advantageous conditions, specifically including the local government's foreign investment policy tendencies, the level of economic development, market size, infrastructure, resource endowment, labor, and its costs, etc. If a foreign market is particularly favorable to the production and operation of the enterprise in terms of the market environment compared with the home country, then this market will be very attractive to the multinational operation of enterprises. In addition, cultural differences in different locations also have a significant impact on the choice of the OFDI approach, as small cultural differences can make it easier for enterprises to obtain the location advantages of the region.

According to Dunning, if an enterprise has the two necessary conditions of ownership specific advantages and internalization advantages, and has location advantages in a host country, the enterprise has the necessary and sufficient conditions for OFDI, and OFDI becomes the best choice for the enterprise, but the theory still does not address the choice of OFDI mode.

In his research, Dunning (1998, 2000, 2001) realized that since the OLI paradigm does not clearly distinguish different modes of entry of FDI, the materials for its analysis is mostly derived from new investment rather than M&As, so it is difficult to explain the phenomenon of cross-border M&As as the norm of FDI in reality and even more so for the phenomenon of giant M&As among MNCs and their joint internalization. For this reason, Dunning further incorporates the M&A factor into the OLI paradigm, which provides a theoretical framework for analyzing cross-border M&A. As long as the three advantageous elements contained in it are combined with the specific methods of cross-border M&A, an analysis paradigm about cross-border M&A can be obtained (see Table 4.1). In fact, the main significance of using the OLI theoretical framework to explain cross-border M&A is the inclusion of the time factor. However, the theoretical essence of this explanation is still one of "motivation" and "existence", which does not answer the questions about the organizational structure of MNCs and the dynamics of their entire production system.

Table 4.1 Cross-border M&A and greenfield investment under the OLI paradigm

Type	Greenfield investment	Cross-border M&A
"O" advantage	Transfer of specific ownership advantages within the company through the forming of new plants, equipment, marketing networks, etc	It is possible to quickly transfer specific ownership advantages within the company as well as to gain external ownership advantages
"L" advantage	The location of the plant is the best match for the "O" advantage used by the company	Rapidly enter the target location, and/or gain an "advantage" within that location
"I" advantage	Overcome the high transaction costs associated with market failures in intermediate products	A more rapid way to internalize to overcome time constraints

Source Based on relevant literature by Dunning (1998, 2000, 2001)

Based on examining the new trends and characteristics of multinational corporations' FDI since the 1990s, Dunning (2000, 2001, 2003) combined the latest development of FDI theory in this period and analyzed the three elements of its OLI paradigm, namely "O", "L" and "I" in its OLI paradigm, and tries to integrate the relevant FDI theory into its OLI paradigm. For the ownership advantage "O" in MNCs' FDI, Dunning combined the latest research results of resource-based MNC organization theory, firm evolution theory, and internalization theory, and argues that the motive of MNCs' FDI is, on the one hand, to use its advantages to maximize profits, and on the other hand, to develop and increase strategic assets. Based on affirming the importance of static "O" advantage, we start to pay attention to the ability of MNCs to obtain dynamic "O" advantage. For the location advantage "L" in MNCs' FDI, Dunning combines the latest research results of location theory, economic agglomeration theory, knowledge-enhancing dynamic location theory, and internationalization theory. While emphasizing the traditional locational comparative advantage at the national level, more attention is paid to the location competitive advantage at the sub-national level, and it is believed that the non-transferable and hard-to-replicate strategic assets formed by the network integration of MNCs' FDI and host countries, such as enterprise clusters, are the competitive advantages of MNCs' FDI. For the internalization advantage "I" in MNCs' FDI, Dunning incorporates the latest advances in traditional internalization theory, dynamic internalization theory, theory of the firm, and knowledge acquisition and sharing theory, and incorporates strategic asset-seeking and increasing FDI such as cross-border M&A and international strategic alliances into his analytical framework. The revisions and additions made by Dunning to his OLI paradigm in recent years have absorbed and integrated many research results of related FDI theories, and to a certain extent, reflected the development trend and characteristics of multinational corporations' FDI in recent years. As he says: "After expansion, an eclectic paradigm with additional dynamic content, which incorporates cross-border investment activities related to asset-augmenting and alliance behavior into a theoretical framework, has strengthened its theoretical status as a major analytical framework for testing the determinants of international production. However, some scholars argue that this revision pays attention to some dynamic features of MNCs' FDI and their competitive advantages, but it is still carried out within the original OLI framework, and the approach adopted is based on integrating the latest developments in related theories, failing to reveal the dynamic features in the interaction of the factors in OLI and their interaction mechanisms in a comprehensive manner.

Based on Dunning's OLI paradigm, many scholars have conducted in-depth research and boldly proposed new theoretical frameworks. Wang Huanxiang (2004) introduced the "factor transaction integration advantage (T)" to construct the T-OLI four-factor diamond model. He argues that the use of Dunning's OLI paradigm to explain cross-border M&A can only use internalization theory to emphasize the transfer or acquisition of resources by MNCs, and does not provide a fuller explanation for the reverse internalization (reverse M&A) behavior of contemporary MNCs. Mainstream FDI theory emphasizes the importance of internalization advantages (intra-firm transactions of factors) based on transaction cost savings, while more importantly, transaction activities (forward and reverse M&As) improve the efficiency of the use and production of a firm's existing factors and reduce total costs (including transaction costs and production costs). He proposed that cross-border M&A should be included in the OLI paradigm as an independent factor that can be integrated according to changes in the relative importance of internal and external factors or advantages in the OLI structure, thus making the existing advantages in the OLI paradigm a dynamic and variable overall advantage.

Huang Zhongwen (2004) combined OLI theory and corporate M&A theory, and he argues that the reason why an MNC with a traditional sense of triple advantage makes a different choice between M&A and new establishments is that M&A investment has a significant speed advantage(s) over new investment and introducing this advantage forms a new theoretical framework for explaining cross-border M&A (OLIS framework), which can remedy the deficiency of the OLI paradigm in explaining M&A.

The Eclectic Theory of International Production explains the conditions for OFDI by enterprises, again without addressing the choice of OFDI approach, but provides some implications for the choice of M&A and new investment, which suggests some influencing factors on M&A and new investment through ownership advantage, location advantage and internalization advantages, such as transferability of strategic assets, corporate management level, previous M&A experience, research and development capabilities of enterprises, project construction speed, and cultural differences.

4.2.3 Analysis of Influencing Factors of Mergers and Acquisitions and Greenfield Investment Choices

Based on the above theoretical analysis, it is concluded that the factors affecting M&A and greenfield investment are enterprise size, enterprise's research and development capability, enterprise's management level and experience in M&A operation, project construction speed, host country market growth, market competition, host country government's policy preference, transferability of strategic assets, and cultural differences, among which enterprise size, enterprise's research and development capability, enterprise's management level and experience in M&A operation, and project construction speed can be categorized as enterprise's ownership advantage and internalization advantage, while the host country's market growth, market competition, host country government's policy preference, transferability of strategic assets, and cultural differences can be categorized as the location advantage of the host country. These influencing factors can be summarized into external and internal factors.

4.2.3.1 External Factors

(1) Market growth status

One of the differences between M&A and greenfield investment is that M&A is adjustment to market stock, while greenfield investment increases market supply. According to the basic theory of Western economics, in the case of a certain market capacity, simply increasing the supply, to achieve a new equilibrium, must reduce the price to expand the demand, and this is what investors do not want to see. Therefore, we believe that when the market growth rate is high, the market capacity is constantly expanding, and it is more inclined to enter the market through greenfield investment at this time. While the market growth rate is low, the market has become saturated. At this time, it is more suitable to optimize the allocation of resources through M&A and adjust the existing production capacity.

Caves and Mehra (1986) conducted an empirical study on the relationship between investment mode and GDP and showed that countries with high GDP growth rates are more likely to have greenfield investment than countries with low GDP growth rates, a result that laterally supports the above inference. The choice of a firm to invest in greenfield investment or M&A is attracted by the industry's sales growth rate, and the higher the growth rate, the more likely the firm is to choose new construction (Mudambi & Mudambi, 2002).

(2) Market structure status

Industrial concentration refers to the scale structure of the distribution of enterprises in an industry, which has two main indicators: Industrial Concentration Index and Summary Concentration Index. Industrial Concentration Index refers to the market share of a few of the largest enterprises in an industrial market, above a certain size (generally with sales, but also with assets, income and labor force, etc.). The commonly used industry absolute concentrations are the largest four- vendor concentration (CR4) and the largest eight-vendor concentration (CR8). After analyzing the concentration of the manufacturing industry, Bain (1959) proposed his basic standard Summary Concentration Index based on market share, which is an index reflecting the relative concentration of enterprises in the industry. It is usually expressed by the Lorenz Curve and the Gi-ni Coefficient based on the Lorenz Curve.

Generally speaking, in industries with high industrial concentration, the first few companies have a relatively high market share, have formed economies of scale, and formed their marketing strategies and customer groups. For investors, if they use the method of new investment when entering, they will face two risks: first, several companies with high market shares will take joint boycott actions against new entrants to avoid profit dilution; second, compared with companies that have already formed economies of scale, new entrants face more intense competition in the initial stage. Based on the above considerations, investors generally use M&A rather than greenfield investment. Therefore, it can be inferred that industry concentration is negatively correlated with the likelihood of firms adopting greenfield investment.

Caves (1976) showed that when entering a market with a concentration of firms, the choice of M&A is more likely to be made to avoid a fall in market prices.

In the choice of foreign investment methods, there is also a trade-off between M&A and greenfield investment, which are embodied in two modes: cross-border M&A and greenfield investment. If FDI investors enter the host country through the greenfield investment model, the market share of the newly established target enterprises needs to be seized from the original enterprises in the same industry in the host country market, so they will face fierce competition; if FDI investors enter the host country through cross-border M&A, since the M&A behavior has not changed the original competition pattern in the host country market, the competition faced by the target company will be weaker than that of the greenfield investment model. Li Shanmin and Li Chang (2013) inferred that overall the future growth of newly built target firms in the greenfield investment model would be slower than those acquired in the cross-border M&A model due to the greater competitive pressure they face. This inference is consistent with the empirical study of Georgopoulos and Preusse (2009).

The investors themselves, as they have often formed a scale advantage, are more inclined to choose greenfield investment rather than M&A when choosing investment methods. And at this point, the influence of industry concentration refers mainly to the characteristics of the enterprise itself. The position of the enterprise in the industry, that is, the market power, can often be reflected by the ranking of the enterprise in the industry.

(3) Preference for government policies

The investment risk of the host country is reflected in the uncertainty of the economic and political conditions and the continuity of government policies which play a key role in the survival and profitability of the enterprise. Government policies include the government's attitude towards foreign-funded enterprises and certain industries, the government's capital control policy on foreign- funded enterprises, the government's asset requisition policy on foreign-funded enterprises, and exchange rate policies. The policies formulated by the host country need to be able to affect the ability of foreign investors to obtain value from the investment target enterprises, and to play a role in guiding the flow of foreign capital. Generally speaking, tax policies (tax reduction or tax increase), restrictions on the maximum shareholding ratio of foreign capital, and prohibition of industry entry are all policy means that can guide the choice of foreign investment entry modes (Li Shanmin & Li Chang, 2013). Changes in government policies may cause difficulties in the recovery of proceeds, or even expropriation of assets in extreme cases (Root, 1987), and some scholars believe that restrictive policies of the host government may prevent inward foreign investment (Rugman, 1979; Stopford & amp; Wells, 1972), in such countries, firms are better not to enter, and even if they enter, they may prefer non-investment models (Agarwal & Ramaswami, 1992).

The government's policy inclination towards a certain industry often also influences investment decisions. The government's regulation of a certain industry may be inclined to a certain investment method, or more conducive to the implementation of a certain investment method. For example, for some industries with weak strength and lack of competitive advantages, preferential policies may be formulated to encourage new investment in this field; while for some industries that tend to be saturated and heavily redundant, they may be encouraged to carry out M&A integration, to further optimize the allocation of resources. Correspondingly, when enterprises in the industry make investments, they will largely consider the government's policy inclination to make their investment decisions more reasonable.

Changes in exchange rates also reflect the policy inclination of the host country's government or the political and economic stability of the host country to some extent. For example, the host country adopts different foreign exchange policies due to the need to attract foreign investment, export or foreign exchange control, changes in the domestic economic prosperity of the host country, or sudden economic crisis, these factors will directly cause exchange rate changes.

When the foreign currency appreciates and the actual purchasing power exceeds the nominal value, foreign investors enter the host country market through M&A and can obtain undervalued assets and realize low-cost expansion. A case in point is the acquisition of American companies in the 1980s when the Japanese yen appreciated against the US dollar.

Davidson (2002) also shows that the difference in exchange rate parity increases the possibility of overseas investment through international M&A. In the 1950s and 1960s, American companies acquired a large number of European companies. At that time, the US dollar was in a strong position.

The undervaluation of the host country's enterprises caused by the exchange rate changes of the host country will have a positive impact on the mergers and acquisitions of enterprises. It is worth noting, however, that the effect of this influence is relatively limited. Firstly, the undervaluation of the target company is a short-term phenomenon, and more often the market mechanism can accurately estimate the value of the company; secondly, in the actual operation of most M&A transactions, the value of the target company is often relatively overvalued. In addition, the company's M&A behavior will consider some strategic factors more. The undervaluation of the target company in the short term only provides an opportunity to enter, and generally does not become a determinant of M&A, but only influences the choice of investment approach of a company at a certain time.

Swedish economist Gustav Cassel in 1916 based on summarizing the previous academic theories, systematically proposed that the exchange rate of the two currencies is mainly determined by the purchasing power of the two currencies. It is called the theory of purchasing power parity (referred to as PPP theory). The purchasing power parity index compiled using this theory can reflect the exchange rate differences between countries. In a certain period, the greater the difference between the nominal exchange rate of the target party and the actual purchasing power, the more inclined the enterprise is to choose M&A, and conversely, the more inclined to invest in greenfield investment.

Moskalev (2010) studied data from 57 countries or regions around the world and found that laws targeting cross-border M&A had an impact on both the number and form of cross-border M&A. Those countries that have deregulated cross-border M&A have significantly increased the number of cross-border M&A.

At the same time, FDI investors in countries with weaker regulatory laws against cross-border M&A are also more likely to acquire host country target firms rather than make greenfield investments or set up joint ventures. The study also found that the host country's enhanced legal supervision of cross-border M&A will lead FDI investors to turn to greenfield investment or joint ventures to avoid regulatory restrictions, and to find entry models that are more conducive to increasing their control over investment target companies. Anwar (2012) analyzed and compared the specific laws and regulations on FDI in China and the United States, Australia, Canada, and the United Kingdom, and pointed out that the policies of these five countries have a very obvious impact on the development of FDI in their respective countries.

(4) Availability of strategic resources

The most important motivation for a company's strategic M&A under globalization is to acquire the strategic assets of the target company through M&A, to maintain and enhance its competitive advantage in the world market. Strategic assets, including research and development capabilities, technical know- how, patents, trademarks, supplier networks, marketing networks, etc.,[1] are an important part of an enterprise's ownership advantage. These strategic assets are either difficult for the acquirer to obtain (such as the commercial reputation of the target company), or difficult for the acquirer to form in a short period time (such as the marketing network in the host country). The acquisition of these strategic assets will enable the company to quickly enter the local market, acquire the technology and marketing network of the target company, realize the combination of management and operational advantages of both parties, achieve worldwide economies of scale, and make the company's global production layout more efficient, or be in a more advantageous position to compete in the product market of the host country, which has a more special strategic significance beyond the target's intrinsic value for the company.

In addition, according to the transaction cost theory, enterprises can save transaction costs from the following aspects: Firstly, in the case of information asymmetry and externalities, it is difficult for enterprises to transfer the market value of knowledge acquired through R&D investment, and even if the transfer is realized, it requires high negotiation costs. At this time, the use of knowledge in the same enterprise through greenfield investment can achieve the purpose of saving transaction costs. Secondly, as intangible assets, enterprises' trademarks and commercial reputation also encounter the problem of externality in their application. Because a certain trademark user reduces the quality of its products, it can get most of the benefits of cost reduction, while the loss of commercial reputation is shared by all trademark users. One way to solve this problem is to increase supervision, and the

[1] In a general sense, strategic assets may also include human capital. However, human capital is both industry-specific and firm-specific. In comparison, industry characteristics have a greater impact because the intensity of human capital often depends heavily on industry characteristics. Thus, we put this factor into consideration in the context of industry characteristics.

other is to adopt greenfield investment to make all trademark users internal members. In the case of external transactions, the cost of supervision will be greatly increased. As an internal member, reducing the quality will only bear the loss but not the benefit, eliminating the opportunistic motivation. Thirdly, some companies need a lot of intermediate product inputs for their production, and the market for intermediate products suffers from uncertainty in supply, difficulty in controlling quality and opportunistic behavior. The above- mentioned problems can be eliminated by enterprises turning their partners into internal members through M&A. Therefore, Balakrishnan (1993) predicted that when the target company and the investment company are in different industries, greenfield investment will be more preferred because of its high transaction cost. Whereas, when both parties are in the same industry, they may be more inclined to choose M&A.

Of all strategic assets, technology holds a special place as the most important part of the ownership advantage. The competition among modern enterprises is mainly expressed in the competition in technology, and enterprises can obtain or play the competitive advantage in technology through M&A to enhance their core competitiveness. Through M&A, the technology, patents and related professional and technical personnel of the acquired company can be directly obtained, which will facilitate the expansion of unfamiliar fields in the acquisition direction, save research and development costs, reduce the time risk and failure risk in technology development, or quickly realize technological upgrading and catch-up. To enter the field of data communication, the famous communication system supplier Lucent Technologies carried out 12 M&A of data communication enterprises from 1996 to 1999, constantly enriching the data network department. In January 1999, Lucent acquired Ascend, a well-known computer network manufacturer in the United States, for US$20 billion, achieving the largest merger of a telecommunications manufacturer and a data network supplier. After the merger, Lucent established a broadband network department composed of Ascend and Lucent's original data network system, optical fiber system, and software department, realizing a major strategic shift from the traditional communication production industry to the expansion of the data communication field.

In the initial stage, there is a certain difference in the technology transfer effect between M&A investment and greenfield investment. Greenfield investment is the establishment of a new enterprise, which generally uses new equipment, technology, and workplace from the very beginning, and can adopt appropriate advanced technology according to the actual development situation of the target company. The new company established through M&A is based on the original business and there is a post-acquisition integration period in which the M&A investment cannot transfer new or better technology and skills as quickly as a greenfield investment while the acquirer continues to use the acquired party's existing technology and equipment. However, if the equipment of the acquired enterprise is outdated or inefficient, the acquirer is likely to invest in new equipment, technology, and production methods, to rapidly enhance the competitiveness of the acquired enterprise and make post-acquisition investments. The study of Hennart (1988) show that when a firm's desired assets are mixed with assets it currently does not need, it is more inclined to acquire these assets through acquisitions. He believes that the digestibility of target assets is the most critical factor in deciding whether to adopt greenfield investment or acquisition, and the research focuses more on the cost of integrating the target company's human resources. Shan's study (1988) shows that a small-scale biological company can incur high integration and management costs for this reason.

Under long-term conditions, M&A are usually the same as greenfield investments, which are industrial investments that focus on long-term development. As a long-term investor, the company has an incentive to improve and enhance the operational efficiency of the acquired company and enhance its competitiveness. Therefore, M&A can also bring advanced production, sales technology, and management methods to the enterprise in the long run.

In most developing and transition countries, foreign investors usually have a stronger presence. Therefore, M&A, especially M&A by companies in developed countries, will improve the level of hard and soft technology and related capabilities of the acquired company. Mergers and acquisitions not only improve the labor productivity of the acquired enterprises, but also improve the total factor productivity of these enterprises, and the increase in productivity of acquired enterprises is generally greater than the increase in productivity of locally acquired enterprises. Even in developed countries, when the technology gap between the two parties is relatively small, M&A often improve the production efficiency of the acquired company.

There are at least two prerequisites for the inference that the choice of M&A is beneficial in enhancing firm performance (Yu ChengYong & Shi Jianjun, 2011). The learning effect is greater than the spillover effect. The learning efficiency of acquiring external complementary knowledge through M&A and the competition effect that may originate from inter-organizational learning are sufficient to offset the profit monopoly or spillover effect between organizations. Due to the enhanced control of complementary external assets and the reduction of interest conflicts between different organizations, M&A are superior to alliances in terms of organizational interest alignment and prevention of opportunistic behavior, and the ultimate development trend of alliances is M&A.

Hennart and Park (1993) applied resource theory and transaction cost theory to conduct empirical research on Japanese enterprises and pointed out that Japanese enterprises with strong technological advantages generally use greenfield investment to enter other countries' markets, and the study concluded that their transfer is generally difficult due to complex technologies, and the difficulty and risk of training employees of the acquired firms are greater. Therefore, high-tech enterprises are more inclined to use greenfield investment to enter foreign markets.

The study of Davidson (1980) shows that the investment enterprises with centralized production technology and famous international brand are more proposing the way of greenfield investment rather than the way of M&A. Curhan et al. (1977) joint research also shows that most companies with a high level of market technology tend to advocate greenfield investment by way of greenfield construction rather than M&A. Our explanation for this phenomenon is that this kind of enterprise has superior technical and marketing capabilities than the invested enterprise and through this advantage can pursue a product differentiation strategy that can substantially reduce the risk associated with the uncertainty of the investor.

According to the research of Stopford and Wells (1972), enterprises with low research and development expenses are more inclined to choose M&A as investment methods, while enterprises with high technology intensity choose greenfield investment methods instead of M&A to avoid losing their competitive advantages.

According to the above analysis, we can see that the more strategic assets investors have, the more inclined they are to use greenfield investment. The more strategic assets the target company has, the more inclined it is to M&A.

4.2.3.2 Internal Factors

(1) Size of the enterprise

Firms need asset strength to expand internationally and successfully compete with host country firms, resources to absorb high marketing costs, strengthen patents and contracts, and obtain economies of scale (Hood & Young, 1979). The size of the firm reflects the firm's ability to absorb these costs (Buckley & Casson, 1976; Kumar, 1984). Empirical studies have shown that firm size has a positive effect on OFDI (Buckley & Casson, 1976; Cho, 1985; Caves & Mehra, 1986; Yu & Ito, 1988; Terpstra & Yu, 1988; Kimura, 1989). In other words, usually firm size is positively correlated with the propensity to enter international markets.

(2) Previous business experience of the enterprise

Po-Lung Yu (1980), a professor at the University of Kansas, pointed out in the study of personal development: "Good intelligence is not as good as good habits." The habitual behavior of an individual comes from its habitual domains, there is a rich habit field is the potential of a person's development, and the enterprise organization as an organic whole is also the same, its mode (method, way) system and culture also come from the habitual domains of its enterprise organization, so the key to reformation, innovation system, and culture is to continuously enrich and improve the enterprise organization habitual domains, and the key to the sustainable development of the enterprise is to have a continuous improvement of the habitual enterprise domains. From this point of view, after completing similar decisions several times, enterprises are more inclined to adopt similar decisions in the process of making decisions in the future. The past decision-making experience is very important, the decision-making thinking of decision-makers has certain inertia, and the past decision-making methods and decision-making results have an important influence on the choice of M&A and greenfield investment (Cho & Padamabanan, 1996). In other words, if an enterprise has made a relatively large number of M&A decisions, its subsequent decisions tend to adopt M&A rather than greenfield investment, thus forming its own enterprise organization's habitual domains (EOHD). Once the habitual organizational domains of the enterprise are formed, if there is no strong external conflict, it is difficult to change it.

Moreover, as a form of investment, whether it is M&A between domestic enterprises or M&A of overseas enterprises by domestic enterprises, the initial purpose belongs to the same category. Therefore, in the process of continuous M&A, enterprises can accumulate corresponding experience and learn from failures, to provide strong support for future M&A decisions.

The results of empirical research show that (Barkema & Vermuelen, 1998; Larimo, 1996; Larimo, 1998; Wilson, 1980; Zejan, 1990), the longer the history of enterprises investing in greenfield construction, the more likely they are to invest in the same way, which corroborates the previous inference from the side.

(3) R&D strength of the enterprise (the ability to develop differentiated products)

The strength of R&D capability and the size of R&D expenditures of enterprises are also important factors affecting the choice of FDI entry methods for multinational companies. If a multinational company enters the host country through greenfield investment, it must pay higher R&D costs to understand the local market, obtain market information, and research market opportunities, the greater the R&D investment of the enterprise, the stronger the R&D capability, and the strong R&D capability can be injected into the new enterprise without much transfer cost, which can reduce the R&D cost of the new enterprise. A study by Andersson and Svensson (1994) concluded that firms with high R&D capabilities tend to invest in greenfield investments.

In addition, when a firm has the ability to develop differentiated products, if it shares this knowledge with the host country firm, the firm faces the risk of long- term loss of revenue, as the foreign firm may use this knowledge in the future as independent corporate management (Van de Ven & Poole, 1989). So when a business has this capability, the high-control model, i.e., greenfield investment, is very effective. Empirical studies have also shown that high levels of product differentiation require the use of high control models (Anderson & Coughlan, 1987; Caves, 1982; Coughlan, 1985; Coughlan & Flaherty, 1983; Davidson, 1982; Stopford & Wells, 1972).

(4) Enterprise management level

In the 1960s, Leibenstein (1966) proposed the theoretical model that non- configurative inefficiencies are widespread in firms and that the difference in managerial efficiency between dominant and disadvantaged firms becomes an important intrinsic motivation for corporate M&A. The core point of the x-efficiency theory based on this model is that corporate M&A have potential benefits for the entire society, and the occurrence of M&A behavior is not only conducive to improving management's operating performance but will also lead to some form of synergistic effects.

According to the x-efficiency theory, the management efficiency of each enterprise is also different due to the different management layers that make up each enterprise. When the management of company A is more efficient than the management of company B, and when company A believes that "exporting" its management efficiency to company B will bring benefits to itself, company A then has an efficiency incentive to acquire company B. The "management spillover" realized through M&A

enables company A's management resources to be fully utilized, and company B's inefficient capital is combined with effective management to increase its efficiency to the same level as company A's, thus achieving management synergy effect.

The theory of the management synergy effect implies three basic assumptions: first, the acquirer has slack management resources, which are efficient and inseparable, or these management resources have economies of scale and can be fully utilized through M&A; second, for the target company, the inefficiency of its management can be improved through the intervention of external managers and increased management resources; third, management synergy is also achieved when the acquirer has the specific experience needed in the target company's industry and is committed to improving the target company's management. Therefore, this argument is more suitable for explaining horizontal mergers. Taking this argument to the extreme, there may be such an extreme assumption that after a series of M&A, there is only one enterprise with the most efficient management in the whole society, and the socio-economic efficiency is also maximized. Obviously, the limited internal coordination and management resources within the company prevent the unlimited expansion of M&A.

The technology transfer effect of M&A is also reflected in the transfer of soft technology to the acquired party in the host country, such as the transfer of information resources including management and organizational methods, etc. Through M&A, based on using the original equipment and production technology, the acquired firm's production efficiency can be improved through the transfer of soft technology. For example, in Argentina's privatization process in the 1990s, private companies acquired some of Argentina's state-owned utilities, and post-acquisition implemented measures such as laying off redundant staff, improving customer records and collection methods, modifying major reforms such as procurement policies and subcontracting policies. The acquirer also improved the organizational technology of the original enterprise and realized the computerization and automation of management. To solve the problem of a low- quality labor force, the company has also carried out a lot of employee training for the acquired subsidiaries. Through the transplantation of M&A soft technology, the production efficiency and quality standards of the acquiree have been significantly improved. Other research evidence also shows that foreign investors have mostly introduced new or improved management techniques in acquired firms, especially in state-owned enterprise acquisitions.

To a certain extent, enterprises with low management levels are more inclined to adopt the method of greenfield investment to avoid the risk of integrating a high-level enterprise.

(5) Project construction speed

Compared with greenfield investment, M&A has the advantage of speed.

When a company expands domestically or overseas, M&A are often the quickest way to reach its goals. Under the conditions of economic globalization, speed not only enables the acquirer to quickly enter the relevant market but also affects the survival and development of the enterprise. The speed advantage is particularly important when companies invest overseas.

Firstly, M&A have the advantage of the speed of entry over greenfield investment. Through M&A, the company can greatly shorten the construction or investment cycle of the project, quickly enter the local market, and seize the opportunity in the fierce competition in the market. While the greenfield investment generally involves different stages of work such as project demonstration, government approval, infrastructure construction, equipment installation, and personnel allocation. The construction period is long, and there are many uncertain factors. It usually takes 1.5–2 years to create a new enterprise from inspection and negotiation to opening. It takes at least 3–5 years to reach a certain scale. In contrast, the acquirer needs only 3–5 months to quickly form a production scale, and even if it is renovated, it only takes 1–2 years at most, which is 2–3 years shorter than that of a newly built enterprise. Under the new economic conditions, the rapid development of science and technology makes M&A avoid the time pressure and risks faced by greenfield investment to a large extent when entering. Li Shanmin and Li Chang (2013) found that in countries or regions with fast construction speed, FDI investors tend to use greenfield investment to enter the host country; on the contrary, in countries or regions with slow construction speed, FDI investors prefer the cross-border M&A model.

Secondly, M&A can enable investors to obtain the ownership advantage of the acquiree at the fastest speed or realize the combination of ownership advantages of both parties, and then quickly occupy the target market. These ownership advantages include the acquiree's existing production equipment, skilled workers, advanced technology and management experience, as well as its brand trademark and sales network. At the same time, through mergers and acquisitions, the market share of the acquired company can also be obtained, reducing competition and consolidating the market position.

Finally, M&A can promote the rapid growth of enterprises. In recent years, technological breakthroughs and major innovations have increasingly relied on exchanges and cooperation between disciplines and industries, and the previous division of disciplines and industrial sectors with clear boundaries has been broken down. A company with extremely limited capabilities and resources can hardly compete effectively by relying solely on its internal research and development efforts. Moreover, product life cycles are shortening, technology is becoming more complex, and research and development expenses have increased significantly due to the increase in labor and capital costs, which not only increases the time urgency and risk but also reduces the potential return on significant research and development. Therefore, enterprises need to grow at the fastest speed in the increasingly fierce market competition. Through M&A in the global market, not only can it be much faster than its development speed, but also can obtain external special assets or resources, and even a new business field, can seize the source of knowledge, and form continuous technology development capabilities. Therefore, the speed advantage of M&A has become the best choice for corporate investment. Among the many network M&A that have occurred in recent years, quite a few are investment strategies adopted by computer manufacturers or software companies to quickly enter the network industry. Numerous empirical studies have also shown that the shorter the time for greenfield investment, the more likely companies will choose to invest in greenfield investment rather than M&A

(Andersson et al., 1992; Andersson & Svensson, 1994). For the choice of foreign investment methods, when the volatility of the host country's market demand is higher, the construction period of greenfield investment projects is shorter, and the culture of the host country is more attractive to greenfield investment, FDI investors are more inclined to adopt the greenfield investment model and conversely tends to cross- border M&A model (Brouthers et al., 2008).

(6) Cultural difference

Due to the geographical distance between the home country and the host country and the difference in traditional culture between the East and the West, multinational companies must fully consider the differences between the host country's regional culture and its own culture when choosing FDI entry methods. The reason is that these types of ownership advantages are context-specific and cease to exist once they leave the environment, or are in an unfamiliar country. To take advantage of these ownership advantages and better internalize them, it must be possible under similar circumstances.

When one company acquires another, integration is difficult due to the cultural differences between the two companies (Jemison & Sitkin, 1986). These cultural gaps may arise from different countries as well as from different industries. Generally speaking, the larger the gap between the two countries, the more likely they are to adopt greenfield investment because it is very difficult to integrate companies from two different cultures.

Kogut and Singh (1988) compiled an index to summarize the gap between the target country and the investor's country for each Hofstede dimension, and concluded that firms with larger index gaps were less inclined to M&A. Dubin (1976) took overseas investment from 1948 to 1967 as the object, and based on the international M&A of American companies, he investigated the determinants of the choice of investment method. He found that the higher the cultural and geographical gap between the investor country and the investee country, the more inclined to choose greenfield investment. However, some scholars believe that the small cultural gap allows enterprises to establish their production and operation systems without the help of local enterprises, so they are more inclined to choose greenfield investment (Brouthers and Brouthers, 2000).

4.2.3.3 Interrelationship Between Internal and External Factors

For ease of presentation, we further categorize internal and external factors. External factors of a firm are divided into market potential (mainly in terms of market growth, market competition, and access to strategic assets) and investment risk (mainly in terms of the host government's attitude toward foreign firms and certain industries, the possibility of capital control and asset expropriation, and exchange rate changes), while internal factors are mainly expressed in terms of ownership advantages such as the size of the enterprise, experience in multinational operations, R&D strength and the ability to develop differentiated products.

(1) Scale, multinational operating experience, and market potential

Corporate strategy has strong explanatory power for the way a company enters the market. Generally speaking, companies that pursue a localized multinational operation strategy are more inclined to choose cross-border M&A, while those that pursue a globalization strategy tend to invest in greenfield investment. (Harzing, 2002).

On the one hand, enterprises with a large scale and high level of multinational operating experience are more likely to choose countries with relatively low market potential for greenfield investment.

Brouthers and Dikova (2010) show that greenfield investment can start from a very small scale, and gradually increase investment and expand the scale when the market conditions improve in the future, so greenfield investment enjoys a positive asset option (deferring option) compared to cross-border M&A. From a market perspective, countries with relatively low market potential are less likely to attract foreign companies, but some large multinational corporations may be interested in such markets to achieve their growth and profit goals. These markets may have sufficient potential and strategic importance to ensure corporate returns, and due to market imperfections, opportunities for additional returns are also high. Only large firms have sufficient resources to take on the risks associated with entering low market potential (Lambkin, 1988). If firms decide to enter a market with relatively low potential, they are more likely to choose a greenfield investment model to meet their strategic needs (Bartlett, 1986; Bartlett & Ghoshal, 1986; Doz et al., 1988). Research on global strategy shows that such firms are concerned with their global strategy rather than transaction costs associated with a particular market (Porter & Fuller, 1986). Exports, M&A, and joint ventures are also suitable for low-potential markets for risk reduction purposes, but they do not have the strategic control, strategic change, and strategic flexibility to ensure long-term global competitive advantage. In special cases, the partners of the joint venture and minority shareholders of the acquirer may create obstacles to the achievement of strategic objectives, and their motivations may be incongruent with those of the investing enterprise, which may cause great difficulties (Prahalad & Doz, 1987). Conversely, a newly established sole proprietorship can take advantage of the strategic choices generated by integrated operations to gain a competitive advantage (Kogut, 1989).

On the other hand, enterprises with a small scale and low level of multinational operating experience are more likely to choose greenfield investment models to enter countries with higher market potential.

Enterprises that are small and inexperienced in multinational operations are not expected to have sufficient resources and skills to enter many foreign markets, so they use the option to new-build strategies and focus their energies on more potential foreign markets due to their high chances of achieving higher returns in such markets. In addition, resource constraints (including scale) make them more inclined to enter into joint ventures with industry leaders (Contractor & Lorange, 1988; Fayerweather, 1982; Stopford & Wells, 1972). Joint ventures enable them to spread risks and costs and complement the assets and skills of the host country's partner enterprise

(Harrigan, 1985). In this way, the joint venture can reduce the long-term uncertainty of the enterprise at a low cost compared with the pure organization or market method (Beamish & Banks, 1987).

(2) Ability to develop differentiated products and investment risk

On the one hand, enterprises with the ability to develop differentiated products are more likely to choose the form of greenfield investment to enter enterprises with high investment risks. Moreover, large-scale enterprises with a high level of multinational operating experience are less likely to choose greenfield investment in such markets.

In a high-investment-risk environment, the best option for enterprises is not to enter, and if enterprises nevertheless have to choose to enter, it is much better to export than to invest. However, the ability of enterprises to handle risk varies across firms due to different ownership advantages, and enterprises with valuable assets and skills in particular may negotiate with host governments to obtain concessions that will give them immunity from high risk (Leontiades, 1986). If they don't get such concessions, they won't get in. Empirical conclusions show that enterprises with their independent products and skills can improve their bargaining position with the host country (Lecraw, 1984; Vernon, 1983). Scale of enterprise and transnationality do not necessarily provide this negotiating advantage (Fagre & Wells, 1982), and the reason for this difference is that host governments can find alternative sources of capital, but not skills, implying that even in countries with high investment risk, the required technology can determine the negotiating position (Ting, 1988). In addition, for the consideration of reducing risk, enterprises with independent products and skills will choose the high control model, because this model can make enterprises change their investment so that if the assets they put in the host country are expropriated by the host country, these assets are not profitable for them (Eston & Gersovitz, 1983). Without controls, these enterprises face the threat of host governments changing their policies in favor of their local enterprises.

4.2.4 Selection Method of M&A and Greenfield Investment

After qualitatively analyzing the various factors that influence the choice of direct investment entry methods of investment companies, we developed an analytical model for analyzing the choice of greenfield investment and M&A of companies using the theoretical models in economics that analyze the equilibrium situation of markets under various market structures to quantitatively analyze the choice of direct investment entry methods. We firstly introduce a simple model of market competition—the Cournot model. The basic assumption of this model is that the competitive strategy adopted by the participating enterprises is pure quantity competition, rather than price competition. Under this basic assumption, we apply the Cournot model to the choice of greenfield investment or M&A entry methods for investment companies. The main idea of model analysis: in the face of three basic market structures, investment companies enter the market through greenfield investment or M&A, whether it has an impact on the original market structure, and whether the profit of the investment company increases or decreases under the new market structure after entering compared with the pre-investment, and the profit increase or decrease becomes the only investment decision indicator. The three basic market structures are perfectly competitive market structure, monopoly market structure, and oligopoly market structure.

4.2.4.1 Model Building

We base our analysis on a simple Cournot model. The Cournot model was proposed by the French economist Cournot in 1838. The Cournot model is usually used as the starting point for the analysis of oligopoly theory, and is often referred to as the duopoly model, but this model can also be used in situations where there are more than two manufacturers, such as pure output changes as competition means of multiple manufacturers. Given the particularity of the comparative analysis of greenfield investment and M&A, we first give the basic assumptions of the model, the variable selection of the model, and the overall description of the model, and then analyze three market structures on this basis.

(1) Basic assumptions

- (i) The products produced by all enterprises are homogeneous, and there is no difference in brands;
- (ii) There are only differences in production and sales costs between different enterprises. The differences in production and sales costs here include all possible differences in costs that exist in the enterprise when the enterprise uses capital, produces products, sells products, and provides services, including a series of differences in the brand effect, technology level, and sales costs of the enterprise;
- (iii) The investment company is free to make investment decisions, i.e., the investment company is not affected by non-economic factors, such as policy influence or other influences in the target market;
- (iv) Investment companies only consider economic interests when making investment decisions, that is, maximizing pure profits;
- (v) Market information and product information are shared;
- (vi) The investment company has sufficient capital to realize any form of investment;
- (vii) In the event of mergers and acquisitions, mergers and acquisitions can only occur between investment companies and target companies, and mergers and acquisitions cannot occur between investment companies or between target companies;
- (viii) The fixed cost of production and sales of the enterprise is zero;
- (ix) Only one investment firm enters the target market;
- (x) The expansion of the investment company is horizontal rather than vertical for its products and services, that is to say, the investment

company only expands the scale of the same product and service without considering the purpose of the investment company to enrich its products and services;

(xi) The determination of the acquisition price of the investment company is based on the actual value of the target assets. We assume that the acquisition price at this time is not less than the actual asset value of the target company;

(xii) Enterprises participate in the market competition by changing their output, without considering other competition methods.

(2) Variable selection for the model

Obviously, the most important variables in this model are the net profit when the investment company enters through greenfield investment and the net profit when it enters through mergers and acquisitions. These two variables become the only criteria for the decision of the investment company's entry method.

Variable parameters to be considered in the model:

(i) Target market size *a*: The market size of product *X* in the target market is described by the market demand curve.

$$P = a - bQ$$

where: *P* is the price, *a* is the market size, *b* is the elasticity of demand, and *Q* is the output.

Intuitively, the size of the market has an impact on the entry of investment companies to a certain extent, and the smaller-scale market is easily changed by the entry of investment companies. Here, however, changes in market size are out of the question.

(ii) Target enterprise's marginal cost of production and sales is c_{ai} $(i = 1, 2, \ldots, n)$, a is the target enterprise.

(iii) The marginal cost of production and sales of the investment company is c_b, *b* is the investment company. Assume that because the investment company has a series of advantages over the target production enterprise, such as advanced production technology and advanced management experience, its marginal cost of producing and selling product *X* is smaller than that of the target production enterprise, that is,

$$c_b < c_{ai} \quad (i = 1, 2, \ldots, n)$$

At the same time, it is assumed that the cost function is a linear function, that is,

$$c(q_i) = c_i q_i (i = 1,\ 2,\ \ldots,\ n)$$

(iv) The actual value of the production and operation assets of the target enterprise is K_i $(i = 1, 2, \ldots, n)$ refers to the available assets of the target enterprise for the production and sale of the produced product *X*, including a series of available resources such as machines, plant buildings, patented technologies, and social network resources.

(v) The competitive price of the production and operation assets of the target enterprise is rk, r is the financing rate and k is the acquisition price. This variable will only be under monopoly market or oligopolistic market conditions, due to the influence of the original market power of the target enterprise, when the company intends to acquire the enterprise, the acquisition price is higher than or equal to its actual asset value, that is $K \leq k$. Suppose the financing rate is r, then the apportionment in a calculation period is rk.

(vi) The cost of fixed assets required for the investment company's greenfield investment rf, f is the total investment.

Assuming that the total investment required by the investment company for the greenfield investment is f, r is the financing rate, then rf is the apportionment of the investment cost over a calculation period for the entire expected duration of the investment.

(vii) The cost of acquiring market information for an investment company to enter a new market is rm, m is the market information fee.

The investment company lacks market information relevant to the target market. To obtain this information, a certain cost must be paid. Assuming that the total cost is m, r is the financing rate, then rm is the apportionment of the cost of obtaining the market information in a calculation period during the entire expected duration of the investment. If the investment company enters the target market through mergers and acquisitions, then this cost is considered negligible because the investment company can familiarize itself with the target market with the help of the relevant information of the target company; if the investment company enters the target market through greenfield investment, then this cost will become an integral part of investment company's familiarity with a new market. which is

$$rm^G > 0$$

$$rm^A = 0$$

where: G is the greenfield investment entry method; A is the mergers and acquisitions entry method.

(viii) The cost of resource integration between the investment company and the target company is rd, d is the integration costs.

Due to different environments, different production technology levels, different management levels, and differences in corporate culture between the investment company and the target enterprise, if mergers and acquisitions occur, the full integration of the two companies will inevitably cost a certain amount of cost. This integration cost is denoted by d, as above, r is the financing rate, then rd is the apportionment of the cost of resource integration in a calculation period during the entire expected duration of the investment.

(3) Model idea

In this model, direct investment activities are divided into two different stages: the first stage is the stage before the investment company enters the target market, which is also the investment decision-making stage of the investment company; the second stage is when the investment company enters the target market and affects many variables in the market.

The first stage: In this stage, the target market is in equilibrium, multiple manufacturers compete perfectly, one firm monopolizes the entire market, or several firms form an oligopoly market, assuming the market demand curve for product X in the target market is:

$$P = a - b\mathrm{Q}$$

To simplify the discussion, we assume $b = 1$ that because the model is static, the slope of the demand function is equal to -1, ignoring changes in the elasticity of demand for income, then the market demand curve is:

$$P = a - \mathrm{Q}$$

Faced with this market demand curve, under different market structures, different manufacturers have different production and sales costs, and their output and profits are also different. We will discuss the different situations separately under different market structures.

The second stage: After the investment company enters the target market, due to the different market structures and the different entry methods of the investment company, it may not only have an impact on the target market structure but also may not have an impact on the current market structure (see Table 4.2). In different circumstances, the entry profit of the investment company will be different.

Here, for the simplicity of analyzing the problem, when considering the entry of an investment company, only two scenarios are considered that may occur:

(i) Investment company enters by way of greenfield investment;
(ii) Investment company enters through M&A.

Table 4.2 Market structure before and after different direct investment methods

Before investment	After investment	
	Greenfield investment	M&A
Perfect competitive market	Perfect competitive market	Perfect competitive market
Monopoly market	Oligopolistic market	Monopoly market
Oligopolistic market	Oligopolistic market	Oligopolistic market

We only consider only one investment company entering the target market. In fact, even if it is assumed that multiple investment companies enter the target market at the same time, their analysis ideas, analysis methods, and final results will be consistent. However, there is a situation that we have to pay attention to, that is, when multiple investment companies are intending to acquire a target company at the same time, the price of the production and operation assets of the target company may be much higher than its actual asset price, causing the investment company's entry decision to deviate from the norm. In this stage, the investment firm's investment entry mode decision depends on the size of its expected entry profit, i.e., the size of the benefit minus the cost. We take the investment company's microeconomic decision as the starting point and take the profit maximization of the new company formed in the target market after the investment company enters as the decision criterion for judging the investment company's entry, regardless of the investment company's other intentions for direct investment.

In Cournot model, since it is assumed that the competition among enterprises is purely the competition of changing their output, the equilibrium price of the market is closely related to the marginal production and operating costs of the competing enterprises. Due to the strictness of Cournot's assumption, we can easily obtain the equilibrium market price, the output, and profit of the investment company according to market parameters such as market size and production and operation costs of each enterprise, and compare the net profit of the investment company under the two entry methods, it can be concluded that which way the investment company chooses to enter is the optimal decision.

4.2.4.2 Comparison of M&A and Greenfield Investment in a Perfect Competitive Market

(1) Model description

In the discussion in this section, the market is assumed to be perfectly competitive. The analysis and conclusions drawn in this chapter will be idealized due to the unrealistic assumption of perfect competition. However, it is because of the idealization of the market that external conditions hardly have any impact on the investment company's investment decisions. All factors will be concentrated within the enterprise, which will instead highlight the internal factors of the investment company when making investments.

(i) Market description before the investment company enters

Suppose the market demand function for product X is:

$$P = a - bQ$$

For simplicity, suppose $b = 1$, then the market demand function is:

$$P = a - Q$$

Enterprises in the original market are D_{ai} ($i = 1, 2, \ldots, n$), the actual value of its assets is K_{ai} ($i = 1, 2, \ldots, n$), the marginal cost of producing and selling product X is c_{ai} ($i = 1, 2, \ldots, n$), and the output is q_{ai}^B ($i = 1, 2, \ldots, n$), then

$$Q_a^B = \sum q_{ai}^B$$

where: B is the state before investment.

This output is the equilibrium output in the equilibrium market. The market equilibrium price of product X is P^B.

The net profit of the target company's production and sales is:

$$\prod_{ai}^{B} = (P^B - c_{ai})q_{ai}^B \quad (i = 1,\ 2,\ \ldots,\ \mathrm{n})$$

(ii) Market description after the investment company enters

Investment companies can enter target markets in two ways: greenfield investments and M&A. Since the market is perfectly competitive, the entry of a single firm cannot change the market structure of the product and the equilibrium price of commodity X in the target market.

The net profit of the investment company through greenfield investment is:

$$\prod_{b}^{G} = (P^G - c_b)q_b^G - (rf + rm)$$

The profit of the target enterprise is:

$$\prod_{ai}^{G} = (P^G - c_{ai})q_{ai}^G \qquad (i = 1,\ 2,\ \ldots,\ n)$$

The net profit of the investment company through M&A is:

$$\prod_{b}^{A} = (P^A - c_b)q_b^A - (rk + rd)$$

The profit of the target enterprise is:

$$\prod_{ai}^{A} = (P^A - c_{ai})q_{ai} \qquad (i = 1,\ 2,\ \ldots,\ n)$$

(2) Investment company decision analysis

Due to the assumption of perfect competition in the market, the entry of investment companies will not have an impact on the target market, so

$$P^G = P^A = P^B$$

And suppose $q^G = q^A$, then there is, $\prod_b^G - \prod_b^A = (rk + rd) - (rf + rm)$.

If $(rk + rd) > (rf + rm)$, then the profit of an investment company entering the market through greenfield investment is higher than that through M&A, and the investment company will choose the greenfield investment; if $(rk + rd) < (rf + rm)$, then the profit of an investment company entering the market through greenfield investment is less than that through M&A, the investment company will choose the M&A. At this time, we can see that due to the perfect assumption of a perfectly competitive market, the investment company's entry decision depends on four factors: the price of the production and operation assets of the target enterprise (rk), the cost of resource integration when entering through mergers and acquisitions (rd), the fixed cost of investment company when entering through greenfield investment (rf), and the cost of obtaining market information required by the investment company after entering through greenfield investment (rm). Therefore, under the assumption of perfect competition, the entry of investment companies does not affect the target market. We can regard this process as a static process, and investment companies only need to consider their entry costs when entering.

From the above analysis we can draw the following conclusions:

If the investment company enters through M&A, and the price of the target enterprise is very high, or the price is much higher than the actual value of the production and operation of the target enterprise, the investment enterprise will consider entering through greenfield investment. The second situation is more likely to occur. This situation may occur when the target enterprise has scarce resources, or certain key technology, or market resources, and the resources owned by the target enterprise of the investment company's M&A has become an ideal target for many investment companies. In this case, for investment companies, M&A may not be successful.

If the investment company enters through M&A, the normal and efficient operation of the new enterprise requires the successful integration of the resources of the investment company and the target enterprise. There are differences between the investment company and the target enterprise in many aspects, especially the differences in the technical level, management level, and corporate culture of the two will have an impact on the normal operation of the company. For a productive enterprise, the existing assets of the target enterprise may not be able to meet the requirements of the investment company to produce new products, which requires a period to spend a certain cost to combine the existing resource advantages of the two, so that it can achieve synergy. If the investment company considers in advance the high cost that these differences may bring to the integration of resources between the two, it will not choose to enter the target market through M&A.

When the investment company enters through greenfield investment, it needs an initial fixed investment. If the amount of this fixed investment is relatively large, the investment company may consider choosing M&A. Because for the same amount of production and business assets, if M&A is adopted, since M&A can adopt a variety of financing methods, the financial pressure on the investment company is relatively small, and this risk can be shared with the enterprise being acquired, unlike greenfield investment that requires the investment company to bear the risk of investment failure alone. Therefore, some large-scale direct investments are carried out in the form of M&A.

When an investment company enters through greenfield investment, because the investment company lacks necessary information about the target market, to make the company's production and operation operate normally, it needs to have a process of understanding the target market from unfamiliar to familiar, and this process also costs time and cost, such as the target's market demand, consumers' consumption preferences, relevant laws and regulations of the target and a series of information related to the company's production and operation. However, if the investment company enters by way of M&A, this cost can be ignored, because the investment company can obtain relevant information about the target market through the target enterprise. Therefore, this cost is also one of the factors that investment companies must consider when choosing an entry method.

4.2.4.3 Comparison of M&A and Greenfield Investments in Monopoly Market

(1) Model description

In this part of the discussion, the market is assumed to be monopolistic. Before the investment company entered, there was only one company that provided product X, and the demand curve faced by this company was the market demand curve, and the company decided on the output to obtain the maximum profit. After the investment company enters in different ways, the market structure of product X will change differently, and accordingly, the profit function faced by the investment company will also be different. The following analyzes the decisions made by investment companies based on profit maximization in different situations.

(i) Market description before the investment company enters

Suppose the market demand function for product X is:

$$P = a - bQ$$

For simplicity, suppose $b = 1$, then the market demand function is:

$$P = a - Q$$

Enterprises in the original market are D, the actual value of its assets is K the marginal cost of producing and selling product X is c_a, and the output is Q. This output is the equilibrium output in the equilibrium market. The market equilibrium price of product X is P^B.

$$P^B = \frac{(a + c_a)}{2}$$

$$Q_a^B = \frac{(a - c_a)}{2}$$

The net profit of production and sales of enterprises in the original market is:

$$\prod\nolimits_a^B = (P^B - c_a)q^B = (q^B)^2 = \frac{(a - c_a)^2}{4}$$

(ii) Market description after the investment company enters

Investment companies can enter target markets in two ways: greenfield investments and M&A. Due to the entry of investment companies, the supply of product X in the market increases, and the market structure may also change, depending on the way the investment companies enter. In this process, we only consider greenfield investments and M&A.

Investment companies enter through greenfield investments. If only one investment company enters in the form of greenfield investment, then the newly entered investment company and the enterprises in the original market form two oligopolies, forming a Cournot equilibrium, and the equilibrium price is:

$$P^G = \frac{(a + c_a + c_b)}{3}$$

The output of the investment company is:

$$q_b^C = \frac{(a - 2c_b + c_a)}{3}$$

The target enterprise's output is:

$$q_a^G = \frac{(a - 2c_a + c_b)}{3}$$

The net profit of the investment company is:

$$\prod\nolimits_b^G = (P^G - c_a)q_b^G - (rf + rm) = \frac{(a - 2c_b + c_a)^2}{9} - (rf + rm)$$

The profit of the target enterprise is:

$$\prod\nolimits_a^G = (P^G - c_a)q_a^G = \frac{(a - 2c_a + c_b)^2}{9}$$

If the investment company enters through M&A, there is still only one enterprise in the target market, which monopolizes the market, and the equilibrium price is:

$$P^A = \frac{(a + c_b)}{2}$$

The output of the investment company is:

$$Q_b^A = \frac{(a - c_b)}{2}$$

The net profit of the investment company is:

$$\prod\nolimits_b^A = (P^A - c_b)q_b^A - (rk + rd) = \left(q_b^A\right)^2 - (rk + rd) = \frac{(a - c_b)^2}{4} - (rk + rd)$$

The target enterprise is acquired with zero profit.

(2) Investment company decision analysis

The investment company's entry decision is determined by the profit of the two entry methods. Due to the impact of the entry of investment companies on the structure of the target market, the two entry methods of greenfield investment and M&A have different profits for investment companies. The impact of $(rf + rm)$ and $(rk + rd)$ on MNC entry decisions has been analyzed under the assumption of perfect competition. Here, the important thing is to compare q_b^G and q_b^A. Therefore, when $c_b < 2c_a - a$, $\prod_b^G > \prod_b^A$, indicated that when the investment company has obvious technological advantages and the marginal cost is low enough, the investment company will choose the greenfield investment method to enter. When $c_b < 2c_a - a$, $\prod_b^G < \prod_b^A$, indicated that when the technological advantage of the investment company is not obvious, the investment company will choose the way of M&A to enter.

It can also be seen from the formula that when the market size is large (that is, a is large enough), investment companies tend to enter through M&A, and when the market size is small, they enter through greenfield investment, because emerging and developing markets are better equipped to accommodate the entry of new businesses, while a relatively saturated market is not conducive to new enterprises.

From the conclusion of this model, the technical level of the investment company and the target company directly affects the marginal cost of sales of both parties, thus determining the profit of the new company under different entry methods; The differential market size also provides an environmental factor for the selection of appropriate modalities for the entry of investment firms. Therefore, the investment company's decision depends on three factors: the target market size, the target enterprise's production and sales marginal cost, and the investment company's production and sales marginal cost.

4.2.4.4 Comparison of M&A and Greenfield Investments in Oligopolistic Market

(1) Model description

In the discussion in this section, the market is assumed to be oligopolistic. In this market, before the investment company enters, several companies offer product X, and they all share a market. After the investment company enters in different ways, the market structure of product X will change differently, and accordingly, the profit function faced by the investment company will also be different. This section analyzes the decisions that investment firms make based on profit maximization in different situations.

(i) Market description before the investment company enters

Suppose the market demand function for product X is:

$$P = a - bQ$$

For simplicity, suppose $b = 1$, then the market demand function is:

$$P = a - Q$$

Enterprises in the original market are D_{ai} ($i = 1, 2, \ldots, n$), the actual value of its assets is K_{ai} ($i = 1, 2, \ldots, n$), the marginal cost of producing and selling product X is c_{ai}, and the output is Q, there are n firms in the market, suppose

$$c = \sum c_{ai} \quad (i = 1, 2, \ldots, n)$$

This output is the equilibrium output in the equilibrium market. The market equilibrium price of product X is P^B,

$$P^B = \frac{(a + c)}{(n + 1)}$$

$$q_{ai}^B = \frac{[a - (n + 1)c_{ai} + c]}{(n + 1)}$$

The net profit of production and sales of enterprises in the original market is:

$$\prod\nolimits_{ai}^{B} = \left(P^B - c_{ai}\right)q_{ai}^B = \left(q_{ai}^B\right)^2$$

(ii) Market description after the investment company enters

Investment companies can enter target markets in two ways: greenfield investments and M&A. Due to the entry of investment companies, the supply of product

X in the market increases, and the market structure may also change, depending on the way the investment companies enter.

In this process, we only consider greenfield investments and M&A.

If the investment company enters in the form of greenfield investment, then the newly entered investment company and the enterprises in the original market form $(n+1)$ oligopolies, forming a Cournot equilibrium, and the equilibrium price is:

$$P^G = \frac{a + c + c_b}{(n+2)}$$

The output of the investment company is:

$$q_b^G = \frac{a - (n+1)c_b + c}{(n+2)}$$

The output of the target market enterprise is:

$$q_{ai}^G = \frac{a - (n+2)c_{ai} + c + c_b}{(n+2)}$$

The net profit of the investment company is:

$$\prod\nolimits_b^G = (P^G - c_b)q_b^G - (rf + rm)$$

The profit of the target enterprise is:

$$\prod\nolimits_{ai}^G = (P^G - c_{ai})q_{ai}^G = \left(q_{ai}^G\right)^2$$

If the investment company enters through M&A, there are still n enterprises in the target market, and these n enterprises form an oligopolistic equilibrium in the market. Assuming the original marginal cost of production and operation of the target enterprise is c_{ai}, the equilibrium price is:

$$P^A = \frac{a + c - c_{ai} + c_b}{(n+1)}$$

The output of the investment company is:

$$q_b^A = \frac{a - nc_b + c - c_{ai}}{(n+1)}$$

The net profit of the investment company is:

$$\prod\nolimits_b^A = (P^A - c_b)q_b^A - (rk + rd) = \left(q_b^A\right)^2 - (rk + rd)$$

The output of the target enterprise is:

$$q_{ai}^{A} = \frac{[a - (n+1)c_{ai} + c - c_{ai} + c_b]}{(n+1)}$$

The profit of the target enterprise is:

$$\prod_{ai}^{A} = (P^A - c_{ai})q_{ai}^{A} = (q_{ai}^{A})^2$$

(2) Investment company decision analysis

The investment company's entry decision is determined by the profit of the two entry methods. Since the entry of investment companies has an impact on the structure of the target market, the profits generated by greenfield investments and M&A are different for investment companies. The impact of the formula $(rf + rm)$ and $(rk + rd)$ on the investment company's entry decision has been analyzed under the assumption of perfect competition. Comparing the profits of the two entry methods is equivalent to comparing q_b^G and q_b^A,

$$q_b^G - q_b^A = \frac{[(n+2)c_{ai} - a - c - c_b]}{(n+1)(n+2)}$$

Similar to the analysis under monopoly conditions, when $c_b < (n+2)c_{ai} - a - c$, $\prod_b^G > \prod_b^A$, indicates that when the investment company has obvious technological advantages and the marginal cost is low enough, the investment company will choose to enter through the greenfield investment; when $c_b > (n+2)c_{ai} - a - c$, $\prod_b^G < \prod_b^A$, indicates that when the technological advantages of the investment company is not obvious investment companies will choose mergers and acquisitions to enter.

It can also be seen from the formula that when the market size is large (that is, a large enough), investment companies tend to enter through M&A; and when the market size is small, they enter through greenfield investment, because emerging and developing markets are better equipped to accommodate the entry of new businesses, while a relatively saturated market is not conducive to new enterprises.

As same as the analysis under monopoly conditions, it can be seen from the conclusion of this model that the technological advantages of investment companies directly affect the marginal cost, which determines the profit of new enterprises; the size of the market affects the difficulty of establishing new enterprises in the target market. Therefore, the investment company's decision depends on three factors: the target market size, the target enterprise's marginal cost of production and sales, and the investment company's marginal cost of production and sales.

If a constraint is imposed on the production and sales costs of target enterprises under oligopoly conditions, and the marginal costs of production and sales of target enterprises are assumed to be equal in size, the oligopoly conditions evolve into monopoly conditions, and the analysis results of the two are completely consistent.

4.2.5 Summary

By revising some preconditions of the original model, the Cournot model starts from the perspective of cost and benefit analysis, studies the difference in profits obtained by investment companies in the face of different target market structures and through different entry methods, this is the criterion for the selection of direct investment methods.

In a perfectly competitive market environment, investment companies have the same returns regardless of M&A or greenfield investments. The choice of investment method depends on four cost variables: acquisition price, integration cost, start-up cost, and information acquisition cost. When the sum of the acquisition price and the integration cost is higher than the sum of the start-up cost and the information acquisition cost, the investment company will choose greenfield investments; when the sum of the start-up cost and the information acquisition cost is greater than the sum of the acquisition price and the integration cost, the investment company is more willing to choose M&A.

In a monopolistic market environment, if the investment company chooses greenfield investments, the market structure will be transformed into a duopoly market, and if the investment company chooses M&A, the market structure will remain monopolistic. In addition to the above-mentioned four factors, the decision-making factors of investment companies in monopoly markets also depend on the size of the target market, the marginal cost of the target enterprise, and the marginal cost of the investment company. If the investment company has significant technological advantages, the marginal cost of the two companies is very different, or the target market is small, greenfield investments become more favorable; otherwise, M&A should be the first choice.

In an oligopolistic market environment, investment companies have a certain impact on the market no matter how they enter, and the factors and basic conclusions of investment companies' investment decisions are consistent with those of a monopoly market. When the investment company has technological advantages or the target market is small, it tends to greenfield investments, otherwise, it prefers M&A investment.

The establishment of the Cournot model has strict assumptions, such as the assumption of freedom of decision-making, which excludes the influence of policy; the assumption of product homogeneity, which ignores the role of brand effects and goodwill, but its conclusions are similar to the previous analysis of influencing factors. For example, the stronger the technical advantages of the investor, the greater the technical difference between the two parties, the more inclined they are to invest in a new company; the greater the cultural difference between the two investors, the higher the integration cost, the more inclined the investment company is to invest in a new company; comparing acquisition price with start-up cost, the investment method with a larger scale tends to be M&A; following the previous investment experience, choosing a market with lower barriers to entry or the investment company itself with strong R&D strength, will save the cost of information acquisition, so that the investment company tends to be low-cost; a large market size often means a high degree of market development, and there are enough target companies to choose, and investment companies tend to be M&A. Qualitative and quantitative analysis, although the methods are different, the angles are different, but the conclusions are convergent.

The fundamental difference between greenfield investment and M&A is whether the investment company establishes a completely new business or acquires or merges an existing company. This determines that M&A have the advantages of quickly entering the market, acquiring strategic assets, and avoiding government regulations, while greenfield investment has the advantages of a reasonable choice of investment location and scale, low investment costs, and easy access to the support of all sectors of the target market. At present, M&A account for the absolute majority of direct investment globally. In developed countries, M&A have grown particularly rapidly. In terms of industry distribution and location distribution, M&A are significantly different from greenfield investments. It should be said that this is due to differences in characteristics between M&A and greenfield investments. However, no one method can occupy an absolute advantage in all situations. When making investment decisions, we should fully consider the actual situation of the enterprise and the surrounding economic environment it faces and combine the characteristics of the two direct investment methods, to realize the goal of strategic investment in enterprises.

4.3 Boundaries of M&A and Strategic Alliances

4.3.1 Introduction to M&A and Strategic Alliances

4.3.1.1 The Concept of Strategic Alliance

Strategic alliance refers to a loose network organization with mutual advantages, risk-sharing, and elements that flow horizontally in both directions or multiple directions, formed by two or more enterprises (or specific undertakings and functional departments) with equal economic strength, through signing agreements and contracts to achieve the strategic goals of jointly owning the market and using resources together. Most strategic alliances are long- term alliances and cooperation, which are spontaneous and non-compulsory. American strategic management scientist Michael Porter (1985) defined a strategic alliance as: "a long-term agreement between enterprises that is beyond normal transactions but does not reach the level of the merger. The alliance does not need to expand the enterprise, and the general approach is to agree with an independent enterprise to carry out value activities (such as supply agreements) or to cooperate with an independent enterprise to jointly carry out some activities". Parkhe (1991) defines a strategic alliance as: "A relatively durable inter-firm cooperative arrangement involving the flow and linkage of resources and government

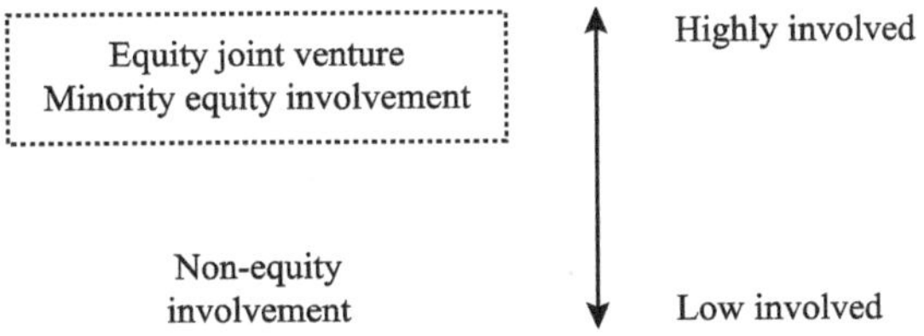

Fig. 4.1 The main forms of participation of affiliated enterprises

structures from autonomous organizations to jointly achieve individual goals related to the corporate mission of each sponsoring firm." Gulati (1995) sums it up to a more succinct definition: "Any independently initiated inter-firm link involving exchange, sharing or exploitation." Dr. Zhang Weiying (2000) regards strategic alliance as "an organizational form between independent enterprises and market transactions, which neither has centralized authoritative control nor is a transaction in the market that pays firsthand and delivers second hand".

Strategic alliances can take many forms, including joint ventures, minority ownership alliances, R&D contracts, joint R&D, joint marketing, supplier partnerships, distribution agreements, and franchise agreements. To better sort out so many forms of alliances, theorists have proposed several classification methods of strategic alliances (Dussauge & Garrette, 1995; Lorange & Roos, 1990; Oliver, 1990; Pisano & Teece, 1998). Most studies classify strategic alliances because of equity versus non-equity. Therefore, we also follow this idea and divide strategic alliances into equity alliances and non-equity alliances. Equity alliances include equity joint ventures and minority equity alliances, and non-equity alliances refer to all other cooperative arrangements that do not include equity transactions. According to the degree of participation of the alliance enterprises, the main forms of alliance participation are divided as shown in Fig. 4.1.

4.3.1.2 Distinguish M&A from Strategic Alliances Based on the Degree of Integration

For a long time, people have thought that there are only two ways of resource allocation: market and enterprise. With the development of the economy, many organizations between the market and enterprise have emerged (Lorange & Roos,1993). Ndsborn and Boughn (1993) called non-equity alliances like strategic alliance agreements as quasi-market, and they called the joint venture form of strategic alliances as quasi-hierarchy, which revealed "the nature of the intermediate organization". M&A activity is a manifestation of the internalization of corporate transactions. According to the degree of integration, the organizational form of resource allocation can be represented as shown in Fig. 4.2, the left side is the market system, the right side is the bureaucratic system of a typical enterprise structure, M&A and strategic alliances are between market price adjustment and enterprise bureaucratic organization, it is a combination of the two, which has both advantages.

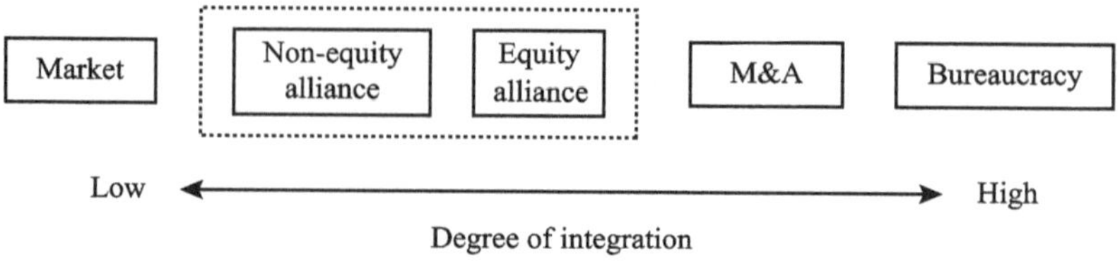

Fig. 4.2 Several forms of resource configuration

To sum up, it is not difficult to find that strategic alliances and M&A are two different concepts. The strategic alliance emphasizes cooperation. The member enterprises of the alliance are independent and equal, which is a "win- win" strategy. Even if the participation of equity is accompanied by the process of allying, there will be no transfer of control. Mergers and acquisitions are different, emphasizing mergers, which are based on the paid transfer of control rights as the basic feature. The difference between the two is not whether there is equity participation, but whether the control right is transferred. We believe this essentially defines the boundary between M&A activity and alliance activity.

4.3.1.3 Comparison of the Advantages and Disadvantages of M&A and Strategic Alliances

(1) Advantages of M&A

First, compared with strategic alliances, the transfer of ownership and control is the most prominent feature of M&A. After the acquisition of the target enterprise, it controls the operating rights and management rights of the target enterprise. The acquirer can integrate the target enterprise according to its strategic intention, and change the behavior of the market and contract into internal organizational management behavior. They have greater initiative and control over their goals, and unlike strategic alliances, all behaviors must be restrained and coordinated by alliance participants.

Second, M&A can quickly enter the target market. Whether expanding domestically or abroad, M&A are often the fastest way to get there. Intensified competition and ever-shortening product life cycles have forced companies to accelerate their adaptability to changing economic conditions. At the same time, when a multinational company successfully invests in a certain area, to prevent the former company from monopolizing the market, other companies will compete to invest in the same market. Currently, M&A are the fastest way to enter. The reason why M&A have this characteristic is that: firstly, M&A can greatly shorten the investment cycle of the project, save the time of building a factory, and enable the company to quickly acquire the current management and technical personnel, production equipment, suppliers, and marketing channels, etc. Secondly, mergers and acquisitions effectively lower barriers to entry into new industries. The entry of a new industry requires a lot of manpower, material resources, time, and faces a series of uncertain factors, such as production expertise, supply of raw materials, geographical location, and host country control. Through M&A, multinational companies can quickly enter a brand-new industry and realize their diversification and industrial transfer.

Third, M&A can also quickly gain market share. The M&A company can directly eliminate its competitors, occupy the original market share of the target enterprise, and make full use of the original enterprise's sales channels, trademarks, original management system, and human resources. In addition, there will be no new production capacity, and it will not affect the balance of supply and demand in the industry. Therefore, the competition structure within the industry will remain unchanged in the short term, and it is unlikely to cause a price war or retaliation.

Fourth, M&A can fully apply the experience curve effect. When an enterprise accumulates more and more experience in production and operation, the unit cost of a product will show a downward trend. When an enterprise develops through M&A, it not only acquires the production capacity and various assets of the original enterprise but also acquires the experience of the original enterprise. Mergers and acquisitions can seize the opportunity to acquire assets cheaply. When the target enterprise encounters problems in its operation, or the stock market price in the target market generally falls, or when a situation that is conducive to M&A occurs, such as taking advantage of the large change in the exchange rate between the two places, the company can use a lower price for M&A.

(2) Disadvantages of M&A

First, valuation is very difficult. Because different countries have different accounting standards, and it is difficult to collect real information about the target enterprise, the evaluation of the target enterprise's value has become the most critical and complex link in M&A.

Second, some of the original contracts and traditional relationships of the target enterprise make the acquirer subject to certain constraints in production and operation. At the same time, the utilization of redundant resources is also a difficult problem. Sometimes a heavy price is paid for the resolution of these contracts and relationships.

Third, the post-merger management integration stage is also a difficult problem. Many M&A fail not at the stage of acquiring control of the target enterprise, but at the stage of integration and management after control is obtained. Due to the different cultural backgrounds and enterprise cultures of the two companies, the management and communication difficulties of both parties have caused many difficulties in production and operation, and sometimes even led to business failure or separation after acquisition. At the same time, the size and geographical location of the target enterprise may not fully meet the needs of the strategic layout of multinational companies.

Fourth, the failure rate is high. Judging from the measurement indicators that can be used at present, the failure rate of subsidiaries established through M&A is higher than that of new ones, and from the perspective of the goal of the company's operation-maximizing shareholder wealth, the shareholders of the M&A company have not much profit is obtained in the merger, while the shareholders of the target enterprise benefit a lot from the merger.

(3) Advantages of strategic alliances

First, the advantages of strategic alliances are mainly reflected in greater flexibility and looseness. The relationship between the members of the strategic alliance is not formal, and the realization of its goals relies entirely on negotiation rather than legal rights and obligations. Once the external technology and market change, this alliance relationship will change at any time. Therefore, the international strategic alliance belongs to a dynamic and open cooperation system.

Second, strategic alliances have changed the traditional, highly confrontational way of competition aimed at eliminating competitors. In addition to adversarial competition among enterprises, there may also be cooperation and alliances. Both sides of the alliance have their own goals, using each other's strengths to make up for their weaknesses, allocating the market defensively, and opening the market offensively. What the strategic alliance emphasizes is cooperation and win–win. All parties in the alliance maintain the independence of the original enterprises, but within the alliance they are required to share responsibilities, coordinate with each other, and take concerted actions to achieve a common goal. Although the alliance companies cooperate in some fields, they still maintain the independence of operation and management outside the agreement and in the overall situation of the company's activities, and they are still competitors. Cooperation is temporary and conditional, while competition is permanent and unconditional. This kind of cooperative competition can be divided into three types: (i) cooperation within the cooperation field and competition outside the cooperation field; (ii) cooperation first and competition after the cooperation is over; (iii) cooperation within the alliance, which competes with enterprises outside the alliance, or the alliance competes with alliances.

Third, implement all-around cooperative organizations to achieve innovation. The strategic alliance has expanded to all-around cooperation in technology, market, capital, talents, information, etc. It combines different enterprises with specific advantages in all aspects of the value chain such as research and development, production and processing, marketing, and after-sales service scattered in various countries, implementing division of labor and cooperation, complementing each other's advantages, utilizing resources, and sharing benefits. In this way, franchisees can not only get what they need from each other but also ensure their independence.

(4) Disadvantages of strategic alliances

An alliance is a loose organizational form, which has limited constraints on each alliance party. So the shortcomings of the alliance are also obvious. Only when both parties have the attitude of cooperation and competition and abide by the agreement can it be effective. The experience of many cooperative enterprises emphasizes that this kind of partnership also has risks and costs. The intention of allying is a long-term cooperation, but the maintenance time of the cooperative relationship is not necessarily long. Overall, strategic alliances do have a high failure rate. Therefore, the risks of the alliance must be fully considered. The risks are mainly reflected in the following aspects:

First, the process of analyzing the strategic and organizational capabilities of potential partners is one of the important steps in a strategic alliance, but it is also the most difficult task. Effective pre-alliance analysis requires not only data on the tangible assets of potential partners (e.g., plant and equipment condition, productivity), but also data on some intangible assets (including brand power, quality of relationships with customers, and level of expertise) and information on organizational capabilities (e.g., management capabilities, employee loyalty, and shared values, etc.). Information that is otherwise difficult to obtain is made even more difficult to obtain due to the short time constraints in which many coalitions are formed.

Second, there is a gap between promise and reality. During the process of affiliate planning and negotiation, some unrealistic requirements or wrong choices may arise. The operation of the alliance will inevitably face potential and hidden difficulties and problems.

Third, whether the definition of the scope of the alliance is reasonable is related to the stability of the alliance. The more complex the alliance, the more attention it needs from management, and the more difficult it is to manage. Cross- functional departments need to be coordinated and integrated, and the number and scope of collaborative activities need to be understood. The scope of strategic alliances and the uncertain environment they are bound to face make it difficult for both parties to understand the nature, extent, and dispersion of rewards or risks that may arise during the evolution of cooperation, or even don't know the role status and tasks of each member of the alliance.

Fourth, the purpose of cooperation between enterprises is to a large extent to obtain technologies and resources that can benefit all parties. The equality of the competitive position of all parties in the alliance is an important factor for the alliance to be maintained. When all parties in the alliance both cooperate and compete, one party in the alliance may use the cooperation to develop its advantages, causing risks to the other party, and eventually leading to the imbalance of competitive position and the disintegration of the cooperative relationship. When the skills and capabilities of one party are hidden in the complex organizational process, it is difficult to learn and imitate, while the skills and capabilities of the other party are relatively clear and easy to learn and imitate. It is entirely possible that in the process of cooperation, one collaborator can protect its technological advantages while learning the technological advantages of the other party. In the end, it is possible to abandon the collaborators and enjoy the benefits brought by the cooperation alone. At the same time, when a party actively invests in product development, manufacturing, marketing, or any kind of value chain of strategic importance, and has more control over major investments than its partners, under the premise of ensuring its independence, it can effectively constrain the other party, cause the other party to rely on itself unilaterally, and then arbitrarily weaken and control the partner. In addition, since the purpose of an alliance is usually to share risks, each cooperating enterprise "externalizes" some tasks to the partner by "learning by doing", and the enterprise almost inevitably loses some interests and shapes the future potential competitors for itself.

Fifth, the complexity of strategic and organizational partnership management is also a disadvantage of strategic alliances. Firstly, its complexity comes from the different management traditions and strategic thinking of the partners. Due to the different management traditions of the parties involved in the cooperation and the differences between Eastern and Western cultures, the alliance has brought different strategic thinking and management practices. With this corporate culture, unique rules and regulations, and management models formed in the long-term practice, cultural conflicts may cause instability in the operation of the alliance. Secondly, the complexity also comes from the uncertainty of the environment. No alliance can predict all possible variables in advance, and the strategic goals of alliances are highly environmentally sensitive. The obligations of both parties are not static but adjusted as the environment changes. This constant monitoring and adjustment increase the risk of the partnership. This additional investment in monitoring and renegotiation also increases the overall risk and cost of the alliance.

4.3.2 Theoretical Explanation of M&A and Strategic Alliances

4.3.2.1 Transaction Cost Theory

Transaction costs are the costs incurred in completing activities necessary for a transaction, such as drawing up and implementing a contract. Ronald Coase's analysis (1937) provides a powerful framework for merger decisions. A fundamental question was raised in his research—what determines the size of a company? The question of why and when companies will engage in horizontal integration or vertical integration. Coase's central point is that a company will face a variety of costs, some internal and some dependent on external suppliers or distributors. He believes that the size and merger of a company should be determined by the relevant internal and external transaction costs of the company. The Coase model provides an important guide for managers to make merger decisions. Coase instructed that managers should weigh the transaction costs of separate and combined entities before entering a merger transaction. If the transaction costs of the two separate entities are higher than the transaction costs of the combined entity, it is appropriate to consider an M&A strategy. Internalization is favored when the transaction cost is high because it can effectively control transaction costs, such as M&A and internal development. Kogut (1988) argues that firm ownership decisions emphasize the minimization of the sum of transaction costs and production costs. The decision-making of internalization such as M&A or internal development is appropriate when transaction costs are high (i.e., higher asset specificity, uncertainty and transaction frequency, higher costs

Table 4.3 Comparison of M&A and strategic alliances based on transaction cost theory

Items	Transaction cost fundamentals
Decision-making principles	Minimize the sum of production and transaction costs (Kogut, 1988)
Market	Low transaction costs and/or high production costs
Strategic alliance	When transaction costs associated with a transaction are moderate and not high enough to warrant vertical integration (Gulati, 1995) The joint venture is formed when the transaction risk shows that the internalization is efficient, but cannot be completely internalized due to the constraints of the conditions … (Rmanathan et al., 1997)
M&A	High transaction costs (i.e., higher asset specificity, uncertainty and transaction frequency, higher control costs) and low production costs (i.e., collaboration and learning) (Kogut, 1998)

Source Chen Yang. Applicable Boundaries Between M&A and Alliance. Beijing: Doctoral Dissertation of Beijing Jiaotong University, 2007

of controlling opportunistic behavior) and production costs (i.e., collaboration and learning) are low.

A strategic alliance is to partially internalize a transaction (such as a joint venture). Therefore, a strategic alliance combines the characteristics of internalization and production transactions to become "an organizational form between an independent enterprise and a market transaction relationship." (Zhang Weiying, 2000). Contracts are still required, but due to the imperfection of contracts, many behaviors need to work together. Therefore, some researchers propose that alliances will be considered when the relevant transaction costs of a transaction are neither high nor low enough to be vertically integrated (internalized) (Gulati, 1995). Even if coalitions are seen as a form of semi- internalization, there is a slightly different view that when internalization is most efficient but constraints prevent full internalization (Ramanathan et al., 1997), the alliance is reasonable.

A strategic alliance based on transaction cost theory is shown in Table 4.3.

From the perspective of transaction cost, the choice of the external growth strategy of the company is mainly affected by the following factors: the exclusiveness of asset investment, the uncertainty of behavior caused by opportunistic, the size and duration of economic synergies, occupancy regime of the asset and management costs.

4.3.2.2 Resource-Based Theory

The basic principle of the resource-based theory is to emphasize maximizing the value of an enterprise by concentrating and utilizing valuable resources. That is, enterprises are seen to find optimal resource boundaries by better-realizing resource value, rather than by other combinations of resources. The resource- based theory proposes that valuable enterprise resources are often scarce, cannot be fully imitated, and lack direct substitutes (Barney, 1991; Peteraf, 1993). In this way, the transaction and concentration of resources become a strategic necessity. When resources are available through efficient market transactions, "enterprises may move forward on their own" (Eisenhardt & Schoonhoven, 1996), relying on the market for development. But even though market transactions are the default mode, efficient transactions often do not develop in the spot market. Since valuable resources are sometimes mixed with other resources, or embedded within the organization (Chi, 1994), certain resources cannot be obtained exclusively through transactions. Thus, mergers, acquisitions, and strategic alliances are used in different situations. Therefore, the resource-based theory regards strategic alliances, mergers, and acquisitions as strategies to acquire resources of other enterprises and to store hard-to-obtain competitive advantages and values for enterprises.

Wernefelt (1980) first defined acquisition from the perspective of enterprise resources. He pointed out that acquisition can be viewed as purchasing a class of resources in a highly incomplete market. Shelton (1988) argued that an acquisition is a combination of the assets of the target and acquirer; value is created when these assets can be used more effectively in the combined enterprise than by the merging parties. Empirical research also showed that the value created by M&A came from the opportunities to utilize specific resources obtained from M&A (Chatterjee, 1986; Jesen & Ruback, 1983; Bradley et al., 1983). Jemison (1988) pointed out that the value creation of M&A came from the transfer of strategic capabilities. Research by Salter and Weinhold (1979) found that there is a positive relationship between key skills and the potential for value creation, that is, value can be created by strengthening skills that are critical to the success of the combined enterprise (the value created will be reflected in the enterprise's stock price).

The resource-based view explains the strategic alliance that no single enterprise can fully possess all the resources needed to develop its core competitiveness, and the human and physical resources required for a technological breakthrough often exceed the capabilities of a single enterprise. Enterprises accomplish the aggregation and combination of resources by finding and cooperating with partners who possess the resources it lacks, which is the main reason for making strategic alliances. Kogut's (1988) organizational learning model, a component of the generalized resource-based theory, provided a refined view of alliance formation, which is based on a firm's resources (e.g., knowledge and technology). Since strategic alliances are essentially the result of the combination of resources among enterprises, resource- based theory can help us better understand alliances. From a resource-based perspective, Eisenhardt and Schoonhoven (1996) viewed alliances as cooperative relationships driven by a logic of strategic resource thirst and social resource opportunities. Van de Ven (1976) noted early on that the process of establishing inter-organizational relationships can be viewed as a flow of inter-organizational resources. For example, joint ventures are formed when two or more enterprises share a portion of resources within a common legitimate organization (Kogut, 1988).

In Kogut's (1988) view, there are two possible reasons for enterprises to construct alliances: to acquire the know-how of other organizations, or to retain their know-how while benefiting from the resources of other organizations. Extending this analysis to all types of corporate resources, enterprises use strategic alliances or M&A for two related but distinct motivations: to acquire the resources of others; to retain and develop their resources by combining their own with those of others.

Enterprises can use alliances or M&A to acquire resources held by other enterprises that are valuable and necessary to gain a competitive advantage. In the international arena, multinational companies can enter a foreign market by acquiring a local company. They can also use the formation of international joint ventures to acquire the resources of their local partners, such as facilities, knowledge, and relationships (Beamish, 1987; Yan & Gray, 1994). In new product development, strategic alliances are used to pool the know-how and expertise of various enterprises (Leonard-Barton, 1992; Teece, 1992). In addition, M&A are often used to create economies of scale in R&D. Although both strategic alliances and M&A can achieve the goal of acquiring the resources of a certain enterprise, the resource-based theory proposes two conditions that distinguish alliances from M&A: First, strategic alliances are more feasible than M&A when all the resources owned by the target enterprise are of little value to the acquirer. Second, due to a certain degree of asset specificity, some valueless or redundant resources in M&A are not easy to dispose of (Ramanathan et al., 1997). Hennart and Reddy (1997) explains that acquisitions inevitably produce useless assets when unwanted assets are mixed with the desired assets and the two assets are difficult to separate. When non-desired assets cannot be easily separated, strategic alliances can allow partner enterprises only to approach desired assets and avoid non-desired assets, thereby increasing overall value. In this way, the obvious advantage of a strategic alliance is to approach the desired assets precisely with a minimum of additional unneeded assets. In support of this view, Hennart and Reddy (1997) found that enterprises favor acquisitions when the desired assets are "digestible".

Given that the motivation for acquiring resources is to get closer to others' resources, the motivation for "retaining resources" is to keep one's valuable resources safely in the enterprise. Kogut (1988) argues that enterprises may want to retain certain resources, but lack the equipment to utilize them. For example, sometimes enterprises are over-staffed with researchers and don't have enough work on hand to do. Rather than with researchers these personnel, enterprises may want to collaborate with other enterprises' resources (such as financial and physical resources) on projects to put these personnel to good use. For this purpose, strategic alliances may help retain internal resources that are not currently being utilized. Nelon and Winter (1982) argue that to prevent the decay of know-how, enterprises sometimes need to utilize alliances that allow them to continuously apply these capabilities. In this case, the choice between strategic alliances and M&A is about whether an enterprise should relinquish its resources over the long term (the M&A approach) or at a given time (the alliance approach). What differentiates strategic alliances from M&A is that the enterprise only briefly relinquishes its resources, which can later be used for internal allocation. Thus, when the future discounted value of the resource allocation exceeds the realized value of the current sale, the strategic alliance will be selected. Otherwise, the enterprise should consider selling.

The difference between acquiring additional resources owned by other enterprises and retaining one's resources is that acquiring resources is more about creating a

Table 4.4 Comparison of M&A and strategic alliance based on resource theory

Items	Resource-based theory
Decision-making principles	Maximize the value of one's enterprise by accessing valuable resources of other enterprises (Madhok, 1997; Ramanathan et al., 1997)
Market	It is more efficient to operate through the market when resource services are purchased from the owner
Strategic alliance	When the key input elements required to seize the opportunity are owned by different subjects, and these input elements cannot be separated from other assets of the owning enterprise (Ramanathan et al., 1997), it is better to choose the alliance. Collaboration is a useful means of increasing knowledge in key areas where the necessary knowledge is lacking and cannot be developed within an acceptable time frame or cost (Madhok, 1997)
M&A	When an enterprise requires assets that are not mixed with other unwanted assets of the acquired enterprise, which can be obtained by purchasing the enterprise or parts of it, then it will favor an acquisition over the joint venture. (Hennart & Reddy, 1997) If the market is permissive or the enterprise is pursuing a broad resource capability strategy, there is little incentive to collaborate. Enterprises are more likely to acquire or develop independently (Eisenhardt & Schoonhoven, 1996)

Source Chen Yang. Applicable Boundaries Between M&A and Alliance. Beijing: Doctoral Dissertation of Beijing Jiaotong University, 2007

competitive advantage quickly while retaining resources is more about protecting future competitive advantages. Beyond this distinction, what the two motivations have in common seems more important. Those resources contributed to the alliance must have a higher realized value than those of selling or utilizing them on their own. Regardless of whether long-term use of another's resources (to acquire resources) or to allow others to use one's resources temporarily (to retain resources), the primary decision-making principle should be the opportunity cost of the resource. The alliance is adopted when the realized value of those resources contributed to the alliance is higher than the value of internal utilization or abandonment. If the internal allocation or sale of resources can create more long- term value, strategic alliances will not be adopted at all.

In summary, a comparison of M&A and strategic alliance based on resource theory is shown in Table 4.4.

From the perspective of resource-based theory, the factors that affect the choice of external growth strategies of enterprises are the enterprise's resource endowment, the absorptive capacity of the enterprise, and the implicit degree of knowledge.

4.3.2.3 Theory of Enterprise Strategic Choice

According to the strategic choice theory, the purpose of M&A and strategic alliances is to improve the competitiveness or market dominance of enterprises, which is mainly divided into four aspects: First, to increase market dominance by setting up barriers to market entry or creating monopoly power. Second, to increase its influence over economic entities. Third, to improve the efficiency of functions such as research and development, production, and marketing. Fourth, to provide differentiation of products or services. However, due to the uncertainty of the external environment of the enterprise, the enterprise's strategy is very flexible, and different environments can affect the enterprise's strategic goals, and then affect the enterprise's choice of M&A and strategic alliances. It can be seen that changes in the external environment faced by enterprises are also one of the factors that affect the choice of enterprise M&A and strategic alliances.

4.3.3 Analysis of Influencing Factors of M&A and Strategic Alliances

From the previous theoretical analysis, it can be seen that when choosing the external growth strategy of an enterprise, different influencing factors are derived according to different theories. Transaction cost theory emphasizes the selection of external growth strategies based on the efficiency of economic activities.

Resource-based theory and strategic choice theory make strategic decisions based on the criteria of the enterprise's competitive advantage. Generally speaking, the internal and external factors of the enterprise are the two basic dimensions of the strategic decision analysis, but considering that M&A and strategic alliances are transactional behaviors between enterprises, the transactional dimension should also be included. Therefore, we construct the decision analysis framework for M&A and strategic alliance from three dimensions: environment characteristics, enterprise characteristics, and transaction characteristics, as shown in Fig. 4.3.

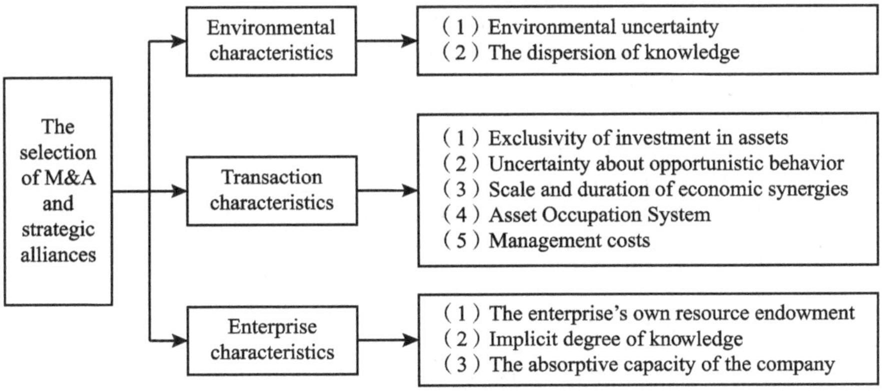

Fig. 4.3 Decision analysis framework for M&A and strategic alliances

4.3.3.1 Environmental Characteristics

(1) Environmental uncertainty

Available statistics show that M&A are more common in mature industries (such as steel, textile, and food), while strategic alliances occur in some emerging high-tech industries (such as biotechnology, multimedia, telecommunications, and computers). Theoretically, enterprises can promote the development of market, technology, and enterprise scale through strategic alliances or M&A. However, when making strategic choices, enterprises must be fully aware of the impact of environmental volatility and uncertainty. Uncertainty of the environment includes uncertainty of market demand, uncertainty of technology, degree of market competition, industrial policy and so on. Uncertainty of the environment leads to the uncertainty of the enterprise strategy, which requires the enterprise to maintain flexibility in their strategy, and then affects the choice of the enterprise's external growth strategy. Generally speaking, as the uncertainty of the enterprise strategy increases, the degree of closeness between the enterprise and the target resources will decrease subsequently when the enterprise chooses the external growth strategy. If the enterprise is not clear about the future dominant development direction of the industry, the enterprise may only master the process of one certain development direction through M&A, and lose other possible development opportunities. This means that in an uncertain environment, if M&A cannot reduce the risk of environmental uncertainty, such uncertainty can be reduced through strategic alliances, because strategic alliances provide enterprises with more cooperation opportunities and flexible strategic options, and enterprises' investment in strategic alliances is relatively small and can be withdrawn. In addition, the uncertainty of cooperation is also a direct factor affecting the transaction cost of cooperation. The higher the uncertainty, the greater the risk, and alliances can be used to avoid risks, conversely the M&A strategy is feasible (Chen Yang & Zhang Qiusheng, 2008). At the same time, the uncertainty of enterprise strategy is also reflected in the lack of understanding of the future market. Through strategic alliances, more market knowledge and experience can be gradually accumulated and risks can be reduced as much as possible. As we all know, when multinational companies enter foreign companies, they are mainly affected by strategic uncertainty, such as lack of knowledge about foreign markets and industrial regulation, and generally adopt strategic alliances (including joint ventures) first. With an in-depth understanding of the local economic system, culture, market and other knowledge, multinational companies may change their strategies and consider adopting M&A. It can be concluded that in the case of a high degree of strategic uncertainty, the requirement to maintain a high degree of strategic flexibility is more beneficial to the strategic alliance.

(2) Dispersion of knowledge

In the high-tech industries with rapidly changing technologies, strategic alliances are more likely to emerge. The reason is that new knowledge and new technologies are constantly emerging, and this new knowledge and new technologies are not owned by a few enterprises. The distribution of knowledge is relatively dispersed, and no one enterprise can dominate. Through strategic alliances, enterprises exchange knowledge with each other and recombine disperse knowledge to create value. At the same time, strategic uncertainty drives enterprises to acquire knowledge and skills quickly and flexibly through strategic alliances. The enterprise's strategic alliance can help the enterprise to acquire the knowledge needed quickly to realize a new business activity within a certain period, without the need to integrate it into the enterprise's operating activity system for a long time through M&A. This leads to the conclusion that strategic alliances are more beneficial in environments where knowledge distribution is more dispersed.

4.3.3.2 Transaction Characteristics

(1) Proprietary of assets input

In practice, proprietary inputs in a transaction have an impact on the choice of alliance or M&A strategy. When an enterprise cooperates with other enterprises to obtain complementary resources, it needs to invest some proprietary resources and skills. When the alliance fails, these proprietary inputs may lose their value or even become worthless. The research of Hoffmann and Schaper-Rinkel (2001) shows that there is a strong correlation between the proprietary of asset inputs and the degree of tightness of inter-firm alliances. If the enterprise needs to invest some resources with a high degree of proprietary in the alliance, the enterprise will face high withdrawal costs and opportunity costs if the alliance fails and cannot find a similar enterprise to form an alliance, and then the enterprises tend to acquire M&A. Proprietary inputs increase mutual interdependence, thereby enhancing the tightness of the union.

(2) Behavioral uncertainty induced by opportunistic behavior

The behavioral uncertainty caused by opportunistic behavior and moral hazard requires the establishment of expensive protection and control mechanisms, which will lead to higher management costs (ongoing transaction costs) and lower economic efficiency. If the benefits of acquiring complementary resources are small and the behavioral uncertainty is high, this will make the alliance cooperation of enterprises a transaction disadvantage. In this case, M&A will be more efficient than alliances.

(3) Size and duration of economic synergy

On the one hand, if the economic synergy effect lasts for a long time and affects a wide range, especially when it can bring economies of scale and scope, M&A may still be an alternative strategy, although the one-time cost is large and irreversible. On the other hand, alliances are appropriate when the complementary resources acquired are short-term, and the one-time transaction costs (costs of search, negotiation, and evaluation) may not be compensated by the cumulative synergies generated by the alliance. The size and duration of economic synergies are not only related to the types of resources to be combined and the relationships established between them, but also closely related to the environment. Changes in the environment can jeopardize the durability of synergies to some extent. If the uncertainty of the environment is high, the enterprise strategy must have a certain flexibility, and in this case, the synergy effect of the alliance will be weakened.

(4) Appropriability regime of assets

Fleece (1996) argues that the appropriability regime of assets determines an enterprise's capability to protect its core resources and capabilities from being appropriated by partners, which is another factor that affects the transaction cost of inter-firm relations. For a particular transaction, the strength of the appropriability regime depends on the isolation mechanisms such as patents and licenses, that is, whether these isolation mechanisms can provide sufficient protection for key resources. In an alliance, the easier it is to protect the competitive advantage derived from core resources, the less risk the cooperation will be. Conversely, if some key knowledge and skills can be obtained by paying certain transaction costs, then it is appropriate for the enterprise to adopt M&A strategy at this time.

(5) Management cost

Both M&A and strategic alliances require investing a certain amount of management costs. If there are large differences between the two parties of the transaction in terms of culture, geography, and industry, the management cost (the cost of integrating the target enterprise) through M&A is relatively high. Strategic alliances can easily avoid the differences between the two parties, reach a consensus on specific aspects, and exert synergies. Higher management costs are not conducive to enterprise M&A activities. For the M&A of target enterprises, enterprises must have high management experience and the capability to reduce management costs and improve the effect of M&A. With the increase in enterprise market knowledge and management experience, the possibility of enterprises choosing M&A also increases accordingly. It can be concluded that if the differences in culture, geography, and industry between the two parties of the transaction bring higher management costs, the strategic alliance is more favorable.

Chen Yang and Zhang Qiusheng (2008) found that the geographical distance between the two cooperating parties also directly affects the size of the transaction cost. It will directly affect the accuracy of communication and information acquisition between the two parties. We do not deny that with the development of information and transportation technology, geographic distance is no longer a difficulty. But it should be noted that geographical distance is not only reflected in time and space, but also in aspects such as cultural differences, and differences in policies and regulations. Therefore, we believe that geographical differences have a significant impact on the transaction costs of both parties. The closer the distance, the lower the risk of M&A, and the alliance should be considered if the distance is farther.

4.3.3.3 Enterprise Characteristics

(1) Enterprise's own resource endowment

The resource-based theory is widely used to explain the relationships between enterprises. In essence, M&A and strategic alliances are enterprises seeking to acquire external resources to improve their competitive advantages. If an enterprise has a strong capability to develop resources internally, the possibility of the enterprise seeking development through external means will be greatly reduced. Therefore, the internal resource reserve of the enterprise affects the decision- making of the external growth strategy to a large extent. M&A and strategic alliances require enterprises to have considerable internal resources, especially financial resources, and human resources. Generally speaking, strategic alliances invest fewer financial resources and can acquire target resources faster. Therefore, from this perspective, enterprises with a shortage of financial resources tend to favor strategic alliances, while enterprises with abundant financial resources may be more likely to choose M&A. In terms of human resources, M&A have much higher requirements for enterprise management than strategic alliances. If there are no professional management talents for the target enterprise, it is difficult to achieve good results. It can be concluded that a strong enterprise resource reserve is more favorable for M&A.

(2) The degree of tacit knowledge

According to the theory of knowledge, an enterprise is a social community in which knowledge is created and transferred due to the continuous interactions between individuals and groups in the enterprise (Kogut & Zander, 1993). From this perspective, the choice of M&A or alliances depends on the speed and efficiency of knowledge creation and transfer within the enterprise, and the speed and efficiency of knowledge transfer mainly depend on the tacit characteristics of knowledge. The higher the tacitity of knowledge, the more likely there will be obstacles for enterprises to use the market to trade knowledge, and the less the effect of the market approach will be. The research of Kogut and Zander (1995) on the regulatory structure decision-making of multinational enterprises shows that the transfer of knowledge with a higher tacit degree between units within the hierarchical structure of multinational enterprises is more effective and faster than the transfer between enterprises in the market, meaning that knowledge transfer costs are lower. This conclusion still holds for general enterprises. Therefore, the higher the tacit degree of knowledge, the more likely for enterprises to choose M&A.

(3) Absorptive capacity of the enterprise

An enterprise's absorptive capacity, that is, its ability to learn and adapt, also affects the choice of alliance or M&A strategies. Alliances are often regarded as "learning competitions", where participating enterprises always want to learn as much as possible from their partners (such as knowledge about products and markets) and disclose their knowledge as little as possible. If an enterprise has a strong learning capability and can effectively protect its core capabilities from being learned faster by alliance partners, it will take the initiative in the learning competition and gain more benefits, and then the alliance is the best strategy choice for the enterprise.

4.3.4 Decision Matrix for M&A and Strategic Alliances

So far, we have put forward the favorable conditions for enterprises to choose external growth strategies from different perspectives through the analysis of three factors: environmental characteristics, transaction characteristics, and enterprise characteristics. There is no absolute criterion for enterprises to choose M&A or strategic alliances. However, when an enterprise chooses an external growth strategy, it must comprehensively consider the above three factors and need an overall decision matrix to guide its strategic choice. The decision matrix we propose is based on the enterprise's requirements for strategic flexibility and control, as shown in Fig. 4.4.

We have found that strategic alliances are particularly suitable in uncertain environments, allowing enterprises to maintain a high degree of strategic flexibility. As analyzed above, factors such as environmental uncertainty, relatively dispersed knowledge distribution, limited resource reserves, and non-durable synergies all require enterprises to maintain a high degree of strategic flexibility. While maintaining a high degree of strategic flexibility, the type of strategic alliance can be selected according to the degree of control required. In the case of low control requirements, strategic alliances based on agreed cooperation, namely strategic alliance I, can be adopted. For those with high control requirements, strategic alliances in the form of joint ventures, namely Strategic Alliance II, can be adopted. M&A are especially suitable for a relatively stable strategic environment, with lower requirements for strategic flexibility, focusing on giving full play to economies of scale and scope, and this form can effectively control uncertainty in behavior due to factors such as asset proprietary, mutual distrust, and inconsistency in strategic objectives. In other words, M&A emphasize the need for enterprises to control the target resources. For general contractual relationships between enterprises, the requirements for both strategic flexibility and control are low.

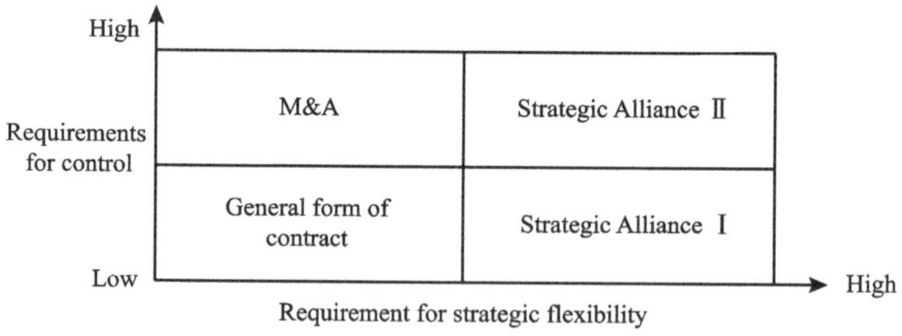

Fig. 4.4 Decision matrix for M&A and strategic alliance

4.3.5 Interconversion of M&A and Strategic Alliance

Strategic alliances are often thought to lead to an increase in the number of enterprises, while M&A often lead to a decrease in the number of enterprises. This view is a bit biased. M&A do not make the acquired party disappear, but may still retain its legal personality. Therefore, M&A do not always lead to a decrease in the number of enterprises. From this point of view, strategic alliances and M&A are not two extremes, and there is an inevitable connection between them. The equity participation among the members of the strategic alliance will eventually lead to an imbalance in equity distribution and may lead to M&A. The ultimate development trend of strategic alliances is basically M&A. American scholars Bleeke and Ernst (1995) research shows that the average life expectancy of the alliance is only 7 years. The joint venture is the most common form of strategic alliance, and nearly 80% of the results are purchased by the alliance partner, that is, the result of a strategic alliance is a transfer of ownership.

Chapter 5
M&A Direction

5.1 Concept and Significance of M&A Direction

5.1.1 The Concept of M&A Direction

To its competitive advantage, an enterprise will formulate a strategic goal and the resources needed to achieve this goal. The gap between the strategic goal resources and the enterprise's resources is expressed as resource surplus or resource gap. Resource surplus is the M&A capability of an enterprise, which is the resource basis and constraint condition of M&A. Resource gap is the resource requirement of an enterprise, and the resource requirement that can meet the constraints of M&A capability is the resource demand, that is, the inherent resource range of the M&A direction. The attributes of these resources in the four dimensions of industry, region, scale, and profitability are the directions of mergers and acquisitions. The M&A direction is essentially the strategic plan for M&A in terms of industry, region, scale, and profitability, which is formulated when the enterprise has the motivation and capability to carry out M&A and decides to do so. It is not only consistent with the enterprise's overall development strategy, but also the refinement of the overall development of strategy.

According to its concept, M&A direction is essentially the strategic direction of M&A, whose internal demand is the shortage of resources of the enterprise, and whose external expression is the attributes of these resources in terms of industry, region, scale, and profitability. The M&A direction specifically expresses whether related M&A (fully related or not fully related) or non-related M&A in terms of industry; whether it is the same-province M&A, cross-province but same-region.

M&A, cross-region M&A, or cross-border M&A in terms of the region; whether it is a large-scale M&A, medium-scale M&A or small-scale M&A in terms of scale; and whether it is a high or low profitability requirement in terms of profitability. We examine the direction of M&A from four dimensions: industry, region, scale, and profitability.

Q. Zhang, *Mergers and Acquisitions*, https://doi.org/10.1007/978-981-92-0122-8_5

The industry is judged according to the products or services provided by an enterprise. The National Standard Industry Classification Standard of National Bureau of Statistics of China subdivides all industries and codes them uniformly. Each industry code is expressed by industry sector, major category, type, and sub-category, and the final expression is a combination of one letter and four digits. The M&A direction of enterprises in the industry can be determined with the help of the national standard industry classification standard, assuming that the national standard code of the target industry selected by the enterprise for M&A is X; and the enterprise may be involved in multi-industry operation at present, we assume that the national standard code of the enterprise's main business industry is $x1$, and the industry codes of the enterprise's part-time business are $x2$, $x3$, … If X = $x1$, the M&A is within the same industry, that is, a horizontal M&A, which is called a fully related M&A; if X is the same as the industry code of part-time business such as $x2$, $x3$, or the industry code of its supply and sales enterprise, the M&A is not fully related M&A, which includes vertical M&A; if the target industry X is different from the company's main business and even the part-time business industry Xn ($n = 1, 2, \ldots$), the enterprise's M&A is a non-related M&A. Lee and Lieberman (2010) pointed out that the main purpose of M&A in the enterprise's main business areas is to improve the existing product system, while the main purpose of M&A outside the enterprise's main business areas is to expand new business areas.

The region is the geographic location of an enterprise. China's Administrative Division Table of the People's Republic of China determines a code for each administrative division and even each province, with a total of six digits, of which the last four digits are all zeros. So this book only takes the first two digits to represent different geographical locations: the first is the region code, the second is the province code, and the two-digit codes of foreign enterprises are represented by zero. In this way, the geographical location of an enterprise can be easily expressed with the help of administrative division codes.

Assume that the target region of M&A determined by the enterprise is Y, the geographic location of the enterprise itself is y, and the geographic location of the enterprise itself is determined according to the geographic location of the enterprise registration. If the codes ofY and y are the same, it means that they are in the same province in China, and the M&A is the same-province M&A. If Y and y have the same first digit and different second digit, it means they are in the same economic region of China, but different provinces and the M&A is the cross-province but same-region M&A. If Y and y are completely different, it means that they are both Chinese enterprises, but they are neither in the same economic region nor in the same province, and the M&A is the cross-region M&A. If Y = 00, y ≠ 00, then the two enterprises are located in different countries, and the M&A is the cross-border M&A. By the same token, the geographical division can also be classified more coarsely or finely.

The scale of the enterprise is measured by the total assets indicator. We divide the scale of M&A into three types: large, medium, and small. Assuming that the current total assets of the enterprise are A, if the scale of M&A is αA–βA, it is regarded as medium-scale M&A, smaller than αA as small-scale M&A, and larger than βA as large-scale M&A, where α and β depend on the specific conditions of the enterprise. In addition to total assets, financial indicators such as net assets, tangible assets, and income, as well as non-financial aggregate or relative indicators such as output and market share can also be used to indicate the scale.

The profitability of the enterprise is expressed by the return on investment, which is a relatively comprehensive indicator. The return on investment of the enterprise after the M&A has great uncertainty, but the enterprise has a minimum tolerance for profitability after the M&A. This book divides the profitability of an enterprise into three cases: high, medium, and low. Assuming that the current return on investment of the enterprise is B, if the return on investment expected by the acquirer is in the range of χB to δB, it is regarded as medium profitability, greater than δB as high profitability, and less than χB as low profitability, where χ and δ depend on the different tolerance of enterprises to profitability.

From the concept of M&A direction, it can be seen that the determination of M&A direction is constrained by two aspects: the enterprise's strategic objectives, the target resources to achieve the strategy, and the enterprise's existing resources. In Chapter 2, it was discussed that the M&A motivation of enterprises should be consistent with the objectives of M&A activities under the framework of the enterprise's strategic objectives; and the enterprise's existing resource surplus relative to the strategic objectives is regarded as an enterprise capability, so the direction of M&A is originated from motivation, and limited by capability.

As far as the enterprise's M&A strategy is concerned, grasping the direction of M&A involves two-level decision-making: to determine the collection that meets the requirements of various dimensions and to search and determine the target enterprise. The M&A direction referred to in this book is the former one in a narrow sense, while searching and determining the target enterprise is the main content of M&A matching. In two-level decision-making, the determination of the collection that meets the requirements of various dimensions is the premise of two-level decision-making. The accuracy of M&A direction decision-making directly affects the accuracy of M&A matching and the selection of target enterprises, and indirectly affects M&A performance and the success or failure of the whole M&A activities. It can be seen that the M&A direction is an important premise for enterprises to effectively implement M&A strategies, and clarifying the M&A direction can help enterprises avoid the blindness of M&A, so that M&A can better obey, and then serve the long-term development strategy of the enterprise, and truly create value for the enterprise.

5.1.2 The Importance of M&A Strategy

With the fifth wave of M&A, more and more enterprises have participated in M&A. Although many advantageous enterprises have been able to expand rapidly through M&A, there are also a considerable number of enterprises whose M&A have ended in failure and do not create value for the enterprise. A McKinsey & Company report showed that 61% of M&A failed because the returns generated were not sufficient to cover the costs incurred (Sirower, 1997). Behind the wave of M&A in China, there is also a crisis of blind M&A. Greed for more, chasing industry hot spots, and lack of careful analysis in decision-making are the great hidden dangers in China's current large-scale enterprise M&A. It is estimated that less than 10% of the M&A transactions in China in recent years are successful (Wang Dong, 1999). There are three main reasons for the failure of M&A: wrong selection of target enterprises, overpayment, and unfavorable integration, and 80% of them are due to the wrong selection of M&A targets (Marks & Mirris, 2001; Orgaton, 1998), that is, in there may be deviations or improper positioning in the direction of M&A. In addition, management tends to attribute M&A failures to incomplete execution rather than their inappropriate strategies (Levitt & March, 1988), and we believe that lack of M&A strategy guidance is also the main reason for the failure of M&A.

For an enterprise that is about to take M&A, the adopted M&A strategy is also undoubtedly important for the choice of target enterprises. In 1990, *Business Week* of the United States conducted a comprehensive review and analysis of the national M&A activities in the 1980s, and the results showed that strategy is the starting point for successful M&A. Only when the enterprise merges according to a clear strategic objective, the merger can bring benefits to the enterprise. And only by understanding its strengths and weaknesses, can the enterprise know what kind of M&A target to choose to enhance its strengths and make up for its weaknesses. It can be seen that clarifying the strategic objectives of M&A and its advantages and disadvantages is the premise basis for selecting target enterprises.

M&A is an investment activity of an enterprise and an unconventional event in the development process of an enterprise. M&A activities should be strategically in line with the enterprise's long-term business development strategy, which shows that M&A strategy is a sub-strategy of business management strategy and an application of business management strategy in the field of M&A. As a specific strategic measure of an enterprise, M&A activities are aimed at achieving the overall strategic objective of the enterprise. The overall strategic thinking of an enterprise determines the motivation, direction, and way of M&A. What kind of overall strategy an enterprise has will lead to what kind of M&A strategy and M&A behavior. Therefore, whether an enterprise uses M&A strategy and what kind of M&A strategy it adopts should be based on the enterprise's development strategy. The enterprise's strategic positioning and objectives affect the various aspects of M&A.

5.2 Review of Related Research and Enlightenment in M&A Direction

5.2.1 Research on Industry Relevance and M&A Performance

The enterprise expansion strategies can be implemented through both M&A (external expansion) and internal growth. Scholars such as Porter (1987) and Weston (1998) found that external expansion was the main way through research. Corresponding to the direction of enterprise expansion, M&A are divided into related M&A (mostly horizontal and vertical M&A, the same below) and non-related M&A (mostly hybrid M&A, the same below). In addition, the research on the expansion of enterprises through M&A has led to the proposition that related M&A are better than non-related M&A, which is known as the M&A correlation hypothesis. For a long time, this hypothesis has attracted extensive attention from domestic and foreign scholars.

In foreign countries, Rumelt (1974, 1977) defined the correlation of two enterprises from three dimensions: (1) using similar channels to serve similar markets; (2) using similar production technologies; (3) using similar scientific research. Rumelt's research found that related diversification strategies generally outperformed unrelated diversification strategies. Although Rumelt's empirical research failed to give a reason for this difference, he certainly found a very meaningful question. Accordingly, scholars who support the M&A correlation hypothesis suggest that acquirers should look for related target enterprises.

Salter and Weinhold (1979), Shelton (1988), and Singh and Montgomery (1987) argue that the benefits of hybrid M&A to enterprises (such as lower cost of capital, increased management efficiency, and increased market power due to increased scale and business) also exist in related M&A, but the synergistic gains from economies of scale and scope, as well as the transfer of core skills between related industries created by related M&A, are difficult to achieve in hybrid M&A, so related M&A should show better performance, that is, the higher the degree of correlation between the two parties of the M&A, the greater the value created by the M&A.

Jenson (1983) argues that hybrid M&A are generally more difficult to succeed than M&A within the industry (horizontal and vertical M&A), because the managers of the acquiring enterprise are not familiar with the business of the target enterprise's industry, or because they waste "free cash flow" on inefficient M&A activities. Mueller's (1969) managerialism theory holds that the motivation of hybrid M&A is to pursue self-interest and blindly expand the scale of enterprises. Efficiency theory also believes that the purpose of hybrid M&A is to reduce the risk of managers themselves and can not improve the efficiency of enterprises. It can be seen that the efficiency of hybrid M&A is relatively low in theory.

However, Montgomery and Wilson (1986) believed that non-related diversification is also one of the tools of strategic planning, where enterprises can enter new industries through non-related M&A and gradually exit industries with limited future development potential; related M&A have great profit potential, but realize the profit also require more effort, and the difficulty of integration and management increases the risk of failure, so related M&A are not as successful as expected.

Seth (1990) believes that compared with related M&A, non-related M&A enable the merged entity to obtain more value-added from coinsurance (because the non-related M&A have a lower correlation between the earnings streams of the two parties, which reduce the risk of enterprise bankruptcy) and financial diversification (through the M&A of non-related businesses, the enterprise's cash flow is more stable and the volatility of returns is reduced). Seth (1990) emphasizes that different types of M&A have different sources of value creation, and it is impossible to determine which source creates more value only at the theoretical level. Therefore, whether related M&A is better than non-related M&A can only be confirmed by empirical tests.

Scholars have done a lot of empirical studies on the differences in the performance of different types of M&A. These studies can be divided into three categories according to the different objects analyzed, that is, from the perspective of the target, the acquirer, or the merged entity of the two parties to examine the performance differences before and after related or non-related M&A. Each of these studies can be divided into three categories according to the different conclusions of an empirical test of the "correlation hypothesis", that is, related M&A can create more value for the enterprise than hybrid M&A, such as Flanagan (1996), Shelton (1988), and Singh and Montgomery (1987); related M&A are not better than hybrid M&A, such as Lubatkin (1987), Seth (1990), and Agraawal (1992); hybrid M&A create higher value than related M&A, such as Elgers and Clark (1980), and Chatterjee (1986). The specific research conclusions are categorized and listed in Tables 5.1, 5.2, and 5.3.

Table 5.1 Specific conclusions of the correlation study: an overall perspective

Type	Author	Analysis conclusion
Support	Shelton (1988)	Coherent and enhanced-related M&A offer numerous opportunities for value creation; Enhanced-related M&A create value with the least volatility; Non-related M&A create the least value; The greater the value of the target relative to the acquirer (larger size), the greater the value created by M&A; If there are bidders, the combined value of the target and the acquirer will increase
Neutral	Seth (1990)	Both related and non-related M&A can create value, and the performance of related M&A is not better than that of non-related M&A; there is an obvious size effect in related M&A, that is, in large-size M&A transactions, the synergistic benefits of related M&A are greater than those of non-related M&A
	Lubatkin (1987)	M&A cause a permanent increase in the value of common shareholders' equity on both sides of the transaction; M&A with related product and market do not outperform non-related M&A as expected

Source Liu Yan. Strategic Selection of Mergers and Acquisitions Based on Industrial Relations. Beijing: Master's Thesis of Beijing Jiaotong University, 2005

Table 5.2 Specific conclusions of the correlation study: the target's perspective

Type	Author	Analysis conclusion
Support	Singh and Montgomery (1987)	The returns in both related and non-related M&A are positive and significant, and the returns in related M&A are significantly higher than those in non-related M&A
Neutral	Flanagan (1996)	Gains in related M&A are not higher than in non-related M&A, but higher in cash-paying M&A transactions
Object	Chatterjee (1986)	Profits from non-related M&A are higher than related M&A, non-horizontal M&A (because horizontal M&A is excluded from sample selection), and the target's returns are proportional to the relative size of the M&A parties

Source Liu Yan. Strategic Selection of Mergers and Acquisitions Based on Industrial Relations. Beijing: Master's Thesis of Beijing Jiaotong University, 2005

Table 5.3 Specific conclusions of the correlation study: the acquirer's perspective

Type	Author	Analysis conclusion
Support	Flanagan (1996)	Gains in related M&A are significantly higher than those in non-related M&A, and in bona fide or cash-paying M&A transactions, the acquirer's shareholders receive higher returns
Neutral	Singh and Montgomery (1987)	Gains are not significant in M&A (including related and non-related M&A)
	Park (2002)	Enterprises in industries with high profitability are more likely to implement related diversification strategies than enterprises in industries with low profitability. If an enterprise has strong profitability in its industry before diversification, it is more likely to implement a related diversification strategy. The enterprise's strong profitability after implementing related diversification is due to the industry in which the company was located before the merger and the company itself was at a high level of profitability, not because the related M&A strategy is more superior
	Chatterjee (1986)	M&A gains are not significant (the reason may be that the acquirer is too large relative to the target)

Source Liu Yan. Strategic Selection of Mergers and Acquisitions Based on Industrial Relations. Beijing: Master's Thesis of Beijing Jiaotong University, 2005

In China, Zeng Ying (1999) took mature enterprises as the research object and analyzed the strategy of enterprise M&A. The research focuses on the corresponding decision-making of enterprise financial management and management accounting and points out that the mature enterprise is in a strong stage of its life cycle, and its strategic conditions and financial characteristics determine the main use of horizontal M&A (for the production sector), vertical M&A and holdings (for purchasing, marketing, and service sectors), and mergers with pre-mature enterprises and invests in R&D consortia (for science and technology development sectors) to consolidate weak links in their value chains and improve flexibility and responsiveness, to acquire innovation capabilities and delay aging.

Guo Yongqing (2000) applied the long-term performance research method to compare the degree of improvement of listed companies'performance by different M&A models. The study used 351 M&A events of listed companies from 1994 to 1998 as samples, and selected main business revenue, main business profit margin, return on net assets, and earnings per share as indicators to measure the performance of M&A. By comparing the comprehensive scores in the year of M&A with the year before M&A, it was found that hybrid M&A have significant effects on improving the operating conditions of listed companies, while vertical M&A have an insignificant effect, and horizontal M&A deteriorated the operating conditions of listed companies.

Gao Jian and Chen Xinwei (2000) paid more attention to the industry correlation of restructuring and conducted a quantitative analysis. The study found that asset restructuring in related industries occurs mostly in enterprises with better operating performance. Enterprises in which asset restructuring occurs in related industries generally have a relatively high return on net assets. However, from the perspective of the effect of asset restructuring on the improvement of operating performance, it does not correlate with whether it belongs to a related industry. They believe that in the Chinese securities market, the performance of asset restructuring has little relationship with whether it is related to the industry, which indicates to some extent that asset restructuring in China has not yet risen to the level of strategic investment from the perspective of capital operation, and there are still many elements of "doing" the subject matter.

Lou Jing and Huang Yuxiang (2001) study the influence of industry structure on horizontal M&A strategy. This study examines the changes in enterprise market power by analyzing the impact of changes in output after M&A on market prices and average costs. The study analyzes the changes in market power when different M&A strategies are adopted in different stages of development of the same industry and in different industries, and use these changes to judge the effect of M&A. The study concludes that, for the same industry, if the enterprise is in the emerging growth stage, the strategy of significantly expanding output after horizontal M&A can easily enhance the market dominance of the enterprise; if the enterprise is in the mature and concentration stage, it is easy to enhance market dominance by adopting the strategy of significantly reducing output after horizontal M&A; for different industries, the elasticity of demand, elasticity of supply, market structure and cost advantages are different, as a result, the more significant the economies of scale of the industry, the more conducive to the enhancement of market dominance by adopting the strategy of maintaining the same output after horizontal M&A; if the scale economy of the industry to which the enterprise belongs is more significant, the market structure tends to be more perfectly competitive, the elasticity of demand is greater, and the elasticity of supply is greater, the strategy of expanding output after horizontal M&A is conducive to the enhancement of market dominance; and for enterprises whose market structure in the industry to which they belong is closer to a complete monopoly, the less the elasticity of demand and the less the elasticity of supply, the strategy of significantly reducing output after horizontal M&A is conducive to the enhancement of market dominance.

Fang Fang and Yan Xiaotong (2002) analyzed the effects of different M&A modes according to the changes in the performance of listed companies before and after M&A. The study selects 80 enterprises from 115 M&A cases in 2000 as the research object, and refines these samples into 46 horizontal M&A, 10 vertical M&A, and 24 hybrid M&A according to the mode of M&A. Nine indicators of profitability, solvency, and growth of the company are selected as comprehensive evaluation indicators for listed companies' M&A performance. The study aims to analyze the effect of different types of M&A according to the changes in the performance of listed companies before and after M&A to illustrate the current misunderstandings of enterprise M&A and the dominant way of effective M&A. The study concludes that the horizontal M&A of listed companies in the stock market in 2000 promoted the development of enterprises, improved their financial situation, and improved profitability, which is beneficial; however, the current hybrid M&A of listed companies whose performance shows a downward trend, and many listed companies that have been merged have a parabolic change in their profits, that is, before the M&A, many companies with average profitability and earnings have significantly improved their performance in the year of the M&A, but then began to experience a decline in growth or even negative growth in the following year.

Liu Xiaoping et al. (2009) found that there is no significant difference in the performance of different types of M&A regardless of industry cycle factors. Considering industry cycle factors, there are significant differences in the performance of different M&A types. Contrary to their conclusion, Raudszus et al. (2013) found that vertical and hybrid M&A reduce enterprise performance, while horizontal M&A improve enterprise performance. Song Shuqin and Dai Shujiang (2015) found that the M&A performance of related M&A is better than that of non-related M&A.

Wu Yuping (2002) applied the long-term performance method to study the long-term performance of different M&A models. The study takes 542 M&A cases from 1997 to 1999 as samples and selects the indicators of total asset income ratio, total asset profit ratio, earnings per share, and net asset profit ratio to form a comprehensive score model to evaluate M&A performance. The study found that the performance of the M&A year and the first year after the M&A showed a positive change, then followed by a downward trend; in the long run, the advantages of hybrid M&A were limited, and the overall performance of horizontal M&A was stable and showed an upward trend.

Empirical findings on the correlation hypothesis have reached mixed conclusions for a variety of reasons. For example, the analysis objects selected by each study are different, the classification methods for related and non-related M&A are different, and the selected performance indicators are different. In addition, the sample of M&A events selected differed in the relative size of the two parties, the time span of the sample, the industries to which the sample companies belonged, and the development stages of enterprise growth. Moreover, their research is based only on the impact of different types of M&A on enterprise performance, without seeing the impact of enterprise strategic target resources and the enterprise's existing resource strength on M&A.

5.2.2 Research on the Choice of Target Enterprises

Fritz and Joerg (2001) first introduced the concept of the value growth matrix, which is a starting point for assessing which companies in an industry would be the best acquisition targets when developing a successful acquisition strategy (see Fig. 5.1). Acquiring the "underperformer" competitors means that you need to make a radical change, because the acquisition target's revenue growth and value growth are below the industry average, and such acquisitions are often very risky unless the acquirer can grow the acquiree's business rapidly and manage the negative impact. "simple growers" and "profit seekers" are more logical targets because they have an established growth base, are inexpensive, and do not involve too much management effort. Finally, "value growers" are usually the best strategic acquisition targets, but they are often very expensive.

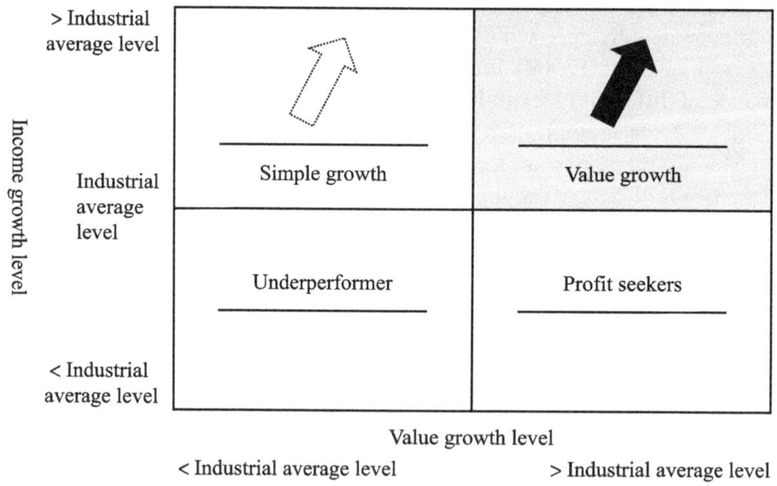

Fig. 5.1 Value growth matrix (*Source* McGrath et al. [2001]. The Value Growers. New York: McGraw-Hill)

Additional foreign studies have suggested a series of factors that should present potential and attractive M&A targets, such as M&A size, firm growth rate, M&A pricing range (Vance, 1969), and acceptable management range (Linowes, 1968), earnings stability, market independence, ownership dispersion, competitive position (Wyatt & Kieso, 1969), and M&A steps that incorporate these factors, among others (Taylor, 1970).

Li Yutian (2002) suggested that the following factors need to be considered when selecting a target company: business factors, financial factors, size of the target company, and other factors.

Qi Ruqing (2001) argues that two factors, industry and enterprise, should be considered when selecting M&A targets. At the industry level, acquirers are faced with three development directions, i.e., same, related, or unrelated industries. At the level of enterprise selection, many factors affect the selection of M&A targets, mainly including the size, equity structure, financial status, geographical location, technical level, market position, special assets, and corporate culture of the target enterprise.

Zeng Ying (1999) used some basic analysis methods of financial management and management accounting, and drew on the value chain analysis framework of enterprise competitive advantage and the diagnosis tools of the corporate life cycle to provide a more scientific and operable specific idea for the formulation and implementation of the M&A strategies of mature enterprises. The study proposes that when formulating the M&A strategies for mature enterprises, the first step is to analyze the value chain of mature enterprises and select the form of M&A. Through the value chain analysis, the authors conclude that the relationship between functional departments generally follows the following principles: (1) production department: horizontal merger; (2) purchasing, marketing, and service departments: vertical merger or holding; (3) science and technology development department: merger with premature enterprises or investing in R&D association. Second, the target enterprise merged with a mature enterprise must meet the following conditions: (1) it has the target factors of the mature enterprises' M&A, and the scale and structure of the target factors meet the requirements; (2) after the adjustment of the asset structure, it can bring long-term net income to the mature enterprise; (3) M&A can be carried out in certain places and with a certain procedure. Finally, the study analyzes the M&A approaches of mature firms. Zeng Ying's discussion points out that the analytical framework of M&A strategies for mature firms is also applicable to firms at other stages of the firm's life cycle. The specific approach used differs depending on each firm's stage of development and industry.

Zhang Yifang (1999) summarizes the basic situation analysis of alternative targets in deciding on M&A strategy as follows: (1) the industrial environment and domestic and foreign competition conditions faced by the target enterprise; (2) the size of market share and strength of the target enterprise; (3) the profit level and prospect of the target enterprise; (4) the ownership and financial affiliation of the target enterprise; (5) the scale of net assets and liabilities of the target enterprise; (6) management level of the target enterprise, etc.

Liu Kexin et al. (1999) proposed the following criteria for judging M&A strategies: (1) industry: Are the businesses in which the possible M&A targets are engaged attractive? (2) geography: Which regions are attractive? Which one should be avoided or are too far away to be conductive to control? (3) price: How much capital is needed to complete the M&A from both internal resources or external borrowing? (4) size: Which is possible to afford when comparing turnover, net assets, number of employees, etc.? (5) funding conditions: How much investment in fixed assets and operating capital is needed to support and develop the acquired company? (6) management: Should the acquiree have a good management model? In the model constructed by Liu Kexin et al. for target firm selection, the prospect description vector A of different target firms are assigned certain weights W to indicate their relative importance. The overall attractiveness $S(i)$ of target firm i, can be expressed as

$$S(i) = \sum_{j=1}^{n} A_i(j) \times W_{ij}$$

where i denotes the ith target firm, j denotes the jth factor considered in the M&A prospect analysis, and n denotes the total number of prospect analysis factors. The different target enterprises can be ranked according to the magnitude of $S(i)$ values, which will be an important decision basis for the acquirer to select the final target.

According to Yu Kai et al. (2003), the selection model is constructed using hierarchical analysis and correlation analysis under the condition that there are multiple target enterprises to be selected as shown in Fig. 5.2.

The set of factors of the same level belonging to the same higher-level factor is set as C′, C′ = (C1′, C2′,..., Cm′). Using a certain algorithm, the relative importance of each element under the same high-level factor within the same level can be obtained hierarchically, and the comprehensive importance Wi of each factor Ci in the key factor set C in the criterion level concerning the target level can be obtained, i.e., the comprehensive importance Wi of each element Ci in C concerning the target level, i.e., the weight set W of C. For example, for any element Ci, with (−2, −1, 0, 1, 2) denote the evaluation set V = {adverse impact, less adverse impact, no impact, more favorable impact, favorable impact}, for any target enterprise i to be evaluated (i.e., the optional solution), the factors can be evaluated by M&A experts and relevant decision-makers, resulting in the evaluation set Vi = {Vi1, Vi2, ..., Vin}, then the evaluation matrix V of the P target enterprises to be selected can be obtained, and the maximum value in Vi is the proposed optimal solution for the target company to be selected in the M&A decision.

In addition, the geographic orientation of the M&A can affect the appropriateness of the target firm selection. For example, reaching an agreement does not guarantee the efficiency of off-site M&A, and the information disadvantage is likely to lead the main merging firm to choose the wrong target firm (Liu Chun et al., 2015; Tu et al., 2013).

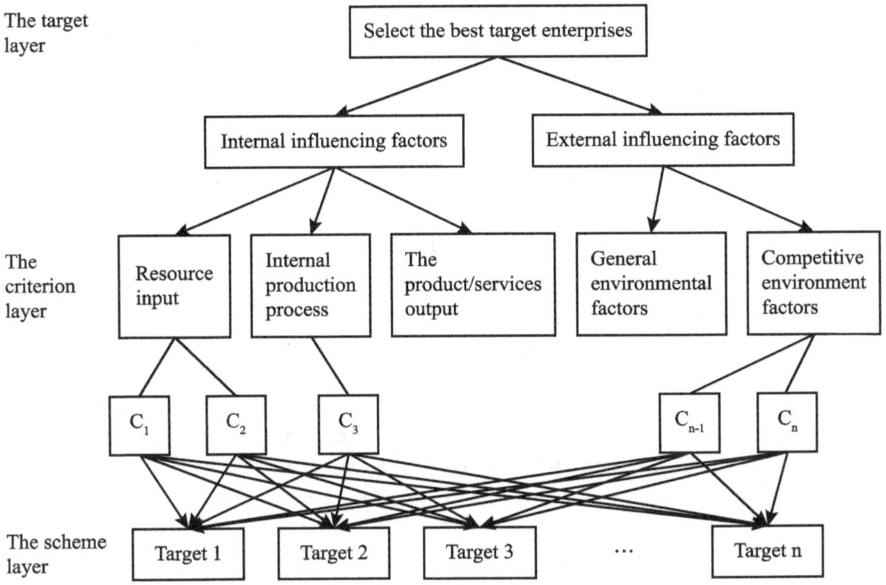

Fig. 5.2 Structure of the key factors related to the target firms selection model (*Source* Yu Kai et al. [2003]. A Method for Constructing A Target Firm Selection Model in Corporate M&A Decision Making. Reform of Economic System, Vol. 2, 58–61)

5.2.3 Research on the Factors Influencing the Choice of M&A Strategy

5.2.3.1 Industry Status

(1) Industry profitability

Industrial economists believe that the average profitability of an industry reflects the attractiveness of the industry. Weston and Mansinghka (1971) argue that when an industry as a whole is less profitable and unattractive, the management of firms in that industry is more likely to implement a defensive diversification strategy (mainly through a mixed M&A strategy) into an attractive industry to counteract the risk of decline in the traditional industries. Rumelt (1974) also suggested that diversification (mainly through a mixed M&A strategy) is one of the effective ways for firms to avoid the prospect of a decline in their original industries. Therefore, if the industry in which the firm was operating before the M&A was less profitable, the firm was more likely to implement a mixed M&A into an unrelated industry.

As the profitability of an industry increases, management's motivation to implement a defensive diversification strategy gradually decreases, and the motivation to implement offensive diversification increases accordingly. Offensive diversification refers to the further expansion and utilization of a company's resources and capabilities in the current industry in which it is currently operating or in related industries.

When an industry is highly profitable or firms in this industry have resources and capabilities that are difficult to replicate and have a strong position, management often has a strong incentive to expand the use of such resources and capabilities in other industries. These capabilities and resources nurtured and developed in the current industry are more likely to be transferred to related industries than to unrelated industries (Lecraw, 1984), so firms in highly profitable industries prefer related diversification mergers and acquisitions by comparison.

It can be seen that the level of profitability of an industry is known to influence the choice of target firms by firms in the industry. If industry profitability is poor, firms' defensive motivation is stronger and they prefer non-relevant diversified M&A to select target firms to avoid the bleak prospect of future industrial decline. As industry profitability increases, firms' offensive motives gradually take over and they prefer relevant diversification to select target firms to expand the use of their established, hard-to-replicate resources and capabilities in relevant industries.

(2) Industry market structure

When choosing which industry to enter, a company must first analyze the market structure of the industry to determine whether it should enter. Market structure refers to the relationship between firms in a particular market in terms of number, share, and size, and the form of competition determined by this. Market concentration and barriers to entry are the two main factors that describe market structure. Market entry patterns are related to the direction of M&A in the industry dimension. In their study of market entry patterns, Lee and Lieberman (2010) state that a firm's market entry pattern depends on whether the new market is within or outside the firm's main business area. The firm makes unrelated M&A enter new markets outside their main business area, while they make related M&As within their main business area to improve their existing product system.

(i) Market concentration

Market concentration reflects the relationship between enterprises in a particular industry and the size and number of distribution characteristics. High market concentration means that a certain industry is controlled by a few large enterprises, and the degree of competition in the industry is low, so large enterprises can obtain high monopoly profits by their control, and the higher the concentration of the market, the more monopoly profits they obtain. Frequent M&A activities in the industry help to increase the market concentration; in turn, the monopoly profits gained by firms due to the increase of market concentration stimulate them to continue horizontal M&A in the industry.

(ii) Barriers to entry

Barriers to entry reflect the relationship between existing firms and potential entrants in a particular industry. Barriers to entry set obstacles to the free flow and optimal allocation of resources. Therefore, when a company considers entering a new industry, it should fully anticipate and consider the possible barriers it may encounter, and the level of industrial barriers that can influence M&A strategic decisions.

First, barriers to economies of scale. Whether an industry has significant economies of scale determines the level of barriers to entry into the industry. On the one hand, if the economy of scale is more significant, the cost advantage of existing large enterprises in the industry is obvious, and it is difficult for potential entrants to compete with the original enterprises if they cannot form a certain scale and obtain the corresponding cost advantage in a relatively short period. On the other hand, the more significant the economies of scale in an industry, the more inclined the enterprises in the industry are to horizontal M&A to obtain greater cost advantages, and the value created by M&A is also greater. It can be seen that the more significant economies of scale in the industry, the higher the barriers to scale and the more concentrated horizontal M&A in the same industry.

Of course, not all industries have the requirements of economies of scale, so not all industries are required to implement horizontal M&A strategies to pursue economies of scale. Take the sub-industries of China's manufacturing industry as examples: textiles, garment, and fur are labor-intensive industries, which do not have obvious economies of scale, and the main goal of their strategies is to innovate technology and establish brand advantages rather than to implement horizontal M&A to expand their scale; while for the home appliance industry (such as washing machines, refrigerators, electric fans, air conditioners, and televisions, etc.), the technology is already relatively mature and has obvious economies of scale, and to face competition from foreign brands, the horizontal M&A strategy should be used to improve the scale and efficiency level and expand the market share; for another example, food, beverage, and other manufacturing enterprises, which are regional, short transportation distance, and not easy to trade, so the implementation of horizontal M&A to expand the scale must consider whether the capacity of the regional market has room for expansion, and the scale of production must match the scale of the market to obtain economies of scale; for capital-intensive and technology-intensive industries and industries with obvious economies of scale, such as automobiles, iron and steel, petrochemicals, and communication equipment, moderate production concentration, and economies of scale are inherent characteristics of these industries, while the current degree of production in these industries in China is not high and the scale of enterprises is too small, so he phenomenon of repeated construction and production should be reduced through horizontal M&A strategy, so as to realize the strategic integration between enterprises across departments and regions and improve international competitiveness.

Second, technical barriers and policy barriers. Industrial organization theory suggests that, in addition to the minimum effective production scale of enterprises, core technologies and government restrictions on an industrial entry will also form industrial barriers for enterprises to enter the industry. If the technical barriers and industrial entry policy barriers are high, then firms can acquire production capacity and technology by acquiring existing firms in the industry to reduce or eliminate barriers and achieve effective entry. It can be seen that vertical M&A and mixed M&A will help companies to overcome technical barriers and policy barriers.

5.2.3.2 Location

The American scholar Green (1990) has studied corporate M&A from a geographical perspective. He found that the more prosperous the economy is, the more frequently M&A activities are conducted and the higher the rate of external control over other regions, i.e., the ratio of the number of acquirers to the number of acquirers in a certain region. After companies in economically developed regions acquire companies in underdeveloped regions, they import capital and technology to the acquiree, improve production and management, increase the productivity of the acquiree, eliminate or reduce regional disparities, produce resource reallocation effects, and promote the overall development of the regional economy and the overall economy. Almazan et al. (2010) conducted a study on the relationship between a company's geographical location, M&A opportunities, and financial structure, and found that companies located in the industry cluster location face more M&A opportunities.

Geographical factors here include physical and economic geographic location, including the distribution of local natural resources, the level of economic development, economic and legal policies, the degree of market development, transportation and communication conditions, environmental conditions, public security conditions, the cultural quality of the public and moral and ethical concepts, and many other factors. The analysis of geographical factors helps the acquirer to judge whether the M&A is feasible, and helps the acquirer to formulate the regional business development strategy comprehensively. Therefore, the acquirer should consider geographical factors as an important factor when implementing the M&A plan.

First, the geographic factors can be used to understand whether the acquirer's market type is national, regional, or a special type of narrow market. If it is a national market, the selection of target companies is not limited to a certain region; on the contrary, regional markets should be considered for M&A in the same region, otherwise, the company's market advantages cannot be reflected in other regions. In contrast, specific type markets are more narrowly adapted, and the range of M&A targets is smaller.

Second, the decision to use vertical M&A should focus on upstream and downstream companies in the same region. One of the main purposes of vertical M&A is to save costs. There are transactions costs associated with trading in the market, and when the market is internalized, the transaction costs are converted into internal organizational costs, and real cost savings can only be achieved by conducting an M&A if the savings in transaction costs are greater than the resulting increase in internal organizational costs. The transportation cost of materials or products is an important part of the transaction costs, so reducing the transportation cost between the two parties of the M&A is an important way to save transaction costs. Because of the similarities of customs, human environment, value orientation, and spiritual of enterprises in the same region, it is relatively much easier to organize and coordinate after internalization, and the increased organization and coordination costs of enterprises for this purpose is much less. Therefore, it is advisable to target enterprises within the same geographical area.

Another reason for using co-located companies as targets is that inter-province mergers need to bear higher costs. The information disadvantage of inter-province mergers is likely to lead the acquirers to choose the wrong target firms (Tu et al., 2013; Liu Chun et al., 2015). It may be easier for local SOEs to obtain government support for M&As in the same place. The probability of inter-province mergers of local SOEs is significantly lower than that of private firms and compared with M&A in the same region, local SOEs receive less government support after inter-province mergers, which leads to negative economic consequences (Pan Hongbo & Yu Minggui, 2011). Fang Junxiong (2009) found that market segmentation is significantly and negatively related to firms' inter-province mergers, i.e., market segmentation raises the cost of inter-province mergers.

In conclusion, if the target company is located in a favorable geographic location, with abundant local natural resources, good economic development, mature market development, infrastructure construction, good ecological environment, people living and working in peace and happiness, and high quality of public culture and open-mindedness, there is more room and opportunity for development after the M&A; otherwise, the acquirer should consider abandoning the acquisition. The current location environment is poor, but the location advantage is expected to emerge soon, and the acquisition conditions are favorable, this kind of target company should also be actively considered for M&A.

In addition, different economic and legal policies affect the choice of M&A region. The main economic policies are industrial policies, financial policies, and fiscal and taxation policies that influence M&A in industry and regional choices. For example, China's financial and credit policies affect the choice of cross-regional M&A by the regional lending system. The fiscal and taxation policies by administrative affiliation can influence the choice of cross-industry and regional M&A due to the protection of local interests by local governments.

M&A rapidly expand the scale of enterprises and easily cause industrial monopolies, and there are generally regulations and restrictions on M&As in foreign developed countries. The regions and countries with relatively well-developed laws and policy restrictions on M&A include the United States, the European Union, Germany, Japan, etc. Anti-monopoly Law of the People's Republic of China has been in effect since 2008. Comparing the differences in these legal factors helps to understand the inherent differences in the regional choices of M&A activities worldwide. Policy and legal factors are increasingly being used as important tools to guide M&A activities in various countries, and the influence of this should also be considered when making decisions on M&A direction. In addition, the macro-legal environment of M&A can also influence the industrial choice of M&A. At present, a series of regulations in China make certain provisions on M&A issues, and the acquirer's choice should avoid target enterprises that involve regulatory restrictions. For example, China's policy on the transfer of state-owned shares stipulates that enterprises involved in national security, national defense, cutting-edge technology and other enterprises that are monopolized by the state and are expressly prohibited from being transferred by the state shall not be transferred; monopolistic or natural monopolistic industries such as energy, transportation, and communication, as well as other important industries related to the livelihood of the nation and the backbone of the development of state support, can selectively transfer part of the property rights (equity) of enterprises, but the state must control the operation. It is difficult for enterprises to achieve the purpose of M&A if they choose the above target enterprises.

5.2.3.3 Enterprise Size

Shelton (1988) argues that the larger the target enterprise, the more assets it provides to the acquirer, and the greater the value created on that basis. Enterprise size is often considered to be a measure of economies of scale and market power. The cost advantage provided by economies of scale and strong market power allows larger enterprises to maintain higher profitability, and therefore Robins and Wiersema (1995) argue that there is a positive correlation between enterprise size and performance.

Park (2002) argues that large enterprises usually have complex organizational structures, a fine division of labor, and formal systems of planning, control, and resource allocation. The complexity of organizational structure and formal management systems and processes may lead to greater resistance to changes in organizational structure and system, and it is believed that the larger the enterprise, the more likely it is to engage in related M&A. While Chatterjee and Wernerfelt (1991) argue that there is no well-established and rigorous theory to predict the effect of enterprise size on the type of diversification. In reality, large enterprises often tend to operate multiple unrelated businesses, and therefore there is a tendency for unrelated diversification to increase with enterprise size. An empirical study by Dass (2000) argues that as enterprise size increases and enterprise inertia increases, the more likely it is that enterprises will make abrupt changes rather than incremental changes to break organizational routines.

The overall strategic thinking of a firm varies depending on its size, which may be expansion or contraction. Taking a step back, even if a company attempts to expand through M&A, its specific M&A path (horizontal, vertical, or mixed) will vary depending on the size of the enterprise. If an enterprise is small in production, has not reached economies of scale, and has a low market share of its products, it often tends to implement horizontal M&A if it wants to approach the lowest point of the long-term cost curve and reach economic scale. In this case, the development of the enterprise is not achieved by increasing the size of the enterprise, but by increasing the number of factories, i.e., by M&A. If a company has already achieved a significant level of scale, realizing economies of scale, and good profitability and management capabilities make it has surplus capital, operating and management resources, it is not wise to consider using these slack resources to invest in the main business to continue to expand the scale of operations. On the one hand, because the remaining market share is already very limited, and limits the space and potential for the development of the market share in the main business. On the other hand, if the scale of production is too large, the original reasonable technical ratio will be disrupted, and diseconomies of scale will follow. In this case, it is a more sensible alternative for enterprises to digest the remaining resources by venturing into other industries through mixed M&A. The above is a study from the perspective of size to industry preference, which only illustrates the choice of the industry by different enterprise sizes, and the empirical findings are not consistent.

The relative size of the acquiree and the acquirer is also a factor that affects the success of M&A. Chatterjee (1986) found that the reason for insignificant M&A gains may be that the acquirer is too large relative to the target when studying the relationship between M&A correlation and performance. On the contrary, if the acquiree is too large for the acquirer, it may lead to unfavorable integration of the enterprise after M&A, or failing M&A, so the reasonable size of M&A is a factor that affects the success or failure of M&A and should also be examined as a dimension of the direction of corporate M&A.

5.2.3.4 Corporate Profitability

The organizational learning literature (Cyert & March 1963; March & Olsen, 1976; March & Simon, 1958) suggests that when firms receive positive feedback on actions they take, they tend to repeat previous actions related to the positive feedback obtained, which usually results in the firm maintaining the status quo. Negative feedback requires firms to look for problems, investigate deeply, and face pressure to make strategic shifts (March & Simon, 1958). So in contrast, highly profitable firms will seek a smaller degree of strategic shift due to the positive feedback received, and poorer performers firms will seek a larger degree of strategic shift due to the negative feedback they face.

Carroll and Delacroix (1982) and Hannan and Freeman (1977, 1984) argue that organizational performance is positively related to inertia. Highly profitable firms tend to have difficulty implementing strategic change due to the presence of strong organizational inertia. For underperforming companies, due to their small organizational inertia, it is possible to implement a greater degree of strategic change. Kahneman and Tversky (1979) argue that the impact of an adverse environment would force enterprises to seek change, even at risk.

In summary, a highly profitable company in a favorable business environment, with strong organizational inertia and constant obtains positive feedback on its decisions and actions, usually does not risk major strategic shifts and therefore prefers to make relevant acquisitions; while a poorly performing company with less organizational inertia, in an unfavorable environment and facing multiple pressures such as negative feedback on its decisions and operations, prefers to take risks in making major strategic shifts, i.e., making non-relevant acquisitions.

5.2.3.5 Other Factors

(1) Corporate life cycle

The corporate life cycle theory divides the corporate life cycle into incipient, growth, maturity, and decline. As the life cycle evolves, the flexibility of the enterprise decreases, while the controllability keeps increasing, peaking at the maturity stage, and then begins to decline and the enterprise enters its demise. Although there is a natural sequence in the life cycle of a company, it is possible to change its state through appropriate measures, and in many cases this help from the "outside" is necessary. In this regard, Charles Handy believed that the secret of corporate longevity lies in how to open up a second curve through diversification or industrial transformation when the existing growth curve is approaching its "parabolic apex". In this way, when the resources on which the old curve is based start to decline, the company has already opened up a new successful track in the new industry and ensures rapid growth of the company. In other words, success is only for one stage. The acquirer should identify which stage of the life cycle it is at to decide on the selection criteria of the acquiree. For example, the success of a company at a certain point in time means that it is close to its "parabolic apex", and a horizontal M&A to expand within the industry on this basis can at best reduce the downward slope of the curve to a certain extent, i.e., slow the rate of decline, but not reverse the downward trend.

Fan Conglai and Yuan Jing (2002) studied the M&A performance of listed companies in growth, mature, and declining industries. The results of the empirical analysis of 336 M&A events of listed companies in China from 1995 to 1999 showed that companies in growth industries performed relatively well in horizontal M&A; companies in mature industries performed relatively best in vertical M&A, and companies in declining industries performed the worst in horizontal expansion. This empirical result confirms, to some extent, the validity of the hypothesis of the relationship between "industry cycle theory and M&A type".

However, this conclusion is not absolute and does not require all companies in growth industries to choose to make horizontal M&A, all companies in mature industries to conduct vertical M&A, and all companies in declining industries to conduct mixed M&A because each company faces a different specific industrial environment, its industrial position, and status in the industry, etc. are not the same. In the early stages of maturity, a company may have a relatively large market share and therefore a high industry position, but because it may be restricted by upstream or downstream bottlenecks in the industry chain, i.e., its industrial potential is relatively low. If the enterprise spends great efforts to expand on a large scale at this time, it seems that economies of scale can be produced, but the actual effect is just the opposite, because the larger the scale at this time, the greater the constraints of upstream and downstream bottlenecks, then the industrial potential will not improve but will be seriously weakened. Therefore, a more reasonable choice is to ensure the current status of the industry and seek to enhance the status of the industry through various methods. When an enterprise has stronger industrial control, it can further improve its industrial position through horizontal expansion (Xu Lin, 2005). Therefore, the premise of horizontal expansion of enterprises to obtain economies of scale is that the development of enterprises is not constrained by industrial bottlenecks and they already have a certain industry position.

According to Fan Conglai and Yuan Jing (2002), if a company is in a growth industry and the industry has obvious economies of scale, then the company can adopt a horizontal M&A strategy to obtain the advantages of economies of scale and expand its market power. Of course, market-expanding mixed M&As are also an option; if the company is in a mature industry because the industry has experienced fierce competition in the growth period, there are only a few evenly matched companies left in the market. At this time, improving the competitiveness of enterprises should be more cost-oriented, so the forward or backward integration strategy can be adopted. However, vertical mergers also mean that companies have to take greater risks. Because the concentration of a large number of assets in one industry after the implementation of a vertical merger will lead to a reduction in the resilience of the company to switch to other industries, the company is bound to be hit hard in case of a downturn in that industry. If the company does not have considerable market power in this mature industry, it can also consider product expansion mixed M&A, using the original sales channels and markets to venture into some new industries related to the original products, to achieve the transition of exiting the original market at a lower cost. If the company is in a declining industry, and the industry is not subject to any policy preferences and protection, then a purely mixed M&A is a wiser choice, as the company can exit the original industry smoothly by acquiring unrelated industries. However, if the company is in a declining industry but has a pivotal position in the market, it may still consider becoming a leader in the industry or maintaining its competitive advantage in a particular market segment, and the M&A strategy may also be a vertical M&A to obtain cost advantages.

Liu Xiaoping et al. (2009) found that there were significant differences in the performance of different M&A types considering industry cycle factors. Diversified M&A performance among declining industries was significantly better than horizontal M&A performance within declining industries. For acquirers, diversified M&A performance between growth industries was significantly better than horizontal M&A performance within growing industries. Diversified M&A performance between declining industries and growth industries is better than horizontal M&A performance within declining industries. For target firms, diversified M&A performance between growth and declining industries is better than that of horizontal M&A performance within declining industries.

Based on enterprise life cycle theory and resource-based theory, Yang Yan et al. (2014) found that there are significant differences in the choice of M&A strategies for firms at different stages of their life cycle with growth stage firms preferring horizontal M&A, mature stage firms preferring horizontal and mixed M&A, and declining stage firms preferring mixed and vertical M&A.

(2) Previous M&A experience of the company

Jin Yunhui and Jia Changjie (2003) studied the effect of inertia on the strategic choice of M&A of listed companies. Inertia theory argues that every organization is controlled by strong inertial forces, and when faced with the shock of a changing environment, they rarely succeed in making fundamental changes in strategy and organizational structure. The study concludes from an event analysis of M&A data from 210 listed companies in the Chinese stock market over four years that there is inertia in the development and implementation of M&A strategies of firms and that firms tend to repeat the types of M&A that they have previously implemented, regardless of whether the environment has changed. The greater the number of previously executed M&A of a certain type, the greater the likelihood that a firm will execute that type of M&A next time. They also consider inertia in M&A activity to be a "double-edged sword". On the one hand, inertia helps managers focus their attention on one M&A strategy and learn from it. On the other hand, inertia limits managers' vision and makes them obsess over M&A strategies that have been proven to be correct in the past, thus neglecting new options and opportunities. Therefore, companies should not only make good use of the positive effect of inertia but also pay attention to cultivating an innovative corporate culture and establishing a dynamic, forward-looking vision of the company to overcome the negative impact of inertia.

5.3 M&A Direction Decision Theory and Method

5.3.1 Competitive Advantage Theory

In the early 1980s, Porter's competitive advantage theory became the mainstream of strategic management. This theory introduced the industrial-organizational theory with the main content of "structure-conduct-performance" into the field of strategic management and provided a reliable basis for economic analysis to explain how enterprises develop strategies and obtain sustainable competitive advantages. The core of the theory is five competitive forces models, namely industrial competitors, buyers, suppliers, substitutes, and potential competitors. The theory assumes that the formulation of an enterprise's strategy is highly related to the external environment (i.e., the market) in which it operates and that the most critical environmental factor is the industry in which the enterprise operates. The structure of the industry affects the rules of competition, and the combined effect of the five competitiveness models varies with the industry, so the result is that different industries or the same industry have different profit stages at different stages of development, which in turn affects the formulation of corporate strategies. Therefore, the basic unit of enterprise strategy analysis is industry, enterprise, and product, and the key point is to determine the reasonable position of the enterprise in the industry through the analysis of five competitive forces, and to influence the five competitive forces through the implementation of strategy, thus affecting the industrial structure, and even can change some competition rules. The attractiveness of the industry and the position of the enterprise in the market then become the source of competitive advantage.

According to the competitive advantage theory, companies should develop and implement strategies based on the attractiveness of the industry and their position in the market. The significance of this theory for the choice of M&A strategy is that: (1) The acquirer analyzes the characteristics and position of the industry in which it is located. If the acquirer's current industry is attractive, it may choose to expand its scale through horizontal M&A or consolidate its position through vertical M&A. If the acquirer's current industry is unattractive, it should implement a strategic shift and retreat through mixed M&A. (2) The acquirer influences the pattern of formation of the five competencies through the implementation of M&A strategies. In some cases, an enterprise may enter certain industries through relevant mixed M&A where it can use affiliation to conquer a competitor of a single business or a competitor with a poor array of business units. (3) The acquirer determines the industries to enter by analyzing the industry attractiveness when deciding to make a hybrid M&A.

However, we believe that the use of Porter's competitive advantage theory in selecting an M&A strategy has its inherent flaws. First, unattractive industries do not mean that there are no opportunities for profitability. It is increasingly clear that the profit gap between enterprises within the same industry is not smaller than the profit gap between industries, that highly profitable enterprises can be found in unattractive industries, and that there are poorly run enterprises in attractive industries. Rumelt's research shows that the dispersion of long-term profitability within industries is much greater than the dispersion between industries and that the dispersion of profitability within industries is four to six times greater than the dispersion between industries. This shows that an enterprise's competitive advantage does not come exclusively from external market forces. Second, the theory implies that enterprises can succeed in any attractive industry. Porter takes the industry as the object of study, and when an enterprise enters a new industry, it first selects an industry based on its attractiveness, then formulates an entry strategy based on a reasonable judgment of its strategy under the assumption that the competitor's rationality, and finally make a strategic investment to compete.

In summary, using this theory alone to guide enterprises in their choice of M&A strategy can easily induce enterprises to enter some industries that seem to be highly profitable, but lack experience or have nothing to do with their competitive advantages for unrelated hybrid M&A. Existing empirical studies have proved that the ability difference between enterprises can better explain the performance difference between enterprises than the structural difference between industries. In addition, comparative advantage theory is more widely applied in cross-border M&A. Brakman et al. (2013) find that cross-border M&A is driven by the comparative advantage in cross-country differences, with acquirers operating in industries in which they have a comparative advantage. Xie Hongjun and Jiang Dianchun (2017) argue that the "competitive advantage hypothesis" cannot explain the rapid growth of China's overseas M&A in recent years and that domestic companies' overseas M&A needs to be explained by combing domestic and foreign asset price factors.

5.3.2 Resource-Based Theory

The resource-based theory paradigm constructs the basic framework of "resource-strategy-performance". The theory assumes that a firm is a collection of resources that each have its purpose. Differences in firms' competitiveness are explained by differences in strategies or, furthermore, by differences in resources. Resource-based theory explicitly makes two assumptions that differ from the industrial organization school: (1) strategic resources possessed by enterprises in an industry are heterogeneous; (2) strategic resources are not completely mobile, i.e., they are sticky, thus making heterogeneity sustainable. Thus, an enterprise's competitive advantage comes from resources that have special properties within the firm. The theory further states that such special resource that forms competitive advantage have characteristics such as value, scarcity, inimitability, and difficulty to substitute. When the resource is valuable and scarce, the enterprise as the owner of the resource can obtain Ricardian rents and gain competitive advantages. When the resource is still difficult to imitate and difficult to substitute, then Ricardian rents are maintained, and the enterprise can obtain sustainable competitive advantages.

The resource-based theory emphasizes that enterprises should develop and implement a resource-based competitive strategy. The significance of this theory for the choice of M&A strategy is manifested in two aspects: (1) Through M&A, to acquire and supplement the resources that a company must possess to have sustainable competitive advantages. When an enterprise does not have or lacks the strategic resources in the industry, and it is also difficult to obtain them in the factor market, the enterprise can choose to make horizontal or vertical M&A. When an enterprise does not have or lacks the strategic resources in the industry, and it is difficult to obtain them in the factor market, and the cost of horizontal or vertical M&A is greater than the cost of obtaining the strategic resources needed to enter other industries, the enterprise can choose to conduct mixed M&A. (2) Choose an M&A strategy based on the characteristics of the enterprise's resources. If the acquirer has strategic resources (e.g., brand, knowledge, reputation, management model, etc.) that can be reused without depreciation and resources (e.g., funds, equipment, raw materials, etc.) that can be smoothly transferred to the target industry, it can expand the scale of the enterprise through horizontal M&A to obtain economies of scale and expand its competitive advantages. If the strategic resources required by the acquirer are highly specific, i.e., lacking transferability from one use to another, then vertical M&A can be used to reduce market transaction costs. In contrast, the acquirers who conduct related mixed mergers generally have abundant reusable resources, and the acquirers that conduct unrelated mixed mergers have rich divisible resources. According to Nath et al. (2010), an enterprise's diversification strategy is constrained by its resources. Therefore, enterprises should implement diversification strategies within a reasonable range of their resources.

It should be noted that the resource-based theory also has the following shortcomings: First, the definition of resources in this school is still not clear enough, and the scope and specific contents covered by resources are also vague, so it is difficult to operate. Second, resources can be obtained through market transactions in a fully competitive market, so resources are not a sufficient condition for generating a competitive advantage for enterprises. Third, the resource-based theory ignores the industrial environment in which the enterprise resources exist. The value assessment of enterprise resources should not be limited to the enterprise itself but should be placed in the industrial environment and compared with competitors to determine the pros and cons. Fourth, the resource-based theory ignores the ability to use resources. In fact, the competitive advantage of an enterprise is not only related to the unique resources possessed by the company, but also related to the ability of the enterprise to allocate these resources in a specific competitive environment, and the ability of resource allocation affects the efficiency of resource operation.

5.3.3 M&A Direction Decision Method

Competitive advantage theory and resource-based theory are the sources of competitive advantage from two perspectives: the external environment and the strategic resources possessed by an enterprise, respectively, and obviously, the two are closely related to each other. The ultimate goal of developing a suitable M&A strategy is to maintain and sustain a company's competitive advantage and achieve its overall development goals, so these two theories should be used together to develop an M&A strategy.

The M&A direction is a sub-strategy of the overall development strategy of the enterprise and is the strategic guide for the M&A activities taken by the enterprise to realize the overall development strategy of the enterprise, which presupposes that the enterprise has already determined the overall development strategy and the resources needed to realize this strategy. Therefore, the acquirer's idea of choosing an M&A strategy is: to compare the company's strategic target resources with its resources to arrive at the enterprise's resource shortages, these shortages are the enterprise's resource needs, which are constrained by the M&A capability (resource redundancy) on the one hand and the enterprise's external competitive environment on the other hand, their combined effect determines the enterprise's resource needs. Then the analysis of resources establishes a decision model of M&A direction and determines the M&A direction of the enterprise in the four dimensions: industry, region, scale, and profitability. According to this idea, the acquirer's choice of M&A strategy is based on a comprehensive analysis of the competitive environment in which the enterprise is located, and the strategic resources it has and needs.

5.4 Enterprise Competitive Environment and Resource Analysis

5.4.1 Analysis of the Competitive Environment Faced by Enterprises

M&A activity is carried out in the general market environment, so it is necessary to analyze the external competitive environment faced by the enterprise before M&A, especially the structural characteristics of the industry, its development prospects, the degree of competition, market conditions, the height of barriers to entry and the product life cycle among many other factors. When analyzing the structural characteristics of the industry, the enterprise should conduct a comprehensive analysis of the technical characteristics of the industry, its life cycle, as well as competitive position, and future trend of the industry. If the technical structure of the industry is highly specialized, the degree of resource specialization in the industry is high, the cost of transferring resources between industries is high, and the value of the enterprise's core competencies is usually locked in the relevant industry, then the enterprise should give priority to the specialized M&A strategy. Similarly, if the industry is in a period of rapid development and the core competencies of the enterprise are in a period of strengthening compared to its competitors, then horizontal and vertical M&A will be the primary choice of the company; if the industry is in a period of decline, then a mixed M&A strategy will be the primary choice of the enterprise.

Usually, we can use two analytical tools, industry attractiveness evaluation tool and industry relevance evaluation, to assist enterprise decision-making. By comprehensively evaluating the attractiveness of different industries and the relevance of the activities of enterprises in the industry to the activities of an enterprise, we can select the industry from which the enterprise has the most competitive advantages and development prospects. Industrial attractiveness can be evaluated in the following four aspects: (1) growth, which can be measured by indicators such as market size, growth rate, stage in the life cycle, international market size, stability of sales, etc. (2) profitability, which can be measured by profit, economic value added, and stability; (3) accessibility, which can be measured by industry concentration, start-up rate, barriers to entry, penetration difficulty, price elasticity, etc. (4) environmental condition constraints, analyzing social and legal constraints and labor constraints. Industrial relevance is mainly reflected by the relevance of the value chain, such as market relevance, production relevance, technology relevance, procurement relevance, basic activity relevance, management technology relevance, etc. In general, selecting an M&A strategy based on the principle of relevance can lead to the following advantages: (1) combine related activities of different operating businesses to operate together and reduce costs; (2) effective transfer of key skills, know-how, or management secrets from one business to another ; (3) share the reputation of a common brand in the new operating business; and (4) implement relevant value chain activities by competitive capabilities and collaboration mode that can create valuable competitive.

5.4.2 Resource Analysis of the Enterprise

According to the resource-based theory, an enterprise is a collection of resources, and no two enterprises can be the same because they cannot have the same resources. However, for an enterprise, many of its resources are general and basic, and other enterprises will also have such resources. At the same time, a competitive enterprise must also have some strategic resources that other enterprises cannot or are difficult to obtain, and such resources largely determine the survival and development of the enterprise and are at the core of its total resources. In each M&A transaction, the strategic resources that the acquirer pays attention to may be different, so it is necessary to identify the strategic resources from the enterprise's resource group and analyze and describe the connection between them. Corporations contemplating M&A need the necessary resources, and a lack of sufficient resources can hinder corporate strategic change (Iyer & Miller, 2008).

According to the research of a large number of scholars on the resource-based theory, the resources that enterprises rely on to obtain sustainable competitive advantages include capital (Penrose,1959; Grant, 1991), physical assets such as machinery and equipment (Barney, 1991; Grant, 1991; Wernerfelt, 1984), skilled employees (Wernerfelt, 1984), technical knowledge (Polanyi, 1962, 1966; Wernerfelt, 1984), strategic planning ability (Michalisin et al., 1997; Powell, 1992), management skills (Castanis & Helft, 1991) and so on. Although scholars hold different views on the definition and classification of enterprise resources, their research conclusions are complementary and closely related, rather than conflicting and contradictory. Zhang Jinxin (2006) constructed a conceptual system of resources applied to M&A research based on summarizing the classic literature on enterprise resource theory, and classified them systematically, including physical assets, financial assets, intangible assets, social capital, human capital, and company culture. Based on a review of the literature related to enterprise resource theory at home and abroad, Su Jingqin and Wang Hechun (2010) reclassify resources within enterprises through three dimensions: the form of resources, the relationship between resources and competition, and the relationship between resources and people, from the perspective of adaptation and taking into account the dominant role of entrepreneurs. Resources are classified into three categories: tangible resources, entrepreneurial resources, and intangible resources, according to the classification of the enterprise resources themselves. Combined with the previous analysis and research, we divide the resources of an enterprise into human resources, financial resources, physical resources, information resources, and the ability to use various resources. Human resources are the knowledge and skills that exist depending on the employees of the enterprise (Becker, 1983; Coff, 2002) and can create future income for the enterprise. Financial resources are assets in the form of financial claims, currency gold, company stocks, etc. Physical resources include the company's factory building, equipment, land, production lines, resource reserves, information systems, etc. Information resources include open information and hidden, subtle know-how. Information includes intangible assets and social capital. Intangible assets are non-monetary assets with no physical form held by an enterprise for the production of goods, provision of labor services, leased to others, or for management purposes, including patents, non-patented technologies, trademarks, copyrights, land use rights, franchise rights, and commercial reputation, etc. Social capital represents the related resources that enterprises or individuals can obtain through social relationship networks. Capability includes general ability and special ability. General ability is the management ability of an enterprise, and special ability includes bargaining ability, supply speed, innovation ability, production ability, quality management ability, serviceability, and so on.

For enterprises, identifying assets and capabilities with the potential to create competitive advantages can be screened one by one from the list of enterprise resources with the help of value chain analysis tools, combined with the characteristics of strategic resources themselves. At the same time, the analysis of the value chains of both sides of the M&A can also clarify the linkages that can be obtained between the two companies and determine the rationality of the value chain organization.

The concept of the value chain was first introduced by Michael E. Porter in 1985 in his book *Competitive Advantage*. He described the value chain as a collection of activities used by a company to design, produce, sell, deliver and play a supporting role in the product, which is a series of activities completed continuously, the process of converting raw materials into a series of final products. It consists of basic activities and auxiliary activities. Basic activities refer to various activities involving the material creation of products and their sales, transfer to buyers and after-sales services, including internal logistics, production operations, external logistics, marketing and services, and auxiliary activities refer to the activities that support basic activities and mutually support each other internally, including enterprise infrastructure, human resource management, technology development, and procurement. In various activities of the value chain, enterprises have corresponding human resources, physical resources, financial resources, information resources, and the ability to use resources associated with them. In other words, it is these resources that support the value chain activities of the enterprise, and the value that the enterprise ultimately creates through product sales or services is the result of the joint action of resources in various functional activities. Zhou Lin (2006) introduced the main components of enterprise resources into the value chain and established a resource-based value chain model, as shown in Fig. 5.3.

The model consists of two parts. At the bottom of the model are various functional activities such as corporate procurement, research and development, manufacturing, marketing, service, etc. Here, there is no distinction between basic activities and auxiliary activities like Porter's proposed value chain, but they are integrated. The upper part of the model is the main component of resources, including human

Financial resources/human resources/general capabilities						
Physical resources	Raw materials	Equipment	Workshop, production line	Product	Stock	Value
Intangible assets		Patent, proprietary technology	Industry, license	Trademark	Reputation	
Dedicated capabilities	Bargaining power, supply speed	Innovation capabilities	Production capacity, quality management	Public relations ability, promotion ability	Service ability, information feedback ability	
Functional activities	Procurement	Research and development	Manufacturing	Marketing	Service	

Fig. 5.3 Resource-based enterprise value chain model. *Note* The value chain model only provides an identification framework in which each row reflects the specific content that each resource may contain, and it does not have a one-to-one correspondence with each column. Products, for example, can be both objects of marketing activities and inputs in the R&D phase (*Source* Zhou Lin, Mechanism Analysis of Resource Synergy in Mergers and Acquisitions, Doctoral Dissertation of Beijing Jiaotong University, 2006)

resources, financial resources, physical resources, intangible assets, general capabilities, and Dedicated capabilities, and this division of resources is consistent with the division of resources (human, financial, physical, information and capabilities) in the M&A capabilities section. As can be seen from Fig. 5.3, different types of resources play an important role in the value creation of the enterprise at each stage of the enterprise's operation process. The right side of the model values, which is not represented by profit as in the value chain proposed by Porter, but is replaced by value with richer content. This model combines the main components of resources with the functional activities of enterprises and provides a concise and effective framework for enterprises to identify their resources.

The analysis of the enterprise's resources is a global approach to the quantitative and qualitative aspects of the enterprise's resources for each functional activity, which forms the business structure of the enterprise and the material basis of its strength. The current situation and trends of the enterprise's resources are the most fundamental constraints for formulating overall strategies and choosing business areas. Because the resources that enterprises can put into business activities are limited. This limitation is twofold. The external resources that can be provided are limited, and this capacity is related to other elements such as supply channels, in addition to the financial limitations. Therefore, in the resource analysis of strategic enterprise management, one is to analyze the status and changing trend of the existing resources of the enterprise, and the other is to predict which resources (resource gaps) should be increased in the strategic period. Table 5.4 provides a framework and ideas for enterprise resource analysis, each of which can be either the actual situation of the enterprise or the demand for resources from the enterprise's strategic plan. The gap between the reality of the origin and the planned demand for resources is the resource gap of the enterprise.

The direction of M&A in the resource gap of the enterprise is determined based on the analysis of resources after identifying its resources through the functional activities of the value chain, and the external expression of these resource gaps is the M&A direction, including the industry attributes, regional attributes, scale attributes and profitability attributes of these resources.

We should firstly analyze the industry, region, scale, and profitability of the enterprise itself, assuming that the industry, region, scale, and profitability of the enterprise itself are represented by x, y, z, and w respectively. The business scope of an enterprise may not be limited to only one industry. We determine the industrial location of the enterprise according to the industry classification used in the registration of the enterprise or the main business of the enterprise; the regional location of the enterprise itself is determined according to the geographical location of the enterprise at the time of registration; the scale of the enterprise is determined according to the total assets of the enterprise; the profitability of the enterprise is measured by the return on investment.

The analysis of the enterprise's resources is carried out under the framework of the "resource-based enterprise value chain model" based on the determined industry, region, and scale. The enterprise's resources are divided into human, financial, material, information, and capability, and the functional activities of the enterprise include R&D, procurement, manufacturing, marketing, and service.

Human resources of an enterprise are divided according to functional activities, including R&D personnel, purchasing personnel, production personnel, marketing personnel, and service personnel. According to the industry, region, scale, and profitability of the enterprise analyzed above, it can be determined that the human resources of the enterprise meet the following conditions: x industry, y region, enterprise size z, profitability w. The scale and profitability of the enterprise limit the

Table 5.4 Enterprise resource analysis

Value chain resources	Research and development	Procurement	Manufacturing	Marketing	Service
Human resources					
Financial resources					
Physical resources					
Information resources					
Capability					

number of personnel in the enterprise. The industry exclusivity of different functional activities personnel is different. For example, the industry exclusivity of R&D personnel is stronger than that of purchasing personnel, so different functional activities of personnel should be expressed separately.

Financial resources are more liquid, less exclusive, and more transferable, so it is not influenced by industry or region, nor by functional activities.

Physical resources are divided according to the functional activities of the enterprise, and physical resources include raw materials, equipment, instruments, factory building, production lines, products, etc. Physical resources of an enterprise can be smoothly transferred between enterprises, with availability and transferability, and will be continuously reduced due to consumption in the process of use. The exclusivity of physical resources in different industries is strong; the scale and profitability of enterprises determine the quantity and quality of physical resources enterprises; at the same time, due to the availability and transferability of physical resources of enterprises, the regional requirements for physical resources are not high.

In the "resource-based enterprise value chain model", information resources are intangible assets, including patents, proprietary technologies, industry licenses, trademarks, reputation, etc., which are reusable and do not depreciate. The information resources of different industries and even different enterprises are more exclusive and less regional, while the scale and profitability of enterprises reflect the quantity and quality of their intangible assets.

Capability resources include industry-specific capabilities and general capabilities. Different functional activities include bargaining capability, innovation capability, production management capability, service capability, etc.

5.5 M&A Direction Decision of the Enterprise

5.5.1 Enterprise Resource Characteristic Analysis

Enterprise resource characteristics refer to the characteristics of human resources, financial resources, physical resources, information resources, and capabilities in terms of industry, region, scale, and profitability. Since resources of the same type in different links of the value chain have the same characteristics, we will not analyze the characteristics of resources in each link for the time being.

(1) Human resources

Non-managerial human capital is exclusive to the production organization of the enterprise (manufacturing personnel), and at most can only be obtained from similar institutions; industry-specific human capital (R&D personnel) can only be obtained through other enterprises in the same or related industries; general human capital can obtained through M&A of companies in unrelated industries.

From a regional perspective, due to the restricted mobility of labor, labor costs in different regions of a country, especially different countries, are quite different. The geographical difference in human capital cost is an important factor that enterprises need to consider when choosing the direction of M&A.

For each industry, there is a certain rule for the amount of human capital that needs to be equipped for different scales. According to this rule and the shortage of human capital in the enterprise, we can determine the size of the enterprise that needs to be acquired.

(2) Financial resources

Financial assets have the highest liquidity and the least exclusivity, so they have strong transferability. There is no obvious preference for the choice of different M&A directions, but the number of financial assets will limit the scale of M&A and even the profitability of enterprises.

(3) Physical resources

Physical resources can be smoothly transferred between enterprises, with availability and transferability, and they will be continuously reduced due to consumption in the process of use.

If the exclusivity of physical assets (raw materials) is high and requires repeated purchases, companies will have a clear preference for vertical M&A to save transaction costs. If the exclusivity is high, there is no need for repeated purchases (R&D equipment) and industry-specific equipment (production lines) has a clear preference for horizontal M&A.

In resource-based industries such as minerals, if the company lacks control over raw material resources, it tends to implement vertical M&A, integrate upstream resources, and is more inclined to implement cross-regional M&A to expand to regions with such raw materials, so as to make up for the resource gap. The number of physical asset shortages can determine the size of a firm's M&A.

(4) Information resources

Intangible assets are resources that can be reused without depreciation, and their transferability and sharing determine that the greater the number of products that share such resources, the smaller the cost allocated to unit products.

The acquisition (relative to the resource gap), extension, and transfer of dominant brand resources have a clear preference for related industries. From the regional dimension, brand resources have a greater preference for cross-regional M&A or even cross-border M&A. The information on the enterprise is directly proportional to the profitability of the enterprise.

If the enterprise has mastered the core technology of its leading industry and is not restricted by the industrial bottleneck, it has a clear preference for horizontal and vertical M&A; otherwise, it has a clear preference for intra-industry M&A.

(5) Capability

General capability can be transferred smoothly between industries and are not bound by industry. Dedicated capabilities such as innovation capabilities in R&D and production quality management capabilities are more industry-specific, and such resources prefer correlation M&A. A firm's capabilities are usually proportional to its profitability.

5.5.2 Evaluate the Strategic Importance of Resources

After identifying the various resources that the enterprise is currently in a non-equilibrium state, it is necessary to evaluate its strategic importance. In the evaluation, the characteristics of the specific industry to which the enterprise belongs and the resource status of the enterprise should be comprehensively considered. The same kind of resources has different strategic importance to enterprises in different industries or different development stages of the same enterprise. For example, in the consulting service industry, human capital that is difficult to imitate is the key to competition; for high-tech industries such as electronic information and biomedicine, the strategic significance of technical resources is even more prominent. For another example, in the early stage of enterprise development, financial resources may become the source of sustainable competitive advantage (Lee et al., 2001), and in the later and mature stages of development, intangible assets such as technology and brand will become the key resources elements for enterprise expansion. Therefore, enterprises in different industries and at different stages of the life cycle should determine the proportion of their weight in resources according to the strategic importance of resources.

The evaluation of the strategic importance of resources can be determined according to the evaluation of the importance of resources by experts in the industry: $W_r = \sum S_{rf}/f$.

Where W_r is expressed as a percentage, representing the important proportion of different resources; r takes the value (1, 2, ..., 5), representing different resources; S_{rf} represents the$f$ th expert's score on the importance of resources; the same expert's scores on different resources add up to 100%f takes the value 1, 2, ... n, representing the number of experts who evaluate the importance of resources.

5.5.3 M&A Direction Decision Model

In the internal resource demand of the M&A direction, the resource range of the corporate M&A is that the resource demand constrained by the M&A capability and the external environment is the maximum value of the resources acquired by the M&A, and the minimum value of the resources required by the M&A is zero.

Therefore, the resource range of corporate M&A is between zero (greater than zero) and internal resource demand. However, some resources do not belong to the scope of total assets, such as human capital, capacity, etc. We believe that there is always a certain rule between the amount of human capital and the scale of the enterprise, so the scope of total assets can be determined through physical assets, intangible assets, and financial assets, namely the scale of corporate M&A.

Based on the analysis of the characteristics of the enterprises, the selected models for M&A in terms of industry, region, and profitability are set respectively.

5.5.3.1 Resource-to-Industry Selection Model

The selection model of resources to industries is: $I_k = \sum i_{rk} \times W_r$. Where, I_k is the weighted average score of resources for industry selection;

k takes the value 1, 2 … n; n is sorted in order according to the GB industry classification criteria;

i_{rk} is the preference scoring of industry k based on resource r, representing the different preferences of resource r for various industries;

r takes the value 1, 2, … n, which respectively represent various types of subdivided resources;

W_r is the strategic importance weight of resource r, $\sum W_r = 1$ and $0 < W_r \leq 1$.

5.5.3.2 Resource-to-Region Selection Model

The selection model of resources to regions is: $G_j = \sum g_{rj} \times W_r$. Where, G_j is the weighted average score of resource to region selection;

j takes the value 1, 2 … n, representing the different preferences of the resource r to the region, and n is sorted in order according to the administrative division criteria;

r takes the value 1, 2, … n, which respectively represent various types of subdivided resources;

g_{rj} is the score based on the preference of resource r for region j;

W_r is the strategic importance weight of resource r, $\sum W_r = 1$ and $0 < W_r \leq 1$.

5.5.3.3 Resource-to-Profitability Selection Model

The selection model of resources on profitability is: $M_h = \sum m_h \times W_r$.

Where,

M_h is the weighted average score of resource selection on ROI;

h takes the values 0.01%, 0.02%, … n; n representing the different preferences of resource r for ROI;

r takes the value 1, 2, … n, which respectively represent various types of subdivided resources;

m_{rh} is a score based on the preference of resource r for ROI h;

W_r is the strategic importance weight of resource r, $\sum W_r = 1$ and $0 < W_r \leq 1$.

According to the established model, calculate the weighted average scores of enterprise resources for different industries, regions, and ROI choices, I_k, G_j and M_h, (max (I_k), max (G_j), max (M_h)), that is, resources for M&A industry, region and profitability preferences, determine the direction of M&A of enterprises, and clarify whether the M&A are related or unrelated, intra-regional, cross-regional or cross-border, large-scale, medium-sized or small scale M&A and require target companies to have certain profitability.

Chapter 6
M&A Fit

The selection of the target enterprise is an important part of the M&A pre- preparation and the basis for planning the M&A plan, but the selection of the target enterprise cannot simply examine the quality of the target enterprise because the value of the target enterprise to different acquirers (the stand-alone value of the target enterprise) is the same purely from the perspective of the value that the target enterprise may bring to the acquirer, and this value will be more available to the shareholders of the target enterprise because of the competitive mechanism in the competitive market (Zhang Jinxin, 2006). Therefore, the selection of the target company should be a measure of the match between the M&A parties.

Through the analysis of the M&A direction, we can clearly understand the M&A demand of the acquirer, which provides us with the screening scope of target companies. This chapter will take the M&A parties as a whole as the research object, and based on giving the definition of M&A fit, it will divide the M&A matching into two stages of operational fit and resource fit with due diligence as the boundary, and then carry out the target company group screening by evaluating the two stages of M&A fit, and finally provide the judgment basis for the selection of target enterprises.

6.1 The Concept of M&A Fit

6.1.1 Concepts Related to M&A Fit

The fit itself is not a new concept but comes from the contingency theory (Ginsberg & Venkatraman, 1985) in the strategy and organization literature, which analyzes whether an enterprise's strategy or organizational structure matches the enterprise's external environment. In the diversification research, the concept of fit focuses on the research on the parent-subsidiary fit relationship, and Amit and Thornhill (2000)

Q. Zhang, *Mergers and Acquisitions*, https://doi.org/10.1007/978-981-92-0122-8_6

divide the parent-subsidiary fit relationship into relational fit and economic fit. Relational fit affects the culture and structure of an organization, while the economic fit is a function of subsidiary demand and parent company resources.

Different from the concept of fit in the field of strategic management, the fit in M&A focuses on the fit relationship between the M&A parties. Jemison and Sitkin (1986) distinguish M&A fit into strategic fit and organizational fit. Strategic fit refers to the degree to which the target enterprise enhances or complements the acquirer's strategy in terms of industry, market, or technology. Organizational fit refers to the fit between the target company and the acquirer in terms of the management system, corporate culture, and employee characteristics.

6.1.2 Definition of M&A Fit

Mergers & acquisitions fit refers to the extent to which the target's resources confirmed by the acquirer meet the acquirer's demand. The essence of the analysis of M&A fit is to solve a problem of supply and demand, that is, whether the existing resource supply of the target party can meet the demand of the acquirer. When there is a large gap between the existing resources of the target and the demand of the acquirer, the acquirer will have a large demand gap. Then, if the target party meets the demand of the acquirer to a lower degree, the M&A fit degree will be lower. Conversely, the target party has a higher M&A fit. Taking due diligence as the boundary, M&A fit can be divided into two stages, namely, the operation fit stage and the resource fit stage.

The main research in the operation fit stage is to determine the scope of M&A according to the direction of M&A before due diligence and to preliminarily screen the target enterprise group by measuring the fit degree of M&A. Before due diligence, the acquirer cannot understand the internal resources of the target in detail, concretely and clearly, so it cannot judge the effect of the interaction between the resources of the target and the resources of the acquirer. However, the acquirer can understand the basic situation of the target through the external information disclosed by the target and confirm whether it meets its basic demand, so as to achieve the purpose of preliminary screening of the target group. Therefore, the operational fit is a macro perspective to analyze the fit between M&A parties.

Resource fit refers to the fit of M&A parties in specific resource categories. The main research at this stage is to determine whether the capabilities of the target party can be preserved, transferred, and developed based on understanding the resource status of the target enterprise after due diligence, for further screening the target enterprise, and analyzing the fit of M&A parties from a microscopic perspective. Resource fit includes asset fit and capability fit. According to the source of capability, we divide it into human capital fit, organizational capital fit, and relational capital fit.

Asset fit means that the combination of the assets of the acquirer and the target party can bring about an increase in scale effect, and the financial capital gains obtained are greater than the sum of the gains when the two are independent. Asset fit may originate from the complementarity or substitutability of the physical capital of the M&A parties, or the complementarity or enhancement of the financial capital of the two parties.

Capability fit means that the combined capabilities of the acquirer and the target party can create value, which is greater than the sum of the value created when the two are independent. Capability fit not only indicates that the external relationship resources of the M&A parties are complementary or enhanced but also indicates that the internal organizational resources of the M&A parties, such as management process and corporate culture, are not conflicted and are compatible. Capability fit means that there is the potential for value creation in M&A, and this value creation is achievable, that is, the M&A parties are strategically and organizationally matched.

It should be noted that, in the basic theory of M&A, the selection of target enterprises spans three links, namely M&A direction, M&A fit, and M&A synergy. The acquirer should comprehensively assess the degree offit between itself and the target enterprise, and this assessment should help the acquirer determine whether the target enterprise's full potential qualities can be combined to produce synergies. If so, this could further assist in developing practical plans to exploit potential synergies (Ahammad & Glaister, 2013). M&A direction will address the area where the potential target enterprises are located, M&A fit will address whether the resources of the potential target enterprises can be preserved, transferred, and developed by the acquiring enterprises, and M&A synergy will address how much value the acquiring enterprises and the potential target enterprises can create after the M&A. Therefore, the study of M&A basic theory will provide systematic and perfect guidance for target enterprise selection. Figure 6.1 provides a brief description of the target enterprise selection process in M&A basic theory to better understand the content of M&A fit research and the relationship with other links.

It is worth noting that Chinese enterprises have their characteristics in the selection of M&A target enterprises, and these characteristics are realized through the identification of M&A targets. Zhang Jinxin et al. (2012) found that M&A target companies in the Chinese market are characterized by high financial leverage, low solvency, poor profitability, weak growth, fragmented equity, and high share liquidity through an empirical study that developed a predictive model of M&A targets.

6.2 Research Status of M&A Fit Theory

6.2.1 Research on Fit Theory

At present, there are few direct studies on M&A fit in the theoretical circle, and the existing literature related to M&A fit mainly discusses the influencing factors of value creation in M&A. The basic idea of the research is to put forward the hypothesis of the relationship between "influencing factors" and "M&A performance" based on theoretical analysis, and then test the hypothesis through empirical research. This

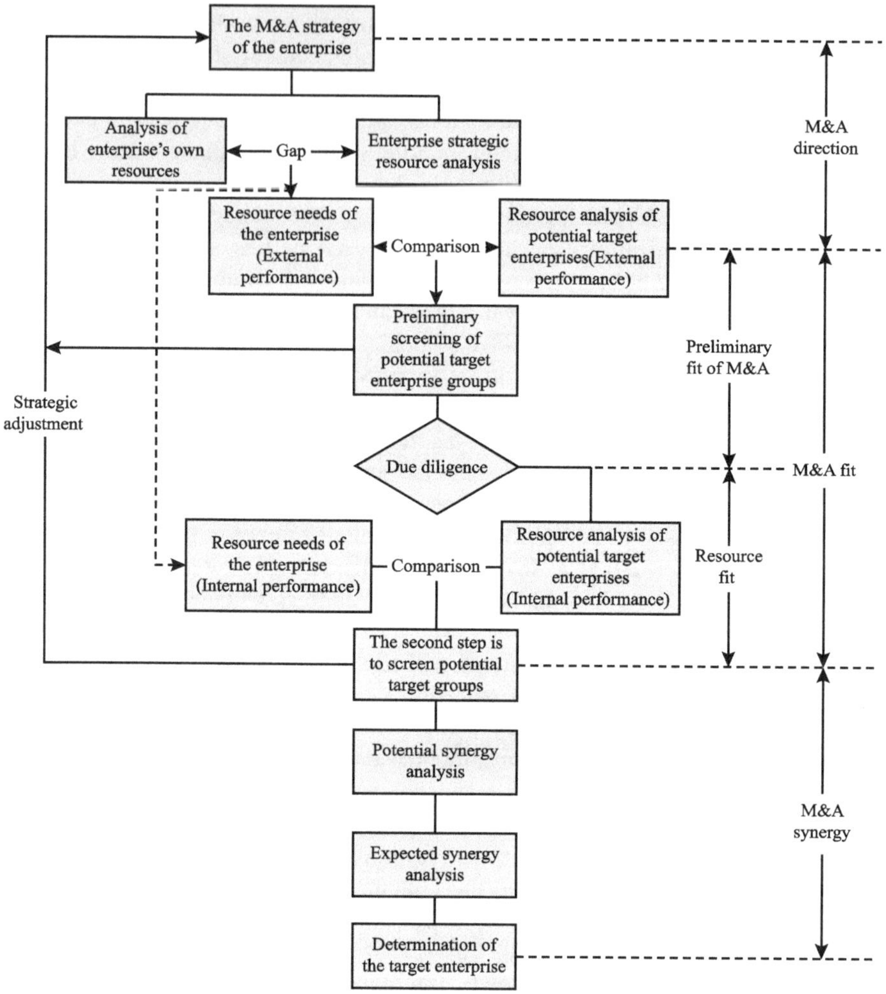

Fig. 6.1 The selection process of target enterprises

literature can be divided into four areas, namely, strategic fit, organizational fit, cultural fit and trade-off fit. Ahammad and Glaister (2013) studied the impact of pre-merger target company evaluation on cross-border acquisition performance using a sample of the UK company acquisitions. Research shows that the more the acquirer knows about the target enterprise, the better the M&A performance. Specifically, the assessment of strategic fit and cultural fit is the factor that affects the success or failure of cross-border M&A. Detailed assessment of target enterprise employees and business capabilities improves M&A performance.

6.2.1.1 Strategic Fit

The concept of strategic fit comes from the research on diversification. Later, Salter and Weinhold (1979) introduced the concept of strategic fit into the field of M&A by studying the strategic relationship between the acquiring company and the target enterprise and classified M&A into relevant and irrelevant M&A according to the strategic fit between the two parties. They considered relevance as a key factor for the success of M&A, which is derived from the transfer of key technologies between enterprises, and they also found a positive relationship between the acquisition of key skills or product market position and value creation potential. Thereafter, Singh (1984) used an event-based analysis, a research method in financial economics, to compare the advantages and disadvantages of correlated and uncorrelated M&A through the movement of stock prices. The results show that the value created by correlated M&A is higher than that of uncorrelated M&A, but the impact on the acquirer is still unclear. Singh's research model became the research paradigm followed by many subsequent scholars, namely relatedness/strategic fit—post-merger performance, scholars put forward theoretical hypotheses by dividing and defining correlated M&A, and testing empirically whether correlated M&A is more profitable than uncorrelated M&A, and whether the target enhances or complements the acquirer's strategy and creates new value. Scholars have drawn three different conclusions from a large number of studies, as follows.

The first research conclusion is that because correlated M&A has a greater possibility of strategic fit, correlated M&A is more profitable than uncorrelated M&A, that is, correlated M&A is better than uncorrelated M&A. Singh and Montgomery (1987), based on Salter and Weinhold's (1979) classification of correlated M&A, defined correlated M&A as having at least one of the three characteristics of similar production technology, similar scientific research, similar products or markets. By using the event study method, the following three conclusions are drawn: (1) the total income of correlated M&A is higher than that of uncorrelated M&A; (2) the gains of the acquiree in both correlated and uncorrelated M&A are positive and significant; (3) the gains of the acquiree in correlated M&A are significantly higher than those in uncorrelated M&A, and the acquirer's gains in M&A are not significant. He suggested that the acquiree should choose correlated M&A to obtain higher returns; the acquirer should pay more attention to how much of the value created by the acquisition can be obtained by the acquirer itself, rather than on how much total value the acquisition can create. Shelton (1988) defined a correlated M&A as satisfying at least three of the four characteristics of the same customer type, the same production technology, the same product type, and the same functional purpose. He proposed four types of strategic fit, namely, complete correlated, uncorrelated, complementary correlated, and alternative correlated. Then he added up the value of the acquirer and the target enterprises, and took the three days before and after the announcement of the news as the inspection period, and came to the following conclusions: complete correlated M&A and alternative correlated M&A offers a lot of value creation opportunities, while alternative correlated M&A creates the least volatility in value and uncorrelated M&A creates the least value. He suggested that target enterprises with large assets, high quality, and popularity could be ideal targets for M&A. Flanagan (1996) uses the combination of SIC and subjective classification method to distinguish M&A into purely correlated M&A and purely uncorrelated M&A. Through the empirical test, it is concluded that in purely correlated M&A, the acquirer's returns are significantly higher than that of purely uncorrelated M&A, and if the M&A is done in good faith or cash, the acquirer's shareholders will receive higher returns. Hopkins (1987) explains the reasons for the higher profitability of correlated M&A than uncorrelated M&A by arguing that strategic fit enhances the synergies ofthe merging firms, so a long-term acquisition strategy that emphasizes strategic fit can result in high returns on assets and equity for the acquirer. More specifically, Tsai (2000) points out that when two business units are strategically correlated, their common interests may motivate them to exchange information and resources in a mutually beneficial way. Given the other circumstances, the higher the strategic relevance of two business units, the stronger their incentive to exchange resources.

The second study concludes that correlated and uncorrelated M&A are similar in terms of creating value for shareholders and achieving synergy. Lubatkin (1987) classified M&A into four categories based on the Federal Trade Commission classification: product-centric M&A, horizontal and market-based M&A, intensive M&A, and vertical M&A. By testing the hypothesis of shareholder value appreciation ranking of acquirers and acquirees in the four categories, it was concluded that the two types of correlated M&A, product-centric M&A and horizontal market-based M&A, were not as superior to uncorrelated M&A as expected. Seth (1990) systematically summarized the previous literature and proposed that the reason for the divergent results of a large number of empirical studies is the difference in study methods, that is, different measures of value creation, different M&A classification systems, and different sample selection criteria. He then adopts two approaches to classify M&A, namely the FTC classification method and Porter's buyer-seller relationship-based classification method, while he empirically tests whether there are synergies between M&A parties as a whole in M&A based on two questions; and whether correlated M&A creates higher synergies than uncorrelated M&A. Empirical results show that both correlated and uncorrelated M&A create value equally, with no results showing that correlated M&A create more value than uncorrelated M&A.

The third study concludes that uncorrelated M&A creates higher value than correlated M&A. Chatterjee (1986) compared the impact of three resources (capital cost, product cost, and price) on M&A value creation and concluded that relevant capital cost would generate financial synergies and the type of M&A associated with it would be uncorrelated or mixed M&A; relevant product cost would generate operational synergies and the type of M&A associated with it would be correlated or vertical M&A; and relevant price would generate complicity synergies and the type of M&A associated with it would be vertical M&A. By randomly selecting 157M&A transactions between 1969 and 1972 with a size of more than US$10 million from the FTC M&A statistical report, and using the event study method to analyze, the following conclusions are drawn: (1) in general, complicity synergies create higher value; (2) resources corresponding to financial synergies create higher value than resources corresponding to operational synergies; (3) uncorrelated targets outperform correlated, non-vertical targets, i.e., uncorrelated M&A have higher returns than correlated M&A; and (4) the returns of the targets are proportional to the relative size of the two parties to the M&A. Elgers and Clark (1980) examined the risk-adjusted common stock returns of 377M&A that occurred between 1957 and 1975 and found that buyers and sellers of stocks received higher returns in mixed M&A than in non-mixed M&A, but the difference was not significant.

In addition, studies have noted that in the 1980s, correlated M&A yielded more returns to acquirers than uncorrelated M&A, but this did not apply in the 1970s (Morck et al., 1990), and some scholars believe that correlated M&A does not affect performance (Fowler & Schmidt, 1989).

There are many contradictions in the research results of the previous literature. Some scholars have analyzed the contradictions, which are roughly divided into two categories: one view, such as Seth (1990), suggests that differences in study methods, different treatment of samples, periods, and control variables, or the existence of loopholes, are the source of the different results. For example, the analysis objects selected by each study are different—some take the target party as the analysis object, some take the acquirer as the analysis object, and some take the merged entity as the analysis object; different methods of classifying related M&A and unrelated M&A—some adopt subjective classification methods, some adopt objective classification methods, and some adopt a combination of subjective and objective classification methods; the relative size of the M&A parties, the period of the sample and the industries to which the sample companies belong differ greatly in the selected M&A event samples; the performance indicators selected are different—the performance indicators used in the event research method are abnormal cumulative returns or monetary returns, while the performance indicators used in regression analysis are mainly return on assets. Another view is that, as Jamison and Sitkin (1986) suggest, strategic fit, while important, is not sufficient to explain M&A and that further research needs to focus on the M&A "process".

Synthesizing the previous literature, we can see that the research on strategic fit considers the value creation of M&A from the perspective of external factors of the enterprise. The contradictory research conclusions show that the research on M&A fit cannot be limited to the business level of the enterprise, but needs to go deep into the enterprise resource level, because in the same industrial environment, the difference in enterprise value creation mainly depends on the difference of resources. The same business may have different modes of operation (business models), which require different combinations of resources. Therefore, only by digging into the composition of the business can we get a clearer understanding of why the same business creates different values.

6.2.1.2 Organizational Fit

Given the inconsistency between strategic fit theory and empirical research results in M&A, in the late 1980s, many scholars began to pay attention to the impact of organizational fit on M&A performance, forming organizational fit—post-merger performance research paradigm, which mainly focuses on the influence of management style, evaluation and compensation system, organizational structure and organizational culture on M&A performance and the realization of the potential value of M&A. Therefore, the studies on organizational fit can be divided into three categories: the first category is the human capital fit problem, the second category is the organizational system fit problem, and the third category is the cultural fit problem.

(1) Human capital fit

A large body of writing has focused on the human resource impact of M&A and the management of such impacts. Schweiger and Walsh (1990) have made a comprehensive review of this, and the two questions examined by human resource researchers involve both pre-merger and post-merger events. Typically, they examine only negative effects, and the positive effects of M&A on employees' career opportunities and improved financial or non-financial rewards are rarely addressed in their research. Instead, these writings focus on typical employee feelings of conflict, tension, isolation, career uncertainty, behavioral difficulties, stress, loss of productivity, financial security, workplace relocation, and trust among colleagues. Although some studies do not address the impact on post- merger retention, some studies address the relationship between M&A and employee turnover. Schweiger and Walsh (1990) note in their review that this complex relationship is neutralized by a large number of contextual variables.

Organizational behaviorists have also studied the question of whether members of the acquired party will accept and identify with the new owners and managers (Graves, 1981). An implicit assumption of these studies is that identifying key human resource issues in M&A will help resolve execution issues more equitably and with less conflict. In addition, based on discussing the negative impact of M&A on human resources, they also put forward a large number of management measures that can be used to reduce labor costs, including strengthening communication, caring for employees, providing psychological counseling, and so on. Chung et al. (2014) proposed a theoretical model to explain the process of employees adapting to cross-border M&A based on an empirical analysis of 174 Chinese employees who experienced unexpected M&A initiated by Western companies. The study found that the relationship between change management practices (i.e., providing training and job security assurance) and post-change performance was mediated by employees' change adaptations. Underlying cultures, such as collectivism and Confucian teachings, influence Chinese employees' attitudes and behaviors toward change.

In addition, studies on organizational fit have shown that the mismatch between the two parties in M&A is likely to cause conflicts between employees of the acquired company and the acquiring company and its employees, resulting in the loss of key management and technical talents, which is very unfavorable for the realization of synergy. If the synergy intention is realized through business process adjustment, the loss of key personnel weakens the effective operation of the business process. If the synergy intention is realized through intangible skills and knowledge transfer, the departure of these people is a fatal blow.

(2) Organizational system fit

Datta (1991) explored the relationship between organizational fit and acquisition performance when examining post-acquisition integration effects. He believes that "organizational fit" affects the ease of assimilation between two organizations after the acquisition and can evaluate organizational fit through multiple dimensions. But from the perspective of post-acquisition integration, two areas that are often mentioned and very important are the management styles of both parties (Callahan, 1986; Davis, 1968; Diven, 1984; Seed, 1974) and organizational systems, especially reward and evaluation systems (Diven, 1984; Ferracone, 1987; Hayes, 1979; Magnet, 1984). Based on 173 acquisitions in the US manufacturing industry, Datta (1991) examines the impact of organizational differences between the two parties on post-acquisition performance. The results show that, regardless of the degree of post-merger integration, differences in top management style will hurt post-merger performance. However, reward and evaluation systems do not have such effects on post-merger performance.

For the possible impact of changes in the reward and evaluation system, Jeomison and Sitkin (1986) believed that the acquirer's imposition of its system on the acquiree would cause adverse reactions. This is caused by the arrogance of the acquirer and the defensive mentality of the acquiree's employees. The logical solution is to have the two systems coexist within the organization.

Another type of organizational behavior scholar's research focuses on the collective experience of individuals of the acquiree. Based on the theory of organizational crisis, this type of research regards the negative impact of M&A as a necessary organizational crisis, at least to a certain extent, and proposes the so-called "merger crisis period", that is, the members of the acquired company will experience several psychological processes such as shock, defensive retreat, recognition of reality and final adaptation (Devine, 1984).

6.2.1.3 Cultural Fit

Many researchers view M&A integration as a culturally driven phenomenon. Acquiring parties should assess cultural fit to increase the chances of a successful merger. This assessment should help the acquiring firm select the appropriate form of integration and determine the degree of change required or the degree of adaptation required to achieve the success of the M&A (Ahammad & Glaister, 2013). Based on the original literature examining cultural differences within and between organizations, these researchers believe that more consideration should be given to cultural compatibility between organizations when making merger decisions. From the perspective of cultural conflict, M&A are a process of cultural conflict, one of the reasons for which is that M&A may lead to a stronger group unilaterally imposing its cultural elements on others, regardless of the resistance of the weaker group (Sales &

Mirvis, 1984). Therefore, the magnitude and scope of change induced by M&A in an organization is an important variable that affects organizational conflict and M&A performance (Napier et al., 1989).

David and Singh (1994) divided the sources of cultural risk in M&A into four levels, namely environmental cultural risk, cross-organizational cultural risk, organizational cultural risk, and operational cultural risk. Nahavandi and Malekzadeh (1993) proposed the concept of "cultural fit" in M&A and pointed out that cultural fit between organizations may take four modes, including cultural assimilation, integration, isolation, and destruction. In addition to company culture, company history is also seen as an influencing factor. To some extent, each employee group's history affects that group's behaviour and its perception of its surroundings. Groups that have had a conflict but are asked to collaborate may have developed severe barriers to collaboration (Blake & Mouton, 1984).

The acquiree's concern centers on how much it can retain its personality. One of the countermeasures to this is to enhance the understanding of the elements of the two companies' cultures and the mutual understanding and respect between the two organizations (Sales & Mirvis, 1984); the other is to communicate about the upcoming changes actively and effectively (Buono et al., 1988).

Although organizational behavior theory is a supplement and revision to the strategic researchers' view of M&A, organizational behavior theory research has gone to the other extreme, that is, viewing the organization as a more important issue than strategy, and the integration of M&A is mainly considered from the perspective of whether individuals accept or adapt to the new environment (Wang Changzheng, 2002). Therefore, a comprehensive assessment of cultural fit should improve the target enterprise's cultural awareness and assist the acquiring firm in choosing the appropriate integration approach (Weber et al., 2011).

6.2.1.4 Trade-Off Fit

Some researchers have discussed how the M&A process affects the realization of corporate strategic goals from both strategic and organizational aspects. Traditionally, M&A performance is seen as the result of achieving strategic fit and organizational fit between two enterprises. However, the reality is that more and more M&A fail to produce the expected performance, leading people to question this view. In this context, the view that the M&A process itself is an important latent variable in determining M&A performance begins to emerge (Jemison & Sitkin, 1986). This view still recognizes the importance of strategic fit and organizational fit but adds to the consideration that the M&A decision-making and integration process affects final performance.

The idea of balancing strategic and organizational factors first appeared in the writings of Mace and Montgomery (1962). Through 275 interviews, the two researchers found the impact of M&A on organizational personnel. They believed that the impact was "obvious and real … Original job worries will be exacerbated by possible changes, while the entire organization may be detached from its day job." At the same time, the researchers did not shy away from the strategic task of the enterprise: "People who report to the executive manager at headquarters must acknowledge his responsibility, and they should take a positive attitude and spend time trying to make the newly added firm part of the overall operating structure." They noted the importance of process, as they said: "The value derived from mergers and acquisitions depends primarily on skills in dealing with integration management issues. Many potentially valuable assets of the acquiree are wasted due to a low level of disposal and negligence during the integration process. Each acquired organization is a unique combination of human and physical assets, and this unique group needs to be motivated and managed to achieve the goal of a good deal."

Since the mid-1980s, many M&A researchers have argued process-related issues and even supported a view of the process. Among them, two researchers have paid great attention to the problems of strategic fit and organizational fit when they study the integration of M&A. Jemison (1988) was the first researcher to link the outcome of M&A (improvement of competitive advantage) with the integration process to achieve the results (the interaction of members of the two organizations that led to the transfer of strategic capabilities). He explicitly proposed the value creation of M&A stems from the transfer of strategic capabilities. Competitive advantage is formed through the interaction between the different organizational levels of the M&A parties. However, he does not distinguish between transferable, flowable, imitable, non-specific, and capabilities in non-fully transferable, non- fully mobile, non-fully imitable, specific, that is, general capabilities and core capabilities. Therefore, the issues of capability protection, accumulation, and development in the process of M&A integration have been neglected by him. Moreover, his concept of "strategic capability transfer", only involves the sharing of business resources, the transfer of functional skills, and the transfer of general management skills, while the important elements such as organizational design, process reengineering, organizational learning, the cultivation and protection of high-quality corporate culture and the accumulation of knowledge as the main source of enterprise capabilities have not been given due attention.

Haspeslagh and Farquhar (1987) proposed for the first time a stochastic framework for merger integration considering strategic fit and organizational fit. Strategic fit (or strategic relevance) refers to the degree to which the target enterprise enhances or complements the acquirer's strategy in terms of industry, market, or technology. Organizational fit (or organizational relevance) refers to the matching between the target enterprise and the acquirer in terms of management, culture, and employees, which may directly affect the integration of daily operations between the two enterprises after the merger. There is a certain connection between organizational fit and strategic fit. Strategic fit determines the value creation potential of M&A, and organizational fit determines the degree of difficulty in realizing potential value creation (i.e., the execution of M&A strategy). In other words, both strategic fit and organizational fit are necessary conditions for value creation. At the same time, according to the requirements of strategic fit and organizational fit, the acquirer can choose among three integration models:

(1) absorption model, (2) protection model, (3) symbiotic model. Considering the factors of strategy and organization at the same time, choosing an appropriate integration mode and method for a specific M&A undoubtedly provides us with an analysis method for integration decision-making, but the improvement of its theoretical basis and analysis method still needs a lot of research work.

Douma et al. (2000) discussed the dynamic process of building a strategic alliance with matching as the core concept in the paper Strategic Alliances: Managing the Dynamics of Fit, arguing that the fit between the two sides of the alliance is the premise that determines whether an alliance can be successful or not. The success of an alliance is affected by five levels of fit, namely strategic fit, organizational fit, cultural fit, human fit, and operational fit. Based on emphasizing that the inadequacy of any match may lead to the alliance's failure, the authors adopted a case study method, focusing on the drivers of the strategic and organizational fit and the ability to manage the dynamics of a fit. The authors discussed the evaluation methods of strategic fit and organizational fit respectively and discussed issues such as the degree offit required for a successful alliance. The conclusion includes: (1) a good fit is the key to a successful alliance, and through effective management, an alliance with a limited fit or mixed fit can be transformed into a good match, thus bringing the success of the alliance; (2) the ability of both sides of the alliance to manage the match over time is a necessary condition to ensure the long-term success of the alliance. The goal of this paper is to provide an effective guiding framework for building successful alliances, and it also provides a good idea for studying matching problems, but all the expositions in the paper are limited to qualitative descriptions, as the authors said that the testing of all these theoretical hypotheses would be the direction of further research.

6.2.1.5 Resource Fit

The concept of resource fit was first proposed by Itami Keiyuki (1987). It mainly refers to matching the company's corporate strategy and internal resources. This fit relationship can be judged from three aspects: whether the company has enough resources to realize the strategy, whether the company's existing strategy can make full use of resources, and whether the company is effectively accumulating resources for the future. Zhang Jinxin (2004) in the article Resource Matching: Strategic Analysis of Matching of M&A Parties, based on identifying the strategic resources of both parties, judges the potential synergy and transfer efficiency of resources and believes that the efficiency of resource transfer is considered to be a key influencing factor in the transformation of potential synergies into expected synergies, the potential synergy and transfer efficiency of strategic resources is the key to matching the two parties in M&A, and it is concluded that the potential synergy of strategic resources determines the potential of synergy, and the transfer efficiency of strategic resources determines the difficulty of realizing potential synergy.

6.2.2 A Summary of Research on M&A Fit Theory

Looking at the existing research on M&A fit at home and abroad, researchers have carried out a lot of theoretical research and empirical tests on strategic fit and organizational fit. They have promoted the development of the M&A fit theory. The importance of strategic fit and organizational fit has been recognized by scholars. However, the existing research is still unable to provide a practical and effective M&A fit theory and analysis method that can guide the practice of M&A, mainly due to the following deficiencies:

First, the understanding and management of strategic fit and organizational fit need to be strengthened. As far as the value creation of M&A is concerned, the most important flaw in the study of strategic performance relationships is that it does not consider the difficulty of strategy execution, that is, it equates or confuses strategic fit and management "dependency". These researchers generally assume that strategic fit determines the range of value creation that can be achieved through "dependency" management, and that this range is the primary objective pursued by M&A. As Haspeslagh and Jemison (1987) pointed out, the strategic fit is only an ex-ante indicator of potential sources of value creation, and it does not determine the nature, scope, and possibility of actual value creation. These researchers overemphasize strategic tasks while often ignoring practical barriers to value creation, such as frictions and conflicts of interpersonal, inter-organizational, and intercultural, even in cases where it is intended to develop strategically matched value creation potential through "dependency" management, the actual results of M&A can also vary widely.

Second, the research methods and means need to be improved. Most of the previous researches have gradually confirmed the factors affecting matching through empirical research or case analysis. This method is valuable for understanding the influence of individual factors, but it is insufficient for a comprehensive understanding of the influencing factors of M&A fit. The systematic analysis of the matching problem should start from the basic elements of the enterprise.

Third, the research perspective needs to be changed. In the past, the perspective of strategic fit analysis was centered on the characteristics of the enterprise, rather than the starting point of the analysis based on the resources of the enterprise. From the perspective of resources, both the same and different resources may produce synergy, and in some cases, the complementary synergy of different resources may contribute more to M&A performance, but these differences cannot be reflected in the overall characteristics of the enterprise. Therefore, the matching analysis based on the overall characteristics of enterprises may blur the differences between enterprises and fail to grasp the most important factors affecting M&A performance. Compared with the theory of strategic fit, the analysis of M&A fit based on efficiency and scale is also particularly important. Shi Hailiu et al. (2015) pointed out that M&A matching is more in line with the rational decision-making of enterprises in terms of efficiency and scale. The reason is that improving efficiency and pursuing economies of scale are important motivations for M&A. Compared with the potential value of enterprises, structural compatibility, and resource complementarity, companies involved in M&A

are more concerned about whether the efficiency is damaged after M&A, and whether the scale is too large.

Fourth, the previous research only paid attention to the internal factors of enterprises and did not fully consider the external factors. Enterprise resource theory believes that competitive advantage depends not only on the endowment of internal resources of the enterprise, but also on environmental factors such as competitors, suppliers, and customers. It is necessary to internalize the relationship between these external factors and the enterprise, as an important type of enterprise information resource, relationship capital. Fit is not only a problem between two enterprises but a matching that considers internal and external factors of the enterprise. Matching should be studied from the point of view of establishing competitive advantage, not in terms of M&A themselves.

Fifth, the influence of intangible assets doesn't get enough attention, especially the influence of factors such as human capital, organizational capital, and relational capital is often neglected. This may be the reason why those scholars were unable to find significant differences between related and unrelated diversification strategies. In the case of M&A, if scholars ignore the impact of intangible assets in empirical research, the performance of M&A is difficult to distinguish from the perspective of relevance.

6.3 Determination of M&A Operation Fit Degree

As mentioned in the first section of this chapter, the merger fit in the basic theory of M&A is divided into two stages based on due diligence. In the process of selecting target companies, it is necessary to evaluate the matching degree of M&A in each stage. The first stage of operation matching is mainly from the analysis of organizational fit and strategic fit, which is the content of the traditional M&A fit analysis framework. The second stage is resource fit, which is to analyze the scale economy, scope economy, and network economy benefits brought by capability fit and asset fit according to the possible relationship between the resources of both parties and their impact on value creation.

6.3.1 M&A Fit Evaluation Criteria

6.3.1.1 The Basic Idea of M&A Fit Degree Evaluation

In the Sect. 6.1, we mentioned that the M&A fit is based on the determination of the M&A direction. Therefore, when evaluating the M&A fit degree, determining the M&A direction also needs to be the starting point. Then, according to the logical relationship between M&A direction and M&A fit, combined with the definition of M&A fit, we determine the basic idea of M&A fit degree evaluation.

First, analyze the acquirer's resources, understand the shortage of resources, clarify the resource needs of the acquiring enterprise, and determine the direction of M&A. When an acquiring enterprise conducts its resource analysis, based on the value chain of the enterprise, according to the functional activities of R&D, procurement, manufacturing, marketing, and service, the existing people, finances, materials, information, and capabilities of the enterprise can be analyzed from the aspects of the industry, region, scale and profitability of the enterprise. Then compare with the resources that the enterprise needs to have to realize its future strategy, to determine the resource gap, so the acquiring company will eventually get a list of its own resource needs and can also get the attributes of these demand resources in terms of industry, region, scale, profitability, etc., that is, the direction of M&A.

Second, according to the direction of M&A, select indicators to measure the fit degree of M&A from the aspects of the industry, region, scale, and profitability.

Third, collect, classify, and organize the information of potential target enterprises, and distinguish the data for qualitative and quantitative analysis. The process of collecting information on target enterprises should be based on the scope delineated by the direction of M&A, which can save costs, shorten time, and improve efficiency.

Fourth, calculate the gap between the acquisition direction of the acquirer and the potential target enterprises in terms of industry, region, scale, and profitability.

Fifth, calculate the comprehensive index gap between the M&A direction and potential target enterprises, that is, the comprehensive M&A fit degree.

Sixth, the calculated comprehensive M&A fit results are sorted from high to low, and combined with other basic information of potential target enterprises, such as the enterprise's development strategy, corporate culture, etc., to conduct a comprehensive evaluation, and filter to obtain the target enterprise group.

Correspondingly, the evaluation steps of the M&A fit degree are shown in Fig. 6.2.

6.3.1.2 The Principle of Selecting Indicators for the Evaluation of M&A Fit Degree

The selection of M&A fit degree indicators should reflect the principles of comprehensiveness, importance, and relevance. Various forms of external information reflect the needs of the acquirer, ranging from product (service) quality, cost, corporate image, and technical level to corporate human resources, marketing, internal management, and the connection with the outside world. The selection of indicators should be aimed at the direction of M&A of the acquiring enterprise, the needs of the acquiring enterprise should be considered as comprehensively as possible, the principle of importance should be emphasized, and the indicators that best reflect whether the two parties to the M&A are matched should be selected. The selection of indicators should measure the matching degree of M&A from different angles and overcome the limitation of measuring from a single angle, to reflect the deep connotation of the matching degree of M&A, especially the determinants of the matching degree of M&A.

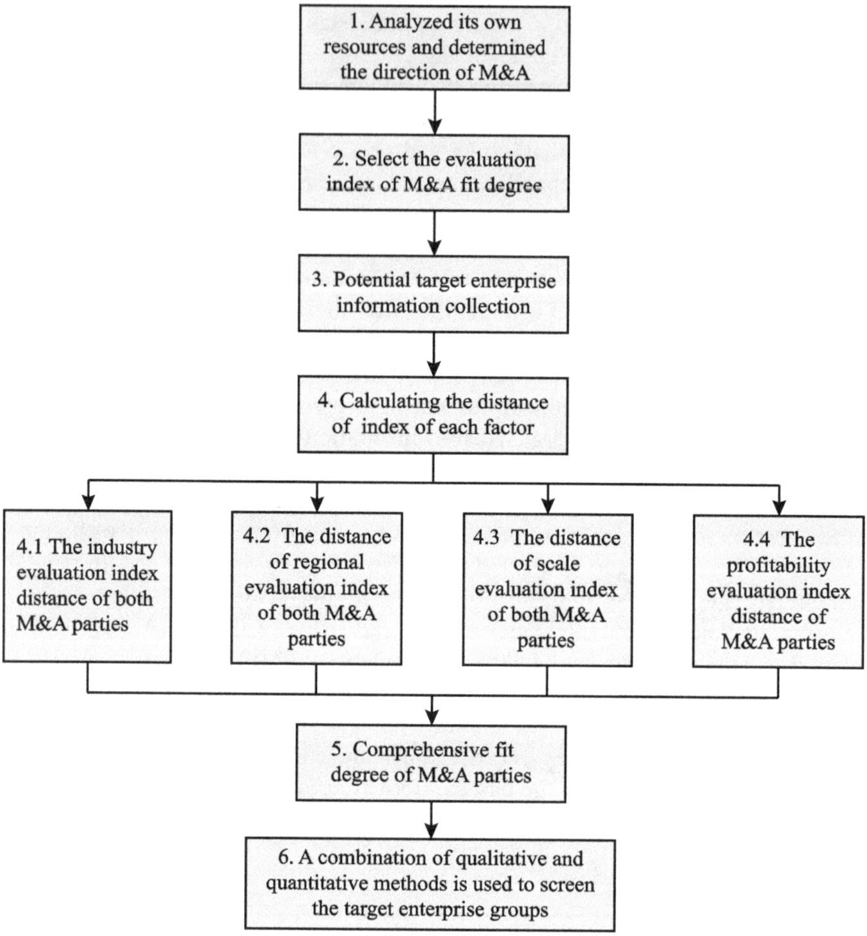

Fig. 6.2 Evaluation steps of M&A fit degree

6.3.1.3 Collection and Screening of Evaluation Data

As the starting point of M&A activities, information collected in the early stage of M&A plays a vital role in ensuring the success of M&A. In M&A activities, a comprehensive collection of M&A information from all aspects will help select target enterprises.

(1) Ways to collect information

M&A fit degree evaluation data mainly refers to information obtained from public and private data sources, including original data, that is, data obtained directly from the target enterprise, and secondary data, obtained from other channels than the target enterprise.

Clemente and Greenspan (2003) proposed five ways of collecting information and data: (1) collecting industry information, which can be obtained from business journals, professional news reports, and industry associations; (2) communicating with key outsiders, which can be a discussion with colleagues in the company and interviews with authoritative observers in the industry; (3) using the "circular chain" method to interview other people, you can sell products to existing customers and ask them what they know may become new customers of the company; (4) examine government documents and learn about the company's financial and operating conditions through official materials; (5) obtain information directly from the target enterprise, and get the latest developments of the target company from some of the materials provided by the target enterprise to the public about the basic situation of the enterprise.

(2) The content of the information collected

After determining the M&A fit degree evaluation criteria, the acquiring enterprise can confirm the information collection content according to the information requirements of the evaluation criteria, mainly including the number, the industry, region, scale, financial status, and the development strategy of potential target enterprises. Since it is the stage of preliminary screening of target companies, the information collected does not need to be too in-depth. Otherwise, it may pay a higher cost of information collection, and further information can be collected after confirming the enterprises that need due diligence.

(3) Screening of evaluation data

There are two main forms of data: one is objective data, such as special surveys and statistics conducted by internal financial, accounting departments, and external independent agencies; the other is subjective evaluation data, which is mainly based on the subjective judgment of the company's management, including the senior management of the acquirer. In the evaluation process, the objective evaluation data should be selected as much as possible, and the proportion of subjective evaluation data should be reduced as much as possible.

6.3.2 The Evaluation Index of M&A Fit Degree

Strategy determination is an important part of strategic management, mainly through the analysis of the enterprise's external environment and its strength to determine the enterprise's development goals and the resources needed to achieve these goals. The external environment includes the general environment and the industry environment, while the enterprise's strength mainly refers to the enterprise's resources. Mergers and acquisitions are important means for enterprises to realize their development strategies. During the implementation process of M&A, it is necessary to constantly analyze the external environment and the strengths of the enterprise, especially when looking for target enterprises that match its development strategies. The acquiring enterprise is even more necessary to consider its strength to determine whether it has sufficient capacity to absorb, digest, and transfer the resources of the target enterprise. Usually, the analysis of the enterprise's resource status focuses on four aspects: industry, region, scale, and financial status, and the result of the company's resource analysis is the direction of the enterprise's M&A, that is, the scope of the target enterprise's choice. Then, we should also consider these four aspects when selecting the evaluation indicators of M&Amatching degree.

6.3.2.1 Industry Factors

Salte and Weinhold (1979) advises on the choice of target enterprises in one of the three models of the enterprise's diversification strategy. They suggested that acquirers should limit their selection of target enterprises to two simple principles:

(1) enhanced relevance, that is, acquiring more of the acquirer's existing resources;
(2) complementary relevance, that is, to obtain resources that can be effectively combined with the acquirer's resources. Rumelt (1974, 1977) defined the relevance of two firms in three dimensions: (1) using similar channels and serving similar markets; (2) using similar production techniques; (3) using similar scientific research. Correspondingly, scholars who support the M&A relevance hypothesis suggest that acquirers should look for relevant target enterprises.

The M&A correlation is first reflected in the correlation between the acquirer and the target party's industry. M&A can be divided into horizontal M&A, vertical M&A, and hybrid M&A according to the industry relationship between the two parties. If the merger is to expand market share, reduce product costs by forming economies of scale, and ultimately achieve monopoly profits, it needs to be achieved through horizontal M&A, then the business of the potential target enterprise must be the same or closely related to the business of the acquiring enterprise. If the merger is to reduce transaction costs, optimize resource allocation, and achieve the strategic goal of vertical integration, it needs to be achieved through vertical M&A. The potential target companies are generally suppliers of raw materials or buyers of finished products, and the businesses of both parties must be irrelevant. If M&A are to diversify business risks and optimize investment portfolios, which can be achieved through hybrid M&A, so the business scope of the potential target enterprise and the business scope of the acquiring enterprise may or may not be related. Therefore, after the acquirer has clarified its development strategy, it can choose whether it is related to its industry for M&A. Then, the industry correlation index is a standard to measure whether the two parties of the M&A are matched.

The business scope of an enterprise cannot be limited to only one industry. Especially for a diversified enterprise, it is sometimes difficult to judge its main business. If it is determined by the industry classification or main business used in the enterprise registration, then it cannot truly reflect the current state of the enterprise. Therefore, we use the number of industries included in the business scope of the enterprise as an indicator for judging the industry correlation between the two parties. The more industries the two parties share in their business scope, the higher the industry relevance of the two enterprises. At present, the National Economic Industry Classification and Code published by the National Bureau of Statistics of China has divided all industries into categories, major categories, types, and subcategories, and unified the coding, so we can easily understand the number of industries included in the scope of business.

6.3.2.2 Regional Factors

A region is a geographic location where a business is located. When the acquirer chooses the target enterprise, it needs to consider the influence of the geographical location of both parties on the M&A performance. Because the natural environment, economic development level, laws, regulations, policies, public quality, and moral cultivation of a region have a great impact on the target market, organizational structure, and cultural atmosphere of the enterprise. If the two parties to the M&A have conflicting corporate cultures, then it will inevitably increase the cost of post-merger integration, and even lead to the final failure of the merger. In addition, if the main purpose of the acquisition by the acquirer is to save costs, then selecting the target enterprise in the same geographical area can reduce the transportation cost of materials or products, thereby saving transaction costs. Therefore, choosing a target enterprise that is geographically close to the acquirer will help improve the M&A performance and achieve the enterprise's M&A goals. Therefore, the similarity of the regions where the acquirer and the target are located is a criterion for measuring whether the two parties are matched.

The geographical location of the enterprise can be determined according to the place of registration or business. At the same time, the administrative division table of the People's Republic of China delineates the regions of the territory of China, and each region has a code. Therefore, We can use the region code as an indicator of the similarity of the regions in which the two parties to the merger are located. In cross-border M&A, the economic zone and continent where the target enterprise is located can be indicators to measure regional factors. The specific regional advantage of the acquirer's country—host country is an important factor affecting the quantity and quality of cross-border M&A (Buckley et al., 2012). Wu Xianming and Xie Weiyun (2016) further studied the influence of the degree of matching between the specific advantages of the acquirer and the specific advantages of the host country on M&A and found that the degree of fit was significantly positively correlated with the entry of M&A into the host country, and formal institutional constraints weakened a positive relationship between the degree of fit and M&A. The institutional environment of different countries has played a moderating role in the impact offit degrees on M&A.

6.3.2.3 Scale Factor

Although with the emergence and rise of high-risk, high-interest rate bonds and leveraged buyouts, corporate M&A are not limited to " big fish eat small fish", and many "small fish eat big fish", but the scale of target enterprises is still an important factor in determining whether a merger can proceed. Some scholars (Park, 2002; Robins & Wiersema, 1995; Shelton, 1988) believe that there is a positive correlation between the size of the enterprise and the performance of M&A, the larger the target enterprise, the more assets it provides to the acquirer, and the greater the value created based on this. However, the theory of economies of scale also tells us that although acquiring enterprises can expand their scale and obtain economies of scale through M&A. But if the size of the enterprise is too large, it will be counterproductive and lead to diseconomies of scale. Chatterjee (1986) found in the study of the relationship between M&A correlation and performance that the reason for the insignificant M&A benefits may be that the size of the acquirer is too large relative to the target, and if the target is too large relative to the acquirer, it may also cause unfavorable integration after the M&A and ultimately leads to the failure of the merger. Therefore, only when the scales of both parties to the M&A are matched, the acquirer will have sufficient capacity to absorb, digest, and transfer the resources of the target party, and the target party will also have sufficient resources to meet the needs of the acquirer. Therefore, in the process of selecting the target enterprise, it must consider the degree of matching of the scales ofthe enterprises ofthe two parties to the merger.

At present, many indicators can be used to measure the scale of enterprises. For enterprises that operate different types of businesses, the indicators are different. For example, for a trading enterprise, its size defined by sales volume can better reflect the true value of the enterprise than the usual amount of assets. In practice, payment costs (the acquisition price that the acquirer is willing and able to bear), market share, and the number of employees are often used as indicators to measure the scale of the enterprise, and listed companies often use the total share capital as the measurement standard.

6.3.2.4 Profitability Factor

Profitability is crucial to the survival and development of an enterprise, and its level will have a greater impact not only on the current period but also on future periods. Profit is not only the starting point and destination of an enterprise, but also the ultimate manifestation of core competence. The stronger the profitability of the enterprise, the higher the return ability to shareholders, the greater the enterprise value, the more cash flow it brings, and the stronger the solvency and financing ability of the enterprise. Therefore, profitability indicators are the primary indicators for evaluating financial conditions. At present, many companies still hope to improve their financial status, profitability, and operational efficiency through M&A. On the one hand, a target enterprise with good profitability can improve the acquirer's asset income level after the acquisition, directly bring a large amount of cash flow to the acquirer, and on the other hand, provide the acquirer with a good financing channel. Therefore, profitability is always an important factor in the process of evaluating itself and potential target enterprises. Many indicators reflect an enterprise's profitability, mainly divided into absolute numbers and relative ratios. Absolute numbers include sales revenue, profit from sales, total profit, net profit, and other indicators. The larger the value of these indicators, the better the profitability of the enterprise, But it is more practical to measure it in combination with the scale of the enterprise. When the number of selected indicators is not large, the selection of relative ratio indicators such as return on equity (ROE) can better illustrate the profitability of enterprises.

6.3.3 *The Evaluation Model of M&A Fit Degree*

6.3.3.1 M&A Fit Evaluation Tool

The quantification of the M&A fit degree is finally realized by the distance function. If the value calculated by the acquirer and the target party according to the distance function is larger, it means that the similarity between them is smaller (the gap is larger), conversely, the similarity is larger. Suppose d is a distance function, the value range is between [0, 1], 0 means that the two enterprises are completely matched, 1 means that the two enterprises are completely mismatched, and other values are in the middle. When the distance is closer to 1, it indicates that the fit degree is lower, and conversely, the distance is closer to 0, which indicates the matching degree is higher. The distance function corresponds to the similarity function, which can be represented by $1 - d(*)$, or $\frac{1}{1+d(*)}$.

Due to the different nature of the indicators for measuring the fit degree of M&A, the representation of the distance function is also different. The following will evaluate the fit degree according to different indicators.

6.3.3.2 Industry Factor Fit Evaluation

To measure the industry correlation between the two parties to the M&A, we use the number of industries included in the enterprise's business scope. Here, we use the Jaccard similarity function[1] to quantify whether there is an industry correlation between the two parties to the M&A.

Assuming that there are acquisition enterprise A and target enterprise T, enterprise A's business scope set is $X = (x_1, x_2, \ldots, x_n)$, enterprise T's business scope set is $Y = (y_1, y_2, \ldots, y_n)$, which x_i, y_i is the industry classification confirmed according to the

[1] The Jaccard similarity function is a traditional and convenient function to measure the degree of similarity of sets. The principle is that if there is a similarity between sets, then there will be an intersection between two sets.

National Economic Industry Classification and Code table, the industry classification should be as detailed as possible, and the elements in set X and set Y are independent of each other. According to the Jaccard similarity function, then:

$$sim(X, Y) = \frac{|X \cap Y|}{|X \cup Y|}$$

Then, the distance function of X and Y is

$$d_1(X, Y) = 1 - sim(X, Y) = 1 - \frac{|X \cap Y|}{|X \cup Y|}$$

When acquiring enterprise A and target enterprise T are more similar in industry, the industry correlation between the two enterprises is greater, and the distance function is smaller. If the business scope of the two enterprises is the same, then the distance function is 0.

Example 1: assuming that the acquiring enterprise A according to the National Economic Industry Classification and Code table divides its business operations into $X = (C_{2710}, C_{2730})$, the target enterprise T_1's business operations are classified as $Y_1 = (C_{2710}, C_{2720}, C_{2730})$, the target enterprise T_2's business operations are classified as $Y_2 = (C_{6470}, C_{6171})$, the target enterprise T_3's business operations are classified as $Y_3 = (C_{1499}, C_{2730}, A_{0110})$, the distance between the acquiring enterprise A and the three target enterprises is calculated as:

$$d_1(X, Y_1) = 1 - sim(X, Y_1) = 1 - \frac{|X \cap Y_1|}{|X \cup Y_1|} = \frac{1}{3}$$

$$d_2(X, Y_2) = 1 - sim(X, Y_2) = 1 - \frac{|X \cap Y_2|}{|X \cup Y_2|} = 1$$

$$d_3(X, Y_3) = 1 - sim(X, Y_3) = 1 - \frac{|X \cap Y_3|}{|X \cup Y_3|} = \frac{3}{4}$$

Then $d_1(X, Y_1) < d_3(X, Y_3) < d_2(X, Y_2)$, so the target enterprise T_1 and the acquiring enterprise A have the closest industrial distance.

From the actual situation, both the acquiring enterprise A and the target enterprise T_1 belong to the pharmaceutical manufacturing industry, and the business scope of T_1 is slightly wider than that of A, so the industries in which the two enterprise are located are highly related. If acquisition enterprise A is too competitive in the industry, it hopes to expand market share and improve sales profits through M&A, undoubtedly, T_1 is the best choice. The target enterprise T_2 belongs to the retail and wholesale industries of pharmaceuticals, which is completely different from the industry in which the acquiring enterprise A is located, so the industries in which the two enterprises are located are not related. If the acquiring enterprise A hopes to build its marketing network through M&A to improve the profitability of the circulation link, to avoid the impact of the decline in sales efficiency caused by the reform of the national pharmaceutical circulation system, then the target enterprise T_2 should be the best choice. The target enterprise T_3 has a wide range of businesses, including the health food processing industry, the Chinese herbal medicine processing industry, and the Chinese herbal medicine planting industry. If acquiring enterprise A wants to diversify its business risks through M&A, the target enterprise T_3 is also a suitable choice. Therefore, in the process of selecting a target enterprise, it is not only necessary to determine which enterprise is suitable for M&A from the calculation results of the distance function but also needs to be determined based on the strategic needs of the acquiring enterprise.

6.3.3.3 Regional Factor Fit Evaluation

We use the region code as the indicator for judging the regional correlation between the two sides of the M&A. However, this indicator cannot be used to determine whether there is an equal or unequal precise relationship between the two parties to the M&A on this indicator through conventional calculation methods, but we still need to determine which target enterprise the acquirer has a closer relationship with in terms of region. Therefore, the measurement method of the semantic distance of Web structure data is borrowed here, and the region code is used as a semantic structure. Then the distance function is established through the semantic path so that the region factors can be effectively quantified.

(1) The Concept of a relational tree

There are several semantic structures in Web structure data, and the relational tree is one of them.

Definition 1 (relational tree): a relational tree is a directed rooted tree $G = \langle V, E, W, r \rangle$, in which $V \neq \phi$ is the set of items, which r is the root of the tree, also denoted as *root* (G). $E \subset \{r\} \cup V \times V$ is the set of directed edges, and W is the function of $E(G)$ to the set of positive real numbers, called the weight function. Only the in-degree of r in G of the node is 0, and the in-degree of the rest of the nodes is 1.

As a weight function, W represents the relative importance of each region, and the weight function can be established through some attributes, such as the transportation cost from the acquired enterprise to the target enterprise. Of course, the weight function can also be a constant, that is, each region is equally important to the acquiring business.

According to the definition of the relational tree, combined with China's administrative area code, we have established the region code tree shown in Fig. 6.3.

From Fig. 6.3, the region code tree can be divided into multiple levels according to the degree of refinement of the area code, and the layers are refined step by step. Each area is a node of the tree. The target enterprise can confirm the location in the region code tree according to the area to which it belongs.

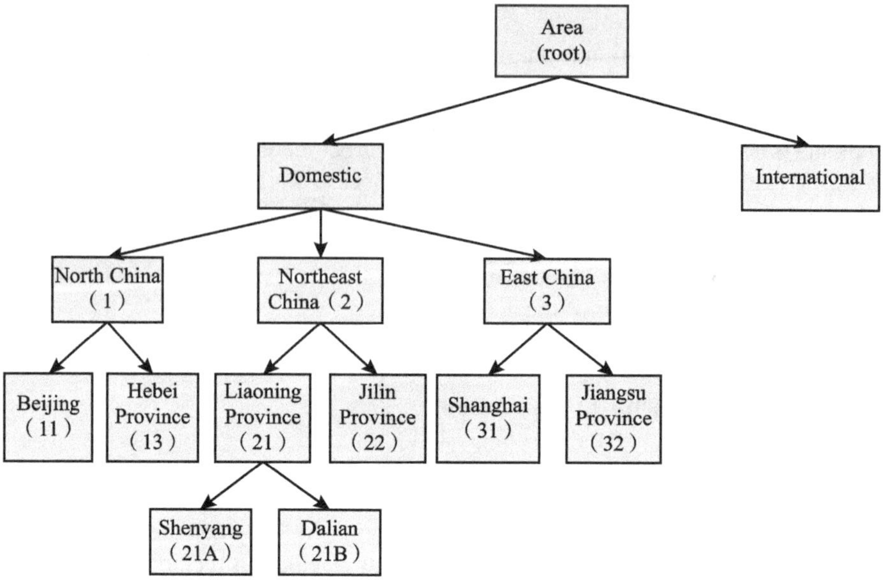

Fig. 6.3 Region code tree

(2) Semantic path

Here, the path in the relational tree is recorded as a sequence of edges.

Definition 2 (path): Suppose $G = \langle V, E, W, r\rangle$ is a relational tree, and $x_0, x_1, \ldots, x_n \in V$, $n \geq 0$ if there is an item with a directed edge sequence $P = (e_1, e_2, \ldots, e_n)$ that satisfies any edge that $e_i \in E(1 \leq i \leq n)$ is x_{i-1} to x_i, then it is called P, which is a path from x_0 to x_n. Symbolically, $W(P)$ represents the sum of the weights of all edges in P. If there is no path between two items, define an empty path, denoted by $\perp$, $W(\perp) = 0$.

Definition 3 (semantic path): There is a relational tree $G = \langle V, E, W, r\rangle$, and a directed path from r to any node $v \in V$ is a semantic path of v, and v has one and only one semantic path, denoted as $\phi(v)$.

Definition 4 (intersection of semantic paths): Assuming that there is a semantic path $P = (e_1, e_2, \ldots, e_n)$ and $Q = (e'_1, e'_2, \ldots, e'_n)$ on the relational tree G, it may be assumed $n \geq m \geq 0$, that the intersection of P and Q is a semantic path, denoted as $P \cap Q$. The specific definition is: if there is a maximum $k \geq 1$ satisfy $e_i = e'_i$, $1 \leq i \leq k, k \leq m$, and $e_{k+1} \neq e'_{k+1}$, then $P \cap Q = (e'_1, e'_2, \ldots, e'_k)$; otherwise $P \cap Q = \perp$.

Example 2: assuming that the acquisition enterprise A is registered in Shenyang, Liaoning Province, the target company T_1 is registered in Dalian, Liaoning Province, and the target enterprise T_1 is registered in Shanghai. The semantic path of the region where an enterprise is in:

- P_1 = (⟨Industry, Domestic⟩, ⟨Domestic, Northeast china, ⟨Northeast china, Liaoning province⟩, ⟨Liaoning province, shenyang⟫), $W(P_1) = 4$
- P_2 = (⟨Industry, Domestic⟩, ⟨ Domestic, Northeast China⟩, ⟨Northeast china, Liaoning province⟩, ⟨Liaoning province, Dalian⟩), $W(P_2) = 4$;
- P_3 = (⟨Industry, Domestic⟩, ⟨Domestic, East China⟩, ⟨East China, shanghai⟩), $W(P_3) = 3$;
- P_4 = (⟨ Industry, Domestic⟩, ⟨Domestic, Northeast China⟩, ⟨Northeast china, Liaoning province⟩), $W(P_4) = 3$
- P_5 = (⟨Industry, Domestic⟫), $W(P_5) = 1$;

$$P_1 \cap P_2 = P_4; P_1 \cap P_3 = P_5$$

The set of semantic paths for each node is:

$$\phi(\text{shenyang}) = \{\text{P}_1\}; \phi(\text{Dalian}) = \{\text{P}_2\}; \phi(\text{shanghai}) = \{\text{p}_3\}.$$

(3) Distance function

The following describes the distance between two regions based on the semantic path, and the GCSM similarity function will be borrowed here.[2]

There is a relational tree G = ⟨V, E, W, r⟩, there are nodes $u, v \in V \cup \{r\}$, and the distance $d2$ between u and v on G is defined as:

$$d_2(u, v) = \begin{cases} 1 - \text{Max}\left\{\frac{2\times W(P\cap Q)}{W(P)+W(Q)} | P \in \phi(u),\ Q \in \phi(v)\right\} & u \neq v \\ 0 & u = v \end{cases}$$

Example 3: following Example 2, calculates the distance between the acquisition enterprise A and the target enterprise T_1 and T_2 as:

$$d_1(\text{Shenyang, Dalian}) = 1 - \frac{2 \times W(P_1 \cap P_2)}{W(P_1) + W(P_2)} = 1 - \frac{2 \times 3}{4 + 4} = \frac{1}{4}$$

$$d_2(\text{Shenyang, Shanghai}) = 1 - \frac{2 \times W(P_1 \cap P_3)}{W(P_1) + W(P_3)} = 1 - \frac{2 \times 1}{4 + 3} = \frac{5}{7}$$

[2] The GCSM similarity function is a function proposed by Prasanna Ganesan et al. based on the traditional similarity function to measure the degree of similarity between items. This function adopts a hierarchical data structure in its derivation, that is, a relational tree, and confirms the degree of similarity of the two nodes by calculating the maximum depth between two nodes in the tree (depth refers to the number of stages from the root to the node, and the maximum depth refers to the maximum number of stages shared by two nodes). The final derivation of the GCSM function results in a spatial similarity function, which is actually an extension of the cosine similarity function. Based on the GCSM similarity function constructed by Prasanna Ganesan et al., Ruan Beijun introduced the semantic path concept into the similarity measurement, and modified the GCSM function. The modified similarity function was not measured from the spatial perspective, therefore, it is closer to the situation in this book, so the actual distance function used in this book is the similarity function that Ruan Beijun re-modified.

Comparing the d_1 and d_2, we can see that the acquiring enterprise A has a higher geographical similarity with the target enterprise T_1. From qualitative analysis, whether the acquiring enterprise A wants to expand the enterprise's scale and achieve diversified development, or save transaction costs and improve operational efficiency, the target enterprise T_1 in Dalian may have greater regional similarity than the target enterprise T_2 in Shanghai. Compared with Shanghai, Shenyang and Dalian are relatively similar in terms of cultural environment, economic environment, local regulations, and policies due to their geographical proximity, which may be beneficial to reducing the difficulty of integration after M&A. At the same time, for acquiring enterprise A's strategy of achieving vertical integration, the proximity of the two regions will also save the transportation cost of raw materials and products, shorten the transportation time, and improve the operating efficiency.

6.3.3.4 Fit Evaluation of Size Factor and Profitability Factor

We use the enterprise's total assets (TA) and ROE as indicators of the fit between the target enterprise and the acquirer in terms of size and profitability respectively. When calculating the distance between the target enterprise and the acquirer, this book adopts the relative value, and to make the value range of the distance function in [0,1], both M&A parties as a whole are used as the benchmark.

Suppose the total assets of the acquiring enterprise A are TA and the total assets of the target enterprise T are TA', then the distance between the total assets of the M&Aparties is:

$$d_3(TA, TA') = \frac{|TA - TA'|}{TA + TA'}$$

Suppose the ROE of the acquiring enterprise A is ROE and the ROE of the target enterprise T is ROE', then the distance between the ROE of the M&A parties is:

$$d_4(ROE, ROE') = \frac{|ROE - ROE'|}{ROE + ROE'}$$

Example 4: assume that before the M&A, the total assets TA of the acquiring enterprise A are RMB2,114.8639 million, the ROE is 4.62%; the total assets TA_1' of the target enterprise T_1 are RMB2,585.3627 million, the ROE_1' is 0.33%; the total assets TA_2' of the target enterprise T_2 are RMB821.4802 million, and the ROE_2' is 5.06%. So the distance between the two parties in terms of size and profitability is calculated separately as:

$$d_3(TA, TA') = \frac{|TA - TA'|}{TA + TA'} = \frac{|2,114.8639 - 2,585.3627|}{2,114.8639 + 2,585.3627} = 0.10$$

$$d_3(TA, TA'_2) = \frac{|TA - TA'_2|}{TA + TA'_2} = \frac{|2,114.8639 - 821.4802|}{2,114.8639 + 821.4802} = 0.44$$

$$d_4(ROE, ROE'_1) = \frac{|ROE - ROE'_1|}{ROE + ROE'_1} = \frac{|4.62\% - 0.33\%|}{4.62\% + 0.33\%} = 0.87$$

$$d_4(ROE, ROE'_2) = \frac{|ROE - ROE'_2|}{ROE + ROE'_2} = \frac{|4.62\% - 5.06\%|}{4.62\% + 5.06\%} = 0.05$$

Comparing these results, the size of the target enterprise T_1 is close to that of the acquiring enterprise, while the profitability of the target enterprise T_2 is more comparable to that of the acquiring enterprise. Acquiring enterprises need to identify the factors that the enterprise is concerned about according to their strategic objectives, and then weigh which target enterprise is a better choice. For example, if the acquiring enterprise only wants to expand the enterprise's size and increase its market share, and does not pay much attention to the profitability of the target enterprise, the acquiring enterprise may prefer the target enterprise T_1. If the target enterprise T_2 is a listed company and the acquirer takes listing as its development goal, then maybe a better shell resource.

6.3.3.5 A Comprehensive Evaluation Model of M&A Fit Degree

In the process of selecting target enterprises, if the acquiring enterprise only measures the fit of each factor that affects the M&A separately, the result of the selection may be one-sided. Therefore, the acquiring enterprise needs to comprehensively evaluate the fit degree of both parties of M&A. Before comprehensive evaluation, it is necessary to calculate the fit degree of each factor, and then confirm the weight according to the importance of each factor to the acquiring enterprise, and finally carry out the comprehensive calculation.

Suppose acquiring enterprise A and target enterprise T, their distances in industry, region, scale, and profitability are respectively d_1, d_2, d_3, d_4, and the weights of each factor are $\alpha_1, \alpha_2, \alpha_3, \alpha_4$, $0 \leq \alpha_1, \alpha_2, \alpha_3, \alpha_4 \leq 1$ and $\alpha_1 + \alpha_2 + \alpha_3 + \alpha_4 = 1$ then the comprehensive distance function of the M&Aparties is:

$$d(A, T) = a_1 d_1 + \alpha_2 d_2 + \alpha_3 d_3 + \alpha_4 d_4$$

According to the definition, we can see that the value range of d is still [0, 1], that is, when $d = 1$, the gap between the two parties of M&A is the largest, and on the contrary, when $d = 0$, there is no distance between the two parties of M&A at all. When confirming the weights, the acquiring enterprise can decide according to its development strategy. For example, if the enterprise's M&A objective is to expand the market, it can assign a higher weight to the regional factor. If the enterprise's M&A objective is to expand its scale, it can assign a higher weight to the scale factor. If the enterprise's M&A objective is to improve its financial situation and increase its profitability, it can assign a higher weight to the profitability factor. Of course, if each factor is equally important to the acquiring enterprise, then the weight can be assigned a value of 1.

As with the previous conclusions, what is provided here is only an evaluation tool based on the distance for fit, and the closer distance does not mean a better fit between the two parties. Fit or not depends on the strategic needs of the acquirer.

6.4 Determination of M&A Resource Fit

6.4.1 Resource Fit Analysis Framework

6.4.1.1 General Framework of M&A Fit Analysis

Figure 6.4 shows the value analysis framework of enterprise M&A fit with resource fit as the core.

In Fig. 6.4, I_A and I_T represent the intangible resources of the acquirer and the target respectively, and T_A and T_T represent the tangible resources of the acquirer and the target, respectively. It is the interaction of resources between the two parties (enhancement, conflict, complementarity, substitution) that drives the fit between the two parties in M&A, which leads to whether the post-merger enterprise system can reach "harmony". The whole framework is divided into three levels. Firstly, the dotted box on the left represents the resource fit between the two parties, including capability

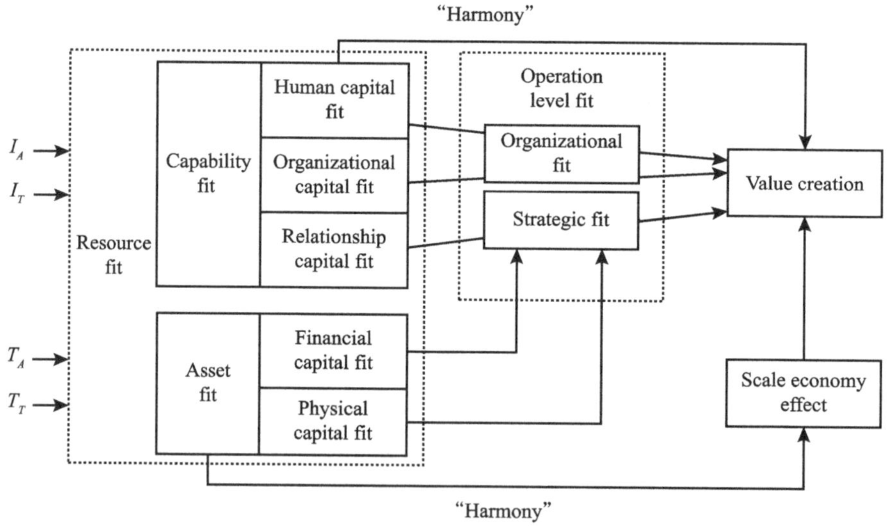

Fig. 6.4 Value analysis framework of enterprise M&A fit

fit and asset fit. Capability fit is driven by intellectual capital and its interrelationships, including human capital fit, organizational capital fit, and relationship capital fit, which are all company's intangible resource fits. Asset fit includes financial resource fit and physical capital fit, which are both tangible resource fits. There is also an interactive relationship between capability fit and asset fit. Secondly, the dotted box in the middle of the graph is the fit at the operational level, including the strategic fit and the organizational fit between the two parties. Operational level fit is driven by resource fit, organizational fit depends on the fit of human capital and organizational capital, and strategic fit is driven by the fit of relational capital. The fit of financial capital and physical capital also affects the strategic fit and organizational fit of both parties. Thirdly, the right side of the figure represents the effect of fit. Capability fit is the main source of value creation in M&A. Strategic fit implies that M&A have the potential to create value and organizational fit implies the difficulty in achieving value creation. Asset fit leads directly to economies of scale, which together with economies of scope and network economies, constitute the value creation of M&A. The two dimensions of operational level fit analysis are exactly the main contents ofthe previous M&A fit analysis.

The resource fit analysis is divided into three steps. Firstly, based on the overall identification of the resources of both parties by using the value chain tool, the mechanism analysis of the resource fit is carried out for tangible assets, human capital, organizational capital, and relationship capital respectively. Secondly, a resource evaluation index system is established to evaluate the pros and cons ofthe tangible assets, intellectual capital, organizational capital and relationship capital of the M&A parties respectively, and then judge the fit of each type of resources between the two parties in conjunction with the business processes in the value chain. Finally, the fit evaluation of the individual resources is used as the basis to evaluate the overall fit of the M&A parties.

According to the basic theory of enterprise resources, enterprise resources are the source of sustainable competitive advantage. M&A activities make two originally independent resource systems merge, and a new resource system is created through interaction, which determines the value creation capability and sustained competitive advantage of the post-merger enterprise. The resources owned by different enterprises are different, and the value of the resources of enterprises with the same kind of resources also varies greatly, which depends on the essential attributes of the resources on the one hand, and the interactions between the resources on the other hand. Since resources and their interrelationships determine the characteristics and functions of the post-merger enterprise and are also the internal driving factors for the fit of the two parties, the correct identification of the resources and relationships between the two parties is the first step in the fit analysis.

6.4.1.2 The Value Chain Model of Resource Fit Analysis

Porter (1985) put forward the concept of value chain when answering the question of the source of competitive advantage of an enterprise, arguing that avalue chain is

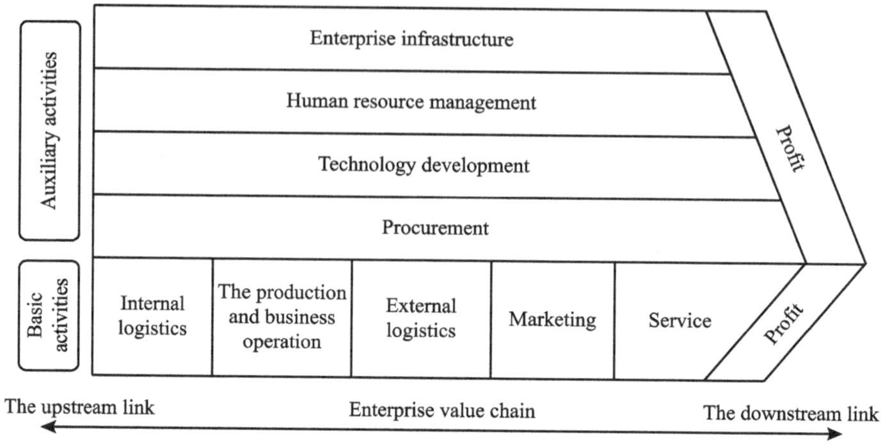

Fig. 6.5 Porter's value chain model

a collection of activities used by an organization to design, produce, market, deliver and support its products or services, including basic and auxiliary activities. The basic activities consist of five types of operations: internal logistics, production and business operations, external logistics, marketing, and service. The auxiliary activities refer to procurement, technology, human resources, and various enterprise-wide functional activities, and infrastructure supports basic activities and the entire value chain. Each of these value activities contributes to the enterprise's relative cost position and creates a basis for differentiation, which together constitute the enterprise's competitive capability. Profit is the difference between the total value and the total cost of engaging in various value activities. Porter's value chain model is shown in Fig. 6.5.

(1) Properties of the value chain

The value chain can become a tool for identifying enterprise resources, partly because it reveals the value creation mechanism of the enterprise, and partly also depends on the properties of the value chain itself. An enterprise's value chain and the way it executes its activities are reflections of its history, its strategy, the way it executes its strategy, and the economics implied by the activities themselves (Porter, 1985). In addition, some scholars believe that an enterprise's value chain is also a reflection of its political and organizational culture (Schweiger et al., 1993).

(i) The basic concept of the value chain

A value chain reflects an enterprise's basic activities and the linkages between them. An important premise that forms the basis of the value chain concept is that an enterprise can build its competitive advantage in the market by developing special integration and linking its activities. Porter believes that value chains exist simultaneously among enterprises with a single business or multiple businesses, and competitive advantage is a function of the structure of an enterprise's value chain. The linkages between activities in a single value chain and the linkages between activities in two or more value chains are how enterprise can build a competitive advantage. Moreover, an enterprise implementing a horizontal integration strategy can use its position in one market to effectively constrain its competitors in another market. Accordingly, if a company is to exchange or share resources within and across its value chain, a large number of linkages may be necessary. Such linkages are most likely required when there are potential operational or collusive synergies; conversely, when M&A are only aimed at obtaining certain financial effects, there may be little or no interdependence, and therefore no need for value chain linkages. For the value chain to become a functioning organization, an enterprise must equip its various units with qualified personnel, and properly supervise and motivate this personnel. This will further require enterprises to establish corresponding processes and improve related structures, systems, and regimes.

(ii) The political properties of the value chain

In any company, in addition to formal organizations, there are informal organizations (fewer formal processes, structures, systems, and rules). Such informal organizations often evolve alongside the formal processes, structures, and systems of the enterprise, and are often heavily political. Informal organizations can affect the competence and enthusiasm of their members, and they may also promote or hinder the formation and development of an enterprise's competitive advantage. An enterprise's value chain reflects not only the "technical" links between units and activities but also the social and political links among its members. The merger of the post-merger organizations will inevitably lead to changes in the original social and political relations to a certain extent. The formal processes, structures, and systems that underpin an enterprise's value chain structure are also influenced by enterprise politics.

(iii) Cultural view of the value chain

Informal processes and systems also imply a certain cultural identity in an enterprise's value chain. The cultural identity of a value chain is mainly reflected in its symbolic forms, such as the language, names, concepts, and categories that people use to give meaning to their work, the behavior of others, and events in their environment. Other verbal cultural form (such as myths, stories, legends, and rituals) and non-verbal cultural form (such as employee dress code, employee skills, habits, preferences, corporate architecture, logos, and art collections) can also reflect important activities of the value chains. In extreme cases, these cultural forms can also transcend themselves and enhance the source of competitive advantage created in the value chain. An enterprise's culture can influence the behavior of its employees. When enterprise culture is translated over time into specific values, codes of conduct, corporate traditions, or consensus, its impact is more immediate and visible. If enterprise culture is widely shared by the members, it can motivate and guide their efforts to engage in value chain activities that may be accepted or desired (Geertz, 1975).

The technical, political, and cultural attributes of an enterprise's value chain correspond with the enterprise's resources (tangible and intangible), which provides an excellent tool for properly identifying and comparing the resources of M&A parties.

(2) Value chain structure of resource identification

Porter's value chain model tells us that starting from the basic strategy selected by the company (total cost leadership, differentiation, or concentration), effectively designing and management of an enterprise's value chain is the fundamental way for the enterprise to obtain and maintain the market competitive advantage. By analyzing the value chain within the enterprise, we can discover the operational links that add value to the enterprise and identify the source of value creation. The essence of basic activities and auxiliary activities is the reflection of the various resources of the enterprise and their interrelationships at the operational level. Each activity has a certain degree of influence on the value creation of the enterprise, but the differences in resource categories determine the roles of these different activities in value creation are different. Among the many operating links in the enterprise's value chain, not all links play an equal role in value creation. Those specific links that play a key role are called strategic links. Although knowledge and capabilities mainly play a supporting role in the operation process of the enterprise's value chain, they are increasingly becoming the dominant elements of these strategic links. The key role of intangible resources in value creation has attracted the attention of scholars, and several value chain models characterized by emphasizing intangible resources or intellectual capital have emerged (Holsapple & Singh, 2000; Lev, 2000; Powell, 2001; Sullivan, 2000).

The resources of an enterprise are like the DNA that determines the physical appearance and personality traits of individual human beings according to the laws of heredity, and the resources of each company are a fundamental component of the value chain that has an independent value contribution to the business output. Given the attributes of different types of enterprise resources, especially the impact of knowledge-based resources on value creation, we incorporate resource elements into the enterprise value chain system, as shown in Fig. 6.6.

Firstly, we extend the basic activities of Porter's value chain into a chain that includes six operational links from strategic planning, R&D, material procurement, manufacturing and processing, and marketing to service. Secondly, according to the different influences of the three types of knowledge resources on the operational links of the enterprise's value chain, connections are established between each type of resource and the operational links. As a result, we can not only identify the key resources that distinguish different operation links in the value chain but also lay the foundation for correctly comparing the fit of resource elements in different operational links between M&A parties. Figure 6.6 reflects the overall situation of enterprise knowledge resources from the perspective of the value chain, which helps us to judge the fit of the overall resources between the M&A parties. Human capital, relationship capital, and organizational capital have commonalities, but the essential differences among the three also determine that each type of resource plays a different role in the value creation of a company. Moreover, in the case of M&A, the possible

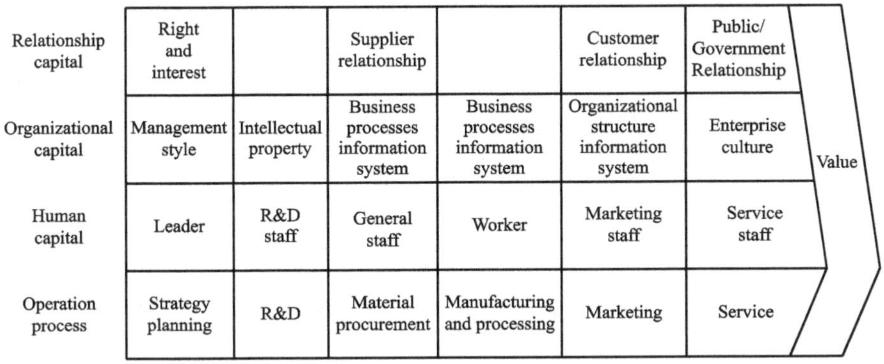

Fig. 6.6 Enterprise resource value chain system

relationships between the human capital, organizational capital, and relationship capital of the two companies, such as complementation, substitution, enhancement, conflict, or independence, are different, resulting in different fit relationships and degrees of fit between the two parties in M&A, so when analyzing the fit of the resources between the two parties, we can compare and judge the specific types of resources in the value chain of both parties.

In conclusion, in the era of a knowledge-based economy, many companies have begun to replace material capabilities with knowledge-based capabilities to enhance product value and obtain excess profits. At the same time, the proprietary nature of knowledge also makes these companies more capable of market value. The advantage of including resources into the value chain system is that the status of knowledge-based resources, the main source of value creation, is highlighted, which is important for identifying resources and their role relationships and thus essentially understanding the potential and obstacles of value creation. Establishing a value chain system by resource category not only allows us to compare the fit of resources of both parties in general, but also helps us to analyze the fit of specific resources according to the value-creating characteristics of different resources.

(3) The basic idea of resource fit analysis

The resource value chain system decomposes the company's source of value creation into a series of interrelated intellectual capital activities, each link interacts with each other and jointly determines the benefits of the entire value chain. M&A have established a close connection between the originally independent value chains of the two companies and formed a new resource network relationship structure.

It is the attributes of these two value chains and their network relationships that determine the functions, characteristics, and benefits of the post-merger enterprise. A single enterprise can't maintain absolute advantages in all links, therefore, an enterprise will only develop its core capabilities in the links with comparative advantages. Enterprises should choose target enterprises with complementary value chains and enhanced structures for M&A to make the overall value chain of the post-merger

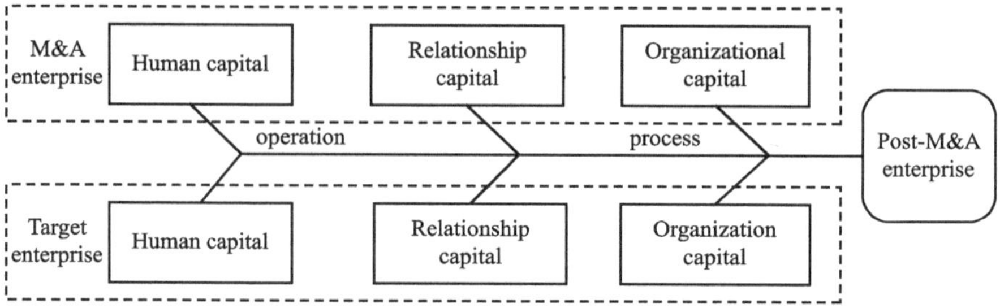

Fig. 6.7 Comparison of value chain systems between M&A parties

enterprises stronger. Moreover, the differences and incompatibility of the two enterprises' intellectual capital value chains must be analyzed. If there is a serious conflict, it may lead to the failure of M&A. Analyzing the fit between the M&A parties can start by comparing the value chains ofthe acquirer and the target enterprise, as shown in Fig. 6.7.

According to the above value chain model, the intellectual capital of the acquirer and the target enterprise can be analyzed and compared. The main steps of the analysis include: First, according to the resource value chain system established in Fig. 6.6, identifying the intellectual capital of the M&A parties according to the value chain operation process. The purpose of this step is to preliminarily judge the capital stock status of both parties and to evaluate whether the acquirer's human capital, organizational capital, and relationship capital are scarce resources and the degree of satisfaction of the corresponding resources of the target party in conjunction with the six operating processes in the company resource value chain. Second, compare the interrelationship between the resources of the acquirer and the target company in the six operation processes of the value chain and judge the complementarity, substitution, enhancement, conflict, or mutual independence of the intellectual capital of both parties. A fit evaluation matrix can be established for each resource in a specific analysis, which will be described below.

The interrelationship of resources between M&A parties determines the fit between their resources, and the fit is the premise and basis for the potential synergy of M&A. Differences in the type of resources and the fit between the two parties will lead to differences in the types of synergies. The fundamental motivation of most M&A is to obtain certain synergies or create enterprise value. Based on the evaluation of the respective value chains ofthe acquirer and the target enterprise, we can judge the fit of the specific resources of the two enterprises by judging the relationship between the knowledge resources corresponding to different operational processes in the value chain of both parties. Based on the possible interrelationships between resources and the similarities and differences between the two value chains, the possible fit effects of the value chains of the acquirer and the target are reflected in the following aspects:

(i) Size increasing fit

When the value chains of the acquirer and the target enterprise are almost identical, the combination of the two value chains will increase the size of the original resources and generate economies of scale. This purely incremental effect may result from cost savings due to the substitution of physical resources, or from increased market power due to the sharing of knowledge resources. Such M&A effects may result in more from asset fit than capabilities or knowledge resource fit, so they are not the best choice for acquiring and maintaining sustainable competitive advantage and value creation.

(ii) Enhanced fit

When the value chains of the acquirer and the target enterprise are the same, but the strength of each corresponding value link is different or the strength of different links is different, the integration of M&A will form a strengthening or complementary effect through the transfer and diffusion of capabilities, and achieve shared competitive advantage and increased value creation. Such M&A may require the rationalization of value chain activities by divesting or unbundling inappropriate and unwanted parts of the acquired enterprise's value chain.

(iii) Transfer and diffusion fit

When the value chains of the acquirer and the target enterprise are different, but some key parts of one value chain are useful to the other value chain, there will be potential transfer and diffusion effects of enterprise M&A. Transfer and diffusion effects can occur in three forms: when the acquirer's skill level in one of its key business activities is lower than that of its main competitors, skills are transferred or diffused from the target enterprise to the acquirer; conversely, skills are transferred or diffused from the acquirer to target company; or skills are transferred or diffused in both directions between two value chains. To obtain a positive net effect, a rationalization of value chain activities similar to achieving the enhancement effect is also required.

(iv) Complementary fit

When the value chains ofthe acquirer and the target enterprise are completely different, there are two situations when M&A will produce complementary effects. Firstly, when the value chains of both parties belong to the substitution relationship between the new (innovative value chain) and the old (original value chain), M&A integration can achieve the sharing of competitive advantages and increase value creation through the transfer and diffusion of intellectual capital. Secondly, when the acquirer and the target company are in different business areas, but for strategic reasons, the enterprise's strategic intent can only be realized by entering new business areas, such as expanding the business area to complementary products or extending the core capabilities of the company, M&A will bring complementary effects.

6.4.1.3 Resource Fit and M&A Value Creation

Based on the comparative analysis of the value chain between the two parties of M&A, enterprises can make judgments on whether an M&A can create value to provide the necessary basis for the selection of the target enterprise and the integration decisions (Wang Changzheng, 2000). The general principle for judging whether an M&A can create value is by evaluating the strengths of the value chains of both parties and then measuring the fit of the value chains of both parties.

(1) Evaluation of the advantages ofthe value chain

The advantages ofthe acquirer and the target enterprise's value chains can be divided into three grades: high, medium, and low. Comparing the value chains of the two parties of M&A, there may be the following three situations:

(i) If both the acquirer and the potential target enterprise have fairly intact and sound value chains, the value chains of these two enterprises have a high level of advantages; if these two value chains can be successfully merged, a real "association between strong enterprises" can be achieved. Otherwise, asset divestiture may be required.
(ii) If there is only one high-quality value chain between the two M&A parties, the value chains of these two enterprises combined are at a medium level of advantage; if the value chain of the acquirer is better, it may inject capital into the target enterprise or transfer and diffuse skills to achieve reorganization; if the value chain of the target enterprise is better, and there is a highly strategically fitted area of activity between the two enterprises, the acquirer may also reduce the disadvantage in its value chain through the transfer and diffusion of skills. However, if potential target enterprises have areas of strength that do not fit the acquirer's, the acquirer may have to consider selling the corresponding assets.
(iii) If the value chains of both M&A parties' organizations have obvious disadvantages, the value chains of the two enterprises should be regarded as low level. In this case, the target enterprise is not necessarily worthless but should be treated with caution. When the two value chains have a high degree of strategic fit, the successful reorganization of the two enterprises' value chains will still bring the desired synergies to the enterprises. In addition, if the two value chains have disadvantages in the same area, the merger may bring a negative effect on M&A and exacerbate the original competitive disadvantage.

(2) The relationship between the fit of the value chain and enterprise value

The strategic fit level of the value chain can also be divided into three grades: high, medium, and low.

(i) If the value chains of the two enterprises are already fitted at present, and the reorganization is not expected to cause serious damage to the enterprise's capabilities, the level of strategic fit is high.

(ii) If the two value chains do not have an obvious fit under current conditions, but have the potential to obtain an appropriate fit in the future, then it is a medium strategic fit. This situation requires an analysis of possible changes in the value chain of a potential target enterprise (such as changes in marketing and sales processes) and a determination of whether the changes in the value chain can achieve a satisfactory strategic fit that will facilitate the mutual growth of both organizations. Such changes may also have external effects, such as bringing in a changed or redefined market.

(iii) If the value chains of the two enterprises do not fit or complement and there is no opportunity to overcome this deficiency through post-merger management, the fitness level of the two value chains can be low. In this case, the fit problem must be viewed as a strategic problem. This strategic problem cannot be solved by relying only on the similarity of value chains.

Using the two indicators of value chain strength and value chain strategic fit, an "M&A fit matrix" can be established, as shown in Fig. 6.8. The horizontal axis represents the strategic fit level of the value chains of the two enterprises in M&A, and the vertical axis represents the comprehensive evaluation of the value chain strengths ofthe two enterprises. Using this matrix, we can evaluate the M&A fit of each potential target enterprise. The target enterprises in the three regions in the lower left corner of the matrix have the lowest level of M&A fit; the target enterprises in the diagonal direction from the upper left corner to the lower right corner have a medium level of M&A fit; the target enterprises in the three regions in the upper right corner have the highest level of M&A fit.

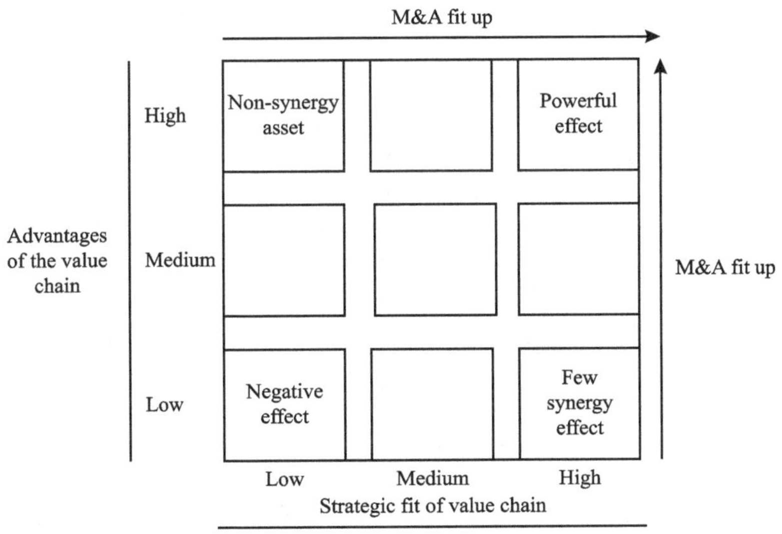

Fig. 6.8 M&A fit matrix

6.4.2 *Mechanism Analysis of Resource Fit*

6.4.2.1 Fit Analysis of Tangible Assets of Strategic M&A Parties

Among the seven elements of enterprise resources, namely natural resources, human resources, physical resources, financial resources, information resources, capability resources and time resources, financial and physical resources, that is, tangible assets, constitute the basic structure of the enterprise and reflect the survivability of the enterprise. Tangible assets are also the carriers of operational activities.

The asset fit of the two M&A parties is that the combination of the assets of the acquirer and the target enterprise can bring an increase in scale, and the financial capital gains obtained are greater than the sum of the gains when the two are independent. According to this meaning, the asset fit affects the comprehensive operational efficiency of the post-merger enterprise, which will bring about the expansion of the size of the post-merger enterprise, and the direct gains generated will bring economies of scale to the enterprise. It can be divided into the fit of financial capital and the fit of physical capital.

(1) Fit analysis of financial capital

The fit of financial capital means that the combination and reallocation of the financial capital of both parties can bring financial benefits to the enterprise, and are greater than the sum of the capital benefits when the two are independent.

Although in the enterprise resource theory, financial capital is not a scarce, inimitable, or non-tradable resource, it has a unique value in M&A for several reasons: (i) Financial capital is a highly liquid and less specialized asset and thus often becomes the resource base for the acquirer in hybrid M&A or the resource base for the target enterprise being attractive. (ii) Financial capital may become the source of sustainable competitive advantage during the development phase in the corporate life cycle (Lee et al., 2001), because in the development phase, an enterprise with richer financial capital will have the opportunity to accumulate more strategic assets than an enterprise lacking financial capital (Dierickx & Cool, 1989). (iii) In a specific financial environment, certain financial capital may have an important influence on the company. (iv) For the consideration of financial security, the acquirer is also willing to take the enterprise with sufficient and stable cash flow as the target enterprise, especially in an industry with high economic volatility. (v) For specific types of industry, financial capital and risk tolerance are closely related. If the acquirer has more financial capital, it tends to have a greater risk tolerance for investments in capital-intensive industries (Zhang Jinxin, 2005).

The analysis of the financial capital fit between M&A parties should not only consider the macro factors mentioned above but also pay attention to the possible micro benefits of financial capital fit. The fit of financial capital comes from the complementary mechanism of resources. The economies of scale brought by financial capital fit may include (i) Reasonable tax avoidance effect. According to the tax shield theory, since different tax rates are levied on assets with different income types, companies can adopt certain accounting treatments to achieve the purpose of tax avoidance. (ii) Stock price expectation effect. According to the signaling theory and undervaluation theory[3] of the financial management principle, the announcement of M&A will change the stock market's evaluation of the stocks of listed companies and cause price fluctuations. (iii) Comprehensive leverage effect. It refers to the financial leverage effect such as the change in the long- term debt-to-capital ratio of companies, the increase in the debt repayment and borrowing capacity of the company, and the reduction of capital costs that may be acquired through M&A (Guo Junhua, 2002). If the combination of the financial capital of both parties can produce one or more of the above effects, it can be considered that the financial capital of both parties is fitted.

(2) Fit analysis of physical capital

Physical capital includes physical resources such as inventories, buildings, machinery, and equipment, and it is an important part of an enterprise's balance sheet that reflects its financial status of an enterprise. If physical resources can be applied to both parties of the M&A, but its full effectiveness is not fully utilized in the original enterprise or is more efficiently utilized in another enterprise, and the intensity of use at different times is different, the economies of scale can be achieved through the full utilization of physical resources. The economies of scale brought by the fit of physical capital are usually reflected in cost reduction or efficiency improvement.

Like financial capital, physical capital is also a non-dominant resource in the enterprise's resource system. Because they are generally acquired directly in factor markets, they are usually not a source of competitive advantage. However, the following reasons should be paid attention to when we analyze the fit between the M&A parties: (i) compared with purchasing from the factor market, M&A can acquire physical assets relatively quickly, thereby gaining time advantages; (ii) due to the volatility of the capital market, there are sometimes cases of undervaluation of the assets of the target, allowing the M&A to obtain a more favorable price advantage than purchasing directly from the factor market; (iii) some physical assets themselves may not be special, but if their effectiveness depends on a specific environment, and their value may exceed the value of general similar assets; (iv) some special equipment developed by the target alone (such as information system developed specially for the enterprise) is actually integrated into the target's proprietary knowledge, and the development of the target's capability cannot be separated from the support of these proprietary assets, so it may also become a unique and valuable resource (Zhang Jinxin, 2005).

[3] Signaling theory: new information is transmitted when the target enterprise is acquired and the capital market will re-evaluate the value of the enterprise. Undervaluation theory: M&A activity occurs when the target enterprise's market value fails to reflect its true or potential value for some reason.

6.4.2.2 Fit Analysis of Human Capital of Strategic M&A Parties

(1) Basic analysis of human capital fit

Human is an important resource element of an enterprise. From the perspective of knowledge management, it is also an important type of intellectual capital.

Human capital is the knowledge and skills that depend on the individual (Becker, 1983; Coff, 2002) and can create future income for the enterprise. Human capital is the basic capability of all intellectual capital, and only individual learning can create knowledge, and only through the knowledge possessed by employees can create and establish various relationship capital and organizational capital. Human capital affects relationship capital and organization capital. The enterprise's internal information technology systems, operational processes, product development, and innovation, as well as the management of relationships with external customers and suppliers, are all affected by employees' knowledge, skills, and experiences. The higher the quality of employees, the more likely they are to develop highly productive operational processes.

Human capital fit means that the human capital benefits of the acquirer and the target enterprise combined are greater than the sum of the human capital when the two are independent. The unfit of human capital between the M&A parties may lead to the failure of the M&A. There may be substitution or conflict between the human capital of both parties, and there may also be complementarity or enhancement. It is the attributes of human capital and the interrelationship between human capital that determines the fit relationship between the human capital of both parties.

Firstly, human capital is the most active asset within an enterprise. Due to the strong autonomous mobility, valuable human capital may occur in unplanned runoff under certain conditions. Such runoff may sometimes bring large losses to the enterprise (especially when the enterprise is a knowledge-intensive enterprise). On the one hand, it may damage the key skills of the target enterprise (especially the small and medium-sized enterprises that are highly dependent on key personnel), thereby reducing the independent and synergy value of the target enterprise (Coff, 2002). On the other hand, in M&A with anti-takeover measures such as "poison pills", the loss of human capital also means paying large compensations. Although partial runoff is also expected to adjust the strategic direction of underperforming targets, it is generally limited to the top management team (Walsh & Kosnik, 1993). However, some studies have begun to question whether replacing the CEO of an underperforming target company can improve subsequent performance (Cannella & Hambrick, 1993; Walsh & Ellwood, 1991; Walsh & Kosnik, 1993).

Secondly, human capital is the carrier of dynamic capabilities. Due to the dynamism of human capital, it is different from the general capability carriers such as financial and physical resources, which can consciously improve or destroy capabilities. In M&A, to guide human capital to play a positive role, it is important to pay attention to reward incentives and cultural incentives. For example, if the relationships between the target enterprise's employees and key customers are the primary driver of sales, it is quite important to develop an incentive plan to retain key employees.

Thirdly, human capital is the foundation of organizational capital. In fact, what is most concerned about in M&A research is not individual human capital, but organizational capital as a collection of human capital. Organizational capital is the information about people-to-people, people-to-things, and people-to-organization fits (Weston, 2001), that is, information about who an employee works with and what they do to achieve the highest efficiency. This unique information is valuable to the enterprise. In addition, due to the long-term cooperation of efficient teams engaged in specific tasks, team members are very familiar with role orientation and even role complementarity. The sense of trust among team members is also strong. This tacit understanding constitutes the basis of organizational capabilities. Unique information and tacit understanding make teams more valuable than individual employees and more difficult to obtain from factor markets. This is also one of the motivations to induce M&A.

(2) Mechanism analysis of human capital fit based on value chain

There may be substitution or conflict between the human capital between M&A parties, and there may also be complementarity or enhancement. To analyze the fit of human capital between M&A parties, we should first clarify the own demand of the acquirer for specific human capital according to the operational process in the value chain. On this basis, we then analyze the possible interrelationship between the specific human capital of both sides in each operational process by judging the strengths and weaknesses of the human capital of both sides of the M&A. For ease of analysis, we extract human capital and operational processes from the resource value chain, as shown in Fig. 6.9.

We will analyze the fit between the human capital of M&A parties based on the six operational processes in Fig. 6.9. The specific analysis steps are as follows:

(i) In terms of strategic planning

The human capital closely related to it is the leader of the enterprise. We first judge the strengths and weaknesses of the leaders of both parties. On this basis, consider the following two situations: First, if the acquirer wants to improve its strategic planning capability and take the acquisition of excellent leaders as an important goal of M&A, it can judge the complementarity of the two parties by analyzing the degree

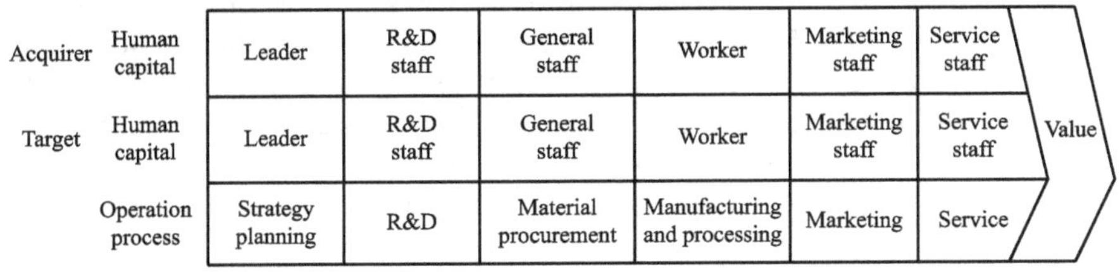

Fig. 6.9 Human capital elements in the resource value chain

of advantage of the target enterprise's leaders. If the leader of the target company has excellent quality, the acquirer also needs to pay attention to the possibility of his or her departure after M&A. Second, the leader of the target enterprise is not a scarce resource, the acquirer needs to determine his or her retention based on the degree of his or her strengths and weaknesses. If the leader of the target enterprise is strong and must stay with the enterprise after M&A, the acquirer must consider the possible conflicts between the two parties and develop a conflict resolution plan, such as arranging appropriate positions that would be accepted. The acquirer should consider abandoning the target if the conflict cannot be resolved.

(ii) In terms of R&D

The directly related human capital is the R&D personnel of the enterprise. It is necessary to evaluate the basic situation of the technical personnel of both parties. Then consider the following situations: First, the R&D personnel of both parties have advantages but have different R&D capabilities, and the merger of the two will enhance the overall R&D capabilities of the post-merger company, so it can be determined that the R&D human capital of both parties has enhancement. Second, the R&D personnel of both parties have advantages but have the same R&D capabilities, and the original personnel of the company has met the needs, then it can be determined that the two parties have substitutability, and the proper placement of redundant personnel should be considered when executing M&A transactions. If both parties' R&D personnel are retained in the post-merger company, the possibility of conflict and its elimination is a problem that the acquirer has to consider. Third, If the enhancement of R&D capability is the M&A objective of the company, and the R&D personnel of the target has advantages, the human resources in the R&D of both parties are complementary.

(iii) In terms of material procurement

Manufacturing, marketing, and service operations, all of them will directly involve two types of personnel in the enterprise: one is the middle managers of each department, such as purchasing managers and marketing directors; the other is general employees, such as production workers and after-sales service personnel. Taking marketing as an example, first, if the human capital of the marketing director of the target party is judged to be excellent, and it is a scarce resource required by the acquirer, then the two parties can be complementary, but their runoff should be considered. If they are not scarce personnel, and stay in the enterprise after the M&A, it is necessary to judge whether there will be conflicts with the original marketing director of the acquirer. If the two marketing directors belong to different regions, the possibility of conflict is very low. Second, if the general marketers belong to the scarce resources of the acquirer, and the target party can just satisfy them, it can be considered that the two parties are complementary, and at this time, it is necessary to further judge the possibility of runoff. If they belong to non-scarce resources, but have strong marketing capabilities, and are willing to stay in the company after the M&A, and do not overlap with the original marketing staff of the acquirer, there will be no direct interaction between the two parties. On the contrary, it is necessary to determine that the human resources of both parties are substitutable. Since the human capital directly involved in material procurement, manufacturing, and service is similar to marketing, the possible interrelationships between the human capital of these three operational processes in the value chain of both parties can be judged in comparison with that of marketing.

6.4.2.3 Analysis of the Organizational Capital Fit Between Acquirer and Acquiree in Strategic M&A

(1) Organizational problems faced in corporate M&A

Organizational resources are the collective knowledge embedded in the organizational structure of an enterprise and are the organizational knowledge and capabilities stored and accumulated by the organization that affects the operation of the enterprise. Individual knowledge must be effectively transferred into knowledge-intensive operating procedures, core competencies, management systems, and strategies in the organization, i.e., employee knowledge can only form an organizational advantage if it is transformed into the collective knowledge of the organization. Individual employees' abilities are like general parts, and if they cannot be coordinated and integrated most effectively so that they can produce positive effects and enhance organizational and relationship capital, then the poor management system, organizational structure, and culture will cause employees to fight with each other, compete for power and profits, not share knowledge, communicate and coordinate poorly and lack team spirit, thus even if there are good employees, it will never mean that the performance of the company will be improved (Lin Dongqing, 2004).

Organizational capital fit means that the combined organizational resources of the acquirer and the target firm produce an effect that is greater than the sum of the effects of their organizational capital when they are separate. The fit of organizational capital will have a direct impact on the overall operational effectiveness and growth potential of companies after the merger. There may be complementary or enhanced effects, as well as substitution or conflicting effects between the organizational capitals of both sides in M&A. Complementarity and enhancement can occur in all types of processes from strategy to business activities. The existence of organizational capital is dependent and non-transferable to the organization and is the corporate personality formed by the interaction of various relationships in the dynamic operation of the organization, then when M&A combines the organizational resources of the two companies, conflict is inevitable to some extent. Analyzing the fit of organizational capital should pay more attention to the conflict. The conflict of organizational resources may be manifested in the following aspects:

(i) Conflict of management styles between the acquirers and acquirees

Management style refers to the management culture or subjective culture of the organization (Bhagat & McQuaid, 1982; Sathe, 1985), including managers' attitudes toward risk, preferences for decision-making methods, control and communication styles, etc. Management styles are unique to different organizations and may vary greatly between organizations. For example, different management groups may adopt very different risk-taking tendencies. Thus, policies and procedures that are considered too reckless and extremely risky by one management group may be the most appropriate approach for another (Davies, 1968; Friedman, 1985). Similarly, one management team may be more tolerant of change than another. Senior management groups may also have different approaches to decision-making.

(ii) Conflict of corporate culture between the acquirers and acquirees

Corporate culture refers to the common values and behavioral norms gradually formed by all employees of an enterprise in the process of long-term development and evolution, which includes the highest goals, management philosophy, historical traditions, etiquette customs, behavioral norms, management systems, etc. as well as the corporate ethos and entrepreneurial spirit expressed therein. Corporate culture emerges and develops in a certain socio-historical and cultural background, and is directly related to the character, entrepreneurial awareness, business thinking, and working style of the founder of the company. The formation of enterprise operation and management style is also a long-term practice and exploration process, and once formed, its influence may exist for a long time, with stability and distinct individual differences, as expressed in the differences in perception of problem perspectives, way of thinking and the judgment standard. Corporate culture conflict is a concentrated expression of the corporate system, mechanism, organization, and psychological conflict. Thus different companies often have different forms of corporate culture, bringing cultural differences to M&A integration.

Correctly understanding the possible organizational resources conflicts between the acquirers and the acquirees is necessary to correctly evaluate the organization fit between the acquirers and the acquirees and thus judge whether the M&A can successfully achieve value creation, as well as to clarify the difficulty of post-merger integration and guide the direction of post-merger integration.

(2) Basic analysis of management style fit

The earliest research on the impact of management style compatibility on organization fit can be traced back to Davies (1968), followed by representative scholars including Datta (1991) and Schoenberg (2004). Based on early case studies, Davies (1968) demonstrated how differences in management styles between acquirers and targets can lead to suboptimal acquisition outcomes. Datta (1991) empirically examined the impact of management style compatibility on M&A performance in a sample of 173 domestic acquisitions in the US, and the results showed a statistically significant negative relationship between differences in management style and acquisition performance between the acquirers and the acquirees. However, Datta does not provide a measure of the differences or similarities in specific management styles between the acquirers and the acquirees. Schoenberg (2004) noted this issue and empirically tested the effect of differences in specific dimensions of management styles on cross-border M&A performance using different dimensions of management styles as independent variables and concluded that in M&A situations, management style compatibility is an important performance determinant.

Mergers and acquisitions bring together the management groups of two firms whose management styles may be similar or different. The apparent differences in management styles can lead to cultural ambiguity, which means that there is uncertainty about which party's management style or culture will dominate after the merger (Buono et al., 1985). Generally speaking, managers of the acquirers tend to eventually impose their style on the acquired firm, which may lead to the loss of the identity of the acquired firm's managers (Hirshch & Andrews, 1983). This results in increased managerial uneasiness, mistrust, and conflict and leads to decreased productivity and post-merger performance (Ivancevich et al., 1987). Compatibility of management styles facilitates the assimilation of both sides after the merger, whereas major differences in management styles and management philosophies can be serious obstacles to the success of M&A (Davies, 1968).

We determine the fit of the management styles of the acquirers and the acquirees by measuring the differences or similarities between the management teams of the acquirers and the acquirees on several dimensions, such as their attitudes toward risk, the way they participate in decision-making, the flexibility of their management, and the degree of formality of their organizational procedures.

(i) Measurement of risk positioning differences

Risk orientation has a critical impact on the M&A decision-making process (Pablo et al., 1996). It has been argued that firms with different risk orientations have different perspectives on post-merger integration. In other words, if acquirers and acquirees process different risk orientations, they develop different understandings of post-merger integration approaches. Such differences in understanding are detrimental to the creation of a harmonious corporate climate, which is essential for the smooth implementation of value creation capabilities (Haspeslagh & Jemison, 1991; Hunt, 1990). Further, differences in understanding may lead both sides to act differently concerning similar events (Rentch, 1990), resulting in conflict and other consequences that lead to organizational dysfunction and ultimately poorer M&A performance. Existing research in M&A organization fit has concluded that there is a relationship between the risk orientation of both sides and M&A performance. Davis (1968), after studying acquisition transactions in the US, concluded that the differences in risk philosophies of both sides affect all levels of decision-making and various functions within the organization. Schoenberg (2004) hypothesized that the differences in attitudes towards risk between acquirers and acquirees are negatively related to the performance of cross-border acquisitions, and his empirical results further support this hypothesis.

(ii) Measurement of differences in the normality of the organization's daily procedures

Differences in the degree of formality of organizational routines between acquirers and acquirees are the second factor that affects the organization fit. Kitching's (1967) path-breaking study argues that reporting relationships and control systems between acquirers and targets may have a significant impact on acquisition outcomes. Subsequent case study literature has documented the conflicts that can arise from differences in organizational routines. After a merger, managers at the target firm may feel alienated and excluded as succession plans for managers are announced and formal control and communication systems gradually replace the target firm's previously comfortable reporting systems and informal institutions (Walter, 1985). Employees of an acquired firm often feel anxious and uneasy when they anticipate a stronger performance orientation in the control and reward systems of the new firm (Cartwright & Cooper, 1996).

(iii) Measurement of decision style variability

Similar to the normative differences in the day-to-day organizational processes, the different decision-making styles of acquirers and acquirees can have an impact on organization fit. For example, a highly centralized versus a democratic decision-making style. Differences in decision-making styles between acquirers and acquirees may hinder smooth post-acquisition integration due to potential conflict and frustration on both sides. Empirical research has been conducted to suggest that acquisitions can exhibit low performance if employees of the acquired firm are aware that their decision-making autonomy is severely limited after the merger (Calori et al., 1994; Cartwright & Cooper, 1996).

(iv) Management style fit and the type of post-merger integration

The management style fit between acquirers and acquirees affects post-merger integration decisions, while the type of post-merger integration also constrains the fit of management styles. The general patterns of post-merger integration include:

First, the symbiotic integration refers to the approach where the acquiring company seeks a balance, aiming to achieve the transfer of strategic capabilities between both parties while maintaining the organizational independence of the acquired company.

Second, the goal of "preservation" integration is to achieve a fully operational, organizational, and cultural merger of the two sides of the acquisition and ultimately eliminate the boundaries between the acquirer and the target.

Third, the "reserved" integration requires a high degree of organizational independence, with little operational management contact between acquirers and acquirees. In this case, the acquired firms are relatively unaffected by the organizational climate of the acquirers (Chatterjee et al., 1992; Datta & Grant, 1990), suggesting differences in the management styles between acquirers and acquirees have little adverse effect on the outcome of the merger.

Conversely, differences in management style are important for absorption- type integration, in which the degree of strategic interdependence between acquirers and acquirees is high, both managers need to work closely together, and common policies and procedures must be adopted to achieve the desired transfer of skills or sharing of activities (Cartwright & Cooper, 1996; Haspeslagh & Jemison, 1991). As a result, absorption-type integration implies a considerable loss of independence for the acquired firm (Haspeslagh & Jemison, 1991), and relies on the power structure of both sides (Sales & Mirvis, 1984), where the acquired firm usually gives up its management style to endorse the management style of the acquirers (Datta & Grant, 1990). In such cases, differences in management style can cause serious internal conflicts and gradually undermine firm performance (Buono & Bowditch, 1989).

(v) Turnover rate of administrative personnel

The relationship between differences in management style and degree of organization fit is also affected by another factor, namely, the turnover rate of the acquired company's executives during the acquisition process. The departure of a large number of executive managers may dilute the advantages initially brought about by the differences in management styles between acquirers and acquirees. It has been argued that management mobility resulting from M&A is an important mechanism for implementing cultural change (Buono & Bowditch, 1989), a means of dismissing those responsible for deviating from desired organizational norms (Sathe, 1985), and a way of replacing pre-existing power and control structures (Cannella & Hambrick, 1993). Similarly, the voluntary departure of managers of the acquired firm may mean that they are dissatisfied with the management style of the acquirers (Krug & Nigh, 2001; Larsson & Finkelstein, 1999). The imposition of the acquirer's management style on a recently acquired target may induce feelings of stress and loss of identity among the target firm's employees (Buono & Bowditch, 1989), which in turn may subsequently lead to higher turnover rates (Krug & Hegarty, 2001). Senior managers are usually the first to leave at the point of acquisition (Krug & Hegarty, 2001), and it is usually the employee collective that plays a key role in delineating organizational attitudes, behaviors, and beliefs (Very et al., 1993). These arguments suggest that higher executive turnover may have reduced both the absolute dominance of the target firm's previous management style and the loyalty of retained employees to the previous management style. This dilution may next reduce the potential for conflict from differences in management styles.

(3) Cultural compatibility analysis

A considerable body of research literature has attempted to explain how the organizational level of the firm affects post-merger firm performance. The study of organization fit is closely linked to several disciplines, including strategic management (Chatterjee et al., 1992; Very et al., 1997), international business (Datta & Puia, 1995; Morosini et al., 1998) and organizational behavior (Buono & Bowditch, 1989; Cartwright & Cooper, 1996). These literatures have focused on the importance of cultural compatibility as a core element of organization fit on acquisition outcomes, and empirical studies have concluded that there is a strong negative relationship between the degree of cultural differences between organizations and the returns to acquirer shareholders.

(i) Cultural compatibility of acquirers and acquirees: theoretical study

Culture is defined as "the beliefs and assumptions shared among members of an organization" (Nahavandi & Malekzadeh, 1988) and "a common scheme of thinking that distinguishes between different group members or ranges of personnel" (Hofstede, 1991). Corporate culture is considered to be an important determinant of organizational behavior (Johnson, 1992), and a strong cohesive culture is strongly associated with superior performance (Barney, 1986; Deal & Kennedy, 1982). Assuming that an acquisition involves combining two separate corporate cultures, most of the literature examining organizational fit in M&A has given attention to the issue of cultural compatibility. What factors determine cultural compatibility? How does cultural compatibility affect the outcome of an acquisition? The former question has been answered by a large body of theoretical research, while the latter question has been tested in various empirical studies. In the following, we will review the existing theoretical and empirical literature.

Acculturation describes the process by which members from one culture adapt to another culture. The acculturation framework of acquisition is formulated based on a contest between personnel rights and property rights (Walter, 1985), is a force-field analysis between the forces of cultural differences and the forces of organizational integration (Elsass & Veiga, 1994), and a distinction between four different modes of cultural adaptation according to an anthropological perspective (Nahavandi & Malekzadeh, 1988, 1994).

"Assimilation" refers to the willingness of the acquired enterprise to abandon its own culture and adopt that of the acquirer. Assimilation implies voluntariness, not coercion, and is therefore associated with a low level of conflict.

"Integration" refers to the acceptance and retention of the basic assumptions and practices of two organizations. It involves both the relative factors of cultural independence and the exchange between selected cultural elements.

"Separation" occurs when the acquired enterprise wishes to maintain the original cultural aspects and rejects another culture autonomously. The desire to maintain independence can cause a considerable degree of conflict and be difficult to implement.

"Deculturation" is when members of the acquired enterprise no longer value the organization's previous culture but also do not want to be assimilated by the acquirer. In essence, such employees find themselves in a state of exclusion, and the culture is associated with the highest degree of conflict and difficulty.

Nahavandi and Malekzadeh (1988) further identified the factors influencing the choice of acculturation model and postulated an integrated model of the acculturation process in acquisition. They argue that the level of potential post- merger conflict, or "acculturation pressure", is both a function of the cultural fit model adopted by the acquirer and derives from the degree of congruence between the models supported by two sides of M&A. For the acquired enterprise, the acculturation model it supports depends on its understanding of how attractive the acquirer's culture is relative to its own. For acquirers, the cultural fit model depends on the degree of cultural diversity that can be tolerated and accepted within the parent enterprise. Acquirers will also be influenced by the acquisition strategy, especially in trying to achieve operational synergies that the acquirer must impose on the target enterprise of its own culture and practices. They argue that relevance acquisition is the best form for forced acceptance cultures, although based on Haspeslagh and Jemison (1991), the integrated form may more accurately describe its strategic impact on the acculturation model. This is because the form of integration takes into account not only the degree of strategic interdependence of the post-merger firms but also the degree of organizational independence of the target enterprise.

It should be noted that acculturation is a dynamic process, and patterns of acculturation and the degree of perceived stress may change over time, for example, a result of gradual familiarity with the culture and behavior of other organizations (Nahavandi & Malekzadeh, 1994). Multiple sub-cultures may also exit within an organization, and therefore, post-merger enterprises may adopt the multiple acculturation model (Elsass & Veiga, 1994).

Implicit in the acculturation model is a link between acculturation pressures and conflicting behaviors and actual M&A outcomes, a relationship that has received support from sever empirical studies. Thus, the model ofNahavandi and Malekzadeh (1988) provides a useful theoretical framework for understanding the various factors that influence the overall relationship between cultural differences and acquisition performance.

(ii) Cultural compatibility of acquirers and acquirees: empirical study

Schoenberg (2000) reviewed the empirical research literature on corporate cultural compatibility and concluded that there are mainly four representative kinds of literature that have empirically studied cultural fit in domestic M&A. Three of them are case studies from a phenomenological perspective (Buono & Bowditch, 1989; Cartwright & Cooper, 1992; Sales & Mirvis, 1984), and one is a quantitative study based on positivists (Chatterjee et al., 1992).

Sales and Mirvis (1984) explored the process of cultural adaptation in detail using the case of an agreed acquisition between a medium-sized US manufacturing firm and a large conglomerate. They detailed the apparent differences between the two companies in terms of corporate philosophy and behavior and documented miscommunications, misunderstandings, and conflicts that resulted from cultural differences over a year. Although no performance evaluation was conducted, Sales and Mirvis' description supports the acculturation model identified by Nahavandi and Malekzadeh (1988) and emphasizes the dynamic nature of the acculturation process. After three years or so, the early "separation" gradually gave way to the integration of management styles and the "assimilation" of reporting and control systems.

Cartwright and Cooper (1992) also adopted the analytical framework of Nahavandi and Malekzadeh (1988). By examining four takeover transactions in the UK, they confirm the assumption that cultural conflict can be minimized if the employees of the acquiree are willing to both abandon their original culture and recognize that the acquirer's culture is attractive. They argue that minimal cultural conflict can be achieved if the acquirer's culture grants similar or greater involvement and autonomy to the acquiree's individuals than their original culture. It was observed that employees of acquirees work harder to achieve successful post-acquisition integration when they recognize that the acquisition will, if not enhance, at least maintain their original involvement and autonomy.

Buono and Bowditch (1989) longitudinally studied three cases of acquisition that occurred in the service industry to illustrate the acculturation pressures that can occur when incompatible corporate cultures combine. In one bank merger, the vision of planned full integration was initially reflected in the choice of a new name, location, and system. But within a year, it became clear that the values, philosophies, and people of the acquirer were taking over the acquiree. This led to the voluntary resignation of a significant number of the acquired company's employees, and those who remained were disgruntled and eventually resorted to "a series of attempts to undermine the merger... and created significant barriers to successful corporate integration during the first four years after the merger". Although to a lesser extent, a similar case, the acquisition of a fast-food chain by a large conglomerate, also resulted in negative acculturation pressures, even though the acquired business was positioned as a subsidiary of the new enterprise. There was a significant difference between the fast-food chain's family-oriented business style and the parent company's systematic, high-growth rate orientation, and senior managers ofthe acquired company experienced strong feelings of stress and frustration as they compromised the skills necessary to master new formal planning systems and procedures. They experience intense stress and frustration. The result is the failure of the new subsidiary to meet strategic growth objectives, along with a planned and proactive exit by the company's CEO.

Chatterjee et al. (1992) conducted a statistical test with a sample set of 30 US M&A transactions, and the results supported the qualitative description of the negative effects arising from cultural differences. Researchers found a strong negative correlation between cultural differences and shareholder returns from acquisitions. Importantly, the introduction of a measure of multicultural tolerance in acquirers did not reconcile this relationship, as predicted by the Nahavandi and Malekzadeh (1988) model. While it is expected that cultural differences may negatively affect aggregate performance, this study is potentially limited by the ex-ante nature of the stock price performance variable. This is similar to earlier correlation studies, as shareholder expectations of future operating performance may not accurately reflect ex-post reality by measuring excess returns 15 days before and after the acquisition announcement date (Nayyar, 1992).

In conclusion, empirical research confirms that differences in corporate culture may lead to acculturation stress, which in turn can have negative impacts on human resources and next cause poorer acquisition performance in firms. Empirical support for Nahavandi and Malekzadeh's (1988) model of the acculturation process, particularly for the extent to which the perceptions of the relative attractiveness of the new cultures and the choice of the form of integration strategies may mediate the impact of cultural differences, has gradually emerged.

The available research literature suggests that the impact of cultural differences is measurable and meaningful. Cultural differences may lead to increased difficulty during the M&A integration period, which in turn may next reduce acquisition performance. However, cultural differences should not be automatically associated with negative effects. Studies have found that mergers with dissimilar cultures exerted a positive effect on performance when the acquirer's culture demonstrates relative attractiveness.

(iii) A theoretical framework for measuring cultural compatibility

A detailed assessment of cultural compatibility has become a necessary component of practitioners' bid planning and value assessment activities (Schoenberg, 2000). However, which specific factors should be given special attention in the assessment remains a question to be explored. Theoretical models predict that potential determinants of cultural compatibility include the acquirer's tolerance for multiculturalism, the relative attractiveness of the acquirer's culture, and post-acquisition integration strategies (Nahavandi & Malekzadeh, 1988; Olie, 1994). The actual impact of these factors has been tested in one or more empirical studies, respectively, but has yielded variable results.

First, it was found that the acquirer's tolerance for multiculturalism did not moderate the effects of organizational cultural variability (Chatterjee et al., 1992). A possible explanation for this result is that tolerance for multiculturalism is viewed as an individual, rather than an organizational attribute (Adler, 1986) and that multinational acquirers typically assign responsibility for acquisition integration to other managers or managerial levels. Thus, there is wide variation in multicultural tolerance within acquirers, which makes the use of this variable to predict the level of organization fraught with doubt. In the absence of further research, practitioners should assess the fit between individual managers' tolerance for multiculturalism and the cultural dynamics ofthe specific acquisitions they will be responsible for.

Second, the effect of integrated form has received multiple empirical supports. While several studies have reported that integrative approaches may mediate the negative effects of cultural differences (Morosini & Singh, 1994; Morosini et al., 1998; Very et al., 1997), others have concluded that the relationship between cultural differences and acquisition performance is independent of the forms of integration (Buono & Bowditch, 1989; Datta, 1991; Schoenberg & Norburn, 1998). Undoubtedly this area needs further research, but the implication for practitioners is that it is dangerous to assume that managing a multinational acquisition (retention-based integration) at arm's length will necessarily soften the negative effects of cultural differences.

Third, the relative attractiveness of the acquirer's culture is considered a key determinant variable of the ease of integration of the two cultures after a merger (Very et al., 1997). The results of two studies suggest that acquisitions achieve superior performance if the culture of the offeror will endorse higher levels of empowerment independence and involvement relative to the culture of the target (Calori et al., 1994; Cartwright & Cooper, 1992). Other studies have also pointed out the specific effects of the relative attitudes of both sides towards formalization and risk (Calori et al., 1994; Morosini & Singh, 1994; Schoenberg & Norburn, 1998). These results suggest that potential acquirers should pay particular attention to the relative attitudes of the acquirers towards participation, formalization, and risk.

Finally, relative cultural attractiveness raises the question of whether attractiveness should be viewed as being based on cultural similarities or cultural differences. Researchers have different views on this issue, with some studies suggesting that cultural differences are positively related to performance (Morosini et al., 1998), yet

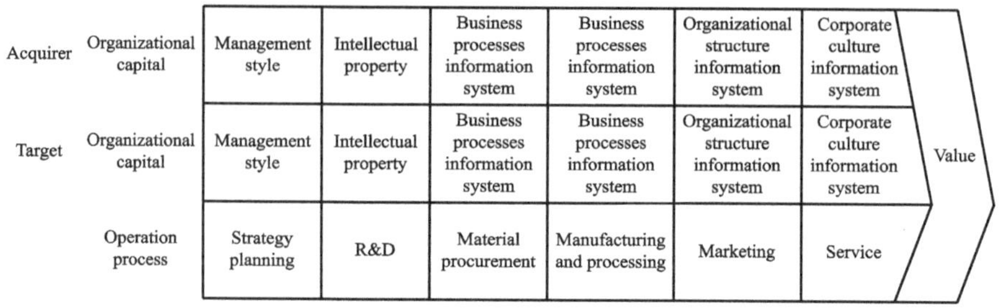

Fig. 6.10 Elements of organizational capital in resource value chain

other studies link cultural similarity to superior performance (Chatterjee et al., 1992; Datta & Puia, 1995). However, these large-sample empirical studies tend to utilize tests of the absolute value of cultural differences between acquirers and acquirees as independent variables. Very et al. (1997) provided a further way to examine this issue by looking at the relative value of the cultural gap between acquirers and acquirees, and the standard cultural values of the acquired enterprise. The results support the key idea that it is relative cultural attractiveness rather than absolute differences or absolute similarity is itself a determinant of performance.

(4) Mechanism analysis of value chain-based organizational capital fit

We will analyze the fit of the organizational capital between acquirers and acquirees for the operation process in the value chain, and then clarify the impact of the fit of organizational capital of both sides on the value creation activities. To facilitate the analysis, we extract organizational capital and operational processes from the resource value chain in Fig. 6.6, as shown in Fig. 6.10.

We analyze the possible interrelationships between the organizational capital of the acquirers and acquirees for each of the six operation processes of the corporate value chain of both sides and lay the foundation for analyzing the comprehensive fit of organizational capital.

(i) In terms of strategic planning

The closely related organizational capital is the management style of the company. The greater the difference between the management styles of the two sides, the greater the possibility of conflict between them after the merger. Therefore, we first determine the differences in the management styles of the two sides. This can be done by designing the same questionnaire for both sides, asking the people involved on both sides to give their answers, and then making judgments by comparing the answers. The questionnaire can be designed around the dimensions of the previous analysis of management style, for example, does the company like to take risks or is willing to avoid risks? Do the organization's daily procedures, such as reporting systems and reward systems, have very formal processes? Does the company have a highly centralized or democratic style of decision-making? Because a significant difference in management style between the two sides will directly affect the strategic planning aspects of the value chain and thus the long-term development of the company, the acquirer should further determine the conflict between the two sides in the context of the acquisition and the possible degree of integration. For example, if the two sides operate independently after the M&A and the management systems will not intersect directly, then the difference in organizational resources will not bring conflict and will not be a factor affecting the match; on the contrary, if the two sides will merge after the M&A and the management systems of both parties need to intermingle, then we must pay attention to the conflict and consider the possibility of conflict elimination.

(ii) In terms of R&D

The directly related organizational capital is the enterprise's intellectual property right(IPR), including intangible assets such as trademarks, patents, know- how, trade secrets, etc. These intangible assets are more in line with intangible assets as defined in the financial statements. The acquirer first needs to assess the basic situation of the intellectual property of both sides. Then the following situations are considered: First, a certain IPR of the acquirees, such as know- how, is a scarce resource of the acquirer and is required for the acquirer's R&D process, then the IPR of both sides can be considered complementary. Second, both sides have high-value IPRs that do not overlap and can enhance the R&D capabilities of the companies after the merger, e.g., the acquirer's know-how in manufacturing new tires and the target's know-how in producing special vehicles can result in an enhanced match. Third, if both sides have the same or different IPRs that can be used to solve similar R&D problems, and there is no need to use both, then substitutability between their resources should be considered. In the case of the R&D segment, there does not appear to be a problem of conflicting IPRs.

(iii) In terms of both material procurement and manufacturing and processing

The organizational resources that will be directly involved include business processes and information systems. First, the acquirer needs to clarify whether it needs the target's business processes and information systems, such as the target's internal information network or corporate knowledge base, etc. If so, and the target happens to be able to meet them, the organizational capital of the material procurement or manufacturing and processing links between the two sides can be considered complementary. Second, for business processes or information systems that are not required by the acquirer, if the greater the differences between the two sides and the fact that each enterprise will not operate independently after the M&A, the greater the possibility of conflict between the two sides, at this time, the acquirer should consider the possibility of conflict elimination, otherwise, the target should be abandoned.

(iv) In terms of the marketing operations segment

The organizational resources that will have a direct impact on it include organizational structure and information systems. The issues to be considered in analyzing the fit of organizational resources in this segment between acquirers and acquirees are similar to those in the material procurement and manufacturing and processing segments. It is also important to focus on the conflict of organizational capital in the marketing segment.

(v) In terms of service links

Corporate culture and information systems are two types of organizational resources that have a direct impact on them. The influence of corporate culture on service operations may be directly reflected in the overall service quality, service attitude, service environment, and many other aspects of the company. For example, Haier's customer-first cultural philosophy directly affects the work attitude and service quality of its service personnel. Thus, it is the unique influence of a corporate culture that makes acquirers and acquirees, which have major differences, face serious conflict problems. In fact, corporate culture is embedded within the company and does influence not only the service chain, but also the whole operation process of the value chain. The compatibility and adaptability of the cultures of both sides is also an important management issue. To evaluate the fit of organizational resources both sides must pay special attention to the clash of corporate cultures. Specifically, it can be similar to the evaluation method of management style, and it can be done by designing a questionnaire to determine the degree of difference between the corporate cultures of the two sides and then making a judgment on the conflict or compatibility of the two sides about the possible forms of integration after the merger. The analysis of the relationship between the information systems of the service links of both sides is the same as the item (iii) above, focusing on complementarity and conflict, but, of course, if the two sides combine, for example, corporate knowledge bases and internal information networks, there may be a mutual enhancement effect.

6.4.2.4 Analysis of Relationship Capital Fit Between Acquirers and Acquirees in Strategic M&A

(1) Basic analysis of relationship capital fit

Corporate relationship capital is a company's ability to invest in, maintain and manage its stakeholders in the external environment, reflecting the company's relationship with its stakeholders in the external environment and reflecting its ability to master and control the relationship with the external environment (Luo Min, 2003). Relationship capital is cultivated and precipitated for a long time in the enterprise development process, which is jointly owned by relationship partners and difficult to be imitated and replaced by other enterprises. It is built and developed gradually through continuous learning, creation, and even accumulation and refinement in the market competition. Its formation is the result of the overall optimization among relationship partners, and it co-exists with its owner and has its specific scope of use, which can benefit the relevant links in the relationship network, and is reflected in all aspects of production and business activities among relationship members.

The fit of the relationship resources between acquirers and acquirees directly affects the industry potential of the post-merger enterprise, i.e., the actual position of the enterprise in the society and the industry it is in, which reflects the influence of the enterprise on the market and society, and is also a reflection of the industry competitiveness.

Relationship capital fit is a combination of the acquirer's and the target's relationship capital that enhances the firm's industry potential and is greater than the sum of their relationship capital when each is independent.

The reduction of post-merger capital may be caused by substitution or conflict between the relationship capital of the two sides, mainly due to: (i) The reduction of customers. Down (1995) estimated that in addition to the reduction rate of existing customers (depending on the nature of the industry, generally 20%–40%), the newly acquired firms will lose another 5%-10% of their existing customers. Moreover, in the process of integrating the relationship capital between the two sides after the merger, the company may voluntarily give up some customers for the need for strategic adjustment to focus on serving the important customers of the company. (ii) The reputations of both sides of the M&A are mixed. Although the poor corporate reputation of one party may benefit from the good reputation of the other party and achieve better business performance than when it operates alone, it may also damage the reputation of the other party, especially the party with a very poor reputation may cause the other party to suffer. (iii) Inconsistent or conflicting product images between acquirers and acquirees. The relationship capital between acquirers and acquirees may also cause an increase in post-merger capital due to complementary or enhancing mechanisms, including the sharing of the brands of both sides increases in the product image and reputation of the company, the increased strength and reputation of the company after the M&A attracts more new customers, the sharing of marketing skills, sales channels, and service networks, the sharing of customer relationships, etc. In fact, the sharing of relationship capital between the two sides is itself an important motivation for M&A (Guo Junhua, 2002).

The match analysis of the relationship capital of both sides should also focus on the substitutability or conflict between the capital.

(2) Mechanism analysis of value chain-based relationship capital fit

We will analyze the fit of relationship capital between acquirers and acquirees for the operational process in the value chain, and then clarify the impact of the fit of the relationship capital between the two sides on the value creation activities. To facilitate the analysis, we extract the relationship capital and operational processes from the resource value chain in Fig. 6.6, as shown in Fig. 6.11.

For the six operating processes of the corporate value chain of acquirers and acquirees, we analyze the possible relationships between the relationship capital of the acquirer and the acquiree item by item and lay the foundation for analyzing the comprehensive fit of relationship capital.

(i) In terms of the strategic planning link

The closely related relationship capital is the equity relationship of the enterprise, including the relationship with external shareholders and creditors. The shareholders exert influence on the strategic planning of the enterprise by exercising their voting

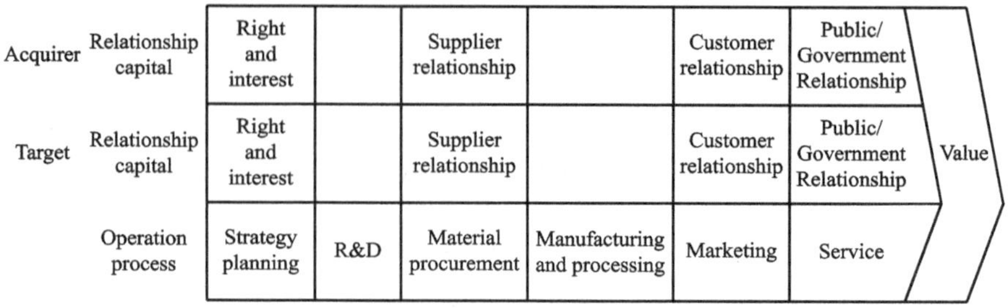

Fig. 6.11 Elements of relationship capital in the resource value chain

rights, etc., while the creditors exert influence on the strategic planning of the enterprise by stipulating some restrictive terms. As the two major sources of financing for a company, the relationship with shareholders and creditors may be directly related to the implementation of the company's strategy to some extent. The acquirer should first analyze whether it sees an equity relationship as a scarce resource for development and if so, the degree to which the target party meets them should be concerned. If the target has a superior equity relationship that can be transplanted to the post-merger company, then the relationship capital of the two sides is highly complementarity and even enhanced. However, if there are obstacles to the transfer of the target company's equity relationship capital, for example, the original creditor may stop cooperation due to the M&A event, then the complementarity or enhancement of the relationship capital between the two sides cannot be realized, so the acquirers must consider this.

(ii) In terms of the material procurement link

The directly related relationship capital is the supplier relationship. Obviously, as the upstream value chain of a company, suppliers are directly related to the smooth implementation of a series of businesses such as production, marketing, and services. Supplier relationship, as an important relationship resource for enterprises, is also an important concern for M&A. First, the acquirer should clarify whether the target's supplier relationship is its scarce resource; if it is and there are no barriers to transplantation, then the capital of the two sides is undoubtedly complimentary. Second, if it is not a scarce resource in itself, but can enhance the strength of the original material procurement chain, then it can be considered that there is an enhancement of the supplier relationship between the two sides. Third, if there is an overlapping supplier relationship between the two sides, and there is no need for them to coexist, and cutting one side can bring cost savings, then there is substitutability in the relationship capital of the material procurement link between the two sides of the M&A.

(iii) In terms of the marketing operation

Customer relationships and marketing operations are the related resources that will have a direct impact on this segment.

First, customer relationship is closely related to the downstream value chain of an enterprise, and is a very important resource for an enterprise. In recent years, customer relationship management (CRM) is a hot issue that has received wide attention from both industry and theoretical circles. Customer relationship resources of a company can be focused on both positive and negative aspects, such as customer satisfaction and customer loyalty on the positive side, and customer complaints and customer churn on the negative side. If the customer relationship of the target company is scarce for the acquirer, then the merger will bring complementarity; if the customer relationship of one party and the other party can complement each other and produce an enhancement effect, then the customer relationship resources of the marketing segment of both sides are considered to be enhanced. There is another situation that the relationship resources of both sides are independent of each other and no relationship will occur, and the merger will still have an independent impact on their respective marketing links. The fit of other resources of both sides should be examined in this case. Of course, there is also the question of whether customer resources can be transferred smoothly.

Second, market operation may include relationship resources such as brand awareness and marketing network. If the acquirer considers brand awareness or marketing network as its scarce resource, and through its judgment of the target's strengths, it believes that the acquiree can provide them, then this resource can be considered complementary between the two sides. Likewise, we should pay attention to the issue of whether the marketing network relationship can be transferred smoothly. If the M&A event will lead to the disintegration of the acquiree's original marketing network, then the acquirer should proceed with caution. If one party has brand awareness and shares this relationship resources with the other party through M&A, it will lead to an increase in the marketing capacity of the post-merger company, and the overall revenue of the company will be greater than the sum of the two independents, then it can be considered that the relationship resources of both sides for marketing have enhancement; if the marketing networks of both sides have overlapping, the coexistence of both sides will increase competition and reduce market share, then if the cancellation of one party brings cost savings, it is considered that there may be substitution or conflict effects between the acquirer and the target.

(iv) In terms of the service segment

It is directly related to resources such as market operation, and relationships with the public and government. Market operations may include customer databases, franchising, etc. Analyzing the attributes of this resource, we can learn that: First, if one or two of these two types of relationship resources are scarce resources for the acquirer and the target happens to be able to satisfy them, then there is complementarity in the relationship resources of the service segment between the two sides, for example, the target has a franchise for a high monopoly business. Second, if these relationship resources are not the acquirer's scarce resources, but the target has such superior resources that can have an enhancing effect on the acquirer's existing resources, then the relationship resources of both sides can be judged as an enhancing fit. In addition, the relationship between a company and external groups such as the public and government constitutes the external operating environment of the company, which can facilitate or constrain the development of the company. The acquirer should select targets with good resources for such relationships.

Although no analysis is done here for the R&D and manufacturing and processing value chain links, once the stakeholders of these two links are found, they can be analyzed and judged concerning the resource relationship between them.

6.5 Evaluation of the Resource Fit Degree

6.5.1 Evaluation Program Design for Resource Fit

6.5.1.1 The Basic Idea of Evaluation of Fit

Assessing M&A fit is a complex task. Firstly, we need to evaluate the strengths and weaknesses of the respective resources between acquirers and acquirees, and the intangibility nature of resources, especially knowledge-based resources, makes it difficult to measure them. Secondly, the fit between enterprises is based on the fit between specific resources, and at the same time, may be restricted by the relationship between different resources. We need to evaluate the overall fit between acquirers and acquirees based on judging the fit between specific resources.

Following this idea, this book designs the M&A fit analysis scheme as shown in Fig. 6.12.

Step 1 to step 5 in Fig. 6.12 belongs to the evaluation of resource fit, and step 6 is a comprehensive evaluation of fit, which is based on the evaluation of resource fit, i.e., the fit of specific resources is an influencing factor of overall fit.

6.5.1.2 Evaluation of Resource Fit

The basic idea of resource fit evaluation: firstly, the operational processes in the value chains of acquirers and acquirees are corresponded to the three types of intellectual capital one by one to establish the resource value chain fit matrix; secondly, an index system is established for the four types of resource elements; thirdly, the basic resource factors of both sides are quantified to evaluate the advantages of the specific resource value chain of enterprises, and the judgment set is specified as specific values (roughly divided into three values: high, medium and low in the following); finally, the value chain of both sides are included in the resource value chain fit matrix for comparison, and a judgment can be made on the fit degree (high, medium, low) of the specific resource value chains of both sides.

The evaluation of the advantages of the resource value chain will be carried out for the four levels of the value chain divided into four categories of indicators, the first is the indicator of tangible resources factors; the second is the indicator of human

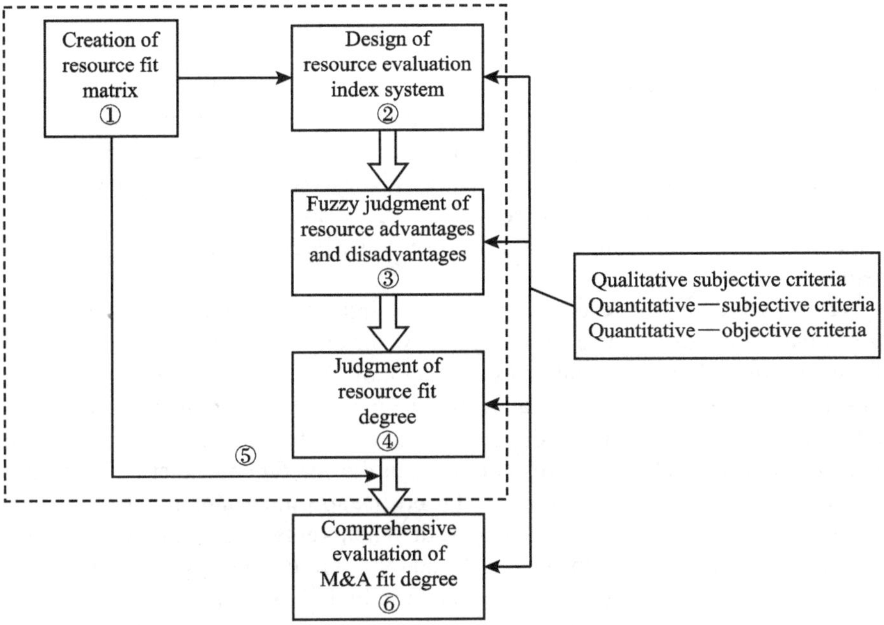

Fig. 6.12 M&A fit analysis scheme

capital; the third is the indicator of organizational capital factors; the fourth is the indicator of relationship capital factors.

These four categories of indicators reflect the resource status of the enterprise from four different perspectives and aspects, and are interrelated, with each category reflecting a different function that supports the healthy functioning of the enterprise. The indicators of tangible resources reflect the material characteristics of the operational process of the value chain and are the material basis for maintaining the integrated operation of the enterprise; the indicators of human capital reflect the knowledge and capabilities stored in the employees of the enterprise and are the basis for determining the development potential of the enterprise; the indicators of organizational capital and relationship capital are the structural capital of the enterprise, the former is the internal manifestation of the organizational knowledge and capability, which affects the enterprise's comprehensive operation efficiency and development potential, while the latter is the external manifestation of the enterprise's organizational knowledge and capability, reflecting the value of the relationships between the enterprise and external stakeholders and affecting the enterprise's industry potential.

By assigning values to the above four categories of indicators through certain channels and using fuzzy mathematics and other tools for a comprehensive evaluation, the quantitative results of the advantages and disadvantages of each category of resources can be obtained. Then, according to the resource value chain fit matrix, the fit of the same resources between acquirers and acquirees is judged according to the six operational processes in the value chain.

6.5.1.3 Basic Methodology of M&A Fit Evaluation

The evaluation of the fit between acquirers and acquirees is based on the identification of specific influencing factors (indicator system design), to quantitatively determine the advantages and disadvantages of resources, and then qualitatively determine the fit of resources based on the "resource fit matrix". Based on the fit of specific resources, the evaluation of the overall fit of both sides will be conducted by a comprehensive evaluation method, and computer simulation can also be conducted by neural network methods.

We first subdivide the resources into various independent items, and then design an evaluation indicator for each category. According to the previous division of resources, we will build a detailed evaluation indicator system for the four subsystems: tangible assets, human capital, relationship capital, and organizational capital, and establish a fuzzy comprehensive evaluation model that can be applied to evaluate the advantages of each type of resources. Then the "resource fit matrix" is used to evaluate the fit of specific resources. By proposing specific evaluation indicators for different types of resources and judging the fit, it helps enterprises grasp the contribution and role structure of each subsystem, and through monitoring these indicators, it can strengthen the management of resource fit by M&A entities.

We use a combination of qualitative analysis and quantitative assessment for the evaluation of M&A fit.

(1) Qualitative subjective criteria. The resource fit matrix is established to qualitatively determine the possible relationship status between the two value chains based on the pros and cons of the resource value chain of the acquirer and the target. These indicators are not conventional quantitative measurement units, but vague indicators such as low, medium, and high.
(2) Quantitative criteria. It can be subdivided into quantitative—objective criteria and quantitative—subjective criteria. The former is mainly some financial indicators, while the latter focuses on non-financial indicators, such as consumer satisfaction.

6.5.2 *Evaluation Mode of Degree of Resource Fit*

The first step of resource fit evaluation is to evaluate the advantages of specific resources on both sides, and we will design indicators for each of the four categories of resources. It should be emphasized that the specific content of similar resources of different enterprises may vary, and our evaluation is conducted for the commonality of resources and the factors that can reflect the value of a type of resource. The design of indicators does not mean that the more is better, or that the more is more comprehensive. It is not necessary to include all indicators with strong relevance in the indicator system. Instead, the indicator system should reflect the focus of the evaluation, i.e., the key resource factors in the value chain.

6.5.2.1 The Conceptual Model for Resource Fit Evaluation

(1) Judgement matrix of enterprise resource value chain

In the above, we established a link between each type of resource and the operation link. We established a value chain system for resource fit analysis, aiming at the different influences ofthe three types of knowledge resources on the operation links of the enterprise value chain.

The first step in resource fit analysis is to judge the scarcity of resources in different value chain operations of the acquirer. The specific method is based on the resource value chain system established in Fig. 6.6, according to the value chain operation process, to identify the respective knowledge capital of the M&A parties, to preliminarily judge the stock status of the capital of both parties, and to evaluate whether the human capital, organizational capital and relationship capital of the M&A party are scarce resources and the degree of satisfaction of the corresponding resources of the target party by combining the six operation processes in the enterprise resource value chain. Accordingly, we establish the judgment matrix of the resource value chain of the acquirer, as shown in Fig. 6.13.

In Fig. 6.13, the scarcity of resources corresponding to different operation processes is represented by o and × respectively. For example, if human capital in strategic planning is scarce, fill in o in the corresponding position of the matrix, otherwise fill in ×. The advantage of resources is represented by high, medium, and low. For example, if the relationship capital of the marketing link does not have an advantage, then fill in low in the corresponding position of the matrix. By filling in the contents in Fig. 6.13, the acquirer can make judgments on the scarcity and advantage of specific resources in different operation links of the value chain. As a result, enterprises can not only clearly know the resource status of their value chain operation links and the key resources they need to obtain from the target party, but also lay the foundation for further judging the possible fit relationship between the specific resources of the M&A party and the potential target party. Correspondingly, to judge whether the resources of the target party meet the demand of the acquirer, we can fill in the judgment matrix of the resource value chain of the target party,

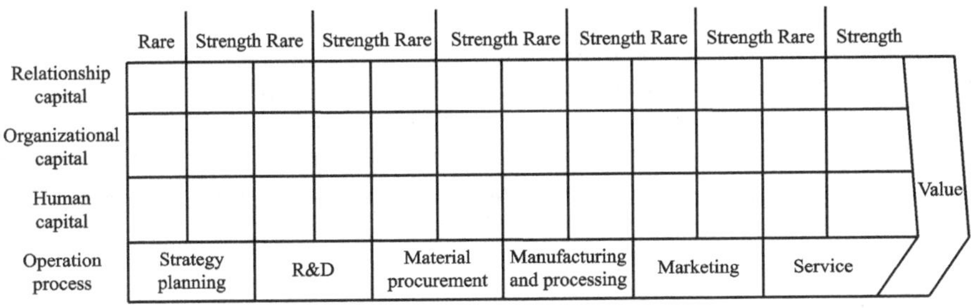

Fig. 6.13 Judgment matrix of the resource value chain of the acquirer

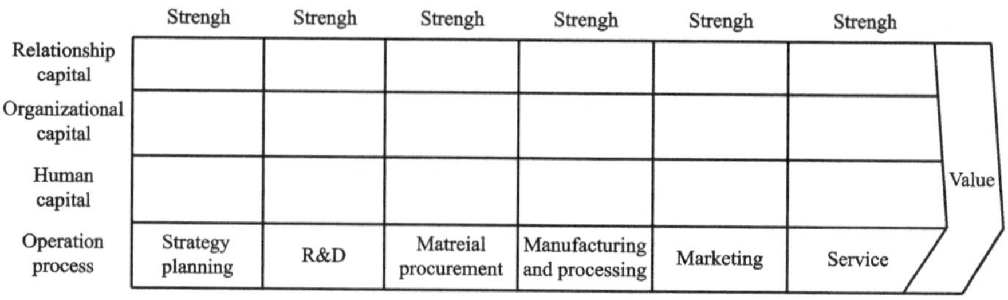

Fig. 6.14 Judgment matrix of the resource value chain of the target

and focus on evaluating the strengths and weaknesses of different resources in the operational links of the target's value chain, as shown in Fig. 6.14.

In Fig. 6.14, the advantages of resources corresponding to different operating processes in the target value chain are also represented by high, medium, and low.

For the six operation processes of the value chain, based on identifying the scarce resources required by the acquirer and the basic resource status of the acquirer and the target enterprise, we can analyze and judge the fit degree of similar resources between the two sides of the M&A in different operational links.

This process requires two steps to complete. First, judge the overall advantages and disadvantages of human capital, organizational capital, and relationship capital of both parties. the judgment matrices in Figs. 6.13 and 6.14 can qualitatively analyze the strengths and weaknesses of the specific contents of the three types of knowledge capital. Second, we will also use quantitative methods to judge the overall strengths of each of the three types of the intellectual capital of the M&A parties, i.e., we use a combination of qualitative and quantitative methods to evaluate the degree of resource fit.

(2) Value chain fit matrix

Based on evaluating the specific resource advantages of the acquirer and the target enterprise, we can establish a value chain fit matrix to make a preliminary judgment on the basic fit of the resources between the two parties of the M&A, as shown in Fig. 6.15.

The horizontal axis of the matrix represents the advantages of the value chain of the target, and the vertical axis represents the advantages of the value chain of the acquirer, and the degree of resource fit determined by the superiority and inferiority of the two value chains is represented by different positions of the matrix. The target value chain corresponding to the column on the left has disadvantages, so they are all areas that do not fit; if the comparison results of the value chains of the two parties fall in other areas, we need to combine the value chain operation process to make further judgments on the fit of specific resources of both parties.

(3) Resource fit judgment matrix for M&A parties

According to the six operational processes in the value chain, the possible interrelationships between the three types of the knowledge capital of the acquirer and the

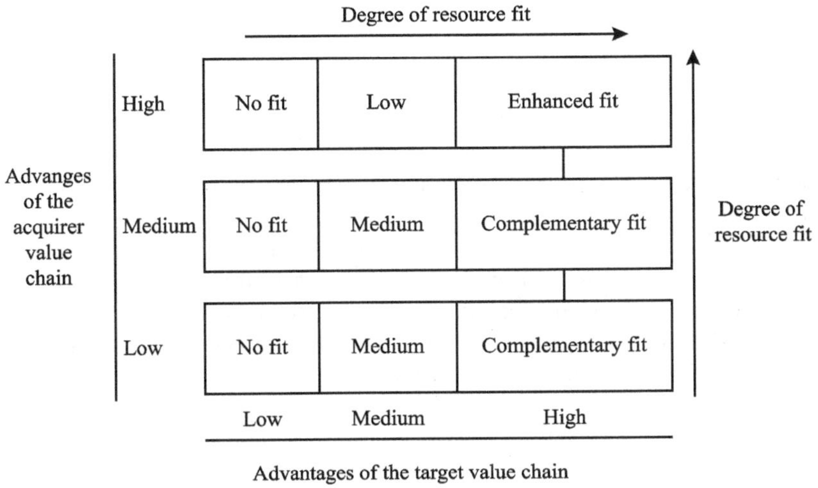

Fig. 6.15 Value chain fit matrix

target enterprise, i.e., human capital, organizational capital, and relationship capital, include five cases, i.e., complementarity, substitution, enhancement, conflict and independence. Accordingly, we can establish a matrix for judging the resource fit between the two parties of M&A. The matrix consists of five rows and six columns, which represent the five types of role relationships of resources and the six operational processes in the value chain, as shown in Fig. 6.16.

Figure 6.16 shows the conceptual model for judging the degree of resource fit between M&A parties, where the matrix values are expressed as 0 or 1, i.e., 1 for complementarity, enhancement, and substitution, and 0 for the opposite; 0 if there is

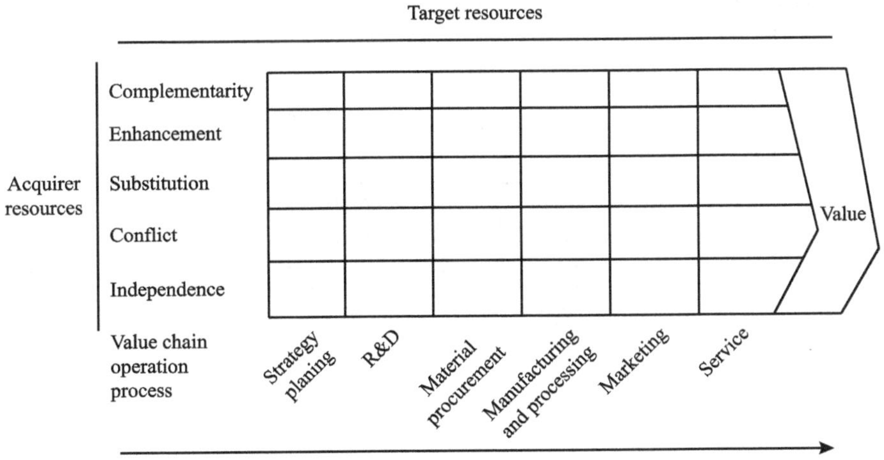

Fig. 6.16 Matrix of resource fit evaluation of both parties in M&A

conflict, and 1 otherwise. Therefore, we can make a judgment on the fit of specific resources, such as human capital. For each type of knowledge capital, a fit matrix can be established separately for the specific analysis.

According to the above analysis, we divide the resources of enterprises into tangible assets and intangible knowledge capital according to their impact on value creation, while the fit of knowledge capital is the main source of value that can be created by M&A.

We believe that the fit of knowledge capital is the key factor that affects and restricts the fit of both parties in M&A. Therefore, we focus on evaluating the advantages and fit of three types of knowledge capital. According to the connotation and influence variables of different capitals, the index systems of human capital, organizational capital, and relationship capital are shown in Fig. 6.17.

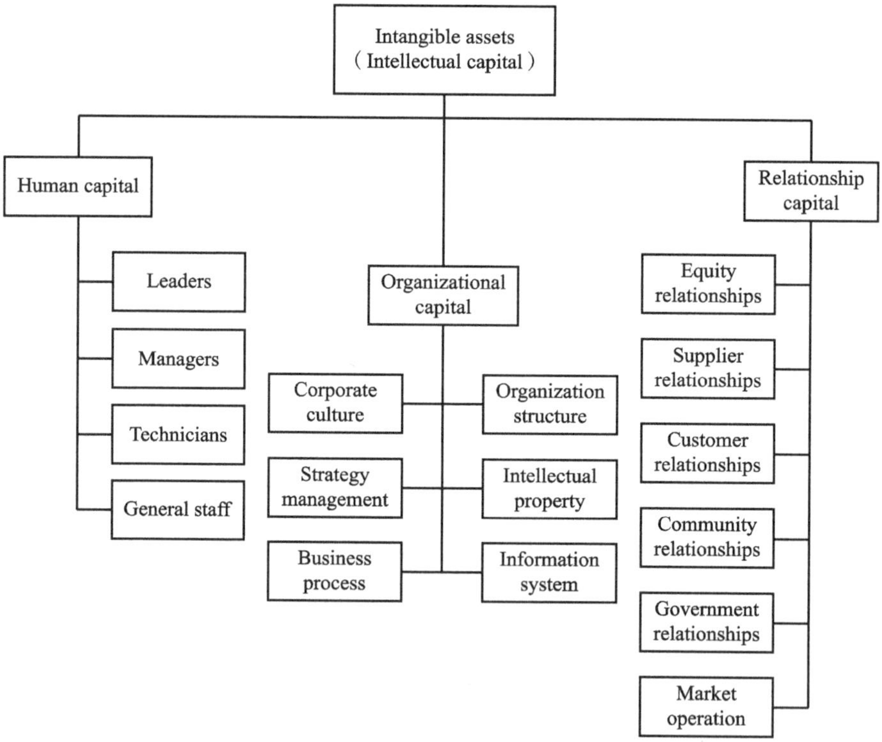

Fig. 6.17 Enterprise knowledge resource index system

6.5.2.2 Fit Evaluation of Tangible Assets

(1) Tangible asset advantage evaluation index

Tangible assets are closely related to economies of scale and capital efficiency. We will evaluate the advantages of corporate assets from two dimensions corporate profitability and market growth.

(i) Profitability and changes in profitability

Although the profitability evaluation will produce misleading results due to changes in the company's strategic arrangement and external environment, the profitability index is the primary indicator that reflects the performance of a company at a certain stage.

(ii) Market growth

Indicators reflecting market growth should include the current market position and the progress of the market position of the evaluated company's products, for example, by using indicators such as market share, relative market share, and market growth rate.

(2) Tangible assets fit matrix

Based on evaluating the strengths and weaknesses of the tangible assets of the acquirer and the target, and comparing the two into a coordinate system, we can establish a fit matrix of tangible assets to measure the fit of tangible assets of both parties, as shown in Fig. 6.18.

In Fig. 6.18, the horizontal axis of the matrix represents the advantage of the target's tangible assets, and the vertical axis represents the advantage of the acquirer's

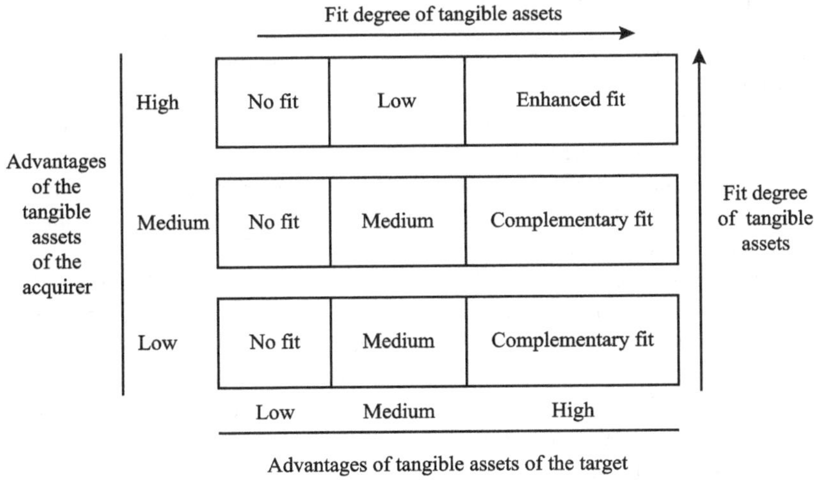

Fig. 6.18 Tangible assets fit matrix

tangible assets. The degree of tangible asset fit determined by the degree of superiority and inferiority of tangible assets of both parties from the lowest to the highest is represented by different positions of the matrix. The tangible assets of the target party corresponding to the column on the left have disadvantages, and if other resources are not considered, the acquirer has no reason to choose such a target party, so they are all areas where tangible assets do not fit. While the target's tangible assets corresponding to the right column have advantages, and if the acquirer's tangible assets are at a disadvantage, the target's superior asset value chain can just make up for its shortcomings, as shown in the lower right corner; if the result of comparing the value chains of both parties falls in the upper right corner, it means that both parties have superior assets and can join forces to obtain economies of scale. The middle column of the matrix is at a medium level because of the tangible asset advantage of the target party, so regardless of the tangible asset advantage of the acquirer, the fit degree of the tangible assets of the two parties is also judged to be a medium level. At this time, the acquirer should focus on examining the fit of the knowledge capital of both parties.

6.5.2.3 Fit Evaluation of Human Capital

The evaluation of the human capital fit between the M&A parties can be divided into three steps: firstly, set up indicators, and evaluate the human capital advantages of the acquirer and the target party respectively using the fuzzy comprehensive evaluation method; secondly, based on the strengths of the human capital of the M&A parties, judge the position of the human capital of both parties in the value chain fit matrix; thirdly, use the human capital fit evaluation matrix (see Fig. 6.19) to evaluate the fit of the human capital of both parties.

(1) Human capital advantage evaluation index

The human capital of an enterprise includes the knowledge, experience, ability of its various personnel, and the degree to which they play a role. According to the difference in the role played in the operation and management, we classify the human capital of the enterprise according to the senior decision-making leader, middle management, technical staff, and general staff, and separately evaluate these four categories of personnel in five aspects: education level, business ability, innovation ability, learning ability, and psychological satisfaction.

Accordingly, the index system of human capital advantage evaluation is divided into three levels. The target level is the human capital advantage, and the first-level indicators include four dimensions of leadership personnel, middle management personnel, technical personnel, and general employees, and each dimension is composed of five indicators to form the second-level indicators, as shown in Table 6.1.

We can use the above indicators and use the fuzzy comprehensive evaluation method to evaluate the advantages of the human capital of both parties, and on this basis, judge the position of the human capital of the acquirer and the target enterprise

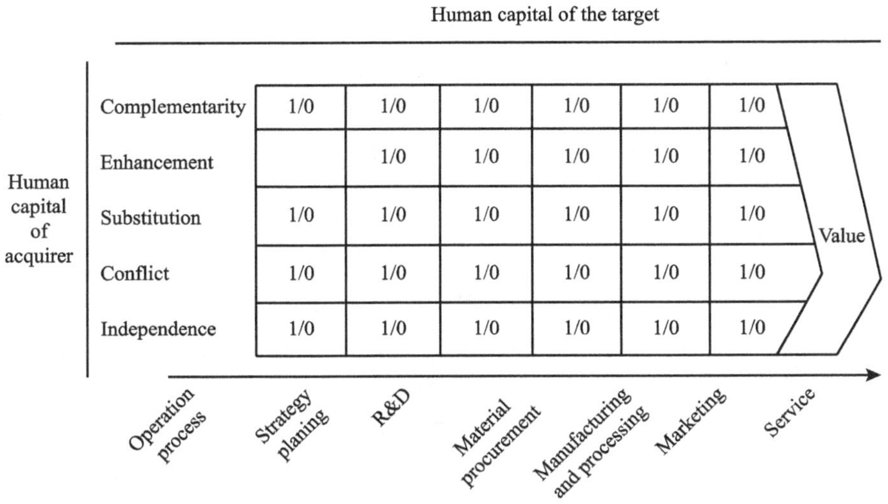

Fig. 6.19 Human capital fit judgment matrix

in the fit matrix of the value chain, and then evaluate the fit of the human capital of both M&A parties.

(3) Human capital fit judgment matrix

According to the six operating processes of the value chain and the possible interrelationship between the human capital of the acquirer and the target, we establish a matrix to judge the human capital fit of both parties. The matrix consists of five rows and six columns, which represent the five role relationships of the human capital of the two parties and the six operational processes of the value chain, as shown in Fig. 6.19.

The value of the matrix is represented by 0 or 1, that is, if the human capital of both parties in the M&A has complementarity, enhancement, and substitution, the value is 1; otherwise, the value is 0; if there is conflict, the value is 0, otherwise, the value is 1. Therefore, by summarizing the value of the specific resource relationship corresponding to the same operation process of both parties, we can judge the fit of the human capital of both parties. For example, in terms of strategic planning, if excellent leaders are a scarce resource for the acquirer, and the analysis shows that the leader of the target party has advantages, and the possibility of leaving after the acquisition is low, then judging that the two parties are complementary, we can fill in 1 in the upper left corner of the matrix in Fig. 6.19. The possible interrelationships between the human capital of both parties in the operation process link have been described in detail in the mechanism analysis of human capital fit, which can be referred to when the model is applied for analysis. After judging the interrelationship between the human capital of the two parties in the value chain, we can evaluate the fit of the human capital of the two parties according to the value (0 or 1).

Table 6.1 Indicators for evaluating human capital advantage

Target layer	Primary indicators		Secondary indicators		Indicator description
Human capital advantage	Leaders	U1	Education level	U11	It is divided into four categories: doctoral, master, undergraduate, and junior college, which are processed by questionnaire
			Business ability	U12	By processing the questionnaire
			Innovation ability	U13	By processing the questionnaire
			Learning ability	U14	By processing the questionnaire
			Psychological satisfaction	U15	Design survey forms, and get data directly from leaders' subjective comments
	Middle management	U2	Education level	U21	It is divided into four categories: doctoral, master, undergraduate, and junior college, which are processed by questionnaire
			Business ability	U22	By processing the questionnaire
			Innovation ability	U23	By processing the questionnaire
			Learning ability	U24	By processing the questionnaire
			Psychological satisfaction	U25	Design survey forms and obtain data directly from the subjective comments of middle managers
Human capital advantage	Technical staff	U3	Education level	U31	It is divided into four categories: doctoral, master, undergraduate, and junior college, which are processed by questionnaire
			Business ability	U32	By processing the questionnaire

(continued)

Table 6.1 (continued)

Target layer	Primary indicators		Secondary indicators		Indicator description
			Innovation ability	U33	By processing the questionnaire
			Learning ability	U34	By processing the questionnaire
			Psychological satisfaction	U35	Design survey forms, and get data directly from technical staff's subjective comments
	General staff	U4	Education level	U41	It is divided into four categories: doctoral, master, undergraduate, and junior college, which are processed by questionnaire
			Business ability	U42	By processing the questionnaire
			Innovation ability	U43	By processing the questionnaire
			Learning ability	U44	By processing the questionnaire
			Psychological satisfaction	U45	Design a survey form, and obtain data from subjective comments by conducting a sample survey of employees

Source The index design refers to He Qingming (2005)

6.5.2.4 Fit Evaluation of Organizational Capital

(1) Organizational capital advantage evaluation index

The status of corporate organizational capital can be evaluated from six dimensions, including corporate culture, organizational structure, management style, intellectual property, business processes, and information system, and each dimension can be examined from five aspects. Accordingly, the index system for evaluating the organizational capital advantage is shown in Table 6.2. The target level is the advantage of organizational capital, and the primary indicators include six dimensions of corporate culture, organizational structure, management style, intellectual property, business process, and information system, and each dimension is composed of five indicators to form the second-level indicators.

Table 6.2 Indicators for evaluating organizational capital advantage

Target layer	Primary indicators		Secondary indicators	
Advantages of organizational capital	Corporate culture	U1	Values	U11
			Willingness to collaborate	U12
			Cohesion ability	U13
			Organizational learning	U14
			Willingness to innovate	U15
	Organizational structure	U2	Corporate governance	U21
			Decision mode	U22
			Project integration	U23
			Institutional integration	U24
			Rights and interests	U25
	Management style	U3	Strategic concept	U31
			Strategic plan	U32
			Strategy implementation	U33
			Strategic resources	U34
			Environmental integration	U35
Advantages of organizational capital	Intellectual property	U4	Patent	U41
			Trademark rights	U42
			Copyright	U43
			Trade secret	U44
			Proprietary technology	U45
	Business process	U5	Order cycle	U51
			Product quality	U52
			Operational efficiency	U53
			Value process	U54
			Reengineering ability	U55
	Information system	U6	Intranet	U61
			Enterprise knowledge base	U62
			Real-time communication network	U63
			IT hardware	U64
			IT software	U65

Source The index design refers to He Qingming (2005)

For the above evaluation criteria index system, the method of "fuzzy comprehensive evaluation" in fuzzy mathematics can be used to quantitatively and comprehensively evaluate the organizational capital advantages of both parties involved in strategic M&A, and on this basis to judge the position of the organizational capital

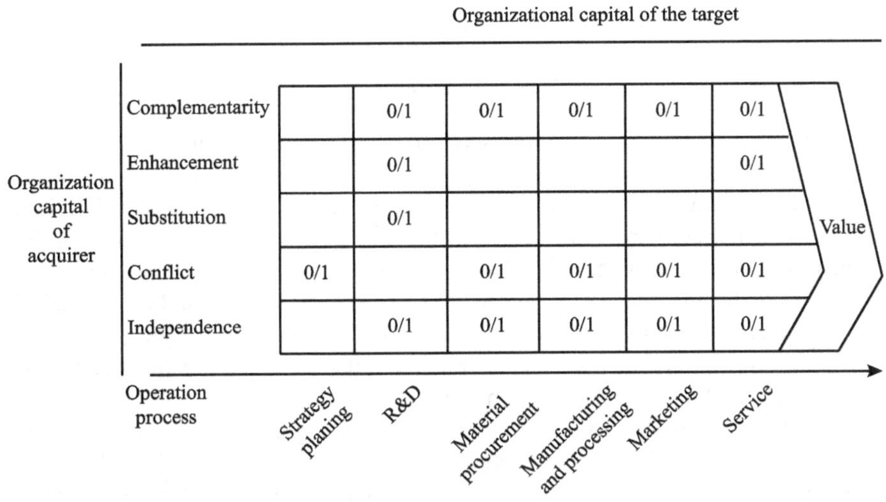

Fig. 6.20 Organizational capital fit judgment matrix

of the acquirer and the target in the value chain fit matrix, and then evaluate the organizational capital fit between the M&A parties.

(2) Organizational capital fit judgment matrix

Aiming at the six operation processes of the value chain and the possible interrelationship between the organizational capital of the acquirer and the target party, we establish a matrix to judge the capital fit of the two parties in the M&A, which consists of five rows and six columns, representing the five role relationships of organizational capital and the six operational processes in the value chain, as shown in Fig. 6.20.

Similar to the evaluation of human capital, the value of the matrix is represented by 0 or 1, that is, if the organizational capital of both parties in the M&A is complementary, enhancement, and substitution, the value is 1; otherwise, the value is 0; if there is conflict, the value is 0, otherwise, the value is 1. Therefore, by summarizing the value of the organizational capital relationship corresponding to the same operation process of both parties, we can make a judgment on the fit of the organizational capital of both parties. The possible interrelationship between the organizational capital of both parties in the operation process has been described in detail in the mechanism analysis of organizational capital fit, which can be referred to in the practical application. After judging the interrelationship between the two parties' organizational capital in the value chain operation process, we can evaluate the fit of the two parties' organizational capital according to the value (0 or 1).

6.5.2.5 Fit Evaluation of Relationship Capital

(1) Relationship capital advantage evaluation index

Relationship capital includes interest relationship, supplier relationship, customer relationship, market operation capability, public relationship, and government relationship, and again the factors included in these items can be further subdivided. Accordingly, the index system of relationship capital evaluation is divided into six dimensions, and each dimension includes five indicators, as shown in Table 6.3, the target layer is the advantage of relational capital, and the primary indicators include interest relationship, supplier relationship, customer relationship, market operation, public relationship, and government relationship, and each dimension is composed of 5 indicators, which constitute secondary indicators.

Given the above evaluation criteria index system, the method of "fuzzy comprehensive evaluation" in fuzzy mathematics can be used to quantitatively and comprehensively evaluate the relationship capital advantages of both parties in the M&A, and on this basis, to judge the position of the relationship capital of the acquirer and the target party in the value chain fit matrix, and then evaluate the fit of the relationship capital of the M&A parties.

(2) Relationship capital fit judgment matrix

Corresponding to the six operating processes of the value chain and the possible interrelationship between the relationship capital of the acquirer and the target party, we establish a matrix for judging the fit of the relationship capital of the M&A parties, which consists of five rows and six columns, representing the five role relationships of the relationship capital of the parties and the six operational processes in the value chain, as shown in Fig. 6.21.

Similarly, the value of the relationship capital fit evaluation matrix is represented by 0 or 1, that is, if the relationship capital of both parties in the M&A is complementary, enhancement, and substitution, the value is 1; otherwise, the value is 0; if there is conflict, the value is 0, otherwise the value is 1. Therefore, by summarizing the value of the relationship between the relationship capital corresponding to the same operation process of both parties of the M&A, we can make a judgment on the fit of the relationship capital of the two parties. The possible complementarity, conflict, enhancement, substitution, and independence of the relationship capital between the two parties in the operation process have been described in detail in the mechanism analysis of organizational capital fit, which can be referred to when applying the model. After judging the interrelationship of the relationship capital between the two parties of the M&A according to the value chain operation process, we can evaluate the fit of the relationship capital of the two parties according to the value (0 or 1).

Table 6.3 Indicators for evaluating relationship capital advantage

Target layer	Primary indicators		Secondary indicators	
The advantage of relationship capital	Interest relationship	U1	Shareholder services	U11
			Shareholders' equity	U12
			Shareholder satisfaction	U13
			Debt service	U14
			Creditor's rights and interests	U15
	Supplier relationship	U2	Supplier complaint	U21
			Supplier churn	U22
			Supplier services	U23
			Supplier satisfaction	U24
			Supplier Loyalty_	U25
	Customer relationship	U3	Customer complaints	U31
			Customer churn	U32
			Customer service	U33
			Customer satisfaction	U34
			Customer loyalty	U35
	Market operation	U4	Customer database	U41
			Market share	U42
			Marketing network	U43
			Brand awareness	U44
			Franchise	U45
The advantage of relationship capital	Public relationship	U5	Local government	U51
			Residents	U52
			Community enterprise	U53
			Relevant departments	U54
			Community network	U55
	Government relationship	U6	Macropolicy	U61
			Industrial policy	U62
			Tax policy	U63
			Financial policy	U64
			Functional management	U65

Source The index design refers to He Qingming (2005)

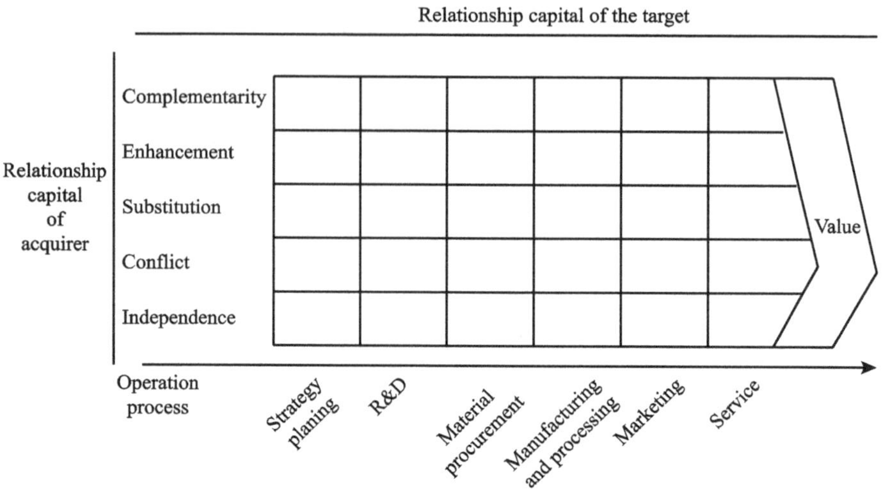

Fig. 6.21 Relationship capital fit judgment matrix

6.6 Comprehensive Evaluation of Resource Fit

For the acquirer, finding an appropriate target company and judging the fit of the two parties is the premise and basis for deciding whether to further execute the transaction. According to the enterprise resource theory, resources are the source of the sustainable competitive advantage of the enterprise; the system theory also emphasizes that the elements that make up the system and the interaction between the elements determine the function and structure of the system. Therefore, we believe that the enterprise is a system composed of resources, whose function and structure are determined by the interaction between enterprise resources and resources. It can be seen from the above analysis that the interaction relationship between resources is nonlinear. M&A activities will inevitably make the two resource systems move from isolation to integration, and the function and structure of the post-merger enterprise will also be determined by the resources of both parties and their interactions, and it is this non-linear relationship of interaction that makes the new functional structure not a simple addition of the original individual functional structure. The whole is greater than the sum of the parts, and a fit between the two parties indicates a successful M&A; conversely, it means a failed M&A. Thus, it is important to understand the interaction between the resources of the two parties after the M&Ato determine whether they are a good fit.

Since the fit of the two parties in the M&A is driven by the resources of the enterprise, especially the intangible knowledge resources and their relationships, the overall fit of the two parties in the M&A should be based on the fit of specific resources, but the fit of similar resources is only a necessary but insufficient condition for the overall fit. The role relationship between resources is complex, not only from the same kind of resources but also the interrelationship between different kinds of resources. Based on identifying the fit between the same resources of both parties in the M&A through the fuzzy comprehensive evaluation method and the fit evaluation matrix, we need to use the fit of resources as an input variable to determine the possible relationship between different degrees of fit of various types of resources and enterprise value, that is, with the overall fit of both parties.

For the judgment of the overall fit driven by this very complex and difficult to identify the nonlinear relationship, Zhang Haishan (2007) used the BP algorithm neural network tool to establish a neural network M&A fit evaluation model and simulated 88M&A transactions that occurred in the US in 2000.

Chapter 7
M&A Synergy

7.1 The Concept of M&A Synergy

Synergy is derived from the Greek word "synergos", which means working together. Karl Marx in *Capital* put forward the view that "cooperative production can lead to higher productivity or save production costs than individual small production", which is rich in synergy ideas. In fact, since H. Igor Ansoff first introduced the concept of synergistic effect in the 1960s, it has been one of the most important basic principles on which large western companies formulate diversified development strategies and plan M&A activities. Specifically, the motivation of corporate M&A mainly lies in obtaining synergistic effects through resource sharing and transfer of capabilities and knowledge between the two parties of corporate M&A, which are the main drivers of corporate M&A value creation (Bruner, 2001). As Stiegler (1996) thought, the process of corporate diversification and expansion is often the process of corporate M&A, so the study of synergistic effects is also the core area of corporate diversification research, which has attracted great attention from western financial scholars and strategic management scholars.

7.1.1 The Concept of M&A Synergistic Effect

From the 1960s to the present, the research on synergistic effect has experienced the evolution from static synergy to dynamic synergy, and from intra- firm synergy to external synergy. Several scholars have defined the concept of the M&A synergistic effect, among which H. Igor Ansoff, Hiroyuki Itami, Robert Bazzell, Bradley Gale, and Mark L. Sirower are the main representatives.

Q. Zhang, *Mergers and Acquisitions*, https://doi.org/10.1007/978-981-92-0122-8_7

7.1.1.1 H. Igor Ansoff's Definition of Synergistic Effect

H. Igor Ansoff, the father of strategic planning, was the first person to use the term "synergistic effect" in management. In the 1960s, a time when many companies were expanding and diversifying their businesses, Ansoff first proposed the concept of synergistic effect in *Corporate Strategy* published in 1965, that is, "the overall value of an enterprise may be greater than the sum of the value of the parts" when it comes to the field of M&A, synergy "is considered to be the ideal state of the fit relationship between the company and the acquired enterprise, and is often expressed as '2 + 2 = 5', which means that one company, by acquiring another company, makes the overall performance of the company better than the sum of the original performance of the two companies". Ansoff introduced the concept of synergy to help managers make better decisions on development and diversity issues. Ansoff's interpretation of synergy emphasizes its economic implications, namely the potential for tangible and intangible benefits and the strong linkage between this potential and the firm's capabilities, and argues that the effectiveness of the synergy model stems in part from the benefits of economies of scale, such as the potential for cost reductions in both firms through improved equipment utilization, shared sales forces, or unified ordering. But synergy also includes other more abstract benefits, such as the possibility that managers can apply their accumulated knowledge and experience in one enterprise to other new enterprises, which Ansoff calls "manager's synergy".

7.1.1.2 Hiroyuki Itami's Definition of Synergistic Effect

Hiroyuki Itami (1987), a Japanese strategist, based on resource theory, broke down Ansoff's concept of synergy into two parts: "complementary effect" and "synergistic effect". Itami's research goal is to hope that managers can make the most efficient use of all the resources of the company and at the same time create sufficient resources. In his mind, synergy is a method to maximize the effectiveness of resources. Therefore, he divides resources into two categories: physical assets, such as production equipment, and invisible assets, which are intangible resources, such as trademarks, customer recognition or technical expertise, or a corporate culture that inspires a strong sense of identity among employees. Itami believes that improving the utilization rate of physical assets is one of the ways to maximize the effectiveness of all the company's resources. He calls the method of improving the utilization efficiency of physical assets or financial assets to save costs or increase sales as "complementary effects". Although this effect is extremely valuable, it is not a real source of synergy because it is very easy to be copied by other companies and does not provide a lasting advantage for the company. Real synergies are only possible when a company begins to use its unique resource, and intangible assets, and because such synergies are difficult to replicate by rivals, they can give the company a more lasting competitive advantage.

Itami proposed two concepts of static synergistic effect and dynamic synergistic effect in *Mobilizing Invisible Assets*. The static synergistic effect comes from the combination of different strategic elements at the same point in time, while the dynamic synergistic effect comes from the combination of two strategies at different points in time. Itami believes that the key to a company's development lies in its ability to obtain the dynamic synergistic effect and establish a basic framework for a dynamic synergistic effect. The reasons are as follows: (1) only through the dynamic synergistic effect, can the invisible resources be accumulated and applied over a long time, and only in this way can the company have the resources needed to actively adapt to the environmental changes; (2) dynamic synergistic effect between two products or markets can also make it easier to achieve dynamic complementary effects on financial resources at the same time. It can be seen that Ansoff's definition of synergy includes both scale and scope effects (which are consistent with Itami's complementary effect) and the sharing of intangible assets such as technical expertise and company image, while Itami's definition of synergistic effect is limited to invisible use of resources. But Itami acknowledges that complementary and synergistic effects often go hand in hand, and he deliberately separates the two to make managers realize that invisible assets are fundamental to a company's growth and prosperity.

7.1.1.3 Robert Buzzell and Bradley Gale's Definition of Synergistic Effect

Buzzell and Gale (1987) explained the definition of synergistic effect from the perspective of the enterprise group, that is, the business performance of the enterprise group as a whole relative to the business performance formed by simply summarizing the individual components. They believe that sustained synergistic effect can create value in four basic ways: (1) sharing resources or activities, where economies of scale are achieved by sharing common business performance (research and development or engineering, procurement, production or operations, a unified sales force, marketing plans, distribution channels, etc.); (2) spill-over effects from marketing and R&D expenditures, where firms in a cluster often benefit indirectly from the marketing and R&D efforts of sister firms, even if there is no sharing of marketing and R&D; (3) similarity of firms, i.e., sharing of technical and managerial knowledge and skills in similar knowledge areas (high- tech industries or certain areas where marketing can play a key role); (4) sharing of corporate image, i.e., being seen as a member of a reputable enterprise group that can enhance the image of an individual enterprise and makes it profitable. At the same time, they combine daily experience and the strategic planning institute (SPI) database to propose a framework for evaluating the existence of synergistic effects between business behaviors across related firms' value chains. They argue that if a group of enterprises has a larger share of the value chain in terms of marketing and R&D expenditures, the group of enterprises can usually achieve an above-average synergistic effect and thus have better profitability than if the individual firms had operated independently. This result reflects not only economies of scale in costs in functional areas, but also spill-over effects in marketing and research and development. In addition, these two scholars also remind managers that synergistic effects can be positive or negative, while most managers and scholars always focus on positive synergistic effects and ignore the existence of the negative synergistic effects.

7.1.1.4 Mark L. Sirower's Definition of Synergistic Effect

Both Ansoff's broad synergistic effect and Itami's narrow synergistic effect concepts, which focus on the synergy of different business units within a diversified business, have obvious shortcomings when applied to explain M&A activities: they do not take into account the original growth potential of both parties to the M&A, and when predicting or testing the effects of M&A, they may confuse the synergistic effects of M&A with the original growth potential of both parties to the M&A. To this end, Eccles Robert et al. (1999) further specify Sirower's definition of synergistic effect by arguing that the value of a firm's synergistic effect is the sum of the net present value of the firm's cash flows resulting from various improvements created by the firm's merger, and they believe that these cash flows exceed the sum of those market expectations for the cash flows that the business would have had if the business were operating on its own, i.e., in the absence of M&A. Since then, Sirower (2001) put forward the dynamic concept of synergistic effect in M&A: "it should be the portion of the combined firm's overall benefits that grow beyond the sum of what the market already expects from the target firm and the acquirer as a stand-alone firm. M&A must meet at least one of the following two points to obtain the synergistic effect and obtain M&A benefits: (1) the acquirer must be able to further limit the competitive threat to the acquirer and the target enterprise from current and potential competitors in the input market, production process, or output market; (2) the acquirer must be able to open up new markets or encroach on its competitors' markets so that competitors cannot respond".

7.1.2 Classification of M&A Synergy

7.1.2.1 Classification of Existing M&A Synergy

(1) Classification of synergy in M&A by foreign scholars

Penrose (1959) explained the synergy by adopting the theory of corporate capability. Although Penrose did not explicitly put forward the concept of synergy, he pointed out two forms of synergy: one is asset sharing caused by the inseparability of resources; the other is asset transfer caused by the surplus of internal resources of the company.

Rumelt (1974) divides synergy into two types: financial and operational. The former refers to the various financial benefits brought by M&A to the enterprise. This benefit is achieved not by an increase in efficiency, but it is a kind of pure cash flow income generated due to the internal regulations of tax laws, accounting standards, and securities transactions. The latter mainly refers to the changes brought by M&A to the production and operation activities of enterprises and the benefits produced by the improvement of efficiency, which is prominently reflected in economies of scale and scope.

A buyer's monopoly or a seller's monopoly is achieved, resulting in lower purchase prices from suppliers. Pursche (1988) believes that there are three types of synergy between the two sides of M&A: the first one is general synergy, which includes economies of scale and management activities, sharing of facilities, etc.

These cost-saving synergy are available to most buyers; the second one is the industry-specific Synergy, which are usually closely related to the characteristics of production, operation, and management of a specific industry, and may arise between the target and several potential acquirers in the same industry; the third one is a specific synergy that exists only between the target and a specific acquirer and cannot be imitated or enjoyed by other companies.

Larsson (1990) believes that the synergy produced by M&A can be divided into the following four types: market power synergy—obtaining higher selling prices from customers by expanding transaction scale or increasing market concentration; operating synergy—through joint operations, expand the scale, scope, gain experience, and reduce production and marketing costs through vertical mergers; financial synergy—through financial market forces, internal capital markets and diversification, joint acquisition and allocation of capital, risk reduction, and realization of capital costs decline; management synergy—gain in the application of additional (additional or similar) and complementary (different but compatible with existing capabilities) management skills and talents through the sharing and mutual exchange of management know-how from different units.

In his book *Takeover, Restructuring and Corporate Governance*, J. Fred Weston (1996), the management synergy is also listed as a kind of synergy that is parallel to the operation synergy and financial synergy and is considered to be an important motive for hybrid mergers.

Singh and Montgomery (1987) and Seth (1990) believe that the synergy after the merger comes from improving the enterprise's operating efficiency, enhancing the market competitiveness, or some financial benefits. Eccles and Robert et al. (1999) mentioned that in the calculation of synergy, the synergy is generally divided into five kinds, namely cost saving, income increase, process improvement, financial engineering, and tax benefit.

(2) Classification of synergy in M&A by Chinese scholars

Chinese scholar Zhu Zhengxuan (1999) divides synergy into three categories according to the different levels of enterprise operation: if two enterprises can reduce the direct production cost or improve the product quality through the merger, they can create the synergy of production and operation; through mergers, enterprises can integrate relevant operation and management functions, on the one hand, reduce the management expenses of unit products, and on the other hand, through the expansion of scale, strengthen the functions of relevant operation and management, make the enterprise more competitive, and create synergy of management and operation; if M&A of the corporate can reduce capital costs through centralized financing, or improve capital investment efficiency through the allocation and mobilization of funds on a larger scale, thereby enhancing financial strength and reducing financial risks, create synergy in capital management.

Wang Changzheng (2000) classified the synergistic of M&A as follows according to the similarity of the value chains of the two organizations and the relationship between them: (i) increase effect. The value chain of the acquirer and the target enterprise is the same, and the integration after the merger is less difficult, mainly through the sharing of the company's infrastructure and other fixed expenditure projects, reducing the company's costs to obtain the synergy of economies of scale. (ii) Strengthen the effect. The value chains of both parties are different, but some parts are similar. By integrating previously independent value chain parts, such as sales force, production capacity, logistics, R&D, etc., to better serve customers and obtain synergy such as economies of scale. (iii) Transfer, diffusion effect. The two value chains are different, but some key parts of one value chain are useful to the other value chain, creating synergy through the transfer or diffusion of skills in a key business. (iv) Complementary effect. The value chains of the two parties are completely different, and they are in different business areas. However, under the consideration of the M&A strategy, the goal may be to enter new business areas to achieve product expansion or extension of the company's core capabilities. Different types of synergy reflect, to a certain extent, the integration methods and difficulties that should be adopted for specific M&A.

Xu Mingbo (1997) briefly discussed the manifestations of financial synergy in M&A (reasonable tax avoidance effect, undervaluation effect, expected effect, etc.); Lu Yuming (1999) emphasized the analysis of potential business synergy in different types of M&A; Liu Wengang (1999) analyzed the impact of intangible assets on M&A of enterprise and believed that the transfer and exertion of the advantages of intangible assets such as brands, patented technologies, and corporate culture in M&A can produce synergy and greatly improve performance of M&A.

7.1.2.2 Classification of M&A Synergy in This Book

At present, the concepts of M&A synergy at home and abroad describe the meaning of synergy as a whole. This book will divide M&A synergy into potential synergy, expected synergy and actual synergy according to the different stages of M&A. Potential synergy refers to the synergy that the acquirer estimates that the merger will produce after the merger transaction is completed and before the integration activities begin. It is under the premise that the resources of both parties to the merger can be fully transferred, and the ex-ante perspective predicts the part of the enterprise entity that realizes value appreciation after the merger through the role of independence, substitution, complementarity, enhancement, and conflict between the resources of the two parties to the merger, which is the maximum value of the synergy that can theoretically be achieved under the condition that the existing resources of

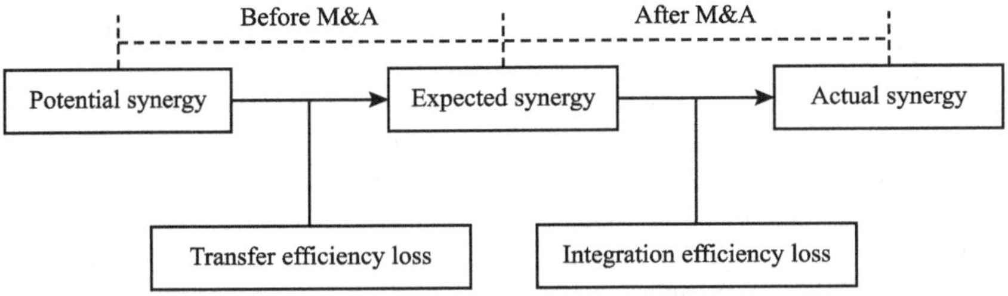

Fig. 7.1 Three synergistic relationships. *Source* Zhang Jinxin. Who Is the Target: Strategic Analysis of Resources Fit Between Mergers Beijing: Economic Press China. 2006

the two parties to the merger can be comprehensively exerted. Expected synergy refers to the synergy that the acquirer estimates after the M&A before the integration activities begin. It considers the transfer efficiency of the resources of both parties based on potential synergy but still focuses on the forecast from the perspective of the ex-ante. Different from the potential synergy and the expected synergy, the actual synergy refers to the synergy that is finally realized after the merger and integration, so it is an after-the-fact study, and in fact, it is the performance part of the M&A. At present, much empirical research at home and abroad is trying to test whether M&A can produce synergistic and measure the size of synergy, and the research object is essentially realistic synergy. The relationship between potential synergy, expected synergy, and actual synergy is shown in Fig. 7.1.

7.2 Identifying M&A Synergy Opportunities

7.2.1 The Identification Method of Synergy Opportunity Proposed by Foreign Scholars

Synergy plays an important role in the strategies of many companies. Many managers may easily find synergy opportunities, but how to analyze and filter these synergy opportunities in depth and detail is confusing to them. Therefore, to find synergy opportunities, consultants and scholars have developed many analytical frameworks.

7.2.1.1 Michael Porter's Approach to Value Chain Analysis

Michael Porter (2006) explores how companies create and maintain a profitable state within an industry or several industries. He believes that a company's various business behaviors are the source of competitive advantage, so he uses value chain analysis to study how each business behavior affects the company's overall strategy. He classified the possible associations between business units into three types, namely tangible associations, intangible associations, and competitive associations.

Porter first explained tangible linkages. He believed that when there are common customers, channels, technologies, and other factors, related business units have the opportunity to share activities along the value chain, and tangible linkages arise. Tangible linkages create competitive advantage if sharing reduces costs or increases differentiation from competitors enough to exceed the cost of sharing.[1] Porter divides the business activities that can be shared into five categories according to the various links in the value chain: production, market, procurement, technology, and infrastructure. Each type is carefully analyzed for the source of the tangible linkages and possible forms of sharing, potential competitive advantages, possible sources of shared costs, etc. He believes that the value of sharing to the enterprise is the sum of the net competitive advantages of the business units concerned.

For the intangible linkages, Porter believes that it stems from the similarity of various basic attributes between business units, such as the same basic strategy, the same type of customers, similar value chain forms, similar important value activities (such as the manufacturing processes of products, relations with the government), etc. It generates a competitive advantage through the dissemination of basic management skills or techniques across different value chains. These skills or techniques are either about how to manage a specific type of activity or how to make a business unit more unique. Intangible linkages can lead to a competitive advantage if the improvement in cost or differentiation of the business unit that acquires the skill outweighs the cost of spreading the skill. Especially when many business units adopt the same basic strategy, the intangible linkages are often reflected, and thus reflect the ability and skill of enterprise management in implementing a specific strategy.

Competitive linkages arise from the existence of actual or potential competitors in multiple countries. Porter believes that because the competitive action taken against a company in one industry often affects the business of the company in other industries, these "multi-domain competitors" must link their businesses in various industries. Although competitive linkages occur with or without tangible and intangible linkages, because these two linkages provide the basis for diversification, competitive linkages often coexist with them. Since a multi-domain competitor may force a company to establish a corresponding linkage to avoid falling to a disadvantage in competition, competitive linkages also make it more important to recognize and develop the use of tangible and intangible linkages.

---

[1] Including coordination cost, compromise cost, and rigid cost. To achieve sharing, business units must coordinate in aspects such as formulating work plans, determining work priorities, and resolving conflicting problems. The cost of time, personnel, and funds involved in coordination is called coordination cost. Sharing an activity requires this activity to operate in a consistent way that may not be the most beneficial way for any of the business units involved. The business units must compromise their needs in some way, and the resulting cost is called compromise cost. Rigid cost manifest in two forms: potential difficulties in responding to changes in competition and increased barriers to exit. Unlike other shared costs, rigid cost is not an always- on cost, it becomes a cost only when elasticity becomes a need.

It is precisely because of the classification of these three types of associations between business units, in Porter's view, there is not only one meaning of synergy, but three fundamentally different meanings. He argues that intangible linkages can be pitfalls and are generally difficult to implement. Although their enormous potential, their role in creating competitive advantage is often uncertain; in contrast, The link between tangible linkages, competitive linkages, and competitive advantage is more attractive and easy to implement.

Porter's contribution is that he developed a method that can identify synergy opportunities, thereby helping managers to make better judgments about potential benefits.

7.2.1.2 "Integration-Responsiveness Grid" by C. K. Prahalad and Yves L. Doz

Prahalad and Doz (1986) discussed the various interdependencies among subsidiaries of multinational corporations. They believe that these enterprises may share a certain technology and may also achieve economies of scale through globalized manufacturing or unified coordination of product distribution and marketing. These connections are complex, and the biggest challenge is to identify which are critical connections, a task that value chain analysis cannot accomplish. They propose an integration—responsiveness grid (IR grid) to identify these key dependencies and help managers understand the balance between increasing the coherence of global management (the need for integration) and maintaining the responsiveness of local management. They give an example if a company believes that technology and the supply of components from within the group are the most important to the success of the company, then the dependency relationship between the company and the component company is the most critical, and the company will move closer to the position of the component company in the IR grid. The strategic focus will be primarily on cost reduction, technology transfer, economies of scale, and standardization of products and product modules. Conversely, if a firm is most concerned with market expansion and believes that sensitivity to customer tastes and preferences is the most critical to firm success, then in the IR grid, firms will move closer to firms with regional market responsiveness. They also evaluate the costs and benefits associated with managing dependencies and build a balance sheet that evaluates dependencies. At the same time, they further point out that Porter's approach of focusing too much on strategic business units is inappropriate. Organizational and administrative costs should not be overlooked in a detailed analysis of economic benefits. Although these costs are difficult to quantify, they have a very substantial impact on interrelated net earnings.

7.2.1.3 "The Four-Category Portfolio Method" by Christopher J. Clarke and Kieron Brennan

Christopher J. Clarke and Kieron Brennan (1990) argue that the failure of many companies in diversification strategies in the 1970s and early 1980s was neither because companies had misjudged synergy opportunities, nor because companies were overly optimistic about the potential benefits of synergy, but due to the company fundamentally ignores the existence of synergy opportunities. They divided the company into four types of portfolios, namely product portfolio, resource portfolio, customer portfolio, and technology portfolio, and then analyzed each portfolio separately based on some specific indicators and using a matrix method. By comparing the results of the analysis, we further identify the potential synergy opportunities among the four types of combinations. For example, when analyzing the portfolio of product and market, it will be analyzed according to the analysis method of the Boston growth/ market share matrix; when analyzing the resource portfolio, the demand growth rate (indicating the business's ability to grow) and relative unit costs can be considered[2]; when analyzing the customer portfolio, the customer's business growth speed and market share are taken into account; similarly, technology portfolio analysis will consider the future importance of each specific technology and the company's technology competition relative to competitors. After completing the above work, by comparing the results of the portfolio analysis, we further identify the potential synergy opportunities among the four types of portfolios. In evaluating acquisition projects, they believe that the acquired company and the parent company should have the possibility of synergy in at least three portfolio areas so that the company can have the opportunity to tap the potential of existing advantages and cultivate new competitive advantages.

7.2.1.4 Three Methods Proposed by Michael Goold and Andrew Campbell

Michael Goold and Andrew Campbell (Goold & Campbell, 2000) divided synergy opportunities into six categories: shared know-how, shared tangible resources, joint negotiation capabilities, coordinated strategies, vertical integration, and new business creation, and proposed three methods that could help discover synergy potential i.e., value chain overlap modeling, group-focused interviews, or designing a corresponding questionnaire to identify each item on a case-by-case basis.

---

[2] In this way, the competitive advantage of a certain resource is expressed as the unit cost of the result of using this resource, and it is also expressed as the impact that the use of this resource may bring to differentiation.

7.2.2 *The Identification Method of Synergy Opportunity Proposed by Chinese Scholars*

7.2.2.1 Wang Qian's Fuzzy Analytic Hierarchy Model

Wang Qian (2003) believes that the key to the success of enterprise M&A lies in how to choose the appropriate target enterprise to achieve maximum synergy. Therefore, the acquirer must master the specific methods of identifying potential synergy before M&A, and also be collaboratively identified and comprehensively evaluated by all enterprises that may become the target of the acquisition, which can be used as the basis for the acquirer to screen the target enterprise before the merger. He believes that the identification methods of M&A synergy proposed by western scholars in the past are all from a qualitative point of view, and focus on a certain aspect, lacking a systematic quantitative identification method. Therefore, based on different identification methods for operating synergy, financial synergy, and management synergy, he proposed an overall evaluation model for identifying potential synergy of the acquirer: the fuzzy analytic hierarchy model.

When proposing the identification method of operating synergy, Wang Qian borrowed the concept of the value chain. Wang believes that when the two parties have related technologies, similar value chain activities, cross-distribution channels, common customers, or some other competitive valuable connection, the enterprise can gain the potential for competitive advantage through M&A. The more businesses in which the merging parties have competitive, valuable strategic synergy, the more potential it has for achieving economies of scope, improving the competitiveness of its products and operations, and using its resources to achieve greater joint performance than would be possible alone. Therefore, if the value chain of both parties does not have many fit relationships, it is necessary to question whether there is synergy between the acquirer and the target and whether this M&A method can truly increase shareholder value.

Wang Qian borrowed the Boston matrix to analyze the identification method of financial synergy. Wang believes that when evaluating whether there is synergy between each other's financial resources and business, two parties should estimate the cash needs of different businesses in the business portfolio of both parties, and decide which are the bulls, which are the problems, which are the stars so that the company can transfer resources between businesses to achieve the best overall portfolio. In addition to considering cash flow, the target company has a good financial synergy when its business contributes to the achievement of the acquirer's business performance goals and can increase shareholder value.

For the identification method of management synergy, Wang mainly emphasized that an enterprise's M&A strategy must consider whether its human resource capability and the competitiveness of other businesses can generate a good synergistic relationship in the target enterprise. When an enterprise's human resources capabilities are very suitable for competition in new industries, it is often easy to win through M&A in these industries to expand the business scope of the company. And conversely, the lack of a very good human resources synergy between the two parties to the merger is often easy to fail.

Based on analyzing the identification methods of operational synergy, financial synergy, and management synergy, Wang Qian used the AHP model to construct an identification and evaluation system for the synergy of M&A. The AHP model of the synergy of target companies is divided into seven levels: the overall target layer A, it is pointed out that the ultimate goal of evaluation and decision is to screen out the best M&A target, that is, to find the target company that produces the maximum total synergy; sub-target layer B consists of expanding existing sales (B1), reducing product costs and expenses and tax-saving effects (B2), reducing investment amount (B3), cultivating new competitiveness in a shorter time (B4), and obtaining new expansion opportunities (B5); criterion layer C, according to the source of synergy is divided into three aspects: financial synergy (C1), operational synergy (C2) and management synergy (C3); sub-criteria layer D, which refines each criterion layer and consists of 10 indicators; the first- level basic indicator layer E, which refines the sub-criteria layer of the operation synergy and composed of 11 indicators; the second-level basic indicator layer F, which refines the first-level basic indicator layer and consists of 7 indicators; The candidate target enterprise layer G, which consists of various companies that may become the target of M&A. Based on this, the constructed target enterprise synergy evaluation index system is divided into five levels: the first level, the sub- target layer B, is divided into the five factors that affect the size of the enterprise synergy; the second level, the criterion layer C, 3 comprehensive indicators to determine the size of each target of the sub-target layer; the third level, the sub- criteria layer D, consists of 10 indicators; the fourth level, the first-level basic indicator layer E, consists of 11 indicators; the fifth level, the second-level basic indicators layer F, consists of 7 indicators (see Table 7.1).

Based on constructing a specific index system of corporate M&A synergy and calculating their weights, Wang also used the fuzzy comprehensive evaluation method to evaluate the potential synergy of target enterprises. It is mainly to ask several experts to evaluate the specific indicators of each target enterprise, which are divided into four grades: excellent, good, medium, and poor, and then combine the evaluation vectors of every single indicator to obtain a fuzzy relationship matrix (R), and multiply the weight of each evaluation index (A) to obtain a comprehensive evaluation result. The target enterprises that can produce the greatest potential synergy are finally obtained after comparison and sorting.

In addition, Wang also put forward two issues that should be paid attention to in the process of identifying synergy. On the one hand, when comparing and judging the synergy brought about by various indicators, not only the benefits of synergy but also the cost of synergy should be considered. Because synergy more or less requires both parties to modify their original behavior patterns in some way. On the other hand, it should be noted that in corporate M&A, the importance of synergy generated by intangible assets and tangible assets of both parties is different, because the synergistic effect created by tangible assets is far less than intangible assets in creating competitive advantages for enterprises, and the use of intangible assets

Table 7.1 Target enterprise synergy evaluation index system

Total synergistic effect (A) (affected by B1 / B2 / B3 / B4 / B5)	Financial synergy (C1)	Tax savings benefit (D1)		
		Internal financing interest (D2)		
		External financing benefits (D3)		
		Diversify the business risk of the enterprise (D4)		
	Operational synergy (C2)	Productive synergy with economies of scale and scope (D5)	Same need for enterprise infrastructure (E1)	
			Common origin of raw materials (E2)	
			Same or similar manufacturing procedures (E3)	
			Same or similar assembly procedures (E4)	
			Identical or similar inspection/ quality control procedures (E5)	
			Same need for factory auxiliary activities (E6)	
Total synergistic effect (A) (affected by B1 / B2 / B3 / B4 / B5)	Operational synergy (C2)	Unproductive synergy with economies of scale and scope (D6)	Economy of marketing (E7)	Common client (F1)
				Common sales channel (F1)
				Common geographical market (F2)
			Economy of Purchase (E8)	Joint procurement (F4)
			Economy of R&D (E9)	Common product technology (F5)
				Common machining technology (F6)

(continued)

Table 7.1 (continued)

				Technology common in other value activities (F7)
		Transaction fee savings (D7)	Technical efficiency (E10)	
			Agency efficiency (E11)	
	Management synergy (C3)	Synergy of general management ability (D8)		
		Synergy of industry-specific management ability (D9)		
		Synergy of enterprise exclusive non-managerial personnel ability (D10)		

to achieve competitive advantages through synergy effects is both substantial and continuous.

7.2.2.2 Zhou Lin's Value Chain Model for Resource Identification of M&A Parties

Zhou Lin (2006) believes that M&A essentially create value through the sharing of assets, the transfer and diffusion of capabilities of both parties, that is, to achieve synergy by relying on the integration and innovative allocation of resources of both parties, therefore, identifying and comparing the resources of the two parties to the merger is the primary link of collaborative analysis. Zhou borrowed Michael Porter's concept of the value chain, introduced the main components of enterprise resources into the value chain, established a resource- based value chain model (see Fig. 7.2), and realized a preliminary analysis of the overall situation of enterprise resources. At the same time, to further identify strategic resources, she also analyzed and summarized the attributes of strategic resources, namely value, uniqueness, specificity, and self-learning. By constructing and filling in the resource value chain and combining several attributes of strategic resources, enterprises can clearly understand the strategic resources they currently have, the resources they lack to achieve their strategic goals, and the need for resource reallocation. On this basis,

Financial assets/human capital/general ability							
Physical assets	Raw material	Equipment, machine	Workshop, production line	Product	Stock		
Intangible assets		Patent, proprietary technology	Industry, licence	Trade mark	Reputation		
Special ability	Bargaining ability, supply speed	Innovation ability	Production capacity, quality management	Public relations ability, promotional ability	Service ability, information feedback ability	Value	
Functional activity	Purchasing	R&D	Manufacture	Marketing	Service		

Fig. 7.2 Resource-based enterprise value chain model. *Note* The value chain model only provides an identification framework, in which each row reflects the specific content that each resource may contain, and there is no one-to-one correspondence with each column. Take a product as an example, it can be the object of marketing activities or input in the research and development stage

Zhou Lin still uses the value chain tool to compare the resources ofthe two parties to the merger.

Zhou believes that the value chain model decomposes the value creation process of an enterprise into a series of different but interrelated value activities, and it is impossible for any single enterprise to maintain an absolute advantage in all links. Different enterprises will inevitably choose to focus on different stages and aspects of the value chain, and even two enterprises that choose the same activities in the value chain may develop completely different enterprise assets or capabilities, so in some strategic links that create enterprise value, the acquirer may have a competitive advantage, and the target may have a more competitive advantage in other aspects. This requires overlapping the value chains of the acquirer and the target, and by comparing the original independent value creation activities horizontally and vertically, analyzing the key value-added links in the business activities of both parties and the strategic resources supporting these links, and preliminarily evaluating their scale and complementarity, and judge possible synergy opportunities. At the same time, the conflict and incompatibility of the resources of both sides are analyzed, and the possibility of collaborative realization is preliminarily judged.

Figure 7.3 is a schematic diagram of the horizontal and vertical comparison of resources between two enterprise value chains. Generally, horizontal comparison occurs between resources supporting the same value creation activity (as shown in Fig. 7.3 (a)), and vertical comparison occurs between resources supporting different upstream and downstream value creation activities (as shown in Fig. 7.3 (b)).

The horizontal comparison makes the resources on the value chain overlap, which increases the thickness of the link of the value chain. The synergy between resources

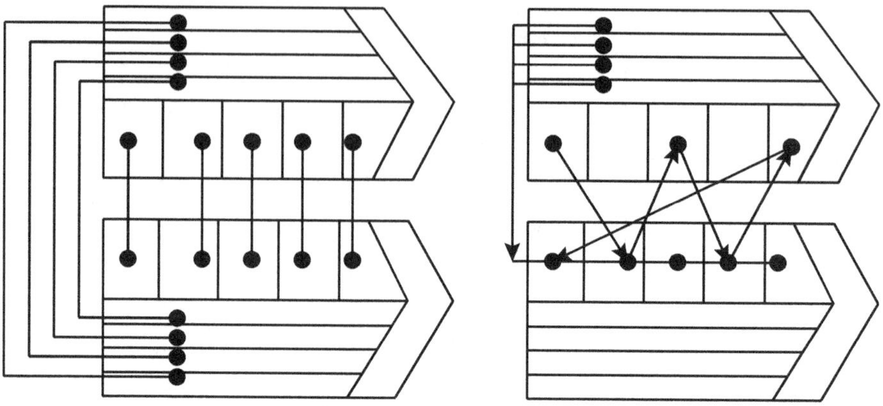

(a) Horizontal comparison (b) Vertical comparison

Fig. 7.3 Horizontal and vertical comparison of the value chains of the M&A parties. *Source* Zhang Qiusheng, Mergers & Acquisitions *Forum 2005*, Beijing: Economic Press China, 2005, p. 304

on the same chain link will promote the quality improvement of the chain link so that the post-merger enterprises will have economies of scale, economies of scope, and learning effects. Vertical comparison interleaves the resources on different upstream and downstream value chain links, so that the post-merger enterprise obtains a larger opportunity set of chain link combinations, extends the original value chain, and promotes the quality improvement and quantitative expansion of the link of the value chain.

In addition, after fully analyzing the possible synergy opportunities between the resources of both parties in the M&A with the help of value chain tools, it is also necessary to consider whether the assets and capabilities of the acquirer can be effectively transferred and diffused to the target party, exerted in the target company, whether the assets and the capabilities of the target party can be absorbed and integrated by the acquirer, that is, the compatibility of the resources of both parties. If the compatibility is not good enough, it is necessary to consider whether this obstacle can be eliminated to determine whether the synergy can be realized. If there is a serious conflict, it may lead to the failure of synergy, and even the M&A activity itself cannot be carried out.

7.3 Mechanism of M&A Synergy

7.3.1 Mechanism of M&A Synergy at the Strategic Level

7.3.1.1 Management Synergy

The management synergy means that when two companies with different management capabilities are merged, the merged company will be affected by the company with strong management capabilities, showing a phenomenon that is greater than the sum of the management capabilities of the two separate companies. Its essence is an effect of the rational allocation of management resources. But the theory has two basic assumptions: (1) If the acquirer has slack management resources that can be easily released, M&A activities will be unnecessary; but if as a team its management is effective and inseparable, or it has economies of scale, then it will be feasible to make full use of the remaining management resources through M&A, which can improve the efficiency of the entire economy. (2) For the target party, the inefficiency of its management can be improved through the intervention of external managers and increased investment in management resources (Yuan Xin et al., 2011).

One school of management theory holds that managerial functions such as planning, organizing, commanding, and controlling can be easily borrowed into all types of operating enterprises and that managers who have the experience and ability to perform the above management functions can operate in any environment to perform these functions, that is, management is transferable across a wide variety of industries or types of organizations. The theory holds that if any two enterprises with different management capabilities are merged, the performance of the merged enterprise will benefit from the influence of the enterprise with advanced management experience, the comprehensive management efficiency will be improved, and the overall performance of the merged enterprise will better than the sum of the two separate parts. This is the most common form of management synergy.

To gain a deeper understanding of management synergy, two concepts must first be clarified—organizational experience and organizational capital. The organizational experience is "the improvement of employees' skills and abilities obtained through the learning of experience within the enterprise". Organizational experience is divided into three types. Rosen (1972) has pointed out that the experience of a situation exists in the field of entrepreneurial or managerial ability to economically organize and maintain complex production processes. This management experience can be divided into general management experience and industry-specific experience. The former refers to the capabilities developed in general management functions such as planning, organization, and command, as well as in finance and control; the latter refers to the development of special management capabilities related to the production and marketing characteristics of a particular industry. The third form of organizational experience exists in the realm of non-managerial labor input elements—production workers' skill level is gradually improved over time through learning from experience. As can be seen from this, organizational experience exists in human capital.

Organizational capital is accumulated gradually through experience in an organization called an enterprise, which may be called a synergistic effect, that is, under such conditions, the role of information is to help companies organize effective management and production teams within its internal. Organizational capital includes information about the characteristics of employees, which enables firms to make effective combinations between workers and jobs, and people with special talents and skills to do some work better; another type of organizational capital is used in the combination of workers. The overall performance of the group, therefore, depends largely on the characteristics of the individual and how well they fit the job and others who are engaged in related work. The types of information included in organizational capital may be firm-specific. The owner or manager of the business may know more about the information of the related worker that produces the synergistic effect than the worker himself, and the transfer of this information to other businesses may just be misinformation, and in such a process a transaction will be generated cost.

The ability of an enterprise is the skill of using resources, including general management ability, industry-specific management ability, and enterprise-specific management ability. In theory, general management ability can even be extended in mergers between companies in unrelated industries. Since their synergistic effects are also important, mergers that preserve these effects are more efficient than the movement of managers as an individual between firms. Usually, in a pure hybrid merger, only general management ability can be transferred, that is, only through the sharing of senior management talents who perform general management functions such as command, planning, control, and finance to improve management efficiency and create management synergy. Many scholars see it as a motive for pure hybrid mergers. However, the author believes that although it is theoretically efficient to transfer general management ability through M&A, due to the extremely limited number of senior management talents an enterprise needs, it is relatively easy to organize a " management team", and the information of senior management personnel is relatively open. It is easily obtained from the market, so for pure hybrid M&A, the more important benefit should be reflected in the financial synergy, which will be described in detail later.

7.3.1.2 Operational Synergy

Operational synergy mainly refers to the changes in efficiency brought by M&A to the production and operation activities of enterprises and the benefits generated by the improvement of efficiency. Zhang Jinxin and Yue Gongzheng (2008) believe that since the acquirer paid a premium for M&A, they have to solve two operational problems: (1) to meet the performance targets already expected by the market; (2) to satisfy higher performance targets required by M&A premiums. If economies of scale exist in the industry, and before the merger, the level of business activity of the firm does not meet the potential requirements to achieve economies of scale, then operating synergy will arise after the M&A.

Yuan Xin, Song Wenyun, and Zhang Qiusheng (2011) applied the theory of diversification to analyze the synergy of M&A. Diversification refers to the situation in which a company owns and operates assets whose returns are less correlated. For a company, diversification can spread risk and stabilize revenue streams. Typically, stakeholders such as company employees, consumers, and suppliers are more willing than shareholders to pursue a company's diversification strategy. This is because, first, shareholders can diversify risks by diversifying their shareholdings in the capital market, while it is difficult for employees to diversify their sources of labor income. Most of their knowledge and skills are useful to the company but not to other companies, so company managers and general employees prefer the company to be stable and do not want the company to take too many risks. Second, companies generally form stable relationships with consumers and suppliers through advertising, research and development, investment in fixed assets, and employee training, thus forming the company's reputation. Diversification reduces the risk of a company going bankrupt and helps preserve the company's credibility, thereby maintaining stable relationships with consumers and suppliers.

(1) Operational synergy and horizontal M&A

A major source of operating Synergy is economies of scale. In Western economic theory, the input of various elements in the production process of an enterprise has an optimal scale. At this point, marginal cost equals marginal revenue, and the average unit cost is the lowest. Until this point, the cost of production will gradually decrease as the scale of production expands, which is known as economies of scale. Horizontal mergers and acquisitions can rapidly expand the production scale of enterprises and achieve the requirements of optimal economic scale through resource complementation, thereby reducing production costs and improving production efficiency.

(2) Operational synergy and vertical M&A

Operating synergy can also be obtained from vertical mergers. Vertical mergers occur between enterprises at different stages of production and operation, and the motive for mergers is generally to control the entire production and sales process of a department or industry. The direct effect of vertical M&A is the saving of transaction costs.

From the perspective of resource allocation, "transaction is the transfer of goods and services between two technically separable units" (Williamson, 1987). This kind of transaction activity is common between two enterprises with a forward–backward relationship. In a non-perfectly competitive market, the conclusion of any economic transaction requires the negotiation of contracts, the supervision of the implementation of contracts, bargaining, etc. In addition, it is necessary to understand the production and demand information of producers and consumers, etc., the costs incurred in these links not only exist but are sometimes so high that the transaction cannot be concluded.

Many people believe that vertical M&A can give companies a cost advantage over their rivals, and companies no longer must pay suppliers the profits that should be included in the price of raw materials, that is, the internal transaction price is only the cost of raw materials, and below the market price. However, this apparent cost saving is a zero-sum transaction, which is the transfer of profits from the subsidiary to the parent company. From the perspective of the post- merger conglomerate, this transfer of profits does not increase the value of the enterprise.

Vertical mergers between enterprises may also generate technical economics, that is, technical cost savings by linking successive production links. This synergy is particularly prominent in some industries, such as iron and steel production, including coking, sintering, iron making, steel making, blooming, and other interconnected production stages. Steel production requires very high temperatures. Through vertical mergers, combining production stages reduces handling and heating costs. Similar thermal energy savings also exist in other industries, such as pulp and newsprint production, which can avoid the cost of drying and re-watering of raw materials through vertical mergers; and the joint production of oil refining often reduces processing costs or other costs.

In addition, a very important point is that a reliable supply of input elements can be obtained through vertical mergers among enterprises, which can reduce some uncertainties in the external environment of enterprises and reduce risk costs. The transaction relationships between enterprises—transaction object, price, time, channel, quantity, method, and responsibility are constantly changing.

The change in such enterprise transaction conditions will inevitably increase the business risk and operating cost of the enterprise. These external business risks can be internalized through corporate M&A, thereby making production and operation more stable and reducing production costs and risk costs.

7.3.1.3 Financial Synergy

Financial synergy refers to the M&A of two or more companies to maximize profits (Zhao Junkai et al., 2016). The various financial benefits that M&A bring to enterprises are not caused by the improvement of efficiency, but by tax laws, accounting conventions, and the inherent laws of securities transactions.

(1) Lower cost of capital

One theory of hybrid mergers states that pure hybrid mergers occur when a business in a low-demand-growth industry (i.e., the industry's demand growth is lower than the growth of the economy as a whole) acquires another business operating in a high-demand-growth industry. Such mergers use the acquiring company's lower-cost internal cash to lower the cost of capital of the combined company, thereby capturing investment opportunities available in the industry of the acquired company. If the cash flow of the acquired business is low, the opportunity to capitalize on the cash flow of the acquiring business increases. Thus, the theory implies a process of reallocation of financial resources—resources are transferred from an industry where the acquiring company is in a slow-growth demand to an industry where the acquired company is in a high-growth demand. Very and Schweiger (2001) emphasized the importance and challenge of assessing assets and liabilities, future revenue and costs, and investment needs of the target company. A comprehensive assessment of investment and financing needs can reveal some issues that may affect the realization of synergy.

The main reason for the decline in the cost of capital may be "coinsurance" effect. That is, when the cash flows of the two enterprises are not completely positively correlated, the possibility of bankruptcy of the joint enterprise after the merger will be greatly reduced, the income flow will become stable, and the possibility of lender suffering losses will be reduced. The direct result of this effect is that the ability of companies to borrow money will increase. Stapleton (1982) presents a more rigorous formulation of this argument in his option pricing model (OPM) framework. In his framework, borrowing capacity is defined as the maximum amount of debt that can be raised at a given interest rate. Most of the earlier studies on the effects of mergers found that merger activity resulted in increased leverage. Among them, Shrieves and Pashley (1984) carefully tested the theory of increasing leverage. After controlling for firm size and industry impact, they found that most hybrid mergers resulted in a significant increase in financial leverage. Zheng Guang (1982) in his doctoral dissertation Investment Opportunities, Synergy, and hybrid Mergers, through many empirical studies, showed that joint enterprises have higher leverage ratios than other manufacturing companies. After a hybrid merger, the systematic rise in leverage is consistent with a fall in expected bankruptcy costs.

In a general sense, the cost of debt financing is usually lower than that of common stock financing, mainly because: first, creditors bear less risk than common stock shareholders, so common stock shareholders require higher risk returns; second, interest is an after-tax cost, while dividends are not deductible before taxes. Therefore, an increase in the debt ratio in the capital structure usually results in a decrease in the comprehensive cost of capital. At the same time, the rising debt/equity ratio makes the post-merger enterprises have the characteristics of "high risk and high return". In financial management theory, when a company's investment rate of return is greater than its cost of capital, with the increase in debt ratio, shareholder wealth will continue to rise, thereby increasing the company's value, which is the financial leverage effect. Zheng Guang's research found that by using a higher percentage of leverage, joint enterprises increased their return on shareholders' equity by 1.3 percentage points more than other independent companies in the same industry (manufacturing). In addition, the issuance of many new bonds after the merger can bring considerable tax savings to the company and increase the company's net cash flow. These are important components of the financial synergy brought about by a hybrid merger.

(2) Reasonable tax avoidance

Taxatiosn is a factor that has a significant impact on business decisions. The tax rates and tax scope of capital gains such as assets, dividend income, and interest income vary greatly among different types of enterprises in different countries. This difference allows enterprises can achieve reasonable tax avoidance through M&A,

thereby increasing their free cash flow, which is also an important source of financial synergy. DeLong (2003) suggested that M&A should consider taxation and legal provisions related to property, employee contracts, and the environment. Lack of valuation may lead to difficulties in post-merger integration and reduce opportunities for synergies. Under the existing tax laws, companies can use the loss deferral clause in the tax law to avoid tax reasonably. Loss deferral means that if a company has a loss in one year, the company can not only be exempted from the income tax for that year, but its loss can also be deferred back to offset the surplus in subsequent years, and the company pays income tax based on the offset surplus. With such a loss deferral clause, a loss-making company is often considered a merger target or considered to merge a profitable business to take full advantage of the loss deferral tax benefits.

The tax avoidance effect is even more pronounced when M&A transactions are not paid for in cash but in the form of share swaps or the issuance of convertible bonds. Take share swap as an example. The transaction is tax-free because the two parties do not engage in a cash transaction, no cash is transferred in the process, and no capital gains are realized. While the transferee of the asset is still subject to capital gains tax when it sells the shares it acquires through the securities secondary market, it is at least "tax-deferred" for a potentially considerable period. Due to the existence of the time value of money, this kind of deferral has an important influence on the enterprise value growth at the initial stage of the merger. The benefit of tax deferral is even more apparent if it takes the form of convertible bonds, in which the shares of the merged company are converted into convertible bonds and then converted into common stock after a period. Because the interest the company pays on these bonds is pre-deducted from income, the tax is determined by multiplying the interest-deducted earnings by the tax rate. At the same time, the company can retain the capital gains on these bonds until they are converted into common stock. The company can pay fewer capital gains taxes due to the deferred repayment of capital gains.

7.3.2 *Operational Mechanism Of M&A Synergies At The Resource Level*

From the perspective of enterprise resources, the value of resources is realized through three stages: resource acquisition, resource utilization, and resource innovation. M&A can directly promote the first two stages, but can only provide resources to be used to innovate for the third stage, and the implementation of innovation depends on the internal capabilities of enterprises (Zhang Jinxin & Wang Qingjian, 2009).

7.3.2.1 Operational Mechanism of the Potential Synergies of Enterprise M&A

(1) Mechanism of intangible assets synergy

In the traditional western synergy theory, the concept of "intangible assets synergy" does not appear. However, with the development of the economy and the rapid progress of science and technology, the key to success in the competition of enterprises relies more on intangible assets such as brand, technology, and culture. Pan Liyun (1999) juxtaposed the intangible assets synergy with management synergy, operational synergy, and financial synergy, and explained its operational mechanism in detail.

Intangible assets synergy refers to the fact that due to some special nature and functions of intangible assets that are different from tangible assets, including high input in formation, long-term performance, deep level, and expansion, inseparability and inimitability in use, integration with tangible assets, and uncertainty in transactions. Inputting intangible assets to transform inferior assets into high-quality assets, and inefficient assets into high-efficiency assets in M&A, can improve the efficiency of production and operation of the acquired party, thus increasing the overall efficiency of the two enterprises after the M&A (Liu Wengang, 1999). Intangible assets can be roughly divided into three major categories, namely, market, intellectual property, and management base. The intangible assets synergy is mainly manifested in the aspects of brand synergy, cultural synergy, and technological synergy.

(i) Brand synergy

Pan Liyun (1999) believed that brand plays an important role in enterprise M&A. Relying on the "famous brand" and sales and after-sales service network that the acquirer has established, the market competitiveness and sales performance of the acquired company's products can be immediately improved. Compared with the long process and huge investment of building a high-quality brand through internal development, it can immediately improve the competitiveness of products and open sales in a relatively short period, so that the efficiency and benefits of the enterprise can be improved rapidly. In addition, instilling a famous brand culture in the employees of the acquired party, can improve their brand awareness and quality, and the cohesiveness and attractiveness of the enterprise can be enhanced, which are all intangible forces to promote the performance of the enterprise. With the expansion of enterprise scale, the enterprise can have stronger strength to carry out technology development, and advertising, and establish a more perfect sales and service network. All these activities will further expand the market influence of the brand and greatly enhance the value of the brand and the competitive advantage of the enterprise, forming a virtuous circle.

At the same time, Pan Liyun also believes that brand synergy is constrained by three factors: the first is the strength of the brand itself. If the brand is a domestic or even an international famous brand, it will have a greater impact on the performance of the acquired party, and the brand synergy will also be stronger; the second is the ability of the acquired party to support the brand, that is, whether the acquired party's technology and management can meet the requirements of the brand; the third is industry relevance, that is, the relevance degree of the acquired party's products to the original dependent products of the brand.

(ii) Technological synergy

Pan Liyun (1999) defined technological synergy as the effect of technological innovation gaining economies of scale and increasing enterprise profits through the low-cost diffusion of patented technology and proprietary technology. This effect can also be called the technology diffusion effect. Under the circumstance that there is a significant difference in the technology level of the two parties involved in M&A, the sharing of technology usually enables the low-tech enterprise to improve the technical level rapidly after M&A until it reaches the level of the more technologically advanced enterprise, thus turning its formerly inefficient assets into efficient assets, improving the production efficiency and benefits of the enterprise. Technological synergy mainly exists in horizontal M&A and related hybrid M&A. In horizontal M&A, since the merging parties produce the same products and use the same technology (the technology level may be different), the acquired party can easily and quickly improve its technology level by acquiring the advanced technology of the acquiring company, thereby saving costs, and increasing the output and quality of products. In related hybrid M&A, the similarity of core technologies allows the new or advanced technologies of dominant enterprises to penetrate and diffuse in adjacent industries.

(iii) Cultural synergy

Pan Liyun (1999) believes that the influence of corporate culture on M&A is achieved through cultural synergy, which is often long-term, deep, and difficult to measure. The generation of cultural synergy is due to the exportability of positive culture to negative culture and the potential for economies of scale. Therefore, the overall quality and efficiency of the acquired party can be improved through the diffusion, penetration, and assimilation of positive corporate culture to negative corporate culture in M&A. The essence of cultural synergy is to establish common value orientation and behavioral standards, thereby forming internal cohesion and external radiation. Although this power is intangible and its formation process may be relatively long, the impact of a company's cultural atmosphere, employees' spirit, and morale is huge and immeasurable on production efficiency, management efficiency, and the overall image of the company presented to customers and investors.

Generally speaking, with the expansion of the scale of M&A, the cultural synergy effect also expands; but when the scale of the enterprise group reaches a certain level and exceeds the tolerance of the corporate culture, the effect will reach its limit due to the sharpness of various cultural conflicts within the group. The size of the cultural synergy depends on the following two factors: The first is the cultural connotation of the merged enterprise. If its corporate culture has a high degree of external recognition and conforms to the trend of the times, it will have stronger vitality, larger development space, and stronger synergy with other cultures. The second is the cultural gap between the M&A parties. Corporate culture is individualistic, and the cultural differences between the two parties of M&A determine the possibility of cultural conflict, thereby affecting the synergy effect of their cultures. The greater the cultural differences between the two parties, the more difficult it is for one culture to assimilate the other, and the smaller the cultural synergy effect will be. Therefore, when selecting M&A targets, it is necessary to analyze and compare the cultures of the two parties, and select enterprises with small cultural differences and conservative and backward cultural properties as targets to maximize the cultural synergy effect in M&A.

(iv) Core competitiveness cultivation effect

The enterprise is physically made up of an organic combination of production factors such as labor, plant, and equipment. When an enterprise can use these factors more effectively than its competitors to complete a certain job, the enterprise has a competitive advantage over its competitors, and the ability of an enterprise to use the production factors effectively is the competitiveness of the enterprise. For a specific enterprise, not every kind of competitiveness is equally important. We regard it as the core competitiveness, which is the most basic of enterprise competitiveness and enables the enterprise to obtain long-term stable competitive advantage and profits higher than the industry average profit rate (Liu Shijin et al., 1999). It takes a long time for an enterprise to establish its core competitiveness through internal development, and the cost is also very high. In contrast, it is possible to acquire the necessary elements of competitiveness in a relatively short period by absorbing external "resources", that is, acquiring the intangible assets of other enterprises.

Pan Liyun (1999) believes that core competitiveness is formed by enterprises through long-term efforts of learning, refining, innovation, and practice. The core competitiveness of an enterprise and its intangible assets have an interdependent relationship, that is, most of the core competitiveness elements are manifested as intangible assets, such as enterprise patented technology, marketing network, brand, and culture. The process of developing and acquiring intangible assets is exactly the process of cultivating the core competitiveness of enterprises. Pan explains the core competitiveness cultivation effect as the process of acquiring intangible assets of other enterprises or injecting intangible assets into other enterprises to form the core competitiveness elements of enterprises in M&A, thereby promoting the establishment of the core competitiveness of enterprises as soon as possible and laying the foundation for joint enterprises to obtain long-term stable and high profits. Whether the core competitiveness of the joint enterprise can be cultivated or strengthened as soon as possible after the M&A determines the success or failure of the M&A to a large extent. Of course, acquiring core competitiveness elements does not necessarily mean that the core competitiveness can be established quickly. For example, in M&A, the acquired party has acquired a certain advanced technology of the advantageous enterprise, but this does not mean that the technological advantage has been established because the real establishment has to go through an internal transformation and learning, such as training of professionals, digestion, absorption and reinvention of technology, and quality control, that is, the post-merger integration must be done well. Usually, it takes some time for the later integration and the generation of core competitiveness.

(2) Mechanism of knowledge capital synergy

In the era of the knowledge economy, the knowledge factor is separated from other production factors and becomes a crucial factor independently, playing a leading role in the value creation of enterprises. Guo Junhua (2002) believes that knowledge capital reflects the heterogeneity among different enterprises and is an important motivation for M&A. Its synergy is the real source of M&A benefits, so she proposed seven mechanisms of knowledge capital synergy, analyzed the internal mechanism of the function of the four modules in the process of M&A integration, established a theoretical model of the evolution of knowledge capital, and analyzed the transformation process of knowledge capital in the open environment.

(i) Seven mechanisms of knowledge capital synergy

Guo Junhua (2002) believes that each enterprise is a system with "individuality", and the comprehensive expression of individuality (difference) is the unique element of an enterprise—knowledge capital. Therefore, the key to achieving synergy between the two M&A parties is the interaction of two knowledge capital systems. Guo divided knowledge capital synergy into seven mechanisms: sharing, learning, transfer, substitution, complementarity, conflict elimination, and creation, and analyzed the operation mechanism respectively.

First, sharing mechanism. The prerequisite for synergy generation is the exchange and sharing of knowledge capital and the effective replication of knowledge capital under the guidance of existing resource allocators is the basis of knowledge capital sharing. Common sharing methods and possible synergy advantages gained in M&A mainly include five aspects: human capital sharing, goodwill capital sharing, technology capital sharing, market capital sharing, and infrastructure capital sharing. After the M&A, both parties of the M&A can improve the organizational experience and the personal quality of the employees by sharing management experience, entrepreneurial capability and employee training to enhance the strategic planning capability; improve the enterprise image and product image of both parties by sharing the enterprise image, brand and trademark to gain brand customer loyalty; obtain a higher level of R&D platform and technological innovation capability by sharing R&D and innovation capability, product interface design, technical know-how and patents to strengthen technical competition barriers and entry barriers and reduce product or processes design costs; broaden markets and increase sales by sharing marketing networks, supply networks, service networks, and customer relationships to reduce procurement and marketing costs and improve service quality; and obtain more efficient information systems and information communication quality by sharing information technology, financial and government relationships, business processes, and corporate standard to improve employee morale and team spirit. Therefore, if the benefits of sharing outweigh the costs of sharing, and this sharing makes it difficult for competitors to imitate and match, a competitive advantage can be created through the sharing of knowledge capital after M&A.

Second, learning mechanism. The accumulation of post-merger knowledge capital can be accomplished through organizational learning. Guo Junhua established a process model of knowledge learning after M&A (see Fig. 7.4). Guo believes that the knowledge learning of post-merger organizations is a closed-loop control cycle process. The greater the gap between the knowledge capital of M&A parties, the stronger the complementarity, and the greater the potential opportunity for learning (synergy). When the types of knowledge capital are different, the learning modes adopted are also different. For the learning of tacit and explicit knowledge, different learning modes such as internalization, externalization, thinking, expansion, and instillation can be selected. In addition, the effect of digesting and absorbing knowledge capital in the learning process is proportional to the adaptability of the organization, the innovation capability of the enterprise, and the degree of new knowledge created. In conclusion, knowledge learning is a multi-stage dynamic cycle process. As long as there are learning opportunities, enterprises will continue to repeat the above process. With the continuation of learning, the knowledge capital gap among enterprises will be gradually reduced, and the stock of knowledge capital will be improved.

Third, transfer mechanism. M&A provide a good opportunity for the "internalization" transfer of knowledge capital of the enterprise. In the value network formed by the acquirer, the transfer of knowledge capital may lead to the increase of intangible value, so the effectiveness of communication and transfer will determine the key factor of value creation. Guo Junhua (2002) divides knowledge transfer into nine ways according to the E-I-E structure (the individual capability, internal structure, and external structure of knowledge capital) proposed by Sveiby (1996), which are:

Firstly, knowledge transfer between individuals means that knowledge transfer is promoted through team activities, job rotation, and other methods based on mutual trust between organizations of M&A parties to achieve the purpose of knowledge sharing.

Secondly, knowledge transfer from the individual capability to the internal structure is mainly to transform the capability and knowledge condensed in individuals, especially tacit knowledge, into a knowledge base that can be shared by the entire organization.

Thirdly, knowledge transfer from the internal structure to individual capability is mainly to improve individual capability using systems, tools, and templates, and

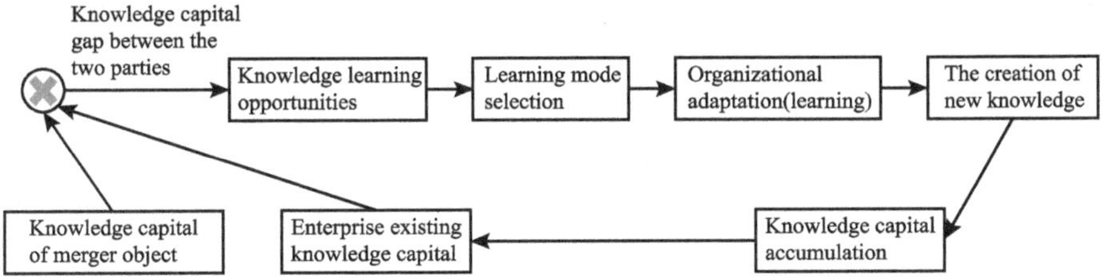

Fig. 7.4 Process model of knowledge learning after M&A

the key is to improve the human–machine interface of the system and to establish an imitative and interactive e-learning environment.

Fourthly, knowledge transfer from individual to the external structure is mainly to transfer employee's knowledge to customers, suppliers, and other stakeholders through the reduction of official procedures, holding product presentations, and other forms.

Fifthly, knowledge transfer from external structure to an individual is mainly to help employees learn from external structure, and the key is to create and maintain good interpersonal relationships between organizational employees and outsiders.

Sixthly, knowledge transfer between external structures is mainly to build bridges between customers, suppliers, and other stakeholders so that they can communicate and improve their capabilities.

Seventhly, knowledge transfer from external structure to internal structure focuses on how the enterprise acquires knowledge from the outside, and how to use the capabilities of stakeholders such as customers to improve the internal structure of the organization.

Eighthly, knowledge transfer from the internal structure to the external structure focuses on how the organization's systems, processes, and products can be used to improve the capabilities of stakeholders such as customers, and the key is to make the enterprise's systems and processes effectively serve customers, external network, product tracking, and e-commerce.

Ninthly, knowledge transfer between internal structures focuses on how to effectively integrate the auxiliary supports such as systems, tools, and processes within the enterprise.

Forth, substitution mechanism. The substitutability between knowledge capital is manifested in the fact that the knowledge capital of both M&A parties makes the use of either one of them sufficient, which makes the use of the other unnecessary. Substitution mechanisms can occur across the components of knowledge capital. As long as the substitution conditions are met, the enterprise will make decisions about whether to substitute. There are two main ways to substitute knowledge capital, one is the substitution between the same type of knowledge capital that achieves the same goal and function, and the other is the substitution between different types of knowledge capital that achieves the same goal and function. Since the transfer of knowledge capital from one side of M&A to the other side requires costs, and the absorption of new knowledge capital by enterprises requires a long process of learning, digesting, and organic combination with other knowledge capital, in addition, the collision of old and new knowledge capital will cause large or small frictional costs in the substitution process, the substitution decision-making of post-merger knowledge capital is a difficult, time-consuming and labor-intensive process.

Fifth, complementarity mechanism. The complementarity of knowledge capital means that the knowledge capital of one enterprise has references and supplements to another enterprise so that the development of another enterprise's knowledge capital shows increasing returns. Complementarity is an important motivation for M&A and the key to synergy realization. It means the correlation and difference of knowledge capital, and indicates the existence of the spillover effect of knowledge capital. The uniqueness and heterogeneity of knowledge capital constitute the basis of complementarity. When both M&A parties have more complementary knowledge capital, greater synergy and combined advantage can be formed through the aggregation of knowledge capital. Such complementarity can occur either between the same type of knowledge capital or between different types of knowledge capital. Complementary mechanisms must be coupled with other mechanisms such as transfer and sharing to be successful. In addition, compatibility is more important than simple complementarity, and the possibility of a successful combination of knowledge capital that is too similar or completely different is very small.

The network clusters formed by highly interdependent enterprises, suppliers, research institutions, customers, and intermediaries through the interconnection of value chains help enterprises acquire new and complementary technologies, learn new skills, reduce transaction costs, overcome market barriers, achieve synergies, and diversify innovation risks (Yuan Xin, 2013).

Due diligence can reveal surprises (Cullinan, Le Roux & Weddigen, 2004) that may lead acquirers not to make acquisitions (Kaden, 2009) or to seek out companies more likely to achieve synergies for acquisition. Ahammad and Glaister (2013) argue that during the due diligence process, acquirers can assess whether they can leverage and integrate the complementary capabilities of both transaction parties to create synergies.

Sixth, conflict elimination mechanism. The two M&A parties are integrated through M&A due to differences in knowledge capital. Although there may be huge potential synergy advantages, conflicts may also arise because of differences. Conflicts of knowledge capital will not only lead to the dispersion of time and energy but also bring a lot of coordination costs. Too intense conflicts can even lead to the failure of the entire M&A plan. Therefore, eliminating conflicts in the process of knowledge capital integration is a key step in the process of knowledge capital co-evolution. The heterogeneity of knowledge capital can be manifested in any of its components, and conflicts may occur as long as an incompatible knowledge capital. Among them, organizational culture, human resources, information systems, goodwill capital, and management systems are the five types of knowledge capital that are most likely to conflict. Both parties of M&A can adopt the temporary avoidance strategy, negotiation and mediation strategy, gradual strategy, and activation of competition and coordination mechanism strategy to achieve the purpose of conflict elimination.

Among them, for goodwill, only when the merging company confirms the outsourcing goodwill in the M&A in order to obtain the self-created goodwill that the acquired company cannot record, or when the merging company expects to form a synergy effect after the M&A. When the outsourcing goodwill is confirmed, the outsourcing goodwill is the pure goodwill in the true sense, which can bring continuous excess profits to the company (Meng Qingli, 2013). Fu Chao (2015) used the "peer effect" theory to analyze the internal logic of inter- organizational imitation that generates huge goodwill from M&A in emerging capital markets. Enterprise is one of the most important organizational forms in modern society, and inter-organizational imitation is a very common organizational behavior. Studies have shown that whether it is the adoption of new products or technologies, the development of new management methods or organizational structures, or the selection of new market entry or investment timing, there is a phenomenon of inter-organizational imitation (Cao Xing, 2011).

Seventh, creation mechanism. The creation of knowledge capital is the ultimate manifestation of synergy. After M&A, as time goes by, the differences between the systems are gradually transformed into synergies and drivers through dialogue, synergy, and resonance, which promotes the coordinated development of both parties and creates new knowledge capital. From the perspective of entity theory, the creation of knowledge capital is achieved through the joint action of the four levels of the system: individual, group, individual enterprise, and different enterprises. From the perspective of epistemology, the creation of knowledge capital is realized in the process of transformation and application of explicit knowledge capital and tacit knowledge capital. Among them, tacit knowledge capital and explicit knowledge capital are mutually transformed through the interaction of four modes: socialization, internalization, integration, and externalization.

(ii) Theoretical model for the evolution of knowledge capital

After analyzing the seven mechanisms of sharing, learning, transfer, complementarity, substitution, conflict elimination, and creation, Guo Junhua (2002) divided them into four modules according to the similarity of their functions, namely, learning, transfer, and sharing mechanism module, substitution and complementarity mechanism module, conflict elimination mechanism module and creation mechanism module.

Firstly, Guo believes that learning, transfer, and sharing mechanisms are the basis and necessary conditions for synergy generation. Organizational learning is the fundamental way of knowledge capital accumulation and synergy. With the help of knowledge learning and dissemination, both M&A parties can realize the transfer of knowledge capital in nine ways in three aspects: individual capability, internal structure, and external structure. In addition, it is possible to obtain greater synergy advantages through the sharing of multiple dimensions of knowledge capital such as human capital, goodwill capital, technological capital, and infrastructure capital.

Secondly, Guo believes that the substitution and complementarity mechanisms are the core mode of knowledge capital integration. M&A combine two huge knowledge capital systems, and to avoid the redundancy of knowledge capital of both parties, improve efficiency, and reduce costs, enterprises must choose and trade-off the knowledge capital that meets the substitution conditions. The complementarity mechanism is the starting point and core of a successful M&A. When both parties have more complementary knowledge capital, greater synergy can be formed. However, these two mechanisms can only be realized under the cooperation of the first and third modules.

Thirdly, Guo believes that the conflict elimination mechanism is the guarantee of the smooth progress of synergy, and it is constantly identifying and eliminating conflicts in the process of other mechanisms functioning to ensure the smooth evolution of the knowledge capital system.

Finally, Guo believes that the creation mechanism is the ultimate manifestation of synergy. Under the joint action of the first three modules, the enterprise continuously absorbs and digests external knowledge capital, and when the accumulation exceeds the threshold, it enters the stage of independent innovation, that is, new knowledge capital is created. It means that the enterprise has gone beyond the simple transplantation stage and reproduced new knowledge capital, making the enterprise's development enter a new platform. The synergy of knowledge capital after M&A is a process of continuous fitting and integration of the knowledge capital strategies of two companies, and it is also the process of continuous action of the seven major mechanisms. According to the viewpoint of system theory, the transformation of knowledge capital in M&A can be regarded as the process of knowledge capital input → knowledge capital processing → knowledge capital output to construct a clear outline of the evolution of the knowledge capital system.

The synergy of knowledge capital is a dynamic evolutionary process. In the early stage of M&A, the relationship between the two knowledge capital systems is very weak, and cannot restrain the spontaneous and irregular independent movements of the subsystems themselves. The system presents a disordered state, and the integration of the seven major mechanisms starts from a lower starting point. Over time, various nonlinear interactions such as sharing, learning, complementarity, and substitution occur continuously between systems, and the coupling between systems is gradually active. After the joint action of the first three modules, the system moves from collision to gradual integration until the creation mechanism takes effect. The creation and accumulation of knowledge capital have brought about a qualitative change in the system, and the seven major mechanisms begin to function on the new knowledge capital platform until the next creation arises. This process proceeds circumstantially leading to an ever- increasing stock of knowledge capital for the M&A entity. After the integration of the two enterprises' knowledge capital systems is completed, the enterprise will develop knowledge capital on a new platform. Currently, the substitution, complementarity, and conflict elimination mechanisms in the four major modules are no longer applicable, but the basic principles of knowledge capital evolution do not change.

The synergy and evolution of knowledge capital after M&A is a complex process. Different types of knowledge capital have different focuses on the seven major mechanisms. Different types of M&A have different focuses and difficulties in the role of synergy mechanisms. In short, appropriate knowledge capital synergy strategies must be adopted for different enterprises and different types of M&A.

(iii) Environment of knowledge capital synergy after M&A

Guo Junhua (2002)'s analysis of the knowledge capital synergy mechanism is not limited to the analysis of the interaction of knowledge capital between the M&A parties within the system. At the same time, the enterprise system is placed in an open environment and analyzes the control and constraints of the external environment of knowledge capital synergy.

Guo believes that the knowledge capital systems of M&A parties breed and develop in four internal shared environments: the source field, the interactive field, the network field, and the training field, while the whole M&A entity is in the external environments of the product market environment, factor market environment, institutional and legal environment, and social and cultural environment. The exchange of knowledge, capital, and personnel, as well as the exchange of explicit and tacit knowledge capital, is constantly taking place between the internal and external environments. In addition, there are many ontological levels in a shared environment, and the combination of environments at a certain level will form a larger shared environment. Therefore, the organic combination between different levels of environments can amplify the process of knowledge capital creation. Knowledge capital synergy is a highly complex process. Maintaining a balance between promoting the transfer of knowledge capital and reducing the conflicts between the two M&A parties is a careful trade-off and choice between the needs of the environment, the evolution model expected by the acquirer, and the specific situation in a specific period. The complexity and dynamics ofthe synergy process require the M&A entity to be in a strong enabling environment. The contingency theory holds that the environment is constantly changing, and the knowledge capital that is most appropriate for a certain environment at a certain point of time may become inappropriate with the change of the environment, and only the knowledge capital that is appropriate for the environment can be developed successfully. Therefore, it is necessary to pay attention to the relationship structure between the acquirer and the external environment, adjust the strategy to the changing environment, and take appropriate control measures.

(3) Mechanism of strategic resource synergy between M&A parties

Zhang Jinxin (2005) examined the synergy provided by strategic resources from a qualitative perspective. Zhang divided the synergy into complementary synergy and scale synergy based on whether each of the merging parties owns a certain resource. The synergy in which one party owns a certain resource and the other party has other resources that can create synergy with the resource is defined as complementary synergy, and the synergy in which both parties in the merger have a certain resource that can create synergy is defined as scale synergy. The classification of resource synergy is shown in Fig. 7.5.

	The target party	
Acquirer	Scale synergy (yes, yes)	Complementary synergy (yes, no)
	Complementary synergy (no, yes)	(no, no)

Fig. 7.5 Classification of resource synergy. *Source* Zhang Jinxin. Who Is the Target: Strategic Analysis of Resources Fit Between Mergers. Beijing: Economic Press China. 2006

Zhang Jinxin (2005) believes that the potential synergy of resources should be judged in the context of the strategic motivation of M&A. If the M&A pursue a scale effect, the judgment of potential synergy should focus mainly on the scale synergy of similar resources; If the M&A pursue cost-saving effect along the value chain, the judgment of the potential synergy should focus mainly on the complementary synergy between different types of resources that can generate synergy effect. He regards whether resources reach economic scale and whether resources are effectively managed as the factors affecting the realization of scale synergy, and regards the non-sharing and resource abuse as factors hindering the realization of complementary synergy.

Based on analyzing the concepts, sources, and influencing factors of scale synergy and complementary synergy, Zhang Jinxin focused on analyzing the potential synergy realization mechanism of property assets, human capital, and social capital in skills and assets.

(i) Mechanism of potential skill synergy

There are two prerequisites for the realization of skill scale synergy, one is the scale space, and the other is the investment guarantee. The scale of the enterprise is matched with the skills of the enterprise. If the scales of the two M&A parties are not comparable, there may be a problem of wasting skills. In addition, when the scale of the newly merged enterprise expands after the M&A, the acquirer may also consider developing some skills comparable to those of large enterprises accordingly, which may make the acquirer face the problem of investment security. Because new skills do not arise naturally as the company expands, managers need to pay special attention and safeguards. There are also many ways to realize the skill scale synergy, which is contained in the large-scale operation of enterprises. There is potential for economies of scale in research and development, procurement, manufacturing, sales and marketing, service, and daily management activities at scale. Therefore, enterprises need to identify whether these pathways are realistic and feasible to achieve economies of scale. In addition, cost savings are the ultimate source of scale synergy, and costs can be divided into transaction costs, production costs, and management costs. Different costs have different shares in the cost structure of enterprises, and those factors that have a greater impact on the cost of the larger share and general share should be paid attention to.

The complementary synergy of skills comes from the economies of scope and learning of the skills of both M&A parties.

There are two prerequisites for the realization of the skill economy of scope: one is the existence of residual skills that can be shared, and the other is the guarantee of the organizational system. The skill economy of scope can be realized through joint research and development, joint purchasing, joint manufacturing, joint sales, joint service, and joint management, and each way saves different costs, and the impact of different costs on the cost structure of enterprises is different. The sources of skills economy of scope are mainly examined in terms of improved linkages and increased utilization. Improving linkages between interrelated skills can improve product performance, and increasing the efficiency of underutilized skills can directly save production costs.

The realization of the skill economy of learning requires two prerequisites: one is that the two M&A parties have close cooperation on the skills, and the other is that the transfer of skills has organizational guarantees. The ways to realize the skill economy of learning can be examined from two perspectives: from the way of communication, knowledge sharing can be achieved through direct and indirect communication; from the level of communication, knowledge sharing can be achieved through the introduction, discussion, application, and development.

The results of the measurement of potential synergy in the skills of both M&A parties are finally summarized in an evaluation table, as shown in Table 7.2, which mainly examines the contribution of synergy to the acquirer, the new company, and the new expansion opportunities in the four functional areas of daily management, operation and business, research and development, and marketing.

Table 7.2 Evaluation of skills synergy

Skill	Business content	Importance in the cost structure	Opportunities for synergy	
			Scale synergy	Complementary synergy
Research and develop	Basic and applied research, mockup and model manufacturing, industrial design and production drawing, production process and technology development, market research	Very low	High	High
Marketing	Product introduction, advertising, promotion, sales, product allocation (including transportation and warehousing), contract management, sales analysis, sales services	Medium	High	Medium
Production operation	Raw material procurement, production planning control, equipment installation and maintenance, manufacturing technology, quality control, inventory management, product manufacturing	High	Low	Medium
Daily management	Strategy development, accounting, human resource management, maintaining public relations	High	Medium	

Source Zhang Jinxin. Who Is the Target: Strategic Analysis of Resources Fit Between Mergers. Beijing: Economic Press China. 2006

(ii) Mechanism of potential asset synergy

First, mechanism of potential property right-based asset synergy. The property right-based assets obtained by M&A can increase the total assets in the balance sheet, but they can only generate potential synergy when they exert the benefits of large-scale production or joint production in specific production links. Before the acquisition, the acquirer should determine the production links to be focused on according to the development strategy, examine whether the target's property right-based assets can enhance its strength in this production link, and then clarify the potential way to achieve it in research and development, procurement, manufacturing, sales or service link.

The purpose of examining the ways to achieve potential synergy is to clarify in which production link the assets of the target party can create synergy with the assets of the acquirer through coordinated production. This examination not only facilitates a more accurate measurement of potential synergy benefits during the valuation stage but also facilitates the development of a clearer integration strategy during the integration stage. In addition, such analysis can help to clearly distinguish strategic and non-strategic resources to focus on the acquisition of strategic resources.

The analysis of potential synergy economic sources should be specific to the cost level. Potential synergy may come from savings in production costs, transaction costs, or management costs, but in the case of property right-based assets, it tends to have a more direct impact on production cost savings.

Second, potential human capital synergy. Acquiring companies should assess employees' capabilities, as these capabilities play a significant role in realizing synergies (Ahammad & Glaister, 2013). New post-merger enterprises require an appropriate ratio of human capital in terms of quantity and quality with different roles and levels. For example, a frequent situation is that the target has excellent technical human capital, but lacks qualified management human capital. At this time, if the acquirer can input a corresponding amount of excellent management human capital, it can fully exploit the target's potential of technological human capital to realize the potential value of the target.

There are both qualitative and quantitative requirements for the human capital synergy between M&A parties, but the qualitative requirements are the main conflict, and the quantitative scale can only be determined on the premise of satisfying the qualitative requirements. The human capital synergy in quality can be examined from two aspects: economies of scale and economies of scope. Economies of scale of human capital are generally manifested in that they can generate specialized division of labor, save costs in the reinvestment of human capital, and improve the capability of technological innovation by the exchange of different types of human capital. Economies of the scope of human capital are generally manifested as improving the utilization efficiency of human capital because a larger scope of activities allows previously unused human capital to be used more fully.

Jiang Jilu and Liu Zhenlin (2010) believe that the synergistic use of human capital and physical capital can bring average market profits to enterprises, which means that fixed assets and current assets cannot bring excess profits to enterprises. At the same time, the impact of the expansion of enterprise scale on management costs may be bidirectional, which may lead to diseconomies of scale or economies of scale in management. On the one hand, if the scale of the enterprise is too large, the management information will be transmitted slowly or distorted due to the wide range of management and too many levels, and various frictions and conflicts will be caused due to the increase of departments within the enterprise, resulting in rigidity of enterprise management and reduced operational efficiency. On the other hand, if the acquirer has excess managerial human capital before the M&A, the expansion of enterprise scale provides an opportunity to make full use of the excess managerial capacity. Moreover, if M&A integration merges the overlapping management functions of the two parties, the expansion of the enterprise scale may also lead to a decrease in the unit management cost from the perspective of average cost. Therefore, the change in management cost is directly related to the management capability, as shown by the fact that the higher management capability can improve the management efficiency of the previously mismanaged business unit and thus reduce the unit management cost (Zhang Jinxin & Wang Qingjian, 2009).

Third, potential social capital synergy. The scale synergy of social capital exists based on the coordination of social network organizations. The coordination of network organizations requires that the related social organizations should be harmonious, and there should be a foundation that can be synergized, such as compatible strategies, organizational systems, and management mechanisms. From the perspective of the source of scale synergy, the scale synergy of social capital mainly comes from the saving of transaction costs. Social capital is based on the exchange or transaction relationship between the enterprise and external stakeholders. Compared with the market transaction relationship, this relationship can save transaction costs such as search costs and negotiation costs, and bring economies of scale. Of course, with the expansion of the enterprise scale after M&A, the newly merged enterprise has the opportunity to expand the scope of its social network and obtain more social capital, which may also bring economies of scale in the production and management of social capital itself.

The complementary synergy of social capital is often the greatest source of social capital gains. The complementary synergy of social capital can be examined from two aspects: social network and resources occupied by network members. Differentiated social networks may have two forms of complementary synergy: the complementary synergy of heterogeneous networks and the complementary synergy of similar heterogeneous networks. Integrating the resources of differentiated networks may save channel development costs and channel management costs, and bring complementary synergy benefits of social capital, but differentiated networks do not naturally generate complementary synergy, and sometimes it is also the source of conflict because complementarity includes two meanings: difference and commonality, and if differentiated networks cannot be common, there is no basis for complementary synergy.

From the perspective of resources occupied by network members, the complementarity is reflected in two aspects: the M&A parties are complementary in status and weakly connected. Status refers to the distance from the network member to the center of the network. Status determines the amount of resources owned, and indicators that reflect status or influence include market share, price influence, etc.

Therefore, the complementary synergy potential of social capital can be captured from two aspects: one is the network differences, including differences in network size and network heterogeneity; the other is the network resource differences, including differences in members' status, the amount of resource owned, and relationship strength.

Lu Changbao (2012) believes that building an enterprise network can acquire and consolidate strategic relationship resources. Enterprises use various contracts to exchange and accumulate social capital among network members, thereby reducing transaction costs, gaining competitive advantages, and achieving greater economic benefits.

(4) Mechanism of resource synergy between M&A parties

Zhou Lin (2006) systematically discussed the operational mechanism of resource synergy (potential synergy) of enterprise M&A from both qualitative and quantitative aspects. In the qualitative aspect, she discussed the interaction mechanism of resource synergy in enterprise M&A from the perspective of strategic management, analyzed the internal and external environment of the M&A entity, and established a model of the resource synergy process in an open environment. Zhou believes that, on the one hand, the resources of both parties after M&A may have various nonlinear effects such as substitution, complementarity, enhancement, and conflict due to differences. On the other hand, the enterprise entity and the external environment will also resonate and fluctuate. Therefore, the difference is the premise and foundation of synergy, and the resources of both parties of M&A evolve precisely in the sequence of difference— selection—nonlinear action—synergy. In terms of the quantitative aspect, Zhou uses the knowledge of synergy theory in systems science, and establishes a matrix model of the interaction of resource elements of M&A parties with the help of the concepts and methods of Boolean algebra, explaining the occurrence of enterprise M&A behavior and the principle of resource synergy between M&A parties. The mechanisms of potential synergy between M&A parties are divided into four categories: substitution, complementarity, enhancement, and conflict, and are discussed from these four aspects respectively.

The substitution mechanism arises mainly from two aspects: cost reduction and efficiency improvement. The necessary conditions for the substitution of the resources of the two enterprises are: (i) the independent application of either of these two resources (or combinations) can achieve the purpose to an equal degree; (ii) mastering the two resources (or combinations) at the same time cannot improve the utility of either resource (or combination) to any extent, that is, there is no complementarity between the two resources (or combinations), and having both at the same time would only result in duplication and redundancy; (iii) the cost of acquiring either resource (or combination) is non-zero, and there is no "cost interaction" (the act of acquiring one type of these resources affects the cost of acquiring another type of resource), or, if such a "cost interaction" exists, the direction of the interaction is such that the acquisition of one type of resource (or combination) increases the cost of acquiring another type of resource (or combination) ("lock-in effect"). Zhou believes that resource substitution usually occurs between similar resources to achieve the same goal or function, mainly in the form of the substitution of physical assets and the substitution of human capital.

The complementarity of resources means that the resources of one enterprise are complementary to the resources of the other enterprise, and the gap in the strategic resources of the enterprise can be supplemented after the M&A so that the overall development of the enterprise after the M&A shows an increase in revenue. Complementary mechanism needs to have two conditions: value and exportability. Correspondingly, complementary mechanism is divided into two categories: (i) The input and effective operation of one resource requires the input and operation of another resource at the same time. If the input of the latter is missing, the utility of the former is almost impossible, while the reverse does not exist. (i) The two resources cannot be invested and operated independently but must be conditioned on the input of the other. Zhou believes that the complementarity of resources between M&A parties can occur either between the same type of resources or between different types of resources. Common types include the complementarity of financial assets and the complementarity of physical assets, financial assets, and human capital.

The promotion mechanism means that when two resources of both M&A parties are not required to be conditioned on each other's input production, the resources of the other party still invested in the production and operation process at the same time, the production efficiency of both resources will be greatly increased. The promotion mechanism is mainly manifested in the diffusion and creation of capabilities. Diffusion of capabilities means that knowledge-based capabilities are mastered and applied by new organizations without changing the original organization's ownership and use of capabilities. The creation of capabilities is an extension of capability diffusion, which refers to the spontaneous and irregular movement of various knowledge in human capital and organizational capability from the initial stage of M&A, to the integration and then amplification through knowledge diffusion within the organization, and the formation of new knowledge through different ways.

Conflict mechanism refers to the mutual restriction and mutual influence of various types of resources, which leads to the use of value or material characteristics of one resource affecting the existence of other resources, and this mutual influence phenomenon will lead to the waste of internal resources and the deterioration of resource conditions. The phenomenon of resource conflict is caused by two subjective and objective factors: the disproportionate relationship between resources and the heterogeneity of things. This is because, on the one hand, if the proportional relationship of resources in the entities formed by the two parties changes after M&A and becomes unreasonable, it will lead to conflicts among various elements of resources, affecting the value benefits of resources and the overall value benefits of the system and hindering the ultimate realization of strategic goals; on the other hand, the heterogeneity of resources determines that any dissimilar resources may conflict. Therefore, in the process of resource synergy evolution, conflicts must be correctly identified and evaluated, and then weakened or even eliminated to achieve a win–win situation for both the acquirer and the target.

Zhou Lin (2006) believes that M&A parties belong to an open system and the process of acquiring resources cannot be separated from the influence of the environment. Therefore, Zhou analyzes the internal and external environment of potential synergy between M&A parties based on detailing the four mechanisms of M&A potential synergy performance. Zhou divides the external environment into product market environment, factor market environment, institutional and legal environment, and social and cultural environment. At the same time, Zhou believes that after the completion of the M&A transaction, under the influence of the internal environment, the resources of both M&A parties breed and develop through different combinations and interactions, while exporting products and services as well as intangible assets with added value (such as patents and brands), while products and services are put into the market to exchange capital and personnel with the external environment, and capabilities are further enhanced in the operation of the enterprise. Therefore, Zhou also gave the dynamic synergy process of the resources of both parties in the open environment (see Fig. 7.6) and pointed out that the process of resource synergy is a dynamic cycle of self- combination, self-transformation, self-enhancement, or weakening of internal resources of enterprises after M&A.

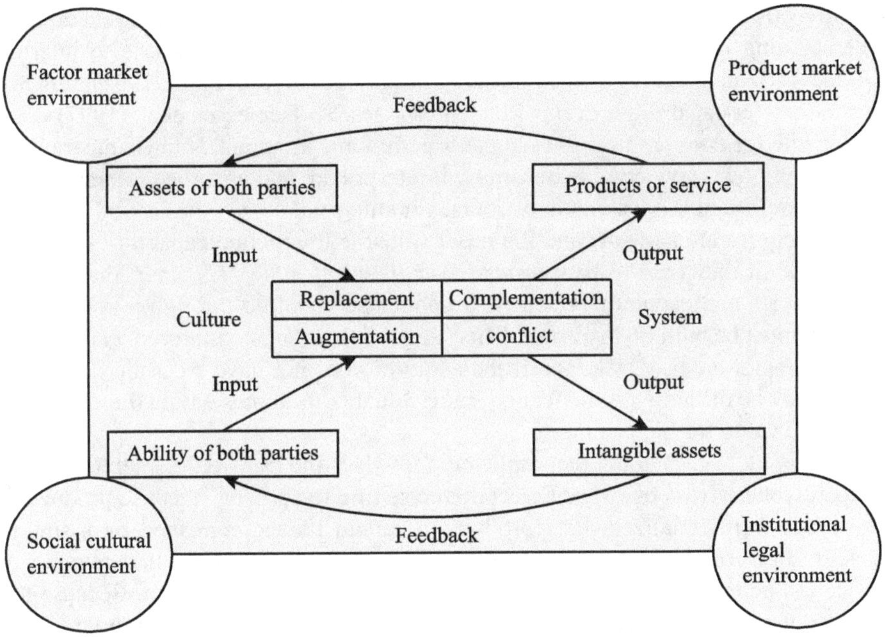

Fig. 7.6 Dynamic synergy process of resources between M&A parties in an open environment. *Source* Zhou Lin. Research on the Mechanism of Resource Synergy in M&A. Doctoral dissertation of Beijing Jiaotong University. 2006

7.3.2.2 The Expected Synergy Mechanism of Corporate M&A

(I) Expected synergy of capabilities

(i) Difficulty in transferring capabilities in M&A

The knowledge-based view of the firm holds that the essence of capability is knowledge. Therefore, analyzing capability transfer from the perspective of knowledge provides insight into the internal process of capability transfer. Studies have shown that four factors may affect the difficulty of knowledge transfer: the characteristics of the transferred knowledge, the source, the recipient, and the context in which the transfer occurs (Leonard & Barton, 1990; Teece, 1977; Rogers, 1995; Szulanski, 1996). While most works on knowledge transfer have focused on the transfer barriers and facilitators of optimal approaches within organizations and knowledge flows between business units (Gupta & Govindarajan, 1991; Kostova, 1999; Szulanski, 1996), it is widely accepted that knowledge transfer initiates and depends on organizational capabilities. For example, the concept of absorptive capacity means that an organization must first possess a certain level of relevant knowledge to acquire and internalize knowledge (Cohen & Levinthal, 1990).

The focus on the acquirer's capabilities also comes from a deepening theoretical understanding of intra-firm capability transfer. Studies show that due to internal stickiness (Szulanski, 1996) or knowledge inertia (Kogut & Zander, 1992), it is not easy to transfer capabilities even within enterprises. So Tiemessen et al. (1997) warn that knowledge does not flow as easily as is commonly assumed. Knowledge transfer depends on how knowledge is transmitted, interpreted, and absorbed (Hamel et al., 1989), therefore, it is not a matter of course for enterprises to get the capabilities they want to acquire after M&A, and the more valuable the unique capabilities are, the more difficult they tend to be transferred, so Teece et al. (1997) assert that unique competencies and capabilities generally cannot be acquired through purchase and that they must be built on their own. This suggests that the integration of capabilities in M&A is not an easy task, and if the acquirer does not have a certain capability base, it may be difficult to transfer and share valuable resources within the enterprise and create value for the enterprise.

Teece et al. (1997) argue that replication involves the transfer and application of competitiveness from one specific economic setting to another. Because productive knowledge is materialized, its reproduction cannot be accomplished by a simple transfer of information. Only when knowledge is fully encoded and understood can replication be transformed into a simple information transfer problem. Because the initial context on which performance depends is often not fully understood, replication actions are generally difficult unless firms have experience replication of their productive knowledge systems on many previous occasions (Teece, 1976).

(ii) The capability to transfer knowledge

The traditional understanding of M&A tends to regard M&A as a way to obtain resources in the same form as the purchase of a factor from the factor market, which is nothing more than the purchase of a set of factors. Therefore, the analysis of M&A naturally tends to look more at the quality and price of the target, and much more cursorily at the acquirer. Perhaps the acquirer thinks that it knows more than enough about itself, so there is no need for a specialized analysis before the merger. However, many cases of failed M&A show that the acquirer's output and absorption capabilities are also key factors in the success or failure of an M&A.

A complete understanding of M&A should be that it is both a way of acquiring resources and a way of exporting resources. Through M&A, enterprises transfer resources from one of the parties to the other to achieve resource reallocation and then realize synergies and value creation. In the process of resource reallocation, the acquirer, whether as the exporter or a recipient of resources, must have the corresponding output capacity or absorption capacity to ensure the efficiency of resource transfer.

First, capability to output. The output capability is the ability of the acquirer to encode, express, and integrate intangible resources to effectively transmit them to the recipient. Such intangible resources may be technology (know- how), reputation, culture, etc. In particular, intangible knowledge resources need to be coded before the transfer, summarized into a form that can be understood by the recipient, and then passed on to the recipient through training, informal communication, written documents, and other expressions. However, the degree of coding needs to be matched with the degree of integration, and the more explicit and standardized it is, the better it is for integration. For example, Singh and Zollo (1998) found based on empirical research that the higher the degree of coding, the better the economic performance of the acquisition in the context of higher integration; however, the higher the degree of coding, the worse the economic performance of acquisitions in the context of lower integration.

In the process of resource transfer, attention should also be paid to creating a suitable environment, such as an incentive to encourage the exporter to take the initiative to export and the receiver to be willing to accept, and the corresponding adjustment of organizational structure. The output of capabilities is often accompanied by the transfer of assets, such as the acquirer's original human resources, technology assets, trademark usage rights, channel relationships, customer relationships, etc. Among them, the efficiency of the transfer of right- to-use assets is also one of the key concerns. On the surface, M&A is about acquiring resources, but from the perspective of whether M&A is successful or not, M&A is first and foremost about exporting resources. The exported resources are not limited to the capital, but also include human capital, relationship assets, capabilities, culture, etc. that may need to be provided to the acquirees. This is consistent with the philosophy of "if you want to take something, you must give it first".

Second, capacity to absorb. The capacity to absorb refers to the acquirer's ability to learn and manage new resources. Especially for knowledge-based intangible resources, only with a certain ability base can the acquirer ensure its understanding, rapid learning, and effective application of new knowledge. The lack of absorptive capacity on the part of the acquirer is the most significant obstacle to knowledge transfer (Szulanski, 1996), because the organization cannot improve what it does not understand (Teece et al., 1997).

The absorptive capacity of an acquirer is mainly related to two factors: the existing knowledge stock and the learning capacity. In discussing the cost of acceptance in the process of knowledge transfer, Wang Kaiming and Wan Junkang (2000) pointed out that the differences in knowledge understanding, time and effort spent in comprehending knowledge by different people reflect the differences in learning costs of the receivers in the process of receiving the knowledge. The initial reason for the differences in learning costs is the differences in individual talents, that is, differences in the ability of different people to comprehend specific types of knowledge, but the most fundamental reason lies in the difference in the accumulation of acquired knowledge. They show that the acceptance cost of inter-individual knowledge transfer depends on learning ability and the existing knowledge stock. The same is true for knowledge transfer between organizations.

In the process of transferring the capabilities of the acquiree to the acquirer, if the acquirer has a certain accumulation of relevant knowledge or has a strong learning ability, they can learn the specific knowledge faster and improve the speed of integrating new knowledge with the knowledge stock and the efficiency of ability transfer.

(iii) Efficiency of skill transfer

Both practice and research have found that there are many thorny issues in achieving capability transfer through strategic M&A. Capability transfer depends on the successful integration of the acquiree (Haspeslagh & Jemison, 1991), but the integration process is subject to a high risk of failure (Jemison & Sitkin, 1986). In other words, there are frequent losses in the transfer of capabilities in M&A that strategic M&A from being an efficient method of transfer of capabilities. Therefore, it is understandable that researchers pay attention to the factors that affect the efficiency of capability transfer. Although there has been considerable research on knowledge transfer within individual firms, between alliance firms, and between independent firms, except for the so-called "process school" (Greenwood et al., 1994; Haspeslagh & Jemison, 1991; Hakanson 1995; Shrivastava, 1986), there is a lack of specialized research on knowledge transfer in M&A (Rumyantseva, Gurgul & Enkel, 2002). The process school of research on M&A based on a strategic perspective, which gradually developed after the mid-1980s, mainly focuses on how to create value through post-acquisition integration. Their contribution to the study of capability transfer is to suggest that knowledge transfer between acquirers and acquirees depends on the development of the partnership, but the process school focuses on how knowledge transfer affects value creation without focusing on the factors influencing knowledge transfer itself. In the following, we will analyze the factors that affect the efficiency of capability transfer in strategic M&A and how they affect the efficiency of capability transfer.

First, the process of skill transfer. Gunnar and Hedhund (1994) classified knowledge into individual knowledge, team knowledge, organizational knowledge, and inter-organizational knowledge according to the carrier of knowledge. Individual knowledge refers to the explicit and tacit knowledge held by individuals. In innovation and product development, much of the transfer and learning of knowledge occurs at the team level, resulting in team knowledge.

Organizational knowledge refers to the explicit and tacit knowledge held by an organization. Inter-organizational knowledge includes knowledge about important users, suppliers, and competitors. They also summarized the transformation process of knowledge at different levels: the process of gradually transferring from individual knowledge to team knowledge, organizational knowledge, and inter- organizational knowledge is called the process of knowledge expansion, and the reverse process of this one is the process of knowledge specialization.

Nonaka and Takeuchi (1995) also discussed the transformation process between individual knowledge, team knowledge, and organizational knowledge. Individual tacit knowledge is the basis of organizational knowledge creation, which is amplified and turned into higher-level knowledge within the organization through knowledge transformation, a process called "knowledge spiral". Among them, knowledge transformation, which plays a key role, includes four basic transformation forms: socialization, representation, synthesis, and internalization of knowledge.

Firstly, the process of obtaining tacit knowledge from tacit knowledge is called "socialization". This is a form of transferring or creating knowledge through shared experiences by specific individuals or teams. It is the sharing and transformation of knowledge through perceptual experiences such as experience, observation, and imitation rather than through language. Through the process of socialization, empathic knowledge is generated.

Secondly, the process of obtaining explicit knowledge from tacit knowledge is called "representation". New knowledge is created based on sharing and integrating individuals and teams tacit knowledge, such as the formulation of new concepts in product development, the literalization of technical know-how, and the specific description of potential customer needs. Through the process of representation, conceptual knowledge is generated.

Thirdly, the process of obtaining explicit knowledge from explicit knowledge, and creating new knowledge by synthesizing various kinds of knowledge by individuals and teams is called "synthesis". For example, knowledge is created using tools such as language, documents, design drawings, databases, and computers. This is the process of combining existing explicit knowledge to systematize explicit knowledge. Through the process of synthesis, systematic knowledge is generated.

Fourthly, tacit knowledge is obtained from explicit knowledge, and the explicit knowledge obtained through the processes of socialization, representation, and synthesis is transformed into tacit knowledge that can only be understood but not communicated. This process is called "internalization". Through the process of internalization, operational knowledge is generated.

In the case of M&A, the transfer of skills is essentially a transfer of knowledge between organizations. This transfer goes through a process from encoding to decoding. After the new knowledge is decoded, it gradually becomes familiar to the new exploiters. Based on this, knowledge exploiters create new knowledge and go through the process of sharing tacit knowledge, creating ideas, confirming ideas, establishing protoforms, and spreading knowledge across levels (Nonaka & Takeuchi, 1995).

Second, influencing factors of skill transfer. The nature of skills is collaborative knowledge, so skill transfer has been explored more from the perspective of knowledge transfer. Studies have shown that even intra-firm transfer of skills is not easy due to internal stickiness (Szulanski, 1996) or inertness of knowledge (Kogut & Zander, 1992). The "noise" in knowledge transfer, the bias in understanding the meaning of both parties, and the cost of transfer determine the inefficiency of multiple transfers of knowledge along interpersonal communication networks (Wang Kaiming & Wan Junkang, 2000). Previous studies have suggested four factors that may affect the efficiency of knowledge transfer: the characteristics of the knowledge being transferred, the source, the recipient, and the context in which the transfer occurs (Leonard-Barton, 1990; Rogers, 1983; Szulanski, 1996; Teece, 1977; Yu Guangsheng, 2000). Badaracco (1991) argues that four conditions must be met for knowledge to move quickly: the first is it must be explicit and in packages; the second is a person or group must be able to unlock, understand, and have the skills to absorb the knowledge; the third is these people or groups must have sufficient motivation to do the above; and the fourth is there must be no barriers preventing them from doing so.

In the context of M&A, the factors influencing the efficiency of skill transfer are mainly manifested in four aspects: the knowledge transferred, the source of knowledge, the recipient of knowledge, and the context of knowledge transfer.

Firstly, the knowledge transferred. Some skills are expressible, and they are relatively easy to transfer. Some skills are not yet encoded, and it is not clear where the exact outcome of the skill lies, these skills are therefore causally ambiguous. Causal ambiguity refers to the difficulty in specifying what factors play a decisive role in the formation of skills, and thus it is difficult to replicate. Causal ambiguity is indicated when the key factors for replicating a skill in a new setting are not precisely identified even afterward, making it impossible to give a clear list of the factors of production needed to replicate the skill, let alone measure their marginal contribution (Rumelt, 1984).

Two factors influence the factor ambiguity of skills: the tacitness of skills and the complexity of skills (Simonin, 1999). Tacitness refers to the ineffable and uncodifiable nature of skills acquired through learning by doing (Reed & DeFilipi, 1990). Tacitness means difficult to communicate and share, highly personal, and deeply rooted in context-specific actions and personally relevant things (Nonaka, 1994), so tacit skills have the characteristics that are characterized by high transfer costs. Zander and Kogut (1995) pointed out, based on empirical research, that the degree to which manufacturing skills can be codified and taught significantly affects the speed of their transfer, and also indicated that tacitness is an obstacle to skill transfer.

The degree of tacitness of a particular skill in a company can be reflected by several indicators. The first is whether the skills are process-based. If there is written information about the description of the skill and a standardized procedure for the execution of the skill, the degree of explicitness of the skill will be higher. The extent to which management information systems are applied is an important indicator of the processability of skills. How much an enterprise relies on the knowledge in the minds of a few employees and how much an enterprise relies on MIS are complementary; more reliance on MIS indicates the enterprise knowledge process, or the degree of disclosure is higher. The second is whether skills are disseminated. If the skills are understood and used frequently by all those who should know them, it reflects that there are fewer barriers to their diffusion within the organization. Conversely, if the skill is possessed only by a few people (relative to the total number of people who should possess the skill), or if the skill was used only a long time ago (e.g., M&A integration capabilities applied a long time ago), it indicates a higher degree of tacitness.

Complexity refers to the number of technologies, norms, individuals, and resources associated with a given skill (Simonin, 1999). As Reed and DeFilipi (1990) point out, the more complex the human and technical system is, the higher the degree of ambiguity generates, and thus the greater the difficulty of imitation is. The information involved in complex skills may involve a large number of individuals and sectors, and there is ambiguity not only in each part of the skill but also in the connections between skills so that the whole picture is not easily grasped by most people, and so hinders skill transfer.

Secondly, the source of knowledge. The factors influencing transfer efficiency from the skill exporters include knowledge organization ability and knowledge expression ability.

Knowledge organization ability refers to the skills of organizing knowledge into knowledge that can be easily absorbed by the recipient according to the characteristics of the recipient of the abilities. This ability requires not only a deep understanding of the output knowledge, but also an in-depth knowledge of the recipient's work habits, knowledge level, learning style, learning attitude, and other background factors.

Knowledge expression ability refers to the ability to effectively communicate knowledge to the recipients. For organizations, the ability to express knowledge involves the issues of who expresses it and how to express it. How to express, i.e., the way of expression, reflects the means of expression that the knowledge exporter can provide and the means of expression that the receiver can easily accept. Who expresses, i.e., the subject of expression, reflects whether the transfer of knowledge is mainly mediated by a few people or by the majority. If the abilities are mastered by everyone in the organization, there will be more subjects of expression; if the abilities are mastered by only a few people, there will be fewer subjects of expression. The number of expressed subjects will affect the frequency and effectiveness of communication.

Previous studies have paid attention to the motivation of the skill exporter, and the reliability of the exported skills (Szulanski, 1996), but not enough attention has been paid to the changes in the number of knowledge expressing subjects when skills are transferred in M&A. Mergers and acquisitions are often accompanied by staff turnover, which can result in a loss of skills, and in particular, the divestiture of the acquiree may damage skills (Capron, 1999). This means that if skill exporters experience significant turnover, the skills they previously possessed will face difficulties in transfer.

For those who remain in the merger, there is a risk that skills will not be transferred effectively, even if they acquire all the skills. In addition to the factors of the skills themselves (skills that work in the context of the skill exporter cannot be fully utilized in the new context, which is related to the causal ambiguity of the skills), it also lies in the new employees' adaptability to the acquirees, that is, the problem of the person-organization fit. The reason for the people-organization mismatch comes from two aspects, one is the mismatch between people and positions, and the other is the mismatch between people and organizational culture. Therefore, it needs to be noted that inappropriate adjustment of personnel in M&A integration will not only affect the performance of individual skills but also affect the transfer of organizational skills.

Thirdly, the recipient of knowledge. Since the transfer of skills is essentially a transfer of knowledge, the ability of the recipient of the knowledge to absorb it becomes one of the key factors affecting the efficiency of skill transfer (Grant, 1997).

Absorptive capacity refers to a firm's skill in identifying the value of new external knowledge, absorbing it, and applying it for business purposes (Cohen & Levinthal, 1990). Absorptive capacity is largely a function of a firm's level of relevant knowledge (Dierickx & Cool, 1989), and lack of absorptive capacity is one of the main significant sources of stickiness (Szulanski, 1996).

The absorptive capacity of the skill receiver is mainly related to two factors: the relevance of the existing knowledge to the knowledge to be absorbed and the learning skills. In the process of transferring skills from the skill exporter to the skill receiver, if the skill receiver has some relevant knowledge accumulated, it is possible to better assess the value of such skills, better understand the gap between the existing skill and the skill, and deal with the interface issues. As pointed out by Lane and Lubatkin (1998), a firm's ability in identifying, assimilating, and utilizing external knowledge depends in part on the knowledge base, organizational systems, and dominant logic of the parties to the transaction. Coff (2002) finds empirically that similar expertise between acquirers and acquirees is particularly important in the acquisition of human capital-intensive target companies, also in terms of understanding of this similarity in terms of absorptive capacity. Coff argues that if the acquirer has similar expertise, its management can be relatively well positioned to evaluate the target's human capital and potential synergies, which can reduce or even eliminate the dilemma caused by information asymmetry. Inkpen (1998) also pointed out that knowledge in familiar domains is generally easier to learn than knowledge in unfamiliar domains.

Another important factor that affects the receivers' ability to absorb is their learning skills. If skill receivers have strong learning skills, they can absorb specific knowledge faster and increase the speed of integration of new knowledge with the knowledge stock and the efficiency of skill transfer.

Forthly, the context of knowledge transfer. The context of knowledge transfer affects both the motivation of the skill exporter to export skills and the motivation of the skill receiver to receive skills, and it is crucial to establish a trusting and intimate relationship between exporters and receivers to form an effective skill exchange mechanism. The evaluation of the skills transfer environment can be considered from the following three aspects:

The first is whether the balance of interests and compensation mechanisms are appropriate. If the transfer of skills causes a loss of benefits to any party, it will affect their enthusiasm for participating in the transfer. Possible losses include loss of superiority, loss of accustomed work style, loss of familiar working environment, etc. Even if there is no profit loss to either party, it makes one party benefit a lot while the other party needs to invest more time, effort, or personnel, which will affect the assessment performance of their team according to the current assessment system and will also affect the knowledge transfer. The imbalance in benefits needs to be adjusted by an effective compensation mechanism. The basic adjustment idea is to allow both parties of skill transfer to get positive incentives, including spiritual incentives.

The second is whether the psychological resistance is serious. If both parties have had unpleasant conflicts before the M&A, and the "us vs. them" opposition is not effectively channeled after the M&A, it will become a psychological barrier to skills transfer. For the recipients, two other factors that may also create psychological resistance: one is arrogance, believing that one's skills are still very good, or not believing that the skills of the other party are better; the other is conservatism, not willing to change the way one is used to.

The third is whether the communication mechanism is effective. The communication mechanism is reflected by the following aspects: the way of communication, especially informal communication and whether face-to- face communication is common; the coordination of communication, such as whether there is a communication coordination group and functions like feedback, suggestions, and organizational communication; the frequency of communication; the motivation of communication. Rumyantseva et al. (2002) pointed out that communication, technical meetings, extensive mutual visits, joint training programs, and other mechanisms help to improve organizational climate and facilitate knowledge transfer. The role of communication is twofold. First, some knowledge (especially tacit knowledge) can often be transferred only through repeated communication. Second, from the perspective of its effect on the knowledge transfer climate, communication helps to eliminate negative psychological factors that affect knowledge transfer, such as anxiety caused by uncertainty about the future, hostility triggered by pent-up resentment, fears, distorted news etc. (Bastien, 1987; Buono & Bowditch, 1989; Haspeslagh & Jemison, 1991; Kogut & Zander 1992; Rumyantseva et al., 2002). Generally speaking, the more formal and informal interactions are, the more efficient the knowledge transfer is (De Meyer, 1991; Haspeslagh & Jemison, 1991). Table 7.3 reflects the characteristics of knowledge transfer in different periods of M&A integration.

Third, skill transfer efficiency evaluation table. Design measurement indicators based on the influencing factors of skill transfer and evaluating these indicators will result in a skill transfer efficiency score table, as shown in Table 7.4. The indicators in the table are scored on a 7-points scale according to their impact on transfer efficiency, from the most negative to the most positive with a score of 1 to 7, respectively.

(2) Expected synergy of assets

(i) Human capital transfer efficiency

Table 7.3 Characteristics of knowledge transfer in different periods of M&A integration

Compare items	Earlier stage	Late stage
Communication direction	One-way	Bidirectional
Communication method	Forced	Interaction
Communication frequency	Less	More
Type of knowledge	Dominant	Implicit

Source According to Rumyantseva et al. (2002)

Table 7.4 Skill transfer efficiency scoring table

Factors affecting transfer efficiency	Metrics	Scoring (1–7 points)
Ambiguity of skills	Degree of skill processization	
	Degree of skill dissemination	
	Complexity of skills	
Output capability	Knowledge organization ability	
	Knowledge expression ability	
Absorptive capacity	Relevance of existing skills to target skills	
	The level of the existing skill relative to the target skill	
	Learning ability	
Transfer environment	Balance of interests and compensation mechanism	
	Psychological counselling	
	Communication mechanism	
Total score		

Source Zhang Jinxin. Who Is the Target: Strategic Analysis of Resources Fit Between Mergers. Beijing: Economic Press China. 2006

Factors that affect the efficiency of human capital transfer can be divided into two categories, factors that affect separation, which relate to whether one party's human capital remains in the new enterprise after the M&A; and the factors that affect human capital incentives, which relate to whether human capital can be effectively utilized in the environment after the M&A.

First, separation in M&A. Studies have shown that the employee turnover rate of acquirees can be as high as 40% to 80% within two years after they have been acquired; however, this rarely happens in companies acquired by Cisco and is only about 6% or 7% at most (Geiss, 2002). Employee turnover rates have become a concern in measuring the success of M&A, especially for human capital-intensive acquisitions.

Employee separation refers to the process by which individuals who derive material benefits from the organization terminate their organizational membership

(Mobley, 1977). Employee separations are usually classified into two types: voluntary and involuntary separation. Voluntary separation means that the decision to leave is made primarily by the employee and includes all forms of resignation. Involuntary separation means that the decision to leave is made primarily by the company and includes layoff and dismissal. Layoff is driven by economic factors of cost-cutting and efficiency, while dismissals are associated with poor employee performance (Abelson, 1987).

Separation content theory and separation process theory have meaningfully examined the causes of separation (Chen Bihui & Li Qing, 1998), and a large number of research models have been developed on the psychological motivation for voluntary separation Hom & Griffeth, 1995; Xie Jinyu & Wang Ying, 1999; (Zhang Mian & Li Shuzhuo, 2002). Among them, the Price-Mueller model incorporates research results of separation from multiple academic fields (such as economics, sociology, psychology, etc.), and has shown good predictive power in explaining the psychological change process of employee separation (Zhang Mian & Li Shuzhuo, 2002). This model contains 4 categories of variables related to separation: environmental variables (opportunity and kinship responsibility), individual variables (general training, job involvement, and positive/negative affect), structural variables (autonomy, fairness of outcomes, job stress, salary, promotion opportunities, job monotony, and social support) and process variables (job satisfaction, organizational commitment, job-seeking behavior, and intention to stay).

Iverson and Pullman (2000) found that the factors influencing voluntary separation and layoff were different. As can be seen from Table 7.5, only age affects both types of separation (but in the opposite direction), while other variables affect only one type of separation.

Table 7.5 Influencing factors and direction of separation

Variables	Voluntary separation	Dismissal
Demographic variables		
Age	–	+
Full time	O	+
Blue collar	–	O
Sociological variables		
Partner support	O	–
Work overload	O	–
Psychological variables		
Intent to leave	+	O
Response to change		
Merger	O	–

Note "+" indicates a positive impact, "–" indicates a negative impact, and "O" indicates no significant impact
Source Iverson and Pullman (2000)

Second, incentives in M&A. The reason for the close relationship between the transfer of human capital and incentives can be found in the property rights characteristics of human capital, which have been clearly emphasized by Rosen (1985), i.e., the indistinguishability of human capital and its owner in terms of its natural properties. Starting from this premise, Zhou Qiren (1996) further pointed out that the natural personal nature of human capital makes it react in a very different way from non-human capital when property rights mutilations occur when the owner of the property right can "shut down" the corresponding human capital to the extent that the asset seems to have never existed, thus making its economic use worthless. Therefore, the extent to which human capital is valued depends on whether it is in a state of effective value release, and this state is derived from the incentives it receives. In other words, the property nature of human capital determines the need for incentives for its utilization.

Motivation theories can be distinguished into content-based motivation theories and process-based motivation theories (Gan Huaming, 2002). Content- based motivation theory mainly studies the reasons that cause people's behavior, i.e., the factors that motivate people to take certain actions. The three most important content-based motivation theories are Maslow's hierarchy of needs theory, McClelland's achievement motivation theory, and Herzberg's two-factor theory. Content-based motivation theories address some important needs but fail to clearly explain why people choose to behave in a particular way when accomplishing work goals. Process-based incentive theory provides a specific explanation for the entire process of behavior elicitation, development, persistence, and termination, and it includes expectancy theory, reinforcement theory, equity theory, and goal-setting theory.

Robbins (1997) proposed an "integrated model of contemporary motivation theories" after summarizing the various motivation theories. Robbins (1997) identified three important factors that affect performance as competence, motivation, and opportunity when discussing the performance dimension, but in the integrated model he described, the opportunity is regarded as an influencing factor of individual effort. In addition, Robbins' integrated model includes an objective performance appraisal system as a factor affecting individual performance (and also performance appraisal criteria as a factor affecting organizational reward), which finds no supporting evidence from existing motivational theories.

In terms of peripheral relationships, the high achievement needs person is not motivated by organizational performance evaluations or organizational rewards, but by the achievement of personal goals. However, the feedback effect of personal goals will affect the level of individual effort, regardless of who it is for. From the perspective of internal relationships, individual efforts, abilities, and opportunities affect individual performance and if individual performance is recognized according to the organization's performance evaluation criteria, the person will be rewarded by the organization, then the individual compares the organization's rewards for the person with the rewards received by others and the person's own needs to generate a certain level of satisfaction, which in turn affects individual goals. The above shows that the utilization efficiency of human capital in M&A is affected by various factors.

The research results on separation and incentives can better examine the efficiency of human capital transfer in M&A. Simply put, the transfer efficiency of human capital can be examined from two perspectives: whether human capital can be transferred to the newly merged enterprise and whether it can perform at no lower level of efficiency in the newly merged firm than before. In concrete terms, the performance of these two aspects in M&A can be assessed based on the professional analysis tools of the psychology of separation and motivation. In addition to this, since most analytical tools on separation focus only on voluntary separations, special attention should be paid to the impact of involuntary separations in M&A analysis, although this is generally the focus of competence transfer rather than human capital transfer. If the employee involuntarily dismission belongs to the same formal organization (such as a labor union) or informal organization as the employee whom the enterprise wants to retain, the disposition of the employee involuntarily dismission may cause other employees to voluntarily leave. Therefore, efforts should be made to identify the relationship between employees in M&A and try to avoid unnecessary negative chain reactions caused by the layoff or dismissal of some employees. Table 7.6 can be used as a reference for evaluating the efficiency of human capital transfer.

(ii) Transfer efficiency of social capital

Table 7.6 Assessing the efficiency of human capital transfer in M&A

Evaluation indicators		Score
Involuntary separation	Impact on employees ready to be retained	
Voluntary separation	Opportunities	
	Relative responsibility	
	General training	
	Work engagement	
	Positive / negative emotions	
	Autonomy	
	Fairness of results	
	Work pressure	
	Salary	
	Promotion opportunities	
	Work monotony	
	Social support	
Motivation	The science of performance evaluation criteria	
	Fairness of organizational rewards	
	The extent to which individual needs are met	
Total score		

The three important factors that affect the transfer of social capital are interests, trust, and norms. Interests are the economic basis for sustainable business relationships, and compromising benefits may destroy the balance of business relationships. Trust is the most critical factor of social capital (Putnam, 2001), which is the psychological basis of business relationships. Norms are the rules of behavior shared by social networks, which are the social basis of business relationships.

First, interests. In sociological or economic sociology works, interests do not seem to be a focus of the examination of social capital, because there are few specializations on interests. However, when enterprises rather than individuals are the object of study, interests should be one of the focal points of social capital research. First of all, this is because enterprises are utilitarian organizations and interests are the prerequisite and motivation for cooperation in such organizations, so if the position and role of interests in the business relationship between enterprises are ignored, the economic attributes of enterprises will undoubtedly be ignored. Secondly, one of the essences of social capital is that it is a resource that can bring benefits to the owners of social capital, which is an important expression of the productive nature of social capital (Coleman, 1990).

If the original interest pattern is broken after the merger, the transfer of social capital will inevitably be affected. This effect may be positive or negative, depending on whether the merger improves or damages the original pattern of interests.

Whether interests are affected can be analyzed by examining whether the agreements linking the commercial relationship have changed. Acquisitions are often accompanied by the integration of social capital, and in the process give rise to the adjustment in various interests relationships. If the adjustment leads to the impairment of one party's interests, the original social ties may be severed. For example, an M&A that changes a previously cooperative relationship between upstream and downstream into a competitive relationship with the same industry can pose a severe test for the transfer of social capital. Conversely, social capital is strengthened when the parties expect greater benefits from the further development of the relationship. There is also the case where although the acquisition establishes a commercial relationship that can be maintained, whether sufficient benefits can be imported to make the business relationship usable also requires attention. For example, if the acquirer expects to leverage the acquiree's sales channel through M&A, there is a question of whether the acquired party's sales channel will be supportive. Because the new product added by the acquirer in the channel may be a substitute for the seller, if the products of another brand he originally sold are more profitable, he may not have the motivation to actively sell the newly added products of the enterprise.

The support attitude of all parties to the M&A also reflects another aspect of whether the distribution of benefits is recognized or not. Some commitments to the new enterprise after the merger, such as signing long-term economic contracts, increasing investment in dedicated assets, and establishing strategic alliance relationships, are meaningful symbols. For example, a higher level of investment in dedicated assets means a greater commitment of the partner to maintain the relationship.

Second, trust. Trust is the perception of the degree of trustworthiness of individuals or organizations to other individuals or organizations acquired through a series of interactions that take place over a certain period of time (Gu Xin et al., 2003). The stability of trust can be examined in two dimensions: the possibility of establishing new ties and the stability of the existing ties, in an acquisition, the acquirer receives the acquiree's social capital and actually joins the acquiree's original network as a new member. The degree of transfer of the acquiree's social capital depends on the degree of trust and acceptance of the acquirer by the acquiree's original network.

The likelihood of establishing new connections depends mainly on the degree of trust that the original members of the network have in the new members, which in turn is influenced by the new members'reputation and action signals. Reputation reflects an evaluation of the new member's historical behavioral record. The acquirer's good reputation helps to gain the trust of the target's stakeholders, and is an important signal, especially for stakeholders who previously lacked ties with the acquirer. And action signals reflect the feelings about the current behavior of the new member, for example, the new member's attitude, commitment, etc. to the original network members will affect the judgment of the new member's behavior orientation and the acceptance of him.

The stability of the original linkage can be reflected by variables such as link duration, level of investment in dedicated assets, and sunk costs. Link duration refers to the time experienced by both parties of a relationship to connect, and it is an important indicator of social capital. The continuity of behavior determines that past behavior has an indelible impact on present and future behavior, and long- term sustained and reliable relationships tend to further strengthen social capital (Chen Feiqiong, 2003). Relationships are formed gradually over time (Anderson et al., 1994, 1998; Dwyer et al., 1987; Håkansson & Snehota, 1995), and trust is formed over a longer contact period is relatively stable.

Williamson (1981) classifies three types of asset specialization: the specialization of plant sites, the specialization of physical assets, and the specialization of human assets. Dedicated assets here refer to dedicated assets invested for a specific linkage, such as a carriage production line dedicated to an alliance partner's car manufacturing, which is shown to be highly dedicated if the carriages produced can only serve this specific alliance partner. Asset exclusivity constraints opportunistic behavior of the alliance partners, such as a casual withdrawal from the alliance for its benefit. Likewise, asset specificity in acquisitions also limits the asset owner's exit from the original social network.

The formation of social capital is the product of a conscious or unconscious investment strategy (Bourdieu, 1997). This strategy first identifies those social relations that are directly useful in the short or long term and that guarantees material and symbolic profits and then transforms these seemingly "accidental" relationships through "symbolic construction" into a durable and institutionally secure relationship that both parties are subjectively willing to maintain over time. For social capital invested consciously, the absence of a corresponding return on prior investment constrains the investor from transferring freely, because the sunk cost formed by the previous investment act as a constraint to a certain extent.

Third, norms. Norms are the rules of action followed by network members, which are not only binding on network members, but also the basis for other network members to judge the direction of actions of a certain network member.

Norms of reciprocity. Sociology places the greatest emphasis on norms as norms of reciprocity (Putnam, 2001), that is, when the recipient is given by the giver, the recipient is also obliged to repay appropriately at an appropriate time, and this obligation is a kind of social capital. Since social capital corresponds to transactions that are different from spot transactions, where the sale is not completed instantaneously and the final balance of interests is often accompanied by a long time lag, the norm of reciprocity is important. Without such norms, social capital is difficult to build.

Punishment mechanism. That is a mechanism for dealing with actors who do not follow the norms. Opportunism prevails in a network without a mechanism to penalize violating participants. This mechanism may be a mechanism that constrains participants from choosing opportunistic behavior through frequent social exchanges, i.e., repeated games, because in frequent interactions, one opportunistic act may be met with retaliatory behavior in subsequent interactions or even ostracized by the group, making the opportunist feel that he or she has more to gain than to lose.

Communication mechanism. Formal and informal communication is an important guarantee for establishing norms. And communication can only increase transparency and reduce unnecessary conflict if it follows mutually agreed rules. A good communication mechanism facilitates the development of shared values among network members or promotes mutual understanding of values.

7.3.2.3 Corporate M&A Network Economy Synergy Mechanism

M&A is a giant venture capital investment for enterprises, and the acquisition of positive synergies implies the excess returns of venture investment. In the research on the synergistic effect of M&A, related scholars have drawn on the theory of enterprise resources to study the basic problems of enterprise theory from the perspective of resource synergy between acquirers and acquirees, and have obtained a more reasonable classification of enterprise resources and studied the general law of inter-enterprise action. However, we find that such inter-enterprise behavior at the micro-level not only changes the organizational structure and behavior of the companies on both sides of the M&A but also has a great impact on the external economic relations and environment of these companies. Isolated studies of individual resource changes on both sides of M&A do not provide a clear picture of the impact on the internal resource network of the companies, much less a clear measure of the impact on the synergy of the economic network formed by both sides.

The efficiency, network, reliability, and other characteristics of the economic network give rise to their unique economic network synergy. The synergy of the economic network not only affects the operational efficiency of these enterprises and industries but also relates to the welfare of the whole society. A comprehensive study of the synergy of economic networks has also drawn some conclusions.

(1) Basic concepts about economic networks

Many scholars have used different terms to summarize this new organizational form from their research perspective, such as "network organization" (Miles & Snow, 1992), "inter-enterprise networks" (Schibany et al., 2000), "network forms of organizations" (Powell, 1990), "strategic networks" (Jarillo, 1988), "hybrid organizational networks" (Williamson, 1991), "social networks" (Rogers & Shoemarker, 1971), "industry with network nature" (Luo Zhongwei, 2000), and "infrastructure industries that require fixed physical networks to transmit their products and services" (Xiao Xingzhi et al., 2003). Although these concepts have different connotations, they all describe a way of organizing socioeconomic resources. Judging from the current economic literature, people still lack a clear and unified definition of an economic network, and generally speaking, it can be roughly divided into two views: narrow and broad. The narrow view sees the economic network as a form of economic coordination between the market and hierarchical firms. These forms of coordination include social networks characterized by inter-enterprise linked decision making, highly aligned hierarchical organizations based on contractual authority, network forms centered on risk sharing, and strategic alliances characterized by power reciprocity. The broad view sees it as an interdependent system of enduring ties in economic activity. According to this theory, the market is not only a mechanism for resource allocation but also an "organized market", which is itself a network structure (Ye Guanghui, et al., 2009). He Huazheng (2012) argues that the network economy is a new industrial model and business operation model with digital information as the main carrier.

The opposite of economic networks is the study of social networks. In the field of sociological research, there are mainly two types of network analysis methods. One is to use network relationship measures to study the individual network, i.e., to analyze the "individual-centered networks". Zhang Wenhong and Ruan Danqing (1999) and Zhang Youqin (2002) use various network measures or statistical variables calculated from these measures as individual-level variables, and then use these variables in "case-invariant" studies, without directly focusing on network structure and network processes. Scholars such as Wasserman and Faust view this analysis as a sub-attribute network study. The other is the study of the overall structural nature of the network, i.e., the study of the overall network, for which no research results have been found. In the study of social networks, the "social structure" is based on "relationship", so the social structure can be revealed through the collection and analysis of relational data. Many scholars have used mathematical tools such as graph theory to describe and analyze the social relationship between groups. White and his team members of the Social Network Research Center at Harvard University have used algebraic models to study the overall relationship structure of networks, and multidimensional list techniques to translate relationships into "distances". These works have made it possible to describe and analyze relationships in social networks in quantitative form.

Duhaime (2002) argues that the relationship between network organization and synergy is not a simple linear relationship, that network organization is not naturally capable of generating synergies, and that it is unreasonable that simply forming a network will naturally generate significant performance. Mao Yunshi (2004) argues that the synergy of economic networks comes from the connectivity of the network structure itself. Chen Shouming (2002) argues that the efficiency of economic networks stems from the institutional arrangements implied behind this form of organization. Zhang Jianhua, Liu Renjun and Wang Chuanying (2005) argue that the advantages of network organization are mainly reflected in the high degree of specialization and division of labor, while the division of labor between enterprises at different stages of production jointly builds a "value system" with increasing marginal rewards and form an overall economy of scale. Enterprise networks have unique advantages over planning, pure markets, and hierarchical organizations due to the complementary activities and resource dependence of firms, which can be coordinated through diverse contractual arrangements among firms to reduce transaction and production costs, promote joint technological development, and provide effective control over related firms (Li Weian, 2003; Pfeffer & Salancik, 1978; Xie Hongming and Lan Hailin, 2004). Since firms are currently in a complex supply chain network, M&A will lead to changes in the entire network, and changes in the network structure will significantly affect the profitability of all parties in the supply chain, including acquirers (Holmen & Pedersen, 2003; Wu & Choi, 2005). Therefore, the M&A evaluation must broaden the perspective from the acquirers to the whole supply chain and consider the interaction of the supply chain parties to grasp and realize the strategic objectives of the M&A. Su Qin and Liu Qiang (2012) considered the impact of changes in the supply chain structure on the profitability of all parties of M&A when M&A occurred. In the single-buyer multi-supplier multilateral negotiation based on profit distribution, they viewed the buyer as the focal firm, discussed the negotiation analysis framework of M&A between buyers and some suppliers, and revealed the mechanism of the impact of M&A-induced changes in supply chain structure on the profits of all parties in M&A. It is found that the change in supply chain structure weakens the positive effect of M&A synergies and reduces the profit gained by the buyer, thus providing a basis for the gap between the reality and the expectation of M&A transactions.

(2) Research on the formation and evolution of economic network

Haksnasson and Snehota (1995) proposed the basic variables (activities, actors, and resources) that influence network organization and the constitutive relationships of networks (firms, relationships, and networks), arguing that network formation is a self-organizing process whose evolution is characterized by path sdependence. Mitchell (1969) pointed out that the understanding of the network process needs to start from the perspective of network morphology and interaction. Johanson and Mattsson (1986) developed Mitchell's research and pioneered a relationship and interaction model, which organically linked the connection between network nodes and their interaction behavior.

There have been two related explanations for the evolutionary model of social networks. The first is the social capital perspective. Social capital is the third type of capital besides human capital and financial capital (Bourdieu, 1984), which reflects the relationship between the organization and other organizations or individuals. The more social capital, the more feasible channels an organization has to acquire resources in a social network. At the same time, the amount of social capital determines its position in the network structure. The relationships in the network are not evenly distributed, some zones are sparse and some zones are dense. Enterprises need to acquire more resources to grow, which prompts enterprises to move from sparse locations to dense locations, thus building a network with a specific structure. At the same time, this movement makes the originally scattered structures in the network continue to concentrate, and the connections between individuals in the network and other individuals and organizations continue to increase, thereby increasing the social capital of the entire network and promoting the growth and evolution of the entire network. The second is the structural hole theory. The theory holds that the locations in a network that are most likely to give an organization a competitive advantage are between, rather than within, densely relational zones and the sparse zones between such densely relational zones are structural holes (Burt, 1992). To grow, the organization in the network constantly develops the structural holes in the network to establish new dense connections, thereby promoting the evolution of the network structure. In a word, the essence of the research on the evolution of the social network is that the growth of enterprises requires more resources, which prompts them to move in the network to seek resources in new and suitable positions, thereby promoting the evolution of economic network structure and economic strength. The idea that economic performance determines the evolutionary structure is an important research method to study the evolution of the economic network.

(3) The formation of economic networks and their synergies after M&A

According to the research on social networks, the most basic components of social networks include the nodes within the social network and the social relationships between the nodes. The organization of an economic network is a complex network formed by multiple nodes according to certain connections. Nodes in the network should not only consider their factors but also be restricted by other nodes when making decisions. The economic network relationship includes not only the economic relationship between network nodes but also the social relationship outside the network node. According to this basic idea, all economic networks can be expressed as the elements constituting the network and the relationship between the elements. When this economic network is specifically an enterprise, it can be expressed as the relationship between the elements and resources within the enterprise and the division of labor and collaboration between the elements and resources formed according to internal management. When the economic network is specific to an industry, it can be expressed as the internal division of labor and collaboration among enterprises in the industry and between enterprises based on opportunity costs or administrative orders.

A new economic network structure was formed after the M&A. In addition to the division of labor and cooperation, the most important relationship in the new network relationship is regulation. The acquirer is the regulator. The regulator adjusts the construction and the operation of the network according to the network environment and network structure, realizes the effective integration and sharing of resources and capabilities within the network, and realizes the rational allocation of resources among network nodes, which not only helps to improve the efficiency of each node and within the network, but also facilitates the full utilization of resources, reduces the redundancy of social resources, helps to improve the welfare of the whole society, and gets the network synergy.

Since the 1980s, some of the literature on network organization has concluded that network organization has significant synergistic effects. The relationship between network organization and synergy economy is not a simple linear relationship, and network organization cannot naturally generate synergistic effects. The most important source of efficiency in a network economy is network synergy, which is not found in other organizational forms. The source of economic network synergy should comprehensively consider the source of network synergy from the aspects of network structure, network relationship, and network efficiency, that is, the tightness of nodes and the efficiency of network organization. Among them, the tightness of nodes comes from the comparison of internal and external transaction costs, which is manifested in the strength of equity and contract; the efficiency of network organization comes from the scope economy, scale economy, and economy and reliability of network operation of network node resources. Reliability means the degree of reliability of economic network transaction completion, and the measure of this reliability contains two parts, one is the realization of economic network economy and the other is the realization of economic network sociality.

The topology of the network affects the tightness of node relationships in the network while influencing the realization of the network economy by affecting the allocation of resources and the reliability of the network by affecting the position of nodes in the network. In different stages of network evolution, the change of network topology affects the degree of tightness of nodes, and also affects the realization of network economy and reliability, thus affecting the composition of network economy synergy from various parts.

The synergistic effect of the economic network not only enables enterprises to share the economic benefits brought by cost reduction and specialized division of labor but also reflects that the economic network reduces the uncertainty of business operations, thereby reducing the corresponding negative benefits. In industries with high socialization such as transportation and communication, the economic and social benefits brought by this reduction in uncertainty even exceed the benefits brought by economic costs. Based on different institutional arrangements and market conditions, the degree of embeddedness of social relations is different, and the definition of synergistic effects in economic networks is also different, which may also have different requirements for reliability in economic network synergistic effects, thus affecting the network structure of the whole economic network.

An economic network is a group, not a traditional intermediary organization between firms and markets. Business units and their interrelationships can constitute a network. An enterprise group, an enterprise alliance, an enterprise corporation, or an industry consisting of several business units within an enterprise can be considered an overall economic network. The overall economic network can be decomposed into several partial economic networks.

The coordinator in the economic network, which can regulate economic resources in the network, should be highlighted in M&A. The formation of coordinators can be due to either a self-organizing process of the market or statutory or other institutional arrangements. With the help of the circuit function of the network and the coordinator's regulatory role, this form of resource organization of the economic network reduces the waste of resources in the investment stage, improves the efficiency of resource utilization in the operation stage, increases the reliability of the occurrence of the effect on stakeholders, and thus forms the economy of the network. The acquisition of network economics, in addition to the operational efficiency of network economics, depends on the topology of the network.

The economic network after the merger may also be uneconomical. In addition to the existing economic explanations such as scale diseconomies, and scope diseconomies, the cost of network organization is higher than the cost of market organization, and excessive concentration leads to monopoly, it may also be caused by the misfit between economic networks and economic and social environments such as finance.

7.4 Evaluation of Synergistic Effects

7.4.1 Discounted Free Cash Flow Method

(1) Fundamental

(i) Definition of discounted cash flow

The discounted cash flow (DCF) method is a method of predicting synergistic effects by discounting the annual incremental cash flows of a post-merger joint venture. This approach examines the value of a company in terms of cash and risk. Under the condition of certain risk, the more cash flow the evaluated company can generate in the future, the higher the value of the company will be evaluated, and the intrinsic value of the company is proportional to the cash flows, while under the condition of certain cash flows, the value of the company is inversely proportional to risk. Discounted cash flow techniques consider the value of a company to be equal to the present value of its future cash flows, plus the present value of the future value, minus the remaining liabilities. Its theoretical basis is the following three assumptions: the value of a certain amount of cash at present is greater than the value of the same amount of cash in the future; the cash flows generated in the future, such as the cash flows generated by production and operation, can be reasonably estimated; the marginal cost of capital of a company's available capital is similar to the convertible return on its invested capital and can be predicted (Smith, 1985).

Cash flow is defined as:

Cash flow = EBIT × (1−income tax rate) + depreciation and other non-cash expenses − (working capital investment + fixed capital investment)

= net profit + depreciation + after-tax interest − (working capital investment + fixed capital investment).

The formula for calculating enterprise value is:

$$V = \sum_{t=1}^{n} \frac{CF_t}{(1 + R_t)^t} + \frac{TV}{(1 + R_n)^n}$$

where, V is the enterprise value; CF_t is the projected value of free cash flow of the evaluated enterprise in year t; R_t is the discount rate in year t; TV is the terminal value of the evaluated enterprise at the end of the projection period (continuous value); n is the projection period.

Using the DCF method usually first predicts the free cash flows of the evaluation target in each future year, then calculates the risk-adjusted cost of capital, and uses it as the discount rate to calculate the present value of future cash flows, plus the present value of the future value of the enterprise, which is the company value.

(ii) Determination of discount rate

In the discounted cash flow model, an appropriate discount rate must be selected when evaluating the value of the post-merger joint venture. Typically, the discount rate is the weighted average cost of capital $WACC_{AB}$ of the post-merger joint venture. According to the capital asset pricing model, the integrated cost of equity capital K_S is given by:

$$K_s = R_f + [E(R_m) - R_f]\beta_{AB}$$

where, R_f is the market risk-free rate of return, *E(Rm)* is the average market risk rate of return, and β_{AB} is the β coefficient of the post-merger joint venture. When calculating, R_f can generally be replaced by the interest rate of treasury bills after adjustment, and *E(Rm)* can be replaced by the average rate of change of the stock market index reflecting the average yield of listed companies. The difficulty lies in determining the β_{AB} value that reflects the market risk specific to joint venture AB, which may be greater than, less than, or equal to the β value of enterprises A and B before M&A, depending on the type of merger and the post- integration operating conditions. The acquirer may obtain this value based on the weighted average of the β values of enterprises A and B, adjusted for historical information and projections of future production and operations, and with reference to the β values of other similar enterprises. Another option is to consult with a consulting firm specializing in the study of β coefficients.

According to the Modigliani–Miller model, the formula for calculating the comprehensive cost of capital after M&A is as follows:

$$WACC_{AB} = K_s S/(B + S) + K_t(1 - T)B/(B + S)$$

where, K_t, S, and B are the average cost of debt, total equity, and total liabilities after integration; T is the corporate income tax rate. It should be pointed out again that Kt has also been a general change before and after the merger. If the credit rating of the post-merger enterprise increases, the borrowing rate decreases and K_t also decreases; conversely, it increases.

(2) Recursive formula cash flow model

When planning and forecasting free cash flow in future periods, subjective judgments are bound to be involved, and most practitioners assume that there is some systematic relationship between periods. In particular, they usually assume that sales revenue and free cash flow will grow at a certain rate and that there is also a fixed relationship between the company's main operating variables.

Alfred Rappaport (1986), an American scholar, proposed a recursive formula cash flow model, also known as the Rappaport model, which is used to evaluate the value of enterprises in M&A.

(i) Rappaport model

The Rappaport model defines cash flow as:

$$CF_t = S_{t-1}(1 + g_t)\ (P_t)(1 - T_t) - (S_t - S_{t-1})(f_t + w_t)$$

where, CF is free cash flow; S is sales; g is the annual growth rate of sales; P is the operating profit margin; T is the income tax rate; f is the marginal fixed capital investment rate; W is the marginal working capital investment rate.

Operating profit margin refers to the ratio of earnings before interest and taxes to sales revenue; marginal fixed capital investment rate refers to the ratio of fixed capital investment increment to sales growth, that is, the additional fixed capital investment required for each additional unit value of sales revenue. Among them, the fixed capital investment increment is the difference between capital expenditure and depreciation, and the formula for calculating the marginal fixed capital investment rate is:

$$f = \frac{\text{capital expenditure} - \text{depreciation}}{\text{sales growth}}$$

The reliability of using historical data on the marginal fixed capital investment rate to estimate a firm's capital expenditure investment demands over the forecast period depends primarily on how quickly and to what extent the firm offsets the impact of increased fixed capital investment with higher product sales prices or efficient use of assets.

The marginal working capital investment rate is the ratio of the incremental working capital investment added by a company to maintain sales growth to the amount of sales growth. Its calculation formula is:

$$W = \frac{\Delta\text{operation capital}}{\text{sales growth}} = \frac{\Delta(\text{liquid capital} - \text{Interest free current liabilities})}{\text{Sales growth}}$$

It should be noted that cash flows in M&A investment decisions are not simply the sum of cash flows during the separate existence of the two parties, but must consider the contribution of the target company to the cash flows of the joint venture under the management control of the acquirer after M&A, which is the embodiment of the M&A synergistic effect.

(ii) Main parameters in the model

The Rappaport model reveals the relationship between various valuation parameters and enterprise value, fully demonstrating how M&A activity as a strategic investment behavior can serve the goal of corporate strategic development. Professor Rappaport also vividly calls these valuation parameters "value drivers". Figure 7.7 illustrates the relationship between value drivers and corporate objectives, such as sales growth, operating profit margin, income tax rate, working capital investment, fixed capital investment, cost of capital, and duration of value growth.

In this model, T_t is generally easier to determine, the additional investment rate f_t and W_t is an artificially set proportional parameter based on the forecasted values of S_t, g_t and P_t, and the future operating conditions of the post-merger joint venture, and can be considered to be constant during the forecast period, while g_t, P_t can be forecasted year by year or divided into two to three forecast periods based on the company's current operating conditions and future market expectations considering three different scenarios of conservative, most likely and optimistic, or it can be simply assumed that g_t remains constant over the forecast period, in this case, it is assumed that the relationship between annual cost and income also remains constant, that is, P_t is also constant, which greatly simplifies the model. In fact, this is the method most often used when forecasting free cash flow for future periods. However, no matter which method is adopted, the following two factors must be considered when forecasting: The first step is the historical growth rate and sales profit margin

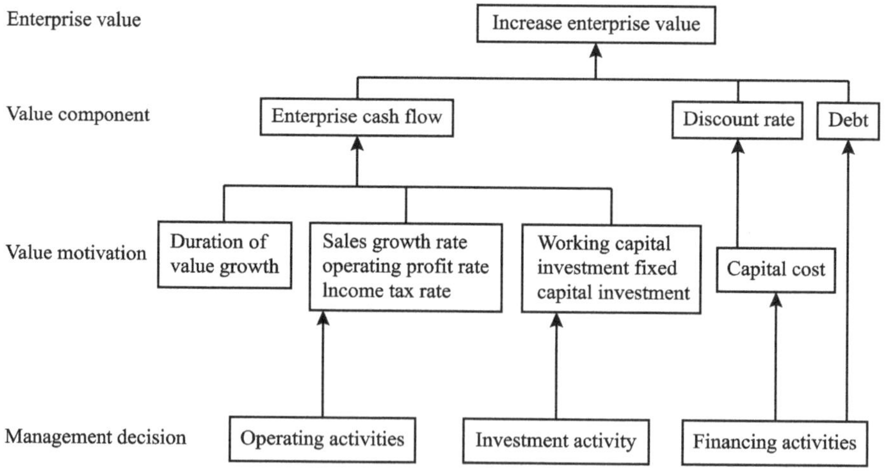

Fig. 7.7 Enterprise value increment. *Source* Alfred Rappaport (1997)

of the sales of both parties to the M&A should be inferred based on the available historical financial information. The former can mainly be determined by calculating the annual compounded growth rate of sales revenue during the observation period, that is $g = \sqrt[n]{\frac{S_n}{S_1}} - 1$, the latter is usually obtained by calculating the weighted average of profit margins in the recent period. However, this is only the basis for predicting the economic and strategic factors that will affect the future of the enterprise. The second and more important step is to fully examine the possible effects of economies of scale, brand sharing, increased market control, technology diffusion, and lower financing costs on the sales revenue and production costs of the combined enterprise, and then, supplemented by the conclusions of the first step, to forecast the growth rate of sales revenue g_t and profit margin P_t of the combined enterprise after M&A, based on the extensive experience of decision makers or specialized consulting organizations. After determining the parameter values of S_O, g, P, f, w, calculate the future cash flows of the joint venture.

(3) Four growth mode models

The Rappaport model implicitly assumes that the target enterprise will gradually slow down its growth rate after continuous development under the control of the acquirer until the growth rate is zero. In real life, almost every enterprise goes through different stages of growth as its life cycle ebbs and flows. Generally speaking, the growth rate in the early stage may be faster, and as the enterprise develops and matures, the growth rate will gradually decrease. But for a particular company, its growth process may evolve into a combination of different growth rates. Based on the above considerations, Weston (1998) put forward an enterprise value analysis model suitable for different growth modes based on the basic principle of discounting future free cash flows, referred to as the Weston model.

(i) Definition of free cash flow in the model

In the Weston model, free cash flow is formulated as:

$$FCF_t = X_t(1 - T_t) - I_t$$

where, FCF is the free cash flow; t is the forecast period; X is the operating profit (earnings before interest and tax); T is the income tax rate; I is the investment. Among them, investment refers to the additional investment including capital expenditure and working capital during the forecast period t, that is, the sum of the fixed capital investment increment and the working capital investment. Therefore, although the expression of free cash flow in the Rappaport model and the Weston model is different, the essence is the same.

(ii) Valuation parameters in the model

Since enterprise value assessment is based on future cash flows, artificial guesses and judgments about the future are inevitably generated. According to the understanding of the relationship between free cash flows and enterprise value, Professor Weston put forward the definitions and assumptions of other valuation parameters and their interrelationships required in the process of value analysis:

(a) Marginal profit ratio r. Since it takes considerable time for a firm to raise additional investment funds and for the additional investment to produce benefits, the additional investment in fixed capital and working capital in the current period may not immediately lead to an increase in the firm's profit in the current period. The effect of additional investment will be deferred to the next period, that is, the additional investment in this period will lead to an increase in profits in the next period, which is the first assumption of the Weston model for additional investment. It is this close relationship between investment and profit that the Weston model defines the marginal profit ratio as the change in after-tax operating profit in period t caused by investment in period t-1, expressed by the formula:

$$r_t = \frac{(X_t - X_{t-1})(1 - T)}{I_{t-1}}$$

A valuation parameter similar to the marginal profit ratio in the Rappaport model is the operating profit rate. The Weston model argues that linking firm profitability to sales revenue, rather than to investment, has at least two disadvantages: first, because capital intensity varies between industries and firms, linking profitability to sales revenue does not make much sense from the view of setting planning and control standards. For example, for capital-intensive industries such as steel and chemicals, the ratio of profit to sales revenue should be much higher than that of wholesale and retail industries, while the ratio of profit to sales revenue of the wholesale and retail industry is often 1%. Second, linking profitability to sales revenue tends to blind managers to the fact that it is impossible to increase sales without investing in fixed capital and working capital. Therefore, the ratio of the operating profit increment of the current period to the investment of the previous period better reflects the profitability of the enterprise.

On this basis, to keep the discussion simple, the Weston model assumes that the marginal profit ratio does not change in each period.

(b) Investment demand b. Investment demand refers to the ratio of investment expenditure in each period to the after-tax operating profit of the current period, which is expressed by the formula:

$$b_t = \frac{I_t}{X_t(1 - T)}$$

Valuation parameters similar to investment demand in the Rappaport model are the marginal fixed capital investment rate and the marginal working capital investment rate. The Rappaport model defines it as the investment in fixed capital and working capital required for each additional unit of sales revenue. While according to the Weston model, although enterprises make additional investments to seek sales growth, and the sales and investment of enterprises reflect the degree of capital intensity that determines the nature of production and operation of enterprises, investment is the source of the firm's products and services and ultimately increase sales revenue, and the disadvantage of linking investment with sales revenue instead of after-tax operating profit is that it ignores that the core of enterprise valuation is free cash flow, which is the same as the definition of profitability as the ratio of operating profit to sales revenue. It can also be seen from the definition of investment demand that investment demand is an opportunity to invest, that is, an additional investment opportunity generated by the current after-tax profit to maintain the survival and development of the enterprise. For simplicity, the Weston model assumes that investment demand does not change in each period.

(c) Growth rate g. Growth rate refers to the growth rate of after-tax operating profit and is expressed as follows:

$$g_t = \frac{X_t(1-T) - X_{t-1}(1-T)}{X_{t-1}(1-T)} = \frac{X_t}{X_{t-1}} - 1$$

By slightly deforming the above formula, we can also get the following important relationship:

$$\begin{aligned} g_t &= \frac{X_t(1-T) - X_{t-1}(1-T)}{X_{t-1}(1-T)} \times \frac{I_{t-1}}{I_{t-1}} \\ &= \frac{X_t(1-T) - X_{t-1}(1-T)}{I_{t-1}} \times \frac{I_{t-1}}{X_{t-1}(1-T)} \\ &= r_t \times b_{t-1} \end{aligned}$$

Since g, b, and r are assumed to be constant over the forecast period, the $g = b \times r$.

(d) Enterprise value under different growth modes. According to the basic principles of capital budgeting and the analysis of the growth stage of enterprises, Professor Weston put forward the enterprise valuation models under the four most basic growth modes, which are listed in Table 7.7 below.

The growth form of any enterprise can be decomposed into the above situations, and the enterprise value is the sum of the value of each stage. Therefore, the Weston model summarizes almost all forms of enterprise growth and is a powerful tool for evaluating and calculating enterprise value.

7.4.1.1 Distributional Summation Model

Zhang Qiusheng and Wang Dong (2001) used various theoretical explanations about the synergistic effect in corporate finance and referenced the "asset source = capital occupation" identity of accounting measurement, and proposed a distributional

Table 7.7 Valuation of four different growth modes under the Weston model

No growth: $V = \frac{X_0(1-T)}{k}$
Fixed growth: $V = \frac{X_0(1-T)(1-b)(1+g)}{k-g}$
Temporarily abnormal growth, then no growth:
$V = X_0(1-T)(1-b)\sum_{t=1}^{n}\frac{(1+g)^t}{(1+k)^t} + \frac{X_0(1-T)(1+g)^{n+1}}{k(1+k)^n}$
Temporarily abnormal growth, and then fixed growth:
$V = X_0(1-T)(1-b_s)\sum_{t=1}^{n}\frac{(1+g_s)^t}{(1+k)^t} + \frac{X_0(1-T)(1-b_c)}{k-g_c} \times \frac{(1+g_s)^{n+1}}{(1+k)^n}$
Where, T is income tax rate; X_0 is the EBIT or net operating income; n is the forecast period; b is the investment demand; r is the marginal profit ratio; g is the growth rate of the after-tax operating profit; k is the weighted marginal cost of capital

Note the subscript s represents g or b in the period of supernormal growth; the subscript c represents g or b in the period of fixed growth
Source J. Fred Weston et al. (1990)

summation model to predict the synergies in M&A. The basic idea is to use the main aspects of operation, finance, and management synergies that may be generated by the M&A of various enterprises as the measurement basis and forecasting ideas, and based on detailed qualitative analysis, to predict the value and the year of each synergy separately and to sum them up after discounting according to their years of effect. Its measuremsent model is:

$$V_{SYN} = \sum_{i=1}^{n}\frac{\Delta R + \Delta C_o + \Delta T + \Delta C_N}{(1 + WACC)^i}$$

where, V_{SYN} is the value of synergies; $\wedge R$ is the increase in operating income (referring to the occurrence of M&A compared to the non-occurrence of M&A, hereinafter); $\wedge C_o$ is the decrease in operating costs; $\wedge T$ is the decrease in tax; $\wedge CN$ is the capital requirement reduction amount; WACC is the weighted average cost of capital of the joint venture; $n = \{n_1, n_2, n_3, n_4\}, n_1, n_2, n_3, n_4$ represent ΔR, ΔC_o, $\wedge T$, $\wedge C_N$ action years respectively, $n_t = (n_{t1}, n_{t2}, \ldots, n_{tr}), (t = 1, 2, 3, 4), n_{t1}, n_{t2}, \ldots, n_{tr}$ represent the years of action that cause the increase in operating income, decrease in operating cost, tax reduction, and capital requirement reduction for various synergies over the years of action, respectively.

The distributional summation approach divides synergies into two categories, one is called "tangible synergies", that is, those synergies whose specific value is relatively easy to measure and evaluate in monetary terms, and the other is those with uncertain or strategic or global, or whose impact is not easily visible in the short term and thus cannot be precisely measured, are called "qualitative synergies". In most M&A, it is often a strong motivation for the M&A and ultimately shows its strong impact on the post-merger performance of the entire business. After identifying

Table 7.8 Tangible reverse synergies

Transaction fees: financial advisory fees, legal fees, administrative costs, publicity fees, etc.
Remuneration for hiring additional managers to oversee M&A
Adjustment of employee salary and welfare policy (level) after M&A
Training for employees of acquired companies
Procedures to execute acquisitions
Additional fulfillment costs
The cost of paying down debt owed by M&A

Table 7.9 Qualitative reverse synergies

Non-cooperation or betrayal by core members of the acquiree
Disperse the time and energy of senior manager
Adverse effects on the people's hearts and morale of the acquiree (especially in a hostile takeover) Commercial conflicts (e.g., the acquirer's customer is precisely the acquiree's competitor)
Image loss (such as the negative impact on the corporate image caused by the adoption of aggressive strategies and the dilution of earnings)
The acquirer and the acquiree's employees do not have a harmonious relationship

possible synergies, several synergy worksheets need to be made, showing the basis on which the synergies are expected to occur, the year in which they will occur, and, if possible, quantifying their impact. This step is critical in the process of assessing synergies. Not only is it critical to assess the value of the target business to the acquirer and thus set the transaction price, but these worksheets will provide decision-makers with a strategic blueprint for the future of the combined business.

While M&A bring positive effects, there are often inevitable costs. These costs include not only one-time transaction fees other than the amount paid to the target company during the M&A, but also some long-term negative effects that are difficult to quantify, such as cultural conflicts. These negative effects of M&A can offset some of the value added by the synergies, and are therefore also referred to as "reverse synergies". They have a much smaller impact on the value of the post- merger joint venture and are therefore often ignored in many valuations (including the overall evaluation method). Table 7.8 and Table 7.9 list the more common "reverse synergies", which can also be divided into two categories: "tangible reverse synergies" and "qualitative reverse synergies".

For the above "reverse synergies", worksheets can also be made separately, quantifying as much as possible, and the format and method are the same as the "synergies worksheet".

7.4.1.2 Stock Return Theory Calculation Model

The stock return theory calculation model is based on the market effectiveness principle from the standpoint of shareholders and analyzes and calculates the synergy effect based on the changes in stock prices and trading volumes caused by the occurrence and disclosure of significant events in the company. Specifically, it is to use the changes in stock prices, the number of stocks, and issuance and circulation before and after the M&A to sum up the net profits obtained by the merging party and the merged party during the event period, to obtain the value of the synergy. Regardless of the changes in the stock attributes of the two parties after the M&A, the value of the synergy can be given by the following formula:

$$V_{SYN} = \sum_{i=1}^{n_{A1}} S'_{Ai}P'_{Ai} + \sum_{i=1}^{n_{B1}} S'_{Bi}P'_{Bi} - \sum_{i=1}^{n_{A0}} e^{\widehat{R}_{Ai}} S_{Ai}P_{Ai} - \sum_{i=1}^{n_{B0}} e^{\widehat{R}_{Bi}} S_{Bi}P_{Bi}$$

where, S_{Ai} and $S_{A,i}$ are the number of the stock i issued and circulated of firm A before and after the merger; P_{Ai} and $P_{A,i}$ are the corresponding price; S_{Bi} and $S_{B,i}$ are the number of the stock i issued and circulated of firm B before and after the merger; PBi and PB,i are the corresponding price; n_{AO}, $nA1$ and $nB0$, $nB1$ are the numbers of stocks issued and circulated by firms A and B before and after the merger; eRAi and eR· Bi are the final value coefficients during the merger period; R_{Ai} and R_{Bi} are the corresponding stock returns calculated with continuous compound interest.

If no new shares are generated after the merger and the original number of stock species is not reduced, the subscript of the above stock species variable is the same for any one firm. More often, the stock of the merged party is no longer listed and traded after the merger, when

$$V_{SYN} = \sum_{i=1}^{n_{AB}} S_{ABi}P_{ABi} - \sum_{i=1}^{n_{A0}} e^{\widehat{R}_{Ai}} S_{Ai}P_{Ai} - \sum_{i=1}^{n_{B0}} e^{\widehat{R}_{Bi}} S_{Bi}P_{Bi}$$

$\widehat{R}_{Ai}$ and $\widehat{R}_{Bi}$ mean the return that the corresponding stock would have had during the period under examination (the short term is often taken as the period from the merger announcement date to the announcement completion date), assuming no merger event occurs. The multiplication of the coefficients $e^{\widehat{R}_{Ai}}$ and $e^{\widehat{R}_{Bi}}$ is done to try to eliminate the effect of systematic risk or general stock market movements on the value of the synergies during the period. There are generally three methods for calculating this rate of return: the mean-adjusted return method, the market model method, and the market-adjusted return method.

In this way, the key to calculating the value of synergy is to predict the changes in stock price and quantity after the M&A. To simplify the analysis, it may be assumed that there is only one common stock in the company before and after the merger, and company A exchanges shares of company B by issuing additional stocks, and at the same time cancels the listing and trading of company B's stocks, then

$$V_{SYN} = S'_A P'_A - e^{\widehat{R}_A} S_A P_A - e^{\widehat{R}_B} S_B P_B$$

In the above formula, $S'_A = S_A + S_B E_R, E_R$ s'A = SA + SBER, ER represents the stock exchange rate, that is, the number of stocks of company B that can be exchanged for the stocks of company A, and then assuming that E is the profit before the merger, and PE is the price-earnings ratio, then

$$P'_A = PE'_A EPS'_A = PE_{AB} EPS_{AB} = PE'_A(E_A + E_B + V_{SYN})/(S_A + S_B E_R)$$

Then there are:

$$V_{SYN} = (S_A + S_B E_R) PE'_A(E_A + E_B + V_{SYN})/(S_A + S_B E_R) - e^{\hat{R}_A} S_A P_A - e^{\hat{R}_B} S_B P_B$$

After finishing:

$$V_{SYN} = [e^{\hat{R}_A} S_A P_A + e^{\hat{R}_B} S_B P_B - PE'_A(E_A + E_B)]/(PE'_A - 1)$$

Under normal circumstances, the price-earnings ratio is always greater than 1, so to make the value of the synergy greater than 0, we must make

$$e^{\hat{R}_A} S_A P_A + e^{\hat{R}_B} S_B P_B - PE'_A(E_A + E_B) > 0$$

which is

$$\begin{aligned} PE'_A &< e^{\widehat{R}_A} S_A P_A E_A/[(E_A + E_B)E_A] + e^{\widehat{R}_B} S_B P_B E_B/[(E_A + E_B)E_B] \\ &= [e^{\widehat{R}_A} P_A/(E_A/S_A)]E_A/(EA + E_B) + [e^{\widehat{R}_B} P_B/(E_B/S_B)]E_B/(E_A + E_B) \end{aligned}$$

Because EPS = E/S, so P/(E/S) = PE, the above formula can be changed to

$$PE'_A < PE_A e^{\widehat{R}_A} E_A/(E_A + E_B) + PE_B e^{\widehat{R}_B} E_B/(E_A + E_B)$$

When the i,and i, are relatively small, $e^{\widehat{R}_A} \approx e^{\widehat{R}_B} \approx 1$, the above formula simplifies to

$$PE'_A < PE_A E_A/(E_A + E_B) + PE_B E_B/(E_A + E_B)$$

The above formula shows that as long as the post-merger price-to-earnings ratio is less than the profit-based weighted average price-to-earnings ratio before the merger, there will be a positive synergy value. Therefore, the key is to accurately estimate the PE'_A of the only unknown post-merger integration joint venture. The calculation of the synergy value is closely related to the period selected for examination while excluding the effect of non-M&A factors on the stock market price.

7.4.1.3 Real Options Pricing Method

Wang Qian (2003) argues that previous studies have ignored the value of real options brought by the synergy between the two parties of M&A, and therefore the synergistic effect is studied in a narrow sense. He points out that the calculation of synergies in a broad sense should not only consider the cash flow increment brought by M&A at present but also consider the real option value implied in M&A, that is, future investment opportunities brought by intangible assets obtained through M&A (growth options) and the value of the target firm's assets when they can be transferred to other uses (flexibility options). For growth options, Wang used the Black–Scholes formula for calculation; for flexibility options, Wang used the binomial pricing model for numerical analysis and the backward-looking method for calculation. Wang believes that only adding the real option value of corporate M&A to the static net present value calculated by traditional valuation methods is a complete assessment of the synergy value of corporate M&A.

7.4.1.4 Synergistic Effect Evaluation Method Based on Synergetics

(1) Potential synergy value evaluation system

The motivation of enterprise M&A is largely based on the expectation of synergies, and one of the most common errors in M&A analysis is the failure to correctly predict synergies. Zhou Lin (2006) analyzed the sources of M&A synergy generation from the perspective of enterprise resources and constructed a M&A synergy value system as shown in Fig. 7.8.

The leftmost part of Fig. 7.8 represents the input of the resources of both parties of the M&A, and*RB, RT* represent the resources of the acquirer and the target party,

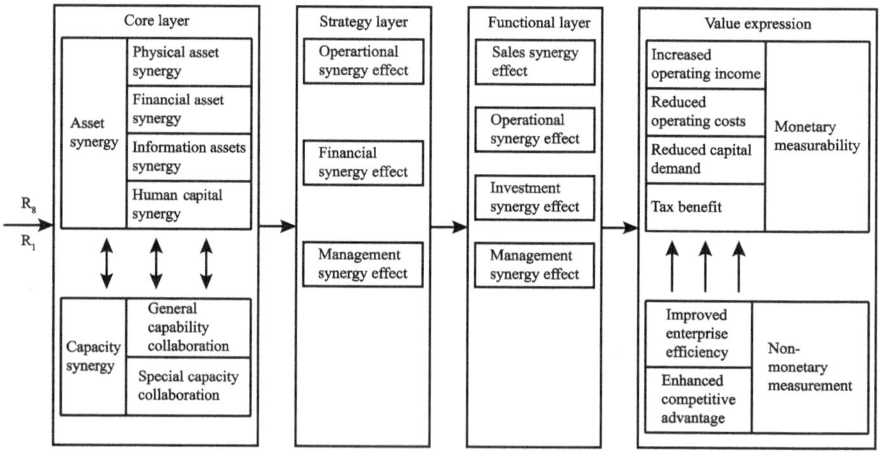

Fig. 7.8 Resource synergy value system of enterprise M&A

respectively. The first box indicates the synergy at the core level of M&A, which consists of asset synergy and capability synergy between the two parties, where asset synergy includes the synergy of physical assets, financial assets, information assets, and human capital, and capability synergy includes the synergy of general and special capabilities. The arrow between asset synergy and capability synergy indicates that there is a close interaction between them. The second box in the figure is the synergy at the strategic level, including operational synergy, financial synergy, and management synergy, which is driven by the core level synergy and directly affects the functional level synergy. The third box in the figure is functional level synergy, which consists of sales synergy, operation synergy, investment synergy, and management synergy, and ultimately realizes its value performance through functional activities, including monetary and non- monetary quantitative values.

(2) Evaluation of capability synergies

Previous studies have mostly evaluated potential synergies from four aspects: the increase in operating income, the reduction in operating costs, the reduction in capital requirements, and gaining tax benefits, which are in essence asset synergies. Since capability synergies are non-monetary and difficult to evaluate directly, their value performance (increased efficiency and competitive advantage) is ultimately reflected through the use of assets, and therefore are often considered an important indirect influence in the estimation of parameters in value evaluation models. It can be seen that the traditional evaluation method describes the result of potential synergy, but fail to effectively portray the synergistic process of capabilities, which is the cause (a mechanism) of this result. Therefore, based on the construction of a potential synergy value assessment system, Zhou Lin (2006) used synergy and self-organization theories as the methodological basis to establish a nonlinear stochastic partial differential equation of capability synergy over time by combining the operational process of resource synergy and the interaction between enterprises and the environment.

Two basic assumptions are made before the model is established, one is that the resource stock is differentiable to the time variable t, and the other is that the external environment in which the enterprise is located can adapt to the development needs of the enterprise, that is, the products or services produced by the enterprise can be successfully traded in the market and then converted into the input factors required for the firm's production and operation.

The purpose of corporate M&A is to obtain key resources for their development (Ginsburg & Baum, 1994), and after selecting, combining, transforming, and accumulating them with the original internal resources of the enterprise, put them into production and operation activities to produce products and services that meet people's needs, thus increasing the value of the enterprise itself. Since the value of an enterprise is expressed as the value of the resources (assets and capabilities) it possesses, the purpose of enterprise management is to add value to its resources (Zhang Zongzhen, 1998). According to the viewpoint of synergy theory, an open system can be regarded as an input and output process, and can be represented by a corresponding model; if a system wants to achieve dynamic equilibrium or a certain dynamic equilibrium, there must be constant input of feedback information.

In typical production and operation activities, enterprises invest labor and capital, and output products or services with added value for people to consume. In this "asset → product" form of business, assets are constantly being consumed and new assets must be invested to sustain business activities. Among them, the assets consumed in business activities can be supplemented from outside the enterprise through market transactions, etc., but due to the corresponding costs, they can only be exchanged at an equivalent value. While the organizational capability cultivated within the enterprise is usually not damaged by use, on the contrary, it is enriched and enhanced by the expansion of the scope of use. Therefore, the source of the value-added of enterprises lies in the value-added of capabilities. The operation mechanism of the enterprise entity after the M&A is the same. When evaluating the effect of resource synergy between the two parties, the substitution and complementarity effects of its assets are limited, and the key lies in the evaluation of the capability synergies. For this reason, we consider the post-merger corporate entity as a collection of human (human capital), financial (financial assets), physical (physical assets), intangible assets, and capabilities (generic and specialized capabilities), and fully consider the influence of internal and external environment on its operation and development, and combine the process of resource synergy in an open environment and the "Brussels reactor" in the synergy theory, and construct a dynamic production function model of the enterprise after M&A. The formula is expressed as follows:

$$H + C \xrightarrow{k} O + I$$

In the model, H stands for human capital, C stands for financial capital, O stands for products or services, I stands for intangible assets (patents, know- how, etc.), and k is the reaction rate.[3] The above formula intuitively interprets the business process of the enterprise, that is, the enterprise invests labor and capital, and outputs products (or services) and intangible assets with added value. The environment in which the enterprise is located (internal cultural environment, external government or regulatory agency policies, etc.) acts as a catalyst, that is, although it cannot directly make the various resources of the enterprise react, it can influence (speed up or slow down) reaction speed, which indirectly affects the reaction results. The model can be further decomposed into three parts: input- output model, capability synergy mechanism, and circulation mechanism, as follows:

Input–output model:

$$H \xrightarrow{k_1} X + Y$$

[3] In chemical reactions, the reaction rate is the amount of change in the concentration of reactants or products per unit of time, i.e., how quickly the reaction proceeds. It is usually expressed as a decrease in the concentration of reactants or an increase in the concentration of products per unit of time. It is influenced by the nature of the participating reactants themselves and the external environment.

$$C + X + Y \xrightarrow{k_2} Y + 0$$

Capability synergy mechanism:

$$Y + X \xrightarrow{k_3} 2X$$

$$X \xrightarrow{k_4} I$$

Circulation mechanism:

$$O + I \xrightarrow{k_5} H' + C' + I'$$

In the whole model, the human capital H and financial assets C invested by both parties in the M&A are the initial reactants, the physical assets O and intangible assets I are the reaction products, and X and Y respectively represent the special ability and general ability of the enterprise, which are the "intermediate products" of the enterprise's production and operation, and k_i (i = 1,2,3,4,5) is the reaction rate, representing the influence of the environment.

The input–output model shows that after the human capital of both parties is put into production and operation, new organizational capabilities are generated after the interaction of substitution and complementation, and the combination of organizational capabilities and financial assets produces physical assets, while the knowledge stock of generic capabilities grows through use and sharing in business activities.

The capability synergy mechanism is manifested as the autocatalysis and mutual catalysis of special capability X in the reaction system, that is, the combination of general capability and special capability contributes to the enhancement of special capability. Here X is both a reactant and a product. Although it participated in the reaction itself, its number increased after the reaction was completed. The rate at which this reaction produces X in unit time is proportional to XY, which is a nonlinear function, and through the allocation and utilization of enterprise assets, the special capability X will eventually produce intangible assets I such as patents and technical know -how.

Since H and C are continuously consumed in the reaction, to maintain the operation and development of the enterprise, it needs to be continuously supplemented by the outside world. Therefore, once O and I are generated, they must be immediately put into the external market for trading to exchange for more H and C to ensure the dynamic normal cycle of production.

The overall mode of reaction depicts the whole process of enterprise operation: "input of assets → synergy of capabilities → output of assets → input of assets → synergy of capabilities → output of assets → …".

We believe that the synergistic effect of capability SYN_x and SYN_y can be expressed as the difference between the stock of capabilities x(t), y(t) at different moments and the stock of capabilities $x(0)$, $y(0)$ at the initial moment when the M&A transaction is just completed, then

$$SYN_X = x(t) - x(0)$$
$$SYN_Y = y(t) - y(0)$$

Still denoting the M&A party by B and the target party by T, X_B and X_T denote the core competencies (measured by the amount of knowledge stock) of both parties before the M&A, and Y_B and Y_T denote the basic competencies of both parties before the M&A, respectively. When the M&A transaction is completed and the resources of the M&A parties are just combined, the core and basic competencies of the post-M&A corporate entity are noted as $x(0)$ and $y(0)$, respectively, then there are:

$$x(0) = x_B + x_T$$
$$y(0) = y_B + y_T$$

With the passage of time and the progress of the integration work, the resources of the two sides are reconfigured under the joint action of various mechanisms such as substitution, complementarity, enhancement, and conflict, and the size of the capabilities continues to change. According to the dynamic production function model, the reaction kinetic equations of "intermediate products" X and Y are the following two-variable differential equations:

$$dx/dt = k_1h - k_2cxy + k_3xy - k_4x$$
$$dy/dt = k_1h + k_2cxy - k_3xy$$

It is worth noting that the value of each asset in the formula is not static, they are also a function of time. The value of assets at different points in time can be obtained from the company's balance sheet, where the value of human capital can be measured by compensation.[4] After appropriate transformation, let the reaction rate k1 = k2 = k3 = k4 = k5 = 1, the following equations can be obtained:

$$dx/dt = h - cxy + xy - x$$
$$dy/dt = h + cxy - xy$$

To sum up, the theoretical evaluation model of capability synergy is as follows:

[4] The difference in the value of the output assets after a dynamic production cycle compared to the stock of assets in the initial state of the acquisition is the potential synergy effect.

$$\begin{cases} SYN_x = x(t) - (x_B + x_T) \\ SYN_y = y(t) - (y_B + y_T) \\ dx/dt = h + cxy - xy - x \\ dy/dt = h + cxy - xy \end{cases}$$

Chapter 8
M&A Performance

In the twentieth century, the world has experienced five waves of M&A. Mergers and acquisitions have become one of the important means for the rapid expansion and integration of modern enterprises, especially large enterprises, and high-tech growth enterprises. What is the performance of the company after M&A? Scholars at home and abroad have done a lot of research from different angles.

8.1 The Overview of M&A Performance

Economists' research before the 1980s mainly focused on the changes in market structure brought about by corporate M&A and the impact of corporate M&A on market monopoly and competition. From the perspective of scientific development, it should fall within the scope of industrial histology. Since the 1980s, scholars have begun to study the performance problems brought about by corporate M&A. Based on these theories, the impact of M&A on corporate performance can be judged.

Referring to the theoretical achievements in M&A of Chinese and foreign enterprises, the performance embodied in M&A can be divided into two different aspects: positive effects and negative effects.

From a macro perspective, corporate M&A performance refers to its social performance, that is, the role of corporate M&A in the allocation of resources in the entire society. For China's listed companies, it mainly analyzes the impact of listed company M&A on revitalizing state-owned stock assets and promoting industrial restructuring and upgrading.

From the perspective of the individual company at the micro level, the establishment of a modern enterprise requires two completely different mechanisms, one is the management strategy mechanism; the other is the company's transaction strategy. The former refers to how to manage the enterprise more effectively and maintain the

Q. Zhang, *Mergers and Acquisitions*, https://doi.org/10.1007/978-981-92-0122-8_8

efficiency of enterprise operation; while the latter refers to how to effectively position the company and design the best corporate structure in a dynamic and constantly changing market economy environment, and make the company "competitive". The former involves the internal accumulation and development of the company, while the latter involves external expansion and development. The micro-level analysis of listed companies in China is mainly to analyze the changes brought about by the M&A of listed companies, such as the expansion of main business, the optimization of product structure or asset structure, the transformation of management mechanism, the improvement of financial indicators, etc.

As far as a single company is concerned, the complete M&A behavior includes two parts: the implementation of the M&A transaction and the integration after the M&A. Therefore, the company's M&A performance can be divided into two parts: one is transaction performance, which exists in the field of financial economics with a market effect. It refers to the performance (value-added status) that the appraisal of the market (investors' expectations) brings to both parties when M&A transaction occur. The other is integration performance, which means that after the completion of the M&A, the target company is incorporated into the bidder company, and after integration, the original intention of the M&A is realized, and efficiency is generated. It is generally reflected through the company's performance improvement over a long period and the cultivation and enhancement of core competitive advantages.

Performance is a general term for the performance and efficiency of an enterprise's activities. It can usually be regarded as the degree of realization of the strategic goals of the enterprise or organization, and its content includes several levels such as the efficiency of the activities and the results of the activities. The performance and effects of M&A activities are collectively referred to as M&A performance.

M&A performance is divided into long-term M&A performance and short- term M&A performance according to the length of time involved. Considering that M&A is a strategic behavior of an enterprise, the M&A behavior of enterprises can be viewed from different perspectives in the short-term and long-term.

M&A performance can be divided into financial performance and non- financial performance according to whether it can be measured. What M&A ultimately brings to the M&A subject can be either measurable financial performance (such as a direct increase in corporate sales revenue, cost reduction, return on equity growth, net profit growth, etc.) or unmeasurable non-financial performance (changes in operating mechanisms, optimization of corporate capital structure, improvement of corporate culture, enhancement of goodwill and corporate image, etc.). However, from a corporate perspective, M&A performance is ultimately reflected in financial performance.

M&A performance is divided into value-creating M&A performance, no value-creating or value-destroying M&A performance, and value-destroying M&A performance according to its impact on value. This classification analyzes whether M&A activities can add value from the perspective of social welfare.

M&A performance is divided into owner M&A performance, operator M&A performance, employee M&A performance, and other stakeholders M&A performance according to the stakeholders involved. After the M&A of enterprises, it will bring different influences on the relevant stakeholders of an enterprise organization. The impact is the performance brought to these stakeholders before M&A. M&A performance of other stakeholders refers to stakeholders other than business owners, operators, and employees, including government, creditors, suppliers, customers and communities, and other business stakeholders.

M&A performance is divided into macro performance, meso performance, and micro performance according to the scope of its influence. Study the M&A performance generated by M&A behavior from the perspective of the whole society, which can be divided into micro-level M&A performance, meso-level M&A performance, and macro-level M&A performance. Micro-level is all about market players, which refers to changes in the performance and efficiency of the company. Meso-level M&A performance refers to the impact of M&A on related industries, such as industrial structure adjustment, industry concentration, etc. Macro-level M&A performance refers to a series of effects brought about by the entire M&A market (i.e., the control market).

The research conclusions and reports on the failure of corporate mergers and acquisitions and the unsatisfactory performance after mergers and acquisitions appear frequently, but corporate mergers and acquisitions are still happening, and the scale and number are constantly increasing. This raises questions for theorists and entrepreneurs: Can M&A not bring about improvements in corporate performance? How do evaluate the performance of enterprises after M&A comprehensively and effectively? The answers to these two questions are related to the development prospects of corporate M&A.

8.2 Evaluation Methods of M&A Performance at Home and Abroad

From the perspective of multi-sample statistics, enterprise performance evaluation can be divided into static performance evaluation (horizontal comparison evaluation) and dynamic performance evaluation (vertical comparison evaluation). Static performance evaluation is to evaluate and compare the performance of different enterprises in the same period. Dynamic performance evaluation is to evaluate and compare the performance of the same enterprise in different periods. At present, the typical dynamic performance evaluation is mostly used in enterprise performance evaluation at home and abroad, which is generally to compare the performance before and after M&A. The following will point out the characteristics of various M&A performance evaluation methods through the comparative analysis of several main methods.

8.2.1 *Evaluation Method Based on Stock Market*

8.2.1.1 Event-Study Methodology

The event-study methodology proposed by Fama, Fisher, Jensen, and Roll (FFJR) in 1969, is one of the most common methods in M&Aperformance testing. This method regards the M&A as a single event, determines an "event period" (e.g., −1 day, + 1 day) centered on the date of the merger announcement, and then the cumulative abnormal returns (CARs) method was used to test the effect of the merger event announcement on the price volatility of the stock market. The choice of the length of the "event period" is very important for the application of this method. In general, the longer the selected "event period", the more comprehensive the impact of the relevant event, but the more likely it is to be disturbed by irrelevant factors.

Madden (1981) and Jensen (1983) and some other scholars early used this method to test the empirical data of the short-term wealth effect of corporate M&A, and their conclusions were the same: (1) The combined returns ofthe shareholders of both parties to the merger in a relatively short period (−1 days, +1 days) is significantly positive, that is, the M&A does indeed create value for shareholders. Over time (−40 days, +40 days), the statistical significance of the portfolio returns created by the event diminishes significantly. (2) Income distribution is not balanced. The target company's shareholder returns are significantly higher than the acquirer's (close to zero). Moreover, the target company's shareholder returns are statistically significant, but the acquirers are not.

Since investors cannot quickly and systematically estimate all the information and effects related to M&A in a relatively short period, many scholars focus on the mid-term and long-term performance test of M&A, such as Mandelker (1974) and Dodd and Ruback (1977) in the early days. After entering the 1990s, more and more attention has been focused on the mid-term and long-term test of mergers and acquisitions. However, the test model (mainly the market model) adopted by the traditional stock event research method has obvious limitations on the mid- term test, because as the "event period" lengthens, the interference of irrelevant events also follows increases, while traditional test models cannot effectively separate the effects of uncorrelated events. Because of this, many scholars tried to revise the traditional stock event research method, the basic idea is as follows: (1) Research from the perspective of methodology. In terms of methodological innovation, research of Franks et al. (1991) is of great significance and put forward an eight-factor method of M&A performance test, thus breaking the previous pattern of using the market model for mid- and long-term test. Subsequently, Agrawal et al. (1992), Barer and Lyon (1997), Kothar and Warner (1997), Fama (1998), and Alon and Brav (2000) have continuously improved the mid-and long-term testing methods, thereby greatly improving the test reliability. (2) Subdivide the M&A samples according to the observable characteristics and separately examine the performance levels of different types of samples to reduce errors.

Many foreign economists have used different samples and measurement intervals to conduct many empirical tests on the abnormal returns obtained by the target party, the acquirer, and both parties, and have come to a similar conclusion: the shareholders of the acquired party are always the absolute winners of M&A; the only difference is the amount of profit. Jensen and Ruback (1983) summarized the research results of 13 research literature and pointed out that a successful merger would bring about 20% abnormal returns to the target enterprise's shareholders, while a successful acquisition would bring about 30% abnormal returns to the target enterprise's shareholders. (Jarrell et al., 1988) summarize the results of a study of 663 successful tender offers from 1962 to December 1985. They found that in successful acquisitions, the target enterprise received an average premium of 19% in the 1960s, 35% in the 1970s, and 30% between 1980 and 1985. Bradley et al. (1988) covered 236 successful tender offers completed between 1963 and 1984 and found similar results: from July 1963 to June 1968, the target enterprise's rate of return was 19%; from July 1968 to December 1980, and from January 1981 to December 1984, the target enterprise's rate of return were both 35%. Schwert (1996) studied 1814 M&A events from 1975 to 1991 and found that the CAR to shareholders of the target enterprise within the event window was 35%, of which the unweighted annual average return rate of all tender offers from 1985 to 1991 was 36.8%.

Empirical research focuses on whether shareholders of the acquirer can benefit from M&A activities, and there are three conclusions: positive returns, weakly positive returns, and negative returns. In their generalization of the evidence, Jensen and Ruback (1983) argue that the CAR of the bidder in a successful tender offer is positive 4%; they also estimate that the CAR of the bidder in merger activity is zero. Jarrell et al. (1988) examined data on returns to shareholders of acquiring enterprises over several decades and found that they got the same results as Jensen and Ruback's study of the tender offer in the 1960s. From 10 days before the announcement date to 5 days after the announcement date, the CAR of successful bidders in the tender offer was 4.4%; when the interval was extended to 20 days after the announcement date, the CAR increased to 4.95%, which is highly significant from a statistical point of view. However, the CAR of successful bidders fell to around 2% in the 1970s, a larger decline from a statistical point of view. In the 1980s, the CAR became negative 1%, but not statistically significant. Bradley et al. (1988) found in their study of tender offer that the acquirer's shareholders could only receive a slightly positive return of about 1%. Loderer and Martin (1992) found that after extensive sampling of M&A on the New York Stock Exchange and the American Stock Exchange from 1966 to 1986, there were negative abnormal returns in the three years after the M&A. But that's not the case in five years. Agrawal and Jaffe (2000) studied 937 mergers and 227 tender offers in the US and found that shareholders of acquiring enterprises lost 10% of their wealth five years after the merger was completed.

Of particular importance is whether the total event return is positive or negative. M. Bradley et al. (1988) once summarized the relationship between synergy and return on equity as "the value created by business combination is the benefit of synergy, which can be seen as the sum of the changes in the wealth of the shareholders of the target enterprise (target) and the shooter enterprise (acquirer). That is, $\Lambda\Pi =$

$\Lambda W_T + \Lambda W_A$. In the formula: $\Lambda \Pi$ is the total synergistic benefit, ΛW_T is the wealth change of the shareholders of the target enterprise, and ΛW_A is the wealth change of the shareholders of the acquiring enterprise." Other economists, such as P. Asquith and E. H. Kim (1992) have also shown the same view. Therefore, by examining the total event benefits of M&A, it is possible to test whether synergies are realized and whether M&A create or destroy value. Scholars have tested several combinations of M&A, both according to the weighted average of the relative size of the two parties to the M&A to test shareholders' average return rate, and some directly test the average return (see Table 8.1). Almost all research results show that the total return of both parties to the M&A is positive, and the M&A activities tend to create value.

The results of Chinese scholars based on the event research method are different from those of foreign countries. As far as the target shareholder's return is concerned, most research results show that it is positive (Chen Xinyuan & Zhang Tianyu, 1999; Gao Jian, 2000; Yu Guang & Yang Rong, 2000; Yu Li & Liu Ying, 2004; Wang Huijuan, 2001; Zhang Wenzhang & Gu Huihui, 2002; Zhu Baoxian, 2003), but researches ofFei Yiwen (2003) and Zhang Zongxin and Ji Lei (2003) on listed companies that have the transfer of controlling rights in different periods all show that the target's shareholder returns are negative (but not statistically significant), even the longer the time, the worse the returns, which has not been seen in similar foreign studies. At the same time, most studies believe that domestic M&A events have strong early reactions and excessive reactions after announcements, which reflects the immaturity of China's stock market.

In the research on the shareholder's return to the acquirer, the proportion of significant positive (Lei Xinghui & Zhang Qi, 2002; Li Shanmin & Chen Yugang, 2002; Zhang Wenzhang & Gu Huihui, 2002) and significant negative (Liang Lanyu, 2002; Yu Guang & Yang Rong, 2000; Zhang Xin, 2003) shareholder return is roughly the same, which is the same as the conclusion of foreign studies. However, these studies are, without exception, the test of short-term abnormal returns before and after the M&A announcement date, and the observation of long-term abnormal returns after M&A is rare.

In addition, due to the relatively few cases of M&A among listed companies in China, only Zhu Baoxian (2003) has investigated the comprehensive income of shareholders of both parties in M&A. Zhu used 12 M&A between listed companies in China's capital market between 1993 and 2002 as a sample, and the market value calculated based on the average stock price of the sample companies was compared using different periods, such as 1 day before and after the merger and 3 years before and after the merger, and based on considering the influence of the merger price and the stock market, it is determined whether the synergy effect between the two parties to the M&A is positive and tested to some extent with financial data. Zhu concluded that M&A created synergies for most of the sample companies.[1]

[1] Of the 12 M&A between listed companies, 3 cases lacked data, and 7 of the remaining 9 mergers successfully achieved synergies.

Table 8.1 Total return to shareholders of both parties of the M&A

Researcher	Cumulative abnormal return	Sample size	Sample period	Event period (days)	Positive earnings percentage	Notes
Bradley et al. (1988)	+\$117MM (7.43%)**	236	1963–1984	(−5, 5)	75%	Tender offer; there was no significant change in the total shareholder returns of both parties during the period
Lang et al. (1989)	+11.3%**	87	1968–1986	(−5, 5)	N.A	Tender offer
Franks et al. (1991)	+3.9%**	399	1975–1984	(−5, 5)	N.A	Mergers and tender offers
Servaes (1991)	+3.66%**	384	1972–1987	(−1, the closing date of the transaction)	N.A	Mergers and tender offers
Bannerjeeand Owers (1992)	+\$ 9.95MM	33	1978–1987	(−1, 0)	N.A	White knight bid
Healy et al. (1992)	+ 9.1%**	50	1979–1984	(−5, 5)	N.A	Largest US merger during the period
Kaplan and Weisbach (1992)	+ 3.74%**	209	1971–1982	(−5, 5)	66%	Mergers and tender offers
Berkovitch and Narayanan (1993)	+\$120 MM**	330	1963–1988	(−5, 5)	75%	Tender offer
Smith and Kim (1994)	+8.88%** +3.79%**	177	1980–1986	(−5, 5) (−1, 0)	79.1% 73.8%	Tender offer
Leeth and Borg (2000)	+\$86 MM	53	1919–1930	(−40, 0)	56.6%	According to US dollars in 1998
Mulherin, Boone (2000)	+3.56%	281	1990–1999	(−1, + 1)	N.A	
Mulherin (2000)	+2.53%**	116	1962–1997	(−1, 0)	66%	Incomplete acquisition
Houston et al. (2001)	+ 0.14% +3.11%** +1.86%**	27 37 64	1985–1990 1991–1996 1985–1996	(−4, 1)	N.A	Inter-bank M&A

(continued)

Table 8.1 (continued)

Researcher	Cumulative abnormal return	Sample size	Sample period	Event period (days)	Positive earnings percentage	Notes
Beitel et al. (2002)	+1.2%**	98	1985–2000	(−1, 0)	65%	M&A transactions between European banks
Kuipers et al. (2003)	+2.99%**	120	1982–1991	(−1, 0)	N.A	M&Aof US companies by foreign companies

Note unless otherwise specified, the M&A announcement date is generally taken as the center of the "event period"; **indicates the significance level of 0.05

Sources Bruner R. F. Does M&A Pay: A Survey of Evidence for the Decision-Maker. *Journal of Applied Finance*. Vol. 12, Spring/Summer 2002: 48–69

8.2.1.2 Stock Price Change Method

The stock price change method is an evaluation method that measures performance by the change of the Tobin's Q ratio, which is a method of evaluating performance by a single indicator. Its calculation formula is Tobin's $Q = (\text{MVE} + \text{PS} + \text{DEBT})/\text{TA}$.

Where, MVE is the market value of the company's tradable stock; *PS* is the preferred stock value; DEBT is the company's net debt value; TA is the book value of the company's total assets.

In a mature stock market, the stock market is the best appraiser of M&A performance, and the market mechanism based on individual decentralized decision-making has a strong ability to interpret and synthesize various information about the company. The change of Q value before and after M&A of listed companies reflects the market judgment of investors on the performance of M&A of listed companies. Therefore, the change in Q value is an objective reflection of the M&A performance of listed companies.

The stock price change method is based on the comparison and analysis of Tobin's Q value before and after the M&A, and the conclusion is drawn. It is suitable for the performance evaluation of listed companies' M&A under the mature and effective stock market environment and requires that the stock price can reflect the future growth of the company. But for the Chinese current stock market, an important question is whether the stock market in China is efficient. If the securities market itself is inefficient, then changes in stock prices cannot measure changes in corporate performance. Although some scholars believe that the Chinese stock market has reached weak efficiency, the development of the stock market is a long-term process. Because China's stock market has not developed for a long time, the integrity, distribution uniformity, and timeliness of information are still far from developed countries, the stock price is easily manipulated by human factors.

8.2.1.3 Summary

Although the use of stock price responses (both short- and long-term) to test the value created by M&A is widely used in empirical research, the shortcomings of this approach cannot be ignored. First, the microstructure of the capital market does not operate completely efficiently, whether in the short term or the long term, so the stock market cannot fully reflect all the relevant information announced by M&A. Second, for stock-financed M&As (including stock swaps), the value-creating effect of stock-financed M&As is underestimated because the stock market's response cannot distinguish between stock issuance and M&A transactions. Third, in a competitive market, when measuring the value created by M&A, we should not only measure the value on investors but also focus on the analysis of various stakeholders, such as the increase in consumer surplus. Finally, due to the expected effect on investors, the stock price changes on the day of the M&A announcement have already been reflected in advance. In addition, investors' psychological expectations will also affect the correctness of stock prices to reflect the value of M&A.

8.2.2 Business Performance Comparison Method

Although the event analysis method has been applied in the test of synergy, its applicability is still restricted and affected by some factors. Therefore, some scholars use the comparative study method of business performance (also known as the accounting event study method) to conduct a mid-to-long-term test of M&A synergy. This method uses financial statements and accounting data and uses operating performance indicators such as profitability, solvency, asset management status, main business status (including market share, sales), and cash flow level as the judging criteria. Compare and examine the changes in operating performance before and after M&A (dynamic performance evaluation) or compared to peers (static performance evaluation method). Among these evaluation methods, M&A financial performance evaluation method mainly examines two types of indicators, the first one is profitability indicators, including return on assets (ROA), return on sales (ROS), return on equity (ROE), earnings per share (EPS), sales growth, return on common stock and other indicators; the second one is cash flow return indicators, including expected discounted cash flow, asset operating cash flow return, operating cash flow return based on the entire market value, etc.

8.2.2.1 Profitability Indicator

The financial measure of profitability is used because some surveys of M&A decisions suggest that managers primarily want to improve profitability through M&A (Ingham, Kran & Lovestam, 1992), where the most used profitability indicator is ROA (return on assets) and ROS (return on sales). Meeks (1977) recommends the use of ROA. He argues that of all the financial measures of profitability, ROA is the least sensitive to estimated deviations, smaller than those reflected by returns on equity (these deviations may be due to changes in leverage or bargaining power after the M&A). Previous studies have generally ignored the impact of industry changes on firm performance. There is much evidence that industry changes can affect the relationship between company strategy and performance. Some studies use ROS rather than ROA because the accounting method for M&A directly affects ROA, while ROS is not affected by the accounting method for M&A. In addition, ROS is an evaluation criterion frequently used by managers.

(1) Single financial indicator method

The single financial index evaluation method is relatively simple and intuitive to use. ROA, ROS, ROE, and EPS can all evaluate the performance of M&A. The most used single indicator is the value of ROE, which can comprehensively reflect the performance of M&A. When evaluating, it is only necessary to calculate the value of ROE before and after M&A and compare them. If the value of ROE increases after the M&A, it means that the profitability of the enterprise after the M&A is higher than that before the M&A, then the M&A is effective, otherwise, the M&A is invalid. However, no matter in the western countries with developed market economies or in China in the primary stage, the goal of enterprises is beyond the improvement of single profitability. For example, enterprises need to expand their scale to enhance their ability to resist risks and control the market.

Therefore, the performance of enterprise M&A needs to use various types of indicators to reflect the changes in the comprehensive strength of enterprises from different angles.

(2) Comprehensive financial indicators method

Given the limitations of the above single index, many scholars have proposed a comprehensive financial index evaluation system. The comprehensive evaluation system involves the determination of the weight between multiple indicators. At present, there are mainly methods such as the proportion score, the entropy method, the principal component analysis, the factor analysis, and the analytic hierarchy process.

(i) Proportion score

The proportion score was originally proposed by Alexander Wole. Wole selected 7 kinds of financial indicators and specified their respective proportions in the comprehensive evaluation so that the sum of the proportions of each indicator was 1000. Then the standard financial indicators were determined, and the actual financial indicators were compared with the standard indicators. The score of each index is obtained, and finally, the final comprehensive score is obtained by using the proportion of each index as the weight. The proportion scoring mainly uses the method of subjective judgment to determine the proportion of each evaluation index. The evaluation results are obtained by analysis lack objectivity, which affects the scientificity and accuracy of the calculation results to a certain extent.

(ii) Entropy method

In 1946, Shannon, an engineer at Bell Labs in the United States, introduced the concept of entropy in thermodynamics into information theory. Entropy is a measure of how much information an event contains. The greater the uncertainty of an event, the greater its entropy. For an inevitable event, its entropy is 0. Therefore, according to the nature of entropy, we can judge the randomness of an event and the degree of dispersion of an indicator. The greater the dispersion of the index, the greater the entropy value. The entropy method mainly starts from the difference between the data. When using multiple indicators to evaluate things, if there is little difference between the individuals of an indicator, the indicator plays a less role in the comprehensive evaluation. Conversely, if for a certain index, the difference in the values between individuals fluctuates greatly, that is, the degree of dispersion of the index is large, it indicates that the index has a very important influence on the comprehensive evaluation. Therefore, the entropy value can be used as the basis for determining the index weight. The entropy method has certain objectivity and scientificity, but this method cannot well reflect the relationship between the relevant indicators.

(iii) Principal component analysis and factor analysis

When discussing the comprehensive evaluation of multiple indicators, the multivariate data analysis method in statistics can be applied to the process of comprehensive evaluation. The principal component analysis is a statistical analysis method that converts multiple indicators into a few comprehensive indicators. In multi-index research, because there are too many variables and there is a certain correlation with each other, which made the information reflected in the observed data overlaps, and when there are many variables, it is troublesome to study the distribution law of samples in high-dimensional space. The PCA can replace the original multi-dimensional variables with a few new comprehensive variables after linear transformation and discard a small part of the information under the premise of ensuring the minimum loss of data information. The PCA analysis method is to find the principal components in multiple indicators, use the principal components to fully reflect the original information, and determine the weights by the principal component scores, the dimensionality reduction effect is obvious, and finally, the comprehensive principal component value is obtained. The results are highly objective, but sometimes the principal components obtained by this method have no obvious practical economic significance.

Factor analysis adopts the elementary component matrix extracted in the principal component method to maximize variance orthogonal rotation, screen out the main factors through the cumulative contribution rate after orthogonalization, then regress to obtain the score function of the factor, and finally obtain the comprehensive factor score value for investigation.

(iv) Analytic hierarchy process

The analytic hierarchy process is an evaluation decision-making method that combines qualitative analysis and quantitative analysis. It mathematicalizes the evaluator's thinking process of evaluating complex systems. The basic idea is that the evaluator decomposes complex problems into several levels and elements, and by simply comparing, judging, and calculating among the elements at the same level, the importance of different alternatives can be obtained, providing a decision-making basis for choosing the optimal plan. The characteristics of AHP are that it can mathematicalize and systematize people's thinking process, which is convenient for people to accept; less quantitative data and information are required. But it requires the evaluator to have a very thorough grasp of the essence of the evaluation problem, the elements included, and the logical relationship between them. This method is especially useful for unstructured systematic reviews and multi-objective, multi-criteria, multi-period, etc. systematic reviews.

8.2.2.2 Cash Flow Indicator

A typical study is Healy et al. (1992) proposed to use pre-tax operating cash flow to evaluate the improvement of operating performance. They define operating cash flow as sales revenue less cost of goods sold, selling and administrative expenses, plus depreciation and goodwill expenses. Use this evaluation indicator to divide the market value of the asset (the market value of equity plus the book value of net debt) to provide a measure of return that can be compared across companies. Unlike the accounting return on book assets, the pre-tax operating cash flow return evaluation excludes depreciation, goodwill, interest expense/income and taxes. Therefore, it is not affected by the accounting method of the merger (purchase method or equity pool method) and the method of payment of the merger (cash, debt, or equity). They argue that operating cash flow performance metrics are not subject to depreciation and goodwill, unlike performance-based revenue metrics. It enables cross-sectional comparisons and time series comparisons (when companies use different M&A accounting methods). Some of the differences in performance before and after M&A should be attributed to economic expansion or industry factors. Therefore, they use industry-adjusted target and acquirer performance as the primary benchmark for evaluating performance after M&A. Industry- adjusted performance measures are obtained by subtracting the median value of the industry from the sample firm value. Data on acquired firms were removed when calculating industry medians. Ramaswamy and Waegelein (2003) continued Healy et al. (1992) used the industry-adjusted operating cash flow indicator for the first time, using the following indicators to evaluate the relationship between the relative size of the target company to the acquirer and post-merger performance:

$$\text{POMDROA} = \alpha + \beta_1 \text{PRMDROA} + \beta_2 \text{SIZE} + e$$

where, POMDROA is the median return on operating cash flow adjusted for the industry in the market asset value of the 5 years after the M&A; PRMDROA is the median return on operating cash flow adjusted for the industry in the market asset value of the 5 years before the M&A; SIZE is the relative size of the target to acquirer based on the market value at the end of the year before the M&A; intercepts α are industry-adjusted abnormal returns; slopes β represent the correlation of cash flow returns between the years before and after the M&A. β_1PRMDROA is used to evaluate the impact of performance before M&A on performance after M&A. So, intercept α is an independent variable of pre-merger returns.

8.2.2.3 Main Empirical Research Conclusions

Foreign scholars have obtained the following results through the M&A performance research expressed by financial performance:

(1) Mergers and acquisitions have improved the financial performance of most target enterprises

A study of 56 hostile takeovers from 1975 to 1983 by Herman and Lowenstein (1988) showed that the return on equity of the offeree rose on average from 14.7% to 19.6% after the M&A. Seth (1990) studied 102 takeover offer from 1962 to 1979 and found that the operating synergies obtained, represented by increased cash flow to the target enterprise, were about 12.9%. Healy et al. (1992) studied the 50 largest M&A in the United States from 1979 to 1984 and found that the return on assets of the company adjusted by the industry increased significantly. Their further research also found that the increase in return rate did not come from labor cost savings that come from firing employees, but rather from the improvement of the company's management efficiency. Parrino and Harris's (1999) research results show that the target enterprise's return rate on operating cash flow after the M&A (operating cash flow divided by the market value of the asset) increased significantly.

(2) The financial performance of most acquirers shows a downward trend or is lower than the industry average

Meeks (1977) study of 233 mergers in the UK from 1964 to 1972 showed that the acquirer's ROA continued to decline in the years following the merger.

Salter and Weinhold (1979) found that the acquirer's average ROE was 44% lower than the NYSE average over the same period, and the ROA was 75% lower than the NYSE average over the same period. Mueller (1985) studied 100 largest companies in the US involved in M&A from1950 to 1992, found that their market shares dropped significantly regardless of whether it was a hybrid merger or a horizontal merge. A study by Dickerson et al. (1997) found that in the first 5 years after the M&A, ROA of the acquirer was 2% lower than that of the companies that did not participate in the M&A during the same period. Serovo (2001) studied 168 merger transactions between 1979 and 1990 and found that the return on investment of the acquirer was on a downward trend, with an average decline of 20% in the fourth year after the M&A.

(3) The financial performance of both parties of the M&A changes over time

Carline, Linn and Yadav (2002) examined 86 merger activities from 1985 to 1994, and their research results show that the comprehensive performance of both parties in the merger of the sample enterprises was lower than that of other enterprises ofthe same size in the same industry in the five years before the M&A, and significantly outperform other companies of the same size in the industry five years after the M&A.

The research results are based on the comparative analysis of business performance and the conclusion obtained by using the event analysis method that "the shareholders of the target enterprise have obtained significant abnormal benefits, the acquirer's benefits are not significant, and the total returns of the shareholders of both parties to the merger and acquisition are significantly positive" are the same.

Chinese scholars have obtained the following results through research on M&A performance:

They believe that the application of the abnormal return method relies heavily on the theoretical assumption of an efficient market, and the effectiveness of the Chinese market is still controversial. Therefore, it is more appropriate to analyze the company's financial data to examine whether the overall performance has improved after the M&A and whether the synergies have been realized. The research conclusions of domestic scholars are different from those of similar foreign research. Many studies show that corporate performance after M&A presents an obvious trend of first rising and then falling.

Tan Xiangqiu (1998) studied 198 restructuring cases of the Shanghai Stock Exchange in 1997 and established a comprehensive performance evaluation system including 9 indicators, such as the profit rate of the main business, return on net assets, and asset-liability ratio, and sharpness ratio of the main business. The conclusion is that the performance of companies undergoing mergers and acquisitions has declined.

Feng Genfu and Wu Linjiang (2001) used a comprehensive scoring model composed of main business income/total assets, the profit rate of assets, earnings per share, and profit rate of net assets (excluding industry factors) to analyze and test the performance of M&A of listed companies from 1994 to 1998, the results show that the performance of listed companies overall has a process of rising first and then falling; horizontal M&A performance is better than hybrid M&A, and vertical M&A performance is the worst.

Fang Fang and Yan Xiaotong (2002) selected 80 companies from 115 cases of M&A in 2000 as the research objects and reached a similar conclusion. The paper compares the total performance score of the year of the M&A, the year after the M&A, and the year before the M&A. The total performance score shows that the decline in horizontal M&A is shrinking, and the overall performance is increasing; the decline in vertical M&A is expanding; the performance of hybrid M&A increased significantly in the year but dropped significantly in the second year.

Shen Huashan (2002) studied 392 listed companies that had a transfer of controlling rights during 1997–2001 and measured the performance of the sample after M&A with the industry-adjusted return on equity as an indicator and found that the magnitude of executive changes during 1997–1998 was small, operating performance showed a typical short-term effect. In the year of M&A, performance temporarily improved, but long-term performance declined; after 1999, changes in executives increased, and operating performance improved long-term.

Zhang Xin (2003) studied 1,216 cases of M&A from 1993 to 2002. He measured earnings per share, return on equity, and profit margins of the main business. The research results show that the performance of listed companies as the target party has improved significantly in the year of M&A and the first year after M&A, but the performance improvement was not sustainable after the second and the third years; the listed companies as an acquirer (22 samples), the performance has continued to decline.

Li Shanmin et al. (2004) took 84 Chinese A-share listed companies that had M&A from 1999 to 2001 as samples and used the operating cash flow total asset return to measure and test the performance of listed companies after M&A. The results show that the performance of M&A of the acquiring firm has been greatly improved in the year of M&A, and then the performance decline has even offset the previous performance improvement. Mergers and acquisitions do not substantially improve the operating performance of the acquiring companies.

There are also a few scholars who hold different views. Zhu Baoxian (2002) studied 67 listed companies whose controlling rights were transferred in 1998, based on the return on equity and the profit rate of the main business in the two years before and three years after the M&A. The results show that the main business of listed companies has been significantly strengthened after M&A, and their performance has gradually improved. Li Xindan et al. (2003) took 103 listed companies that had M&A in Shanghai and Shenzhen stock markets in 1998 as samples and used data envelopment analysis (DEA) to systematically analyze the performance of the sample companies in the three years before and after M&A. Studies have shown that M&A activities have generally improved the operational and management efficiency of listed companies and continued to maintain the trend of steady improvement in performance in the years after the M&A. In particular, listed companies as the acquiring companies have greatly improved their performance after M&A; while listed companies as the target are not significant.

8.2.2.4 Summary

The difference in the research results of M&A performance is largely related to the difference in research methods, sample selection, and performance evaluation benchmarks used by scholars. In addition, Calomiris and Kaiseki (1998) also revealed the shortcomings of this method from other perspectives: (1) The vast majority of public financial data are cumulative values, and it is difficult to independently distinguish the impact of a single small event. (2) Financial data is historical data that reflects past performance, not expected future returns. (3) The influence of time delay is investigated. They argue that for cost-saving-motivated M&A, the costs of M&A may increase in the first year after the M&A due to some special processing fees or layoff subsidies and other integration costs. For M&A transactions driven by strategic factors such as synergies or diversification, cost reductions can take 3 years or more to materialize. (4) Contrast the influence of benchmark selection. For example, when using non-M&A samples in the same industry as a benchmark, these samples may have or will have M&A before and after the sample is selected, and non-acquisitors can also achieve the same effect as M&A through development strategies such as green field investment. (5) Influence of accounting treatment method. The same M&A transaction has lower revenue after M&A under the purchase method than under the pooling of interests method. The purchase method increases the expense of post-acquisition depreciation, cost of goods sold, and goodwill. In the year of the M&A, the company's income under the purchase method is lower because the period of the income of the target enterprise of the M&A of the purchase method is shorter than that of the target enterprise of the M&A of the pooling of interests method. The lower revenue reported under the purchase method is entirely due to differences in M&A accounting methods, not differences in economic performance. Due to the increase in the book value of assets under the purchase method, the book assets of the post- merger under the purchase method will be larger than those under the pooling of interests method. Accounting treatments differ in the extent to which they affect profitability and affect cash flow from operations.

Therefore, it is quite difficult to construct a reliable benchmark for performance comparison. Andrade et al. (2001) further pointed out that in the new wave of M&A led by the consolidation of industrial development in the 1990s, the phenomenon of industry shock or M&A industry concentration more acutely highlighted the existing problems in the selection of performance benchmarks, which are further exacerbated by time-lag effects. With the gradual deepening of methodological research, some scholars try to integrate and expand the above two basic analysis methods, such as Pillof (1996) and Akhavein, Berger and Humphrey (1997), and so on. They study the correlation between changes in accounting data and abnormal returns by analyzing the correlation between corporate M&A, accounting data, and stock market returns. They found that the extended research method can accurately predict changes in performance after M&A through the market, and to a certain extent, answer whether the market can distinguish the impact of the activity of M&A on business performance.

8.2.3 EVA Performance Evaluation Method

Economic value added (EVA) refers to the value added by a listed company after deducting the opportunity cost of investors. It first appeared in the model of Nobel laureate Merton Miller and Franco Modigliani on the value of companies, Stern and Stewart, the founders of Stern Stewart & Co. in the United States, first used the concept of EVA and promoted it as an evaluation tool. However, the application of Coca-Cola to the reorganization of the company allowed EVA to achieve a breakthrough at the practical level. There are three main advantages of using the EVA performance evaluation method: First, The EVA is based on the income generated by business activities, which can restrict and regulate the M&A activities of listed companies, and is of great benefit to industries that inhibit listed companies from manipulating profits by using M&A transactions. Second, the accounting research method does not consider the cost of capital of the company and cannot accurately reflect the value created by the company for shareholders, while the EVA considers the cost of capital of the company, making the company value closer to reality. Third, EVA performance evaluation method can actively mobilize all business departments of the enterprise to participate in the whole process of M&A, to alleviate the confrontation between the two sides of M&A, and improve the effect of M&A.

In recent years, inspired by the existing literature research, scholars at home and abroad have begun to evaluate the performance of M&A from a new perspective of corporate EVA. Xiao Xiang and Wang Juan (2009) took the M&A of A-share listed companies in 2002 as the research object and studied the EVA and EVA rates ofthe companies of M&A. The results show that in the short term, M&A performance has improved, while in the long term, M&A performance is not significant. Lu Guixian (2012) took 37 M&A cases of listed companies in Shanghai Stock Exchange and Shenzhen Stock Exchange in 2005 as a sample, calculated the EVA value change trend of enterprises in the selected cases from 2004 to 2009, and found that in the year of the transaction, the value of most companies has improved compared with before the transaction, however, within two years after the completion of the M&A, the value of the vast majority of companies deteriorated, and the performance will not improve until three years later. Wang Songtao and Tu Bin (2012) selected the M&A events ofA-shares and B-shares in Shanghai Stock Exchange and Shenzhen Stock Exchange from 2002 to 2004 as the research objects and analyzed the EVA indicators ofthe acquirers. The results show that in the short and even long term, M&A have improved the EVA of the acquirer and brought benefits to the acquiring company.

Existing literature studies on the effectiveness of economic value added mostly use empirical methods. For example, Uyemum et al. (1996) found that the explanatory power limit of traditional indicators is far lower than that of EVA indicators, the former is only 13%, while the latter is 40%. Biddle et al. (1996) also found that the explanatory power of EVA indicators is higher than that of traditional indicators. The research results of Hu Jizhi and Lyu Yifan (2000), Wang Xigua et al. (2003), Qu Shaofa and Wang Jianwei (2003) show that the explanatory ability of EVA to the stock price fluctuations of listed companies in China is better than that of traditional indicators. Xiao Xiang and Wang Juan (2009), Sun Xifu and Zhang Xiaolei (2012) used the method of empirical research to study the effectiveness of EVA and EVA rate. The results showed that the positive correlation between EVA rates and other indicators was more significant than that of EVA, and believe that the EVA rate is more effective as an indicator of M&A performance evaluation.

The specific method is as follows: the difference between the average REVA of the acquirer in the three years after the M&A and the REVA of the M&A in the year before the M&A is selected as the dependent variable of this book. At the same time, to eliminate the time effect, the acquirer's annual REVA needs to deduct the industry average REVA of the year. The specific formula is as follows:

$$EVA = NOPAT - TC * WACC$$

$$REVA = EVA/TA$$

$$REVA_{ab} = \frac{(REVA_1 - IMREVA_1) + (REVA_2 - IMREVA_2) + (REVA_3 - IMREVA_3)}{3} - (REVA_{-1} - IMREVA_{-1})$$

where, NOPAT is net operating profit after tax; TC is total capital; WACC is the weighted average cost of capital; TA is total assets; REVA is acquirer's total asset EVA rate; IMREVA is the average value of the industry's total asset EVA rate. The meaning and calculation formula of EVA-related indicators are shown in Table 8.2.

8.2.4 M&A Performance Evaluation Methods Based on M&A Motivations

In recent years, some scholars have begun to try to evaluate enterprise M&A performance from the perspective of M&A motivation to explain the reality of unsatisfactory M&A performance and the upsurge of M&A events.

The following are more classic ones. Keith et al. (1998) proposed an M&A performance evaluation method based on multiple motivations, key success factors, and multiple performance measures, which directly divided M&A motivations into three categories: economic motivations, personal motivations, and management motivations. Kitching (2001) also proposed that the key to evaluating the success of an M&A business is to determine a comprehensive performance evaluation method, which must link the management's satisfaction level with the current operating performance to the original acquisition motivation, that is, the basis for judging the success of enterprise M&A is the degree of realization of the M&A motivation.

Liu Wanli (2002) analyzed the various motivations and effects of enterprise M&A. The M&A motivations include managers' economic and psychological motivations and the M&A effects include market share effect, low-cost expansion effect, financial synergy, and operational synergy. Xie Yatao (2003) pointed out that Chinese enterprises have different M&A motivations from foreign ones due to their special background. The direct M&A motivations of Chinese enterprises can be summarized as M&A driven entirely by the government, the motivation of obtaining resources, the need for expansion, the need for obtaining preferential policies and legal tax avoidance, and the motivation for obtaining more market opportunities. Yang Xiaojia and Chen Shou (2005), from the perspective of maximizing the interests of stakeholders

Table 8.2 EVA-related indicators meaning and calculation formula

Variable name	Variable symbol	Meaning and calculation formula
Net operating profit after tax	NOPAT	Meaning: the investment income of the total after-tax comprehensive capital of the enterprise, the calculation result truly reflects the profitability of the enterprise's assets Calculation formula: *NOPAT* = operating profit + investment income + financial expenses + increase in various reserves + amortization of goodwill + increase in deferred tax credit balance + capitalized research and development expenses-amortization of capitalized research and development expenses-EVA tax adjustment EVA tax adjustment = income tax on the income statement + tax rate * (financial expenses + non-operating expenses − fixed assets/intangible assets/preparation for construction in progress − non-operating income)
Total capital	TC	Meaning: the size of the book value of the total capital invested by the enterprise owner to the enterprise, which is composed of two parts: debt capital and equity capital Calculation formula: total capital = debt capital + equity capital Debt capital = short-term borrowings + long-term borrowings + long-term liabilities due within one year Equity capital = common stock equity + minority shareholders' equity + deferred tax credit balance + accumulated goodwill amortization + various reserves + capitalized amount of research and development expenses-construction in progress
Weighted average cost of capital	WACC	Meaning: the total cost of capital is calculated by the weighted average of the capital costs of various long-term funds with the proportion of each capital of the enterprise in the total capital of the enterprise as the weight Calculation formula: *WACC* = cost of debt capital * (debt capital/total capital) * (1 − tax rate) + cost of equity capital * (equity capital/total capital)

and using the multi- objective optimization theory, attribute the M&A motivations to the motivation of protecting the listing qualification to maintain the financing function, the motivation of correcting the illegal behavior to maintain the company's reputation, the motivation of gaining the favor of leaders to maintain personal status, the motivation of pursuing maximum profits to maintain competitive advantage; the motivation of diversifying business risks to maintain investment security; the motivation of establishing industrial alliances to maintain a leading position in the industry. They qualitatively analyze of the degree of matching between M&A motivations and M&A results and regarded it as the basic performance of enterprise M&A. At the same time, an evaluation index system of listed companies' M&A

operation performance is established based on nine quantitative indicators of profitability, asset management capability, debt servicing capability, market share status, learning, and development status, and social responsibility commitment status to evaluate the substantial improvement of performance after M&A, that is, operating performance, and the M&A performance comparison index is used to measure the improvement of operating performance before and after M&A. Jiang Yehua and Chen Hongli (2006) proposed a matrix evaluation model of listed companies' M&A performance to evaluate the overall performance of listed companies' M&A, while the M&A performance matrix evaluation model of listed companies needs to consider the M&A motivations of the acquirers, and reflect the actual situation of the current M&A of listed companies by examining the extent to which the M&A results of listed companies achieve the motivations. Song Jianbo and Shen Hao (2007) studied the relationship between enterprise M&A motivations and M&A performance, taking 138 listed A-share companies in 2002 as the research objects, using the financial index method, and divided M&A motivations into two categories: principal-agent motivation and synergy motivation. It is concluded that the M&A performance was negative under the principal-agent motivation, the M&A performance was positive under the synergy motivation, and conducting diversified M&A has the most significant impact on the performance of M&A enterprises. At the same time, Xia Xinping et al. (2007) used the multi- discriminant method to study the M&A performance of enterprises under principal-agent motivation and synergy motivation, and the results also showed that principal-agent motivations would lead to lower performance, while synergy motivation would increase shareholders' wealth and create value for M&A enterprises. Yang Shuai and Li Weining (2007) analyzed the enterprise M&A motivations based on game theory and proposed a comprehensive evaluation model of enterprise M&A performance using a four- dimensional balanced scorecard (four dimensions include financial dimension, operational synergy dimension, management synergy dimension, and financial synergy dimension with twelve indicators.) combined with the entropy method to evaluate the performance of enterprise M&A. Zhang Xinrong et al. (2010) divided M&A motivations into policy-oriented and market-oriented motivations, and then analyzed M&A behaviors under different motivational orientations, and examined the impact of M&A behaviors on enterprise M&A performance. Zhou Shaoni et al. (2013) divided the M&A motivations into gaining market share, obtaining scale effect, enhancing the core competitiveness of enterprises, and diversifying risks, and argued that M&A motivations are largely influenced by their industrial environment, that is, the stage of industrial evolution. Therefore, the evaluation of M&A performance should follow the logic of "industrial evolution stage— enterprise M&A motivation—M&A performance evaluation". On this basis, the thesis analyzes the M&A motivations at each stage of the industrial revolution and designs a corresponding index system to evaluate the realization of the M&A motivations at each stage as the basis for the M&A performance evaluation of enterprises. Zhang Xuewei (2015) refers to the M&A classification of the WIND database: it is divided into 12 categories according to the specific content of the acquirer's M&A motivation. On this basis, the M&A motivations are divided into five categories: resource-based view, industrial organization theory, industry shock theory, transaction cost theory, and internal capital market. Based on the data envelopment analysis model (DEA) and two-tier stochastic frontier model (TSFA), Zhang analyzed the M&A performance under different M&A motivations. Song Lin et al. (2016) divided enterprise M&A motivations into market motivations, technological motivations, strategic asset motivations, and resource motivations, and took the values of quaternary discrete variables with 1, 2, 3, and 4 respectively. The Logit model was used to empirically study the influencing factors of Chinese enterprises' overseas M&A motivations.

Zhou Shaoni et al. (2013) proposed to use the different M&A motivations and realization degrees of enterprises in each industry evolution stage as the evaluation criteria of M&A performance. The industrial evolution theory agrees with the viewpoint of the diversification of enterprise M&A motivations. Enterprises in different stages of the industrial evolution curve will have significantly different M&A motivations due to the different industrial environments they face. According to the industrial evolution theory, the M&A motivations of enterprises in different industrial evolution stages are analyzed as follows:

In the start-up stage of the industry, there is no enterprise M&A in the early stage due to the large growth space of the industry and more opportunities in the industry, and only at the end of this stage, to gain a firm foothold in the industry, some forward-looking companies start acquiring other companies to rapidly expand their market share. At the same time, the high growth of the industry also attracts companies at the end of the industry evolution curve to enter the industry through M&A. Therefore, from the perspective of the acquirer, the main motivation for M&A at this stage is to enter the industry and gain a firm foothold by increasing market share.

In the scale-up stage of the industry, as the overall growth space of the industry is very limited, it will inevitably lead to intensified competition within the industry. At the same time, excessive competition brings about a decline in profit margins. The growth of enterprises can only be achieved through the internal integration of the industry. In this stage, the decline in profit margins makes economies of scale extremely important. Therefore, there will be many M&A in this stage, with significant characteristics of horizontal M&A, whose motivations are mainly to eliminate their competitors, achieve their growth, and gain economies of scale.

After the fierce struggle in the scale-up stage, the enterprises that can successfully enter the agglomeration stage have strong comprehensive capabilities and strengths. In order not to lag behind other enterprises in the same industry, they will pay more attention to improving the core competitiveness of enterprises. Therefore, how to realize the optimal allocation of resources has become an important task for enterprises at this stage. Enterprises usually focus on their advantageous businesses by divesting non-core businesses to achieve an overall increase in enterprise value and shareholders' wealth.

At the stage of balance and alliance, due to the high degree of industrial concentration, the status within the industry is established, but industry risks will have a significant impact on the enterprise. Therefore, at this stage, enterprises pay more attention to spreading risk, and there are more non-related M&A at this stage. In addition, since there are few opportunities and possibilities for intra-industry M&A

in a country, some enterprises have adopted the method of expanding their sales market by acquiring overseas enterprises to reduce risks.

Zhou Shaoni et al. (2013) summarized the motivations of enterprise M&A at different stages of industrial evolution as shown in Table 8.3.

Once the motivations of M&A are clarified, it is necessary to design performance indicators corresponding to the motivations of M&A to evaluate the performance of M&A, through which the realization degree of the motivations of M&A is reflected.

The enterprise M&A performance evaluation system based on industrial evolution theory constructed by Zhou Shaoni et al. (2013) requires to evaluate of enterprise M&A performance in stages, which is divided into four levels: M&A performance evaluation in the start-up stage, M&A performance evaluation in the scale-up stage, M&A performance evaluation in the agglomeration stage, and M&A performance evaluation in balance and alliance stage. Due to the different motivations ofM&A at different stages, the measurement and evaluation indicators of M&A performance at each stage are also different.

In the start-up stage, no matter what form of M&A, the purpose is to gain a place in the market, and the main consideration of enterprises is the problem of "getting bigger", including getting bigger in absolute scale and relative scale. Therefore, the growth of the enterprise's own operating income before and after M&A can be used to measure its absolute scale expansion effect, and the growth of market share can be used as its scale expansion effect relative to the industrial market to realize the complementarity of the two. At the start-up stage, the M&A can be considered a success if the company's operating income and market share are increased after M&A, while the opposite is considered a failure.

In the scale-up stage, what the company needs to consider and achieve is growth and growth healthily. For measuring its growth, it can continue to use the market share growth metric achieved through M&A. Healthy growth is to build a unique competitive advantage for sustainable growth and long-term profitability in the future. Therefore, M&A players currently focus on those companies with unique, proprietary, and complementary values when selecting targets to create real synergies, including operational synergy, financial synergy, and management synergy. The operational synergy is mainly reflected in the reduction of costs, which is measured by the gross profit rate in this paper. The financial synergy is mainly reflected in the centralization of capital raising through M&A, which can reduce the cost of capital, therefore, the cost of capital can be used as the measure. The management synergy is to realize the integration of management functions through M&A, which can reduce the management

Table 8.3 Motivations for enterprise M&A at each stage of industrial evolution

Industrial evolution stage	M&A motivations
Stage I: start-up stage	Gain market share
Stage II: scale-up stage	Gain economies of scale
Stage III: agglomeration stage	Improve the core competitiveness of enterprises
Phase IV: balance and alliance stage	Spread risk

cost-burdened by unit income, so it is reasonable to adopt the change of management cost income rate. That is, the measurement and evaluation of M&A performance in the scale-up stage are mainly based on market share growth and synergy acquisition. If the synergistic development of the two is achieved, the M&A is effective; otherwise, the M&A fails.

In the agglomeration stage, enterprises focus on how to optimize the allocation of their resources and enhance their core competitiveness. M&A are more often manifested as divesting non-core businesses and exiting weak industries, which directly improve enterprise profitability and value. The improvement in profitability can be reflected by the increase in the net operating income margin index. Usually, it requires the method of value evaluation to verify whether the value of the enterprise has been improved. However, the evaluation of enterprise value requires a considerable understanding of the enterprise and its industry, which cannot be separated from a lot of specific data, while its process is quite complicated. The evaluation results can be affected by too many subjective and objective factors, so there is the problem of huge differences in the results evaluated by different methods and different people, which affects the operability of M&A performance evaluation. Given that enterprise value is the result driven by the two core elements of income and risk, ROE can reflect the level of income that affects enterprise value, and the company's beta coefficient can reflect the level of risk that affects enterprise value. This paper adopts the change in the ratio of income on net assets to beta coefficient before and after M&A to reflect whether the enterprise value has been improved. In this way, the evaluation of M&A performance in the agglomeration stage is based on whether the M&A improves the company's profitability and realizes the improvement of enterprise value, and if the two have improved, the M&A is judged to be effective, while the opposite is considered a failure.

In the balance and alliance stage, it is very difficult for enterprises to achieve sustainable growth in a mature industry, and they can only spread their risks by creating new profit growth points. On the one hand, it can avoid over-reliance on existing products by identifying potential opportunities in the existing market or sub-sectors that can add value to the company. On the other hand, it can be achieved by further expanding the market for existing products, but since it is difficult to continue expanding the market of the industry in a country, the only way to do so is to expand overseas. Therefore, at this stage, the growth rate of new brands or products and the percentage of overseas operating income are two indicators that can be used to judge M&A performance. As long as the M&A achieves an increase in the number of brands and product types or an increase in the percentage of overseas operating income, the M&A is considered a success; while the opposite is considered a failure.

In addition, since the evaluation of any enterprise M&A performance involves two or more indicators, specific indicators are selected using ratio-type indicators for the comparability of the indicators, and all of them should reflect the rate of change after M&A relative to that before M&A. According to the industrial evolution theory and the M&A practice of Chinese enterprises, the M&A performance evaluation indicators are designed for different M&A motivations in each industrial evolution stage, as shown in Table 8.4.

Table 8.4 Design of M&A performance evaluation indicators based on M&A motivations under different industrial evolution stages

Industrial evolution stage	M&A motivation	M&A performance indicator	Indicator description
Stage I: start-up stage	Gain market share	Increase in market share	Post-M&A market share/pre-M&A market share − 1
		Growth in operating income	Post-M&A operating income/pre-M&A operating income − 1
Stage II: scale-up stage	Gain economies of scale	Increase in market share	Post-M&A market share/pre-M&A market share − 1
		Gross margin improvement	Post-M&A gross profit margin/pre-M&A gross profit margin − 1
Stage II: scale-up stage	Gain economies of scale	Increase in management cost income ration	Post-M&A management cost income ratio/Pre-M&A management cost income ratio − 1
		Reduction in cost of capital ratio	1—post-M&A cost of capital/pre-M&A cost of capital
Stage III: agglomeration stage	Improve the core competitiveness of enterprises	Enhancement of enterprise value	Post-M&A beta ratio of ROE/pre-M&A beta ratio of ROE − 1
		Increase in operating income net profit rate	Post-M&A operating income net profit rate/pre-M&A operating income net profit rate − 1
Stage IV: balance and alliance stage	Spread risk	Increase in the number of brands or products	Post-M&A number of brands or products/pre-M&A number of brands or products − 1
		An increase in the percentage of overseas operating income	Post-M&A ratio of overseas operating income/pre-M&A ratio of overseas operating income − 1

Note (1) Management cost income ratio = operating income/management cost

(2) Since the cost of capital is a reverse indicator, when calculating its changes specifically, the data of 1—post-M&A cost of capital/pre-M&A cost of capital is used to realize the positive relationship between it and the realization of M&A motivation

(3) Beta ratio of ROE = ROE/β

Among the above-mentioned M&A performance indicators designed for different M&A motivations in each industrial evolution stage, financial indicators are mainly used, and there are also a small number of non-financial indicators. For financial indicators, they can be calculated from the relevant data of the company's financial statements or annual reports. Non-financial indicators can be calculated by obtaining relevant data from the company's production, sales, and related economic activities.

8.2.5 Case Study Method

The case study method is a new development of the original M&A performance research method in recent years. This method is to analyze and understand individual cases, seek case explanations, and deeply observe the dynamic change process of performance of specific M&A cases to judge the effect of M&A events when the M&A performance of all samples cannot be determined comprehensively and accurately.

The significant advantages of the case study method in practical application are as follows: (1) linking the examination of M&A performance to the characteristic information of the individual case, and applying characteristic information such as M&A motivations and industry differences as a set of conditional variables to econometric analysis, which can be used to examine the influence of M&A motivations and other characteristics on M&A outcomes. However, the previous research methods are quite different in terms of performance evaluation indicators, sample size, and period. Without considering the subjective and objective conditions (including motivations) of the M&A subject, the sample results are used in a biased manner to confirm or deny the M&A's effectiveness. Therefore, the case study method has more potential and is more convincing in deepening the research effect. Kearney Consulting selected 115 giant M&A cases that occurred between 1998 and 1999 for study and found that 42% of the companies achieved their expected goals and were regarded as successful M&A. (2) The ability to effectively distinguish between the proper function and result of M&A. As long as the result of the M&A under specific conditions is consistent with the original motivation of the M&A subject, the M&A behavior can be considered reasonable and effective. Tetenbaum (1999) believes that the previous method confuses the evaluation of the actual results of M&A with the evaluation of the proper results of M&A, thus disputing the role of M&A, and it is difficult to explain why M&A activity continues to flourish despite the high failure rate (60%-80%) of M&A as measured by indicators such as stock price changes and performance. (3) Case studies pay more attention to the dynamic evolution process of M&A behavior rather than simply adding up the successful or failed cases that have occurred, which can artificially exaggerate or reduce the effect of M&A. Calomiris and Karceski (1998) analyzed the nine major M&A completed by the US midwestern banks from 1992 to 1994 one by one, and refuted the original conclusions about the inefficiency of bank M&A.

The case study method is a new development of the original M&A performance research method in recent years. This method is to analyze and understand individual cases, seek case explanations, and deeply observe the dynamic change process of performance of specific M&A cases to judge the effect of M&A events when the M&A performance of all samples cannot be determined comprehensively and accurately. Some scholars in China also use this method to test the synergy of specific M&A transactions.

Chen Xinyuan and Li Dongping (2000) analyzed the case of the merger between Tsinghua Tongfang and Luying Electronics through a share swap in 1998 and found that the tradable shareholders of Luying Electronics received about 96% of the cumulative abnormal return, with an average increase of RMB4.28 per share; the tradable shareholders of Tsinghua Tongfang received about 2.5–5.88% of cumulative abnormal return, with an increase of RMB0.77-RMB1.84 per share. The market reaction shows that the market welcomes mergers that do have the combined effect of resources.

Hong Xixi and Shen Yifeng (2001) empirically studied the eight acquisitions of Shanghai Shenhua by Shenzhen Jun'an and Guangzhou Sanxin from October to December 1996 based on the theory of the western corporate control market. The results show that under the current market conditions in China, secondary market acquisitions cannot bring significant positive returns to the target company's shareholders.

Xu Runping and Li Yinzhu (2001) examined two cases, the acquisition of Sichuan Changzheng by Sichuan Top and the acquisition of Shanghai ACE by Dagang Oilfield in 1998, in terms of main income, main profit, net assets per share, earnings per share, and return on equity, and found that the performance indicators and asset quality indicators ofthe two listed companies have maintained continuous growth and improvement after the M&A, which proves that substantial M&A help to enhance the value of listed companies.

Liu Feng et al. (2002) studied the case of Yantai Xinchao Industry absorbing and merging Shandong Xinmou and concluded that the shareholders of Shandong Xinmou obtained an average of RMB0.43 per share (up to RMB0.965) in excess profit, but the wealth of Yantai Xinchao Industry's shareholders has not increased or decreased significantly.

Yang Xu et al. (2002) took Founder Technology as a typical case and analyzed the impact of three M&A and five shareholding reduction announcements on the target enterprise's shareholder earnings. The results show that even though China's stock market is immature at present, company acquisitions still bring benefits to the target enterprise's shareholders.

Tu Qiaoping (2005) empirically studied the Livzon equity acquisition case, and the results show that the battle for the control of Livzon Pharmaceutical Group brought 23.81% of extraordinary returns to the shareholders of the target company, while the shareholder's return of the acquirer, Taitai. Pharma, is -17.49%, indicating that the M&A did not bring benefits to the acquirer's shareholders. Considering both parties of M&A as a whole, the average market value growth rate before and after M&A is getting higher and higher with time, with an average growth rate of 15.52%, which shows that the comprehensive effect of M&A is significant.

8.2.6 Other Research Methods

8.2.6.1 Self-Reported

When analyzing the long-term performance of the acquirer, the respondents are asked through a designed scale. The long-term performance of the acquisition is evaluated by a self-reported measure of post-merger market share, sales revenue, intrinsic profitability, and profitability relative to the industry average to study the impact of external technology acquisitions on company performance.

8.2.6.2 Academic Group Evaluation

Bruton et al. (1994) analyzed 51 distressed companies that were acquired between 1979 and 1987 and proposed to use the subjective evaluations by academic groups to evaluate the performance of M&A. They argue that strictly performance-dependent financial evaluations are inappropriate because they reflect overall company performance and not just acquisition-related performance. Bruton, Oviatt and White's evaluation group had three members from three universities.

The academic evaluation group devised a subjective evaluation methodology for the performance of each acquisition. The group members studied strategic management, strategic marketing, and finance and were unfamiliar with all other parts of the study. They evaluated the success of each acquisition on a 7-level scale ranging from 1 "very unsuccessful—the acquirer has no significant financial or strategic benefit from the acquisition" to 7 "very successful—the acquirer has significant financial or strategic benefit from the acquisition". The academic group's evaluations were based on available excerpts of publicly published financial data from industry experts, stock analysts, and business writers. They assumed that because people buy the research of these competing authors and sometimes invest based on their advice, these authors want to preserve their reputations by ensuring that their articles provide the most accurate publicly available information about the acquisition. All excerpts relate only to the subject of the study—acquisitions, not to the overall performance of the company.

8.2.6.3 Expert Ranking

Cannella and Hambrick (1993) used the expert ranking method to evaluate the company's post-M&A performance when analyzing the influence of the executive departure of the target on the target's performance in 138 M&A between 1980 and

1984. They believe that since the public information on the post-M&A target's performance cannot be effectively obtained, the evaluation using shareholders' earnings cannot reflect the true post-M&A performance of the target. For each M&A, they selected six top executives of the acquirer and six securities analysts specializing in acquirer securities analysis as surveyed experts. These experts were asked on a 7-level scale, "How would you rate the target's profitability at the time of M&A"; or "profitability four years later".

8.3 Research on Factors Affecting M&A Performance

8.3.1 M&A Payment Method

According to the company finance theory, M&A payment methods include cash and securities. Different payment methods will have an impact on the shareholders' income of both M&A parties, which is mainly manifested in three aspects: (1) Tax factors. Eckbo (1983) put forward the idea of tax synergy, arguing that M&A can make better use of tax avoidance means, such as taxation, capital gains tax, and increasing assets. When using securities (mainly stocks) as a payment method, the target enterprise's shareholders can delay tax payment and engage in tax substitution, which is beneficial to the target enterprise's shareholders; while when using cash as a payment method, the acquirer increases its assets, thereby expanding the amount of depreciation tax avoidance, so the acquirer is also willing to pay a higher price. (2) Information asymmetry factor. Leland and Pyle (1977), Mrers and Majluf (1984), Travlos (1987), and Louis (2002) all argued that when a company realizes that it is overvalued, management will use its private information to issue securities to finance the M&A, so the stock price does not accurately reflect the information about the M&A, which leads to a decline in the company's stock price in the long run. Rau and Vermaelen (1998) also pointed out that stock-financed M&A can lead investors to expect that the acquirer is overvalued. As a result, when M&A news is announced, the acquirer's share price tends to fall as investor expectations return. (3) Signal factor. The theory suggests that the choice of payment method reveals future investment opportunities or cash flow situations. Cash-financed M&A show that the acquirer's existing assets can generate large cash flow or that the acquirer can take full advantage of the investment opportunities owned by the target enterprise or create by the M&A; on the contrary, stock financing is a poor signal. Therefore, theoretically speaking, the excess returns of the acquirer with cash-financed M&A are usually higher than that with stock-financed M&A; while the target companies experience positive returns with both types of M&A, but generally, the return of stock-financed M&A is significantly lower than that obtained with cash-financed M&A.

From the empirical test results, Gordon and Yagil (1981) and Travlos (1987) found that cash M&A can generate more excess returns than stock M&A. Pranks, Hards and Mayer (1987) and Linn and Switzer (2001) also confirmed that the excess returns of cash M&A are relatively high from the perspective of target companies. Bruslerie (2012) discusses the relationship between M&A payment methods and company earnings from the perspective of asymmetric information. Cash will be the payment method for most M&A if the expectation of M&A benefits reaches a certain level; if the acquirer is concerned that the M&A assets may be overvalued, the M&A that uses a certain percentage of shares is a feasible option. From the perspective of the wealth effect of M&A, the payment method of M&A transactions has both short-term and long-term effects (Dube & Glascock, 2006; Ismail & Krause, 2010). Loughran and Vijh's (1997) analysis of a sample of 947 M&A that took place in the UK from 1970 to 1989 shows that the stock returns of shooters in cash acquisitions are as high as 61.7% within five years of the acquisition, while company mergers using stock swaps caused shooters to suffer a 25% share price drop. In contrast to the above research conclusions, Chang (1998) verified the short-term effects of 281 M&A transactions that occurred in the US from 1981 to 1992 and found that among M&A of publicly held companies, the excess returns of cash acquisitions were almost zero, and the return for stock acquisitions was 2.64%. Eckbo and Thorburn (2000) classified the sample of M&A that occurred in Canada from 1964 to 1983 according to the payment methods of M&A and found that the M&A payment methods in equity, cash, and equity combination resulted in significant positive returns to the acquirer. Louis (2002) found that the acquirer's long-term excess return was zero and no significant difference when cash M&A were adopted, while the return of stock M&A was significantly negative.

Researches in China on this aspect mainly include: Zhu Baoxian and Wang Yikai (2002) used the two indicators of return on equity and profit rate of the main business to compare the performance of uncompensated and compensated M&A of listed companies in China, and the results showed the benefits of compensated transfers are generally better than those of uncompensated transfers on the whole. Lyu Aibing et al. (2004) believe that the M&A in which the acquirer obtains control through a joint venture with the parent company in cash can improve profitability through industrial integration, while the stock exchange M&A can save the acquiring company from facing huge financing pressure and immediate payment constraints, thus facilitating effective integration and rapid development of companies after M&A. Gao Minghua (2008) conducted a comparative analysis of the performance of asset acquisitions and stock acquisitions from 1999 to 2001 and found that the performance of stock acquisitions only increased in the year of M&A, and declined in the rest of the years, while the performance of asset acquisitions declined in all years. Wang Meng (2011) analyzed the M&A events of listed companies in 2007, showing that the performance of stock and cash payment methods increased significantly in the year of M&A, while the performance of asset payment methods increased fastest in the later years of M&A. Zhao Libin and Zhang Qiusheng (2012), Yu Pengyi and Wang Mansi (2014) took the listed companies that carried out cross-border M&A from 2005 to 2010 as samples to investigate the influencing factors of M&A performance, and found that the cash payment method was significantly and positively related to the M&A performance of the acquiring company. Zhou Shaoni and Wang Huitong (2015) discussed the impact of different M&A payment methods on M&A performance from the perspective of company governance. The study found that M&A performance in stock payments is significantly better than that of cash payments because stock payments can optimize the shareholding structure and enable strategic investors to play an active regulatory role.

From this point of view, the existing empirical test results generally support the theoretical research, but there is still disagreement on the issue of the extent to which the acquirer obtains excess returns. Shleifer and Vishny (2001) believe that this is mainly due to the different background conditions for studying the impact of payment methods on M&A performance. Under the condition of a strong and efficient stock market, the results of payment method theory and empirical research should be consistent; while under the condition of an ineffective stock market, the market value of the acquirer and the target enterprise deviate from their true value, and both M&A parties decide which payment method to adopt according to the value of their respective stocks. Therefore, the payment method itself does not affect the return of both parties, and what affects the returns of both parties is mainly the extent and direction of the deviation of the market value of their respective stocks from their true value.

8.3.2 M&A Industry Relevance

Singh (1984) divided M&A into related M&A and non-related M&A based on the strategic fit of both parties in M&A. The link between related M&A and M&A performance can be explained by efficiency theory and organizational capital theory. Efficiency theory believes that the higher the correlation of the M&A industry, the better the synergy between the two parties of the M&A can be realized, and the economies of scale can be achieved, thus reducing the production and operating costs. From the perspective of organizational capital theory, M&A with a high degree of industry correlation is more likely to achieve the transfer of exclusive management capabilities to target enterprise, thereby improving M&A performance. Non-related M&A cannot do this, but they can be compared in terms of the acquired economies of scope and reduce the company's operational risk.

The earliest comparison of related and non-related M&A was conducted using the stock event study method. The test results show that for the acquirer, the value created by the related M&A is higher than that of the non-related M&A, but the impact on the target enterprise is still unclear. Later, following Singh's research ideas, many scholars roughly adopted four different segmentation criteria to strictly define the correlation of the M&A industry: (1) hybrid and non-hybrid; (2) horizontal, vertical, and hybrid; (3) level of industry overlap; (4) change in corporate focus. Using these different measures, scholars draw three different conclusions: (1) Related M&A outperformed non-related M&A. For example, Healy et al. (1992) took the level of industry overlap as the test standard and found that M&A with a high level of industry overlap had better performance than those with a low level of industry overlap. Studies by John and Ofek (1995) and Desai and Jain (1999) show that the long-term performance of increasing corporate focus by divesting non-core assets is significantly positive, and these findings are generally consistent with theoretical inferences. (2) There is no significant difference between related M&A and non-related M&A in terms of long-term performance and shareholder value creation. Ghosh (2001) and Linn and Switzer (2001) took the corporate focus as the standard and found that there is no positive correlation between the corporate focus and long-term business performance. (3) The value created by non-related M&A is higher than that of related M&A. Agrawal et al. (1992) used hybrid and non-hybrid as the test standard and found that the long-term stock price level of hybrid (diversified) M&A was higher than that of non-hybrid (concentrated) M&A. In addition, John et al. (1992) and Lang and Stulz (1994) have examined the short-term stock price response to M&A, and have also come to very inconsistent conclusions. Megginson et al. (2002) believed that the underlying reasons for the above-mentioned differences in test results were differences in samples, periods, control variables, and research methods. Therefore, Megginson et al. proposed to use the Herfin index to measure the changes in the correlation degree of the M&A industry, and empirically tested a sample of 204 strategic M&A that occurred between 1977 and 1996. They found that the magnitude of the change in corporate focus before and after M&A was significantly and positively related to the long-term M&A performance. Within 3 years after M&A, each 10% decrease in the focus would lead to a 9% decrease in shareholder wealth, a 1% decrease in operating performance, and a 4% shrinkage in enterprise value, and a 1.2% decrease in operating cash flow. Chatterjee et al. (2014) believe that the degree of synergy obtained depends on the degree of similarity of the industries in which both parties of M&A are located. The relationship between the degree of M&A industry correlation and M&A performance can also be found in the M&A direction. Although the degree of correlation or strategic fit of the M&A industry is important, it is not sufficient to explain the different M&A performances. Moreover, whether the diversification of enterprises after non-related M&A can increase the enterprise value is still a debatable issue.

Yuan Hongqi and Wu Xingyu (1998) used the financial indicator method to study the relationship between industry correlation and M&A performance earlier in China. They conducted an empirical study using a sample of restructured companies in 1997. The study compared four accounting indicators before and after the company's restructuring and found that the earnings per share (EPS), return on equity (ROE), and investment income as a share of total profits increased in the sample companies in the year of restructuring compared to the year before restructuring, while the company's asset-liability ratio has declined. The magnitude of changes in these accounting indicators was related to the way of restructuring and the relationship between the parties involved in the restructuring. Gao Jian et al. (2000) found that the return on equity of industry-related M&A activities was higher than that of non-industry-related return on equity. Feng Genfu et al. (2001) adopted a comprehensive evaluation method based on financial indicators to measure the M&A performance of China's listed companies from 1994 to 1998. They selected four indicators: main business income/total assets, net profit/total assets, earnings per share, and return on equity. It was found that the performance of the second company has improved after

M&A, while from the second year of the M&A, the M&A performance has shown a downward trend year by year. Overall, the integration of the listed companies after M&A was not successful.

Another conclusion is that there are certain differences in the performance of different types of M&A. The performance of hybrid M&A is more significant in the first year; while the performance of horizontal M&A is not significant in the first year after M&A, but then increases; vertical M&A performance was the least significant. Fan Conglai et al. (2002) analyzed the industries in which the M&A parties are located and found that companies in growing industries perform relatively best in horizontal M&A; companies in mature industries perform relatively best in vertical M&A; companies in declining industries perform relatively poor in horizontal M&A. Jiang Xianling et al. (2013) believe that, whether it is cross-industry or cross-regional hybrid M&A, the operating performance of enterprises will decline significantly after the completion of M&A.

8.3.3 Acquirer's Growth and Value Characteristics

The relationship between the growth and value of the acquirer can be explained by the performance extrapolation hypothesis, which is strongly supported by Franks et al. (1991) and Fama and French (1992). According to the performance extrapolation hythopesis, both market investors and other stakeholders evaluate the value created by the M&A based on the historical performance of the acquirer, and people usually use the net market price ratio (the ratio of book-to-market asset value) as an approximate measure of historical performance. A company with a high net market price ratio is called a value company, and a company with a low net market price ratio is called a growth company. It can be inferred that (1) in the period of M&A announcement, growth acquirers will achieve more excess returns than value acquirers, which is caused by the excessive expectations of market participants; (2) in the long run, the market will gradually adjust the initial overvaluation of the acquirer, so the value acquirer's excess return is higher than that of the growth acquirer; (3) the growth acquirer will pay more acquisition premium, which is in line with the target company's shareholders' interests. Therefore, based on the inferences of these three levels, the hypothesis draws the conclusion that the "net market price ratio is inversely proportional to short-term M&A performance and proportional to long-term M&A performance". Lang et al. (1989) found that the acquirer's announcement period return was positively related to Tobin's Q ratio, thus verifying the first level of the hypothesis. Anderson et al. (1993) used the net market price ratio for the first time to conduct a long-term performance test on 670 M&A samples that occurred from 1966 to 1987 and reached the same conclusion. Rau and Vermalen (1998) tested bank samples and confirmed the latter two levels of the hypothesis. They found that growth acquirers had an excess return of -17.3% in three years after the acquisition, while value acquisitions had an excess return of 7.6%. However, the latest empirical results of Louis (2002) show that the significant positive relationship between the net market price ratio and the long- term M&A performance is only established in the bank sample, which is due to the high net market price ratio of the bank itself. When the bank sample is excluded, long-term excess returns for growth acquirers (−10.1%) are higher than for value acquirers (−18.5%), but are not significant.

It is clear that the empirical test results do not fully support the performance extrapolation hypothesis. This is because the hypothesis is based on the measurement of past performance, and whether M&A can create value depends not only on the past but more on the market for expected returns from M&A, so the persuasiveness of this hypothesis is limited.

8.3.4 Acquirer's Initial Shareholding

Until the M&A news is announced, only the acquirer has the inside information about whether the M&A will take place. Therefore, the acquirer will buy the stock of the target enterprise through the secondary market before bidding, establishing a "toehold" in the target enterprise, and the stock price will gradually rise to the level of the offer price so that the acquirer can obtain more income and improve its performance level. Kyle (1985) and Shleifer and Vishny (1986) show that with the increase of the initial equity held by the acquirer in the target enterprise, the probability of successful M&A will increase, and the expected profit of the acquirer will also increase. However, Bradley et al. (1988) refute this point. They believe that most acquirers do not own the shares of the target enterprise at the time of the M&A, and even if the acquirer owns the shares of state-owned enterprises, the potential profit the acquirer can obtain from these shares is very small compared to the cost ofthe M&A. The main reasons are: (1) It is impossible to secretly buy stocks of target enterprises on a large scale in the secondary market, the number of which is limited by law. (2) There are many investors who discover undervalued stocks in the stock market. When the market transaction is very thin, the acquirer's large-scale purchase of stock will expose its private information, so that the stock price will rise rapidly to the offer price level, making it difficult to obtain sufficient profit. Jennings et al. (1993) empirically found that the average initial shareholding of all US acquirers is very low (only 3%), and only 15% of the acquirers hold initial shares ofthe target enterprise. But in a subsample of multiple bidders, the acquirer's average initial shareholding increased to around 18%. Hay et al. (2001) also pointed out that in the early stage of competitive M&A, it is easy for the acquirer to secretly buy stocks under various names to establish a foothold in the target enterprise. However, with the prevalence of regulation today, once the stakeholder holds more than a certain proportion of the stock, they must make sufficient information disclosure as required, so it is not easy to obtain profits from this.

8.3.5 Economic Environment

For studies on FDI, there are many macroeconomic variables as control variables, or as part of measuring political risk, which is closely related to the cost of capital and therefore to cross-border M&A performance. Higher economic growth rates and higher interest rates can generate high returns for companies and thus attract more foreign capital (Oxelheim et al., 2001). Dunning (2009) emphasized the importance of macroeconomic factors in cross-border M&A. Bai Xueyuan (2011) believes that in the historical period of the global financial crisis and the transformation of China's economic development mode, enterprise M&A are affected by the economic environment due to its strong co-movement properties with the economy. The performance of the sample M&A companies in 2008 was poor, but the wealth creation capability of M&A has recovered from 2009 due to the enjoyment of policy dividends. In the post-crisis period, the M&A market should change its original appearance, further improve the corporate governance system of state-owned enterprises, enrich M&A and its financing forms, deepen market-oriented reforms, and provide the impetus for economic development with its intended market vitality. Li Shanmin (2014) analyzed the regulatory system of the foreign M&A security review in the US by examining and analyzing the US administrative authority's review of the acquisition of Ralls Corporation and compared the differences in the security review of foreign M&A between China and the United States. It is believed that the US regulations on national security review and the domestic political and economic environment are the decisive factors for the rejection of the Ralls acquisition case, and the political connection of Chinese enterprises has become one of the focuses of the US national security review. Hu Jiewu (2015) took 94 cross-border M&A events of Chinese listed companies from 2006 to 2012 as samples and used the event study method to study the shareholder wealth effect of the main merging company in cross-border M&A, and the results showed that cross-border M&A does bring significant positive wealth effect to the shareholders of the main merging company in China. The research on the influence of the host country's macroeconomic factors on the wealth effect of cross-border M&A found that GDP was significantly positively related to the shareholder wealth effect, CPI was significantly negatively related to the shareholder wealth effect, and there was no significant relationship between exchange rate and the wealth effect.

8.3.6 Other Factors

Some Chinese and foreign researchers have studied other factors affecting M&A performance, such as:

Managerial arrogance and M&A performance. If the company operates well before the M&A activity, its managers are more likely to make the mistake of over-optimistic evaluation of M&A opportunities by blind arrogance, resulting in overpayment and failure to realize the expected synergies of M&A (Roll, 1986). In the context of lower management shareholding ratio and lower managerial marketization level of listed companies in China, scholars have conducted relevant research, and most of the empirical findings show that there is a negative relationship between M&A performance and profitability before M&A activities. There may be a more serious managerial arrogance situation in China, and the arrogance hypothesis can provide a stronger explanation for China's M&A (Li Shanmin, 2005; Wu Chaopeng, 2008). Xie Linghong (2012) abandoned the assumption of managerial rationality in traditional corporate M&A theory and proceeded from the behavioral corporate finance theory. The results show that managers in group decision-making are generally overconfident; managerial overconfidence is significantly and negatively related to the long-term performance of M&A, and it is also negatively related to short-term performance, but not statistically significant. Zhang Xizhen (2014) studied the impact of managerial overconfidence on M&A performance from the perspective of behavioral finance and found that managerial overconfidence was negatively related to M&A performance. Song Shuqin (2015) studied the influence of managerial overconfidence and M&A type on M&A performance. Through empirical research and analysis, the following conclusions are drawn: (1) Managerial overconfidence can significantly reduce the financial performance and market performance of post-merger companies. (2) The performance of related M&A is better than that of non-related M&A. (3) The influence of managerial overconfidence on M&A performance is different in different M&A types. Managerial overconfidence in related M&A can significantly improve M&A performance, while managerial overconfidence in non-related M&A can significantly reduce M&A performance.

Social capital of executive team and M&A performance. Qi Jipeng and He Xiaoming (2015) analyzed the relationship between the social capital of the executive team and M&A through the data of listed companies. The results show that the social capital of the executive team embedded in the financial network has a promoting effect on the performance after M&A, while the social capital of the executive team embedded in the alumni network is detrimental to the post-merger performance of the company. The social capital acquired by the executive team due to its political network has two effects on post-merger performance: the social capital acquired by the executive team due to its work in government departments has a positive effect on post-merger performance; the social capital acquired by the executive team due to its membership in National People's Congress or Chinese People's Political Consultative Conference is not conducive to the performance after M&A. At the same time, regional factors are introduced to add moderating variables to further explore the relationship between social capital and M&A performance. The research shows that regional factors have a positive moderating effect on the relationship between the social capital embedded in the alumni network of the corporate executive team and M&A. Regional factors have a negative moderating effect on the relationship between the social capital embedded in the financial network of the executive teams and the M&A performance. Therefore, it cannot be generally assumed that the social capital of the executive team has a promoting effect on performance after M&A because of the information and resources it embeds. In the M&A process, the existing social capital should be used reasonably to promote the integration and performance of corporate M&A. At the same time, enterprises should also fully consider the influence of regional factors on the M&A performance in the process of M&A target selection and should consider the portability of the social capital of the executive team to further improve the M&A performance.

The relative size of M&A and M&A performance. The size of M&A parties has a certain impact on M&A performance. Some scholars believe that the larger the size of the target relative to the acquirer, the easier it is for economies of scale to be realized, which makes the transaction price more reasonable, avoiding a higher M&A premium, and therefore contributing to the improvement of M&A performance. Shelton (1988) found that if the M&A is relatively large in scale, the target can provide more assets to the acquirer, and the value generated on this basis is also more. But Chinese scholars Li Shanmin and Zheng Nanlei (2008) concluded through discussion that the "big eating small" model has better performance than the "strong and strong alliance" model. If the relative size of M&A exceeds a certain percentage, it will have a dampening effect on the M&A synergy. Shams (2013) argues that smaller non-public companies can achieve better M&A performance, while larger public companies can achieve better M&A performance. Song Xiaohua (2016) studied the effect of whether the target enterprise is a public company and the impact of its size on M&A performance. The study shows that relative size has different effects on M&A of different types of target enterprises: when the target enterprise is a public company, relative size is positively related to the short-term M&A performance, but not significantly related to long-term M&A performance.

Related M&A and M&A performance. For historical reasons, many companies in China have related relationships, so it is necessary to study their effects on M&A performance. The overall findings show that related M&A has both positive and negative effects on M&A performance. From the perspective of positive impact, because the two parties of related M&A have a better understanding, it can reduce the uncertainty and risks of the transaction, which is conducive to promoting synergy and improving the company's operating efficiency. Yang Kangyu (2003) used the accounting research method on 99 M&A transactions that occurred in China in 2000 and found that among the enterprises with improved M&A performance, the number of related M&A was larger than that of non-related M&A. In addition, Pan Jin and Chen Hongmin (2005) also concluded that the performance of related M&A is better than that of non- related M&A. From the perspective of negative impact, because the equity of Chinese companies is generally more concentrated, as a type of related business, controlling shareholders may use related M&A to capture private interests and plunder the interests of small and medium shareholders, so related M&A cannot bring about the essential improvement in company's performance. Li Zengquan et al. (2005) used the hollowing-out and support theory to study the related M&A of listed companies in China and found that M&A performance cannot be continuously improved by M&A. Huang Haiyan and Li Yue'e (2009) also found that the performance of non-related M&A in China is better than that of related M&A. Wu Chaopeng (2012) examined whether a CEO's political affiliation affects the probability of being changed after a failed M&A and the market reaction when a politically affiliated CEO is changed. The empirical results show that: (1) The worse the M&A performance of the CEO, the easier it is to be changed, but the politically affiliated CEO is not easy to be changed even if the M&A performance is poor. This phenomenon is less obvious in the provinces with less government intervention. (2) When the politically affiliated CEOs are changed, the market reaction is better than other CEOs being changed, and the worse their M&A performance, the more serious the government intervention in the place where their company is located, the better the market reaction is when they are changed. Li Shanmin (2013) used the DEA-SFA quadratic relative effectiveness model to evaluate the performance of Chinese listed companies in related M&A and to estimate the effect of influencing factors on the performance of related M&A. The empirical results show that related M&A can significantly improve the short-term performance and long-term performance of enterprises, rather than the characteristics of "upward and then downward" as traditional viewpoints call it. Yan Xueqin (2016) studied the impact of Chinese company political affiliation on their cross-border M&A performance. The results show that the relationship between the acquirer's political affiliation and its cross-border M&A performance is affected by the degree of government intervention, that is, the higher the degree of government intervention, the lower the M&A performance when the political affiliation of the M&A party is certain.

The proportion of independent directors and M&A performance. The shareholding of listed companies in China is relatively concentrated, and corporate governance is affected by the proportion of small and medium shareholders, resulting in different M&A integration outcomes. Firstly, the higher the shareholding ratio of small and medium shareholders, the more effectively they can supervise corporate M&A decisions, in addition to enhancing effective competition for corporate control, thereby improving the rationality of managers' M&A decisions (Bai Chongen et al., 2005). Secondly, the higher the shareholding ratio of small and medium shareholders not better. When the company's shareholding structure is too scattered, it may weaken the controlling shareholders' enthusiasm for supervision and the incentive and restraint mechanism, and it will also expand the intervention cost and delay the integration time. In the short term, this will not contribute to the improvement of M&A performance, so there may be a positive relationship between the percentage of first largest shareholder ownership and M&A performance in the short term. Li Shanmin and Zhu Tao (2004) also reached a similar conclusion, arguing that the percentage of first largest shareholder ownership is positively related to the M&A performance in a short period, but negatively related to M&A performance in the second year after the transaction is completed. Some scholars believe that the proportion of independent directors will have an important impact on M&A performance. Yang Yuan (2012) and Feng Fugen and Wu Linjiang (2001) found through research on M&A events in China that the percentage of executive shareholding was not significantly related to M&A performance, while the concentration of acquirers' equity, the proportion of independent directors, and the size of the board of directors were all significantly and positively related to M&A performance.

There are many other factors that affect M&A performance, and different conclusions can be drawn from different perspectives, so we won't introduce them one by one here.

8.3.7 Summary

In general, foreign empirical studies on the relationship between corporate M&A performance and its influencing factors have not yet reached a consistent conclusion. The reasons for this are mainly the following: (1) Difference in sample selection and research methods. In terms of sample selection, there are certain differences in sample size, industry category, and period; in terms of research methods, there are differences between short-term and medium- and long-term stock market event research methods, and there are also differences in the selection of accounting indicators and comparative benchmarks in business performance comparison research methods, as well as issues such as the authenticity of accounting data. These differences or issues lead to different research calibers. (2) The influence of enterprise attributes, industry characteristics, and external environment. Many scholars regard M&A as an enterprise's pursuit of profit maximization, do not link their characteristics such as corporate motives for M&A to M&A performance, and do not consider the characteristics inherent in different industries, thus their studies lack causal links. In addition, the external environments such as stock market trends and changes in capital prices may also be variables that affect M&A performance, and there are also differences between the market's perception of the acquirer's share price level before the acquisition and the firm's intrinsic value. (3) The integration of the M&A process is also an important variable that affects M&A performance. In general, payment methods, industry relevance, the growth, and value characteristics of the acquirer all need to be studied before M&A transactions, while the effective integration of the acquirers and acquirees in terms of management style, organizational structure, and organizational culture affects the realization of potential value. (4) The influence of country-specific factors. In China, M&A is to a certain extent a passive government-led activity, which often deviates from the motivation of corporate interests, thus greatly restricting the breadth and depth of asset restructuring and optimization of resource allocation by companies. The performance of M&As motivated by such motives is inevitably different from that of M&As motivated by market factors.

8.4 Theoretical Explanation of M&A Performance

8.4.1 Positive Evaluation of M&A Performance

Hypotheses about the impact of M&A on enterprise performance can be divided into two categories: positive evaluation and negative evaluation. Positive evaluations suggest that M&A helps improve firm performance and operational efficiency, with several theoretical explanations such as synergistic effects, market power, corporate control market, and access to resources.

8.4.1.1 Synergistic Utility Hypothesis

The hypothesis states that mergers can reduce firm costs. Horizontal mergers can reduce costs by combining sales outlets and functions. Vertical mergers can reduce negotiation and transaction costs (Arrow, 1975). The company expands through mergers to achieve economies of scale in the scope of production, thereby reducing production costs. Mergers will also bring financial synergies, for example, some companies have surplus cash flow but few investment opportunities, while others have more investment opportunities but lack funds, and by merging to make up for both sides, the merger brings benefits since internal financing is less costly than external financing (Myers & Majiluf, 1984).

8.4.1.2 Market Power Hypothesis

Stigler (1950) argues that mergers between firms can increase control over the market. First, mergers between industry giants can create a monopolistic situation in the market, and monopolies allow firms to price above the level at which they would earn normal profits. Second, even if a monopoly does not form, the economies of scale that result from the expansion of M&A can drive costs down, pricing products above marginal costs and below the average market profit price, thus forming market entry barriers. Third, M&A can enhance the bargaining power between suppliers and customers, and improve the company's position in the sales market.

8.4.1.3 Corporate Control Market Hypothesis

Corporate control market hypothesis, which originated from Manne (1965), views M&A as a struggle for control of the firm by managers, who acquire the firm and gain the right to control the firm and operate its resources. Therefore, poorly run companies are vulnerable to the threat of external takeovers, and poorly run managers are at risk of being replaced (Jensen, 1988). It is the existence of an objective competitive market that weakens the principal-agent problem so that managers cannot do whatever they want, but act in the interests of maximizing shareholders, and therefore M&A objectively becomes an effective mechanism for monitoring the behavior of managers and contribute to the improvement of the company's business performance.

8.4.1.4 Access to Resources Hypothesis

Mergers and acquisitions allow the acquirer to access the readily available resources of the acquiree. Porter (1980) argues that through vertical mergers, the acquirer secures key resources and reduces external uncertainty. In addition to acquiring raw materials, intermediate products, and distribution channels, M&A can also be used as a means of acquiring technology, patent rights, and management experience.

Compared to the R&D-only approach to developing new technologies, mergers yield faster and less risky results, indirectly enhancing firm value, and improving post-merger performance, which are the non-financial reasons for M&A performance.

8.4.2 Negative Evaluation of M&A Performance

Along with these above positive evaluations, negative evaluations of M&A performance are mainly explained by insider interests and arrogance.

8.4.2.1 Insider Interest Hypothesis

Jensen (1986) argues that due to the existence of the principal-agent problem, the goals of managers and shareholders are aligned, and managers, driven by maximizing their benefits, may expand their firms beyond the optimal size. Managers tend to expand their companies to obtain personal benefits such as managerial allowances, power, prestige, etc. since the above benefits are usually positively correlated with the growth in company size and sales. External expansion through M&A is more likely to result in growth in company size and sales than internal expansion. In order to pursue the maximization of personal interests, insiders adopt the M&A behavior, and the M&A performance is not based on the profit maximization of the company entity.

8.4.2.2 The Hubris Hypothesis

The hubris hypothesis, proposed by Roll (1986), argues that most mergers are decisions that managers think are right but are wrong. In an efficient market, the stock price has adequately demonstrated the intrinsic value of the company, and many managers often believe that they can uncover companies that are undervalued by the market. This type of investment is usually a bad decision by managers who believe too much in themselves and underestimates the market. Both management's arrogance and behavior can lead to poor decisions and M&A performance that does not meet the expected expectations.

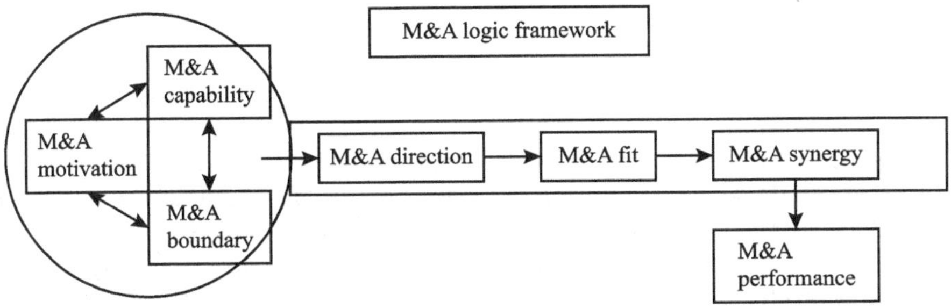

Fig. 8.1 A logical framework for M&A performance

8.5 Factors Influencing M&A Performance Based on the Logical Process of M&A

The authors believe that the analysis of M&A performance must be linked to the motivations for M&A. The motives of corporate M&A vary widely and there are different decision makers for M&A motives as analyzed in the previous section on the M&A motive system. It can be argued that M&A performance is to the extent to which different M&A subjects achieve their M&A motives. Taking M&A motivation as the starting point, M&A performance also depends on M&A capability and M&A boundary; in addition, M&A activities follow the path of M&Adirection, M&Afit, and M&A expectation synergy before the final M&A performance is realized. The logical analysis framework of M&A performance is shown in Fig. 8.1.

M&A motivation, M&A capability, and M&A boundary are the preparatory stage of M&A decision making, which is a system of interaction and mutual constraints. First, decision-makers identify opportunities and gain insight, of course, different decision makers have different motivations, which provides ideological preparation for M&A. Second, decision-makers establish the strategic behavior of taking M&A by comparing the trade-off between M&A and the new investment, M&A and alliance. This trade-off process is the selection of M&A boundaries, and the confirmation of M&A boundaries kicks off the strategic behavior of enterprise M&A. Finally, enterprises usually consider the previous M&A experience, existing M&A manpower, financial resources, material resources, etc., whether they are sufficient to support the enterprise M&A behavior, which is the feasibility consideration of M&A. These three functional processes provide sufficient preparations for M&A. The consideration of each of these functional processes affects the final confirmation of the M&A strategy or not. We call this the first stage of the strategic behavior of M&A, which completes the identification of the development opportunities and the determination of the development approach of the enterprise.

As shown in Fig. 8.1, the next three interlocking functional processes of M&A are M&A direction, M&A fit, and M&A synergy, which are unchangeable in a logical sequence, unlike the first M&A preparation phase mentioned above, which we refer to as the execution phase of the M&A decision. Determining the criteria of the acquiree, screening and finally determining the target enterprises, and integrating the resources of both parties to pursue synergy. The three processes of this phase have been elaborated on in the previous chapters and will not be discussed too much here.

The preparation stage of the M&A decision solves the questions of why do M&A, whether it can do so, and whether it is the best way to do so, while the execution stage of the M&A decision answers the questions of what to do and what will happen after M&A. They are explained in the previous chapters as independent elements to explain M&A performance, but a systematic study of these elements in combination to answer the degree of influence of these independent elements on M&A performance in the M&A market environment requires deeper theoretical and empirical research.

Chapter 9
Corporate Control Market

M&A starts with motivation and ends with a performance. The new performance then induces new M&A to occur, so that the reciprocation from the end to the beginning creates an ebb and flow of M&A activities. A large number of M&A activities constitute the M&A market, and different periods of the M&A market contain unique laws of operation of the M&A market.

9.1 Control Rights, Control Market, and Control Market Performance Definition

9.1.1 Control Rights and Controlling Interest

"Controlling interest" can be understood from two perspectives: the power to own stocks, and the controlling position obtained by owning a majority of stocks. The ownership of shares, no matter what kind of assets it corresponds to, is ultimately a representation of an asset, and the ownership of shares is essentially the ownership of the asset, i.e., the right to possess, use, earn and transfer shares (or other given property). At this level, ownership of the property is equivalent to property rights—how much shares you own is how much property you own. However, at the same time, the controlling interest is also a part of the ownership of the firm, and if the controlling share is understood as the holding position obtained by owning most shares, it belongs to the category of enterprise ownership. This is because a relatively dominant controlling interest can lead to relatively dominant vote rights and thus a relatively proportional residual claim.

In the early literature of business theory, economists defined business ownership in terms of the residual claim. Here, "property ownership should not be confused with business ownership".

Q. Zhang, *Mergers and Acquisitions*, https://doi.org/10.1007/978-981-92-0122-8_9

While the concept of"control" is more complex.

First, from the perspective of economics, the control of modern enterprises, like many other complex economic concepts, has never been able to have a clear definition that tends to be consistent and accepted in the theoretical literature of economics ever since Berle and Means (1932) proposed the theory of "separation of ownership and control" of the company, academic attention to this area has never ceased. According to the classic definition of Berle and Means (1932), the so-called control separate from ownership refers to the power to select members of the board of directors or a majority thereof, either by exercising legal rights or by exerting pressure. However, later on, this concept was still considered to be inadequate and "more a description of a phenomenon than a definition" because it could not reveal the control "why and how control affects the choice of board members". So, since the 1970s, Demsetz and Alchian (1972) have studied the enterprise as a team production unit with various interests, arguing that control in modern firms is a system of mutual ownership and coordination of interests between shareholders and operators. Subsequently, Jensen and Meckling (1976), based on the contract theory, advocated that the decision-making power of management should be transferred to the operator through the principal-agent system within the enterprise, while the owner had the right to supervise the operator, and the operator is disciplined and motivated by performance measures and rewards and punishments. In the 1980s, Fama and Jensen (1983) assumed that the separation of the decision-making management functions from the residual risk-taking functions would lead to the separation of decision-making management from decision-making and control, so that subdividing the decision-making power into management decision-making power and decision-making control power, which are separated by contractual structure within the enterprise organization, that is, the approval and monitoring of decision-making are separated from the proposal and execution of decision-making. This separation means that the agent cannot exercise exclusive management rights and control over the same decision-making. In the late 1980s, Grossman and Hart (1988) proposed that the control right of an enterprise is the residual rights of control in addition to the specific control right stipulated in the enterprise's property rights contract, and its essence is the right to control the material assets of the enterprise. At the same time, Hart further argues in his 1995 book that residual claim is a concept that is not well defined, compared to residual control, which is more clearly defined.

If ownership is defined in terms of residual claims and residual control of the enterprise as defined by Zhang Weiying (2000), then the second dimension of "controlling interest" (residual claim) and the meaning of control rights (residual control rights) as described above precisely illustrate the separation of residual claim rights and residual control rights, in another word, the ownership of a company is a "state-contingent ownership": the existence of controlling rights gives the shareholder a proportionate share of the residual claim rights (balance or profit claims), but not necessarily a proportionate share of the residual control rights (decision-making rights or authority over activities not specifically provided for), or obtains a greater proportion of residual control. Corporate control can be transferred not only among shareholders, but also among shareholders, creditors, managers, and employees, and may even be distinguished by formal control and real control, i.e., "the ability to use and cooperate with critical resources" (Rajan & Zingales, 1997; Tirole, 2000). It is clear that from an economic point of view, even though control can be defined, its precise measurement is still very difficult.

Second, from a jurisprudential perspective, the definition of control under US corporate and securities law derives primarily from the holding of shares and voting rights in a company, which is divided into at least two forms depending on the number of shares held: (1) "absolute or complete control"; (2) "working control". Among these, "absolute or complete control" is defined as the control that arises when a majority of the voting shares issued by a company are held by a single shareholder or a group of shareholders acting together, while a significant minority stake can also constitute absolute control if the shareholding is sufficiently diversified. The former, such as when a single person (or a group of people) holds more than 50% of the equity (the same as the domestic definition of absolute control), and the latter, such as when only 10% of the equity is held but the remaining 90% of the equity of the issuing company is dispersed among thousands of shareholders (a broader definition than the domestic definition of relative control). "working control" means that the minority shareholders have sufficient ability to vote with a sufficient number of other shareholders to elect or remove directors, and this provision indicates a degree of uncertainty about control (Black, 1990). The Securities Act of 1933 and the Securities Exchange Act of 1934 of the United States have provided a literal definition of "control", but they do not address specific criteria for determining it, and it is not until the Holding Company Act of 1935 that a shareholder with a 10% shareholding is determined to be a controlling shareholder (unless he can show that he is not), while in some exceptional cases, the Securities and Exchange Commission (SEC) may consider a person to be a controlling person even if he does not have a 10% shareholding, as long as he exercises controlling influence, either alone or in conjunction with others (Seligman, 1995). The situation becomes more complicated when a person has the status of a director or officer of the company, making him a "controlling person", and in this regard, the Investment Company Act 1940 under "the exercise of power to control influence is only a consequence of the functional relationship" denied the existence of control, but in 1946 the in the case of Transit Inv. Corporation, the SEC stated that "a person is a person in control when he is the president as a result, not the cause, of the power he exercises." It can be seen that, in US law, "control" is not an easy category to define except in the most obvious cases. The SEC generally does not allow lawyers to comment on the existence of a control relationship (Seligman, 1995). As the court stated in a 1964 decision: when there is less than 50% ownership, what percentage of ownership constitutes substantial control is a matter of fact. What is important may not be the shareholding, but its controlling influence, for which precise measurement can only be analyzed on a case-by-case basis.

The Laws in the UK is similar to those in the US in that. The City Code on Takeover and Mergers provides that a shareholder owns 30% or more of the voting shares of a listed company to have control. Although the UK and US differ in whether they impose "mandatory general offer obligations", there are similarities and differences in their regulation of control.

"Definition" 6 of the Hong Kong Code on Takeovers and Mergers states that control is defined as holding or holding in aggregate 35% or more of the voting rights of the target company. Article 47(2) of the Interim Measures for the Supervision of Listed Companies in Shenzhen promulgated by the Shenzhen Municipal Government on April 4, 1992, states that control rights refer to the ownership of more than 25% of the shares or voting rights of a listed company. In contrast, the Measures for the Administration of Takeover of Listed Companies promulgated by the China Securities Regulatory Commission(CSRC) in October 2002 followed the British standard and considered that an acquirer has one of the following circumstances, it constitutes effective control of a listed company if it (1) holds the largest number of shares in the register of shareholders of a listed company (except where there is evidence to the contrary, the same below); (2) the shareholder who is able to exercise and control the voting rights of a listed company in excess of the largest number of shares in the company's shareholder register; (3) the shareholding or control of shares or voting rights of a listed company reaches or exceeds 30%; (4) through the exercise of voting rights can determine the election of more than half of the members of the board of directors of a listed company; (5) other circumstances as determined by the CSRC.

To sum up, ownership of an enterprise is only state-dependent ownership, and there is a possibility of separation of controlling interest and control rights, residual claim rights and residual control rights from each other, and control can not only be transferred between shareholders, but also among shareholders, creditors, managers, and employees, so the precise measurement of control is very difficult. This confusion is also reflected in national laws, and the criteria for determining the proportion of so-called control rights vary. Nevertheless, we still believe that equity is the ownership of the business in its normal state, that "shareholders remain owners of the business in its normal state", and that "this normal state, in terms of time, should account for more than 90%". Moreover, the purpose of studying corporate governance itself is to achieve the maximum match between corporate control and residual claim, therefore, "there is no need to bring about a greater misalignment to eliminate the 10% misalignment between residual claim and control in the existing governance structure" (Zhang Weiying, 2000). According to this line of thought, when conducting an empirical study of corporate control, it is not inappropriate to assume that control rights are a natural derivative of controlling rights in the absence of a better measure of control. At the same time, considering the existence of controlling influence and the differences in the proportion of controlling shareholding across countries, it is too far-fetched to force a 30% shareholding as a criterion for corporate control. Therefore, in the empirical measurement, the actual transfer of the largest shareholder is used as an approximate proxy for the transfer of corporate control, so that, although it does not completely solve the problem, it is still hoped to obtain 90% accuracy.

9.1.2 Control Market and Control Market Performance

Having defined the concept of control, let's focus on the "market". From the perspective of linguistics, the market has two meanings: (1) a place where commodities are bought and sold; and (2) the relationship between the supply of commodities and services, etc., and the demand for them with the ability to pay in a certain area (Ci Hai[1], 1999). Economics explains the market as a mechanism by which buyers and sellers interact and jointly determine the price of goods or services and the number of transactions (Samuelson, 1999). It is evident that whether it is a place, a relationship, or a mechanism, a market is formed whenever there are certain buyers (demand) and sellers (supply) interacting with each other for a given good. Economists believe that there is a market for almost everything, from art to pollution. Markets can be centralized, such as the stock market, or decentralized, such as the real estate market or labor market. It can even be electronic, such as when many financial assets or services are traded via computers. The most critical feature of a market is that it brings together buyers and sellers to jointly determine the price of a commodity and the quantity traded (Samuelson, 1999). When dividing markets, the criteria are generally based on the subject matter of market transactions, such as commodity markets (including cotton yarn, grain, gold, and other markets), factor markets (including technology, capital, labor, information, and other markets), foreign exchange market (such as US dollar market, Hong Kong dollar market), etc., and there should also be a market for corporate control of buying and selling companies.

As for the "corporate control market", Manne (1965) originally proposed the concept to discuss mergers and antitrust issues, but he also pointed out that this analysis (of the corporate control market) is relevant to many economic issues.

Of these, the so-called separation of ownership and control in large corporations is perhaps the most significant. Unfortunately, Manne did not give a precise definition of the corporate control market at the time, nor did he conduct a more in-depth analysis. It was not until 1983 that Jensen and Ruback, in their famous article Corporate Control Markets: Evidence from Science, based on a systematic review of the theory and practice of M&A activity over the years, proposed the much-debated definition of the market for corporate control: We view the corporate control market (also commonly referred to as the takeover market) as a market in which various management teams compete with each other for the management of corporate resources. In this context, Jensen and Ruback's understanding of corporate resource management as corporate control, and the market in which control of the firm is contested, is the market for corporate control. This point should be consistent with the previous understanding of corporate control rights from the perspective of the criteria for dividing the market. As for what Jensen and Ruback call the "takeover market", it is two sides of the same coin: the so-called "takeover" is "the transaction of transferring the ownership of the enterprise" (Hirshleifer, 1992). It is a transaction, and the takeover market is a market named after this kind of transaction, just like the market for buying and selling and the leasing market. The market for corporate control is a market named

[1] An unabridged, comprehensive Chinese dictionary.—*Tr.*

after the subject matter of the transaction, which belongs to the same classification as the product market and the factor market, but the division of these two markets is not contradictory, its connotation and extension should be basically consistent.

According to our definition of M&A, i.e., transactions that are subject to business control, the M&A market equals the corporate control market. Literally, the corporate control market deals with corporate control, while M&A includes not only corporate M&A but also business M&A through asset acquisition. But there is no evidence to exclude the acquisition of assets, a form of M&A, from the corporate control market.

The so-called "performance of the market for corporate control" mainly refers to the overall performance and performance of the corporate control market, which includes not only its impact on the future value of the enterprise within the market operation, but also, and more importantly, whether its expected market role is fully exploited, and creates positive total social welfare. For the former, we define it as the "corporate performance" of the corporate control market, and the impact of this performance may be reflected in two aspects: first, the market's impact on the company's stock price; second, the impact of the market on the trend of the long-term financial indicators of enterprises. Most of the empirical studies on M&A or corporate control market performance at home and abroad have been conducted from this perspective. For the latter, there is not yet a mature test method. From the existing foreign literature, Manne (1965) first argues that "the market for corporate control rights is relevant meaningful to many economic issues, perhaps most significantly to the so-called separation of ownership and control in large firms". Subsequently, Jensen (1983), Easterbrook and Fischel (1991), Martin and McConnell (1991), Hirshleifer (1992), Hirshleifer and Thakor (1994, 1998), Lowenstein (1999), and others have also addressed the role of corporate control markets from different perspectives, respectively, and have gradually focused the topic on the discussion of its impact on both the optimal allocation of resources and corporate governance. However, there are also some studies in this field in China, such as Zhu Wuxiang (2000), who argues that "although the Chinese corporate control market is also optimizing resource allocation, it mainly performs the alternative function of direct listing"; Shen Huashan (2002), who argues that "the takeover activities after 1999 are related to the replacement of corporate executives", etc. However, there are large gaps in the breadth and depth of these studies. Therefore, we adopt the evaluation made by Zhou Xiaochuan (2002) on the "50-Person Forum" in Beijing on the proper role of the control market of Chinese companies from three perspectives: whether it has achieved "strategic restructuring of the national economy, optimized resource allocation, and improved governance of listed companies", and the comparison of the impact of the special forms of corporate control market (management buyouts, proxy contests, and all-share segments) on corporate performance to examine the role of corporate control market in China. Using a sample of 933 M&A events in which control was transferred from 2007 to 2011, Yu Jiang, Zhang Qiusheng, and Wang Yi (2014) explore the causes of M&A failures based on the perspective of ultimate controlling shareholders' interest capture and find that (1) Ultimate controllers are more inclined to use the cash of listed companies in the group for asset acquisition rather than for distribution. To facilitate the smooth implementation of M&A transactions and capture private benefits, the greater the separation between the ultimate controlling shareholder's cash flow rights and the control rights of the listed company, the higher the M&A premium paid by the listed company in unrelated M&A, while the opposite is true in related M&A. (2) The greater the separation between the ultimate controlling shareholder's cash flow rights and control rights of listed companies, the lower the cumulative excess return of the M&A and the worse the performance after M&A. Further empirical evidence is provided to reveal the management agency hypothesis, pride hypothesis, and market timing hypothesis of M&A failure.

With the in-depth study of equity structure, scholars found that within the group under the pyramid structure, the ultimate controlling shareholder controls the listed company through smaller cash flow rights, so the ultimate controlling shareholder has the motivation and ability to transfer the listed company's resources through asset transactions, and this private gain of such control is often greater than the gain obtained through a dividend distribution. Yu Jiang, Zhang Qiusheng, and Wang Yi (2014) explore whether the causes of M&A failures are triggered by the ultimate controlling shareholder's motive of benefit appropriation under the pyramid structure from the perspective of listed companies conducting M&A. In response to this problem, Bae et al. (2002), Zhu Dongqin and Chen Wenhao (2010), and Chen Hong and Yang Lingxiao (2012) did related research. Bae et al. (2002) research found that when a listed company in the Republic of Korea acquires a target with poor performance in the group, it will have a poor market response, which proves that the listed company's M&A often does not maximize the value of the enterprise. Zhu Dongqin and Chen Wenhao (2010) explored the effect of cash flow rights and control rights separation on the M&A performance of private listed companies in China from 2004 to 2005. It was found that the effect of cash flow rights and control separation on M&Aperformance was U-shaped. Chen Hong and Yang Lingxiao (2012) explored the effect of pyramidal shape characteristics on the level of benefit encroachment by the ultimate controlling shareholder using the bulk equity transfer of Chinese firms from 2008 to 2010 as a sample and obtained the finding that the degree of cash flow rights and control rights separation is positively related to the private gain of control rights.

We talked about M&A performance and its interpretation in the chapter on M&A performance, more along the lines of the micro-performance of M&A activity. The control market performance or M&A market performance, discussed in this chapter unfolds more in terms of the performance of M&A as a socioeconomic activity. The performance of the control market is a summary of the pattern of past activities in the M&A market, and more importantly, the control market is the market environment for firms' micro M&A activities, as well as the object of the state macro management's intervention in the market and macroeconomic regulation.

9.2 Control Market Theory

Since the 1960s, Manne and the followers continued to create various theories that attempted to explain the value of the existence of the corporate control market, including Manne's (1965) and subsequent discipline theory, Ansoff's (1965) synergistic theory, Leibenstein's (1966) X-inefficient theory, Jensen's (1986, 1988) free cash flow hypothesis, Williamson's (1988) corporate governance structure theory, Pelikan's (1989) evolutionary theory, Roe's (1999) political theory, and Instefjord's (2001) agency paradigm model, which together provides the classic economic theoretical foundation for the mainstream school ofthought on corporate control markets. However, the rise of counter-mainstream theories following the second wave of antitakeover legislation in the United States has also presented a strong challenge to the soundness of the market theory of corporate control.

9.2.1 The Mainstream Theories of the Corporate Control Market

Shen Yifeng (2000) has summarized the three most representative views of the mainstream theories of the corporate control market, and in fact, these views are invariably scattered in the following scholars' theoretical studies on the corporate control market.

9.2.1.1 The Discipline Theory of Manne and the Followers

The disciplinary theory is a set of theoretical clusters and is also the most mainstream theory of the market school of corporate control. Not only Manne, but also a large number of economists and jurists, including Jensen and Ruback, Dodd,

Easterbrook and Fischel, et al., believe that the primary role of the market of corporate control is to discipline incompetent managers, and it is the "court of last resort" for shareholders. The control market mechanism proposed by Manne (1965) was not originally aimed at the agency conflict between major shareholders and minority shareholders, but rather between shareholders and management, but the control market can play a disciplinary effect on the controlling shareholder's short-selling (Chen Yugang et al., 2013) and play an equally important role in resolving the agency conflict between controlling and minority shareholders. The transfer of control rights will greatly reduce the private gains of controlling shareholders, so strong controlling shareholders will be defensive against M&A (Brickley et al., 1988; Gompers et al., 2003; Li & Qian, 2013). With the research of scholars, especially after Jensen and Meckling discussed the meaning of the agency problem in 1976, the theoretical basis to explain the disciplinary effect from the perspective of agency theory was more established and spawned the financial contract theory, free cash flow hypothesis and corporate governance structure theory in 1980. Deangelo and Rice (1983) pointed out that anti-takeover provisions may increase or destroy the wealth of shareholders, and the effect of anti-takeover provisions is manifested as the trenching effect. Under the framework of the trench hypothesis, the controlling shareholder sacrifices the interests of investors, and the establishment of the anti-takeover clauses facilitates the maintenance of the controlling shareholder's control, which may have the following effects on the minority shareholders: On the one hand, controlling shareholders' disciplinary threat from the control market is weakened, which may intensify the agency conflict with minority shareholders, and controlling shareholders' benefit appropriation behavior will increase, ultimately damaging investors' wealth and interests. On the other hand, the establishment of the anti-takeover clause reduces the threat of punishment from the control market, and objectively reduces the pressure and constraints of the market on the controlling shareholder, who will improve their short-sighted behavior and focus more on improving the long-term performance and growth opportunities of the company, thus also reducing the benefit-encroaching behavior of minority shareholders, and the short-selling will be curbed to a certain extent, while minority can also benefit from the company's long-term growth benefits. Easterbrook and Fischel (1991) further developed the disciplinary theory by arguing that if the company is a contract, the takeover is a mechanism to control contract costs (i.e., the cost of monitoring and replacing management). When the market has accurately reflected the inefficiency of the assets of the target enterprise under the incumbent manager, the acquirer's proposal to take over at a premium indicates that it is confident that it will achieve the purpose of improving efficiency by reorganizing the asset structure and management of the target enterprise, and once this goal is achieved, the acquirer wins the spread, the target company's shareholders receive a premium, and management who is incompetent or those who violate their duties of loyalty and prudence are replaced and disciplined, and the benefits of the entire society will be improved. At the same time, they argue that corporate mergers all lead to scaled-up production operations, more efficient use of information, synergies, and adjustment of slack management and that while benign mergers are less costly than hostile takeovers and enjoy the same favorable tax policies, hostile takeovers can follow if management intentionally avoids the business opportunities of benign mergers, which have inherent characteristics that allow them to disregard management attitude. Even in companies that have never been a takeover target, shareholders benefit from a takeover market, as potential attackers and threats of takeover force management to strive to improve operating performance, which in turn drives up the company's share price. The unqualified approbation of takeovers and hostile takeovers held by these two scholars serves as the theoretical basis for their argument that legislation and executive management should be permissive to M&A activity. However, the disciplinary theory also has some important flaws, for example, it's difficult to explain why the former management of the target enterprise is retained in some acquisitions of giant companies, and it's even more ineffective in explaining management buy-outs.

9.2.1.2 Ansoff's Synergy Theory

Ansoff (1965), a scholar of strategic management, was the first to introduce synergies into M&A research, believing that synergies may exist in the operation, investment, or management activities of enterprises (Campbell & Lukes, 2000) and that the emergence of a hostile takeover may be unrelated to the low performance of the target company's management, and the premium paid by the acquirer is the result of synergies it achieves with the target enterprise in all aspects of management, operation, and finance. In other words, some tangible or intangible assets owned by the target enterprise may be of unique value to the acquirer, and when the assets of the acquirer and the target enterprise are integrated, the value generated will be much greater than the value of the assets when the assets are separated, or even exceed the premium. However, questions have also been raised about: (1) The difference between a hostile takeover and a benign merger cannot be explained; in other words, why would an acquirer initiate a hostile takeover when both can generate synergies? Or why would the target company's management not accept a benign merger? (Easterbrook & Fischel, 1991) (2) Whether synergies exist. Serovo (2001) shows the conclusion that "most of the so-called synergies are just a disguise of a dangerous trap" by analyzing the pressure of M&A premium.

In reality, there are indeed many M&A that pre-declare the existence of synergy (Weston, 2000). Michael Porter, a proponent of synergy, argues that "the main reason for synergy failure is that companies fail to understand it and correctly implement it, rather than the concept itself is flawed" (Campbell & Lukes, 2000). However, even if we agree with Porter, the difficulties in measuring synergy give us reason to believe that it is not a perfect concept.

9.2.1.3 Leibenstein's Theory of X-inefficiency

Leibenstein (1966) studied the inefficiency of resource allocation within firms and introduced the concept of so-called "X-efficiency". He pointed out that protection from competitive pressure not only leads to inefficiencies in resource allocation at the market level but also generates X-inefficiencies at the enterprise level, i.e., companies that are protected from competitive pressures have significantly higher unit production costs. Leibenstein found through a large number of studies that the X-inefficiency in the allocation of internal resources in an enterprise is largely attributable to human factors within the enterprise, that is, human bounded rationality, human response to the objective environment, human effort, etc., while entrepreneurs, in turn, are at the top of the coordination mechanism of enterprises and their behavior will affect the efficiency of resource allocation to the greatest extent. Therefore, entrepreneurial dynamics play an extremely important role in reducing X-inefficiency. In this case, Leibenstein proposed two ways to reduce X-inefficiency within the enterprise: first, to establish a talent mobility mechanism, so that people with specialized talents can direct the allocation of enterprise resources; second, to establish an incentive and restraint mechanism to influence the behavior of managers who have been given the power to allocate resources, so that they can form an incentive or pressure to reduce X-inefficiency. And the existence of the corporate control market not only provides an incentive for corporate management (due to the threat of takeover) but also provides a last resort for the replacement of corporate managers with more severe X-inefficiency. Leibenstein's X-inefficient theory is essentially the same as disciplinary theory of Manne et al., and the X that Leibenstein could not explain in detail in 1966 may be largely the agency problem proposed by Jensen and Meckling (1976). Thus, the flaws of this theory are as described above.

9.2.1.4 Jensen's Free Cash Flow Hypothesis

Jensen (1986, 1988) introduced the concept of "free cash flow (FCF)" to explain the conflict between management and shareholders when the company has a large amount of cash flow and the agency costs it entails, defining FCF as the portion of a firm's cash that exceeds the amount needed to finance all projects which $NPV > 0$ discounted by the associated cost of capital. Jensen argues that if the firm is efficient and wants to maximize value, this cash flow should be distributed to shareholders. The distribution of FCF will help reduce the scale of resources under management's control, thereby reducing agency costs. When the company needs funds again, the management has to raise funds through the capital market, which makes it subject to the supervision and restriction of the capital market to a greater extent. However, in reality, management often does not distribute FCF to shareholders for personal self-interest, preferring to invest it in low-yield projects, which may trigger the takeover(sale) of the company when the firm's internal control system does not effectively address this issue. From this perspective, Jensen boldly regarded leveraged buyouts (LBOs) as an important innovation in corporate governance. Jensen (1989) even asserts that "these debt-ridden companies with a high concentration of equity will run better than traditional companies".

Harford and Hall (1997) found that cash-rich companies are more likely to engage in the acquisition, while cash-richness can be a valuable predictor of the probability of being acquired, thus strongly supporting the free cash flow theory. Table 9.1 shows that cash-rich companies have higher probabilities of starting acquisitions, increasing acquisitions, and making large-scale acquisitions than other companies.

Unfortunately, Copel and Lee's (1988) study contradicts Jensen's theory by finding that the companies that swap debt for equity to increase leverage are precisely growth companies (with zero or negative free cash flow), whereas Jensen declares that such companies do not need to swap debt for equity to ensure future cash outlays. Servaes' (1994) study using a sample of 700 target enterprises in the US also found no evidence of systematic overinvestment, thus further contradicting the free cash flow theory. Liu Wentong (1997) argues that using the method of increasing liabilities to restrain management's behavior may itself increase the risk of the enterprise and that this approach, even if effective for some industries (such as the petrochemical industry used by Jensen's study), may not be feasible for other industries. Pinkowitz's

Table 9.1 Acquisition characterization of cash-rich companies

Project	The market value of equity (RMB million)	Market value/ book value	Leverage ratio	Cash/ sales	Acquisition start	Acquisition add	Large-scale acquisition
Cash-rich companies	961.224	1.754	0.306	0.259	0.136	0.226	0.073
Other companies	1,204.916	1.658	0.317	0.098	0.102	0.178	0.038

Notes (1) Leverage ratio = book value of debt/(market value of equity + book value of debt);
(2) Large-scale acquisition refers to acquisitions whose value is greater than 1/10 of the acquirer's assets.
Source Quoted from Liu Shengjun. On the Corporate Governance Effects of Takeovers. Doctoral Dissertation of East China Normal University. 2001

(1999) doctoral dissertation reached the opposite conclusion from Harford and Hall's (1997).

9.2.1.5 Williamson's Theory of Corporate Governance Structure

Williamson (1988) proposed the doctrine of corporate governance structure, arguing that bonds and stocks are best viewed as different governance structures: bonds are governance structures designed by treaty, called "rule-based governance", while stocks are governance structures that allow certain rights of disposal, called "discretionary governance". At the same time, Williamson also summarizes the various roles of liabilities, including the controlling role of Grossman and Hart (1982) and Jensen (1986), and supports Jensen's view of "leveraged buyout as a tool to restrain management's discretionary power", except that Williamson "considers the problem from an asset perspective rather than a cash flow perspective, which is not contradictory". In short, the corporate governance structure theory regards the corporate control market as an external control force to improve the corporate governance structure, but whether internal or external governance is better or worse is precisely the focus of confusion and debate among many financial economists.

9.2.1.6 Parel Pelikan's Evolutionary Theory

Parel Pelikan (1989) extended Alchian's (1950) evolutionary analysis of product markets to capital markets in his article Evolution, Economic Competition, and the Market for Corporate Control by showing that the corporate control market connects the configuration of two key economic competencies into a closed circle by creating a two-way choice between operators and owners, which enhances the social dynamic efficiency. He argues that incumbent managers, directors, and capital owners do not always have optimal economic competence, and the corporate control market can eliminate such inefficiency and that while the corporate control market also has failures, they should be further facilitated (rather than hindered) by rulemaking. Thus, although the corporate control market itself may be costly, its social value lies in its role as an evolutionary tool that improves the economic competitiveness of other resource allocations. This view still does not jump out of the circle of the punishment theory and X-inefficient theory.

9.2.1.7 Roe's Political Theory

Mark. J. Roe pioneered the political theory of takeover in his book *Strong Managers, Weak Owners* (1999), which opened up the study of the market for corporate control. Roe argues that American democracy has affected American finance, which in turn has affected American corporate structure, which has created the current governance model of predominantly external governance. It is the deliberate weakening and dismantling of institutions and organizations because of Americans' deep aversion to a dictatorship that ultimately led to the formation of decentralized ownership structures, prompting strong management and fostering an active market for corporate control. Here Roe analyzes the role of cultural factors in the formation of the corporate control market, thus providing a new explanation for the corporate control market theory.

9.2.1.8 Norvald Instefjord's Agency Paradigm Model

Norvald Instefjord (2001), in Corporate Control Markets and the Agency Paradigm, established a model to analyze the characteristics of takeover behavior driven by the agency paradigm. He argues that there are two paradigms to explain takeovers behavior: the first is "corporate restructuring paradigm" restructuring, in which the market for corporate control is regarded as a mechanism for corporate restructuring or synergies; the second is the "agency paradigm", which is the takeover behavior caused by agency conflicts, including the "constraint effect" and the "hubris effect". The shortcomings of existing models, such as the Grossman and Hart (1980) and Scharfstein (1988) models, are discussed based on the assumption that corporate restructuring generates absolute positive value, and once this assumption is not valid, the assumption that takeovers can create value is not valid either. Therefore, Instefjord uses a new model and assumes that corporate restructuring is value-free, thereby defining the transfer of corporate control as a takeover that occurs independently of the assumption that there is value in corporate restructuring, and thus concludes that takeovers can create value for shareholders even without the benefits of corporate restructuring. He emphasized that, in general, the investment process of companies involved in M&A is more effective than those not involved in M&A, which is contrary to Jensen's free cash flow theory. The reason why takeovers bring value to shareholders in the absence of corporate restructuring gains is that "wealth creation is manifested in the form of reduced agency costs", i.e., the corporate control market generally has a "constraint effect" on corporate managers (takeover threat). The negative performance of post-merger companies, which contradicts the "corporate restructuring paradigm", is consistent with the new model of the "agency paradigm", which compensates for the shortcomings of the existing "corporate restructuring paradigm" and forms an empirical study. Thus, Instefjord argues that doubts about takeover behavior are not necessarily correct if they are simply because synergies are not reflected on paper, as in Treynor (1993).

9.2.2 Counter-Mainstream Theories of the Corporate Control Markets

With the development of the mainstream theories of corporate control markets, the voice of doubt has never ceased. In particular, the "second wave of anti-takeover legislation" in the US in the late 1980s brought a strong challenge to the mainstream theory of corporate control markets from the legal profession and practice.

9.2.2.1 Mueller's Theory of Managerialism

Mueller (1969) believes that acquisition may not be a recipe for agency problems, but rather a manifestation of them. He assumes that managers' compensation is an increasing function of the size of the company, and thus believes that managers have the motivation to expand the size of the company (i.e., build a management empire) while demanding only a lower rate of return on investment, and uses this argument to explain the hybrid M&A that prevailed in the 1960s. But Lewellen and Huntsman (1970) criticize the basic premise of this theory, arguing that empirical results show that managers' compensation has no significant correlation with a firm's sales, but is highly correlated with a firm's profitability.

9.2.2.2 Roll's Arrogance Hypothesis

Roll (1986) argues that the takeover premium is just an error, a mistake made by bidders in their valuation. The arrogance hypothesis assumes that markets are efficient, that stock prices reflect all information, that reallocation of productive resources cannot bring abnormal returns, and that new value cannot be created through reorganizations and mergers among firms. The flaw in this theory may be that the market is not efficient and it is the existence of transaction costs and information asymmetries that create the possibility of undervaluation of firms, and it is also true that the ability to create value varies between managers of different firms, so that it is possible to create new value through M&A. Most companies pursue short-term profit maximization, while companies that make long-term investments have low evaluations, resulting in such companies' stock prices falling and becoming targets of takeovers.

9.2.2.3 Masulis et al.'s Exploitative Stakeholder Theory

The so-called exploitative stakeholder theories are a set of theories. Scholars who hold these views believe that the existence of a market for corporate control will bring extraordinary returns to target company shareholders, but that such extraordinary returns are based on the exploitation of other corporate stakeholders rather than value creation. Masulis (1980) first discovered that the exchange of debt and common stock may lead to a decrease in the value of non-convertible bonds. Based on this, he proposed that the target enterprise's shareholder returns come from wealth redistribution. McDaniel's (1986) study further supports this view, which has caused widespread debate in economics and legal circles. Shleifer and Summers (1988) believed that considering the specificity of employees' human capital, to attract employees to work unreservedly, in fact, every company has an implied term for its employees that the company will treat its employees fairly every conscientious employee, and the existence of the acquisition breaks this term, resulting in the exploitation of the target enterprise's employees. Other scholars argue that extraordinary post-merger returns come from tax benefits and interest deductions.

As with other theories, mainstream scholars have refuted the "exploitative stakeholder theories". Coffee (1988) pointed out: "In the process of M&A, the loss of stakeholders is far smaller than the premium obtained by shareholders, and it is difficult to think that the excess premium is obtained from the exploitation of stakeholders". Asquith and King (1982) reported that the average returns on bonds of the merged firm and the merging firm were 0.495% and – 0.178%, respectively, after the announcement of the merger proposal, and none of the tests proved that the bondholders involved in the M&A gained or lost anything in the merger, nor was there any evidence of wealth transfer between shareholders and bondholders (Shen Yifeng, 2000). The statistics of Romano (1992) prove that after the hostile takeover is completed, the welfare level of the target enterprise's employees, on the whole, does not decline but increases. Auerbach and Reishaus (1987) also proved that, during 1968–1983, most large-scale M&A did not generate tax benefits for shareholders. And Jensen, Kaplan and Stiglin (1989) even demonstrated that "leveraged buyouts increased the present value of federal tax revenues by 61% under the 1986 US Tax Code".

9.2.2.4 Matin's Theory of Exploitation of Shareholders of Target Enterprises

Matin (1988) argues that a "two-tier bid" is used by the acquirer party to obtain a controlling share in a target enterprise, in which the offeror acquires 51% of the enterprise's shares at a higher than market price and then acquires the remaining 49% at a very low price, averaging the two, so that the total offer price of the offeror is lower than the true price of the target enterprise's stock. And in this kind of acquisition, the shareholders of the target enterprise face the so-called "prisoner's dilemma", that is, they have to scramble to sell their shares to the offeror to avoid the disadvantage of a second-stage takeover, so the exploitation is even more pronounced. However, Jensen (1993), interpreting Grossman and Hart (1980), argues that in fact "price discrimination" mechanism adopted by M&A against shareholders who sell first and sell later is conducive to overcoming the free-rider psychology of small and medium shareholders, so that the takeover can play its due role, incentivizing management to maximize shareholder wealth. Esaterbrook and Fischel (1991) also believed that "precisely because the design of this system ('two-tier bid') is conducive to the success of efficient acquisitions, it should also be efficient". As Tang Xin (2003) remarked, the "true price" of the target company's stock itself is a very vague concept, at least it has not been realized, so the offeror's acquisition of a non-existent "exploitative amount" cannot be called "exploitation"; if there is a "true price", the shareholders of the target company can completely reject the offeror's take-over offer and pursue that true price (such as making a self-acquisition, or accepting bids from risk arbitrageurs), thus leading to the failure of the previous acquisition; even in a two-tier bid, there may be bidding situations where the offeror must ensure that its bid is higher than the true price of the target company's stock to ensure a successful acquisition. For the two-tier bid, scholars who favor corporate takeovers argue that it is inherently efficient because it facilitates the success of an efficient takeover.

9.2.2.5 Brickley's Short-Sighted Market Theory

Brickley et al. (1988) believe that the market for corporate control is short-sighted, because, in the market for corporate control, most companies pursue short-term profit maximization, while companies that make long-term investments are poorly evaluated, causing the stock prices of such firms to fall and became the subject of a takeover. However, Romano (1992) empirically found the opposite results, arguing that (1) the stock market usually has a positive attitude towards long-term R&D projects, and the stock price of companies that announce R&D plans generally rises; (2) companies taking anti-takeover measures instead spend less on R&D; (3) there is no significant difference in the growth of R&D investment between M&A and non-M&A companies. Ma (2001) also proved in his doctoral dissertation that "managers who are interested in maintaining control may prefer long-term investments because the high uncertainty associated with these investments increases the expected takeover price and therefore reduces the likelihood of takeover". He argues that this finding differs markedly from the extant theoretical conclusion that takeover pressure leads to short-term behavior.

In conclusion, from the perspective of the existing literature, the mainstream theory of the corporate control market emerged in the 1960s, gradually occupied the dominance of academia from the 1970s, and reached its peak in the 1980s. However, the anti-mainstream questioning never ceased, and the "second anti-takeover legislation wave" from the late 1980s to the early 1990s dealt a heavy blow to the mainstream theory. In the mid and late 1990s, the mainstream theories showed signs of rising again, especially the great development of corporate governance theory, which also provided a good stage for the mainstream theories of corporate control market to focus on external governance. Overall, this mainstream vs. anti-mainstream debate is far from over. The results of its debate will undoubtedly play an important reference role in how other countries (including China) determine their respective corporate control market development strategies.

9.2.3 Research on the Market Theory of Corporate Control in China

9.2.3.1 Liu Wentong's Hypothesis of Quasi-Merger of State-Owned Enterprises

Liu Wentong (1997) put forward the quasi-merger hypothesis of state-owned enterprises in his doctoral dissertation, arguing that on the one hand, the residual income of state-owned enterprises is divided between the central and local governments, and on the other hand, the residual control rights of state-owned enterprises are also in different parties. Therefore, the residual claim rights and residual control rights of Chinese state-owned enterprises are separated. The administrative hierarchical structure of state-owned property rights of "all people—the central government—local governments—state-owned enterprises" has led to the fact that the property rights transactions between state-owned enterprises did not lead to the flow of property rights in the final sense so that the M&A among state-owned enterprises lost the characteristics of enterprise M&A in the true sense, and correspondingly brought poor M&A performance. In this regard, he called it the "quasi-merger hypothesis of state-owned enterprises". However, he has not yet distinguished the similarities and differences between the M&A behaviors of Chinese listed companies and non-listed companies, and has not seen the alienation of listed companies' behavior due to market segmentation, but has only given a general explanation using the theory of property rights and corporate M&A. Moreover, he has not adopted the empirical evidence to prove the correctness of this explanation.

9.2.3.2 Sheng Hong,s Theory of Property Rights Barriers

Sheng Hong (1997) pointed out that the M&A activities of Chinese enterprises face three obstacles: First, it is difficult to find out who is the real negotiator. Enterprise managers, heads of competent departments, and even leaders at different levels of government are only agents of state-owned property rights, so in M&A practice, it is often awkward to know who to approach for negotiations, or if negotiations do begin, they face great uncertainty because of different opinions from various departments. Second, the implicit lifetime employment contracts of state-owned enterprises for employees and the employment rate requirements set by the government for social stability often make it difficult for the new owners of the companies to handle the placement of personnel after M&A. Third, the problems of "risk aversion" and "rent-seeking" in the process of selling state-owned assets are difficult to solve, especially if the agent of state-owned assets is risk-averse, then, to avoid the notoriety of losing state-owned assets, the agent is likely to exclude non-state-owned enterprises from the negotiations, thus leading to the "second-best choice" of property rights transactions. Sheng Hong's theory of property rights barriers is a good explanation of the difficulties faced by state-owned enterprises in general M&A. Like Liu Wentong, Sheng Hong has not yet been involved in the control market of Chinese listed companies, and his analysis and judgment on M&A of Chinese companies, or the market for control of Chinese companies, is still incomplete.

9.2.3.3 Zhang Daohong et al.'s Theory of Shell Resource Utilization

Zhang Daohong et al. (2002) believed that "from the perspective of economics, the utilization of shell resources is essentially an activity of the capital market to reconfigure shell resources of listed companies, and it is a Pareto improvement. Shell resource utilization has great practical significance in China, which can improve the quality of listed companies and promote the healthy development of the capital market; it can also effectively expand the scale of enterprises and truly establish a standardized corporate governance structure; it can also broaden the financing channels of enterprises." Zhang Daohong et al. used a lot of space to demonstrate the shadow price of Chinese listed companies' shell resources, the game pricing model, the quality fuzzy clustering evaluation model (taking listed companies in Shaanxi Province as an example), the attributes and efficiency of shell resources, etc., but in the process of their argumentation, they fail to consider the current situation of equity separation of Chinese listed companies, only simply substitute the characteristics and models of mature markets into the Chinese reality. Their analysis of the special causes of underperforming shell resources in China only considers the "low quality of listed companies" caused by historical reasons and believes that "administrative intervention is an important reason for the formation of shell companies", but at the same time, they also believes that, as a "strong government during the transition period", administrative intervention can improve the performance of the capital market.

9.2.3.4 Zhu Xiaosheng's Over-The-Counter Agreement Acquisition Can Solve the Problem of Reduction of State-Owned Shares

In his doctoral. dissertation Efficiency Analysis of Corporate Control Transfer, Zhu Xiaosheng (2002) demonstrated the efficiency of corporate control transfer under both centralized and decentralized ownership structures through rigorous mathematical derivation, and concluded that "centralized ownership structure is better than decentralized ownership structure in promoting efficient corporate control transfer; but decentralized ownership structure is better than centralized ownership structure in preventing inefficient corporate control transfer ". However, because Zhu ignores the inherent role of market segmentation in China's corporate control market, Zhu believes that "the high concentration of state-owned shares and state-owned legal person shares of listed companies is the internal source that restricts the efficiency of the transfer of control rights of Chinese companies", thus obtaining the "the problem of reducing state-owned shares in China can be solved by transferring state-owned shares to non-state-owned enterprises with good development prospects and business performance".

9.2.3.5 Zhang Xin's Hypothesis of Value Transfer and Redistribution Under Institutional Factors

In 2002, Zhang Xin argued in the Shanghai Stock Exchange joint project Value Creation, Financial System, and Economic Growth and his article Administrative Measures for the Acquisition of Listed Companies: Value Orientation and Operational Process published in *New Fortune* that "since China is in transition, there is still a lot of room for improving economic efficiency, and there are obvious directions for improving the industrial structure, it is easier for acquirers to find undervalued companies to acquire and potential industries to restructure their main business, so (M&A in China) should be able to create value". At the same time, he collected 1,176 cases of M&A from 1990 to June 2002 for empirical research, and the conclusions supported his hypothesis. Zhang Xin's point of view has changed. In 2003, in his other Shanghai Stock Exchange joint project Whether M&A and Restructuring Create Value: Theoretical and Empirical Study of China's Securities Market and his article of the same name published in *Economic Research Journal*, he further stated that "the classical theory of M&A motivation has some explanatory power for the Chinese phenomenon … but 'the hypothesis of value transfer and redistribution under institutional factors better explains why M&A in China do not create net social value". In the article, Zhang Xin analyzed in detail the relationship between the interested parties involved in the M&A transactions of Chinese listed companies, insisting that China's M&A and reorganization "can indeed bring value to the transaction parties", but the sources of value may exist in two aspects: (1) the restructured company has produced incremental benefits by improving the efficiency of operation and management and exerting synergistic effects, improving performance, and creating value for shareholders and stakeholders; (2) the acquirer/reorganizer seeks compensation from primary market refinancing or secondary market stock speculation, which mainly comes from future small and medium shareholders. Therefore, this M&A is a "zero-sum" game of wealth redistribution. Compared with rigorous empirical research, his theoretical analysis of the "hypothesis of value transfer and redistribution under institutional factors" is slightly insufficient, and the core content of "institutional factors" is unclear.

When considering the interests of small and medium shareholders, with the in-depth study of the ownership structure, scholars have found that the relatively concentrated ownership structure causes the agency problem to gradually shift from the conflict of interests between management and shareholders to the conflict of interests between controlling shareholders and other small and medium shareholders. Especially within the pyramid-structured group, due to the separation of the ultimate controlling shareholder's cash flow rights and control rights over the listed company, the ultimate controlling shareholder has the motivation (small cash flow rights) and the ability (substantial control) to encroach on the resources of the listed company through related transactions and equity transfers, which harm the interests of other small and medium shareholders (Yu Jiang et al., 2014).

9.2.3.6 Wu Xiaoqiu's Speculative Restructuring Theory

Wu Xiaoqiu's views are also gradually evolving. In April 2003, in his book *China's Listed Companies: Capital Structure and Corporate Governance*, he mainly focused on the relationship between financing methods, capital structure, and corporate governance, and did not deal much with the issue of corporate control market. However, at the Global M&A Summit Forum jointly held by the State-owned Assets Supervision and Administration Commission of China and the United Nations Industrial Development Organization on November 20, 2003, he put forward the "speculative restructuring theory" of Chinese listed companies, arguing that "speculative restructuring is an important feature of M&A restructuring under China's special shareholding structure", and the financial risks it may bring are: firstly, it will harm the interests of shareholders in circulation and cause a crisis of confidence in the market; secondly, it will not help to improve the management level and undermine the function of industrial integration; thirdly, the asset price will rise and fall sharply and damage the stability of the financial market.

9.3 Analysis of Corporate Control Models in Various Countries

9.3.1 Market-Oriented Control Markets in the United States

If divided by the occurrence of control transfer transactions rather than by the time when the concept was proposed, the corporate control market in the US should have formed in the late eighteenth century and experienced five "waves" of frequent control transactions in the twentieth century. Early American economists viewed the growth of companies like Standard Oil, US Steel, and DuPont through acquisitions as a natural and helpful process for economic efficiency. For most of the twentieth century, the US government and public attention to corporate control transactions focused on the interplay of monopoly and economies of scale, and the introduction of a series of laws, such as the famous Sherman Antitrust Act of 1890, which reflected the focus of attention on control transaction behavior at the time. By the 1950s, academic attention had turned to M&A strategies, financial issues, and restrictions on managerial privilege. From the 1960s, the economic literature had moved beyond the monopoly to examine the transfer of corporate control, including the implementation of corporate strategy, the realization of financial synergies, the satisfaction of management's desires, etc. From the 1970s, hostile takeovers began to flourish in the US and were booming throughout the 1980s, with 364 hostile takeovers in the US between 1976 and 1990 alone (Jensen, 1992), and a large number of"corporate raiders" were keen to make hostile takeover bids. It's on the academic research of the 1950s and 1960s. But since the 1990s, hostile takeovers in the once volatile US market for control have declined dramatically until the end of the twentieth century, when the so-called fifth wave, with record transaction volumes, was seen as "an evolution from barbarism to civilization" due to the gradual "financial to strategic transformation" of M&A.

In addition, the shareholding structure of American companies is relatively scattered. From the perspective of the number of natural shareholders, the proportion of the total population has risen from 4% in 1952 to 14% in 1992, and if the number of indirect stockholders is added, this share will reach about 60%, and the amount of their shareholdings also occupies a considerable proportion. The shareholding structure of American companies shows the following outstanding characteristics: first, the shareholding is relatively scattered, and the proportion of individual family shares is relatively large, especially under the individual property rights system, the shareholding of any enterprise can be specifically reflected in each natural person; second, institutional shareholding is mainly dominated by non-bank financial institutions such as mutual funds, pension funds, and insurance companies, and direct shareholding of commercial banks is restricted by law restrictions, at the same time, the proportion of mutual shareholding between corporate companies is smaller; third, it can be seen from the shareholding structure of American companies that because companies, institutions, and individuals are less constrained by each other, the market for corporate control is easier to form and play a role.

The early American legislation on the corporate control market mainly focused on opposing various forms of monopoly and the US sense of fairness and freedom was well implemented in the legislation in many acts. Among them, the securities laws of 1933 and 1934 in the US have the most stipulations on the trading behavior in the market of corporate control, which established the basic development framework of the market of corporate control in the US. After the emergence of a large number of listed companies, part or all of the company's ownership has been transferred to the public. Therefore, legislation is bound to place more emphasis on safeguarding the legitimate interests of the public as business owners. In this regard, the US legislation on public takeovers mainly emphasizes two principles: the principle of full disclosure and the principle of equal treatment of shareholders.

Individual liberalism is the most representative core of American culture, which is also the common view of philosophers after research. Yu Hongjun (1997) summed it up as "Christian culture with individual liberalism as the core". The trend of economic liberalism nurtured by the cultural background is bound to run through the main feature of survival of the fittest, making competition among enterprises a common phenomenon and driving force for development in society, and creating a uniquely American environment conducive to corporate control of market transactions.

9.3.2 Institution-Oriented Control Markets in Japan

Although Japan's corporate control market is not very active, M&A had a long history in Japan. Yoshihiko (2003) argues that Japan's earliest M&A began in 1874 during the Meiji Restoration when a huge zaibatsu purchased a mining company from the government and turned it into the coal industry. Since then, M&A activities run by this zaibatsu and other zaibatsu have gradually shifted from coal mining to steel, textiles, electronic machinery, and even personal accident insurance, which constituted the prosperity of these chaebols and the Japanese economy before World War II.

After World War II, the general headquarters of the allied forces in Japan forcibly dissolved the Japanese zaibatsu and sought to Americanize the Japanese corporate governance model by implementing measures to democratize the economy and achieve public shareholding, supplemented by employee ownership. However, due to the subsequent depression of the Japanese stock market and the efforts of managers to prevent control by outsiders, as well as the apparent conflict between the visions of the general headquarters and the Japanese government in various aspects of corporate ownership structure, institutional investor shareholding, and corporate financing structure, gradually led to the formation of a bank-centered corporate group governance model featuring mutual shareholding among related companies, especially the mutual shareholding between former zaibatsu companies developed rapidly during 1949–1955 (Miyajima, 1994, 1995), after that, the funds needed by Japanese companies were no longer obtained from the stock market, but mainly provided by their "main banks", and this mutual shareholding and "main bank" system somewhat curbed the development of the control market for Japanese firms (Reed, 1996).

In Japan, this "main bank" system worked quite well for a time. Once a company is in financial difficulty, the main bank will often prompt its other customers or assist in person, usually without letting the company go bankrupt. At the same time, mergers between companies are very rare, and if there are, they are often led by the main bank, through negotiation and stock exchange to achieve the goal, hostile takeovers are few and far between. However, because Japanese main banks do not always support companies based on efficiency, corporate mergers led by the main banks are more about rescuing the target company from financial distress, and thus such support can be sustained when their economic strength is large enough, but during the continued weakness of the Japanese economy in the 1990s, the main bank system was strongly challenged because the banks itself was also at risk.

Since the 1990s, the Japanese government has begun to adjust relevant policies through the reform of the legal and taxation systems to promote rational M&A activity and the development of the market for corporate control. These reforms included the lifting of the ban on purely shareholding companies in 1997; the start of allowing share exchanges and transfers in 1999; the introduction of a share split system in 2000; and the relaxation of the use of authorized capital funds related to new share purchases and the introduction of tax incentives policies designed to encourage corporate restructuring in 2001. At the same time, Bankruptcy Law of Japan, which refers to that of the US, also came into effect in April 2000, providing a strong impetus for the rapid growth of Japan's M&A activities in recent years (Yoshihiko, 2003).

The biggest feature of the shareholding structure of Japanese companies is the mutual shareholding between legal persons. Before World War II, the economy was dominated by the zaibatsu. After World War II, there was a shift from zaibatsu families to diversified entities such as business corporations, governments, financial institutions, and individuals. Since the 1950s, the current phase of mutual shareholding among legal persons began.

From the perspective of Japan's legal environment, Japanese legislators have experienced a process from discouraging or even restricting the corporate control market, to gradually relaxing and promoting the corporate control market to a certain extent, which is consistent with the entire Japanese society, which is in line with the development of the whole Japanese society and economy in the second half of the last century.

9.3.3 *Family-Governed Control Market in the Republic of Korea*

Although the Republic of Korea adopted a government-led economic development model from the early 1960s and became one of the "Four Little Dragons" in Asia and a newly industrialized country in just two to three decades, the family-oriented nature of companies of the Republic of Korea is still its main characteristic: On the one hand, the influence of family capital is everywhere, not only small and medium-sized enterprises are owned by families or individuals, but even many large consortiums are often directly or indirectly controlled by a certain family. This control usually takes two forms: one is that the family directly controls the subordinate enterprises; the other is that the family realizes indirect control by controlling core companies and non-profit consortiums, which makes the management model of companies of the Republic of Korea mainly show a highly centralized model. On the other hand, to expand family interests, large family-owned conglomerates always try to expand themselves and crowd out other small and medium-sized enterprises. The market for corporate control has not been active enough in the Republic of Korea. Due to the influence of family businesses and the lag of the stock market, it is difficult to directly acquire the Republic of Korea (including acquisitions between Korea) in the securities market through tender offers and other means. In terms of financing, companies of the Republic of Korea rely more on indirect financing from banks; in terms of corporate governance, companies of the Republic of Korea also rely more on family internal monitoring. Only after the Asian financial crisis in 1997 did the acquisition of companies of the Republic of Korea become a reality and fashion due to the rupture of the capital chain and the increase of companies on the verge of bankruptcy.

Although the promoter families of companies of the Republic of Korea do not hold a high percentage of shares, they often control another 30%-40% of the company's shares through cross-shareholdings and other means, so the controlling shareholders often serve as the company's general manager and have the right to choose the executive directors, thus establishing a relatively strong base of control.

The ratio of own capital of companies of the Republic of Korea is very low, with the average ratio of own capital of the top 10 listed companies being 9.4% and nearly half of them having less than 5%, which naturally corresponds to the generally high debt ratio of companies. On the one hand, it reflects that the government of the Republic of Korea has indeed provided many favorable lending conditions so that the cost of debt management is much lower than the cost of own capital; on the other hand, the transitional debt financing will also bring very high operating and financial risk to enterprises, at the same time, reduces enterprise value and increases the risk and difficulty of M&A.

Corporate culture of the Republic of Korea is highlighted by the following five characteristics: (1) emphasis on personal integrity; (2) pride in being loyal to the company; (3) strong hierarchy concept; (4) emphasis on special relationships such as blood, geographical, and academic relationships; (5) emphasis on long-term training and education of employees, etc. (Wu Shukun, 2001). This corporate culture has its unique characteristics not only in operation, but also in internal control, social atmosphere, and interpersonal relationships. However, corporate culture of the Republic of Korea inevitably has many negative effects, some of which may be quite serious. For example, overemphasizing academic, geographical and blood relationships to various factions and "party struggles" in the enterprise; overemphasizing loyalty to the enterprise is not conducive to the rational flow and allocation of talents; overemphasizing the concept of hierarchy is not conducive to talents standing out; overemphasizing on the reverence and authority of entrepreneurs, it is difficult to form innovative ideas, etc. The survival of an enterprise is entirely dependent on the "core" wisdom, which is prone to deviations or extremes. After the financial crisis in 1997, the large number of bankruptcy of companies of the Republic of Korea companies is directly related to their capital structure, but at the same time, it is not unrelated to their business methods. Therefore, in the context of this corporate culture of "taking the factory as home" and "pulling together in times of trouble", both owners and employees feel deep shame about their companies being acquired, which greatly increases the difficulty of M&A and is not conducive to the development of the corporate control market.

9.3.4 Insider-Controlled Control Market in Russia

Strictly speaking, Russia does not have a complete market for corporate control. What it has is the transfer of corporate control in the process of institutional transition, that is, the nationwide privatization movement led by the Russian government after the collapse of the Soviet Union in 1990, which makes the control of state-owned enterprises transfer to other forms of ownership (especially private) in large quantities, resulting in transactions or gifting behavior regarding corporate control.

The privatization (transfer of corporate control) in Russia mainly adopts three methods: the first is to issue privatization vouchers to the public free of charge, which mainly exists in the first stage of the privatization process; the second is the direct sale of state-owned enterprises in various forms, which existed mainly in the second stage; and the third is the management buy-out and employee stock ownership plan that runs through the two stages, that is, the original management and employees of the state-owned enterprise become the new owner of the enterprise by subscribing for the shares of the enterprise. However, unlike the typical MBO and EBO methods in the UK and the US, Russia's MBO and EBO are large-scale "MBO movements" with the main purpose of withdrawing state-owned assets, which lack the necessary market environment, legal environment, and operational mechanisms, thus bringing great drawbacks. Among them, an important consequence is the formation of the enterprise's "insider control" situation.

The impact of "insider control" on the market for corporate control after the privatization campaign was significant. Because there is no set of good institutional guarantees, especially when the market environment is distorted and the prospects are uncertain, companies controlled by insiders are more likely to be "plundered" rather than "built", and even less likely to be a situation of "transferred", which shows that the company's financial situation has fallen sharply, and the company's control transactions are extremely inactive. Especially in the later stage of privatization, when free privatization is transformed into paid privatization, the right of employees to buy shares in the enterprise is actually, because when employees try to buy more shares over the limit, they were faced with a transaction price several hundred times higher than the original price. Take the Sverdlovsk region as an example. The state stipulates that the employees of the enterprise have the right to purchase 10% of the common stock of the statutory fund of the enterprise according to the asset valuation on July 1, 1992, but if they purchase the rest of the shares, they will be treated at 600 times higher than the original price(Yu Sinian & Cui Qiming, 1997). In this way, the control of ordinary employees over the enterprise is weakened, the management's con ability is correspondingly enhanced, and the company is more likely to be "plundered" and less easily transferred.

Later, the Russian government also learned from some Western experiences, and tried the merger and union of domestic enterprises, trying to take this as a new way to get rid of economic and financial difficulties. The main work is to form a financial-industrial group integrating financial and industrial functions through the union of banks and enterprises in more developed industries, such as energy, chemical, automobile, aviation, and shipbuilding, to achieve the optimal combination of capital, resources, and assets, etc. There are four main modes: the first is the "joint by the department" represented by Arhangus Shipbuilding Industry Group and Russian Aviation Industry Group; the second is the "joint by production process and distribution chain" represented by the Russian Textile Industry Group; the third is the "joint by region" represented by the Volga Valley Industrial Group and the Altai Jinsui Industrial Group; the fourth is the "cross-border union" that attracts the participation of foreign enterprises. However, due to the influence of "insider control" and other factors, this kind of union is either a kind of compulsory behavior of the government, or it will greatly increase the cost of a merger due to the existence of "insider". According to Brown (1996), "For Russian firms, if employees are not allowed to share ownership after a takeover when they have acquired a critical minority of shares, the takeover by outsiders can only result in inefficient changes in control; if they are allowed to share ownership, some efficient takeover activity is blocked."

During the transition economy period, the laws of Russia were quite confusing. The old laws of the planned economy period are no longer suitable for business practices after privatization, while the new laws are either difficult to implement, conflicting, or changing due to the uncertainty of government behavior, people's expectations were not adapted, and many people were short-sighted, and "frequently swapped transactions" and "one-time deal without long-term plan" deals are everywhere, resulting in more "looting" than "building" or "dealing" of businesses. It makes the transaction cost of the whole society very high, and the normal and market-based M&A between companies almost unsustainable.

Russia spans both Europe and Asia and combines the characteristics of Eastern and Western cultures, which is the most important unique feature of its cultural background. Berdyaev (1995), a famous Russian philosopher, once pointed out: "The contradiction and complexity of the Russian spirit are related to the collision of the two world-historical trends of the East and the West in Russia, in the interaction between them, the two elements of the Russian spirit are always competing with each other: authoritarianism and laissez-faire, state supremacy and anarchism, the tendency to violence and humane docility, a strong sense of individuality and impersonal collectivism, etc. ... often coexist in the depths of the Russian soul." The ideological confusion of the Russian people during the transition period and the current ideological status hesitant about reform have affected the development of the economy and the establishment of the market for corporate control.

A comparison of the four corporate control market models described above is shown in Table 9.2.

9.4 Analysis of China's Control Market

China's state-owned enterprises are naturally plagued by principal-agent problems and at the same time face an urgent need to improve control efficiency through recapitalization. The gradual marketization of the economic system has made the market system experience a development process from the simplest commodity market to the more advanced control market. The reform of state-owned enterprises, the marketization of the economic system, and the creation of the control market should logically be synchronized. However, the path dependence on institutional changes makes the development process of the corporate control market in China extremely difficult and the control market has taken a specific shape with many inefficient structural features (Wang Gangyi, 2003).

9.4.1 The Initial State of China's Control Market

After 1949, China established a socialist economic system with enterprises owned by the whole people as the main body. As many Chinese economists have pointed out, enterprises that are nominally owned by the whole people can only be controlled by the state (the central planner), and the way the state exercises control must be by assigning control to government officials at all levels. The most obvious feature that distinguishes state-owned enterprises from capitalist enterprises is that the principals of state-owned enterprises are the state rather than natural capitalists and that the government appoints, supervises, and disciplines managers and provides financing for enterprise projects. Due to the inherent flaws of the government as the administrator of the hierarchy system, the main problem of Chinese state-owned enterprises is the principal rather than the agent.

The huge difference between the principal-agent relationship of traditional state-owned enterprises and the principal-agent relationship of enterprises under market economy conditions determines that state-owned enterprises are not independent economic entities established based on contractual relationships, and there is not and cannot be a clear distinction between the ultimate control of property owners and the control of enterprise managers. There are agency problems in state-owned enterprises, but there is no differentiation of control rights in the sense of economic analysis, so the concept of residual control rights in contract theory cannot be used to explain corporate behavior. At the same time, the principal-agent relationship of

Table 9.2 Comparison of four corporate control market models

Corporate control market model	Historical changes	Shareholding structure	Legal environment	Cultural background	Affect the result
Market-oriented (the US)	Five “waves”	Individual shareholding	Full disclosure	Individualism	The market for corporate control is active
		↗	↗	↗	
Organization-oriented (Japan)	Progressively active	Cross-shareholding	Gradually relax	Collectivism	The market for corporate control is relatively active
		↘	↗	↘	
Family governance (the Republic of Korea)	Gradual development	Family holding	East mix West	Familism	The market for corporate control is inactive
		↘	→	↘	
Insider Control (Russia)	Privatization wave	Insider control	Legal “vacuum”	Contradiction and complexity	After the privatization wave, the market for corporate control is inactive
		↘	↘	→	

Source Gao Yuxiang. *Study on the Control Market of Chinese Listed Companies*. Beijing: Economic Press China. 2004

traditional state-owned enterprises will inevitably lead to an administrative allocation of enterprise control rights.

The agents at all levels of the enterprise are not equal contract subjects, but the relationship of administrative orders. The control of the enterprise may be disposed of by agents of different levels due to the size of the assets and the severity of the social problems involved. The division of control is not clearly defined as in modern joint-stock companies, and the division of control between agents at all levels is based on the division of real power at the administrative level. In the principal-agent relationship of state-owned enterprises, the manager, as a first-level agent, has certain control over the enterprise, but this control is an appendage of administrative control.

9.4.2 *The Development of China's Control Market*

Regarding the development stage of the corporate control market in China, there are several divisions, such as a three-stage division and a five-stage division. Among them, the research group Research on Enterprise Mergers and Bankruptcy (Zheng Haihang, 1997) is divided into three stages: the first stage is the administrative shutdown and transfer before the 1980s; the second stage is the semi-enterprise and semi-administrative joint M&A of enterprises at the early stage of enterprise reform; the third stage is the corporate M&A characterized by corporate form after the implementation of the market economy system. Zhang Qiusheng and Wang Dong (2001) used the five-stage division method to discuss the market of corporate control in China, namely the initial stage (1984–1987), the first climax of control transaction activities (1987–1989), the trough period of corporate control transaction activities (1989–1992), the second climax of control transaction activities (1992–1996), the third climax of control transaction activities (1997 to present).

Based on the development of China's corporate M&A practice, and referring to more mature research conclusions abroad, China's corporate control market is divided into three evolutionary stages: fully government-led, financial M&A, and strategic M&A.

9.4.2.1 The Stage of Fully Government-Led M&A for "Traversing the Difficult Position of State-Owned Enterprises" (1984–1992)[2]

The first M&A case took place in July 1984 when Baoding Textile Machinery Factory in Hebei Province merged with Baoding Knitting Equipment Factory by assuming

[2] Cui Yongmei. Research on the evolution of corporate control market based on ecology. Doctoral Dissertation of Beijing Jiaotong University, 2008.

all the debts and liabilities of the merged party. This is also the first case of corporate M&A among Chinese state-owned enterprises. Since then, the phenomenon of corporate M&A has appeared in other regions of China one after another.[3]

After 1987, the government issued a series of policies and regulations to encourage M&A. In January 1988, the State Council's Economic and Technological Social Development Research Center and the Wuhan municipal government jointly held the Seminar on the Reform of Enterprise Property Rights Transfer. In March of the same year, the Government Work Report passed at the First Session of the Seventh National People's Congress pointed out that it was necessary to "encourage enterprises to contract enterprises and lease enterprises" and "realize the conditional transfer of enterprise property rights for a fee" as two important measures to deepen enterprise reform. In May of the same year, Wuhan established the first enterprise property rights transfer market in China, making enterprise M&A on the track of formalization, publicity, and procedure. On February 19th, 1989, the State Commission for Restructuring Economy', the Ministry of Finance, and the State Administration of State-owned Assets jointly issued the Interim Measures on Enterprise Mergers, which stipulated the relevant content of enterprise mergers. At the same time, the Interim Measures for Selling the Property Rights of Small State-Owned Enterprises was jointly promulgated, pointing out: "selling the property rights of small state-owned enterprises in a planned and step-by-step manner is an important part of adjusting the ownership structure and deepening the reform of enterprises." Overall, this wave of enterprise M&A, as an attempt to reform state-owned enterprises, originated in enterprises, was recognized from the bottom up, and then promoted from the top down under the active advocacy of the central and local governments at all levels.

According to statistics from relevant departments, in 25 provinces, municipalities, autonomous regions, and 13 cities under separate state planning, 2,559 enterprises were merged in 1989 alone, transferring a total of more than RMB2 billion in assets, reducing 204 loss-making enterprises, and reducing losses by RMB130 million. Throughout the 1980s, 6,966 enterprises across the country were merged, transferring assets of RMB8.252 billion, reducing 4,095 loss-making enterprises and reducing losses by RMB522 million. In addition, property rights trading markets have also been established in Baoding, Nanjing, Fuzhou, Chengdu, and Shenzhen, which signifies that the corporate control market has entered a preliminary stage of standardization. Beginning in the second half of 1989, due to macroeconomic tightening and a shortage of corporate funds, the economy entered a stage of comprehensive governance and rectification. With the development of governance and rectification, loss-making enterprises increased. For this reason, the government increased its role in the transfer of property rights, administratively compulsory business mergers have

[3] In September 1984, Baoding Steel Window Factory bought Baoding Coal Ash Brick Factory for RMB1.1 million, which was the earliest record of collective enterprises merging with state-owned enterprises in China. In December 1984, Wuhan Milk Company bought Hankou Sports Restaurant for RMB120,000, which was an earlier case of state-owned enterprises merging with collective enterprises for a fee. By 1987, Wuhan and Baoding had each implemented different forms of paid transfer of property rights for more than 20 enterprises, and M&A of state-owned enterprises had also occurred in nine other cities, including Beijing and Shenyang.

appeared in some regions and the increase in mergers within the same region and sector with no compensation transfer.

During this period, the transaction activities of corporate control have the following characteristics: the number of corporate M&A was small. Corporate M&A activity was limited to a few companies in a few cities across the country. The spontaneity of transactions and government intervention coexisted. On the one hand, the expansion of the advantageous enterprises was restricted by sites, factories, and equipment, while the disadvantaged enterprises were suffering from long-term losses and debts, and the wages and benefits of employees were not guaranteed, so both parties had the motivation to merge. On the other hand, the government actively intervened in M&A activities as an owner, thus making most of the M&A actions in this period compulsory. Avoiding compartmentalization, M&As were conducted in the same region, industry, or sector. The government's involvement in M&A was motivated by the elimination of loss-making enterprises. Most of the M&As were debt-bearing and capital purchases. Among the 11 cases of property rights transfer in Baoding from 1984 to 1987, 6 cases were debt-bearing and 3 cases were capital purchases. In Wuhan, almost all the M&A cases were in the form of capital purchases.

9.4.2.2 The Financial M&A Stage Based on Reporting Restructuring and Shell Listing (1992–2005)[4]

In 1992, China's economy established the reform direction of the market economy, and property rights reform became the focus of state-owned enterprise reform. Property transactions have leaped forward in size and form. The establishment and improvement of the capital market have had a profound and long-term impact on the development of M&A of Chinese enterprises and promoted the evolution of mergers of enterprises to a deeper level. At this stage, with the development of the property rights market and the stock market, the forms of M&A in China have become more abundant, and the phenomenon of listed companies, foreign M&A of state-owned enterprises, and cross-border M&A of Chinese enterprises have appeared, marking the marketization and formalization of Chinese enterprise M&A.

On November 14th, 1993, the Third Plenary Session of the 14th CPC Central Committee passed the Decision of the Central Committee of the Communist Party of China on Several Issues Concerning the Establishment of a Socialist Market Economic System, pointing out: "Continuing to deepen the reform, we must solve the deep-seated contradictions and focus on innovation of the enterprise system." "According to the requirements of the modern enterprise system, the existing national industry head offices should be gradually reorganized into holding companies. Develop several large-scale enterprise groups across regions and industries with public ownership as the main body and property rights as the main link." "Generally small state-owned enterprises... can also be sold to collectives or individuals." In

[4] Cui Yongmei. Research on the evolution of corporate control market based on ecology. Doctoral dissertation of Beijing Jiaotong University, 2008.

1993, more than 2,900 enterprises in China were merged, with a turnover of more than RMB6 billion, and 240,000 workers were relocated.

Beginning in 1997, with the reform of China's investment system, the financing structure of enterprises has gradually shifted from relying on a single bank to raise debt to both indirect and direct financing. The securities market has become an important place for enterprises to obtain long-term financial support.

Corporate M&A and asset restructuring events in the securities market have seen a rapid upward trend. The number and transaction value of control rights transactions also showed an upward trend year by year.

According to the statistics of the Asian Business Research Center, from 1999 to 2001, there were more than 1,700 M&A of domestic enterprises in China, and the M&A involved reached RMB173 billion, including more than 400 listed companies, the amount of the M&A is about RMB90 billion. In 2014–2019, the compound annual growth rate of China's M&A transaction value has been 60%. The rapid growth of M&A transaction value indicates that China has become a major M&A country and one of the most active M&A markets in Asia. Despite the rapid growth of M&A transactions, a study by the Asian Business Research Center with a sample of 345 restructuring events shows that there is little industry correlation between enterprises in China's securities market for asset restructuring, although the impact of asset restructuring on distressed enterprises is higher than that on non-distressed enterprises, in general, the effect of restructuring on improving business performance is limited. This is because most domestic M&A in the past were not based on corporate strategy. Because the financial M&A of listed companies became the main form at that time due to the specific institutional environment and company development stage, 80% of listed companies'M&A are related to the acquisition of shell resources.

At this stage, it is difficult for the secondary market acquisition commonly used in foreign securities markets to achieve the holding goal. In this case, the transfer of unlisted state shares and legal person shares through agreement transfer, to gain control over listed companies, has become the most practical way to gain control of listed companies in China's stock market (see Table 9.3).

All in all, the evolution of corporate M&A in China in the modern sense is just the beginning, or, as some domestic scholars have said, is a kind of "quasi-merger" behavior (Liu Wentong, 1996), but the major impact of M&A on the establishment of China's market economic system is an indisputable fact.

9.4.2.3 The Stage of Strategic and Speculative M&A Focuses on Industrial Integration, Optimal Allocation of Resources, and Strengthening of Core Competitiveness (Since 2006)

In 2005, China started the share-trading reform of listed companies, and in 2006, the China Securities Regulatory Commission issued the Measures for the Administration of Mergers and Acquisitions of Listed Companies and Measures for the Administration of Disclosure of Equity Changes of Listed Companies, which fundamentally removed the obstacles that hindered China's listed companies from M&A, laying

Table 9.3 Overview of the means of transferring control of listed companies

M&A method		1997	1998	1999	2000	2001	2002
Free transfer	Quantity	7	18	30	27	25	29
	The proportion (%)	21.2	25.7	35.7	26.3	21.0	17.3
Judicial auction/court ruling	Quantity	0	0	1	3	14	10
	The proportion (%)	0	0	1.2	2.9	11.8	6.0
Agreement to purchase shares of listed companies	Quantity	26	47	46	68	70	104
	The proportion (%)	78.8	67.1	54.7	66.0	58.8	61.9
Buy equity in parent company	Quantity	0	4	5	2	4	11
	The proportion (%)	0	5.7	6.0	1.9	3.4	6.5
Parent company transformation	Quantity	0	1	2	2	6	14
	The proportion (%)	0	1.4	2.4	1.9	5.0	8.3

Source Cui Yongmei. Research on the evolution of corporate control market based on ecology. The Doctoral dissertation of Beijing Jiaotong University. 2008

the foundation for large-scale industrial integration. Strategic and speculative M&A characterized by industrial integration resource optimization and enhancement of core competitiveness will become the mainstream of the M&A market. At the end of 2007, China's share-trading reform was completed. Most of the shares of listed companies can be circulated, and there is a good internal basis for competing for company control. In addition, the revision of the Measures for the Administration of the Takeover of Listed Companies in 2006 also reduced the cost of the acquirer, created better external conditions for acquiring the control rights of listed companies through acquisition, and activated the market of corporate control rights in China. As an important external corporate governance mechanism, the corporate control rights market can, on the one hand, punish the hollowing behavior of controlling shareholders; on the other hand, this punitive effect is also affected by whether the company's internal articles of association have corresponding antagonistic clauses (Li Shanmin, 2016).

In recent years, China's industrial map is undergoing a far-reaching reorganization. The industrial integration based on the industrial value chain has been fully launched. International companies, large state-owned enterprise groups, and private enterprise groups have begun to compete head-on. It constitutes the three mainstream enterprises of China's industrial integration in the global economic environment. Mergers and acquisitions are no longer simply a means of restructuring state-owned enterprises, nor are they merely a means of low-cost expansion of private enterprises, but are based on the transformation and integration of the industrial value chain.

For corporate M&A, the motivation is an important issue. At present, the two basic environmental factors that Chinese enterprises are facing are industrial structure adjustment and integration and institutional changes. The low industrial concentration in China has created huge space and opportunities for industrial integration. Most strategic M&A refer to the M&A in the same industry or related industries that are strategically oriented, that is, the M&A are regarded as an organic part of the company's strategy. In this case, the purpose of M&A is usually not to achieve speculative gains. It aims to obtain or strengthen the core capabilities of enterprises through M&A, expand the market size of enterprises, improve industry status, or optimize resource allocation. The core of a successful M&A transaction is not only to complete the value transfer from the target to the acquirer but to create value through system integration based on completing this value transfer, including enhancing the competitive position, expanding market share, and creating new competitiveness.

There are two forms of strategic M&A: one is strategic M&A with the participation of international capital, and the connotation of the concept of foreign M&A that is currently being hotly hyped belongs to this type of strategic M&A; the other is the internal integration of important Chinese industries. This is a market behavior to improve the core competitiveness of the domestic industry.

The landmark case is the contractionary restructuring strategy of Sinopec and PetroChina: Sinopec, the controlling shareholder of Hubei Xinghua Co., Ltd. (600,886), transferred all 57.58% of its equity to the State Development and Investment Corporation. PetroChina, the controlling shareholder of Samsung Petrochemical (600,764), transferred all of its 51.6% stakes to China Electronics Corporation. PetroChina, the controlling shareholder of Petroleum Long Champ (600,772), transferred its shares to Xi'an Feitianke Industry and Trade Group Co., Ltd. and Wuhan Oasis Enterprise (Group) Ltd. Tibet Summit Industry (600,338) invested RMB265 million to transfer 50% of the shares held by the legal entity in China of Zhuzhou Nanfang Yamaha Motorcycle Co., Ltd., which is a strategic M&A in the industry.

Speculative M&A are a type of speculative behavior. Many listed companies prefer equity financing (known in the industry as "money misappropriation"), cater to or take advantage of short-term speculative trading preferences in the stock market, and are keen to hype conceptual themes, in the name of seeking new profit growth points and maximizing shareholder value. For capital operation, randomly search for irrelevant hot investment opportunities from outside, and engage in industrial speculation, conceptualization, and short-term investment. Speculative behavior can be affected by the problems of over-investment and under-investment caused by market inefficiency, but it does not mean that as long as there is market inefficiency, it will lead to managers' speculative behavior. Wang Zhengwei and Zhu Wuxiang (2010) believe that when managers engage in speculative activities, they will gain gains in financing due to market inefficiency, but at the same time, they will also face the loss of long-term interests. Speculation will only be carried out when the gains from speculation exceed the losses in long-term value. Then, once the inefficiency in the market is high enough to induce managers to speculate, how much will managers speculate, and what factors will affect their degree of speculation? The first factor is the degree of market inefficiency, which is reflected in the average output rate of speculative activities; the second factor is the average productivity of the investment target after additional investment; the third factor is the difference between the amount of financing separated from the amount of investment in the hypothesis, that is, the amount of excess financing; the last factor is the investment amount, which is completely used for investment after being obtained from financing. It is the financing amount that is necessary to improve the output rate of the investment target.

Recently, there have been many cases of speculative M&A of game companies and film and television companies, and a large proportion of M&A are aimed at short-term market value management and capturing hot spots around the so-called reduction of holdings of large and small locked-up shares.[5] In the past, M&A could only be discussed with one company at a time, but now three companies can be discussed at a time, making it more difficult to integrate. Now many companies are suspended from trading. Previously, the trading suspension was only for the sake of a company that was the target of an acquisition. But now that the deal has been negotiated, it may disclose information about another company. Future rational investors are worried about speculative M&A, because strategic M&A may not be successful. If there are mistakes in execution, it will lead to problems in the next few years, not to mention this kind of purely speculative M&A. Therefore, information disclosure will receive more and more attention from regulators. The eighth rejected M&A case in 2017 was that Zhongtong Guomai planned to purchase 100% equity of Shanghai Gongchuang by issuing shares and paying cash. The transaction price was RMB413 million, and the raised funds did not exceed RMB220 million. There are two main reasons for the rejection: first, the valuation premium of the asset of the target reaches, as high as 1,362.55%, and the regulators focus on its goodwill; second, the information disclosure of revenue and gross profit margin forecasts is insufficient, and the regulators question the reasonableness of the forecast results. This shows the importance of information disclosure.

9.5 Influencing Factors in the Control Market

9.5.1 M&A Wave

There is a large body of literature describing the M&A wave in the United States, and here is a brief review. Mergers and acquisitions appeared in the early stages of Western industry, at the end of the nineteenth century. Over the past century and a half, the West has experienced seven huge waves of M&A. The first wave of corporate M&A at the end of the nineteenth century, starting from mangroves in the west (the west coast of the United States) and reaching the Gulf of Mexico in the east (the east coast of the United States), created a group of national giants in the fields of metals, oil, railroads, and consumer goods. By the 1980s, corporate snipers in stiff suits were using junk bonds to finance hostile takeovers of big companies. In 2017, the latest wave of M&A is about to ebb.

(1) The first wave of M&A (1897–1904): horizontal M&A

[5] Non-tradable shares can be circulated due to share changes.—*Tr.*

In terms of science and technology, the construction and development of the electric power, coal, and railway industries are the economic backgrounds of this wave of M&A. From the perspective of the enterprise, after decades of accumulation after the American Civil War, the enterprise has accumulated the necessary resource support for M&A and has also generated the need to develop from a regional enterprise to a national enterprise. Therefore, the expansion of scale is an important characteristic of this M&A, small and medium-sized enterprises in the same industry unite with each other to form giants, thereby gaining economies of scale and market advantages. The establishment of the United States Steel Corporation is the most typical case of M&A during this period. Corporate M&A at this stage has accumulated experience, and explored and established rules for the subsequent development of the M&A industry in the United States. At this stage, due to the insufficient development of the US stock market and the absence of the central bank, individual important investment bankers played a huge role in M&A. From a corporate point of view, this wave of corporate M&A has undoubtedly achieved great success. This stage of M&A also played a role in promoting the introduction of the anti-monopoly law in the United States and attracted the attention of the American society to monopoly enterprises, which also confirmed the great success of this M&A wave.

(2) The second wave of M&A (1916–1929): vertical M&A

Mergers and acquisitions at this stage focused on utilities ranging from the emerging auto industry, and retail chains to electric power, and were mutually reinforcing with the boom in the US stock market. This M&A is mainly vertical, and a pyramid-type holding company appears, which further lays the foundation for the development of larger enterprise groups. With the advancement of integration brought about by vertical M&A, enterprises have entered more abundant production fields, and the demand or dependence on managers has begun to increase. The company's internal organizational structure transitioned from a U-form to M-form. The previous single-product enterprise gradually became a large group with multiple products, scale, and complexity through vertical integration. The disadvantage of the unitary structure was gradually reflected. The multidivisional structure first appeared in the automotive enterprise in the early twentieth century. As a product that conforms to the era of vertical integration, the multidivisional structure has made great contributions to the further innovation of the corporate system of large American companies.

(3) The third wave of M&A (1955–1973): conglomerate M&A

The theoretical basis of the third wave of M&A is the diversification of management and the prevention of enterprise management risks. In this wave of M&A, most companies believe that superb management skills can be applied to any company in any industry. Efficient production and rational allocation of resources mean that a professionally trained manager can apply his / her skills to any business and make it profitable. The new financial portfolio theory that emerged at this stage, that is, a variety of securities portfolios can reduce the risk of income fluctuations on the premise of guaranteeing returns, and have an impact on business operations, thereby promoting enterprises to continuously merge enterprises in different industries to maintain performance stable and reduced performance fluctuations. Judging from the final effect of this M&A, especially the occurrence of the next M&A wave, it proves that the so-called diversification in this M&A wave may not achieve the expected effect.

(4) The fourth wave of M&A (1980–1989): leveraged M&A

The direct cause of this wave of M&A is the economic stagflation in the 1970s and 1980s. On the one hand, economic stagnation has led to a long-term bear market in the United States, and inflation has led to a serious undervaluation of the value of listed companies recorded at historical costs. On the other hand, the failed companies in the third wave of M&A are under pressure to divest the failed acquisition business. In this context, active investment bankers have carried out M&A of undervalued listed companies and the integration of divestitures of large diversified companies. The re are three major characteristics of this stage of the wave of M&A: the first is the huge leading role played by investment bankers, such as Michael Milken; the second is the emergence of many hierarchical financing tools such as junk bonds, which have promoted the continuous emergence of leveraged buyouts of"snake swallowing elephants" of poorly managed enterprises by highly efficient enterprises; and the third is the parallel M&A and divestiture. For companies with low valuations, some investment bankers for the acquisition of the company, or business restructuring to improve efficiency and then re-listed, or directly to the spin-off sale, in the process, there has been a competition for control of the company, and hostile acquisitions have continued to appear. For enterprises that fail to diversify, specialization has become an important guiding theory for enterprise operation in this period. In the process of stripping off non-core businesses of large enterprise groups, management buyouts appeared. Compared with the last wave of M&A, this wave of M&A has greatly stimulated the improvement of economic efficiency and the development of the economy in the United States and has also made M&A integrated enterprises reborn. A typical M&A case at this stage is KKR's acquisition of RJR Nabisco.

(5) The fifth wave of M&A (1994–2000): the global wave of cross-border M&A

This wave of M&A takes the development of the Internet economy as the most important foundation. In the process of driving up the stock market, the M&A companies are getting bigger and bigger, crossing national borders, and combining powerful forces, reflecting the latest stage of corporate development. The characteristics of this wave are: First, the scale is very large. Mergers and acquisitions of more than US$100 million were 94 in 1980, 369 in 1988, and an annual average of more than 300 in the 1990s. Second, hostile M&A are no longer mainstream. Seeking strategic cooperation through M&A is the original intention of many large enterprises to carry out M&A, so the fifth wave of M&A reflects the characteristics of strong alliances. Hostile M&A accounted for only 5% of the share. Strategic M&A are also reflected in the spin-off of many large companies. The spin-off is a strategic attempt made by large companies to better enhance their competitiveness. Strategic M&A are also reflected in complementarity. Although the two parties are in the same industry, there are differences in the market, technology, and industrial chain links.

Through M&A, they can complement each other and enhance their overall competitiveness through synergy. Third, cross-border M&A. In 1996, American companies acquired 501 European companies, with a total transaction value of US$35.7 billion; at the same time, European companies also set off a wave of M&A of American companies. Cross-border M&A itself is a response to economic globalization, but in turn, promotes integration. Cross-border M&A also further intensified competition between countries.

(6) The sixth wave of M&A (2003–2008): the re-emergence of leveraged M&A

This wave of M&A is the increase in the US business community's confidence in economic recovery, which has led to the growth of M&A. After three years of silence, the M&A market became active again in 2003 and reached its peak in 2006, with the total amount of domestic M&A in the United States exceeding US$1 trillion. It gradually subsided after the global financial crisis in 2007. The wave of M&A is characterized by: First, increased scale. The scale of both parties to M&A is larger than the previous fifth wave of M&A. Second, M&A valuations are more pragmatic, that is, this M&A wave is less overvalued than the fifth. It is also rare that the acquirer's valuation is much higher than the target's valuation. Third, double the share of cash as a means of payment. The share of payment in stocks has dropped significantly. The reason for this change is related to the low-interest rates at the time and the company's higher cash reserves. Forth, the battle for control of listed companies is relatively mild. The aggressiveness of M&A initiators has weakened, indicating that M&A decisions are driven less by managers' overconfidence. At the same time, hostile M&A decreased significantly. Fifth, M&A premiums fell significantly. In this M&A wave, the premium ratio is relatively low, indicating that the acquirer can obtain more potential benefits from the transaction and create more value for shareholders at the same time. But in turn, the shareholders of the target company's profits fell. Sixth, private equity funds are growing rapidly. In terms of corporate governance structure, institutional investors represented by private equity funds vigorously promote shareholder activism, which is accompanied by the re-emergence of leveraged M&A. During the sixth wave of M&A, private equity funds showed explosive growth in both quantity and scale.

(7) The seventh wave of M&A (2012–2017): the diversification of global M&A

This wave of M&A began in 2012. The emergence of Chinese buyers as one of the main forces in cross-border M&A transactions is one of the important events. The participation of Chinese buyers has brought diverse characteristics to global M&A. The post-financial crisis world economy is slowing, funding is cheap, and markets are wary, all of which have prompted traders to react. The United States seeks to cut spending, increase market share, and reduce taxes and fees. For example, the US healthcare industry is very keen on "tax inversion" (that is, US companies acquire European companies to change their legal domicile to save tax). The characteristics of Chinese enterprises in this wave are unique transaction logic, China's premium valuation logic, distinctive transaction risk allocation, new transaction practices created by Chinese buyers, transaction certainty problems caused by China's foreign exchange control and so on. These are all meaningful practices that China has made during this ongoing M&A wave and are worth tracking and observing for a long time.

Patrick Foulis (2017) once predicted that the seventh M&A wave would come to end in 2017 for three main reasons: First, antitrust regulation will be tightened, as more and more analyses show that weakening competition is one of the reasons for low growth. Second, populism will make it harder to make deals. This hostility manifests itself through technocratic barriers. For example, the US Treasury Department is trying to end tax inversion, and the European Union is cracking down on corporate tax avoidance. Third, the return on investment of multinational enterprises has declined. At a time when globalization is starting to roll back, investors will be nervous about creating global giants through M&A, especially given the lackluster performance of multinational corporations. The return on investment of US multinationals has fallen from 12% in 2008 to 8% in 2017. In 2007–2017, without Wall Street people brokering deals, those tech star companies have gone global. Google, Apple, and Facebook, which generate most of their profits overseas but have not made any major cross-border deals, are among the five most valuable companies in the world. At the same time, Patrick Foulis (2017) also pointed out that China's foreign investment will have a blowout. Chinese buyers have bought Italian football clubs, Swiss seed companies, and American sausage makers. However, for Chinese savers and Chinese companies, the incentive to allocate overseas assets to diversify risks remains enormous.

China's capital market is open, and the M&A market has been affected by foreign investors (Zhao Xiaofang et al., 2021).

9.5.2 Driving Force of M&A Wave

9.5.2.1 Technological Revolution and Operational Efficiency

In his book *Takeovers, Restructuring and Corporate Governance*, Weston summarizes the transformative forces affecting merger activity in terms of key technological and economic conditions. Among all these forces of change, the most important is technological change, which includes advances in computer technology, computer service technology, software, servers, and many information systems including the Internet. Advances in communications and transportation have produced economic globalization. Many countries have adopted international agreements, such as the General Agreement on Tariffs and Trade (GATT), which lead to freer trade. The euro, issued in 1999, became the sole currency of the 12 participating member states in 2002 and has continued to bring about the opening of borders and constraints throughout Europe. The growth of competitive forces has led to the deregulation of major industries such as financial services, aviation, broadcasting, and medical services.

In addition, the change factor is related to operational efficiency. Economies of scale allow many units to share large fixed-cost investments in machinery or computer systems. Economies of scope refer to the reduction of operating costs for related activities. In the information industry, economies of scope are represented by the economicalization of microcomputer hardware, microcomputer software, server hardware, server software, the Internet, and other related business activities. Another type of efficiency is achieved by merging complementary businesses, for example, merging a company that is good at research and development with a company that is good at marketing. While AT&T's series of acquisitions in the 1990s were about mergers to keep up with technological change, AT&T has been trying to peel off or split many of its businesses in the early 2000s.

9.5.2.2 Deviation of an Enterprise's Market Value from Its Intrinsic Value

When the target enterprise's market value for some reason does not reflect its true value or potential value, M&A activity will occur. There are several reasons why enterprises are undervalued:

(1) The operation and management of the enterprise failed to give full play to its potential.
(2) The acquirer has internal information about the true value of the target enterprise that the external market does not have.
(3) Due to the difference between the market value of assets and the replacement cost caused by inflation, the phenomenon of underestimated enterprise value appears.

When the market value of the acquirer's enterprise is overvalued, the enterprise has an incentive to make its equity overvalued, so that the enterprise can use the overvalued stock for acquisition. Under normal circumstances, enterprises with overvalued equity may survive and develop through M&A, while enterprises with undervalued equity may become acquisition targets. The benefits of M&A in which stocks are overvalued can even create incentives for enterprises to manipulate profits to boost stock prices.

9.5.2.3 Industrial Organization

Industrial structural adjustment and reorganization is a state that always exists in the process of economic development. Although the reasons for structural adjustment and reorganization may be due to excess, technological change, the natural decline of the industry, lack of competitiveness, etc., the choice of "do something, don't do something" often occurs. The adjustment and reorganization of the industrial structure is essentially the withdrawal and reuse of limited resources. There are various ways to adjust the industrial structure, and the existence of a market for company control makes it easier to exit.

Corporate control transactions, as part of the capital market, purchase shares of another company through cash or debt or other means, or acquire control of other companies through proxy competition, directly or indirectly contribute to the exit of resources. The external takeover market plays an important role as a final bailout market. The controlled market provides an early warning mechanism for enterprises, it promotes the early adjustment of the industry, and to a certain extent avoids the waste of enterprises being forced to exit when the product and factor markets fail (Jensen, 1988, 1993). Hu Ruyin (2003) also believes that without the development of the corporate control market and managerial market, a country's industrial structure and industrial organization cannot achieve the best. The efficiency of "big and complete" and "small and complete" is very low. As one of the main ways of corporate control market transactions, corporate M&A is a way to effectively allocate resources among industries.

Scale is not a favorable way to solve excess production capacity but advocates the transfer of new investment and original investment capacity to industries and enterprises with market prospects. Mergers and acquisitions are an effective way to realize the transfer of resources among industries, which is the result of the natural selection of enterprises in the market economy. The industrial characteristics of corporate M&A (vertical M&A, horizontal M&A, and hybrid M&A) are closely related to the life cycle of the industry, that is, the industries are in different life cycles, and the characteristics of corporate M&A are different. During the period of the industrial recession, enterprises conduct horizontal mergers and hybrid mergers to survive, tending to merge enterprises in emerging industries and growing industries. At this level, M&A are essentially the processes of transferring enterprises from mature or declining industries to emerging industries. Therefore, after M&A, industrial integration must be handled properly. After enterprise M&A, the focus of industrial integration is to optimize the industrial organization of an enterprise or enterprise system or enterprise group while improving the industrial structure.

The existence of a market for corporate control is especially important for industries and companies that are in a recession. For example, the oil industry was in a period of contraction in the 1970s and 1980s, and managers of oil companies tried not to reduce their income (their income was positively related to the size of the company), pouring large sums of money into other areas they were unfamiliar with, rather than rewarding shareholders, and the wave of corporate mergers and restructurings (scrambles for corporate control) in the mid-to-late 1980s suppressed the spread of this ineffective investment. However, the market for corporate control is not always efficient. If the manager owns a larger share of the company, the manager can use position as a major shareholder to prevent the "raiders" from making M&A. In addition, current managers can also use a variety of anti-merger measures (such as "golden parachute", "poison pill plan") to increase the cost of M&A, and even make M&A of "raider" unprofitable.

As an external mechanism for overcapacity exit, the corporate control market can exit overcapacity through M&A. In the process of expanding of capacity with the growth of demand, the company has entered a monopolistic competition pattern with no difference in operating efficiency after frequent price wars. However, in the context of overcapacity and monopolistic competition, exit is conducive to the value-added of competitors. Therefore, companies often exit excess industrial capacity through horizontal M&A. Zhu Wuxiang (2000) pointed out that the excessive industrial capability of exiting through the corporate control market can solve the problem of revenue externality caused by the exit of a single enterprise, but it requires a functionally effective corporate control market. Both theory and practice show that the effectiveness of the resource allocation function of the stock market includes the effectiveness of three specific economic functions, such as the dynamic accumulation and distribution of social funds according to risks, the provision of evaluation and price information, and the transfer of corporate control rights. Among them, the ability to exit excess is the most significant economic function of M&A of corporate control in the western stock market.

9.5.2.4 Legal Control

The transfer of company control involves all stakeholders of the company, so it is very necessary to have a law on the transfer of control of listed companies as a formal system. The legal system is the behavioral rules of various stakeholders in the process of the transfer activity, and it is the basis for adjusting and dividing the interests ofall parties. Only under the regulated legal system and legal environment can the market for the transfer of corporate control rights run smoothly and the functions of the market for corporate control rights can be brought into full play. A benign control transfer market can replace bad managers, the talents of efficient managers can be fully demonstrated, and the legitimate rights and interests of various stakeholders in the company can be effectively protected. Coupled with the considerable complexity of the corporate control transfer market, various countries have formulated a considerable number of laws to regulate the transfer of corporate control. These laws, which are formal systems, are a system consisting of the company law, the securities law, the measures for the administration of takeovers of listed companies, and the measures for information disclosure.

At the same time, foreign countries have two main conclusions about the impact of anti-takeover clauses in the company's articles of association on the control market. The first is that anti-takeover clauses are mainly used by insiders to defend against M&A, thereby increasing the possibility of insiders' encroachment on interests, which is not conducive to protecting the interests of small and medium shareholders (Bebchuk et al., 2009; Atanassov, 2013); the second believes that anti-takeover clauses provide managers with more negotiating power in M&A and reduce managers' short-sighted behavior, some anti-takeover clauses can protect the interests of small and medium investors. For example, corporate compensation terms are positively related to M&A premiums (Sokolyk, 2011), and tiered board terms are positively related to target company M&A performance (Ertugrul, 2015).

The corporate control market will evolve towards a more open and efficient direction under the combined effects of technological and transportation advancements, capital market value discovery, industrial organization changes, and continuous improvement of legal supervision.

Bibliography

Acemoglu, D., Johnson, S., & Mitton, T. (2009). Determinants of vertical integration: Financial development and contracting costs. *Journal of Finance, 64*(3), 1251–1290.

Agarwal, S., & Ramaswami, S. N. (1992). The choice of foreign market entry mode: Impact of ownership, location and internalization factors. *Journal of International Business Studies, 23*(1), 1–27.

Agrawal, A., Jaffe, J. F., & Mandelker, G. N. (1992). The post-merger performance of acquiring firms: A re-examination of an anomaly. *Journal of Finance, 47*(4), Article 160521.

Ahammad, M. F., & Glaister, K. W. (2013). The pre-acquisition evaluation of target firms and cross border acquisition performance. *International Business Review, 22*(5), 894–904.

Alfred, M. (1965). *Principles of economics* (Y. Guo, Trans.). The Commercial Press.

Allen, J. (1998). Capital markets and corporate structure: The equity carve- outs of Thermo Electron. *Journal of Financial Economics, 48*(1), 99–124.

Almazan, A., De Motta, A., Titman, S., & Uysal, V. (2010). Financial structure, acquisition opportunities and firm locations. *The Journal of Finance, 65*(2), 529–563.

Amidon, M. (1998). *Innovation strategy for the knowledge economy* (F. Miao, Trans.). Xinhua Press.

Amihud, Y., & Lev, B. (1981). Risk reduction as a managerial motive for conglomerate mergers. *Bell Journal of Economics, 12*, 605–617.

Amiryany, N., Huysman, M., de Man, A. P., & Cloodt, M. (2012). Acquisition reconfiguration capability. *European Journal of Innovation Management, 15*(2), 177–191.

Amit, R., & Schoemaker, P. J. H. (1993). Strategic assets and organizational rent. *Strategic Management Journal, 14*(1), 33–46.

Anand, B., & Khanna, T. (2000). Do firms learn to create value? The case of alliances. *Strategic Management Journal, 21*(3), 295–315.

Anand, J., & Delios, A. (2002). Absolute and relative resources as determinants of international acquisitions. *Strategic Management Journal, 23*(2), 119.

Andersen, O. (1997). Internationalization and market entry mode: A review of theories and conceptual framework. *Management International Review, 37*(1), 27–42.

Anderson, E., & Coughlan, A. T. (1987). International market entry and expansion via independent or integrated channels of distribution. *Journal of Marketing, 51*(1), 71–82.

Anderson, E. M., & Gatignon, H. (1986). Modes of foreign entry: A transaction cost analysis and propositions. *Journal of International Business Studies, 17*(3), 1–26.

Andersson, T., & Svensson, R. (1994). Entry modes for direct investment determined by the composition of firm-specific skills. *Scandinavian Journal of Economics, 96*(4), 551–560.

Andrade, G., & Staford, E. (1999). *Investigating the economic role of mergers*. Harvard Business School Working Paper. Available at SSRN: https://ssrn.com/abstract=47264orhttps://doi.org/10.2139/ssrn.47264.

Q. Zhang, *Mergers and Acquisitions*, https://doi.org/10.1007/978-981-92-0122-8

Andrew, C., et al. (2000). *Strategic synergy* (T. H. Ren et al., Trans.). Machinery Industry Press.

Ang, J. S., & Cheng, Y. (2006). Direct evidence on the market-driven acquisition theory. *Journal of Financial Research, 29*(2), 261–286.

Anwar, S. T. (2012). FDI regimes, investment screening process, and institutional frameworks: China versus others in global business. *Journal of World Trade, 46*(2), 213–248.

Argote, L., Beckman, S. L., & Epple, D. (1990). The persistence and transfer of learning in industrial settings. *Management Science, 36*(2), 140–154.

Arrow, K. J. (1962). Economic welfare and the allocation of resources for invention. In R. R. Nelson (Ed.), *The rate and direction of inventive activity*. Princeton University Press.

Arrow, K. J. (1975). Vertical integration and communication. *Bell Journal of Economics, 6*(2), 173–183.

Arthur, W. B. (1988). Competing technologies, increasing returns, and lock-in by historical events. *The Economic Journal, 99*(394), 116–131.

Asquith, P., & Kim, E. H. (1982). The impact of merger bids on the participating firms' security holders. *Journal of Finance, 37*(5), 1209–1228.

Asquith, P. (1983). Merger bids, uncertainty, and stockholder returns. *Journal of Financial Economics, 11*, 51–83.

Atanassov, J. (2013). Do hostile takeovers stifle innovation? Evidence from antitakeover legislation and corporate patenting. *Journal of Finance, 68*(3), 1097–1131.

Atkinson, J. W. (1964). *An introduction to motivation*. Van Nostrand.

Bae, K. H., Kang, J. K., & Kim, J. M. (2002). Tunneling or value added? Evidence from mergers by Korean business groups. *Journal of Finance, 57*(6), 2695–2740.

Bai, G. (2004). *Looking at the governance structure of listed companies in China from the control market* (Master's thesis). Tsinghua University.

Bai, X. Y. (2011). Research on China's M&A market under the background of financial crisis. *China Business and Market, 25*(6), 89–93.

Bain, J. S. (1968). *Industrial organization*. John Wiley & Sons.

Baker, W. E. (1990). Market networks and corporate behavior. *American Journal of Sociology, 96*(3), 589.

Baldwin, J. R., & Caves, R. E. (1997). *International competition and industrial performance: Allocative efficiency, productive efficiency and turbulence* (Harvard Economics Discussion Paper, no.1809).

Barkema, H. G., & Vermuelen, F. (1998). International expansion through start-up or acquisition: A learning perspective. *Academy of Management Journal, 41*(1), 7–26.

Barner-Rasmussen, W. (2003). *Knowledge sharing in multinational corporations: A social capital perspective* (Doctoral dissertation). Swedish School of Economics and Business Administration.

Barney, J. B. (1991). Firm resources and sustained competitive advantage. *Journal of Management, 17*(1), 99–120.

Bartlett, C. A., & Ghoshal, S. (1986). Tap your subsidiaries for global reach. *Harvard Business Review, 64*(6), 87–94.

Beamish, P. W., & Banks, J. C. (1987). Host national attitudes toward multinational corporations. *Journal of International Business Studies, 18*(2), 1–16.

Bebchuk, L. A., Cohen, A., & Ferrell, A. (2009). What matters in corporate governance? *Review of Financial Studies, 22*(2), 783–827.

Bergen, M., Dutta, S., & Shugan, S. M. (1996). Branded variants: A retail perspective. *Journal of Marketing Research, 33*(1), 9–19.

Bertrand, O., & Zuniga, P. (2006). R&D and M&A: Are cross-border M&A different? An investigation on OECD countries. *International Journal of Industrial Organization, 24*(2), 401–423.

Betrand, O. (2005). On the effects of economic integration on greenfield investments and cross-border mergers and acquisitions location patterns. *Journal of Economic Integration, 20*(1), 26–51.

Bitzer, J., & Gorg, H. (2009). Foreign direct investment, competition and industry performance. *World Economy, 32*(2), 221–233.
Bleeke, J., Ernst, D. (1995). Is your strategic alliance really a sale? *Harvard Business Review*, January–February, 97–105.
Borghese, R. J., & Borgese, P. F. (2004). *M&A from planning to integration*. China Machine Press.
Borys, B., & Jemison, D. B. (1989). Hybrid arrangements as strategic alliances: Theoretical issues in organizational combinations. *Academy of Management Review, 14*(2), 234–249.
Bourdieu, P., & Wacquant, L. (1992). *An invitation to reflexive sociology*. Polity Press in association with Blackwell Publishers.
Bradley, M., Desai, A., & Kim, E. H. (1988). Synergistic gains from corporate acquisitions and their division between the stockholders of target and acquiring firms. *Journal of Financial Economics, 21*(1), 3–40.
Brakman, S., Garretsen, H., van Marrewijk, C., & van Witteloostuijn, A. (2013). Cross-border M&A activity and revealed comparative advantage in manufacturing industries. *Journal of Economics and Management Strategy, 22*(1), 28–57.
Brickley, J. A., Lease, R. C., & Smith, C. W. (1988). Ownership structure and voting on antitakeover amendments. *Journal of Financial Economics, 20*(88), 267–291.
Brouthers, K. D., & Brouthers, L. E. (2000). Acquisition or greenfield start- up? Institutional, cultural and transaction cost influences. *Strategic Management Journal, 21*(1), 89–97.
Brouthers, K. D., & Dikova, D. (2010). Acquisitions and real options: The greenfield alternative. *Journal of Management Studies, 47*(6), 1048–1071.
Brouthers, K. D., Brouthers, L. E., & Werner, S. (2008). Real options, international entry mode choice and performance. *Journal of Management Studies, 45*(5), 936–960.
Bruner, R. F. (1988). The use of excess cash and debt capacity as a motive for merger. *Journal of Financial and Quantitative Analysis, 23*(2), 199–217.
Bruner, R. F. (1999). An analysis of value destruction and recovery in the alliance and proposed merger of Volvo and Renault. *Journal of Financial Economics, 51*, 125–166.
De La Bruslerie, H. (2013). Crossing takeover premiums and mix of payment: An empirical test of contractual setting in M&A transactions. *Journal of Banking & Finance, 37*(6), 2106–2123.
Buckley, P. J., & Casson, M. C. (1976). *The future of the multinational enterprise*. Holmes & Meler.
Buckley, P. J., Nicolas, F., & Surender, M. (2012). Host-home country linkages and host-home country specific advantages as determinants of foreign acquisition by Indian. *International Business Review, 21*(5), 878–890.
Burt, R. S. (1992). *Structural holes: The social structure of competition*. Harvard University Press.
Byrne, J. A. (Irvin, J. A.), & Michaels, E. W. (1989). Core skills: Doing the right things right. *The McKinsey Quarterly* (4), 35–46.
Campbell, A., Goold, M., & Alexander, M. (1995). Corporate strategy: The quest for parenting advantage. *Harvard Business Review, 73*(2), 120–132.
Cao, X., Wu, C. F., & Nie, Y. W. (2011). Research on the influencing factors of implicit incentives on fund managers'herd behavior. *China Soft Science* (7), 111–122.
Casson, M. C. (1996). *The theory of the firm*. Edward Elgar.
Caves, R. E. (1982). *Multinational enterprise and economic analysis*. Cambridge University Press.
Caves, R. E., & Mehra, S. K. (1986). Entry of foreign multinationals into U. S. manufacturing industries. In M. E. Porter (Ed.), *Competition in global industries* (pp. 449–481). Harvard Business School Press.
Caves, R. E., & Murphy, W. F. II. (1976). Franchising: firms, markets, and intangible assets. *Southern Economic Journal, 42*(4), 572.
Celikyurt, U., Sevilir, M., & Shivdasani, A. (2010). Going public to acquire? The acquisition motive in IPOs. *Journal of Financial Economics, 96*(3), 345–363.
Chang, S. (1998). Takeovers of privately held targets, methods of payment, and bidder returns. *Journal of Finance, 53*(2), 773–784.
Chatterjee, S. (1986). Types of synergy and economic value: The impact of acquisitions on merging and rival firms. *Strategic Management Journal, 7*(2), 119–139.

Chen, H. (2005). Research on the allocation mode of control right and governance efficiency of listed companies: Based on the premise of shareholding structure. *Investment Research* (6).

Chen, H. M., Li, Q., & Li, K. Z. (2004). An empirical study on the performance of unrelated assets restructuring of listed companies in China. *Systems Engineering—Theory & Practice*, 24(10), 59–66.

Chen, H., & Yang, L. X. (2012). Pyramid shareholding structure, equity check and balance and embezzlement by ultimate shareholders. *Investment Research, 31*(3), 101–113.

Chen, J., Xi, Y. M., & Guo, J. E. (2005). A review of research on performance evaluation methods for foreign mergers and acquisitions. *Contemporary Economic Sciences* (5).

Chen, K. (2006). *A preliminary study on mergers and acquisitions capability of enterprises* (Unpublished working paper). China Mergers and Acquisitions Research Center, Beijing Jiaotong University.

Chen, L. T. (2004). Research on the mechanism and effect of the control market on improving the governance of listed companies. *Productivity Research* (12).

Chen, X. Y., Ye, P. F., & Chen, D. H. (2003). Opportunistic asset reorganization and rigid control. *Economic Research* (5).

Chen, X. Y., & Yuan, H. Q. (1998). Research on financial accounting issues of asset reorganization of listed companies. *Accounting Research* (10).

Chen, X. L., & Zhou, S. P. (2002). Capital structure and corporate governance performance. *Enterprise Economics* (2).

Chen, Y. (2006). *Research on the applicable boundary of enterprise M&A and new investment* (Master's thesis). Beijing Jiaotong University.

Chen, Y. (2007). *Research on the applicable boundary of M&A strategy and alliance strategy* (Doctoral dissertation). Beijing Jiaotong University.

Chen, Y. G., Chen, W. T., & Li, S. M. (2013). Can M&A reduce the hollowing out behavior of target companies? *Journal of Management Science in China, 16*(12), 57–67.

Chen, Y. G., & Li, S. M. (2007). An empirical study on value sources in M&A. *Academic Research* (9).

Chen, Y. G., & Li, S. M. (2007). The predictability of mergers and acquisitions: A study based on the perspective of transaction costs, *Economic Research* (4).

Chen, Y. G., & Li, S. M. (2008). Research on value decomposition and key value drivers in mergers and acquisitions. *Statistics and Decision-Making* (20).

Chen, Y. H., & Zhang, Q. S. (2006). Analysis of influencing factors of mergers and acquisitions and new investment decisions. *Journal of Beijing Jiaotong University* (*Social Science Edition*) (4).

Chen, Y. H., & Zhang, Q. S. (2008). An empirical study on the applicable boundary of M&A strategy and alliance strategy. *Journal of Beijing Jiaotong University* (*Social Science Edition*) (1).

Cheng, G. S., Chen, H. M., & Sun, W. J. (2005). Analysis of network externalities and vertical mergers of enterprises. *Chinese Management Science* (6).

Cheng, G. S., Chen, H. M., & Sun, W. J. (2006). The choice of enterprise merger mode with network externalities. *Chinese Management Science* (5).

Cheng, H. W. (2002). On financial management ability. *Shanghai Accounting* (2).

Chi, T. (1994). Trading in strategic resources: Necessary conditions, transaction cost problems, and choice of exchange structure. *Strategic Management Journal, 15*(4), 271–290.

Cho, K. R., & Padmanabhan, P. (1995). Acquisition versus new venture: The choice of foreign establishment mode by Japanese firms. *Journal of International Management, 1*(3), 255–285.

Chu, Y. H., & Song, X. L. (2006). Analysis on the characteristics, motivation and synergy effect of Qingdao Hisense's acquisition of Kelon Electric, *Finance and Accounting* (18).

Chung, G. H., Du, J., & Choi, J. N. (2014). How do employees adapt to organizational change driven by cross-border M&As? A case in China. *Journal of World Business, 49*(1), 78–86.

Chung, K. H., & Pruitt, S. W. (1994). A simple approximation of Tobin's Q. *Financial Management, 23*(3), 70–74.

Ci Hai Editorial Committee. (1980). *Ci Hai*. Shanghai Lexicographical Publishing House.

Coase, R. H. (1937). The nature of firm. *Economica, 4*(16), 386–405.

Coleman, J. S. (1990). *Foundations of social theory*. Harvard University Press.

Comanor W. S. (1967). Vertical mergers, market powers, and the antitrust laws. *The American Economic Review*, 254–265.

Conner, K. R., & Prahalad, C. K. (1996). A resource-based theory of the firm: Knowledge versus opportunism. *Organization Science, 7*(5), 477–501.

Contractor, F. J., Lorange, P. (1988). Competition vs. cooperation: A benefit/cost framework for choosing between fully owned investments and cooperative relationships. *International Strategic Management*. Routledge.

Coughlan, A. T. (1985). Competition and cooperation in marketing channel choice: Theory and application. *Marketing Science, 4*(2), 110–129.

Criado López Duarte, C., & García-Canal, E. (2002). The effect of firm and host country characteristics on the choice of entry mode: Empirical evidence from Spanish firms, *Journal of Management and Governance, 6*(2), 153–168.

Cui, Y. M., Shi, X. D., & Chen, Y. H. (2008). An empirical study on the applicable boundary of mergers and acquisitions and greenfield investment. *Productivity Research, 19*, 65–67.

Cui, X. G., & Jing, X. (2006). Research on the prediction of control transfer of listed companies. *Accounting Research* (1).

Cui, Y. (2008). *Research on the market evolution of corporate control rights based on ecology* (Doctoral dissertation). Beijing Jiaotong University.

Cui, Y. M., Ye, G. H., & Gao, Y. X. (2007). An empirical analysis of the influencing factors of the market economy of control rights: A case study of the American market from 1970 to 1999. *Journal of Beijing Jiaotong University (Social Science Edition)* (1).

Cui, Y., & Zhang, Q. S. (2002). An empirical study on the impact of equity changes on stock prices. *Economist* (2).

Cui, Y. M., Zhang, Q. S., & Ye, G. H. (2002). An empirical analysis of the influencing factors of the market economy of control rights. *Journal of Beijing Jiaotong University (Social Sciences Edition)* (10).

Cullinan, G., Le Roux, J., & Weddigen, R. (2004). When to walk away from a deal. *Harvard Business Review, 82*(4), 96–104.

Das, T. K., & Teng, B. S. (1998). Resource and risk management in the strategic alliance making process. *Journal of Management, 24*(1), 21–42.

Das, T. K., & Teng, B. S. (2000). A resource-based theory of strategic alliance. *Journal of Management, 26*(1), 31–61.

Davidson, W. H. (1980). The location of foreign direct investment activity: Country characteristics and experience effects. *Journal of International Business Studies, 11*(2), 9–22.

De Man, A. P. (2005). Alliance capability: A comparison of the alliance strength of European and American companies. *European Management Journal, 23*(3), 315–323.

DeAngelo, H., & Rice, E. M. (1983). Antitakeover charter amendments and stockholder wealth. *Journal of Financial Economics, 11*(1–4), 329–360.

DeLong, G. (2003). Does long-term performance of mergers match expectations? Evidence from the US banking industry. *Financial Management, 32*(2), 5–26.

Deng, R. L. (1999). Enterprise asset reorganization and capital operation. *Petroleum Enterprise Management* (12).

Deng, R. L. (1999). Enterprise merger and economic development. *Economics* (6).

Deng, R. L. (2001). Reading shell resources: The theory and cases of mergers and acquisitions of Chinese listed companies. *Management World* (5).

Deng, R. L., & Guo, W. W. (1999). Management Problems in Enterprise Merger, *Nankai Management Review* (4).

Deng, R. L., Liu, J. S., Lu, Y., et al. (2008). Chinese-style cross- border M&A integration. *China Petroleum Enterprises* (5).

Deng, R. L., & Zou, Y. S. (1997). Mergers and acquisitions: An effective approach to resource allocation. *Economics* (6).

Deng, T. S., Pi, A. P. (2001). Analysis of economic conditions of mergers and acquisitions based on synergistic effect, *Journal of Quantitative & Technological Economics* (11).

Devine, M. (2004). *Guide to successful mergers and acquisitions* (S. Han, Trans.). CITIC Publishing House.

Dierickx, I., & Cool, K. (1989). Asset stock accumulation and sustainability of competitive advantage. *Management Science, 35*(12), 1504–1511.

Deans, G., Kroeger, F., & Zeisel, S. (2004). *Winning the merger endgame: A playbook for profiting from industry consolidation* (K. Zhang, Trans.). China Machine Press.

Ding, Z. H., Zhang, Q. S., & Chen, Y. (2007). The motivational deviation of management buyouts in China and its theoretical explanation. *Journal of Beijing Jiaotong University (Social Sciences Edition)* (1).

Dodd, P., & Ruback, R. (1977). Tender offers and stockholder returns: An empirical analysis. *Journal of Financial Economics, 5*(3), 351–373.

Draulans, J., de Man, A. P., & Volberda, H. W. (2003). Building alliance capability: Management techniques for superior alliance performance. *Long Range Planning, 36*(2), 151–166.

Duan, J. S., Zhang, J. X., & Zhang, Q. S. (2008). A brief introduction to the research on arbitrage strategy of foreign mergers and acquisitions. *Productivity Research* (2).

Dube S., Glascock J. L., & Klock M. (2006). Is hostility in the merger and acquisition market wasteful? Empirical evidence of the economic costs of hostility. *Social Science Electronic Publishing.*

Dunning, J. H. (2009). Location and the multinational enterprise: John Dunning's thoughts on receiving the Journal of International Business Studies 2008 decade award. *Journal of International Business Studies, 40*(1), 20–34.

Dunning, J. H. (1998). Globalization and the new geography of foreign direct investment. *Oxford Development Studies, 26*(1), 47.

Dunning, J. H. (2000). The eclectic paradigm as an envelope for economic and business theories of MNE activity. *International Business Review, 9*(2), 163.

Dunning, J. H. (2001). The eclectic (OLI) paradigm of international production: Past, present and future. *International Journal of the Economics of Business, 8*(2), 173–190.

Dussauge, P., & Garette, B. (1995). Determinants of success in international strategic alliances: Evidence from the global aerospace industry. *Journal of International Business Studies, 26*(3), 505–530.

Dutton J. M., & Thomas A. (1985). Relating technological change and learning by doing. In R. S. Rosenbloom (Ed.), *Research on technological innovation, management and policy* (Vol. 2, pp. 187–224). JAI Press.

Easterbrook, F. H., & Fischel, D. R. (1991). *The economic structure of corporate law*. Harvard University Press.

Eccles, R. G., Lanes, K. L., & Wilson, T. C. (1999). Are you paying too much for that acquisition? *Harvard Business Review, 77*(4), 136.

Eckbo, B. E., & Thorburn, K. S. (2000). Gains to bidder firms revisited: Domestic and foreign acquisitions in Canada. *Journal of Financial Quantitative Analysis, 35*(1), 1–25.

Eicher, T., & Kang, J. W. (2005). Trade, foreign direct investment or acquisition: Optimal entry modes for multinational corporations. *Journal of Development Economics, 77*(1), 207–228.

Eisenhardt, K. M., & Schoonhoven, C. B. (1996). Resource-based view of strategic alliance formation: Strategic and social effects in entrepreneurial firms. *Organization Science, 7*(2), 136–150.

Elango, B. (2004). The influence of plant characteristics on the entry mode choice of overseas firms. *Journal of Operations Management, 23*(1), 65–79.

Elango, B., & Sambharya, R. B. (2004). The influence of industry structure on the entry mode choice of overseas entrants in manufacturing industries. *Journal of International Management, 10*(1), 107–124.

Elgers, P. T., & Clark, J. J. (1980). Merger types and shareholder returns: Additional evidence. *Financial Management, 9*(2), 66–72.

Ertugrul, M. (2015). Bargaining power of targets: Takeover defenses and top-tier target advisors. *Journal of Economics and Business, 78*, 48–78.

Eston, J., & Gersovitz, M. (1983). Country risk: Economic aspects. *Managing international risk*. Cambridge University Press, pp. 75–108.

Ethridge, D. (1998). *Research methodology in applied economic* (G. Zhu, Trans.). Economic Science Press.

Fagre, N., & Wells, L. T. (1982). Bargaining power of multinations and host governments. *Journal of International Business Studies, 13*(2), 9–23.

Fahy, J., & Smithee, A. (1999). Strategic marketing and resource based view of the firm. *Academy of Marketing Science Review, 1999*(10).

Fama, E. F., Fisher, L., Jensen, M. C., et al. (1969). The adjustment of stock price to new information. *International Economic Review, 10*(1), 1–21.

Fama, E. F., & Jensen, M. C. (1983). Agency problems and residual claims. *Journal of Law and Economics, 26*(2), 327–349.

Fama, E. F., & French, K. R. (1993). Common risk factors in the returns on stocks and bonds. *Journal of Financial Economics, 33*(1), 3–56.

Fan, C. L., & Yuan, J. (2002). An empirical analysis of the M&A performance of listed companies in growth, mature and decline industries. *China Industrial Economy, 8*, 65–72.

Fan, H. Y., & Zhao, G. T. (2006). Share reform catalyzes the control market. *Shanghai Securities News*, 2nd March.

Fang, F., & Yan, X. T. (2002). Mergers and acquisitions performance and thinking of Chinese listed companies. *Economic Theory and Economic Management* (8).

Fang, J. X. (2009). Market segmentation and damage to resource allocation efficiency: Evidence from corporate mergers and acquisitions. *Finance and Economics Research, 9*, 36–47.

Fang, R. S. (2004). Competency-based theory and its limitations. *Research Management, 25*(7).

Fang, Y. Q., Xia, L. J., & Li, M. C. (2006). Analysis of the influencing factors of corporate performance changes after control transfer: An explanation based on efficiency theory and control theory. *Journal of Finance and Economics* (1).

Fayerweather, J. (1982). Host national attitudes toward multinational corporations. *International Executive, 24*(2), 5–7.

Feng, F. G., & Sun, C. J. (2001). An empirical study on the utilization performance of "shell" resources of listed companies in China. *Finance & Trade Economy* (6).

Feng, F. G., & Wang, H. F. (2002). Review of the performance theory and empirical research of listed companies. *Journal of Northwestern University (Philosophy and Social Sciences Edition), 32*(2).

Feng, F. G., & Wu, L. J. (2001). An empirical study on the M&A performance of listed companies in China, *Economic Research* (1).

Franks, J., Harris, R., & Titman, S. (1991). The post-merger share-price performance of acquiring firms. *Journal of Financial Economics, 29*(1), 81–96.

Fu, C., Yang, Z., & Fu, D. G. (2015). Does companion effect affect M&A goodwill? Based on the empirical evidence of high premium M&A on China's ChiNext. *China Soft Science, 11*, 94–108.

Furubotn, E. G., & Richter, R. (2005). *Institutions and Economic Theory: The Contribution of the New Institutional Economics* (2nd ed.). University of Michigan Press.

Gao, J. (2003). A preliminary study on the micro- and macro-economic functions of the corporate control market. *Journal of Sichuan Administration Institute* (5).

Gao, J. (2005). *Market research on corporate control* (Doctoral dissertation). Sichuan University.

Gao, J., & Chen, X. W. (2000). Analysis of the effects of asset restructuring in China's securities market. *Econimic Science, 1*, 66–77.

Gao, L. H., & Luo, J. C. (2004). The influence of the corporate control market on the efficiency of the securities market. *Journal of Chang'an University, 6*(3).

Gao, L., & Song, S. L. (2006). Transfer of control right of listed companies and market response, *Finance and Economics* (3).

Gao, M. H. (2008). *Research on the financial effects of mergers and acquisitions by Chinese listed companies*. Xiamen University Press.

Gao, Y. X. (2004). *Research on the control market of Chinese listed companies*. China Economic Press.

Gao, Y. (2004). *Research on the control right market of Chinese listed companies: Theory and empirical research* (Doctoral dissertation). Beijing Jiaotong University.

Gao, Y. X., Zhang, Q. S., & Yang, H., et al. (2004). An empirical analysis of corporate governance effects in China's listed companies control market. *Journal of Beijing Jiaotong University (Social Science Edition), 3*(2).

Ge, W. J., Zhang, Q. S., & Zhang, Z. Q. (2014). Residual resources, government intervention and mergers and acquisitions. *Journal of Beijing Jiaotong University (Social Science Edition), 13*(2), 42–48.

Ge, W. J., Zhang, Q. S., & Zhang, Z. Q. (2015). Research on efficiency-based enterprise M&A capability measurement. *Finance and Economics, 3*, 82–89.

Gilson R. J., Scholes M. S., & Wolfson M. A. (1988). *Taxation and the dynamics of corporate control: The uncertain case for tax-motivated acquisition*. Oxford University Press.

Global Mergers and Acquisitions Research Center, Economic and Technical Committee of All-China Federation of Industry and Commerce. (2002). *Mergers and acquisitions handbook*. China Modern Economic Publishing House.

Gompers, P., Ishii, J., & Metrick, A. (2003). Corporate governance and equity prices. *The Quarterly Journal of Economics, 118*(1), 107–155.

Granovetter, M. S. (1985). Economic action and social structure: The problem of social embeddedness. *American Journal of Sociology, 91*(3), 481–510.

Grant, R. M. (1991). The resource-based theory of competitive advantage: Implications for strategy formulation. *California Management Review, 33*(3), 114–135.

Grant, R. M. (1997). The knowledge-based view of the firm: Implications for management practice. *Long Range Planning, 30*(3), 450–454.

Green, M. B. (1990). *Mergers and acquisitions: Geographical and spatial perspectives*. Routledge.

Gregory, A. (1997). An examination of the long run performance of UK acquiring firms. *Journal of Business Finance and Accounting, 24*(7), 971–1002.

Grossman, S. J., & Hart, O. D. (1986). The costs and benefits of ownership: A theory of vertical and lateral integration. *Journal of Political Economy, 94*(4), 691–719.

Gu, X., Guo, Y., & Li, J. (2003). Social capital and its role in knowledge chain. *Research and Development Management, 24*(5), 44–48.

Gu, Y., & Wu, C. F. (2002). An empirical test of M&A motivation and stock price response of listed companies. *Systems Engineering—Theory & Practice*, 22(2).

Gugler, K. P., Mueller, D. C., & Yurtoglu, B. B. (2006). *The determinants of merger waves* (WZB Markets and Politics Working Paper No. SP II 2006-01). Social Science Research Network. http://srn.com/abstract=507282

Gulati, R. (1995). Does familiarity breed trust? The implications of repeated ties for contractual choice in alliances. *Academy of Management Journal, 38*(1), 85–112.

Guo, J. H. (2002). *Research on the synergy theory of knowledge capital in mergers and acquisitions* (Doctoral dissertation). Shanghai Jiao Tong University.

Guo, W. (2005). Research review of accounting index method for mergers and acquisitions performance evaluation. *Journal of Wuhan University of Technology (Information and Management Engineering Edition), 27*(4).

Hagedoorn, J., & Duysters, G. (1999). *External appropriation of innovative capabilities: The preference for strategic alliances or M&As* (MERIT Research Memorandum No. 2000-008). http://www.merit.unu.edu/publications/rmpdf/2000/rm2000–008.pdf

Hale, G., & Long, C. (2011). Did foreign direct investment put an upward pressure on wages in China? *IMF Economic Review, 59*(3), 404–430.

Hart, O. (1995). *Firms, contracts, and financial structure*. Oxford University Press.

Harvard Business Review. (2004). *Mergers and acquisitions* (J. Shi, Trans.). China Renmin University Press.

Harzing, A. W. K. (1998). *Acquisitions versus greenfield investments: Both sides of the picture* [Paper presentation]. Academy of International Business Annual Meeting, Vienna, Austria.

Harzing, A. W. K. (2002). Acquisitions versus greenfield investment: International strategy and management of entry modes. *Strategic Management Journal, 23*(3), 211–227.

Haspeslaph, P., & Jemison, D. B. (1991). *Managing acquisition: Creating value through corporate renewal*. Free Press.

Haspeslaph, P., & Farquhar, A. (1987, October 14–17). *The acquisition integration process: A contingent framework* [Paper presentation]. The Seventh Annual International Conference of the Strategic Management Society, Boston, MA, United States.

Hatch, B. C., & Johnson, S. A. (2002). The impact of specialist firm acquisitions on market quality. *Journal of Financial Economics, 66*(1), 139–167.

Hayn, C. (1989). Tax attributes as determinants of shareholder gains in corporate acquisitions. *Journal of Financial Economics, 23*(1), 121–153.

Hayward, M. L. A. (2002). When do firms learn from their acquisition experience? Evidence from 1990–1995. *Strategic Management Journal, 23*(1), 21–39.

He, H. Z. (2012). Divide or bridge: A moral philosophical criticism of network economy. *Business Research* (5).

He, J. (2006). Analysis on the characteristics of the transfer of control rights of listed companies. *Group Economic Research* (1).

He, Y. K. (2003). *Research on the influence of cross-border mergers and acquisitions on the industrial competitiveness of the host country* (Master's thesis). Graduate School of Chinese Academy of Social Sciences.

Healy, P. M., Palepu, K. G., & Ruback, R. S. (1992). Does corporate performance improve after mergers? *Journal of Financial Economics, 31*(2), 135–175.

Hennart, J. F., & Larimo, J. (1998). The impact of culture on the strategy of multinational enterprises: Does national origin affect ownership decisions? *Journal of International Business Studies, 29*(3), 515–538.

Hennart, J. F., & Park, Y. R. (1993). Greenfield vs. acquisition: The strategy of Japanese investors in the United States. *Management Science, 39*(9), 1054–1070.

Hennart, J. F. (1988). A transaction cost theory of equity joint ventures. *Strategic Management Journal, 9*(4), 361–374.

Hennart, J. F., & Reddy, S. (1997). The choice between mergers/ acquisitions and joint ventures: The case of Japanese investors in the United States. *Strategic Management Journal, 18*(1), 1–12.

Herriott, R. E., & Firestone, W. A. (1983). Multisite qualitative policy research: Optimizing description and generalizability. *Educational Researcher, 12*(2), 14–19.

Hitt, M. A., & Ireland, R. D. (1985). Corporate distinctive competence, strategy, industry and performance. *Strategic Management Journal, 6*(3), 273–293.

Hofer, C. W., & Sehendel, D. (1978). *Strategy formulation: Analytical concepts*. West Publishing.

Hoffmann, W. H., & Schaper-Rinkel, W. (2001). Acquire or ally? A strategy framework for deciding between acquisition and cooperation . *MIR: Management International Review, 41*(2), 131–159.

Hoffmann, W. H., & Schlosser, R. (2001). Success factors of strategic alliances in small and medium-sized enterprises—An empirical survey. *Long Range Planning, 34*(3), 357–382.

Holl, P., & Kyriazis, D. (1997). Wealth creation and bid resistance in UK takeover bids. *Strategic Management Journal, 18*(6), 483–498.

Holmen, E., & Pedersen, A. C. (2003). Strategizing through analyzing and influencing the network horizon. *Industrial Marketing Management, 32*(5), 409–418.

Hood, N., & Young, S. (1979). *The economics of multinational enterprise*. Longman.

Hu, F., & Yu, X. D. (2003). Comparison of cross-border mergers and acquisitions and new investment, *Financial Research* (2).

Hu, J. W. (2006). On the construction of potential collaborative research framework in strategic mergers and acquisitions. *Journal of Dongbei University of Finance and Economics* (5).

Hu, J. W., & Han, L. (2015). Macroeconomic factors and shareholder wealth effect of cross-border mergers and acquisitions. *Journal of Beijing Jiaotong University (Social Science Edition), 14*(1), 60–69.

Hu, J. W., & Zhang, Q. S. (2006). Research on the efficiency of resource transfer in strategic mergers and acquisitions. *Journal of Zhengzhou Institute of Aviation Industry Management* (5).

Hu, J. W., & Zhang, Q. S. (2007). Classification and transfer of corporate resources under the background of mergers and acquisitions. *China Soft Science* (2).

Hu, J. W., Zhang, Q. S., & Xie, J. G. (2008). An empirical study on the long-term wealth effect of Chinese listed companies' management buyouts. *China Soft Science* (9).

Hu, J. W., Zhang, Q. S. & Xie, J. G. (2008). Research on the pricing of Chinese listed companies' management buyout equity. *Productivity Research* (16).

Hua, B., Chen, H. M., & Pan, X. J. (2003). Dynamic game model of enterprise merger in upstream market entry. *Journal of Shanghai Jiaotong University, 37*(4).

Hua, B., Chen, H. M., & Weng, Y. C. (2003). Analysis on the long-term effect of horizontal mergers of different firms. *Chinese Journal of Management Engineering* (2).

Hua, B., & Chen, H. M. (2003). Research on enterprise horizontal merger based on product difference. *Forecast* (1).

Huang, F. M. (2004). Systematic analysis of mergers and acquisitions integration based on core competencies. *Journal of Henan University of Science and Technology* (*Social Science Edition*) (9).

Huang, S. Z. (1997). Fair value accounting: A measurement model facing the 21st century. *Accounting Research* (12).

Huang, S. Z. (2005). Comparison of differences in asset impairment standards and policy suggestions. *Accounting Research* (1).

Huang, S. Z., Chen, J. S., Zhang, X. Z., et al. (2004). Analysis of economic consequences of business combination accounting: Also on the integration of measurement attributes in China's accounting standards system. *Accounting Research* (8).

Huang, S. Z., & Meng, P. (2001). Discussion on some theoretical issues of consolidated accounting statements. *Accounting Research* (5).

Huang, Z. W. (2004). A new interpretation framework: The eclectic theory of cross-border M&A. *Academic Forum* (1).

Ismail, A., & Krause, A. (2010). Determinants of the method of payment in mergers and acquisitions. *Quarterly Review of Economics and Finance, 50*(4), 471–484.

Itami, H. (1987). *Mobilizing invisible assets*. Harvard University Press.

Iyer D. N, & Miller K. D. (2008). Performance feedback, slack, and the timing of acquisitions. *Academy of Management Journal, 51*(4), 808–822.

Jackson, G., & Höpner, M. (2001). *An emerging market for corporate control? The Mannesmann takeover and German corporate governance* (MPIfG Discussion Paper No. 01/4). Max Planck Institute for the Study of Societies. http://ssrn.com/abstract=285232 or https://doi.org/10.2139/ssrn.285232

Jemison, D. B., & Sitkin, S. B. (1986). Corporate acquisitions: A process perspective. *Academy of Management Review, 11*(1), 145–163.

Jensen, M. C. (1986). Agency costs of free cash flow, corporate finance, and takeovers. *American Economic Review, 76*(2), 323–329.

Jensen, M. C. (2011). Takeovers: Their causes and consequences. *Journal of Economic Perspectives, 2*(1), 21–48.

Jensen, M. C., & Ruback, R. S. (1983). The market for corporate control: The scientific evidence. *Journal of Financial Economics, 11*(1–4), 5–50.

Ji, N. Y., & Zhang, J. X. (2007). Strategic analysis and prospect of CNOOC's merger of Sinochem Construction and Sinochem Supply. *Hebei Enterprises* (8).

Jiang, J. L., & Liu, Z. L. (2010). Goodwill information system: A measurement model based on new excessive return theory. *East China Economic Management, 24*(12).

Jiang, R. C. (1995). On intangible resources and intangible assets of enterprises. *Journal of Beijing Business School* (4).

Jiang, X. L., Qin, Z. P., & Li, C. Y. (2013). The diversification strategy and operational performance analysis of China's listed companies: An empirical study based on conglomerate mergers and acquisitions. *International Trade Issues, 1*, 158–167.

Jin, X. R., & Yu, L. Z. (2002). Lack of control right and impediment to property rights of private enterprises. *China Rural Economy* (8).

Jin, Y. H., & Jia, C. J. (2003). Inertia and M&A strategic choice. *Financial Research* (12).

Kaden, K. (2009). Due diligence challenges in today's financial market. *High Yield Report, 20*(1), 5–12.

Kale, P., & Singh, H. (1999). *Alliance capability and success: A knowledge—based approach* (Knowledge@Wharton Working Paper).

Kale, P., Dyer, J. H., & Singh, H. (2002). Alliance capability, stock market response, and long-term Alliance success: The role of the Alliance function. *Strategic Management Journal, 23*(8), 747–767.

Kang, R. P.,& Ke, Y. B. (2005). An important way for Chinese enterprises to go global: Cross-border mergers and acquisitions. *Economics Affairs* (3).

Kapferer, J. N. (1992). How global are global brands? In ESOMAR (Ed.), *The challenge of branding today and in the future* (pp. 199–215). ESOMAR.

Kaplan, R. S., & Norton, D. P. (2005). *Strategy maps: Converting intangible assets into tangible outcomes* (J. Liu & W. Sun, Trans.). Guangdong Economy Publishing House.

Kaplan, S. (1989). Management buyouts: Evidence on taxes as a source of value. *Journal of Finance, 44*(3), 611–632.

Kim, E. H., & McConnell, J. J. (1977). Corporate mergers and the co- insurance of corporate debt. *Journal of Finance, 32*(2), 349–365.

Kimura, Y. (1989). Firm-specific strategic advantages and foreign direct investment behavior of firms: The case of Japanese semiconductor firms. *Journal of International Business Studies, 20*(2), 296–314.

Kogut, B., & Zander, U. (1992). Knowledge of the firm, combinative capabilities, and the replication of technology. *Organization Science, 3*(3), 383–397.

Kogut, B. (1988). Joint ventures: Theoretical and empirical perspectives. *Strategic Management Journal, 9*(4), 319–332.

Kogut, B. (1989). The stability of joint ventures: Reciprocity and competitive rivalry. *Journal of Industrial Economics, 38*(2), 183–198.

Kogut, B., & Singh, H. (1988). The effect of national culture on the choice of entry mode. *Journal of International Business Studies, 19*(3), 411–432.

Kostopoulos, K. C., Spanos, Y. E., & Prastacos, G. P. (2002). The resource-based view of the firm and innovation: Identification of critical linkages [Paper presentation] . The 2nd European Academy of Management Conference, Stockholm, Sweden. http://ecsocman.edu.ru/images/pubs/2003/01/05/0000035682/rb_view.pdf

Krüger, W., & Homp, C. (2004). *Winning the merger endgame* (K. Deans, Trans.). China Machine Press.

Kumar, M. S. (1984). Comparative analysis of UK domestic and international firms. *Journal of Economic Studies, 11*(3), 26–42.

Kumar, V., & Subramaniam, V. (1997). A contingency framework for the mode of entry decision. *Journal of World Business, 32*(1), 53–72.

Laamanen, T., & Keil, T. (2008). Performance of serial acquirers: Toward an acquisition program perspective. *Strategic Management Journal, 29*(6), 663–672.

Lai, B. H., & Zhang, Q. S. (2006). *Foreign direct investment and China's railway human capital accumulation* [Conference presentation]. 2006 Annual Meeting of China Association for Science and Technology, Beijing, China.

Lai, B. H., & Zhang, Q. S. (2008). Enterprise vertical boundary under supply chain management. *Logistics Technology, 31*(10).

Lambkin, M. (1988). Order of entry and performance in new markets. *Strategic Management Journal, 9*(S1), 127–140.

Lambrecht, B. M. (2004). The timing and terms of mergers motivated by economies of scale. *Journal of Financial Economics, 72*(1), 41–62.

Larimo, J. (1993). *Foreign direct investment behaviour and performance: An analysis of Finnish direct manufacturing investment in OECD countries* (Acta Wasaensia No. 32). University of Vaasa.

Larimo, J. (1995). The foreign direct investment decision process: Case studies of different types of decision processes in Finnish firms. *Journal of Business Research, 33*(1), 25–55.

Larson, K. D., & Gonedes, N. J. (1969). Business combinations : An exchange ratio determination model. *The Accounting Review, 44*(4), 720–728.

Lecraw, D. J. (1984). Diversification strategy and performance. *Journal of Industrial Economics, 33*(2), 179–198.

Lee, G. K., & Lieberman, M. B. (2010). Acquisition vs. internal development as modes of market entry. *Strategic Management Journal, 31*(2), 140–158.

Leenders, R. T. A. J., & Gabbay, S. M. (1999). CSC: An agenda for the future. In R. T. A. J. Leenders & S. M. Gabbay (Eds.), *Corporate Social Capital and Liability* (pp. 482–491). Springer.

Leibenstein, H. (1966). Allocative efficiency vs. x-efficiency. *American Economic Review, 56*(3), 392–415.

Leonard-Barton, D. (1992). Core capabilities and core rigidities: A paradox in managing new product development. *Strategic Management Journal, 13*(S1), 111–125.

Leontiades, M. (1986). *Managing the unmanageable: Strategies for success within the conglomerate*. Basic Books.

Levitt, B., & March, J. G. (1988). Organizational learning. *Annual Review of Sociology, 14*(1), 319–340.

Lewellen, W. G. (1971). A pure financial rationale for the conglomerate merger. *Journal of Finance, 26*(2), 521–537.

Lewellen, W. G., & Huntsman, B. (1970). Managerial pay and corporate performance. *American Economic Review, 60*(4), 710–720.

Li, X. (2004). See enterprise merger and integration from enterprise ability. *Market Weekly* (4).

Li, D., Li, Q. H., & Wang, X. (2005). Defects in enterprise capability: Contingency analysis model and corresponding path analysis. *Journal of Southeast University (Philosophy and Social Sciences Edition), 7*(5).

Li, J., & Qian, C. (2013). Principal-principal conflicts under weak institutions: A study of corporate takeovers in China. *Strategic Management Journal, 34*(4), 498–508.

Li, Q. H. (2004). Research on the mechanism of enterprise capability engagement. *Journal of Southeast University (Philosophy and Social Sciences Edition)* (6).

Li, R. H., Chen, H. M., & Zou. L. R. (2005a). An empirical study on the gains from the transfer of control right of Chinese listed companies. *Journal of Shanghai Jiao Tong University*, 39(10).

Li, R. H., Chen, H. M., & Zou. L. R. (2005b). An empirical study on the leading forces and leading motives of Chinese enterprises' mergers. *Economic Theory and Economic Management* (8).

Li, R. H., Chen, H. M., & Zou. L. R. (2005c). An empirical study on the stock price performance of different mergers. *Research on Financial Issues* (9).

Li, R. H., Chen, H. M., & Zou. L. R. (2006). An empirical study on the macro factors affecting Chinese enterprise mergers. *Management Review, 18*(5).

Li, S. M., & Zhang Y. C. (2007). Control interests and exclusive management ability: An analysis based on the perspective of transaction. *China Industrial Economics* (5).

Li, S. M., & Wang, C. P. (2003). Analysis of Greencool's acquisition of Kelon Electric. *Economic Theory and Economic Management* (11).

Li, S. M., & Wang, C. P. (2005). Asset divestment based on value creation: A case study of Shenzhen Vanke Co., Ltd. *Journal of Guangzhou Finance and Trade Management Cadre College* (4).

Li, S. M., & Ye H. (2007). Research on the private benefit of control right, agency problem and enterprise M&A process. *South China Journal of Economics* (12).

Li, S. M., & Zheng N. L. (2007). The influence of shareholder-stakeholder game on the shareholder wealth effect of the acquirer. *Journal of Financial Research* (8).

Li, S. M., & Zheng N. L. (2008). Scale of target companies and mergers and acquisitions performance: A comparative study on industry integration strategies of Tsingtao Beer and Yanjing Beer. *Securities Market Herald* (1).

Li, S. M., & Zhou X. C. (2007). An empirical study on company characteristics, industry characteristics and M&A strategy types. *Management World* (3).

Li, S. M., & Zhu T. (2005a). Long-term performance of mergers and acquisitions of listed companies in China: A research based on the securities market. *Journal of Sun Yat-Sen University (Social Science Edition), 45*(5).

Li, S. M., & Zhu T. (2005b). Research on the relationship between managerial motivation and mergers and acquisitions performance. *Economic Management* (4).

Li, S. M., & Zhu T. (2006). Can diversified M&A create value for shareholders? Also on the factors affecting the long-term performance of diversified M&A. *Management World* (3).

Li, S. M., Chen, Y. G., & Zhu, T., et al. (2004). Prediction model of market response for asset restructuring. *Management Review, 16*(7).

Li, S. M., & Chen, Y. (2002). The wealth effect of mergers and acquisitions of listed companies. *Economic Research* (11).

Li, S., & Chen, Y. G. (2004). Mergers and acquisitions: A preliminary study based on the perspective of relative transaction cost. *Journal of Sun Yat-Sen University (Social Science Edition), 44*(6).

Li, S. M., Hu, Z., & Xia, Y. (2007). Successful well-intentioned strategic M&A under the competition for market control: An analysis of Mrs. Pharmaceutical's acquisition of Livzon Group. *Economic Management* (23).

Li, S. M., & Li, C. (2013). Cross-border M&A or greenfield investment? A study on influencing factors of FDI entry mode selection. *Economic Research, 48*(12), 134–147.

Li, S. M., & Li, H. (2003). Research on asset restructuring performance of Chinese listed companies. *Management World* (11).

Li, S. M., Li, H., Wang, C. P., et al. (2003). Performance evaluation system of asset restructuring of listed companies in China. *Management Review, 15*(1).

Li, S. M., Wang, C. P., Zeng, Z. Z., et al. (2004). Research on long- term performance of asset restructuring of Chinese listed companies. *Management World* (9).

Li, S. M., Wang, D. Y., & Zhu, T. (2006). The separation of control rights and cash flow rights and the performance of listed companies. *Journal of Sun Yat-Sen University (Social Science Edition), 46*(6).

Li, S. M., Xi, C., & Wan, Z. Q. (2014). The Rolls Corporation acquisition case and the U. S. security review: The U. S. regulatory framework for foreign mergers and acquisitions and its enlightenment to China. *Journal of Sun Yat-Sen University (Social Science Edition), 54*(1), 199–208.

Li, S. M., Xu, J. H., Zhang, D., et al. (2016). Do anti-takeover provisions protect the rights of minority investors? Evidence from China's A-share listed companies. *Nankai Management Review, 19*(4), 49–62.

Li, S. M., Yu, J. W., Zhong, L., et al. (2005). The correlation analysis between the nature and institution of asset reorganization. *Research on Economics and Management* (6).

Li, S. M., & Zeng, Z. Z. (2003). Quality differentiation and product complementary enterprise merger. *Journal of Management Science* (6).

Li, S. M., & Zeng, Z. Z. (2003). Research on the background of control right transfer and the characteristics of control right transfer companies. *Economic Research* (11).

Li, S. M., Zhou M. T., & Yu P. Y. (2006). Research on the influence of ultimate ownership and governance mechanism on enterprise performance. *Journal of Management Sciences, 9*(5).

Li, S. M., Zhu, T., Chen, Y. G., et al. (2004). An empirical analysis of the performance of the paired portfolio of acquirers and target companies. *Economic Research* (6).

Li, W., & Song X. L. (2007). Discussion on the financial strategy of screening target enterprises in mergers and acquisitions. *Productivity Research* (5).

Li, W. (2007). Strategic positioning of group mergers and acquisitions based on resource network technology. *Logistics Technology, 26*(9).

Li, W., Liu Y., & Zhang Q. S. (2006). Inquiring about foreign mergers and acquisitions. *National Conditions and National Strength* (11).

Li, X., & Zhang Q. S. (2003). There is a growing market for corporate control. *Talents Magazine* (1).

Li, X. W. (2006). *Operational research on dynamic capability theory: Identification.* Economic Science Press.

Li, X. D., Zhu, H. L., Zhang, B., et al. (2003). Research on M&A efficiency of listed companies based on DEA. *Economic Research* (10).

Li, Y. J., & Zhang Q. S. (2006). Research on accounting elements based on enterprise resources. *Accounting Research* (1).

Lintner, J. (1971). Expectations, mergers and equilibrium in purely competitive securities markets. *American Economic Review, 61*(2), 101–111.

Lipton, M. (1987). Corporate governance in the age of finance corporatism, *University of Pennsylvania Law Review, 136*(1), 1–72. http://www.jstor.org/pss/3312044

Liu, C., Li, S. M., & Sun, L. (2015). Do independent directors have consulting function? An empirical study on the function of independent directors in different places in mergers and acquisitions. *Management World, 3*, 124–136.

Liu, K. X., Yang W. M., & Xuan G. L. (1997). A petri net model for establishing enterprise M&A strategy. *Journal of Shanghai Jiaotong University, 31*(4).

Liu, X. P., Huang, X. W., & Guo, H. Y. (2009). An empirical study on industrial cycle, M&A type and M&A performance. *Journal of Financial Research, 3*, 135–153.

Liu, Y., & Zhang Q. S. (2008). The linkage and integration between logistics industry and basic industry from the perspective of merger and acquisition. *Logistics Technology, 27*(11).

Liu, Y. (2004). Leveraged buyout and its financing issues. *The Accountant, 10*, 38–40.

Liu, Y., Li, W., & Zhang, Q. S. (2006). *Research on M&A direction decision based on resource perspective* [Conference presentation]. The 9th Annual Meeting of the China Association for Science and Technology, Beijing, China.

Lommerud, K. E., Straume, O. R., & Sorgard, L. (2005). Downstream merger with upstream market power. *European Economic Review, 49*(3), 717–743.

Long, W., Zhang, H., & Zhang T. (2005). Research on the ownership structure and transaction characteristics of China's listed companies' control market. *Journal of Guangdong Polytechnic Normal University* (3).

Lorange, P., & Roos, J. (1993). *Strategic alliances: Formation, implementation, and evolution.* Blackwell Business.

Lorange, P., & Roos, J. (1990). Formation of cooperative ventures: Competence mix of the management teams. *Management International Review, 30*, 69–86.

Loughran, T., & Vijh, A. M. (1997). Do long term shareholders benefit from corporate acquisitions? *Journal of Finance, 52*(5), 1765–1790.

Lu, C. B. (2012). A new framework of relationship marketing practice: A research based on enterprise network and social capital. *China Business and Market* (10).

Lu, D. B. (1997). Promoting enterprise merger and accelerating the reform of state-owned enterprises. *Economic Theory and Business Management* (6).

Lu, D. B. (1998). The road to growth in the age of knowledge economy: On the asset reorganization and mergers and acquisitions of high-tech enterprises. *China private economy of science and technology* (8).

Lu, D. B. (2003a). Corporate culture in mergers and acquisitions: Respecting differences and shortening distances. *China Finance* (23).

Lu, D. B. (2003b). Merger and reorganization between giants: A strategic choice for private enterprises to become bigger and stronger—A case study of the establishment of Stoutness Group Co., Ltd. and its enlightenment. *Economic Theory and Business Management* (12).
Lubatkin, M. (1987). Merger strategies and stockholder value. *Strategic Management Journal, 8*(1), 39–53.
Luo, M. (2003). *Organizational management*. Southwestern University of Finance and Economics Press.
Maijoor, S., & Witteloostuijn, A. V. (1996). An empirical test of the resource-based theory: Strategic regulation in the Dutch audit industry. *Strategic Management Journal, 17*(7), 549–569.
Makadok, R. (2001). Toward a synthesis of the resource-based and dynamic-capability views of rent creation. *Strategic Management Journal, 22*(5), 387–401.
Marshall, A. (1965). *Principles of economics* (Z. Zhu & L. Chen, Trans.). The Commercial Press.
Manne, H. (1965). Mergers and the market for corporate control. *Journal of Political Economy, 73*(2), 110–120.
Mark, L. S. (2001). *The synergy trap: How companies lose the acquisition game* (J. Yang, Trans.). Shanghai Far East Publishing House.
Marks, M. L., & Mirvis, P. H. (2000). Managing mergers, acquisitions and alliances: Creating and effective transition structure. *Organizational Dynamics, 28*(3), 35–47.
Mattoo, A., Olarreaga, M., & Saggi, K. (2004). Mode of foreign entry, technology transfer, and FDI policy. *Journal of Development Economics, 75*(1), 95–111.
Melicher, R. W., Ledolter, J., & D'Antonio, L. (1983). A time series analysis of aggregate merger activity. *Review of Economics and Statistics, 65*(3), 423–430.
Meng, F. P., & Linghu W. C. (2004). International comparison of tender offer system. *Journal of Beijing Jiaotong University (Social Science Edition), 3*(2).
Meng, Q. L. (2013). Measurement and empirical test of synergistic effects of mergers and acquisitions. *Statistics & Decision, 24*, 173–175.
Miller, D., & Shamsie, J. (1996). The resource-based view of the firm in two environments: The Hollywood firm studios from 1936–1965. *Strategic Management Journal, 39*(3), 519–543.
Montgomery, C. A., & Wilson, V. A. (1986). Mergers that last: A predictable pattern? *Strategic Management Journal, 7*(1), 91–96.
Moskalev, S. A. (2010). Foreign ownership restrictions and cross-border markets for corporate control. *Journal of Multinational Financial Management, 20*(1), 48–70.
Mowery, D. C., Oxley, J. E., & Silverman, B. S. (1996). Strategic alliances and interfirm knowledge transfer. *Strategic Management Journal, 17*, 77–91.
Mudambi, R., & Mudambi, S. M. (2002). Diversification and market entry choices in the context of foreign direct investment. *International Business Review, 11*(1), 35–55.
Mueller, D. C. (1969). A theory of conglomerate mergers. *Quarterly Journal of Economics, 83*(4), 643–659.
Muscarella, C. J., & Vetsuypens, M. R. (1990). Efficiency and organizational structure: A study of reverse lbos. *Journal of Finance, 45*(5), 1389–1413.
Myers, S. C. (1984). The capital structure puzzle. *Journal of Finance, 39*(3), 575–592.
Myers, S. C., & Majluf, N. S. (1984). Corporate financing and investment decisions when firms have information that investors do not have. *Journal of Financial Economics, 13*(2), 187–221.
Nath, P., Nachiappan, S., & Ramanathan, R. (2010). The impact of marketing capability, operations capability and diversification strategy on performance: A resource-based view. *Industrial Marketing Management, 39*(2), 317–329.
Nelson, R. L. (1959). *Merger movement in American industry, 1895–1956*. Princeton University Press.
Nelson, R. R., & Winter, S. G. (1982). *An evolutionary theory of economic change*. Harvard University Press.
Nonaka, I. (1991). The knowledge-creating company. *Harvard Business Review, 69*(6), 96–104.
Nonaka, I., & Takeuchi, H. (1995). *The knowledge-creating company: How Japanese companies create the dynamics of innovation*. Oxford University Press.

Oliver, C. (1990). Determinants of interorganizational relationships: Integration and future directions. *Academy of Management Review, 15*(2), 241–265.

Osborn, R. N., & Baughn, C. C. (1993). Forms of interorganizational governance for multinational alliances. *Academy of Management Journal, 36*(2), 259–267.

Oxelheim, L., Randøy, T., & Stonehill, A. (2001). On the treatment of finance-specific factors within the OLI paradigm. *International Business Review, 10*(4), 381–398.

Pan, H. B., & Yu, M. G. (2011). The supporting hand, the plundering hand and foreign mergers and acquisitions. *Economic Research Journal, 9*, 108–120.

Pan, L. Y. (1999). *Analysis of the synergistic effect of corporate mergers and acquisitions* (Master's thesis). Beijing Jiaotong University.

Pan, Y. G., Tao, Z. G., & Lu, J. Y. (2005). *When to ally and when to acquire: Expansion strategies of multinational firms in China* (HKIEBS Working Paper No. 1124). Hong Kong Institute of Economics and Business Strategy, The University of Hong Kong. http://www.asia-studies.com/HIEBS.html

Parkhe, A. (1991). Interfirm diversity, organizational learning, and congvity in global strategic alliance. *Journal of International Business Studies, 22*(4), 579–601.

Pennings, J. M., & Lee, K. (1999). Social capital of organization: Conceptualization, level of analysis, and performance implications. *Corporate social capital and liability* (pp. 43–67). Springer US.

Pennings, J. M., Lee, K., & Van Witteloostuijn, A. (1998). Human capital, social capital, and firm dissolution. *Academy of Management Journal, 41*(4), 425–440.

Penrose, E. T. (1959). *The theory of the growth of the firm*. Basil Blackwell.

Peteraf, M. A. (1993). The cornerstones of competitive advantage: A resource-based view. *Strategic Management Journal, 14*(3), 179–191.

Poole, M. S., & Van de Ven, A. H. (1989). Using paradox to build management and organization theories. *Academy of Management Review, 14*(4), 562–578.

Porrini, P. (2004). Can a previous alliance between an acquirer and a target affect acquisition performance? *Journal of Management, 30*(4), 545–562.

Porter, M. E. (1985). *Competitive advantage: Creating and sustaining superior performance*. Free Press.

Porter, M. E. (1997). *Competitive advantage* (X. Chen, Trans.). Huaxia Publishing House.

Porter, M. E. (2002). *The competitive advantage of nations* (X. Chen, Trans.). Huaxia Publishing House.

Portes, A., & Sensenbrenner, J. (1993). Embeddedness and immigration: Notes on the social determinants of economic action. *American Journal of Sociology, 98*(6), 1320.

Portes, A. (1998). Social capital: Its origins and applications in modern sociology. *Annual Review of Sociology, 24*(1), 1–24.

Prahalad, C. K., & Doz, Y. L. (1987). *The multinational mission: Balancing local demands and global vision*. Free Press.

Prahalad, C. K., & Hamel, G. (1990). The core competence of the corporation. *Harvard Business Review, 68*(3), 79–91.

Putnam, R. D. (1995). Bowling alone: America's declining social capital. *Current, 373*, 3–9.

Qi, J. P., & He, X. M. (2015). Can the social capital of the executive team change the performance of corporate mergers and acquisitions? *Research on Financial and Economic Issues, 12*, 111–118.

Qin, Y. L., & Tong J. (2008). Motives of M&A in international shipping industry and its enlightenment to Chinese shipping enterprises. *Logistics Technology, 27*(4).

Qin, Y. L., & Wang, L. Y. (2008). Research on earnings management of listed companies transferring control in China. *Productivity Research* (12).

Qin, Y. L., & Zhou, S. N. (2004). Control right market and resource allocation. *Liaoning Economy* (1).

Qu, T., & Li, S. M. (2004). Corporate governance structure and cross- border M&A. *Journal of Guangdong University of Business Studies* (3).

Ramanathan, K., Seth, A., & Thomas, H. (1997). Explaining joint ventures: Alternative theoretical perspectives. In P. W. Beamish, & J. P. Killing (Eds.), *Cooperative strategies: North American perspectives* (pp. 51–85). The New Lexington Press.

Rau, P. R., & Vermaelen, T. (1998). Glamour, value and the post- acquisition performance of acquiring firms. *Journal of Financial Economics, 49*(2–3), 223–253.

Raudszus, M., Schiereck, D., & Trillig, J. (2013). Does vertical diversification create superior value? Evidence from the construction industry. *Review of Managerial Science, 8*(1), 1–33.

Reddy, S. K., Holak, S. L., & Bhat, S. (1994). To extend or not to extend: Success determinants of line extensions. *Journal of Marketing Research, 31*(2), 241–262.

Rhodes-Kropf, M., & Robinson, D. T. (2004). *The market for mergers and the boundaries of the firm* (AFA 2005 Philadelphia Meetings Paper). http://ssrn.com/abstract=547183

Riad, R. (2005). The power of organizational culture as a discursive formation in merger integration. *Organization Studies, 26*(10), 1529–1554.

Richardson, G. B. (1972). The organisation of industry. *The Economic Journal, 82*(327), 883–896.

Robert K. Yin. (1994). *Case study research: Design and methods* (2nd ed.). Sage Publications.

Roberto, B. (2004). Acquisition versus greenfield investment: The location of foreign manufacturers in Italy. *Regional Science and Urban Economics, 34*(1), 3–25.

Robinson, D. T. (2008). Strategic alliance and the boundaries of the firm. *Review of Financial Studies, 21*(2), 649–681.

Roll, R. (1986). The hubris hypothesis of corporate takeovers. *Journal of Business, 59*(2), 197–216.

Rondinelli, D. A., & Black, S. S. (2000). Multinational strategic alliances and acquisitions in Central and Eastern Europe: Partnerships in privatization. *The Academy of Management Executive, 14*(4), 85–98.

Rossiter, J. R., & Percy, L. (1997). *Advertising communications & promotion management* (2nd ed.). McGraw-Hill.

Rubin, P. H. (1973). The expansion of firms. *Journal of Political Economy, 81*(4), 936–949.

Salter, M. S., & Weinhold, W. A. (1978). Diversification via acquisition: Creating value. *Harvard Business Review, 56*(4), 166–176.

Sappington, D. E. M., & Wernerfelt, B. (1985). To brand or not to brand? A theoretical and empirical question. *Journal of Business, 58*(3), 279–293.

Selznick, P. (1957). *Leadership in administration: A sociological interpretation*. Harper & Row.

Shelton, L. M. (1988). Strategic business fits and corporate acquisition: Empirical evidence. *Strategic Management Journal, 9*(3), 279–287.

Shen, Y. F. (2000). The modern evolution of the market theory of corporate control (Vols. 1–2): The theoretical significance of anti-takeover legislation in thirty-five states in the United States. *China Economic Studies* (2).

Shen, Y. F., Shen H. T., & Hong X. X. (2004). The formation and development of post-capital structure theory: Capital structure management control theory and its verification. *Journal of Xiamen University (Arts & Social Sciences)* (1).

Shi, D. H. (2003). An empirical study on the value of control rights of listed companies. *Economic Science* (6).

Shi, H. L., Wang, Y. M., & Chen, S. Q. (2005). Mergers and acquisitions matching strategy considering efficiency and scale. *Journal of Systems Science and Mathematical Sciences, 25*(6), 695–706.

Shleifer, A., & Vishny, R. W. (1989). Management entrenchment: The case of manager-specific investments. *Journal of Financial Economics, 25*(1), 123–139.

Shleifer, A., & Vishny, R. W. (2003). Stock market driven acquisitions. *Journal of Financial Economics, 70*(3), 295–311.

Shocker, A. D., Srivastava, R. K., & Ruekert, R. W. (1994). Challenges and opportunities facing brand management: An introduction to the special issue. *Journal of Marketing Research, 31*(2), 149–158.

Shughart, W. F., II, & Tollison, R. D. (1984). The random character of merger activity. *TheRAND Journal of Economics, 15*(4), 500–520.

Singh, J., & Montgomery, C. A. (1987). Corporate acquisition strategies and economic performance. *Strategic Management Journal, 8*(4), 377–386.

Sirower, M., & Harrigan, K. R. (1997). *The synergy limitation paradox* (Columbia Business School Working Paper). Columbia University.

Sleptsov, A., Anand, J., & Vasudeva, G. (2013). Relational configurations with information intermediaries: The effect of firm-investment bank ties on expected acquisition performance. *Strategic Management Journal, 34*(8), 957–977.

Sokolyk, T. (2011). The effects of antitakeover provisions on acquisition targets. *Journal of Corporate Finance, 17*(3), 612–627.

Song, H., Shang, Y. (2000). New trends in human resource management: From job-based to competency-based human resource management. *Frontiers of Science and Technology of Engineering Management* (4).

Song, S. Q., & Dai, S. J. (2015). Managerial overconfidence, types of M&A and M&A performance. *Macroeconomics, 5*, 139–149.

Song, X. L., Zhang, Q. S., & Chu, Y. H. (2008). An empirical study on the performance of share swap M&A of listed companies in China. *China Industrial Economics* (7).

Srivastava, R. K., Shervani, T. A., & Fahey, L. (1998). Market-based assets and shareholder value: A framework for analysis. *Journal of Marketing, 62*(1), 2–18.

Stalk, G., Evans, P., & Shulman, L. E. (1992). Competing on capabilities: The new rules of corporate strategy. *Harvard Business Review, 70*(2), 57–69.

Stigler, G. J. (1950). Capitalism and monopolistic competition: I. The theory of oligopoly. The *American Economic Review, 40*(2), 23–34.

Su, Z. W. (2012). A review of research on dynamic capabilities of firms based on M&A perspective. *Foreign Economics & Management, 34*(10), 48–56.

Su, J. Q., & Wang, H. C. (2010). Discussion and definition of enterprise resource classification framework. *Science of Science and Management of S.& T, 31*(2), 158–161.

Su, Q., & Liu, Q. (2012). A framework for M&A negotiation based on supply chain perspective. *Journal of Management Sciences in China, 15*(1), 77–86.

Sun, M., & Zhang, Q. S. (2008). Analysis of the efficiency of splitting and restructuring of railroad transport enterprises. *Productivity Research* (22), 145–146, 153.

Tang, X., & Xu, Z. Z. (2008). The legality test of anti-takeover measures. *Tsinghua University Law Journal* (6).

Tang, X., & Zhu, Y. Y. (2006). Anti-takeover measures under the new EU company law directive: Centering on the principle of establishing a fair competitive market. *Tsinghua Law Review* (0).

Tang, X. Y. (2006). Analysis of the impact of financing structure on the market of corporate control. *Contemporary Economics* (1).

Tang, X. (2001). *The value debate and legislative orientation of corporate acquisition*. China Renmin University Press.

Tang, X. (2008). "Economic security" and foreign M&A review. *Contemporary Law Review* (1).

Teece, D. J. (1992). Competition, cooperation, and innovation. *Journal of Economic Behavior & Organization.*

Teece, D. J., Pisano, G., & Shuen, A. (1997). Dynamic capabilities and strategic management. *Strategic Management Journal, 18*(7), 509–533.

Terpstra, V., & Yu, C. M. (1988). Determinants of foreign investment of U. S. advertising agencies. *Journal of International Business Studies, 19*(1), 33–46.

Tian, F., Zhang, Q. S., & Zhang, J. X. (2008). Research on the trend of M&A in China's control market after the stock split reform. *Journal of Beijing Jiaotong University (Social Sciences Edition)* (4).

Tong, W. (2005). Reflections on China's corporate control market. *Economic Review Journal* (6).

Tu, G. Q., Lin, B. X., & Liu, F. (2013). Political connections and privatization: Evidence from China. *Journal of Accounting and Public Policy, 32*(2), 114–135.

Uzzi, B. (1996). The sources and consequences of embeddedness for the economic performance of organizations: The network effect. *American Sociological Review, 61*(4), 674–698.

Vandeburg, J. M., Fulton, J. R., Hine, S., et al. (2000, December 13). Driving forces and success factors for mergers, acquisitions, joint ventures, and strategic alliances among local cooperatives [Paper presentation]. *NCR-194 Annual Meeting*, Las Vegas, NV, United States.
Van de Ven, A. H. (1976). A framework for organization assessment. *Academy of Management Review, 1*(1), 64–78.
Very, P., & Schweiger, D. M. (2001). The acquisition process as a learning process: Evidence from a study of critical problems and solutions in domestic and cross-border deals. *Journal of World Business, 36*(1), 11–31.
Wada, T. (2001). *Equity joint ventures and the scope of knowledge transfer between diversified firms: Evidence from U. S.-Japan alliances* (Gakushuin University Working Paper). Retrieved from http://emlab.berkeley.edu/users/bhhall/wada829.pdf
Wakeam, J. (2003). The five factors of a strategic alliance. *Ivey Business Journal, 67*(4), 1–4.
Wan, X. L., Li, R. H., & Chen, H. M. (2007). An empirical study on the influence of industrial factors on the frequency of corporate mergers. *Systems Engineering-Theory & Practice* (12).
Wang, C. (2000). M&A integration: Creating value through competence management. *Foreign Economics & Management* (12).
Wang, C., Wang, Q., & Tang, T. (2001). Corporate governance and corporate control market. *Economy* (5).
Wang, D. M., & Jin, Z. M. (2003). Human resource management in the era of knowledge economy. *Science-Technology and Management* (4).
Wang, D., & Li, H. (2004). Corporate culture differences in foreign investment M&A in China. *Journal of Henan University of Animal Husbandry and Economy* (4).
Wang, D., & Zhang, Q. S. (2004). *Corporate mergers and acquisitions: A case study*. Beijing Jiaotong University Press.
Wang, D. (1999). *Enterprise value assessment in M&A* (Master's thesis). Northern Jiaotong University.
Wang, D. (2004). A successful example of Chinese enterprises going global: Beijing Oriental's acquisition of Hyundai's TFT-LCD business in Korea. *Accountant* (10).
Wang, F., Xuan, G. L., & Fan, W. (2000). Resource-based view and its application to the theory of enterprise. *Economic Theory and Business Management* (4).
Wang, G. Y. (2002). Corporate control market and securities market efficiency. *Finance & Economics* (8).
Wang, G. Y. (2003). *Analysis of the shape and efficiency of corporate control market in China* (Doctoral dissertation). Fudan University.
Wang, G. S., et al. (2006). *Theory of the firm: Contract theory*. China Economic Publishing House.
Wang, H. C. (1991). Asset valuation in corporate M&A. *Friends of Accounting* (2).
Wang, H. X. (2004). *On the advantages of M&A-based factor transaction integration in MNCFDI* (Doctoral dissertation). Zhejiang University.
Wang, H. L. (2005). Exploring the classification of corporate M&A performance research methods. *Modern Economic Science* (1).
Wang, J. F. (2005). Bayes network-based enterprise capability assessment. *Journal of Lanzhou University of Finance and Economics* (2).
Wang, K. M., & Wan, J. K. (2000). On the transfer and diffusion of knowledge. *Foreign Economics & Management* (10).
Wang, L. J. (2006). *Analysis of firm growth and entrepreneurial activities: Also on the path sependence of firm growth and its transcendence*. Economic Science Press.
Wang, M. (2011). Analysis of M&A performance of listed companies with different payment methods. *Communication of Finance and Accounting* (5), 9–10.
Wang, Q. (2003). *Research on the synergy effect of corporate M&A* (Doctoral dissertation). Huazhong University of Science and Technology.
Wang, Y., & Zhang, Q. S. (2005). A comprehensive assessment method for measuring the contribution of M&A to corporate sustainable development. *Journal of Beijing Jiaotong University (Social Sciences Edition)* (3).

Wang, Y., Chen, J., & Xu, Q. R. (2000). Core competencies of enterprises: A theoretical tracing and logical structure analysis. *Journal of Management Sciences in China* (3).

Wang, Z. (2005). A theoretical review of corporate control gains. *Economic Exploration* (9).

Wang, M., & Wong, S. (2009). What drives economic growth? The case of cross-border M&A and greenfield FDI activities. *Kyklos, 62*(2), 316–330.

Weber, Y., Tarba, S. Y., & Bachar, Z. R. (2011). Mergers and acquisitions performance paradox: The mediating role of integration approach. *European Journal of International Management, 5*(4), 373–393.

Wei, J. (2002). *New thinking of corporate M&A strategy: A management model of corporate M&A and integration based on core competencies*. Science Press.

Weimer, C. M. (2009). Foreign direct investment and national security post-FINSA 2007. *Physical Review, 114*(1), 209–214.

Wen, F. (2004). *Cultural integration in corporate M&A* (Doctoral dissertation). Huazhong University of Science and Technology.

Wen, H. T. (2008). A review of western M&A performance theory. *Journal of Beijing Jiaotong University (Social Sciences Edition)* (1).

Weng, Y. C., Chen, H. M., & Ni, S. Y. (2003a). A review of the motivation of corporate mergers and their social welfare theoretical models. *Systems Engineering-Theory & Practice* (1).

Weng, Y. C., Chen, H. M., & Ni, S. Y. (2003b). A study of horizontal mergers based on network externalities. *Journal of Systems Engineering* (2).

Wernerfelt, B. (1984). A resource-based view of the firm. *Strategic Management Journal, 5*(2), 171–180.

Wernerfelt, B. (1985). Brand loyalty and user skills. *Journal of Economic Behavior and Organization, 6*(4), 381–385.

Wernerfelt, B. (1989). From critical resources to corporate strategy. *Journal of General Management, 14*(3), 4–12.

Weston, J. F., Mitchell, M. L., & Mulherin, J. H. (2006). *Takeover, Restructuring and Corporate Governance* (Q. Zhang, H. Zhang, & Y. Chen, Trans.). Peking University Press.

Weston, J. F., & Susan, H. (1998). *Mergers*. Economic Science Press.

Weston, J. F., Zheng, G., & Su, Y. (2000). *Takeover*. Northeast University of Finance and Economics Press.

Williamson, O. E. (1981). The economics of organization: The transaction cost approach. *American Journal of Sociolgy, 87*(3), 548–577.

Williamson, O. E. (1985). *The economic institutions of capitalism*. Free Press.

Wilson, B. D. (1980). The propensity of multinational companies to expand through acquistions. *Journal of International Business Studies, 11*(1), 59–65.

Winter, S. G. (1987). Knowledge and competence as strategic assets. In *The strategic management of intellectual capital* (pp. 165–187). Routledge.

Woodcock, C. P., Beamish, P. W., & Makino, S. (1994). Ownership- based entry mode strategies and international performance. *Journal of International Business Studies, 25*(2), 253–273.

Wright, P. M., Dunford, B. B., & Snell, S. A. (2001). Human resources and the resource based view of the firm. *Journal of Management, 27*(6), 701–721.

Wu, Z., & Choi, T. (2005). Supplier-supplier relationships in the buyer- supplier triad: Building theories from eight case studies. *Journal of Operations Management, 24*, 27–52.

Wu, C. P., Wu, S. N., & Zheng, F. B. (2008). A theoretical and empirical study of managerial behavior and sequential M&A performance. *Journal of Management World* (7), 126–133, 188.

Wu, Q. (2004). Marketization of corporate control, equity diversification and governance of listed companies. *Journal of Zhejiang Business Technology Institute* (2).

Wu, X. M., & Xie, W. Y. (2016). Matching of firm-specific advantages, host country-specific advantages and OFDI patterns—The moderating role of institutional environment. *Economy and Management* (3), 90–96.

Wu, Z. G., Han, Y. Q., & Zhou, Y. Z. (2004). Research on enterprise capability index measurement model. *Operations Research and Management Science* (1).

Wu, Z. G., Han, Y. Q., Zhou, Y. Z., et al. (2004). Research on the mechanism of enterprise capability evolution in complex environment. *Science of Science and Management of S.& T.* (4).
Xia, Q. H. (2002). From resources to capabilities: A theoretical review of competitive advantage strategies. *Management World* (6).
Xie, H. J., & Jiang, D. C. (2017). Competitive advantage, asset prices and Chinese overseas mergers and acquisitions. *Financial Research, 1*, 83–98.
Xie, J. G., Tian, F., Ren, Q., et al. (2009). M&A management capability: A new perspective to explain the failure of corporate M&A. *Zhongda Management Research, 4*(4), 71–89.
Xie, J. G., Zhang, Q. S., & Chen, Y. (2008). Market reactions to the Chinese securities market holdings. *Productivity Research* (18).
Xie, L. H., Liu, S. C., & Qiu, W. H. (2012). The impact of managerial overconfidence on M&A performance: Analysis and empirical evidence based on group decision perspective. *Mathematical Statistics and Management, 31*(1), 122–133.
Xiong, D. W. (2002). The market function of control rights. *Finance and Economics Science* (7).
Xiong, P., & Wang, F. (2004). Capital structure, equity structure and the market for corporate control. *Journal of Shandong University of Science and Technology* (11).
Xu, C. Y., & Cai, G. N. (2004). The three-dimensional principle of strategic M&A model selection and its application. *Journal of Guizhou University of Finance and Economics* (6).
Xu, C. Y., & Cai, G. N. (2005). Research on risk-based strategic M&A model. *Soft Science* (1).
Xu, C. Y., & Gao, G. (2007). An empirical analysis of horizontal M&A performance of listed companies: Based on 2004 data from Shenzhen and Shanghai. *Journal of Wuhan Institute of Science and Technology* (12).
Xu, C. Y., & Shen, B. (2007). Strategic mergers and acquisitions, resource reallocation and economic growth. *Business Research* (11).
Xu, C. Y., & Shen, B. (2008). Research on the welfare effects of large firms' mergers and acquisitions of substitute manufacturers. *Management Science* (3).
Xu, C. Y., & Zhou, W. Y. (2004). Segment identification and systematic control of corporate M&A risk. *Science and Technology Progress and Countermeasures* (6).
Xu, C. Y. (2001). Investment perspective analysis of M&A of listed companies. *Management Modernization* (6).
Xu, C. Y. (2004a). *Risk management of corporate mergers and acquisitions* (Doctoral dissertation). Huazhong Agricultural University.
Xu, C. Y. (2004b). The application of grey correlation method in enterprise M&A risk measurement. *Journal of China Academy of Metrology* (3).
Xu, C. Y. (2005). System characteristics and process structure of M&A risk management. *Business Research* (10).
Xu, L. P., Chen, G. M., & Xin, Y. (2005). Research on property rights reform, control transfer and its market reaction, *Audit Research* (5).
Yan, A., & Gray, B. (1994). Bargaining power, management control, and performance in United States-China joint ventures: A comparative case study. *Academy of Management, 37*, 1478–1517.
Yan, S. S., & Zhang, R. J. (2005). Identification of enterprise resource- based theory and enterprise capability-based theory and their logical evolution. *Science and Technology Progress and Countermeasures* (5).
Yang, H. (2004). *The game structure of control market* (Doctoral dissertation). Hunan University.
Yang, Y., Deng, L., & Chen, S. (2014). Corporate life cycle, political affiliation and M&A strategy. *Management Review, 10*, 152–159.
Yao, W. X. (2005). Full circulation will detonate the M&A market. *New Finance* (6).
Ye, G. H., Zhang, Q. S., & Lai, B. H. (2009). A review of the literature on economic network synergy in M&A. *Productivity Research, 24*, 251–253.
Ye, H., & Li, S. M. (2008). A review of corporate M&A theory. *Journal of Guangdong Institute of Finance* (1).
Yip, G. S. (1982). Gateways to entry. *Harvard Business Review, 60*(5), 85–92.

Yu, P. L. (1980). Behavior bases and habitual domains of human decision/behavior—concepts and applications. *Lecture Notes in Economics & Mathematical Systems, 177*, 511–539.
Yu, C. Y., & Shi, J. J. (2011). External learning, technology acquisition frontier and innovation in the perspective of industrial upgrading. *Journal of International Trade, 6*, 128–141.
Yu, C. M. J., & Ito K. (1988). Oligopolistic reaction and foreign direct investment: The case of the U. S. tire and textiles industries. *Journal of International Business Studies, 19*(3), 449–460.
Yu, G. S. (2000). A new theory of enterprise (below): The theory of enterprise knowledge. *Foreign Economics and Management* (3).
Yu, J., Engleman, R. M., & Van de Ven, A. H. (2005). The integration journey: An attention-based view of the merger and acquisition integration process. *Organization Studies, 26*(10), 1501–1528.
Yu, J., Zhang, Q. S., & Wang, Y. (2014). Research on the causes of merger and acquisition failure: Based on the perspective of ultimate controlling shareholders' interest capture. *Securities Market Herald, 11*, 21–28.
Yu, P. Y., & Wang, M. S. (2014). An empirical analysis of factors influencing the performance of cross-border mergers and acquisitions of domestic listed companies. *Accounting Research, 3*, 64–70.
Yu, T. M., Gao, Y. X., & Zhang, J. X. (2004). Industry lifecycle and M&A types: An examination of the efficiency of Chinese corporate control market. *Journal of Beijing Jiaotong University (Social Science Edition)* (4).
Yu, Y., & Chen, Q. W. (2001). Industry concentration and control market efficiency. *Contemporary Economic Science* (2).
Yu, Y., Jiang, Y., & Yuan, M. J. (2004). *Strategic mergers and acquisitions: Three principles of managing risk*. Economic Science Press.
Yuan, H. Q., & Wu, X. Y. (1998). An empirical study on the impact of asset restructuring on financial performance. *Shanghai Securities News*, 26th August 1998.
Yuan, X. (2013). *Research on M&A synergy based on network perspective* (Doctoral dissertation). Beijing Jiaotong University.
Yuan, X., Song, W. Y., & Zhang, Q. S. (2011). Analysis of the synergistic mechanism of mergers and acquisitions in economic networks. *Productivity Research, 1*, 18–20.
Zejan, M. C. (1990). New ventures or acquisitions. The choice of Swedish multinational enterprises. *Journal of Industrial Economics, 38*(3), 349–355.
Zeng, Z. Z., & Li, S. M. (2008a). Major shareholder control, private profits and corporate performance. *Journal of Shanxi University of Finance and Economics* (5).
Zeng, Z. Z., & Li, S. M. (2008b). The influence of control transfer of state- owned holding listed companies on operational performance and agency costs. *Technological Economy* (5).
Zha, J. Q., Zhang, Q. S., & An, Z. R. (2008). Influence of internal control on enterprise value evaluation by income method. *Audit and Economic Research* (6).
Zha, J. Q., Zhang, Q. S., & Hu, J. B. (2008). Research on the current situation and problems of M&A valuation methods. *Productivity Research* (21).
Zhang, A., & Aldridge, D. (1997). Effect s of merger and foreign alliance: An event study of the Canadian airline industry. *Transportation Research Part E: Logistics and Transportation Review, 33*(1), 29–42.
Zhang, B., & Zhang, Q. S. (2002). Establishing competitiveness in electricity market in restructuring. *Journal of Beijing Jiaotong University (Social Science Edition)* (1).
Zhang, D. D. (2004). A brief discussion of corporate financial management capabilities. *Economist* (8).
Zhang, H. S. (2007). *The matching of strategic M&A parties* (Doctoral dissertation). Beijing Jiaotong University.
Zhang, H. S., Zhang, Q. S. (2005). Building an enterprise M&A decision support system: Realizing knowledge-based management of M&A activities. *Journal of Beijing Jiaotong University (Social Science Edition)* (2).

Zhang, H. S., & Zhang, Q. S. (2005, July 1). *Dynamic matching of strategic M&A based on value chain* [Paper presentation] . 2005 National Doctoral Academic Forum (Department of Transportation Engineering). Beijing, China.

Zhang, J. X., Han, R. (2004). Chinese companies' overseas acquisitions. *Accountant* (10).

Zhang, J. X., & Wang, Q. J. (2009). Sources of synergy in strategic M&A. *Finance and Accounting Research, 21*, 56–58.

Zhang, J. X., & Yue, G. Z. (2008). A study on the difficulties of measuring synergies based on M&A. *Statistics and Decision Making* (22).

Zhang, J. X., & Zhang, Q. S. (2007). Advances in corporate M&A matching research. *Productivity Research* (14).

Zhang, J. X. (2003). *Research trajectory of M&A theory* (Working paper). China Center for Corporate Mergers and Acquisitions, Beijing Jiaotong University.

Zhang, J. X. (2005). *Resource matching: A strategic analysis of M&A parties matching* (Doctoral dissertation). Beijing Jiaotong University.

Zhang, J. X., Wang, F., & Zhang, Q. S. (2005). A review of M&A integration research. *Business Research* (9).

Zhang, J. X., Zhang, Q. S., & Li, X. (2007). The empirical research method of M&A performance. *Journal of Beijing Jiaotong University (Social Science Edition)* (4).

Zhang, J. X., Zhang, Q. S., Cui, Y. M., et al. (2004). Classification of enterprise resources in the context of M&A. *Journal of Beijing Jiaotong University (Social Science Edition)* (1).

Zhang, J. X., Zhang, Y. Q., & Xie, J. G. (2012). M&A target identification: Evidence from the Chinese securities market. *Accounting Research* (3), 78–84, 95.

Zhang, J., Chen, H. M., & Sheng, Y. (1999). Corporate mergers and industrial restructuring strategies. *Journal of Systems Engineering* (2).

Zhang, L. Y., Zhang, Q. S., & Wang, L. C. (2007). Research on M&A financing decision model. *Journal of Quantitative Economics and Technical Economics* (6).

Zhang, M. B. (2005). Research on the relationship between manager turnover and control market governance efficiency. *Modern Management Science* (7).

Zhang, Q. S., & Wang, A. H. (1998). On the "privatization" of public capital and the "publicization" of private capital. *Economic Research Reference* (59).

Zhang, Q. S., & Wang, D. (2001). *Mergers and acquisitions.* Northern Jiaotong University Press.

Zhang, Q. S., & Zhou, L. (2003). Research and development of synergistic effect of mergers and acquisitions. *Accounting Research* (6).

Zhang, Q. S. (2004). Integrating human nature. *New Finance* (6).

Zhang, Q. (2005). Who moved the "cheese" of China's M&A market. *New Finance* (3).

Zhang, Q. S. (2005). *Research on the basic theoretical framework of mergers and acquisitions* (Working paper No. 2005–01). Research Center for Mergers and Acquisitions of Chinese Enterprises, Beijing Jiaotong University.

Zhang, Q. S. (2006). Banks should support corporate mergers and acquisitions. *Chinese Financiers* (9).

Zhang, W., & Qi, A. T. (2002). A review of the theoretical research on corporate mergers and acquisitions. *Nankai Management Review* (2).

Zhang, W. S. (2005e). *Research on enterprise strategic capability.* Science Press.

Zhang, X. Z., & He, L. (2014). A study on the correlation between corporate governance, managerial overconfidence and mergers and acquisitions performance. *Journal of xi'an University of Finance and Economics, 27*(3), 17–22.

Zhang, X. (2003). Does M&A and reorganization create value? Theoretical and empirical research on China's securities market. *Economic Research* (6).

Zhang, X. (2004a). How to study and carry out M&A and reorganization. *New Finance* (9).

Zhang, X. (2004b). Play the role of control market in restructuring. *Securities Times*, 27th February, 2004.

Zhang, X. (2007). There is no substantial progress in the restructuring of SST Language. *First Financial Daily*, 6th June, 2007.

Zhang, Z. X., & Ji, L. (2003). Are the interests of stakeholders balanced in company acquisitions? *Economic Research* (6).
Zhang, Z. L., Hu, X. N., & Song, L. F. (2004). *Mergers and acquisitions financing*. China Financial and Economic Press.
Zhao, J. (2004). Theory, assumption and model of enterprise capability. *Journal of Beijing Jiaotong University (Social Science Edition)* (4).
Zhao, J. K., Liu, Q., & Zheng, M. X. (2016). Research on the synergistic effects and factors of mergers and acquisitions. *Productivity Research, 1*, 134–137.
Zhao, L. N., & Zhang, Q. S. (2003). Offset treatment of internal production fixed assets transactions in consolidated accounting statements. *Shanghai Accounting* (4).
Zhao, Y., & Zhu, W. X. (2000). The predictability of mergers and acquisitions of listed companies. *Economic Research* (4).
Zhao, Y. D. (1998). Review of "social capital" theory. *Foreign Social Sciences* (3).
Zheng, H. H. (1997). An investigation on the emergence and development of enterprise mergers and acquisitions in China. *China's Industrial Economy* (9).
Zheng, J. Z. (2002). A brief discussion on the transformation of intellectual capital and core competence. *Journal of Harbin University* (3).
Zheng, Y. F., & Chen, H. M. (2006a). Market structure effect of foreign mergers and acquisitions under the condition of host country government intervention. *Industrial Economics Research* (3).
Zheng, Y. F., & Chen, H. M. (2006b). Review and prospect of empirical research on the impact of cross-border M&A. *Contemporary Economic Management* (4).
Zheng, Y. F., & Chen, H. M. (2006c). The selection of foreign mergers and acquisitions under the condition of multinational corporation bidding. *Journal of Shanghai Jiaotong University* (9).
Zheng, Y. F., & Chen, H. M. (2007a). Analysis of motivation and social welfare effect of foreign investment-driven industry restructuring. *Chinese Journal of Systems Engineering* (4).
Zheng, Y. F., & Chen, H. M. (2007b). Market condition recognition of the motivation of expropriating M&A by foreign capital. *Journal of Shanghai Jiaotong University* (7).
Zheng, Y., & Chen, H. M. (2007c). The stock market effect and financial performance of foreign mergers and acquisitions and their relationship. *Journal of System Management* (1).
Zheng, Y. F., & Chen, H. M. (2008). Recognition of market conditions for "eliminating foreign capital mergers and acquisitions". *Chinese Journal of Management Engineering* (3).
Zhou, L., & Xu, R. P. (2005). The value evaluation model of target enterprises in M&A based on EVA. In *The 2005 Academic Annual Conference and the 12th Annual Conference of the Higher Engineering College Branch of the Accounting Society of China* [Conference session]. Hefei, China.
Zhou, L., & Zhang, Q. S. (2001). Research on target enterprise valuation and determination of share exchange ratio in stock mergers and acquisitions. *Quantitative and Technical Economic Research* (2).
Zhou, L., & Zhang, Q. S. (2003). A review of value evaluation methods in corporate mergers and acquisitions. *Transportation Finance and Accounting* (7).
Zhou, L. (2004). Doubts on the Weston model in the value evaluation of mergers and acquisitions. *Journal of Beijing Jiaotong University (Social Science Edition)* (1).
Zhou, L. (2006). *Mechanism analysis of resource synergy in corporate mergers and acquisitions* (Doctoral dissertation). Beijing Jiaotong University.
Zhou, L. S. (2006). Share structure reform accelerates the formation of control market and industrial integration. *Shanghai Securities News*, 2nd March 2006.
Zhou, L., Lu, A. H., & Zhang, Q. S. (2003). The option hypothesis of controlling premium in mergers and acquisitions. *Research on Technology Economics and Management* (5).
Zhou, L., Zhang, Q. S., & Wang, X. X. (2003). On the risk of overpayment in mergers and acquisitions. *Research on Technological Economy and Management* (4).
Zhou, L., Zhang, Q. S., & Zhou, S. W. (2003). Problems and countermeasures in Chinese enterprise mergers and acquisitions. *Economics and Management* (11).

Zhou, R. L., & Chen, H. M. (2005). A review of empirical research on enterprise mergers: Methods and results. *Chinese Journal of Systems Engineering* (4).
Zhou, R. L., & Chen, H. M. (2005). An empirical study on the stock price response of listed companies' mergers and acquisitions. *Price Theory and Practice* (8).
Zhou, R. L., Chen, H. M., & Chen, L. (2006). An empirical study on the performance of target companies in my country's control transfer M&A. *Industrial Engineering and Management* (3).
Zhou, S. N., & Wang, H. T. (2015). Payment methods, corporate governance and mergers and acquisitions performance. *Journal of Beijing Jiaotong University (Social Science Edition), 2*(2), 39–44.
Zhou, S. N., & Wen, H. T. (2013). Research on M&A performance evaluation system based on industry evolution and M&A motivation. *Accounting Research* (10), 75–82, 97.
Zhou, S. N. (2004). Research on accounting problems of business combination in my country. *Accounting Research* (12).
Zhu, B. X., & Zhu, C. H. (2003). Analysis of factors affecting M&A premium. *China M&A Review* (2).
Zhu, C. H. (2002). Analysis of the current situation of enterprise merger and acquisition performance research. *Learning and Exploration* (6).
Zhu, D. Q., & Chen, W. H. (2010). The influence of control rights, the degree of deviation of control rights and cash flow rights on mergers and acquisitions: Empirical evidence from Chinese private listed companies. *Financial Research, 36*(2), 121–131.
Zhu, D. M. (2003). Extension analysis of resource contradiction in enterprise reorganization. *Industrial Engineering* (6).
Zhu, G. Z. (2002). Multiple regression analysis of the M&A performance of listed companies in China. *Journal of South-Central University for Nationalities* (3).
Zhu, W. X. (2000). Rational corporate behavior and inefficient corporate control market. *Securities Market Herald* (9).
Zhu, W. X. (2007). Case: Mittal's capital market M&A battle. *Capital Market* (12).
Zhu, Y. S. (2002). *Efficiency analysis of the transfer of company control right* (Doctoral dissertation). Graduate School of Chinese Academy of Social Sciences.

FSC
www.fsc.org
MIX
Papier | Fördert gute Waldnutzung
FSC® C083411

Kolibri 360 GmbH
Ferdinand-Jühlke-Straße 7
99095 Erfurt, Deutschland
produktsicherheit@kolibri360.de